The
John W. Campbell
Letters

Volume 1

Editors
Perry A. Chapdelaine, Sr.
Tony Chapdelaine
George Hay

Kelly Freas Cover: *John W. Campbell, Jr.*

Library of Congress Cataloging Number 84-071553

ISBN 0-931150-15-9

AC Projects, Inc., Rt. 4, Box 137, Franklin, TN 37064, *(615) 646-3757*

Limited Edition: <u>   69   </u> of 750 copies

Preface

Criteria for Selection

Considering the representation of such a vast galaxy of glittering ideas, it was difficult to follow consistent guidelines while poring over tens of thousands of brilliantly written, thought-provoking letters by John W. Campbell.

To the best of my ability, and over years of reading them, I have selected these first volume letters based on (1) whether or not the letter addressee was a published author, (2) if so, whether or not the author is well known, (3) if the science fiction story mentioned is well known, (4) if the content of the letter reflects on John W. Campbell, his personality, life and times, (5) whether the letter is non-duplicative of others selected, (6) whether it is the only letter available of a certain author or genre, (7) if the letter content is interesting, (8) whether more than one author is mentioned, (9) and whether or not the letter avoids *exceedingly* technical content (for example, detailed description of radio circuits).

Acknowledgement

Of course, without the many writers who have corresponded with John Campbell, there would have been no John W. Campbell book. But aside from that obvious fact, we are all deeply indebted to a certain few. Without their help and patience *The John W. Campbell Letters* probably would not have come about.

We owe special thanks to members of the John W. Campbell family, both living and deceased, for their blessing, patience and help.

Lester del Rey, Harry Harrison and Willis E. McNelly are owed thanks for their part in securing John Campbell's personal letters.

Thanks to Tim Bolgeo, Ken Moore, Valerie Proctor and James Tollett for securing interested fan artists.

Initial financial assistance from Forrest J. Ackerman, Isaac Asimov, L. Ron Hubbard and A.E. van Vogt helped immensely.

Forrest Ackerman's assistance purchased a microfilmer permitting us to safeguard the Campbell letters in several depositories.

Asimov's, Hubbard's and van Vogt's financial assistance opened the door to purchasing Conde' Nast services when securing the bulk of the letters written under *Astounding/Analog* authority. Conde' Nast, then, over a period, furnished all letters in John W. Campbell's file for duplication.

L. Ron Hubbard spent considerable effort, *free gratis*,

i

duplicating all copies from John W. Campbell's private files (provided by Peg Campbell) and Conde' Nast's work files.

Considering the absolute bulk of these papers, I seriously doubt that this project would have gotten anywhere for years without all of the above dedicated people.

Final financing of the printing of this collection is being shouldered by my children who have always had great faith in my own wild dreams — bless 'em!

PERRY A. CHAPDELAINE, SR.

Table of Contents

The 1960's

The 1970's

Artists

John Wood Campbell, Jr.

by

PERRY A. CHAPDELAINE, SR.

I first met John W. Campbell, Jr. through the pages of *Astounding Science Fiction*[1] magazine when I was fourteen, having already depleted the city's library of every fairy story-book and readable science-book. Like happened to many youths of that vintage era, parents, teachers and other authorities frowned on both fairy stories and pulp magazines, the first being presumed too fanciful for building the stuff that faces economic depressions, and the latter being too sexy or trashy or filled with improper morals (as judged solely by covers). In this long-ago era, getting to know the biological facts of birth became an embarrassing *tour de force* especially when convincing librarians that you are old enough to check out books on being born, and that your parent's signature is indeed genuine.

My parents' friend, Robert Blue, Great Northern and Pacific Railroad electrical engineer, subscribed to *Astounding*. When he finished reading his monthly copy, I sometimes received it. Waiting through four weeks was a terrible, anxious, frustrating period. When he forgot and threw away his copy, I was all gloom and doom. Unfortunately at that time I knew nothing of fandom, being quite isolated from any chance meeting with other fans, or my future life's course might have been quite different.

Campbell's influence, through both story content and editorials, eventually steered me into mathematics and a bubbling interest in math and science.

I began routine purchases of *Astounding* in February 1944, and still have most issues. I read *Astounding* regularly until the time of Campbell's death in 1971.

There gradually grew on me a delight in reading his editorials, usually composited of the most outrageous, irrational "rational" argumentations, where he deliberately sought out the most controversial issues and took umbrage at the "wrong" side, thus making those who sided with "motherhood" issues fighting angry.

He had no peer when reasoning by analogy.

I greatly admired John's ability to find emotional buttons of the "every-one-knows" kind, and he would press them in ways that forced differentness of thought. That side of his nature has already been told, as in Harry Harrison's lovely *John W. Campbell Collected Editorials from Analog*[2].

I also came to realize that John's story selection, or development of story-line through authors, held substrates that were completely apart from anything else in literature. Where literary experts were

1

still struggling to reconcile a mystical philosophy called Freudianism with story value, Campbell was setting about to counterpoint story-line by means of totally different and highly creative "what if" underpinnings. Freudianism dwelt on Id, Ego, and Super-ego so that antagonist and protagonist were boxed in likewise. Campbell simply took man's most basic assumptions about self and reality and turned them, again and again, so that one was forced to mirror his own image — whether ego or culture derived. Where Freudianism insisted on sexual substrates and death-wishes as the endall of life, Campbell showed that life is infinitely varied, most probably found everywhere where exists matter and energy, and that its implications must be at least as complex as reality itself.

Therein, according to my adolescent mind, lay John's second genius: his ability to take outright fairy tale and make its principles apply to reality in all manifestations — meanwhile not neglecting hard science which, after all, might be construed to be the very apex of all fairy tales.

Science fiction, he once said, is an interesting story told within the framework of real or possible science. If you cannot use real science, then write in such a way that the reader thinks it is real. Meanwhile, get across your point, your perspective of reality, in such a manner that it slips into the story silently, an unseen partner with the pleasure of vicarious adventures coupled with unusual mental stimulation.

He also said that science fiction is the only true literature because it permits premises to be chosen and embellished so that it encompasses all possible pasts, presents, and futures! — in effect, all literature!

But again, as with John's editorials, that side of him is well known and can be found in literature everywhere.

My first encounter with the man was during a series of classes at Elizabeth, New Jersey, at the *Hubbard Dianetic Research Foundation, Inc.*, where in 1950 I achieved a Hubbard Dianetic Auditor certificate.

Because he could envision difficulty when selling *Dianetics*®[3],[4],[5] to the public, he set out to teach a class of would-be "auditors" on how to handle a crowd that is heckling you while you are explaining *Dianetics*® to them.

He would set us before the class one at a time, and he would join in with the hecklers.

When we could not counter-argue immediately and with vehemence, he would point his finger at us and shout, "You lose! Sit down!"

I lost every turn. I couldn't help myself. He was so serious about the principles-of-haranguing-the-crowd-that-harangues-you, that I simply had to burst into laughter, and *that* was not the correct well-reasoned, spontaneous, putter-downer that I was supposed to use.

Later correspondence with John grew out of personal tragedies, whence I found him emotionally responsive, a side that many never saw and probably would not believe if they did, for such was the self-assurance, even arrogance, of his proferred image.

After Frederick Pohl purchased my first story, John purchased my second, and thereafter between Pohl and Campbell I begin to learn writing, an ambition sensed and unrealized from age six.

By 1971, at John's death, I'd developed a strong father-fixation with John as my nexus, and cried openly on his death. He'd been part of my "real" world since 1939, a man of so many attributes and talents that even at this writing I feel great sense of loss. I knew him to be brilliant, ethical, honest, open with all men, approachable. . . .

With this *John W. Campbell Letters* series, I have learned that John was a most remarkably creative man of virtually sheer genius, and one who must nevertheless have pits and cracks as would any of the human genetic code.

I am reminded of Sir Isaac Newton, one who sat astride the old and new of mysticism and science. To this day — or so goes the story — each fifty years or so the British government will "discover" a chest all-filled with Newton's unpublished writings. The chest is opened and examined by academia, "true-scientists", who gasp with horror on learning that Newton wrote as diligently and seriously about astrology and numerology as he did about the calculus.

Horror of horrors!

They must not tarnish the man's image, and so again they slam shut the chest for another half century.

Newton's image shimmers like a brilliant star among hundreds of thousands, and he is declared one of the greatest of all mathematicians. No school book stays itself from telling the story on how this remarkable creative genius overnight, so to speak, and from sheer instinctive reasoning, so to say, developed the key to modern mathematics and scientific reasoning.

Hogwash!

Newton, being of a similar genetic code to Campbell and other men, was also man, was a product of his age and culture, was subject to his own pitfalls and errors and certainly equally guided by his own internal motivations.

So it was with my dear, departed John W., who was of the human genetic code, was man, was a product of his age and culture, and was subject to his own pitfalls and errors, and certainly was equally guided by his own internal motivations. Furthermore it is hardly likely that *any* truly creative individual can develop ideas outside of traditional cultural frameworks without also creating some chaff.

Only now, on reading and re-reading tens of thousands of John's letters have I come to realize just how great was this man on the totem pole of brilliance and creativity. Where John would prod mankind by means of story and provocative editorial and verbal argumentation into believing in the existence of unseen, unfelt parapsychological phenomena, he would also insist that scientists act like scientists and test hypotheses before leaping into blind prejudisms. Where he would tout some carefully selected patent (from the U.S. Patent Office) as being the first feeble step toward understanding anti-gravity, he would also convince some science fiction writer to develop a story where belief in the existence of such machines causes hard-nosed scientists to re-examine their reality structures.

Can anyone seriously believe that by running a finger along a photograph of a circuit diagram, or picture of an electronic assembly, the thought and act will affect objects at a distance? Apparently John did, when he promoted eloptics, the combination of electronics and optics derived from another patent.

Or did he?

After reading and re-reading letters I come off with the conviction that John always knew what he was doing, and why — yet perhaps he *was* more the modern Sir Isaac Newton, standing at the threshold of development of true scientific method combined with mystical hazarding.

But even so, what can be so bad about being a modern Sir Isaac Newton of modern literature, and literature of the future?

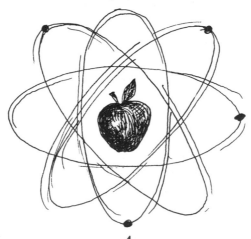

The John Wood Campbell Letters
by
GEORGE HAY

"I was in the hands of the future; I never swerved; I went on my way. I had to judge man as I judge you; to corrupt, as I corrupted you, I cajoled; I bribed; I held out hopes; and with everyone, as with you, I succeeded. It is in that power that the secret of the greatness which is virtue, lies. I had to set about a work of art, of an art strange to you, as strange, as alien, as the arts of dead peoples. You are the dead now, mine the art of an ensuing day. All that remains to you is to fold your hands and wonder, as you wondered before the gates of Nineveh. I had to sound the knell of the old order; of your virtues, of your honours, of your faiths, of . . . of altruism, if you like. Well, it is sounded. I was forever on the watch; I foresaw; I forestalled; I have never rested."[6]

The above passage from Joseph Conrad's little-known science fiction novel, *The Inheritors*, expresses something about John W. Campbell that seems to have been passed over. Admirers may be puzzled . . . *corrupt*? Well, this novel — which was in fact largely the work of Ford Maddox Ford — dealt with a very specific late nineteenth-century psycho-political issue, and I have wrenched the words from their context. Let them stand; I believe they are a true epitaph. The man was ruthless in his own way and, I think, knew himself to be so. Only saints can afford to ignore the needs of ego, and John was no saint. Consider this account by John Brunner:

"John was a man who knew how to hold a grudge, as I can personally testify. I first met him in London at the 1957 World SF Con; then when I first visited him in New York in 1964; but it was at the 1965 Worldcon in London that I think I got to know the *real* JWC.

"For some while, through his editorial columns, he had been trumpeting his conviction that 'the only truly immoral act is to order someone to do the impossible!'

"On a panel with him at the 1965 Worldcon I heard him say precisely that, and was moved to observe that I found it curious for someone to make such a statement in the context of a Christian culture (he had previously defined himself as 'if anything a Unitarian', admittedly) whose Founder had adjured his followers, *'Be ye perfect, even as your Father in heaven is perfect!'*

5

"In other words, he had dug himself a trap, and I happened to be the person who came up behind and pushed him in.

"Not once, not twice, but three times during the next few months I received a note from my New York agents saying John was going from desperate to frantic in his quest for publishable short stories. Each time I wrote one for him, because he had published my work before, and it was still a mark of prestige to appear in *Astounding/Analog*. All three stories sold elsewhere, so they can't have been that bad . . . but he rejected each of them so fast I doubt he took the time to read them.

"Like I say: a guy who knew how to hold a grudge. But after our encounter at the 1965 convention it was his ex-wife who came to tell me it had been a pleasure.

"So he was probably good at teaching other people to hold grudges, too."[7]

Barry Malzberg has recounted how, meeting that great man for the first time, he was left completely speechless and, so to speak, shell-shocked. Noting which, Campbell offered, "Don't worry about it, kid. I just like to shake 'em up."[8]

If I have started off in this somewhat backhanded manner in my approach to Campbell it is because, looking over what has been written by those who knew him or wrote for him there is a serious danger of making him appear not only larger than life — which he was — but more perfect than life, which he was not. Against John Brunner's statement that he could hold a grudge are endless accounts of his generosity of mind and spirit. The comments that follow are typical:

"As a source of inspiration to scientists, Campbell ranked with Verne and Wells, . . . was a great man . . . he was the kind . . . who draws a circle which includes you, even if the circle excludes him" (John Bangsund[9])

" . . . He had extraordinarily free, spontaneous flow of ideas. He seemed to have the ability to focus all his attention on a particular idea and extrapolate it in every possible direction, without looking for ways to chop it at the outset. He had a vivid encylopaedic memory that seemed to hold the past alive and immediately available to him all the time. . . . The stimulus he imparted to practically all the leading writers in the science fiction field was incalculable, . . . was indisputably one of the greatest

6

masters of controlled imagination." (Wynne White-ford[10])

"The man who drives minds to the end of their tether,"   Miscellaneous   press-cutting,   London, 1965[11]

"He can cruelly stab us from our torpor with his shocking declamations, statements that can flagrantly run counter to the most popularly held conceptions . . . . There is nothing mean or tentative about his jabs. He is a first-rate psychologist and he sinks his barbs in just the right places . . . and derives great pleasure from listening to the resultant howls. . . . He makes people think. This is his aim. His *motive* is not to win. . . . We are urged to cease swallowing wholesale the thinking of others, to instead do our own thinking, that we might come to truly have our very own arrived conclusion, to know personally and why. He creates opinions where none before exist, . . . Yes, he is criticized, and a lot more than most — because he is the biggest, he has the greatest stature, the toughest hide, the gall, the nerve, the cheek — the knowledge, the wisdom, the sensitivity, and shrewd insight to wield his power as a rapier rather than as a claymore. . . . He is a Churchill in this SF field." (Jack Woodhams[12])

"To the didactic Campbell the journal's most imporant role was that of subterranean educator, shatterer of conventional thought patterns . . . [he] hammered that man must be forever on guard against the blinkering effects of his education . . . that the innocent may sometimes probe more swiftly to a puzzle's nub than the expert. One fruit of Campbell's propaganda was the Rand Think Tank . . . ," (Herman Oberth[13])

"We have Campbell to thank for the whole modern adult fantasy bit," (Jock McKenna[14])

"The essential difference between Mr. Campbell and all the other editors and controllers of supposed science fiction publications was that his educational qualifications were technological, not literary," (Henry Couchman[15])

"What John W. Campbell brought to *Astounding* . . . was not editorial experience. It was something far more important — a new and more sophisticated conception of science fiction, derived from a new and more sophisticated conception of the nature of the universe," (Alexei and Cory Panshin[16])

You see how it goes? One could fill a monograph with the praises of John W. Campbell. Yet already I feel him leaning over my shoulder, and hear him saying, "Now, hold on there a moment. How would it be if we looked at it on the basis that I were really a very *destructive* personality? Maybe an alien, sent to speed the breakup of earth culture. . . . Looking at things that way, what do you suppose. . . . ?"

See how the man tends to take over? *Go away, John!*

Something — not enough — has been written about what Isaac Asimov has called John Campbell I and John Campbell II. The former could be summed up as the author of "The Mightiest Machine," and the latter as the author of "Forgetfulness," and the other great 'Don A. Stuart' stories, which first brought mood and magic into science fiction in the west. John Campbell II was also, of course, the editor of the pioneer fantasy magazine, *Unknown Worlds*. The distinction is, of course, between the writer as technocrat and galaxy-basher, and the writer as poet, the common factor between them being the desire to bring into question basic premises. John Campbell I questioned the premises of science, as when, for example, in "Uncertainty," he enquires what happens when the laws of probability break down under man-made pressure. Don A. Stuart questioned the premises of life itself. To quote his own words about "Cloak of Aesir" . . . .

> "It's always handy to set up someone like the Sarn Mother. Make her six thousand years old, emotionally remote from her own kind by time, intellectually akin to any intellect. Let her look at two conflicting cultures, and see each dispassionately for what it is."[17]

I would like to go on from this point and suggest that there was, finally, a John W. Campbell III, whom we might consider as some sort of God in the Machine, trundled on-stage by destiny to alter the ways of men. Alter them he did, for like it or not — and many do not — he single-handedly and, as one might say, of malice aforethought, created modern science fiction in the west as vehicle for new ways of thought. In this context he acted, as I have said as an agent of destiny. The concept of destiny is not a very popular one in the west at this time, but an examination of Campbell's fiction and writings may help us to consider if, in this case at least, the term is not being used in a valid sense.

To do this, it is necessary to disabuse oneself of the widespread belief that the man was purely and solely concerned with the hard sciences. The belief is understandable, since the whole progression from *Astounding* to *Analog* was away from 'space westerns' and

8

towards hard science. But one does not have to look very far to see that John's interest in science was due to the fact that science itself is the area where rigorous thought is best demonstrated. Or at least — in deference to theologians and logicians — most widely demonstrated. It was thought itself that John was after. See, for example, in his letter to Perry A. Chapdelaine, Sr.:

> "The essence of *Analog* stories is *not* heavy science — it's hard, detailed, integrated, and internally consistent thinking. No fuzzy-headed generalities, with soft-focus pictures of a slapped-together social or physical world-picture . . . *Analog seems* to be hard-science, simply because most people who have learned to think hard, clear, internally consistent, and defined thoughts learned to think this way while studying science. In the Arts courses, they hold that any opinion is as good as any other; in the science courses they hold that the opinion that makes the experiment work is the better."[18]

So much for the myth of Campbell, the fanatical devotee of science. . . .

It was this devotion of the man to the pursuit of thought to its ultimate conclusions that gave him, I believe, his power to dominate. If he had the quality of genius, it lay here, though I believe that this quality lies far from the built-in arcane device or computer that many seem to imagine the owner to possess, and consists rather that of a supremely simple mirror-like mind that reflects exactly what it sees before it. From this arises the odd belief that genius is 'inconsistent' or 'unpredictable.' All that this exposes is the mental poverty of most of us, who, having arrived at a belief or supposition, allow it to remain soldered-in for life. Naturally, when we mention to the superior man this belief of ours, we are surprised, if not pained, when he looks at it as if for the very first time, and, so doing, derives from it conclusions quite other than our own. We may be even more pained to find that, returning to the conversation in the belief that we now 'know' what the other 'believes,' we find that he has 'changed his mind.' We then accuse him of inconstancy, instead of admitting, even to ourselves, that we would like nothing better than to be able to 'change our minds' — alas! the bloody things have got stuck in bottom gear and won't budge. . . .

There comes back to me a moment when Campbell was participating at a panel at the 1965 British-held World sf convention. The subject of the panel escapes me — I rather think it was something to do with racialism — but I do recall the absolute aplomb with which the man expressed some extreme view. Having spoken, he sat down, passing the microphone along to the speaker next to him, who happened to be Michael Moorcock. There was a long silence while Mike's lips moved in silent struggle. Eventually, he uttered one word — "Christ!" — and passed the microphone along. . . . From my position at the back of the hall, I had a good view of audience reaction to Campbell's words. The spectacle was fascinating. Here, remember, were supposed to be concentrated the most far-out minds of the world. One might have supposed, therefore, that this audience would have received Campbell's mental sallies with the delight of the truly open-minded. What a hope! Some few did, of course, enjoy what was happening, but for the most part expressions seemed to vary between incomprehension and blind rage. One well-known author near me actually loosened his tie, for all the world like some outraged retired Colonel from Bournemouth. "Do you actually *mean* —?" he managed to get out, and then choked on his own words.

It is hardly to be wondered at that, as Peg Campbell told me years later, she and John sometimes found themselves quite alone at conventions, when they would have welcomed company and conversation. One can price oneself out of the market. . . . Still, it is doubtful if this *enfant terrible* aspect of the man was preserved undiminished through his life accidentally, at least from the point of view that regards him as an agent of destiny: this is something one needs if one is to act on behalf of pure reason. As Berthold Brecht — another from the same mould — once remarked: to have got to the stage of conceding, "well, that's just natural" is to have given up. John Campbell *never* gave up, and, what is more to the point, he never, if he could help it, allowed others to do so.

Very well. Having considered Campbell the writer and Campbell the editor — as revealed in both his editorials and in the correspondence you are about to read — let us now look at John Campbell III, the agent of destiny, the magician.

What does a magician do? He breaks down the walls of time and space: lets the waters of eternity flood in. "Eternity," of course, does not mean "a great length of time," it means "the absence of time." We are speaking of something quite beyond physics. John Campbell II had gone as far as any man could with physics: it was time for the archetypes to appear. They came: the city at the world's end in "Twilight" and "Night," the jet-black light-absorbing figures in "Cloak of Aesir" and elsewhere: the *sorgan* field in "Forgetfulness." Consider this latter:

> "In the first revolution it made, the first day it was built, it circled to the ultimate end of time and the universe, and back to the day it was built. And in all that sweep, every *sorgan* unit tuned to it must follow.

That was the master unit; from it flowed the power of the generator, instantaneously, to any ship in all space, so long as its corresponding unit was tuned. It created a field rotating" [19]—
and the minds of his hearers refused the term —
"which involves, as well, time.

"In the first revolution it made, the first day it was built, it circled to the ultimate end of time and the universe, and back to the day it was built. And in all that sweep every *sorgan* unit tuned to it must follow. The power that drove it died when the city was deserted, but it is still making the first revolution, which it made and completed in the first hundredth-of-a-second it existed . . . it rotates still, and will rotate when this world dissolves, and the stars die out and scatter as dust in space." [20]

Follow *that!* Of course, in the pre-World War II days when that was written most scientists would have written that off as mystical twaddle: the position would be rather different now, I think. In any event, though, my point is not to do with physics, but with metaphysics: whether he knew and intended it or not, John Campbell III was here presenting an archetype of eternity. Archetypes such as the shape-changer, eternal city and the all-knowing seer showed up in other stories, respecting science, but transcending it.

Through Don A. Stuart, John W. Campbell took his writing as far as it could well go in matters — what shall I say? — transcendental. However, he saw no reason for stopping at that. A whole stable of writers were to his hand — young, ambitious, science-oriented and — let us be truthful — only too glad to accommodate John's ideas in exchange for the joy, experience, fame and financial reward of access to the pages of *Astounding Science Fiction*. Is it surprising then, that in the years that followed turned up yet further godlike archetypes. Consider — just to take those in the forefront — James Blish's *Cities in Flight* tales, Jack Williamson's *And Searching Mind* (better known now as *The Humanoids*), Asimov's *Foundation* series and Clifford Simak's *City*.

According to A.E. van Vogt, a science fiction legend in his own right:

"His conversation could be — and generally was — overwhelming. At his home in October 1953 he introduced me to his second wife . . . and then he took me into his workshop in the basement. During this entire period of time he had been talking steadily, with me getting in only a few yeses and noes, and other acknowledgements limited to one word. That was the way it was."[21]

Yes, Campbell corrupted his writers, and, through them, his readers. Only, true to what he would probably have referred to as "his cockeyed philosophy," he corrupted them *upwards*. I mean no slightest disrespect to these writers when I say that without John Campbell III not only would these stories not have appeared: that even if they had appeared — say in some other hypothetical magazine — they would not have been that *kind* of story.

Such glimpses of Campbell as can be caught via the accounts of his friends and family confirm, what one might have expected, that his qualities of mind and heart were integral — that he was not just a large-hearted man with a good mind, or a clever man who remembered to be kind, but a man who was all of a piece. Perhaps integration *is* genius. Perhaps, too, the kind of approach to life of such a man tends to be upsetting to others not thus integrated, and who prefer to take life apart and tackle it bit by bit.

Consider this advice from Campbell to Joseph Goodavage, a regular correspondent, who had suffered a heart attack:

"Comes to a very simple question: Are you going to be smart, and learn a new way of living, or die of stupidity?

"Suppose a five year old kid has a heart attack. You can understand that the first necessity is to make the kid slow down, stop trying to run everywhere he goes, instead of walking, stop trying to climb all the trees in sight, stop chasing the dog around the yard — stop all the things that have been his way of life.

"What chance do you think you'll have of getting a five-year-old to understand the necessity of slowing down for six months or so?

"Children almost never survive a heart attack.

"*Really* rest, and the damage can heal. Then accept that you decided, some years ago, to be a typewriter jockey, not an athlete — and accept the *full* consequences of that decision.

"Incidentally, after your wife told me you'd been clobbered, I was darned curious and asked my friend Ralph Hall about how come the doc hadn't spotted the trouble after your first attack — how come the EKG test then didn't show it?

"Answer: the electrocardiograph records electrical pulses due to heart-muscle action — but it has to pick them up through skin, subcutaneous fat, the rib cage, the pericardium, etc., the voltages are pretty darned small to begin with. The voltages it can detect are all those on the *front* surface of the heart. The *rear* parts of the heart can't be picked up; there's all the lungs, the heavy back muscles, the spine etc. between the heart-backside and the skin of the back.

"The result is that an EKG can't detect what's going on at the rear of the heart. You can have a fairly serious damage at the back of the heart, and the EKG won't detect a thing — because there *isn't* anything wrong with the front of the heart. Like a guy could have the back of his head stove in with a baseball bat, but a full-face photograph wouldn't show a thing wrong with him, except he looked sorta dead.

"(Incidentally, an electrocardiograph is an EKG because es war ein Deutscher who introduced the gimmick, and *he* called it, of course, an elektro-kardograf.)"[22]

And so on, for quite a while.

How many editors, one wonders, would go to that trouble, and, those who would, how many would display, not just sympathy, but that enormous curiosity in the malady under discussion? Of course, Campbell did know Goodavage personally, but I don't think that that alone is the answer — though it did give the latter the chance to give to me in a letter a pen-picture of the man in action:

"I can see him now, on one of his luncheon excursions with five or six engineer/scientist types, examining the excavations of Consolidated Edison on Lexington Avenue in New York, talking to the workmen, asking questions and even climbing down into a hole to study the structural material of the underground cables being laid for a new building going up. . . ."[23]

The integral nature of Campbell's interests and affections shows itself equally in the memories of his daughters, Leslyn Randazzo and Philinda Hammond:

"He made growing up difficult, in a great many respects, because *no* authority existed. He insisted that there was at least one alternative to every-thing. . . .

"He refused to allow a point to be won because it was in a book. *He* wrote books, and knew he could be wrong. Therefore, the printed word proved little. Logical thinking, *that* was the key. Proper, organized thinking was the epitome of achievement. He cared

13

not what we thought, so long as, by God, we thought . . . .

"A simple physics project immediately turned into an extensive course in trigonometry. No simple pin-hole camera in a shoe box was acceptable. *My* camera was a 180° pin-hole camera! When distortion occurred at the corners, the film support system had to be redesigned to eliminate the problem.

"Father enjoyed watching us develop, grow and mature. I recall the strange grin on his face when his youngest daughter went out on her first 'real' date. I also recall that it was close to 9:00 p.m. when they managed to leave the house, way too late for the 7:15 p.m. movie!

"College students came constantly during school breaks, our dates learned to come early knowing still that we'd be late, ministers from the church (although Father never attended church himself, he insisted that I did) came frequently, even after being advised of my transfer to a church near college, 'Oh, we know, but we fight for the opportunity to see your father.' No matter what you believed, no matter how strongly you believed it, he had another side and he could have you doubting your beliefs before you parted his company . . . yet the ministers came, and loved it!

"The words 'yes' and 'no' did not exist, alone, in his vocabulary. To this day I can remember as a youngster wanting a simple 'yes' or 'no' answer. Oh, the frustration of wanting a 'yes' and getting a *long* lecture on the why's and wherefores which lead, *eventually* to a 'no.'

"John W. Campbell never let anger show. He never spoke unkindly of anyone to my knowledge. He dealt with facts, alternatives and logic, and usually by the time he was through they were somehow undisputable whether I liked it or not!

". . . to read 2,500 words per minute and *remember*: 'I have to, my love. If I rejected a story from an Englishman and five years later he comes into the office and asks, Why?, I have to know.'"[24]

Well, John W. Campbell the man is gone from us now. But he was more than a man, he was a way of life all on his own. Now, if a way of life is recorded, it can, to some degree at least, be brought back into being. Looking around today, at a world of mental and ethical chaos, one can say that never was that way of life more urgently needed.

That is not the only reason these letters of John are being made available. But I think it is a reason the man would have appreciated. . . .

A thing done has an end. John Campbell is dead, his magic with him, and there is no slightest point in lamenting the fact, or in dwelling unduly on the absence today of that peculiarly heroic quality he represented in himself and sought out and encouraged in others. Others have built on the foundation he constructed so long and so well, and that is reward enough — if, indeed, other reward were needed beyond John's work itself. On the other hand, that work should itself be kept available. It is Frimbulwinter now, when men are mainly concerned with short-time survival, and memories are even shorter than usual. The best of Campbell's stories — though by no means all of them — are available in the United States and in Great Britain: some of the editorials have been reprinted in a Doubleday hardback edited by Harry Harrison — the rest of them are at the mercy of magazine collectors and such libraries as have complete runs of *Astounding* and *Analog*. Hopefully, they will one day be made more widely available, along with the other stories and novels. Here, through the heroic efforts of Perry Chapdelaine and the generous support of many writers and readers we present the correspondence of the man whom posterity may well judge to have had the most challenging mind and the most constructive influence on the United States from the nineteen-thirties up to the end of the nineteen-sixties. If you consider these sweeping claims — well, read the correspondence — before you decide against them. You may be surprised. . . .

John Wood Campbell

by

PERRY A. CHAPDELAINE, SR. AND GEORGE HAY

According to *James Gunn*, Professor of English, University of Kansas:

> . . . .the directions in which science fiction has developed have been largely determined by such editors as Gernsback and, in particular, John W. Campbell. . . .[25]

Isaac Asimov writes:

> There are many people whom one might cite as being the "father of science fiction."

> Johann Kepler wrote the first story that sounded like science fiction and that paid attention to actual scientific fact. Edgar Allan Poe first caught the idea of inevitable social change through advances in science and technology. Jules Verne was the first to specialize in science-fiction writing. Herbert George Wells was the first to make it a recognized branch of literature. Hugo Gernsback was the first to publish a magazine devoted exclusively to science fiction and created the beginnings of the first mass market.

> But all these, put together, only laid the foundation. The man who took that foundation and built the structure of modern science fiction upon it and shaped it to what we now accept as such, was a tall, broad, light-haired, crew-cut, bespectacled, overbearing, overpowering, cigarette-holder-waving, opinionated, talkative, quicksilver-minded individual named John Wood Campbell, Jr.

> He was born on June 8, 1910, in Newark, New Jersey, and remained a Jerseyite almost all his life. He had a difficult childhood, for he was born into a world that had not been designed to his scale.

> He began reading science fiction not long after he began reading. He bought the first issue of Gernsback's *Amazing Stories*, read it regularly, and was profoundly impressed by the trailblazing serial "The Skylark of Space" by E.E. Smith, which began in the August 1928 issue. Inevitably, he began to write science fiction himself in the style of Smith.

> He made his first sale when he was seventeen, but his first published story appeared in the January 1930 issue of *Amazing*. It was entitled "When the Atoms

Failed." In the month that it appeared, a new science-fiction magazine was launched entitled *Astounding Stories of Superscience*. That this was an astonishing coincidence could only be understood in hindsight.

Before 1930 was over, Campbell had launched the Wade, Arcott & Morey series of stories which clinched his fame in the science-fiction world. This series joined him with E.E. Smith as the great exponents of the super-science epic in which men of more-than-heroic mold fought each other with suns and leaped over galaxies in single strides.

But there was this difference between Smith and Campbell. Smith, having found his metier, never left it. To the end he wrote the super-science epic, changing it only to make it ever larger, ever more colossal. Campbell had no metier he wished to call his own; or, rather, having found one, he could not help looking about for a better one.

Perhaps a change in his personal life helped him do so. He attended M.I.T., where he had no trouble with science but was laid low by the German language. He passed on to Duke University in North Carolina, where he completed his work for his degree. (However, it was always M.I.T. which remained his spiritual home in later years, and he visited it regularly.) As though to mark the change from M.I.T., the super-school of science, to Duke University, where psychology was important and where Joseph Banks Rhine (who later put parapsychology on the map) was already an instructor at the time, Campbell began to switch from tales in which super-science blasted the readers minds to those in which human emotion wrung their hearts.

He wrote "Twilight," a low-key poignant tale worth all his super-science adventures put together. "Twilight" appeared in the November 1934 issue of *Astounding*, which was then edited by F. Orlin Tremaine. For various reasons it appeared under a pseudonym. The best reason was that had it appeared as a Campbellesque production, the readers would have been set for super-science and would have missed the wonder the story really was. So it appeared as having been written by Don A. Stuart, a name which was almost identical to the maiden name of Campbell's first wife (Dona Stuart).

For the next four years Campbell, under that pseudonym, pioneered in what came to be the "new wave" of that era. He wrote stories in which science and scientists were what they really were, and combined that with human emotion and human foibles. The climax came in the August 1938 issue of *Astounding*, which carried Campbell/Stuart's "Who Goes There?" surely one of the greatest science-fiction stories ever written, which was made into "The Thing from Outer Space," surely one of the worst movies ever made — [a second version was produced in the 1980's which, it is said, follows story line more closely. Ed.]. But by that time Campbell had made his second metier sufficiently his own to abandon it. He had written all, or almost all, he intended to write. He was going to be an editor.

In September 1937 he had joined Street & Smith, which then published *Astounding*, and in May 1938 he succeeded Tremaine as editor of the magazine. He remained editor thirty-three years and two months — to the day of his death (at home, quietly, quickly, painlessly, as he sat before his television set) on June 11, 1971.

I once asked him, years ago (with all the puzzlement of a compulsive writer who can imagine no other way of life), how he could possibly have borne to leave his writing career and become an editor. I had almost said *merely* an editor. He smiled (he knew me) and said "Isaac, when I write, I write only my own stories. As editor, I write the stories that a hundred people write."

It was so. By his own example and by his instruction and by his undeviating and persisting insistence, he forced first *Astounding* and then all science fiction into his mold. He abandoned the earlier orientation of the field. He demolished the stock characters who had filled it; eradicated the penny-dreadful plots; extirpated the Sunday-supplement science. In a phrase, he blotted out the purple of pulp. Instead, he demanded that science-fiction writers understand science and understand people, a hard requirement that many of the established writers of the 1930s could not meet. Campbell did not compromise because of that: those who could not meet his requirments could not sell to him, and the carnage was as great as it had been in Hollywood a decade before, when silent movies had given way to the talkies.

Campbell went to work to fill the gap left by the forced retirement of some of the best-known names in the field. He began to develop new talents in a new generation of writers, those plastic enough to learn a set of newer and much harder skills, and he succeeded. Those who flourished under Campbell's tutelage and learned to write in his uncompromising school lifted the field from minor pulp to high art.

Not all writers before Campbell were poor; not all writers after Campbell were great — yet the change was large enough and dramatic enough to make it clear that science fiction as adult literature had a name and that name was John Wood Campbell, Jr.

I met him in June 1938, just a month after he had become editor. I was eighteen and had arrived with my first story-submission, my very first. He had never met me before, but he took me in; talked to me for two hours; read the story that night; mailed the rejection the following day *along with a kind, two-page letter telling me where I had gone wrong.*

Over the next four years I saw him just about every month, always with a new story. He always talked to me, always fed me ideas, always discussed my stories to tell me what was right and what was wrong with them.

It was he who gave me the skeleton of "Nightfall," including the opening quotation, and sent me home to write the story.

It was he who considered my third or fourth robot story, shook his head and said, "No, Isaac, you're neglecting the Three Laws of Robotics which are —" and that was the first I heard of them.

It was he who took the idea for a short story which I brought to him and put it through a rich sea-change that transmuted it into the *Foundation* series.

I never denied, or even tried to diminish, the debt I owed him, and told him flatly that everything in my writing career I owed to him; but it was characteristic of him that he never accepted that. He admitted he fed me ideas, but he said he kept on doing so only because I brought them back changed and improved. He denied he had made up the Three Laws of Robotics and insisted he had found them in my stories and merely put them into words.

He watched many of his writers take their instructions from him and use them to go on to fame outside *Astounding* and outside science fiction. He rejoiced in that and stayed behind to teach a newer generation.

Only once did I manage to get him to recognize his value openly. I asked him to what he attributed his editorial ability, and he answered, "To an unteachable talent." I asked him what talent that was, and he said, "The talent which made it possible for me to see writing ability in a hungry teen-ager named Isaac Asimov who had brought me in a completely hopeless first story."

Yes, indeed!

It has always been my pride that of the writers developed by Campbell, I was one of the very first (in time, at least, if not in ability).

Nor did he ever settle down. To the end of his life he was always experimenting, always changing, always trying to find the new and exciting. Others grew stodgy and rut-ridden with age; not Campbell. Many science-fiction writers did; not Campbell.

He tried *Astounding* in different sizes; he tried it with rotogravure sections; he changed the letter columns this way and that; he introduced new departments and dropped them; let word rates depend on readers' votes. Changes didn't always meet with approval, but he wasn't looking for surface approval, but for something he felt and knew to be right — and to the end of his life, he kept *Astounding* first in sales and prestige. he even changed the revered name to *Analog Science Fact-Science Fiction*, over the loud outcries of many readers (including me), but saw it through unwaveringly because he felt the new name no longer smacked of the juvenility of science-fiction's magazine beginnings.

Campbell championed far-out ideas: dianetics, the Hieronymus machine, dowsing, psionics. He pained very many of the men he had trained (including me) in doing so, but he felt it was his duty to stir up the minds of his readers and force curiosity right out to the border lines.

He began a series of editorials in his magazine in which he championed a social point of view that could sometimes be described as far right. (He expressed

21

sympathy for George Wallace in the 1968 national elections, for instance.) There was bitter opposition to this from many (including me — I could hardly ever read a Campbell editorial and keep my temper).

Yet criticism never angered Campbell, nor strained his friendship, and however idiosyncratic his views on science and society, he remained, in person, a sane and gentle man.

I saw him last at a science-fiction convention in New York City, the Lunacon, in April 1971, and spent an evening in his hotel room. While Peg Campbell (his second wife, with whom the last decades of his life passed in happy serenity) worked on a hooked rug, Campbell lectured us all on medicine and psychiatry.

It never occurred to me when I shook hands in farewell that I would never see him again. How could that occur to me when I had never once thought (*never*) that death and he had anything in common, could ever intersect. *He was the fixed pole star about which all science fiction revolved, unchangeable, eternal.*

And now that he is dead, where can we find thirteen people who by united effort might serve as a pale replacement for the man who, in the world of science fiction, lived a super-story more thrilling than any even he wrote.[26]

Professor *Jack Williamson* (Eastern New Mexico University), says:

His topic was science, with science fiction for a metaphor. Though he was too completely himself to be easily defined, I think he was most of all a voice for what Snow calls the culture of science. He was absorbed with technology transforming the world. A canny optimist, he understood the process better than most of us do, and he regarded it with more wonder and hope than fear.[27]

. . . .

At Street and Smith, the way to his office ran past rumbling presses, through gloomy tunnels walled with enormous rolls of pulp paper, back to the cluttered den where his assistant, Kay Tarrant, presided over manuscripts and artwork. He came in only once or twice a week, but nearly always, there or at the family home across the Hudson in New Jersey, writers were welcome.

22

No editor was ever more helpful. He read every story submitted. Those he rejected came back with useful comments, and many a letter accepting one story also included ideas for another. (The mechanical ants in my . . . novel . . . "The Moon Children," were an invention of his.)

Too few of us heard his stimulating talk, but his monthly editorials were the man himself, always outspoken, sometimes deliberately outrageous. In the latter years his opinions made enemies. He was attacked and ridiculed, I think most unfairly.

Though I could never quite accept all his pronouncements on the possible future of science and the best order of society and our proper human roles, I could always accept his candor and good will. So could most of his readers. . . .

Campbell enjoyed a good duel of fact and logic for its own sake, but he held no grudges. No dogmatist, he was rather the Socratic teacher, eager to test every position with shrewd debate but striving always to establish new truth. Beneath all the talk, I think he was inwardly shy. In the course of the years, to paraphrase Poul Anderson's tribute in *Locus*, I found him warm, gentle, often humorous, always kindly, ever eager to share the miracles he had found in a world that now has one miracle the less.

Although *Astounding/Analog* stands as his major monument, he created another magazine, short-lived but not forgotten. That was *Unknown*. Perhaps the inspiration came from H.G. Wells, but he transformed it. Seen through his clear intelligence, the purely unbelievable became a new sort of literature: the fantasy rationalized by means of its own strict internal logic.

But science fiction was his life. For him, as for most of us, it was something more than just another minor sub-literary genre. It was and is international, climbing above all our tribal quarrels to see the world whole. It is at least sometimes intelligent, looking through confusion and indifference to explore our possible futures with some sanity. In its own rising voice, which has strong accents of John Campbell, it speaks for our survival.

As an innovative writer, but chiefly as a great creative editor, he filled a place in science fiction that nobody else can occupy. It was Wells who established and defined the genre. Hugo Gernsback named it. John W. Campbell is the third major name in its history. He reshaped it and taught a whole generation of its ablest craftsmen.

As an old friend of John Campbell, and an old science fiction fan, . . . I am personally in debt to Campbell, not only for years of good reading, not only for editorial inspiration, but for part of what I am. Because of him, I know the art of fiction better, and I can see the changing world more truly. In the whole domain of science fiction, we are all his debtors. In his death, we have lost something of ourselves that we will never find again.[28]

A.E. van Vogt says:

JWC, Jr. was to me, originally, a name on a magazine editorial page. In 1938, I had, evidently, come to accept that such people existed; for, after reading the July, 1938, issue of *Astounding*, I wrote him, outlining a story idea in one paragraph, and describing to him my — up to then — 6 year writing career, first, as a confession story author (for the MacFadden *True Story* magazine group) and radioplay writer (for Canadian radio stations) as evidence that mine was not just a casual inquiry.

His reply urged me to write my story with plenty of "atmosphere." That came natural in my "system" of writing; and so I started to receive checks for one cent a word from a man whose age was, initially, unknown to me, but whose judgment and advice I accepted as if his was the voice of age and experience.

Of course, it was the time of the Great Depression. And I lived in a city that was, surely, in those days about as remote from NYC as a writer could get: Winnipeg, Manitoba, Canada. During the Depression, in Winnipeg, if there was a reasonably steady source of money, we treated its source with respect and, yes, obedience. So what happened to John Brunner, when he, in effect, contradicted JWC, Jr. during a convention panel discussion, could never have happened to me.

You might ask, what kind of caution was involved? Well, I once, without the slightest anxiety or fear, argued with a prowler and, in effect, persuaded him, now that he was discovered, to depart. That kind of incident had nothing to do with a possible threat to annual income in those early days.

When, one night in 1971, JWC, Jr. suddenly slumped in his chair while watching TV, and when, presently, his wife discovered that at that moment of sagging he had died of a heart attack, one of the people she called was Robert Bloch, and one of the persons RB phoned was me.

The man who died at that moment left his mark on a portion of the world, and his name and career was still remembered with kindly thoughts by at least a million persons — in my opinion. I have a feeling — in regard to Brunner — that it is well for an author to realize that editors have to set up a defense mechanism against writers, some of whom bring their stories to his office, and let him know they need the money so they and their families can eat that night, and they sit there waiting while he reads the story.

If life has any meaning, then it could be that somewhere in our great universe JWC, Jr. has been evaluating the new data — something which he always did without fear or favor.[29]

And others have said:

A. Bertram Chandler:

John could talk . . . He could have been an outstanding school-teacher. He could make anything simple. . . . Every writer who ever worked for him learnt much from him. He was a perfectionist. If he wanted a story, and if it fell short of his standards, he would say, take it away and do so-and-so and such-and-such; this is your story, your idea and I want it from you! The end result of all the rewriting was always worthwhile.[30]

Alfred Bester:

Campbell gave science fiction character, rescuing it in the 1930's "from the abyss of space pirates, mad scientists, their lovely daughters (wearing just enough clothes to satisfy the postal authorities) and alien fiends."[31]

John Pinkney:

For a pulp magazine, *Astounding Science Fiction* commanded a remarkably prestigious audience. Albert Einstein was a devoted subscriber. So were Edward Teller and Werner von Braun.

(*Astounding* magazine's) effect on our present

starward-looking world has proved profound . . . became a cerebral playground for engineers, physicists, philosophers . . . circulated most widely in universities and American "technology towns" . . . L. Sprague de Camp, whose oxygen-system designs incorporated into the astronauts' moonsuits; Professor Isaac Asimov; Arthur C. Clarke, inventor of the tv satellite . . . [32]

George Turner:

With the death of John Campbell Science fiction loses the most towering and influential figure of its erratic, fascinating and vociferous career. Like him, hate him, praise him, he remains at stage-centre, commanding your respect even while you finger your overripe egg.

John Campbell as a writer was completely unimportant in literary terms. As an innovator, as a man who had a profound effect on what came after him, he was of vast importance.[33]

John Foyster:

But one thing that Campbell did do by his domination of his own magazine, and thus of the field of science fiction, and in this way speculative thinking in general, was to impress the general public with some of the notions of the importance of futurology — which perhaps might never have got off the ground without the basis provided by sf.

It is ridiculous to talk about sf without John Campbell, simply because sf as we read it today is almost entirely a product of his mind. The changes he made in sf are so revolutionary and widespread that there will never be a time while sf is still being written when his influence will not be felt.[34]

John W. Campbell directly influenced academic careers in creative writing and in the sciences through his publications, letters, and dialogues. Writers are often euologized after their death by literary analysts, publication of their various works, or their personal letters and by other means. Seldom, if at any time, has an *editor* (with Campbell's past influence) been shown to have inspired the careers and many of the basic story ideas which eventually brought fame to writers. Letters of Campbell's will be fundamental in showing how would-be writers (fans) were encouraged and stimulated, and then little by little how they became publishable writers, and even later became famous writers. All of John W. Campbell's letters bear directly on story content and ideas, such ideas forming the basis to a writer's reputation and career; i.e., Isaac Asimov's three laws of robotics, and his "Nightfall" story line; Hal Clement's "Needle" and "Mission Gravity"; and so on.

In short, the ideas and stories that made certain modern writers famous are clearly traced, and often attributed to John W. Campbell.

Also John W. Campbell was a popularizer of scientific projects so that laymen, and young children, could understand the modern, technological world better. He was a thought provocateur, causing many reputable scientists to challenge basic assumptions, or rethink their positions. These letters contain the basis for many such ideas which were subsequently used somewhere in science fiction literature as well as in science itself. The telling of the atom bomb project projected by *Analog*, through author Cleve Cartmill, during World War II was an occasion when the FBI was compelled to force retraction of the story on security grounds, and this before Campbell or the public was aware of the Manhattan project!

Also the first article proposing use of three equidistant satellites for use as communications satellites (Arthur C. Clarke) occurred under Campbell's editorship, and this feature is now commonplace above our skies and integrated into our worldwide communications network.

When John W. Campbell began editing his original pulp magazine, its literature was not quite acceptable to English instructors in high school or college. School children had magazines of such kind taken away or torn up by offended English instructors. Interestingly, now virtually every college, university, and many high schools routinely teach the very same stories and call them "acceptable literature," although their present appearance is usually disguised by hardcover anthology editions instead of "pulp" covers of the early genre.

Professor *James Gunn* (University of Kansas) has further traced science fiction history in the United States:

> The first college course in science fiction was taught at Colgate University in 1962 by Professor Mark Hillegas, now at Southern Illinois. Since then science fiction has spread like a plague from space, not only through the college classroom but into high schools and junior high schools and even primary schools as well.
>
> Nobody knows exactly how many college courses there are. Jack Williamson, who may have taught the second science fiction course at Eastern New Mexico University in 1964, collected course descriptions for

several years and came up with 240. A better estimate today might be some 2,000 — or at least one course for every college and university in the nation. Some, like the University of Kansas, have several.

Science fiction has come a long way since the day in 1950, when a professor at the University of Kansas said about my proposed thesis topic, "Science Fiction is at best subliterary." That may have become the only thesis ever serialized in a pulp magazine.

Science fiction was considered subliterary and beneath academic consideration for more than half a century. Mary Shelley, Poe, Verne, and Wells got the whole business started in the 19th-century, with the help of several dozen other writers. . . . The scientific romance, as it was sometimes called, was welcomed into the pulp magazines, beginning in 1896, along with other kinds of adventure stories about war, the Wild West, the sea, spies, and foreign intrigue. . . .

Then came the creation of the category pulps . . . and science fiction got its own pulp ghetto in 1926 when Hugo Gernsback, an inventor and publisher of popular science magazines, founded *Amazing Stories* and gave the category a name. . . . Other magazines followed, in particular *Astounding*.

. . . .

The magazine period was important. During the 20 years and the succeeding 20 years of tentative emergence, science fiction evolved its own techniques, traditions and conventions, created its own writers out of the unique fan movement that sprang up, and developed its own assumptions about the nature of man, his ethics and his ultimate destiny. It is a fiction concerned with change and humanity's response to it, and as the facts of change produced by man's discoveries and inventions became more apparent, more people began to read the stories seriously.[35]

James Gunn further says:

Tremaine began the trend toward idea-orientation that Campbell continued and combined with his own ideas to produce a magazine that in itself defined SF. SF was what Campbell published in *Astounding* — idea-centered, pragmatic, science-oriented, irreverent, iconoclastic, engineer-fascinated — and what was published in the other magazines (by 1940 they had grown to 18) was something less. It was more adventure, more fantastic, more romantic, and less rigorous — or simply not good enough to meet *Astounding's* standards. Since there was no book publication of any consequence, Campbell was the gatekeeper. What he admitted to the pages of *Astounding* was SF; what he rejected, wasn't.

But the process was not simply a matter of acceptance and rejection; that had been done before. Campbell perfected a method that may have been used first by Weisinger: he actively sought particular kinds of stories. He proselytized for new kinds of writers; he encouraged and redirected more established ones; in editorial and letter and personal conversation he inserted irritating ideas into the oyster shells of author's minds, and he repeated his requirements for good SF so often it was like chiselling them into stone. Such as : "Grant your gadgets, and start your story from there. . . . I want a story that would be published in a magazine of the twenty-fifth century."[36]

And,

In *Astounding* between 1937 and 1950, SF was shaped and re-shaped by the writers attracted to the vision Campbell held up for them and by Campbell himself, and out of this intense experience of creating and shaping and debating came the conventions and the methods that mark SF to this day and which later generations of writers would use, often unconscious of their origins, or react against.[37]

Lester del Rey says:

Back in the early days of science fiction, everyone knew it was impossible to make a living in the field. There were only two SF magazines being published each paying somewhere around $200 for a long novel and perhaps $25 for an unusually good short story. Even when a story was accepted, a writer might have to wait months after publication before he was finally paid for his work. Furthermore, no science fiction *books* were being published; so once a story appeared in a magazine, there would be no further income from it.

Writing science fiction was a hobby, not a career, and nobody questioned that obvious fact — nobody but John W. Campbell! Against all logic, he not only determined to make science fiction his life's work, but he succeeded. It took three careers to achieve his goal, during which he became almost single-handedly the creator of modern science fiction. And eventually, others with less genius or less folly found it possible to follow the trail he blazed.

Campbell's first sale was made while he was still in college, studying for his science degree. (Later, he used to joke about it, saying that he only graduated because his English professor couldn't flunk anyone who was already selling to a professional magazine.) It appeared in January 1930, six months before his twentieth birthday. Within a year, he had become one of the best-liked writers in the field.

In only ten years, John Campbell had become two of the greatest writers of science fiction. And then (except for one short fantasy novel written to fill a magazine he edited) both careers came to an end, as he began a third which was to be even more influential than any amount of writing could have been — so influential, indeed, **that a crater on Mars has now been named** *Campbell* **to honor him.** [Ed. emphasis.]

Toward the end of 1937, he was asked to be the editor of *Astounding Stories* (soon to be renamed *Astounding Science Fiction* and later *Analog Science Fact/Fiction*). He continued as its editor for thirty-four years, until his death in 1971. As a writer under either pen name, Campbell had been one of the best; but as an editor, he quickly became *the* greatest. If that is a personal judgement, it is one shared by most writers and editors in the field.

When he took over as editor, the magazine had settled into a dull routine; and other magazines were folding or turning to blood-and-thunder stories. Old authors were leaving the field and few new ones of any talent were coming in. There seemed no new hope that science fiction would ever become a generally accepted category.

Campbell rapidly changed all that. He had a clear vision of what science fiction should become, and he began teaching that vision to all the established writers capable of learning it. He also discovered a host of new writers within the first few years of his editorship. Most of the leading science-fiction writers today are ones he discovered and trained: Asimov, de Camp, Heinlein, Sturgeon, van Vogt, and many others.

Writers were developed, too, not merely discovered. Faulty stories went back with pages of detailed criticism of plot and technique that meant more than any dozen courses in how to write. Ideas for stories poured out from Campbell to his writers, and many of the best-loved stories in the field came from those ideas. He had the marvelous talent of suggesting just the right idea to a writer and putting it into a form that writer could best handle.

In my own case, he repeatedly forced me to continue writing when I would normally have turned to other things; and he supplied the ideas for many of my best works. Most writers I know had the same experience. Even when a story was not right for him, Campbell was generous with his help in improving it for submission elsewhere. The result was the so-called Golden Age of science fiction — the beginning of modern science fiction, which was capable of reaching beyond a small readership of gadget-loving hobbyists and science buffs. When the book publishers finally began turning to this new category for material, it was only because there was already a body of respectable novels waiting in the back issues of *Astounding*. Even today, a rather large percentage of the most successful books are still produced by the writers Campbell discovered. Without him, the current acceptance of science fiction would almost certainly have been impossible.

To my surprise, many of the writers and fans seemed to consider Campbell a hard man to know well. He was held in some awe and in a measure of affection; but most people complained that he lectured at them, rather than talking to them. This was probably true in many cases. Campbell was somewhat shy, particularly about his personal feelings; and he hated to make conversation, something most people do automatically to fill time. He had no fund of small talk. He was a man passionately in love with ideas, who wanted to chase such ideas back to their beginnings and forward to the furthest possible extension. To him, that meant an all-out, no-holds-barred argument.

His mind was like a rapier, darting out instantly to find any unprotected spot in an opponent's thinking. He was a quick master of the fundamentals of any area of knowledge and he came armed with an amazing fund of information. Apparently he was intimidating to many. But to those who would return his passionate love of argument as mental exercise, he was a wonderful human being. And his delight was as great in losing an argument as in winning. Over the years there were many areas where he and I remained in total opposition. His eternal quest for undiscovered fields of knowledge led him into what I considered cultist beliefs, and I fought against those both privately and publicly. But our clash of ideological attitudes didn't matter. I always found him a warm and generous friend, whose loyalty was unshakable.

His editorials in the magazine were always a source of controversy, as he meant them to be. He was using his editorial page to stir up thinking, to say, "Yes, but how do you know your obvious truth is so darned obvious? Now let's try a different assumption." He refused to accept any set idea of what might be good or bad. And some of his writings on politics or on our current mores infuriated a great many readers. But other editorials were more future-oriented. And there he was always in advance of his writers. . . .In any career, John W. Campbell was always ahead of his time.[38]

When writing about Campbell's background, and influence in science fiction, *Theodore Sturgeon* says:

. . . .in less than a couple of years [after assuming editorial chair of *Astounding Science Fiction*], he attracted to himself and the magazine (the same thing, really) a nucleus of extraordinary writers. A few had been around for a while — Simak, Leinster, Lieber; the others he discovered or invented or, it sometimes seems, manufactured. Pratt and deCamp, L. Ron Hubbard (yes, *that* Hubbard), van Vogt, del Rey, Heinlein, Hamilton — Campbell, through these men, created what has been called a Golden age of SF.

He was a superb and provocative teacher of science and of fiction. "Give me a story about aliens," he would challenge, "in which they think as well as a man but not like a man." He would return a story because it turned upon the fission of light metals or a compound of argon, and would explain to you in five or six or seven single-spaced pages why this was not possible — and give you something which would really work, and which in some cases, as with our nuclear energy technology, ultimately did. He conveyed his preoccupations with power (all kinds), superiority (*our* kind) and scientific probability up and down and across the disciplines, so forcefully to his disciples that they produced a body of Campbellian literature on which the entire field pivoted, and which profoundly affects it to this day. The same pressures which produced that first golden explosion also seem to have squirted, like appleseeds, his early converts into other areas; no matter — he discovered/invented/manufactured more, and as *Astounding* became *Analog* (and Street and Smith, the publishers, dissolved and were replaced by Conde' Nast) the magazine went right on being what it had been since Campbell took over: Campbell[39].

Mrs. John W. Campbell (deceased) said:
My first inkling of the sacerdotal character of science fiction came shortly after John and I were married in 1951. We had moved into a new house in a new neighborhood, and one evening I answered the doorbell to find three young men on the doorstep. The spokesman said, "Does the Great Man live here?" "You must have the wrong house," I said; "this is the Campbell residence."

Just shows you, doesn't it?

For the next twenty years we had an ever-normal granary of youth supply. First, there were my son's and daughter's college friends, who would come in without a "Hello" but with a well-thought-out refutation of some point of an argument begun during a previous holiday months before. They brought new people with them each time, to refuel the discussions and arguments that would last for days.

Later on came the beaux John's daughters brought home. Many's the time I had to interrupt one of those marathon debates to suggest that the girls might like to go out on their dates, rather than fidgeting, all dressed up, in the background.

After the children were grown up and gone, we still had the neighborhood young people to be cudgeled with electronics and chemistry and goodness knows what else. John had an inexhaustible supply of data and loved sharing it, much to the discomfit of his own children, who, after one foray, would cease asking for help on science-fair projects, models of molecules, or, on anything else. What with all the fascinating ramifications, by ways, and side issues John could think of, it took him at least twice as long to convey the information. He also was unnerving about their textbooks and about the accepted authorities. The exceptions to any rule were pointed out; and just at the time when one should develop respect for the written word, the children would be told: "It's only a book. I write books, my friends write books, and we can be wrong." This can be rather unsettling, especially when one is up against a superior arguer.

No one writes about John without mentioning the office arguments — starting at eleven A.M., continuing through lunch, and ending at train time in the afternoon. I have yet to hear anyone who understood the reason for them. But somehow John felt compelled to take a person's own data and bring it through the logical development; to a logical conclusion then he would sit back and say: "You see, you didn't really think that at all."

I really can't know personally what John was like in the years before I met him, though by reputation he was always a great talker and explorer of ideas. But I must take some credit for his well-known prodding of unreasoned convictions and his unraveling of an individual's undesirable viewpoint. John and I had an agreement to try to discover what we thought, how we thought, and why. Now, this can be vastly uncomfortable, because if you take a dearly beloved concept back to its sources, it might turn out to be (1) somebody else's idea, (2) in direct conflict with another equally pet theory, or (3) not what you really thought at all. The trouble is, not everyone wants to play this game — to have his theoretical inconsistencies pointed out to him and to be left with the feeling of being anchorless. I would like to be able to discuss the question of personality balance with John right now, to see whether it's sort of like the binocular viewpoint — that major untenable theories are necessary to maintain stability.

Our own private discussions were remarkable, and

we even gave titles to some of the arguments. Early on, I wanted to have a linen closet built for place mats, tablecloths, and the like. I had it well designed (I thought), and then came his questions: function, practicability, logistics, importance — the works. Our "Linen Closet Argument" lasted for a good ten years and never was solved; but the design, intact and unchanged, was used when John built a storage cabinet for electronic parts. I — on the other hand — never did get the linen closet.

"I *know* what it's like to live in a small town" began another marathon discussion. After days of marshalling every argument I could think of, I suggested using our new tape recorder to get down the facts. The system was awkward at first. But never let it be said that we would be cowed by a machine; so shortly the argument was flourishing. Finally we decided to play back the tape, ending for good and all that type of discussion. I sounded shrewish and petulant, and John sounded patronizing and smug; and neither of us thought we lived up to our self-images to any attractive degree. Humbling, to say the least. Let it be said that we continued to discuss, for the rest of John's life — but not *that* way.

People used to ask me, at science-fiction conventions, what it was "like" to live with John. Interesting, I'd say then. I say now, it isn't in every household, where in trying to get an accurately cooked breakfast egg on the table (7.5 minutes, according to John's timer) one would have to cope with a gent with shaving lather asking, "Now, on the question of the limiting factors of free will. . . ." Nor having the piano tuner coming into the kitchen to ask, "Pardon me, but I'd like to know just how long have you been married?" When we said it had been twelve years, he said, "My God, you talk together as though you'd just met!"

John had no time for string quartets (tweedledum and tweedledee), cocktail party chitchat, the theater, Milton, non-representational art, lobster, tuxedos, hard rock music, liquor, mowing the lawn, going antiquing. He loved his job — it was the only one in the world where someone was paying him for his hobby: reading science fiction. There were recurrent parental questionings about trying to influence John into a "respectable" nine-to-five spot in a lab of some sort. He knew absolutely that he was doing exactly what he wanted to be doing. I once made the suggestion that perhaps he should be teaching, since he was so inspirational and helpful. That was about the only time that I got a sweet, sad smile, all forgiveness: "What do you think I'm doing, with 100,000 students a month?"

People continully urged him to read this, that, or the other thing. But he maintained that he read for a living and that it was high time to integrate the facts he already had, rather than cluttering up the works. As to the manuscripts he received, he read every single word of every one. For there could be the tiniest germ of an idea that he might miss otherwise.

When we were in Cambridge once, where John was to give a talk at MIT, we were watching a TV program and the words "Live from the Moon" flashed on the screen. "I feel validated," John said, and that was all. There were so many unpopular and nonrespectable ideas that he espoused, that he earned himself such epithets as screwball, crackpot and worse — with the consequent loss of friends. . . .This used to worry me, but somehow he coped with it. He never carried a grudge or acted vindictively — He was not smug, but had some tough quality of mind that viewed ideas as fascinating and always worth processing through his mental computer, no matter where they led. This I observed, but could not understand or emulate.

We early came to the conclusion that we handled concepts differently, by methods unacceptable to one another. Women used to become livid when he would say: "Men and women don't think alike," believing he was denigrating the female thinking process. But he was not disrespectful, only marveling at the usefulness of having someone around to double-check with. He often said, "I don't care what people think, just so long as they, by God, think!"

John liked steak, wrestling on TV (best dramatic program on the air), Victor Herbert, his friends (whom he thought were remarkable), comfortable chairs, dogs, kittens, endless discussions, trees, clear thinkers, time to himself, precision machinery and the people who make it go, peach orchards in bloom, anything with garlic, staying home and visits to

Cambridge. The business of going to Cambridge was often accompanied by much bad language, *sotto voce*, and grumbling over the idea of wearing a suit and tie every day — but then one could never get him to go home.

He was a very good father, and the girls have all kept letters — pages and pages of his philosophy of living. They used to bait him by proposing imaginary problems to him because he simply could not bring himself to write brief, chatty notes.

There is no effrontery to equal the statement "I understand him" — although I'm sure he thought I did. I didn't understand that putting up a shelf meant an hour's discussion of torque. I didn't comprehend that a door bell worked better on a storage battery, or that the door to the downstairs cupboard could be worked from upstairs, utilizing the flap-lifting mechanisms from a World War II aircraft; or that it was absolutely necessary to disembowel every new piece of mechanical equipment the second it came into the house, so that days would go by before it could be put into service. Nor that it was necessary to tell the same story over and over again, until it was explained to me that "that's the way to shape and polish the idea before it gets into print." Nor that he wouldn't be lynched one fine day because of some of his appalling ideas.

Yes, indeed, that was one interesting man![40]

. . . .

References

1. *Astounding Science Fiction*, (*Analog Science Fiction/Science Fact*), Davis Publications, Inc., 380 Lexington, Ave., New York, N.Y. 10017.
2. Harrison, Harry, Ed.; *John W. Campbell Collected Editorials from Analog*, Doubleday and Company, Inc., Garden City, New York, 1966.
3. Hubbard, L. Ron; *Dianetics: The Modern Science of Mental Health*, Publications Organization, 4833 Fountain Avenue, East Annex, Los Angeles, California, 90029, 1950.

4. _____; *Science of Survival*, Publications Organization, 4833 Fountain Avenue, East Annex, Los Angeles, California, 90029, 1951.

5. _____; *Advanced Procedures and Axioms*, Publications Organization, 4833 Fountain Avenue, East Annex, Los Angeles, California, 90029, 1951.

6. Conrad, Joseph; *The Inheritors*, _____

7. Brunner, John; Personal Communication to George Hay.

8. Malzberg, Barry; Personal Communication to George Hay.

9. Bangsund, John, *John W. Campbell: An Australian Tribute*, "Introduction," Ronald E. Graham and John Bangsund, Canberra Australia, Parergon Books, P.O. Box 357, Kingston ACT 2604, Australia, pp. 1-2.

10. Whiteford, Wynne; *Ibid*, "Science Fiction After John Campbell," pp. 8-9, 69-73.

11. Johnson, Robin; "Miscellaneous Press Clippings," *Ibid*, "Robin Johnson," London, 1965, p. 11.

12. Woodhams, Jack; *Ibid*, "Jack Woodhams," pp. 12-13.

13. Oberth, Herman; *Ibid*, "John Pinkney," p. 14.

14. McKenna, Jock; *Ibid*, "Jack McKenna," p. 19.

15. Couchman, Henry D.; *Ibid*, "John W. Campbell Educator," "Henry D. Couchman," pp. 66-68.

16. Panshin, Alexi and Cory; *Starship (Algol)*, "John Campbell's Vision," Spring 1979, p. 19.

17. Campbell, John W.; _____ "Cloak of Aesir," _____.

18. Chapdelaine, Perry A.; Personal Communication to Perry A. Chapdelaine, January 19, 1970.

19. Campbell, John W.; *Op. Cit.* "Forgetfulness," _____.

20. Campbell, John W.; *Ibid*.

21. van Vogt, A.E.; Personal Correspondence to George Hay.

22. Goodavage, Joseph; Personal Correspondence to George Hay.

23. Goodavage, Joseph; *Ibid*.

24. Randazzo, Leslyn and Philinda Hammond; Personal Correspondence to George Hay.

25. Gunn, James; *Publishers Weekly*, "Teaching Science Fiction," June 14, 1976, pp. 62-64.

26. Asimov, Isaac; *Astounding John W. Campbell Memorial Anthology*, "Introduction," Harry Harrison, Editor, Random House, New York, New York, 1973, p. ix-xiv.

27. Williamson, Jack; *John W. Campbell, An Australian Tribute*, "Foreward," John Bangsund, Editor; Published by Ronald E. Graham & John Bangsund, Canberra, Australia, Parergon Books, P.O. Box 357, Kingston ACT 2604, Australia, "Foreward" has no numbered page.

28. Williamson, Jack; *Ibid*, "Foreward," "Foreward" has no numbered page.
29. van Vogt, A.E.; Personal Communication to Perry A. Chapdelaine, Sr., June 10, 1984.
30. Chandler, Bertram A.; *Ibid*, "A. Bertram Chandler," pp. 5, 7.
31. Bester, Alfred, *Ibid*; "Wynne Whiteford," p. 8.
32. Pinkney, John; *Ibid*, "John Pinkney," pp. 14-15.
33. Turner, George; *Ibid*, "John W. Campbell, Writer, editor, Legend," "George Turner," pp. 29-36.
34. Foyster, John; *Ibid*, "John Campbell: The Editor," "John Foyster," p. 51-62.
35. Gunn, James; *Op. Cit.* "Teaching Science Fiction,"
36. _____; "The Gatekeepers," *Science-Fiction Studies*, SFS Publications, No. 29, Vol. 10, Part 1, Montreal, Quebec, Canada, p. 18, March 1983.
37. _____; *Ibid*, p. 19, 1983.
38. del Rey, Lester; Editor, *The Best of John W. Campbell*, "Introduction, The Three Careers of John W. Campbell," 1976, p. 1-6.
39. Sturgeon, Theodore; *National Review*, "I List in Numbers," March 10, 1970, p. 266.
40. Campbell, Mrs. John W.; *The Best of John W. Campbell*, "Postscriptum," 1976, pp. 304-307.

The 1930's

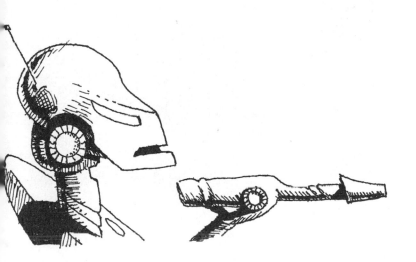

HUBBARD SNUBBARD:
HUBBARD SNUBBARD:
HUBBARD SNUBBARD:

When I was a little boy, on me fodder's knee, he says to me, says he to me, (yes, I was a little boy, and I did have a fodder, and he did have a knee, and he did say to me): "Never take offense, where offense isn't meant."

So thata is data in a hurry. But what did **Doone** mean by keeping that information from me? True, **Art** did tell me to call you at the St. Francis, but that was after you'd been here for weeks, and after many complaints from me. Naturally I couldn't call you then, not knowing anything about your request to have me call, you see. Anyway, the whole thing sounds all screwed up: my address was on file in the **Burks'** house. I didn't move till long after you left. I arrived at the **Burks'** on several occasions and received the news that you had just been there. No word from you to me; naturally I felt slighted. Wouldn't you? Especially after I had specifically requested word from you, through **Doone** or through **Art**, on several occasions. In fact until I finally decided I was deliberately being ignored.

Why **Doone's** son-in-law actually told me he passed my house on several occasions, with you in the car! They didn't know where I lived? Rubbish. Long after you left town, they once called for a visit. Once.

Sir: it looks to me as if I was not considered an personage of sufficient importance, either by one or the other of the **Burks'** household, to bother about. If you wish to be charitable, set it down to a bad memory (collective). I do think a lot of **Art**, and do not think he would deliberately forget anything of so personal a nature.

If you will match notes with **Art**, you will discover that I have submitted to him a plan whereby I propose to publicize me frands. Here's the dope: I have just done an article on **Jerry Forman**, and one on **Art Burks**, for a Sunday magazine. Now that that's over, and I am still, strange to relate, still in favor at the said Mag, I intend to write another article, this time embracing as many departments in the pulp mag industry as possible. I shall include a few writers, yourself, if you like, and such boys as **Ernst**, **Tinsley**, et. al.

Now: — There is a good likelihood of working this so that instead of embracing all departments in the one article, I shall take a few writers for one article, a few agents for another, a few editors for still another, and, if the boys are willing, we'll publicize the forgotten man of the pulp industry, the writers' best friend, and ladies home companion — the reader; not the public reader, but the one who sits in a mousetrap inside the magazine office, and gnaws hardtack, spilling the crumbs all over some guy's masterbate, giving rise to the popular saying among unpopular authors that so-and-so's MSS are positively crummy.

We'll have to have personal anecdotes, as I am explaining the letter to **Burks**. Like the story about the guy who's secretary sent a pulp story to *Colliers* and received a check for $4,550.28, instead of just the 28¢. P.S. The gal was not fired for the mistake.

The reason I want you guys to do your own publicity is mainly because I don't want to go to the trouble of inventing bad stories when you can give me (what you consider) good ones. Besides, don't be lazy when it's for your own good. This mag has a paid circulation of 350,000, besides an awful large stand sale. Mostly among people who do not know the meaning of pulp. It will help gain new friends for the pulp industry, put the writer's name before a new public, and do good in general, for the pulp paper magazine field.

My fran: I hope all your children are acrobats. How is your wife and family? Any new additions? If not, would you consider an adoption? I am looking for a home for a cute little rascal named Yon Clemons.

My best to your wife and kiddies. I am now about to sign off. By the way, forgive the bad copy; I only learned to type a couple weeks ago, and can't control the engine sometimes.

Addio,   John

L. Ron Hubbard   *January 23, 1939*

Dear Ron:

I'm damn glad you'll be with us on the Arabian Nights stuff — and you needn't worry about having it yours. I've been telling a few of the boys to read Washington Irving as an example of pure fantasy and complete acceptance of magic, enchantment, et cetera, and adding that they aren't to do Arabian Nights because the field is preempted by you. It's been held open for you.

As soon as I can get hold of a few office copies of *UNKNOWN*, I'll send one on to you for perusal. "Sinister Barrier," "Trouble With Water" and "Where Angels Fear —" are down the alley. "Death Sentence" and "Dark Vision" are pretty fair ideas. The other two are filling space for me acceptably. I'm having a hell of a time with it, because the genuinely first-rate fantasy I demand is hard to get: if it isn't genuinely first-rate, I'm not going to have the magazine I intend to, but just another fantasy magazine.

Basically, this is the philosophy I'm applying: All human beings like wishes to come true. In fairy stories and fantasy, wishes do come true. Adults with childish minds (average "adult" has the mind of a 14-year old) don't dare to read "fairy stories," because their minds are afraid to acknowledge their interest in anything childish — they subconsciously realize their mental immaturity, and, as a defense mechanism, avoid childish things.

Your true adult, with fully developed mind, can enjoy fantasy whole-heartedly if it's written in adult words and thought-forms, because, being absolutely confident of his own mental capacity, he doesn't have any sense of embarrassment if caught reading "childish stuff."

You get the same effect in the physical world where you find the big, powerful, capable man pretty generally peaceable, friendly, and willing to take ribbing easily because of an assured and unquestionable power. The little runt is apt to be belligerent, spiteful and bitterly resentful if ribbed.

And every human being likes fantasy fundamentally. All we need is fantasy material expressed in truly adult forms. Every author who honestly and lovingly does that makes a name on it. Lord Dunsany, Washington Irving, Stephen Vincent Benet. In view of this, I have absolute confidence that this magazine will inevitably become more or less of a fashion among truly adult people — and will be despised by the 14-year-old-minds.

I don't, personally, like Westerns particularly, and, in consequence, haven't read your western stuff. But I'm convinced that you do like fantasy, enjoy it, and have a greater gift for fantasy than for almost any other type. The fact that editor after editor has urged you to do that type seems to me indication that you always have had that ability, and that, in avoiding it heretofore, you've suppressed a natural, and not common, talent. There are a lot of boys that run out readable Westerns, but only about three or four men in a generation that do top-notch fantasy.

And, as I say, I'm reserving the Arabian Nights to you entirely.

Regards,   John

45

The 1940's

A.E. van Vogt   *June 11, 1942*

Dear Mr. van Vogt:

One reason I thought I'd send that check on "Recruiting Station" along right away was that I hoped you'd be able to break loose and really do some writing with that cash as a starter. I need "Ptath," need more *Unknown Worlds* writers badly. You can, you know, use up to 50,000 words on *Unknown* lead novels now, since we are going to the large size, carrying about 110,000 words.

The break in "Recruiting Station" will come on Page 67, I think. If you'll write a synopsis for the first part and send it along, it'd help. In doing it, you'd better tie in directly, without the break the direct story shows, to the switch-over from Norma to Garson. Otherwise synopsis readers are going to wonder what the hell they missed. Was there an intervening installment, or what —?

I piked the break rather than the Page 78 break, because the Page 67 point about bisects the yarn. Page 78 would give a long and a too-short installment.

If you're doing an article on the metallurgy of magnesium why not do one for us, too? I'd love it. I've been tearing my hair trying to get some good technical articles on metallurgy — metallurgy of all the elements wanted. There's room for reams and reams of stuff, and the light metals are particularly interesting. If you can catch hold of some on Beryllium to throw in with the material on Mg, and add some dope on Al, comparing their properties, I think we could nicely absorb 5,000 to 6,000 words on the Light Metals. One angle might be on the queer fact that Li, Mg, Al, Na and Ca are among the softest of metals, as well as the lightest. But Be, in glaring and inexplicable exception, is very light, and extremely hard — steel hard, and steellike in its resistance to fusion. Yet Be, in the periodic table, is smack between Li, and B, just above Mg.

What I'd really like would be a discussion of the thing in a series of such 5,000 word articles. Age-hardening and precipitation hardening — what it is, how it works, the almost miraculous things accomplished by it (such as dural that's soft as wax when first made, and hard, tough and strong twenty-eight days later. Such as that dural airplane rivets are made, and popped immediately into dry-ice boxes, where they remain soft until put in place and allowed to warm. Then they become hard and strong.)

But I need "Ptath" more than articles.

Regards,   John W. Campbell, Jr.

A.E. van Vogt   *March 3, 1943*

Dear van Vogt:

I just took "The Beast"; it's on its way through the accounting department now, and you should get a check shortly. I still need, and need badly, more short stories; novelettes I'm reasonably well provided with now. Serials also seem to be taken care of. Shorts for *Unknown* are needed at last, also. And I'll be wanting another lead novel for *Unk* in about 6 weeks. How's "Ptath" coming — or is it permanently shelved?

I think your five-years-more prediction is on the pessimistic side. I believe Hitler will go down in 1944, and Japan will be finished off in 1945. The great problem of the United Nations right now is the submarine, of course — but that's a problem of getting destroyers and other escort vessels on the sea. We're doing right well at that now; we're producing destroyers not quite as fast as the Nazis build subs, but we approach that speed. Four went down the ways in one day this week from one New Jersey yard. They don't hold the launching of a destroyer back until more are ready just to make a simultaneous show; they're building them so fast the coincidental completion of four at once reached a probability of one.

I think that the reason for England's survival is double; the channel was no minor hindrance, nor was the opposition of the RAF; together with the British Navy, they made the channel some of the highest priced liquid real estate in the world. (The whole damn channel could be turned into a sea of blazing oil, too, which rather stymied the Nazi intentions to send barges over. The British had God knows how many sunken tanks of oil laid like mines ready to spread oil on troubled waters — and ignite it.) The various forms of hell on waves, wheels, and wings the British had to offer was one item. Joe Stalin tugging his moustache was the other. Neither Hitler nor Stalin ever had the slightest doubt that there was going to be war between them, that each was waiting the most opportune moment. If Hitler had committed his army to the job of taking Britain, he might have gotten a landing, but at a cost out of all proportion in the first beacheads. He'd have lost at least fifty divisions of men, and tied down another fifty to the job of holding those beacheads. Joe would have waited till about a third of England was taken, but before the British Army or Air Force was knocked out, given his moustache an extra tug, and said "Now." In 1940, Hitler had — and had to have — a big force of men tied up in newly occupied countries. He'd have had an extremely badly mauled Army in the west, a depleted reserve in Europe, a holding force in the East — and the Red Army rolling down through East Prussia.

That would probably have been a shorter war, at that. It would certainly have been to Russia's advantage.

The situation was to England's advantage. Hitler never dared to sustain the clawing his Army would have gotten trying to take

50

beacheads in England. The British Lion, like a real lion, was in a position to do some nasty clawing, and land some terrific wallops, though it didn't have any staying power, or the sheer brutal force for crushing action. It takes a bear for that sort of crunching — not slapping — power.

The United States is in a difficult sort of position. It's advantageous and disadvantageous at once. Our factories are practically immune to attack — and they can outproduce the rest of the world put together, once they're organized. (Ever think what would have happened if Hitler had somehow been an American Fuehrer? There would, then, have been no way to prevent world conquest. He would have had a hemisphere to work with as a base and source of supplies before the slightest effective resistance could have been offered, and with that base, Africa would probably have been taken as the next operations base.)

But our immunity-by-distance works against us, too. It's a hell of a job to apply that production power to the necessary points. Also, that immunity has tended to make military and naval establishments so much of a stepchild of American governmental policy that we have a lot to do to get started.

But I'm betting on the American tendency to "figger a way". Like that trick alloy they use in the armor. If the Russians had a decent rail network across Siberia it would help a lot; you can't sink railroad trains, and it's only 5 miles from U.S. to Siberia.

Americans are never, never, never going to understand British imperialism. First, admittedly, is the old fact that — well, you know the story about the definitions of "firm", "stubborn" and "muleish"? I am firm, you are stubborn, he is muleish. Same tendency creeps into any human evaluation. But —

The United States has never wanted to own any non-contiguous real estate. We wanted to get rid of the Phillipines; the Army and Navy saw their value as bases — but we were in process of getting rid of them. Most Americans did not fully realize that the Hawaiian Islands were American territory. I assume they do, now. But you've heard, perhaps, that famous double-talk oration — I've forgotten what comedian does it — about an Isolationist senator? Supposed to be an Isolationist going strong, double-talk of the usual sort with occasional typical isolationist phrases shining through, and winding up with a magnificent, "— but what I wanta know is, what were the Hawaiian Islands doing way out there in the Pacific anyway?" It's a comedian's way of crossing up a not unheard of American little-man's reaction. He — and the Isolationist — would really mean, what were we doing owning real estate way out in the Pacific, anyway.

Since any average-IQ man mistrusts anybody who thinks

differently than he does, there is an inevitable mistrust of anybody that insists on holding on to distant real estate. Since we have, historically, had more frontier than we could readily handle, there's been no dearth of positions for career men, sons of good families, etc. English aristocracy definitely did have a tendency to hold colonial posessions in the fold as an excellent place to station younger sons.

From my point of view, India is right in trying to get freedom now, because in peacetime England isn't so busy she can't devote her whole attention, if need be, to holding on. England is right in refusing it now, because she's too busy to work out practicable measures for simultaneously increasing her military establishment there and relinquishing political control. The answer is to give India a schedule of freedom, to function automatically after the war. But India can't accept that, because she definitely feels that England pulled a stunt like that in the last war — and, once free of that mess, backed down on the promise and restored her full power. It's a complete dilemma, with all roads blocked. But I have a basic feeling that England got herself (and India) into that dilemma by a calculated policy of internal division.

As for distrust of British leaders, both U.S. and Russia have reasons for that. I don't know whether you know about it, but in the last War, British naval and shipping people gave the advice on which our war shipping designs were based. The ships so built were convoy freighters, we found after the war. They were too big for use as tramp steamers — had too great a cargo capacity and engine equipment for economical service. They were too small and too slow for transatlantic shipping trade, too short-range and slow for trans-Pacific work. They rotted for years — till Japan bought them for scrap steel — because of this. The British shipyards were building, at the same time, larger-faster and smaller-slower ships both. Britain retained dominance of the world's merchant marine after the war.

The British leaders were, in the period 1933-1937, in a position to stop Hitler. Before that, they'd been in a position to stop Japan. Our Navy was sailing west of Hawaii with the ships alert for battle operations, expecting surprise attack in 1933. They expected and were ready for war with Japan then. There would have been war then and there, too, if England had stiffened up. Japan would have had its ears slapped down around its knees, Mussolini wouldn't have gotten fancy ideas in Ethiopia, and Hitler would have been a minor nuisance if there had been.

By 1938 of course England had to sell Czechoslovakia down the river — though nobody loved them for it. But Mussolini could have been stopped in the Ethiopian venture.

We don't like imperialism, probably primarily because we don't understand the why of it. And we don't trust British leaders in general, because we're convinced they tend to be wrong, and tend to hornswoggle us and anybody else they get hold of. The latter two points I'm absolutely convinced of. The only difference between my conviction and the general feeling to that effect is that I know damn well it's true — and true of anybody else on Earth, too.

Actually, I think, the American's greatest objection to the Englishman and his ways — concentrated with respect to the English leaders — is the undoubted fact that the English tend to impress people with a twin conviction: that the Englishman feels he is necessarily and inevitably right in all he does, and that he feels any other way whatsoever is silly and amusing. I do not say the man actually feels that; I do say that he has succeeded in convincing a large portion of the world that he feels that.

Oh, yes. Most people don't consciously remember the famous War Debts, but a good many years of conditioning to that thought hangs on. The proposition seems so simple and straight forward — "they hired the money didn't they?" — that a conviction of bad faith hangs on like a pall. Try some time to explain to some IQ 100 man why paying an international debt is any different than paying his debts. Even try it with an Englishman, who has a subconscious willingness, not unwillingness, to understand.

If you succeed, they still want to know why England couldn't sell us some of her real estate in settlement. It rankles deep to feel you've been subtly gypped somehow, and can't quite figure out how it was worked. That's the only feeling you can arouse, if you do convince him an international debt can't be paid with a check on the First National Bank. And he does understand that he has to pay taxes to pay off the National Debt that represents those War Debts.

Ten-fifteen years of that in the background takes considerable eliminating. While it's there, there's a background conviction that you've got to keep a close eye on those English slickers. And one step deeper in the subconscious background is the added comment, "— and maybe we can get even this time." He's human too. And a great and glorious part of the American tradition has to do with hoss-trading, the same being a game without rules or mercy, based on the concept that he who does his fellow man in the eye is smarter — until he gets done. He who gets done is then expected to figure out how the doing was done, improve on it, and do it back. Yeah, Artur Blord is an outgrowth of that purely American tradition. Canada has a common heritage on that, naturally.

I suspect it is not quite understandable to a European that an American could distrust every move a man made and still hold that

53

man as a good friend — just as — a fact I am well aware of — it drives a true German or other European completely bughouse to find it impossible to tell a man's friends from his acquaintances. (The only sure way to tell is that a man is reasonably curteous to acquaintances, and calls only his friends insulting names. Remarkable outgrowth of Western Frontier days.)

I think Americans (U.S. variety) are quite capable of distrusting everything the British leaders do, and still being thoroughly willing to get in and help slug along with them.

My great fear is that Americans are going to continue to distrust *and dislike* the Russians after the war. That will be a world calamity. The United States and Russia, as a team, outweigh any other possible team on Earth. With a three-way partnership of England and the Empire added, the preponderance of power would be so terrific no possible challenge could arise. The United States is apt to have a different and more world-wide angle on things after this war, too. We'll have about as big a stake in Australia as Britain has, for instance. A hell of a lot of American boys are getting married down there, and are going to stay: that's the only kind of stake that will hold American attention. Americans have a reputation for dollar-chasers, of course — as ununderstandable to Europeans as hoss-trading in general. That chase is comparable only to the English fox-hunt; it's a traditional sport, with the result that Americans will not fight as hard for an economic investment as a European would. If he gets beaten on a human stake in a region, the attitude will be different. If we can just get Americans to appreciate Russians as people — they can go right on loathing cheerfully their form of government — there's a real chance for a real peace. Even German militarism would be overawed by a combination of Russian, English and American military power; even the insane Jap militarism would be paralyzed before that deadly combination. There's only one way to keep peace among men; the way a police force does. It is organized on a scale of armed force immensely greater than any gangster group can bring against it, and perfectly ready to jam offenders into jail *right now*, and then investigate whether or not they should be released. The Pax Romana kind of Pax — "Wiggle your ears and you'll get 'em slapped off so fast you'll wonder where they went." — is the one kind that works. But it takes a multilateral enforcement of such a Pax to keep it decently restrained. However, too-multi an enforcement won't work, either. France and democratic Germany were paralyzed that way; they had so many parties nobody could do anything. The two or three party system can be made to work; two-party is best, I honestly believe. A balance of power between three parties means that there will never be a single, decisive, completely responsible party; with two parties, one or the other is always in a position of responsibility-and-authority, of suffocation, not lack of attendance. It takes more than one, so that there is constant restraint — hence the undesirability of the Nazi and Bolshevist one-party systems.

We probably won't have peace, though, till other planets are opened to colonization. Then we'll have peace on earth — and war in heaven!

Regards,   John W. Campbell, Jr.

L. Ron Hubbard   *November 21, 1945*

Dear Ron:

My correspondence is roughly six months behind; **Dona's** is about three and a half months behind. I'm snowed under and have been, by such things as atomic bombs, people wanting me to do books about same, new magazine I'm trying to start, articles I have to do for same because I can't show anybody what I want in the magazine because there's nothing in the magazine till I put it there, doing articles for *Pic* —.

Oh, two or three things have been keeping me hopping.

Meanwhile, everybody, simply everybody, is taking a vacation, including all the authors who were keeping *Astounding* going. **Isaac Asimov's** in the army, now of all times, and the **Kuttner-Padgett-Moore-O'Donell** corporation has moved west for a rest. **Heinlein & Hubbard** are both holding out on me. *Astounding* is in a mell of a hess.

I need — and but bad — stories. Any length. Suggested novelette, for the typer of **L. Ron Hubbard**:

The psychological reaction of a guy who was marooned on an outpost planet when the human forces were overwhelmed by the invaders, and has spent five years listening to alien news broadcasts, hiding from alien soldiers, and wondering what the hell's the use? when the human fleet sails in to take over again. He's got a small model detector, and there are so many pips on its PPI scope, and there's so much stuff visible, that he can't believe it. Where . . . in . . . the, name . . . of, God . . . did . . . all that stuff come from?!?!?! Just don't make his *name* Tweed.

Item: the boys are suggesting that "Final Blackout" referred to the *next* war — not this last one.

Currently, *Unknown* is still a question; it may or may not come back. There's a good chance though, as soon as I can get straightened out from several layers of overburden. I need an assistant, and am having a hell of a time finding someone competent and available.

Your back fantasy, my friend, ain't to be had from *S & S*. We've got the copies in our bound volumes, and we are not parting with 'em. But you can get 'em from **Mr. Julius Unger**, 6401 24th Ave., Brooklyn, N.Y. **Unger's** a fan who makes 2nd hand scf. mags a paying hobby. If you want a Vol. 1, No. 1. *Unk*, you'll pay about $5 for it though.

In the meantime, I'm starting proceedings to make *S & S* disgorge your two bucks; those processes have the speed of a spavined snail.

I can't have a general off-hand note releasing rights to you made out on all the stories you did for us — but *S & S* will make assignments, on request, for any particular stories. Currently, as **Bob Heinlein's** probably told you, we're sort of renting out book rights in anthologies for 1/2¢ a word for 6 months exclusive. Several of the yarns have been so rented; when the final papers go through, **Bob** should be in receipt of a fair hunk of change.

Dona and family are doing fine; **Dona**, in particular, has improved markedly since she had a vacation. She had a noble case of Grade A jitters. **Leslyn**, the smallest fry you've never seen, is our angel child — she'll try to smile even when she's suffering from a nasty cold, the only baby I've ever seen go that far to try to be pleasant. She resents being ignored, but instead of crying about it, starts gurgling and laughing so uproariously you have to pay attention. If she keeps that attitude through life, she's bound to be a success.

Peeds is as usual, only more so. Instead of oscillating at about one cycle an instant, she's up to at least 1.5, now that her legs are a bit longer, and she has — with school teaching her things — so many more ideas to carry out simultaneously.

I've been electronicking along as usual, with some marked improvements in technique and accomplishment. I've got an automatic record changer that I really went to town on. I got a high-grade, broadcast-station quality crystal pick-up, buggered the output with filters, resister-condenser type, until the damn thing lay down on its back and obeyed orders. It's flat, plus or minus 1.5 db, from 10,000 to 50 cycles. The amplifier, rebuilt, improved, and enlarged, is flat from 30 to 12,000 plus or minus 0.3 db, with 15 watts output, and plus or minus 1 db from 30 to 11,000 cycles at 22 watts output. No distortion detectable on the scope at 22 watts; 5% distortion at 34 watts.

I have also given up making radio receivers; the mechanical problems are beyond the home workshop. I bought a Hammarlund "Super-Pro", on the assurance of several knowledgeable people that that was the best there was. It does tricks. One reason I wanted it was that I'm particularly anxious to get the

Moscow English broadcasts, and all the other foreign broadcasts in English that I can. I think it's an excellent idea to know what's being said, and our papers can't report it all.

Incidentally, I hope to God Russia takes over all of Europe — particularly Czechoslovakia and Belgium. I'm not afraid of Russia with an atomic bomb; Russia wants only one thing — peace and time to develop. I am scared to blazes that Czechoslovakia, where they have everything necessary to make one, will get one. Boy, do those Czechs hate the Poles, Magyars, Germans, Yugos, Italians, Swiss, French, English, Russians, Greeks, Bulgars, Romanians, Slavs, and including the Scandinavian. The Belgians, on the other hand, have all the needed facilities, and hate only the Germans, French, Dutch, and English, with a mild dislike of Russians, Danes, and Poles.

And just try scaring a Belgian by telling him his city might be devastated in an atomic war! Like trying to scare an Egyptian peasant with a threat that the land might be flooded.

There's plenty of room for stories about the young men of the United Nations Atomic Inspection Service — Russians and Americans and English and Dutch — keeping tabs on atomic work. The danger of such an organization is that those young men will inevitably get a truly international world picture a generation ahead of the rest of the world, and have a tendency to live in a cultural pattern of their own, apart from ours — tend to view themselves as the Chosen People whose God-given task is to lead — i.e., drive — the world into the right path.

Ask **Bob** what he thinks would be the result of an enforced U.N.O. order that between Jan. 1, 1947 and June 1, 1947, a new international currency, based on a new unit, the *terra*, would be co-valid with national currencies at a fixed rate, but that, after June 1, no national currency of any kind would be valid. Just that and no other economic regulations. Would tarrifs be able to continue?

Science fiction better get stepping if it wants to lead the world!

Regards,   John

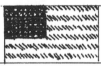

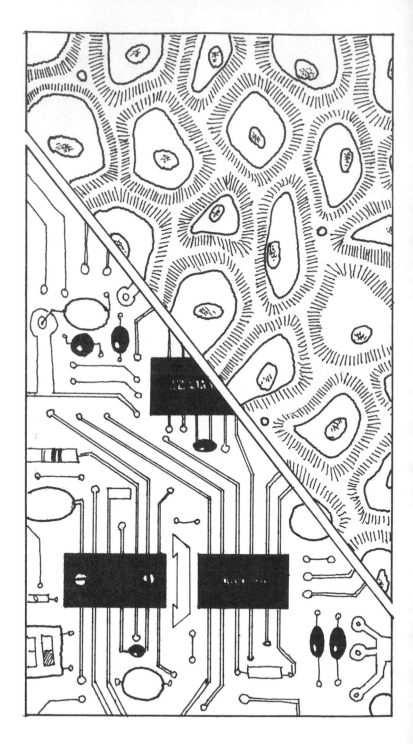

58

The 1950's

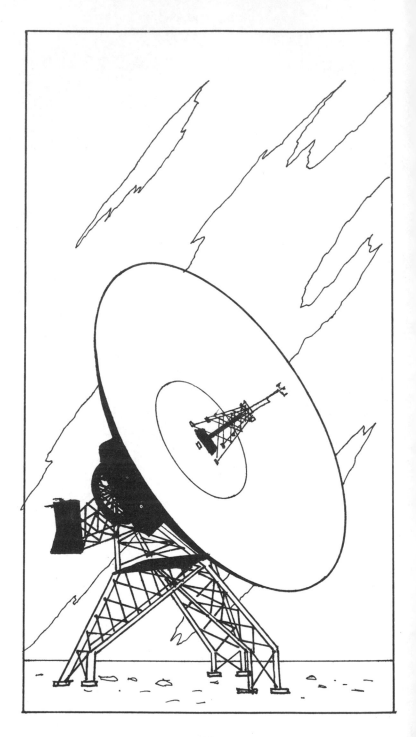

James G. Cooper, III   *February 8, 1951*

Dear Mr. Cooper:

The reaction to "The Hand of Zei" was by no means uniform. Some, like yourself, condemned it heavily; many others reported it as best in its issues. With respect to material of this type, there is only one way an editor can find out whether his readers enjoy it or not and that is to present it to get their reactions directly. The general reaction has been that "The Hand of Zei" represents a type of story our readers do not particularly favor.

But I had no way of being sure until I had actually tried it and given them the opportunity to comment.

In introducing *Dianetics*™ to *Astounding Science Fiction* I was doing two things. First, *Astounding Science Fiction* has long tried to spot at the laboratory stage the technical forces which will over the next decade or so have marked influence on the course of man's development. The article on *Dianetics* was published with that thought in mind. It was not published until I had personally investigated the practical results of *Dianetics* for over a year.

No one who has studied and observed *Dianetics* over a period of months has failed to agree that **Hubbard** has the entering wedge of an enormously important new approach to man's greatest problem: the understanding of his own mind. There is now available at the *Hubbard Dianetic Research Foundation*, P.O. Box 502, Elizabeth, New Jersey, a little booklet of case histories showing psychosomatic changes produced by *Dianetics* and showing the medical effects resulting from reduction of engrams and locks.

There's a lot of opposition to *Dianetics*, but none of it comes on the only admissible scientific basis of "I tried **Hubbard's** technique for six months on a dozen cases and obtained no results or equivocable results." Actually, all opposition has been based on the proposition: "Your theory disagrees with my theory and you must be wrong." People have argued on such data for thousands of years with no satisfactory results. We don't argue that way. Try it and see.

Sincerely,   John W. Campbell, Jr.

William Rotsler   *February 8, 1951*

Dear Mr. Rotsler:

I think it best that I, as a professional editor, refrain from speaking as the professional author might on the subject of "Wish I had written that." The editor is in a somewhat different position. And such a discussion on my part might tend to indicate a degree of favoritism, so I will decline your offer of this opportunity. There are a lot of stories I wish I had written — some of **Heinlein's,** some of **Kuttner's**, some of **Van Vogt's** and one by **Robert Willy** — each for a different reason. The only thing I can do in justice and fairness is refrain from a public statement.

Sincerely,   John W. Campbell, Jr.

L. Sprague de Camp   *February 28, 1951*

Dear de Camp:

Your article on mad genie is one hundred per cent fine business stuff. Very good job indeed. And you are, incidentally, getting our new 3¢ rate on it.

One of the items that delayed the return of your "Glory That Was" was that **Miss Tarrant** was swamped under the responses on our small, retiring mention that we had a few back copies. (Telegraph money order demands for $75.00 worth at a clip. Air Mail Special Delivery checks, with long-distance telephone calls to nail down the copies.) She was working till 10:00 P.M. trying to get unsnowedunder.

The change in buying policy is very easily explained. We do not want to buy Pocket Book rights; it is not our intent to control pocket books. The Pocket Book is now recognized by the public as a legitimate separate channel of distribution, and as such we're willing to co-operate.

But what **H. L. God** [sic] calls a "pocket book" is a magazine, and he's been using Second Serial Rights, in effect, without our permission by calling it a "pocket book," which it isn't. Further, instead of paying royalties, like the legitimate pocket book outfits, he makes a flat payment. A legitimate pocket book I find pays between $1500 and $2500 in royalties; he pays $500, which is less than we pay for a novel, by a long shot.

I don't mind competition; it helps the field. But I have a very deep resentment when some guy starts a magazine and tries to make his reputation not by using stories *like* those I helped build up, but by using the stories that I worked on. That I consider with an extremely jaundiced eye. I don't mind a competitor who sets out to imitate my magazine (he's actually ruining himself thereby; a mimic necessarily puts himself in second place) but I intend to take all possible measure to stop a bird who starts using Second Serial Rights by calling his magazine a book. If you've got a pocket book sale, and not a Second Serial Rights sale, fine. **Gold's** recent bleat about how we swindled the poor author didn't appeal to **Harry Stubbs** or **Eric Frank Russell**. **Eric** was boiling mad; he got only a pared down cut of $500.00 for "Sinister Barrier." The actual rates

God [sic] pays weren't so freely mentioned in his virtuous editorial. He's actually paying regular 1¢ rates for Second Serial Rights.

It's a nice deal from his view; he's beating the magazine competition by saving nearly $1000 on manuscript costs by using in effect Second Serial Rights. And he's beating the pocket books by saving $1000 to $2000 by not paying royalties.

I'm not accustomed to dealing that way, and I'm going to block his tendency to do so in any way I can. At least, by blocking him from getting "Needle" I made him buy an honest First Serial Rights!

Anyhow, what we're really buying is *All* serial rights, including the **Gold** version of Second Serial Rights.

Regards, John

Nelson S. Bond   *May 25, 1951*

Dear Nels:

I was quite well pleased with the movie "The Thing"; it definitely wasn't "Who Goes There." It was a good movie done with considerably more sincerity than most science fiction pieces have been. The boys who did it were all making a genuine effort to produce a good picture and I think they may be right in feeling that the proposition in "Who Goes There" is a little strong if presented literally in the screen.

I am glad you have been having good results from your dianetics and getting real psychosomatic relief. I have been in dianetics now for about two years with some twenty-five hundred hours of processing and research. As you go along, **Nels** you will find that dianetics leads far deeper into the problems of humanity than **Hubbard** or anyone else suspected. **Hubbardian** dianetics asks the question "What happened?" You have progressed far enough in dianetics now to shift your emphasis to "Why did you believe that?" Engrams are important because they serve as false sources of motivation — but if they are the false motivations what are the true motivations? These are the true basic questions which must be answered and understood.

Dianetics, per se, makes no effort to attack that problem and it must be attacked and solved for complete self understanding.

The Foundation has pretty well dissolved at this point, but the necessary function has been served. The understanding of dianetic technique is now widespread and many hundred sincerely competent men are at work developing it. If you do get up in June or July, by all means contact me and I'll see that we have an opportunity to discuss everything from dianetics to the latest in science fiction.

Sincerely, John

Edd Cartier *June 21, 1951*

Dear Edd:

I wish you would make a heading for our book review department.

Here's what I had in mind:

Title: "The Reference Library"

Drawing: A library bookshelf with a man and a woman in the foreground; down at the end of the bookshelf something that isn't quite human — not just something that's really weird, but something you take a second look at and realize it isn't human.

Size: About one third of a page deep.

Sincerely, John W. Campbell, Jr.

Jesse Charney *October 4, 1951*

Dear Charney:

I'm returning "The Captives" for two reasons. Number One reason is a very simple one; inventory's too big. Number two reason is decidedly more complex.

Send the yarn in again in about three or four months; it's a good yarn, a good idea, and a nice presentation. But there's a change I'd genuinely like to have you make.

The major errors of psychoanalysis are very clearly expressed in this story; what you have clearly stated concerning the impact of one culture on another is precisely applicable to a human individual. A new cultural (individual philosophy) orientation can not be imposed from without successfully. It leads to breakdown. If, by authoritarian-power methods, a culture is *made* to behave according to another's opinions, it disintegrates, and becomes a pale, unambitious imitation of the forcing culture.

If an individual is forced to accept the concepts of another individual, he will be a broken man. If the psychoanalyst ever succeeded in forcing a patient to accept his psychoanalytic opinions, the patient would be a well-adjusted person — like a well adjusted machine, which can carry out the little pattern it's been adjusted to.

As in straightening out the neurotic cultures, forces *within the individual* must be realigned so that the individual straightens himself out. It's been a heartbreaking task; the analyst can see so clearly what the errors of the patient are — and that is so utterly useless. The analyst can point out those errors, and if the patient does accept the analyst's instructions, and follows his corrective suggestions, those specific errors will be corrected. But the forces that lead him to make the errors remain, and he will, under new circumstances, make new errors, based on old misconceptions.

Pennington tells Lloyd what's the matter with him. It's precisely as though Lloyd told one of the neurotic planets what was wrong with it. In the words of the old song, "It ain't whatcha do, it's the way thatcha do it." If Pennington is *really* successful, Lloyd can tell Pennington what *was* wrong with him — as a wondrous self-discovery Lloyd has made. (You're quite right in the comment you made about that)! If Pennington has to tell Lloyd, Lloyd's just as fouled up emotionally as ever — only a little more so, because he will now have an added internal conflict. The conflict of intellectual realization of the validity of Pennington's remarks, versus the still unchanged (because un-self-admitted) emotional conflict. When, *and only when*, Lloyd tells Pennington, the conflict will be resolved. When Lloyd can go through the emotional confusion inherent in resolving the problem, swivel around mentally sixteen times a second for a minute or two, then laugh — real, deep, honest belly-laugh — at his own foolish self-importance, he will be able to proceed happily to straighten out that silly little contretemps.

Incidentally, have you ever considered what a magaificent social adjustment an incipient-psychotic paranoid can make by simply becoming a Security Officer? Or by becoming an attendent in the homicidal ward of an institution for the insane? The paranoid is so convinced *somebody's* trying to do him in and has a terrible time allocating it. But as a Security Officer. . . !

Regards,   John

Jack Williamson *April 25, 1952*

Dear Williamson:

Once upon a time, you did a story about a robot horde that menaced man by doing all his work for him. Maybe you could do a job playing with a different story attack on that problem. If the ideas appeal, let me know; if not, or if you're too busy now, let me know and I'll try it on someone else.

Suppose somebody decides war is bad business, but not too bad so long as we don't do it in the present super-powered way. So they develop a new kind of war-machine, a new kind of robot.

This robot is small — but it's living, in the sense that it can reproduce itself, avoid destruction, and is self-repairing within limits. Actually, it consists of a robot ant hill, with robots a few inches long as its worker ants.

And they're parasites. But they parasitize industry, and industry only. They steal metal, and small quantities of plastic. They can build self-duplicates, in an ant hill sort of place, where a robot-maker and robot-servicer are hidden, supplied and fed and serviced by worker-robots.

They can't melt metals from ores, but they can and do attack metallic structures, and use them for construction of more robots.

The result of their built-in urge to make more robots without limit is devastating. They won't harm a human being, of course, or any animal. But they'll take gold, silver and copper for conductors, and steel and aluminum for construction.

They're immortal, of course, because they can simply shut down for an indefinite period if there isn't any metal to gather.

So men can live happily and without trouble — provided they don't try to use metals.

The idea of turning loose such a plague is nonsensical, as crackpot as the robots in the "Humanoids." The problem is someone *has* turned them loose, and they've created a situation which has to be solved. The solution, however, could be any of a number of things. One being to teach them how to melt from ores, and then periodically raiding their nests for supplies of metal! Another answer would be "lesser bugs to bite 'em," or producing an unnatural enemy of the same order.

But I think there's fun in the idea!

Regards,   John

Robert Moore Williams   *August 14, 1952*

Dear Bob:

This is a good yarn, I want it. I'm sending it back for some minor changes, if you agree with me. As you may know, I don't believe in changing a man's story; he made it, and it's his, and editing changes are for him to make or it wouldn't remain his story.

A good many years back, you started selling yarns that had a lot of "mood," and they went pretty well. They were in a way, rather like the Gothic horror story the "Fall of the House of Usher" sort of thing, built up with *Roget's Theasaurus*, and various sources of adjectives. **Lovecraft** did the same kind. I did some of 'em myself. As of the time and the slant of the field, they were right.

That was a dozen years ago, and the field's changed far and fast since then. We're older, too, you and I and we've got to change with the change.

In this story, you have, 95% of the way through. But some of the older style still lingers — and to the extent the adjectivies,or *Roget's* Disease, lingers, the whole is weakened.

The best writing is simple, clear, highly definite, and has the general characteristics of a fishnet. Each string is separate, clearly related to each other, cleanly fixed, and cross-connected by clearly defined cross-cords. It's very effective in netting the reader's attention and his sympathy.

The older style, the yarn suffering from *Roget's* Disease, can also trap someone, much as you can get all fouled up in a snarl or yards and yards of string. The thing has no definite structure, no clear connections, but can be very effective in trapping the mind.

This yarn here is good, because the threads and cross-cords are fairly clear-cut. But it does show touches of the older style.

It's worth noting that some of the most powerfully moving statements men have ever made have been very brief, but very, very clear and keenly defined. "Sighted sub; sank same." "Praise the Lord — and pass the ammunition." "Fourscore and seven years ago, our fathers brought forth on this continent. . . ." "Gold and silver have I none, yet such as I have I give thee."

Words never have conveyed emotion, and never will. The feelings do not lie within the lines — but between them. Therefore, make the lines clear cut and clean, and leave plenty of room between the lines for large emotions. You don't fish for minnows when you use a net woven of a 1/2 inch nylon cord with a 2″ square mesh.

Since the emotion is going to lie between the lines the needs for the most powerful and moving stories are not as easy to meet as the needs of a story for minnow size emotions.

Regards,   John

Enc.: "Peach Blossoms Blowing By the Dark Canals"

Will F. Jenkins   *August 25, 1952*

Dear Will:

I've got an Idea that would, I think, make a lovely story. The only trouble is that it takes an extremely deft touch to handle the thing. Maybe you'd like to play with it, and I hope you would. You're the only one I know of who could do it; as I see it, it would be somewhat similar, in tenor and mood, to that "Historical Note" item you did.

The idea, essentially, would be this: Nature will, you know, answer any question anyone asks. Nature has no race, political, or religious biases, so far as anyone has detected to date. Further, Nature invariably answers the question correctly.

Now let's imagine that Nature can be communicated with directly. For our story, we have a nature-talker machine invented, whereby a direct wire to Nature can be set up. Only we won't refer to Nature as such.

You teletype into the machine any questions, any problems, and immediately get the answer. Naturally, military defense takes over the teletyper. There is a certain amount of confusion, because the answer is always exactly correct for exactly the question you ask, but you may be asking a question other than the one you think you are. For instance, if a chemist in the old days has asked something about "phlogiston" he'd have gotten the correct answer to what he actually meant, which wouldn't have been what he thought he was getting.

In other words, the only limitation on the teletyper is that you must know exactly what you're asking.

Some limitation is clearly necessary, or the story goes haywire.

The essence of the thing is that, naturally, the Russians get plans of the machine, and they, too start asking questions. Nature had to be taught to answer questions in English, of course; somebody suddenly discovers that Nature talks Russian, now, too.

The repercussions of Security are wonderful at that point naturally.

But then Nature responds with a neat detail of how-to-do-it with some remark that "as tried out at Borschtograd" and given freely and without stint of Russia's most secret work. Nature's most useful as a computing machine, outstripping the best electronic devices by six orders of magnitude, everybody's feeding their secret weapons figures into the teletypers for answers.

I think it would be rather wonderful the way Security tempers would rise. The howls of anguish when it was discovered that Nature wouldn't keep a secret. Tsk, Tsk. Ain't it awful.

I think we could have fun and hilarity with this item. The "teletyper" is, of course, the poor physical scientist. But in this guise the problem of what to do about science would suddenly loom somewhat different!

Regards,   John

Eric Frank Russell   *October 1, 1952*

Dear Eric:

First off, let's get the business of **Mark Clifton's** story straightened away, as to why it's what I want.

I'm trying to introduce the proposition of sciences beyond those currently known and accepted.

But **Eric** PLEASE believe me; **Charles Fort** made a mistake. The error was his. He *insisted* that the scientists understand him when he explained it all to them in Swahili. He even repeated it in Hindustani, and still the dolts wouldn't listen to him. The one thing he didn't try was to explain it in their stupid old language; it was obviously up to them to learn *his* language, because he had something important to say.

So his words weren't actually Swahili or Hindustani; they were just as remote from the language the scientists speak. The words of a high Episcopal prayer are English also, but they still do *not* constitute proper form of expression for publication, as a communication of intelligence, in the *Physical Review*.

Also, **Fort** began screaming at the scientists, and calling them names. Now if a man starts screaming at you, and calling you and your company names, your first reaction is, I imagine, that the gentleman has a psychological problem. As a matter of good business, in your line of work, you'll attempt to placate him, sooth him, calm him down, and get intelligence out of him. Difficult — sometimes impossible — but it usually can be done.

I have an idea on how to build a nuclear reactor that will be a power producing breeder reactor, giving 98% or better utilization of neutrons. Very simple design too. I should, then, go down to the AEC office and demand that they listen to me, and scream names at them, pointing out that they are dolts, imbeciles, and dishonest, unwilling to listen to a really brilliant intellect?

Fort refused to take the trouble to translate his observations into coherent language — language of science. He made the mistake. If you have something to say, it's up to *you* to say it right. I have hundreds of letters every year saying "I have a wonderful idea for a story; it just needs to be written up. I'd like to get in touch with someone who can write it down, and we can share the proceeds on a 50-50 basis."

If you feel that merely pointing out that something exists constitutes half or more of the work, I'll gladly put you in touch with a few score people who'd be happy to point out that something exists and you can "write it down" for them.

Look, **Eric**: Maybe Copernicus and astrophysics are all wrong. Suppose, just for the sake of the argument, that they're right.

Then: The stars and planets have been visible from Earth for some 1000 million years. (Assuming it took the first 2000 million to develop eyes that could see them.) The stars were pointed out long, long before villages existed. The moon was pointed out before that. There's the data; look at it. Anybody with a single eye can see it.

After many, many millenia of hard thinking, people finally worked out a scheme of interrelating the obervations to a point where they made intelligible sense. And now some ages-gone caveman can say "Ugh. The dumb fools. I told 'em stars were things to look at. Important. Dumb bastards should of done it when I said so."

There are three steps to making a real authority:
1. He must be able to communicate to another mind, the understanding he has in his mind.
2. He must be able to think clearly and cogently, manipulating his data honestly and usefully.
3. He must have data to manipulate.

The British Museum has more data than any single human being who ever lived. That makes it smart?

The mystic who thinks things through and gets an answer that works is smart; since he can't communicate it, however, he doesn't benefit mankind much.

It counts when you can reach an understanding that is valid, and communicate that understanding to others.

Fort couldn't. He did it wrong. He angered the best thinkers, the clearest, straightest-thinking minds who could have helped most. His writings appealed largely to muzzy-minded people who went in for fortune-telling, crystal-ball readings, and the like; they were the bulk of his audience.

Fort's attitude was just as ineffective as **Hubbard's**; **Hubbard** angered the psychiatrists by his belligerence. True; he may well have had reason for being angry at them — but it didn't get him anywhere to make them refuse to listen to him for two reasons instead of for one, did it?

Now: The scientists today will *not* accept psionic phenomena as valid data. They won't fit anywhere in his universe, and his picture of things is, as it stands, fairly coherent and integrated. (The psionic effects actually belong at a level below the sub-nuclear; physical science simply was *not* ready to study them when **Fort** was yammering so insistently. It was like somebody yammering at a kid in school, who's just learned his multiplication tables, that he should immediately start studying differential equations. The kid is apt to rebel.)

Since they won't fit into his cosmology, he can ignore them while he busily does some damned useful things with what he has. **Fort** was insisting that someone else do the work of integrating them, and refusing to organize and interpret the data into intelligible stuff himself. For that, **Fort** should have been shown the door. He was too lazy to do the hard work; he wanted it done for him, and was very petulant because no one would. It was too damned much of a case of "Let's you and him have a fight, huh?"

His data was valid. It contained important understandings, and important clues. In that, he was right. But why didn't *he* do some of the hard work of integrating it and finding the pattern, instead of frothing about how everyone else wouldn't do that work?

For your information, **Peg** and I have done it, We have the basic understanding of what the psionic functions are, and how they work. It took us over two years of damned hard work. The reason why I'm now starting it in the magazine is that I do have some integrated understanding of what we're dealing with. I'm not yet ready to say a damned thing about it, either, because I recognize that **Fort** *was* wrong, and why he was wrong, and what the right answer is. Until I can demonstrate the phenomena myself, and communicate the exact nature of the mechanisms involved, with demonstrations of each step, I'm not ready to talk. When I've done that, though, by God the physical scientists *will* gladly pitch in and help. I know the general concept of teleportation, levitation, and a few other spontaneous psi phenomena — also telekenesis, etc. In addition, I know the general basic laws which can permit precognition, and an absolute barrier of pure force that will block passage of *any* force now known to physical science. The fundamental clues are to be found in many places; among the places are the sort of data **Fort** collected — but was too stinking lazy to dig into and integrate himself.

I am not kidding.

I am not cracked, either.

Those forces are real, and I have a theory of their structure. I haven't developed methods of setting up an experiment however, and until I can demonstrate it at an experimental level, it simply doesn't count. I've only progressed as far as the theory level. This is for your private information and to let you know part of the reason for the attitude I am now adopting.

I have a hunch that **Fort** was scared blue with pink polka-dots of getting anywhere near those forces; he probably contacted some of it accidently during early childhood, got smacked down by it, and wouldn't ever go near it again himself. Those forces lie beneath the sub-nuclear particles; uranium fission is a gentle release of a side-swipe of a minor readjustment of those forces. Get careless, or frisky with them, and you'll get your come-*way*-uppance.

So. The principle point is this; the *Fortean* approach was invalid, because it demanded that somebody else do the work. To hell with that; roll up your sleeves, if you think its important, and git in and pitch.

The approach I'm planning on is entirely different. It's based on a fundamental law of life: Do not waste energy on an unproductive task. It's corollary is that if a task promises adquate reward, it's worth attempting.

Fort didn't point out the rewards; he pointed out the task. "What's in it for me?" is a valid question. What reward does this task promise, and what's the probability of earning that reward?

So; the first step toward getting interest in psionics started is to establish *that there is a reward to be earned.*

Now since, at the present time, people don't want to learn about psionics, there's still an earlier task facing us, if we want to get them to learn. We have to estabilish that learning about them has an adequate reward.

So how do we do that?

We have a very amusing story about a plant psychologist all tangled up with a bunch of psionic operatives. Reward for considering, for the moment, that psionics might be real: amusement.

Reward for repeatedly considering — and discussing — the possibilities and possible useful applications of psionics: more amusement.

Reward for considering that psionic forces are real, and actually constitute a level of forces below the sub-nucleonic; amusement, plus a hint of satisfying, yet intriguing, possibility.

Reward for getting hold of the idea and actually accepting it; anti-gravity; teleportation, which makes the concept distance and velocity alike meaningless; psychokinesis; absolute physical health, and death only when and as chosen as a conscious desire.

But do not mention those last rewards. Makes it look too much like a gold-brick. The rewards to mention are the little things, the just-over-the-edge-of-the-known items like anti-gravity.

O.K. we are advancing at a creep instead of a march. When you're climbing a vertical cliff, trying to rise from one level to the next higher, you creep if you want to get anywhere.

Want to creep along with us?

I've been looking into my own aberrations right along. One I found the other night will, I'm sure, interest you. I have been consistently refusing to see the undesirable and unpleasant in people. I've idealized and gilded people, at the conscious level. I'm going to have to do a lot of reevaluating of people, in consequence, and I have already changed a number of opinions in some degree.

Some evidence, however, is lacking; I'm not sure whether it is possible to take a normal intelligence and raise it; I am sure that it is possible to take any normal human intelligence and raise it — if the guy wants to take the trouble to do it for himself.

You know that psychosomatron story idea I sent? That's the problem; it means changing your entire personality, and being not the man you are, but the man-you-could-develop-into. Some of the characteristics of that man-you-could-be are anathema to the man-you-are. The essential problem will be whether an individual is *willing* to choose to work — and brother, it's the hardest work there is! To become his maximun possible self.

The brain, as it is, is not perfect — but has the inherent capability of perfecting itself. It's like a servo mechanism that, when started up is way off zero, but has built into it such characteristics that, no matter where it starts, it's capable of adjusting itself to zero. The mind has that characteristic.

Essentially, it achieves it by a recycling process, and the method of successive approximations. The actual logical thinking is *not* done by the brain, it's done by a psionic structure, of pure force. It's instantaneous in action, and complex enough to handle a billion equations in a billion unknowns in a microsecond. The consequence is that an immense number of recyclings can be done in a very short time; the successive approximations can get very close indeed to exact data fact — *provided* no blocks have been nailed down solid. If you have a nailed-down, riveted home, and capped in place proposition that Sex is Nasty, and Thinking about Sex is also Nasty, you can then think very consciously and rationally that sex is *not* nasty — but the psionic computers still have the postulate that sex is nasty, and they won't touch the problem. One consequence of that is that when the Victorian orientation moved out, couples found they were sleeping three in a bed; the woman, the man, and the psychiatrist's ghost, lecturing them both, very consciously, on how they should engage in intercourse.

This intereferes with conjugal bliss.

Eventually we'll get the psychiatrist's ghosts out of our bedrooms again, I imagine. It used to be the priest's ghost, back in the days when the Church taught that the ideal was chastity though married.

But once you pull the false postulate out — really get it out — the automatic computers start recycling all problems involving that concept. And lordeee! Do they run the stuff in a hurry.

I recognize different levels of competence in human beings. But the inherent self-perfection capability is also there; I don't yet know, but suspect, that the ability actually leads to a self-expanding system that allows any mind over a certain level to become whatever it chooses to become.

And it's not necessary to use surgery to cure a twisted mind; a mind can be twisted by actual brain damage, but most twists are caused by a far simpler, and more basic thing — a false idea.

Take this one; A lot of people hold that if you are happy, it means you're not being ethical, but are yielding to your own pleasure drives. This makes "being unhappy" equal to "being ethical." Such a twist makes a man impose unhappiness on himself, and that inevitably include his wife and children, his employees and his friends. He will make them unhappy for the good of their souls, so they too, can have the satisfaction of being ethical.

Now there's nothing wrong with his *brain* his only trouble is that he has the false postulate that it is essential to be unhappy. Many people judge the state of their ethics, and how well they are following them, by how unhappy they are making themselves. This type is the long-suffering-patient-man, type.

But there isn't a thing wrong with his brain, and surgery is totally unnecessary. It is only necessary for him to find out what in God's name ever gave him that cockeyed idea? It certainly isn't sense, but he has never checked on himself deeply to see just how he does determine whether a thing is ethical or not. It's apt to shock him when he finds out!

On problem solving:

There are two general motivations people display for solving problems:

1. To keep from being hurt.
2. To achieve pleasure.

A human being who operates on the avoid-pain drive is not enjoying life adequately. Something's bothering him severely, and he hasn't located it.

The right answer is to enjoy problems, and solve them *for reward of satisfaction*.

Both **Peg** and I had that aberration; I think nearly everyone in our civilization operates on the avoid-pain drive. To keep from starving. To avoid loss of my honor. To pay off the mortgage.

Too little "To see what's beyond the hill. To find out why it works that way. To see if I can make the darned thing work. Just for the hell of it."

It has made an enormous difference to us since we cracked that aberration. I *was* doing the work involved in straightening out my mind in order to be able to handle life. To escape the feeling of incompetence and stupidity. I *am* doing it because nothing I ever tackled before had anywhere near the zest, the high, fine sense of discovery and accomplishment that this has. It's the damndest adventure anyone ever tried — and it's available as near as the nearest quiet room, where there is a fully sympathetic and understanding co-adventurer.

You might try looking and seeing if maybe someone hasn't planted on you, very solidly, the idea that solving problems is a *you must or else* proposition.

In any case, I can assure you — it's a damned lie. You don't have to solve problems — but there's no satisfaction like that that comes from a nicely cracked problem, as the pieces go trickling down into the appropriate mental files.

Regards, John

Dear Harry:

I've just filled out the voucher on "Mission of Gravity." It is the second story I have bought under our new bonus-rate system; 85,000 words at 4¢ figures to $3,400.00 — and I feel this yarn is one of the finest pieces of science-fiction that's been written. And as you may know, my personal opinion is that science-fiction is a very genuinely important field of human development.

You've been doing a marvelous job with the handling of totally alien viewpoints; it's *not* the physical situation that you've actually been working with, but the viewpoint of an intelligent mind that has made your stories in each case. Both "Needle" and "Iceworld" for instance, used the normal, terrestrial environment as their millieu; the strange and terrible world you have in this one is made important only by the intergity of viewpoint you've maintained with Barl.

As you know, **Peg** and I have been trying to understand what intelligence and mind, and the fundamental nature of thought is; some while back we came to the realization that the fact people have two eyes is very important — and that we must, equally, have two minds at work for basically the same reason.

You can't achieve depth-perception with a single viewpoint.

A single viewpoint will produce some peculiar results, unless the most elaborate efforts are made to circumvent its limitations.

Consider this question: Does the Southern Cross exist?

The answer is, necessarily, both "Yes" and "No"; the reality of the Southern Cross can be demonstrated with photographs. Its reality can be demonstrated by the fact that an interstellar navigator could use its reality as a guide-mark in his work. He might say "If you can see the Southern Cross, and the Great Dipper, and . . . , *then* you are in the vicinity of Sol." The Southern Cross, then, has a real existence.

But in a scale model of the Galaxy, no stars would be found which are in the relationship of the Southern Cross.

The only adequate statement of the total situation, then, is that there do-in-fact exist *two* types of absolute realities — a view-reality, or viewpoint reality, and an ab-reality, a reality which can be ascertained *only* by integrating many different view-realities.

Each view-reality is itself a geniune and indisputable *reality;* it has purpose and effect and produces manifestations that can be detected physically.

It follows that no adequate understanding of Totality can be obtained from a single viewpoint.

It also explains the difference between "subjective" and "objective" reality.

Claude Shannon's mathematical analysis of Information Theory has shown that no *true* smooth curve can exist in fact; a smooth curve implies that an infinity of knowledge exists between any two points on the curve — while this is never the case in fact.

One of the aspects that comes out of his work is that the aperture of a lens determines the quantity of information actually available in the image produced, and that the bandwidth of a communication also determines the information available.

More accurately, bandwidth times time-of-continuation gives the information actually transmitted.

Hmmm — pardon if this sounds like rambling jottings; it isn't. I have a point to make, and am trying to assemble the factors leading to it.

"Aperture" of the lens can be compared to time-span-of-study. The "aperture" of a 1-year-old baby is not adequate to supply the degree of discrimination necessary for understanding the world. The "aperture" of an adult is better.

But — the aperture must not be a distorted lens, nor may it be a non-functioning (dirty) lens if it is to actually transmit the maximum information possible to a lens of the given aperture.

Equally, the individual's actual information-available is a function of his clarity of thought (non-distortion), his acuity of observation (no clouding of the lens) and his time-aperture.

Now imagine that there was a nation, a culture, that grew up on Hawaii, and were great at mathematics and philosophy, and lousy as explorers. They develop a high science of astronomy, and make large telescopes, and very accurate observations of the planets. They determine the distances of the planets from the Sun with high precision in terms of Astronomical Units.

Meanwhile, on Cuba, we'll say, another civilization does the same thing.

Then they both discover radio, and get in touch with each other thusly.

Now both cultures have the accurate observations necessary to start figuring out the distances of the planets in miles — but while they are aware of each other, and know that they have two viewpoints, and that these two viewpoints will allow determining the value of 1 A.U. in miles — they do *not* know the distance between their two viewpoints, So they are no better off than before.

Item: One of the major flaws of human civilizations is that it is generally admitted that men and women are different, and have different viewpoints. (It's not so generally admitted, but is actually true, that there is a basic difference in method of thinking between men and women.) The flaw arises from the fact that the *measure* of that difference has never been determined. Under those circumstance, the *fact* of that difference of viewpoint cannot be used to advantage.

You have a wife, now, who has an intelligence as great as yours, a power of personality — determination, honesty of thought, etc. — equal to yours. But the maximum results of you-two-as-a-team can be attained *only* when you two *do think differently*. The "binocular viewpoint" can provide both of you with a depth of understanding that neither of you has.

Mankind's gotten himself loused up by failure to recognize that difference of viewpoint must exist for best penetration of the Universe — but that the difference must be acknowledged, and measured.

Barl would have a depth of philosophical understanding that no human scientist has; he would be able to span a range of viewpoints from 700G down to 3G.

In the magnificently meticulous description of his experience in this yarn, you've expanded your own "aperture" and that of the reader. That's part of what makes it a hell of a good yarn.

And incidentally, your characterization of Barl and Don were both excellent.

I don't know what else you have in mind, what new novels, but you're one man who should stick to novels. Only in this length can the meticulous development be achieved — and only so can the effect be achieved.

One thing I do want you to do though: We'll need synopses, naturally, and I suggest that it would be extremely valuable and interesting if you'd do an article for us, describing the working out of the planet — tell us what your astrophysical problems were, and what you considered and rejected, and how you came to this set of conditions. Then describe the conditions you finally selected in considerable detail. True, the reader can pick them up by inductive thinking, but I, for one, would like to see if I've got the thing all straight.

The Coriolis force on the Planet (I can't recall the spelling of the name you gave it!) would be something rather potent. The equatorial velocity I get is nearly 300 miles a second!

I'm a little confused on the business of the gliders, by the way; there's one sentence to the effect that the atmosphere is less dense than Earth's, but you specify 8 atmospheres pressure. That is true only in the sense that, if it's pure, or nearly pure, hydrogen, with a molecular weight about 29. But the situation isn't too readily understood on a one-sentence explanation. Am I correct in my interpretation?

How about the viscosity, which would have a vast effect on the weather, as well as on the gliders.

One item I'm afraid may be open to kicks; the nature of the wood of the *Bree,* and of the tissues of Barl & Co. You make the valid point that a canoe won't work, that a hollow boat will collapse when subjected to the 700 gravity type enviroment. But the lightness of terrestrial woods is due almost entirley to trapped gas-cells.

Liquid methane is a light liquid; I have a feeling that no organic (carbon-hydrogen-oxygen) compound can be appreciably lighter; I know most are far denser. Vide polystyrene, which is nearly 4 times as dense.

I have a suspicion that Barl & Co. wouldn't float in their seas; they'd be bottom-crawlers. (We don't have to change a line of the story; this is just counter-speculation, because the thing intrigues me.) Also, I have a strong hunch that methane is a damn poor fluid for a metabolite base, ammonia or water are a hell of a sight better. Methane has no detachable H bonds; NH_3 and H_2O does. That's why they are such remarkably potent solvents.

Another horrible item; the things that happen to gases under that fantastic gravity stress.

But the whole conception of the story is wonderful. The idea of the rocket studying gravity, and its 2 billion dollar investment is a lovely one. But the knowledge of organic products of the fantastic structural strengths involved in life-forms on that planet would be worth even more, actually!

The whole job is lovely; by all means, do that article. I'll pay you the regular 3¢ a word on that — so you'll get an extra bonus on the work you did for the background of this story.

Regards,   John

L. Sprague de Camp   *October 14, 1952*

Dear Sprague:

Your information re Street & Smith is correct with a recent change in the rates division. We now pay a 3-1/2¢ and 4¢ bonus rate. The rate is determined by the story quality, and is paid on individual stories.

This you'll have fun trying to express succinctly in a book; the system is that I'll pay according to my judgment — *but* the story that places first in reader opinion is *always* a 4¢ story, and the one that places second is *always* either a 3-1/2¢ or 4¢ story. If I guessed wrong and paid 4¢ on something the readers place last — well, that'll learn me. If I guessed wrong and paid the standard 3¢ on a yarn that the readers put in first place — my error, Sir Author, here's the other 1¢ a word you earned. This lab-determining program begins with the April 1953 issue, although stories that may have received the 3-1/2¢ and 4¢ rate may appear earlier.

The game now is to see whether I can outguess the readers, or the authors can outfox me. No matter what happens, we'll all learn!

As for personal information about me: Born June 8, 1910, Newark, New Jersey. Education: M.I.T. & Duke University. Previous Condition of Servitude: Worked for an Air-Conditioning engineering outfit. Also in Mack Truck Research department. Wrote books with a group under **Carleton Ellis,** the chemical patents collector. But I was a free-lance writer before, during, and after. I started while a freshman at MIT, and never got over it.

Other books: "The Incredible Planet," and "The Moon Is Hell," and "Cloak of Aesir." (Second of the "Who Goes There?" **Don A. Stuart** books.)

Other magazines Street & Smith publishes: *Charm, Mademoiselle, Living For Young Homemakers, Air Trails* and *Baseball Yearbook-Football Yearbook.*

The others were dropped in the fall of 1949.

Hubbard and **van Vogt** are out of science fiction for now, at least. Both engaged in dianetics.

Robert M. Williams is working after a lapse.

Ray Cummings is, I think, finally out.

Cartmill is writing something occasionally; he's mostly newspaperman though, and doesn't try very much in this field.

Now to your previous letter re the social sciences.

My friend, you are an optimist, albeit a somewhat blind one. Psychologists have been talking about sex for some time; everybody else knows it exists, and are busy saying it shouldn't. Their attitude is that murder, insanity, sadism and sex all, unfortunately, do exist. Against the psychologists we find:

The Baptist Church. The Catholic Church. The Presbyterian Church. The National Association of Women's Clubs. The Parent-Teachers Association. All adult females who were "well adjusted young ladies" more than forty years ago. All adult males who were "well adjusted young men" more than forty years ago. (The latter two classes, may, possibly, be motivated much as the Fox in the Aesop Fable, who recommended that all foxes should give up their tails.)

Inasmuch as the groups I have named vastly outnumber the psychological fraternity, and the Post Office is far more sensitive to the loudness, than to the quality, of a voice, please be reasonable. Either we handle sex and don't publish the magazine, or we don't handle sex and do publish the magazine. One might say, "Heads I win, the other way I lose."

Our Society has a number of important postulates; now logical manipulation of *any* postulates is logically acceptable. The postulates don't have to be sensible. I can draw logical conclusions from "The Moon Is Made Of Green Cheese. There is a cheese shortage in Switzerland."

Our Society has, among its basic postulates, the following rare gems of thought:

1. There should be no difference between individuals. (The fact that there is will be sternly fought).
2. There should be no sex. (The fact that there would then be no Society is merely an annoying fact; we can still say there *should* be no sex, can't we?)
3. Society is invariably right, righteous, and sane. (Therefore any individual who disagrees with Society is wrong, evil, or insane. See the cases of Society vs. J. Christ. Society vs. G. Galileo. Society vs. M. Luther. It will be observed that Society was right in each instance. Each individual paid severely for his failure to adjust to reality.)

Now in view of this situation, leave us be prudent. We will not stick our necks out. But it *is* possible to set up a civilization among the Gobblehonks of Deneb IX, who everybody knows are *not* human, and are therefore *not* as enlightened as we are, and inquire what happens in their silly and specifically non-human society.

We will also carefully refrain from discussing the sore points. Sex is so sore a point that it is futile to discuss it; let's instead, attack the purpose behind this business of biting ourselves on the back of the neck. It might turn out that it was the self-biting that was causing the trouble and the said self-biting wasn't necessary after all.

Why does our Society hold that sex should be eliminated?

Could it be that, in a male-oriented society which does not understand women, a major portion of the social conflicts will center in that area? And that the postulate "There should be no difference between individuals" is handicapping efforts to understand the female half of society?

Could it be that that no-difference postulate is not phrased quite correctly? As it stands, it's caused a bit of trouble, here and there. Foreigners shouldn't exist because foreigners are different and there should be no different individuals. Jews should not exist because. . . . Negroes shouldn't. . . . Russians shouldn't ex . . . .

Maybe that postulate could be changed to advantage.

And then maybe sex would not be so inadmissable.

And then, maybe, we. . . .

80

But no. A society that accepted differences as being rational couldn't exist. It would explode, or get into civil war. Or. . . .

Nope, There's Only One Right Way To Do It.

Or is that just another social postulate?

Regards, John

Mr. Irish (From **Marc Alpert** files, MIT.) *October 23, 1952*

Dear Mr. Irish:

First, I'll make a deal with you; I'll come up to MIT to give a talk, but you'll have to pay me for it. In this case, the pay I want is a small stick of dynamite, a JATO unit, or some satisfactorily potent arrangment that will somehow succeed in getting an article out of **Prof. Arnold**, complete with some pictures, on the Product Design Engineer course he runs, using the science-fiction planet idea. If you and/or your members, who are on the spot there, can induce him to do an article for me, I'll guarantee to give the MIT Science Fiction Society a talk, and **Dr. Arnold** 3¢ a word for his article — about $150, I hope, for I'd like about 5000 words on it.

When I was up there I told him I very much wanted the article.

I am afraid that science-fiction and psychiatry doesn't go well together. I would have suspected something of the sort of reaction you got from **Dr. Harris**.

Remember that the basic orientation of the psychiatrist is that the individual must adjust himself to society-as-it-is. The society actually holds that any man who disagrees with things Society believes in is neurotic or insane, and the Society reacts to suppress the deviant. The psychiatrist seeks to get the deviant to cease deviating, and accept the nature of things-as-they-are.

The basic flaw in this attitude is that the Society then has a tendency to hold that Jesus was neurotic because he could not adjust himself to the money changers in the temple, and to other phenomena of his society. By psychiatric definition, Jesus *was* neurotic. So was Galileo; he, too, failed to adjust to the society of his time, and insisted, instead, that the Earth went around the Sun.

I have, at times, amused myself considering what a psychiatrist might have held Galileo's delusion to be. Obviously he was badly adjusted to his Society; his strange idea that the Earth went around the Sun must have been a neurotic fantasy — a projection of his inner conflict. Earth, a Freudian psychoanalyst might have held, was a symbol of the mother — Mother Earth — and poor neurotic Galileo was wishing that the Mother would revolve around the *Son.* Pure neurosis, no doubt.

The psychiatrist's bounden duty in the Society is to induce the deviants to reaccept the structure of Society-as-it-is; inevitably, then, science-fiction, which is the literature based on considering adjusting Society to the needs of the individual says "Society is wrong, and my idea is right!" a decision must be made as to whether the individual is a far-seeing genius, a Jesus, Galileo, Luther or Fulton — or simply another crackpot. But on what basis can we determine that?

Society has always used the easy way: 50,000,000 people can't be wrong. And besides it's easier to change one man's ideas (or eliminate him so he stops bothering us) than to change the opinions of 50,000,000.

The difficulty is that our present society displays the familiar symptoms of a homicidal paranoid. Like a homicidal maniac, it insists on seeing all its neighbors as plotting against its life, and storing guns, knives, and other weapons in its house. It is extremely logical, as are many paranoids, but not very rational. Periodically, it displays fits of homicidal rage.

The impracticability of such a manner of behavior suggests that Society is not facing reality, and adjusting itself to cooperative mutual understanding.

I think history provides some reason for holding that Society is more paranoid than the individuals who compose Society. And that, most certainly, Society is not truly rational.

Therefore, it is a very real and important question, this problem of "On what basis shall we determine whether Society or the individual is right?"

The psychiatrist, however, is somewhat like the policeman; he does not judge society, but instead seeks to enforce Society's rules. From such a viewpoint science-fiction is disturbing, because it constantly discusses changing society. And the psychiatrist is human first, a psychiatrist second; like any human being, he, too, has his basic beliefs and orientations. It's disturbing to a physicist to suggest to him that the concept "distance" is not a valid concept — that it is an artificial and arbitrary way of looking at things, only approximately true under the limited conditions of Earth. For instance, the "distance" from the Earth to the Moon is the same as that from Moon to Earth — but the *action* of actually making such a trip is not equivalent in both directions.

Think of the vast revision of physical formulas required if the idea of "distance" were ruled out! The law of gravity itself would have to be expressed in a totally new manner.

To the scientist, an attack on the basic concepts of his science is disturbing. To the psychiatrist, attacks on the basic concepts of the society-individual relationship are equally questionable.

A friend of mine has an unfortunate problem right now; his aged father is slowly dying of cancer; it's started to affect his brain. The old man has recognized that something has gone wrong in the relationship between himself and his son — and has decided that his son has become insane.

The conclusion that there is insanity between them is correct; the only flaw is that the old man has assigned the locus of insanity wrongly. He is the one whose mind is cracking.

The problem of deciding "Who is insane in this disagreement of opinions?" is a darned tough one. As I say, by definition, both Jesus and Galileo were neurotics; they were unable to adjust themselves to their respective societies.

Sincerely,   John W Campbell, Jr.

Poul Anderson   *October 25, 1952*

Dear Poul:

I'm returning the carbon of your novel to **Meredith;** I can't use it just now. Can't in fact, buy a novel before June, 1953. I just bought a doozey of a novel — 4 parter — from **Hal Clement.** Incidentally, we now have a bonus rate structure; 3¢ a word standard, 3-1/2 ¢ or 4¢ bonus. I bought your sequel to "Double Dyed Villains" at 3-1/2¢. But — if that novelette places first in the reader opinions, I made a mistake, and I owe you another 1/2¢ a word; you've earned the 4¢ rate if you place first in the reader votes. I think your yarn will probably make about second place; that's what the 3-1/2¢ rate means. If I'm wrong — you win. If it places last on the reader votes — I'm wrong then, too, but you've still got the 3-1/2¢.

Hal Clement's novel, by the way, is one you'll enjoy a lot, I think. His central character is an explorer-sea-captain in a civilization about equivalent to Earth's in the 15th century. But the hero is 18 inches long, and 2 in diameter, a caterpillarish creature, and the sea is liquid methane. The storms hurl sleet of frozen ammonia, and the surface gravity of his planet ranges from 3G at the equator to *700G* at the poles! The planet's equatorial diameter is 48,000 miles, its polar diameter 22,000 miles, and the equatorial rotational speed 300 m.p.s.! The day is 9 *minutes* long. The hero's a caterpillar. His tissues are just slightly on the tough side.

Hal Clement is exploring an area of science fiction quite different from the area you're exploring — and from the area ASF is exploring generally. He's exploring, with a new and detailed care, the area of other physical environments. And doing a wonderful job of it.

You're exploring the mental-philosophical aspects.

I couldn't use this novel of yours as is, anyway. Not just now. The world isn't ready for this approach. Science-fiction is far more

83

advanced in understanding than the general culture — but even science-fiction isn't fully ready for this yarn. It needs to be built up to it. We're trying hard to do that now, **Poul** — and I want you to help do it. I've got **Ray Jones** and **E.F. Russell** and **Isaac Asimov** and **Chad Oliver** working on different aspects of it. We are, in essence, trying to teach the most thoughtful, speculative and philosophical group of Mankind — the science-fiction readership — a quite new viewpoint. It isn't something they know they want to learn; therefore we have to do it by entertaining them enough so that they'll accept the new ideas for the *sake of the entertainment,* rather than for the *sake of the idea.*

But actually, in the long run, it makes little difference why they originally accept the idea — for fun, or for serious education; in either case the idea has been entered, and thought about, and will have effect on the individual's total philosophy. I drink orange juice in the morning because it tastes clean and sweet and fresh — because it makes my mouth feel good. I don't drink it because my system needs glucose after the night fast, and because my system needs the organic acid to maintain the pH buffering effects, nor because ascorbic acid is vital to my nerve-system metabolism. What difference? I drink sugar and citric and ascorbic acids; I didn't know I wanted them, but they make me feel good.

As you know, **Peg** and I are doing research into the nature of Man and Man's mind. The following is a theory we've worked up — and your novel seems to me to be simply a deep realization, on your part, of precisely the problem we ran across.

Just imagine the following situation:

Some 10,000 years ago, a mutation appeared; *Homo inquisitivus* was born.

Now let us consider the following circumstances: Most animals are controlled by instinct. Instinct is simply the trial-and-error how-to-do-it data that has been learned by 2,000,000,000 years of field testing. Instincts aren't "good" or "bad," "moral" or "evil," "sane" or "insane." They are simply the genetically transmitted data on what worked successfully through 2,000,000,000 years. It didn't work with absolute success; there have been mistakes — but no very bad ones. If there were very bad mistakes, the race carrying that mistaken instinct — died.

Instinct is, largely, what-works-in-the-long-run. Intelligence originated to select the applicable-instinct-at-the-moment.

The characteristic of instinct is that it's stable, it's a long-term proposition — and it's rigid. It won't bend, it can only break.

The characteristic of intelligence is that it's unstable, it's protean, it's not rigid, and cannot be broken.

Instinct cannot adapt; intelligence can.

The jellyfish cannot be broken; there is no rigidity in him. The clam is either intact — or shattered.

The exoskeletal creatures, the heavily-armored dinosaurs, the turtle — these have been tried down the ages, and they've all failed, essentially. They've never been tops; they work, after a fashion, but they've always been a third-rate life-form.

But the jelly-fish is a fifth-rate life-form.

The best system seems to be a combination of rigidity with joints, and flexibility; elastic muscle of great toughness seems to be a better armour than the hardest shell. Rubber tires will stand wear that would shred a hard steel rim.

The ideal seems to be the combination of a fairly rigid skeleton, and a flexible outer surface.

The same applies to intellect.

There are two forces in primitive man, *Homo sapiens*, instinct and intelligence. And the two are about balanced; instinct is somewhat the stronger force, however.

We are now working with a two-phase system; the two phases are mutually reinforcing, but have basically different characteristics.

Imagine we have a piece of coal, and we heat it with a small gas flame. The coal alone will not burn in air; the gas flame can heat it red-hot, but the instant the gas flame is removed, the coal begins to cool off, and goes out. A single piece of coal is not self-sustaining in air.

But the coal-heated-by-gas gives off more total heat than the gas flame alone.

Intelligence, in a dog, is not adequate to sustain the animal. But instinct-plus-intelligence produces far more results than could instinct alone.

Let's add a second piece of coal; the gas flame plus coal can now give off much more heat than the gas flame alone — though the gas flame controls the amount of heat given off, because turning down the gas will cool off the whole mass, since the coal is not self-sustaining.

There is, on the other hand, a certain critical mass of coal which, once heated by the gas flame, becomes self-sustaining. Thereafter, the gas flame has no control over the operation.

There is a critical level, then, where the gas-flame-coal system is just at the ragged edge — the gas flame can still control the situation, but the control is rather sloppy. Yet that is the point at which the gas flame gets the maximum possible amplification of effect.

I think *H. sapiens* represented the critical point. What you've referred to in this story as the IQ 100-150 region. It's the highest point at which intelligence serves as an amplifier for instinct.

85

Beyond that — intelligence becomes a self-sustaining flame. And it's self-sustaining in the sense a chain reaction is. It can increase without limit by its own action!

Homo inquisitivus, I think, came along about 10,000 years ago. Physiologically, he appears identical with *H. sapiens*. But he has an intelligence that's just a bit beyond the critical point. When his full intelligence is attained, at adolesence, he switches over into self-sustaining powers.

Let's imagine the world of 9,000 years ago, then.

H. inquis. I so call because he has a new characteristic; intelligence wants to know *why* as well as *how*. Instinct only wants to know how.

H. inquis. isn't controlled by his instinct; he's capable of unlimited development. For a monent, let's imagine he has godlike powers. Let's consider that *H. inquis* is the source of the God-legends — and also the demon legends. We'll talk about Zeus.

Zeus, we'll say, was an example of *H. inquis.* He could do teleportation; control minds, do levitation, had telepathy, and could use the poltergeist phenomena. He was a pyrotic (hurled thunderbolts) and so on. He had, futhermore, total racial memory, and could consciously recall everything that the entire race had experienced back to the Carboniferous swamps.

Now Zeus sets out to build a new and finer world. He is practically immortal; his intellectual control so exceeds his instinct patterns that he can force a wound to heal almost instantly. He can change the pattern of instincts to such a degree that he can change his own appearance and shape.

In other words, let's give Zeus everything the legends said — the works, without any limit whatever. We'll make him the Almighty God of all Gods — and then we'll see just how helplessely crippled he is!

He knows everything that's ever happened. He can do anything on the physical level. He can read minds, and change men's motives.

But he can't change the intelligence level of *H. sapiens*.

And because of Heisenberg Uncertainty, even a God can't really read the future to any extent.

He knows all that has happened. But an empire has never happened in all the 2,000,000,000 years of life's history.

He doesn't know about science; it's never happened.

He doesn't know the nature of the complex organization needed to establish a big city, and doesn't know that that's necessary.

He has immense intelligence, enormous physical powers, a life-span of a dozen centuries or more if he wants it. But he has no data. And he can't get the data. He can try by introspection — i.e., by searching the 2,000,000,000 year past — but the data isn't there, either.

He knows all that *has* happened — but practically nothing of what will happen.

And he's lonely. He's a mutant — and I'll show that mutants normally occur in the male line, not the female. Reason: any mutation of the 24th chromosome will *invariably* produce a male who displays the mutated characteristic — he has no paired 24th chromosome from the other parent to block it or blank it out. A female having a mutated 24th chromosome has a paired 24th from the other parent which will block it out or weaken its effect.

Any characteristic appearing in the 24th chromosome will produce a phenotype (an individual displaying the characteristic) in a male, but only a genotype (an individual genetically carrying the characteristic) in a female.

An instance is haemophilia; men have it, but females carry it.

Poor, unhappy, lonely Zeus — he's doomed to lack a true, understanding mate. He can have hand-maidens. He can breed on the daughters of *H. sap.* But he can't find a female of his own type.

All the history of the past tells him nothing of genetics; he doesn't know, therefore, that breeding to his own daughters would hasten the production of a female phenotype of his line.

He could probably produce Minerva-Athena, who sprung full-formed from the brow of Zeus, by auto-hypnosis, and with his ability to control minds, might even induce others to see-hear his own delusion.

But there would be more of the children of Zeus coming along. They'd be hybrids, of course — but the males would be phenotypes frequently. They'd be demi-gods. And they'd be demons, too.

Which are the Gods and which are the demons?

What is right and what is wrong? Who is to judge? If the most intelligent in the world are to be the judges — what if they disagree?

Should *H. inquis.* protect and care for *H. sap?* Should Lucifer, demi-god, bow down to — i.e., respect — a stupid creature like *H. sap.*, a being with the general intelligence level of a primitive tribesman, a Mexican peon who doesn't even want to learn anything new?

Or should Lucifer consider the peon an animal for his use?

The stupidity of the instinct-dominated *H. sap.* must have driven the intelligent-dominated *H. inquis.* frantic. *H. sap.* could *not* be made to be interested in *why* a thing worked; he only wanted to know how.

H. sap. learned that the Gods needed handmaidens; in return for the teachings of how-to-do-it that the Gods offered, the village tribe would select their best daughters as hand-maidens of the Gods.

And when the Gods grew so weary of the futile fight against their own ignorance, and the ignorance of *H. sap.*, and the slow, slow march of time that had to elaspe to get the data they needed to think with — they quit living. They passed to a higher plane or something. And the ancient ritual of selecting the village daughters who were to be handmaidens to the Gods had to be continued, but now the girls, too, had to be sent on to a higher plane.

Moloch may simply have been an *H. inquis.* who's special and favorite ESP or psi power was pyroticism — he threw things into flame. Charging lions and the like. So his handmaidens had to follow him by being burned alive.

And suppose Lucifer wanted to conduct an experiment, and needed someone to hold the other end of a string while he measured something, or some equivalent service. *H. sap.* wouldn't understand *what Lucifer was trying to do*.

So Lucifer might, wearily, say, "All right, Blurpub. You want that stupid female Weblup, and she doesn't like you because she thinks you're ugly. She's right, you are. Also you're incredibly selfish, which is the main reason she loathes you anyway. I'll fix it so you're sure of getting Weblup, if you'll just help me with this experiment. Now I want you to do *exactly* as I say. No bright ideas from you; do *exactly* what I tell you. And don't ask questions; you're too damned stupid to understand any explanation anyway."

So Blurpub has dealings with the demon, and Lucifer does a little psychosomatic reorientation on Blurpub. Blurbup winds up with an altered face — and, horrors of horrors, he's lost his Soul! He's no longer as selfish as he was; he's had his mind straightened out to the point where his old gang finds he's a different being. Weblup, also, incidentally, gets a little psychotherapy from a telepathic being of stupendously greater intellectual power. She marries Blurbup.

Now each individual, at any point in life, considers that his way of thinking is perfect and ideal, or nearly so. Anyone who changes your life-attitudes has stolen your soul. It's what we call the "Spinach Mechanism" in honor of the story about the Irish member of parliament who during a debate on vegetable taxes, was overheard to say, "I don't care how they tax spinach; I hate the damn stuff." An Englishman MP near him said, "I say, have you ever tried it?" "No, I haven't and I'm not going to. If I tried it I might like it, and I *hate* the damn stuff."

Who are the Gods and who are the Demons?

Was God a totalitarian dictator of an absolutionist state, and Lucifer a democratic entity, seeking freedom of the individual?

Who is to judge?

"On what basis shall judgment be made?" is the saner question.

And 9,000 years ago — there was no data on which to judge!

Now down through the ages, it has been held that mystic powers have certain limitations:

1. They work by faith, and by faith alone.
2. They cannot be inspected by logical processes without loss of the power.
3. They cannot work in the presence of a powerful opposed faith.

And these make sense. Suppose A believes deeply and strongly that telekenesis is possible, and that he can do it. And he demonstrates before a group of friends that he can. (This has been done repeatedly.) Then a group of physical scientists wants to investigate; they set up rigorous scientific controls, see to it that he has no accomplices aiding him, and sit down to watch. They have a deep and abiding faith in the laws of physics as they know them; they have a powerful faith, held by powerful and able minds, that the object will not move.

They demonstrate conclusively the power of faith; their faith holds the objects immovable against the power of the medium's faith!

Now since the physicist's faith is not-p type, while the medium's is an is-p type, mutual balance and cancellation will yield no-p. Since "P" can, and usually does, stand for "an interruption in the normal course of events," no-p equivalent to not-p, and appears to invalidate is-p.

The Gods died when logic was invented. Logic constituted a not-p type of faith, and centuries of contact between the magicians of native tribes, who *can* do things while science cannot, as explorer after explorer testifies, has shown that Logic can defeat Magic.

But that doesn't disprove the reality of magic.

In a powerful magnetic field, iron will fall upwards. That doesn't disprove the Law of Gravity. It proves that magnetic fields can be stronger than Earth's gravitational field.

Now it happens that our Logic today is highly defective; it contains immense holes, holes so huge that we can't plug them, and holes through which our whole civilization can fall.

For instance, I can, using the rules of present logic, prove that it is anti-social to be a physicist. Just suppose every one decided to be a physicist; there'd be no one to care for the sick, no one to protect us against criminals, no one to run the farms and the railroads. Clearly, it is illogical and selfish to be a physicist.

Now precisely the same "suppose everybody. . . ." argument can be used against any occupation.

BUT THERE IS NO FORMAL LOGICAL METHOD OF INVALIDATING THAT ARGUMENT.

Logic is irrationally used here — we know it, we feel it — but we can't quote a Law of Logic that invalidates it.

Read Socrates; he was a sunuvvabitch, a nasty, destructive, morale-breaking louse. He ruined Athens, by producing three brilliant pupils who achieved high places in the City — and proved absolutely amoral. He had three prime tactics for destroying any man's belief.

1. Any general rule can be challenged and "disproved" on the basis of a special case.
2. Any special case may be challenged and "disproved" on the basis of a general application.
3. Refused to introduce any theory of his own, while demolishing anything anyone else offered.

Above, I used the general application of something intended to be specific. I can argue against the law of gravity by saying that obviously the attraction of a million suns is greater than the attraction of one, and therefore if the stars were all suns, like ours, Earth would evidently be torn away from the Sun.

Or I can quote the special case against the law of gravity, and point out that a balloon doesn't fall, it isn't attracted, but is repelled.

In the very simple realm of physical science, the answers to those propositions are easy to come by.

Now consider the argument that since a million men are wiser than one, obviously, any idea you alone hold must, obviously, be wrong if it doesn't agree with the million. You're trying to say that the regiment is out of step.

Our system of logic has the vast hole in it that it *cannot determine relevances*!

In this story, should your hero leave Sheila for Dagmar just because Sheila is incompetent in the new world? A man should protect and care for his wife, but he should find a mate suitable to him. Dagmar must remember a woman has no right to break up another woman's home, but a woman must find a mate suitable to her, whom she can help and encourage adequately.

You should not lie, but if some girl asks what you think of her new hat, you must not tell her you actually think it looks like an overflowing garbage pan.

Our logic contains *no measure of relevancy*.

There is a war in Korea. How relevant is that to my thinking about whether or not to have a shade tree installed in my front lawn?

A logic without a method of determination of relevancy is nearly useless! But it will defeat a mind almost completely!

Your novel here, it seems to me, is simply bringing up the

problem ancient *H. inquis.* faced when he first appeared — but with a difference. *H. inquis.* today does have data on what has been done and he has a vast new technique of gathering data. He can solve the ancient problems today — if only he can get a way of handling the data properly!

And one of the things he most needs to learn is that he has powers that he is reacting to, without acknowledging. That he has abilities he is denying himself. That he actually has a — well, let's not use the idea of intelligence quotient, because psychology has missed the boat by about 160 degrees on that one. Let's use the term "competence level" — a competence level of about 1000 to 10,000 instead of the 100-150 he pretends he has. That is, the topmost minds are 10 to 100 times as brilliant as they pretend to be — and have the inherent capacity of using the intelligence chain-reaction to increase that power literally without limit.

There is, somewhere, an undiscovered law of evaluative logic; the missing parameter of the Universe is that undiscovered law. When we find it, we'll have the three Natural Units: h, c and i — i being the unit of intelligent relationship. Then nothing in the Universe need be measured in arbitrary terms.

But to prepare the world to accept that new orientation, we must — steal their souls. We must steal their fixed opinions, alter their evaluations. Like Lucifer, we must take away their deepest beliefs in selfishness, their very souls that know that Tradition is Good and Intelligence is Evil.

Many an intelligent man hates God for a sound reason; if God is omniscient and omnipotent — why does he allow this hell to go on?

My answer: God is omniscient only with respect to the past; He, too, must wait to discover the future. He, too, does not know what the right answers for the future are. He cannot terminate any line of action Man undertakes, because He himself does not know on what basis the final judgment should be made.

What we must do, now, is to try to open up, a little, the fixed limitations of human thinking. And Science Fiction is a fine way to do it.

You're doing it with the idea of the "Double Dyed Villains." That story holds that evil lies only in the results, not in the process. That no act is evil — only consequences are good or evil. But that *all* consequences, not just some of them, must be considered.

Life is *not* simple — and we must have a new slant on what "good" is. I, personally, have thrown out all idea of good and evil, of right and wrong; the only basis I can see for sane judgment is "sensible." Not merely logical, but truly rational, including human feelings, and the long run as well as the immediate results.

But for that, of course, we do, have, and forever will lack total data. That's why we do, have, and forever will make mistakes.

But a man who makes the same mistake several times is unsane.

Regards,   John

Bill Bade: *November 6, 1952*

Dear Mr. Bade:

Hmmmm — physicist interested in macromolecules interested also in anthropolology. And **Chad Oliver** is an anthropologist interested in psychology. And **Norbert Weiner** is an physicist-mathematician interested in cybernetics and neutral systems.

It's a damn shame you're not in this area; I'd like a chance to talk to you, and really kick things around. I've been working on those problems of anthropology and sociology and physics and chemistry for some time — and I have an enormous advantage over you. I'm married, and my wife is a woman who's been trying to solve the same problems from her totally different viewpoint for some 40 years also. We are making progress; we have done work that is showing very marked indications of being both logically correct, and, more important, meaningful. The social scientists have been failing for a number of reasons, no one of which is among the reasons they've listed! The reason I have a great advantage over you is this: the female of the human species does *not* think like the male. When she is permitted the full, free use of her special thinking abilities, and the results of her different thinking are sincerely and genuinely accepted and integrated with male thinking, results are obtained that can Not be obtained otherwise.

Consider this: one eye can percieve pattern only two-dimensionally; it takes two eyes, seeing from inherently different viewpoints, to percieve the three-dimensional aspect of the world. In a similar fashion, two *different* methods of thinking, based on fundamentally different principles, are essential to understanding.

Any biologist holds that the ability to reproduce is essential if we are to consider that we have a living organism. But Man can *not* reproduce; neither can Woman. Only the team of man-and-woman then constitutes a *true human being*. It is essential that the organism be split into two separate sub-units; just as three-dimensional vision cannot be achived by any single optical system, no matter how designed, so full-understanding cannot be achieved by any single thinking unit.

Man is characterized by logical processes; woman is characterized by a non-logical process called "intuition" — but one that has never been defined or studied seriously.

Since Man has dominated society, logic has been dominant, and

92

has been socially considered essential to the discovery of and demonstration of truth.

It isn't.

The reason the Social Sciences — anthropology, psychology, sociology — have failed to progress lies therein; their field happens to have many of its fundamental laws lying in the field of non-logic, laws which, because of the social orientation, cannot be accepted because they cannot be demonstrated to be logical.

The result is that those sciences are in somewhat the position of a computing machine given the order: "Find the sum of 4 and 5, but the answer 9 is not acceptable."

After some seven thousand years of trying, the mathematical logician Goedel has finally developed a logical proof that logic is not itself a continuous function — that there are propositions which are true, but which are not demonstrable by logic.

Heretofore, no proposition has been considered true unless it could be shown to be logical; Goedel's Theorem demonstrates that we must accept that illogical truths exist, in precisely the same sense that irrational numbers were finally admitted to be real.

Until that truth was recognized, only logical truths were acceptable; so long as that situation maintained, it was impossible to establish the illogical, but rational, laws of the Social Sciences.

With that factor added in, we can now see that the mystic, the magician, have been operating in the field of nonlogic. The water dowser doesn't use logical truths — but that he does in reality use something and does in fact find water, can be demonstrated by the nonlogical process of experimentation.

Experimentation, you must recognize, is not a *logical* process. It is absolutely legitimate to say "I know this is not logical, but it works." The validity of the operation can be demonstrated, even if it cannot be logically explained.

The field of human relations occupies the Forbidden Area of non-logical rationality; it is the area that has, therefore, been most severely handicapped.

It is the field in which we will have the maximum difficulty in thinking clearly; we have been specifically, and powerfully conditioned to reject as nonsense any idea which is non-logical. Now we are seeking to overcome a lifetime of conditioning, and accept non-logical ideas — but we do not have the laws of non-logical rationality formulated to a point where they are usable.

Actually, all creative thinking appears to be non-logical, and only when we learn the laws of non-logical rationality will we be able to be creative thinkers at will, and without limit. When Newton worked up the law of gravity, he gave a logical demonstration of the validity of his idea *after* he had derived the postulate of the inverse square law attraction. But no one has ever given a *logical* process whereby he originally derived that postulate that he logically demonstrated.

It's somewhat like a group of men coming to a broad, swift stream; it can't be swum, jumped, or forded. There are no boats, or boatbuilding equipment, but they have ropes. How do they cross?

Well, one of them catches a stone thrown across to him, and pulls over the string tied to the stone, then pulls over a rope, and then heavier ropes, and a rope bridge is built. Simple.

Only how did that first guy get over there?

How did Newton get over to the other side so he could build that logical bridge?

Magic. Certainly not logic.

Logic has been a vastly overrated item. In the first place, it's long been known that logic can be correct, but meaningless. Given the propositions "The Moon is made of green cheese" and "There is a cheese shortage in Wisconsin," you can draw perfectly correct, logical conclusions. But since the postulates are meaningless, the conclusions are meaningless too — however correct they are.

Anyhow, the failure of the social sciences stems from the effort to apply a system of thinking that is inherently unsuitable to the nature of the material.

Soooooo — we have to work out the laws of nonlogical thinking. The chances of the society doing it are exceedingly poor; the Society holds that only logical thinking is true thinking.

India accepts nonlogic somewhat better — but they don't simultaneously insist on *both* nonlogical and logical thinking. We haven't either. We won't get answers till we do.

Incidentally, physics has now reached the furthest extent possible without the use of nonlogical, or hyperlogical, or metalogical whichever you want to call it — methods. They haven't been able to resolve the nucleus, because metalogical factors become important at that level, and logical methods can't resolve it.

Metalogical methods are essential in handling structures of high orders of complexity; your macromolecules are in that class. The reproduction of protein molecules involves metalogical laws, and you can't handle it on a logical basis, any more than you can determine the value of pi if you insist that it be a rational number.

Metalogical methods, however, can direct the application of logic with exceedingly powerful results. Like Newton's law of gravity.

Actually, logic is a fraud of the first water; we never have been logical, and never could have lived on a logical basis. Logic actually works when, and only when, *all* relevant data is known and evaluated. Name the logical method of determing that you do in fact have all relevant data — and if you can't what's your justification for claiming that you are being logical?

Suppose we are discussing automobile storage batteries. I introduce the proposition that the high price of metallic calcium seems to be going down. What's that got to do with automobile batteries, for Pete's sake?

As of 1936 — nothing.

As of 1952 — it's relevant. But if we had known all the relevant data in 1936, we'd have known that it *should* have been relevant. Reason: It's been found that Ca added to the Pb alloy used in the battery plates increases the toughness, hardness, and reactivity of the battery.

How do you know what isn't relevant?

We've been getting highly interesting results that boil down to this; the basic laws of physics are the basis laws of the Universe. Man is a function of the inherent structure of the universe; he must, then, be congruent to those basic laws, and the manifold derivations of those basic laws can be expected to obtain in human behavior.

Consider the basic problem of impedance matching; if your physics didn't include the concept, look it up. If it did, and you've forgotten it, for Christ's sake dig it out; it's basic. Physics hasn't discovered how basic! And neither has psychology, sociology, or anthropology.

If there is a junction at which there is a poor impedance match, some of the incident energy will be reflected, and some transmitted. See what happens at a glass-to-air interface with light.

Where there is a good impedance match, energy is freely transmitted. (Take a glass "diamond" and immerse it in glycerine. It becomes invisible, because of the good impedance match of the glycerine-to-glass interface.)

The United States has a society with certain postulates, certain characteristic properties. Canada has a society having highly similar characteristics. It could be predicted from elementary physics that the two systems would constitute a good impedance match, and that free transmission of information would result.

The recent work in the Theory of Communication has shown that information *is* energy — that information is negative entropy.

The social postulate system of Russia is very different from ours; naturally there is a very poor impedance match, and the interface, consequently, reflects nearly all the incident information back to its source. They can't communicate outward to us, and we can't communicate inward to them.

When a physicist wants to interconnect two systems having

different impedances, he uses an impedance matching transformer. In an automobile, handling mechanical energy, he uses a transmission gear box impedance matcher. In 60-cycle power lines, he uses an electromagnetic transformer. At radio frequencies, he uses either transformers, or resonant lines. At light frequencies, he uses resonant thicknesses — see the effect of a quarter-wave coating on a lens.

Question: What would happen if we established a buffer state on the Russo-Western border?

Answer: Neither side will permit it, because to do so would establish a free flow of information in both directions, and both sides are utterly unwilling to permit that. Their unwillingness, incidentally, has *logical* basis. When they learn how to think metalogically, they'll open up again.

You can get some fascinating questions going; currently we're rejecting relativity and Newtonian ideas, and trying out a completely and totally new thesis. Its results are consistent with observational data, but wildly contrary to present theory. It starts with a third explanation of the Michelson-Morley experiment. Essentially, the experiment tested the proposition "The Earth moves through the ether." The experiment said, in effect, "Your idea is wrong."

One explanation: The Earth does not move, because it is the center of the Universe, and the Universe moves around it.

Rejected.

Second explanation: **Einsteinian** relativity; the Earth does not move through the ether, because there is no ether.

Currently accepted.

Third explanation: The Earth does not *move* through the ether, because we have an invalid conception of the meaning of "move." Distance is not a valid concept as we now use it.

The one we're playing with.

That explanation allows for the universal constant c, but does not contain velocity as a concept. It allows for a number of observed phenomena which have never been explicable before.

The concept "distance" can be shown to be meaningless in its standard usage in the following way: A concept that cannot be demonstrated to have physical validity is not useful, and should be replaced. Consider the "distance" from the Earth to the Moon; by definition that distance is exactly identical with the distance from the Moon to the Earth. But name one, single physical process for which it is true that Earth-to-Moon is equal to Moon-to-Earth. Certainly it isn't for a rocket ship. Equally, it's not true for light, for we know that light is affected by gravitational fields, and the Earth-Moon ray will be affected differently than a Moon-Earth ray.

Perhaps distance has some validity on an isopotential and frictional surface, but it has no physical reality in interplanetary or interstellar space.

Then maybe this, rather than relativity, is the angle of attack to find the meaningful explanation of the Michelson-Morley experiment!

Incidentally, developments along the line suggested here lead to the possibility of hyperlightspeed transportation. It also demonstrates the impossibility of backward time-travel, and the consequent futility of foreward time-travel.

I am not kidding on those latter two items; I think you can see that the attack on the concept of "distance" is bound to have terrific and wide-spread consequences in any picturization of the physical universe.

Some of these concepts lead to a reintegration of what Man is, necessarily, and to what Man's relation to God, Man and the Universe is.

Incidentally, since you're interested in anthropology, note this item: no civilization that has remained stable for more than 3 generations has failed to have three basic factors; no civilization that did not have those three factors has remained stable for more than 3 generations. The number of factors that have been present in human civilizations is almost endless — yet of all that endless motley, three, and only three, seem to be universally necessary.

A food producing economy is essential; that's logical and we understand it.

A recognition and regulation of sex is essential; that, too, we understand logically.

But a non-human God conception is essential — and that is non-logical.

But check it and see if what I say above is not true.

And that, my, friend, is from an agnostic of 30 years standing!

When Rome deified the emperors, it actually humanized the Gods — and broke down the hyper-human aspect of the Gods. Rome fell.

Our civilization, by the way, does NOT stem from Rome, as the history books tend to indicate. Most of the achievements of our civilization stem from Islam! Allah be praised! Also *al*cohol, *al*gebra, *al*chemy, Arabic number systems, and a basic orientation of the scientific method. The Romans were engineers who despised and demeaned philosophy; the Greeks were philosophers who hated experiments. The Islamic civilization produced the world's first philosophical engineers — the scientists. After Christianity got booted out of the Holy Land four times running, Christianity finally got it through its thick skull that it took more than pious wishes to get things done.

97

Unfortunately, at that point Islam decided that they'd proven conclusively that they knew everything anybody needed to know. A couple of centuries of contemplation of their great achievements followed.

Only in the last century or so has the Western Civilization bothered to go back and pick up the ruins of Islam — and then largely the oil fields Islam never found.

When is a man — or a culture — dead? When the body stops moving — or when the mind stops growing?

Regards,   John

Poul Anderson   *December 6, 1952*

Dear Poul:

The trouble with historians is that they'd rather be traditional than be right. It's practically axiomatic; the guy wouldn't be a historian if he weren't all wrapped up and deeply reverent about the traditions of man. There are exceptions, of course — but they're exceptional, and kept well under control by the Traditionalist Authorities.

If you think I'm kidding on that, you're wrong. I know whereof I speak.

Item: **Wallace West,** scf writer, is also a professional history text writer. But he's a researcher, and *not* a traditionalist. He dug out some papers which quoted Washington and Jefferson, separately, as saying that our constititution was based largely on the constitution of the Iroquois Nations, as originally drawn up by Hiawatha, the truly great American statesman. Washington & Jefferson each said that was the case — because the contributions W. & J. themselves made to the contribution was derived from that source. And, dammit, they ought to know where they got their ideas! Franklin, too, paid the highest respect to the Iroquois constitution.

Wally West wrote that into an American History text he was doing.

The School Boards cut it out. They didn't question its authenticity, but pointed out that it wasn't traditional.

So with that wild tradition-inspector **West** well under control, the history text will appear with all the traditions — and no unpleasant new ideas.

Item: The Western Culture we know is based almost entirely on *Semitic* achievements.

Evidence: The Christian culture, post about 500 AD, hated Rome and all things Roman with a virulent hatred. Vide what the Bible has to say about the harlot city. The Romans took baths;

98

bathing was therefore unchristian. Etc. The early Church did everything possible to suppress Roman culture — but Rome, as the head of the church, had to be maintained. A completely non-roman tradition of Rome, therefore, was established.

The new tradition was Christian, of course — which means it was a modified branch of the Jewish culture.

The Christian Church, through the Dark Ages, rejected everything of Pagan Rome and Pagan Greece. We most certainly did NOT get our understanding of Greece and Rome through *that* channel — it was plugged just as hard and tight as the Church Fathers could possibly plug it.

The Dark Ages ended when the Church Fathers got their noggins cracked, but good, trying to bust into Islamic territory — Jerusalem, to be precise. They got clouted, hard, solid, and unequivocably, four times running. They got their pants kicked off.

At this point it was driven into their exceptionally hard heads that the Western Christian culture did NOT have all the answers anybody needed. So they learned a little something new.

Islam, in the meantime, had taken that bunch of fairics and disputation experts, the Greeks, evaluated them for what they were, and come to some conclusions. They'd also looked at Rome — which they had no reason to hate particularly, as the Christians did — and evaluated them. The Romans could do things, by Allah! And the Greeks could explain things. But the Romans couldn't explain why what they did worked, and the Greeks couldn't make their explanations work for them.

So Islam invented science. (We definitely did not; the Semitic Islamic Empire did. They were the first *scientists*.) They invented *al*chemie, *al*gebra, *al*cohol and quite a few other items. Which was, of course, why they kicked those Christian dogs out of their way. They had every reason to consider the Christians a bunch of dirty barbarians, too. The Christians were uneducated, unlearned, dirty, slovenly, brutal, amoral, illogical, and unskilled. Their weapons were clumsy, and they had no understanding of anything beyond their stinking bodies. They were a bunch of hairy barbarians, with all their small attention turned to body and soul — and they had no intellect whatever.

So the Semitic-based culture of Western Christianity, having been soundly booted by Semitic Islam, went home, licked its wounds — and for the first time in ages cracked a book other than the Holy Bible.

It wasn't until Galileo came along, however, that the Christians *finally* got the idea; you're not supposed to study the *books*; you're supposed to study the *real world*, and simply use the books as guides.

99

This idea is now dying out rapidly.

Climb out of your history textbooks, **Poul**, and look see what the real-world evidence is.

Did we get our civilization from Greece and Rome directly?

Is the Islamic invention, science, made up of the combination of Greek philosophy and Roman engineering, properly either Roman or Greek?

Is salt, made up of sodium and chlorine, simply a mixture of a metal and a gas?

Sure, historical *facts* are beyond argument. But the *meaning* of those facts needs a lot of looking into. You wouldn't expect a Western Christian Cultural historian, enamoured of the Great Traditions, to refer to our crusading ancestors as a bunch of stinking barbarians, who were seeking to assault a civilization far higher than their own, would you? Those Western Christian cultural forebearers of ours were the same gang that ruined the original Roman Empire; they were the same gang of barbarians, and they were just as barbarian when they assaulted Islam. But you wouldn't expect a Western Christian historian to recognize *that* would you?

My point: Don't trust an historian's interpretation of facts — and don't trust him to put all the facts available in. He's too interested in the Great Traditions.

Ever read Aristophanes' plays "The Birds," "Lysestrata" or "The Clouds"? They're part of the Great Books series. They're old, all right, but so far as being Great goes, they're just old and to a modern skit. They are *not* good; they're just old and famous. They're no more philosophical — less so, probably — than *Tarzan of the Apes*. Give me 100 high-power philosophers, though, and I'll find 100,000 deep comments of philosophical understanding in Tarzan! Burroughs may not have put it in there — but the philosophers can!

Historians do not like discontinuities — and they don't mind distorting the evidence. That's part of their regular business. Find the U.S. history, for instance, that explains in detail how the infant US got its bloody pants kicked in the War of 1812. The British walked all over us, and walked on because they were busy elsewhere. But the US histories all say that the US never lost a war!

Now let's recognize that historians are men who have pet theories, and are about as unreliable as any other group of men who believe in a dogma, and look at the facts of the real world on which the various dogmatists of history agree.

Egypt's Nile Valley and the Tigris-Euphrates system had been in existence for a LONG time. It was in existence in very much the present condition before the recent glaciation; man was around before, during, and after that glaciation.

Why didn't the Nile valley have that effect on man before?

Now look, **Poul**, it's all right to say it took some time. But my God, man, Man's been around for not less than 100,000 years — and probably, according to a number of anthropologists, nearer 250,000.

Also, *since* the first Empires appeared, empires have sprung up all over the damn planet. The Incas had one, and so did the Aztecs — without help of Egyptain Nile Valleys. There were empires all over the blasted planet. AFTER X happened. Whatever X was, we don't know. The historians have been trying to decide that, and insisting on the ancient Western Christian Cultural tradition that There Is No Difference Between Individuals.

I propose a simple new factor; introduce a mutation and its consequences. The mutation that caused a type that says "Why?" instead of "Oh; I'll do it that way."

The type Oh can go on for 200,000 years, and very, very rarely some oaf will stub his toe on something and fall with his mush in a new invention. Once tell him what to do though — and he'll do it faithfully. He'll keep on doing it, too, until somebody tells him to stop.

The Type Why will get himself into trouble; he'll make Type Oh heartily dislike him, by saying, "Yes, I know you've always done it that way — but why?" Type Oh has no answer to this; to him the question has no meaning whatever. But Type Oh has an excellent traditional answer to the *individual* if he hasn't an answer to the problem; slug him till he stops bothering. "There; now I guess he knows why!"

This same type of Physiological Argument is still used; "Now I guess those Japs know better than to try that again!"

"Let's make a bigger bomb, we'll show those Russkies what to do!"

Somewhat, however, the Physio-logical argument never seems to satisfy. Type Why is a *very* persistent breed.

Look, **Poul** — instead of studying the *fact* of change in the level of culture, study the *rate* of change. A velocity of 100 miles an hour never hurt anyone; it's the deceleration at the end when you hit that stone wall. It isn't the velocity — it's the rate of change of velocity.

Try plotting an acceleration-of-civilization curve for the last 100,000 years, and see if there isn't indication of something of a different order of magnitude.

Item: Our whole science has started off from the proposition that "The whole is equal to the sum of the parts."

That happens to be wrong. The sum of the parts is a mixture; the whole is a compound. Two volumes of hydrogen plus one volume of oxygen gas, mixed at room temperature, equals a small volume of water? Eleven men equal one football team? The dictionary contains all the literature of the English language? One carat of graphite plus one carat of graphite equals two carats of diamond?

A chemist can analyze a magnet, but he won't find the magnetic field — and the magnetic field, is *not* a part of the whole, but is a property of the whole. The magnetic field is an extrinsic property — it's a relationship to the Universe, and *not* a part of the whole.

Take the word "warm" the meaning of the word is *not* a part of the word, and yet is a property of the word-as-a-whole.

A science that is based on not-differentiating between the sum of the parts and the whole isn't going to get valid answers to most of the major questions of the Universe. Such a science can operate *only* on the lowest levels of organization, where extrinsic properties have minimal importance. Even so, organic chemistry was stopped until they recognized that not only the kind of atoms, but the relationship of the atoms was important.

The theory that progress is made by failures interests me. Progress was, I am sure, greatly aided by the organisms which were failures — but in the following way. The land, I think, was first invaded by some hyper-tough organism, of the Alexander-the-Great school of thought. Unquestionably, the first land-living organisms had a tough time. This is where the failure-organisms aided progress. They got chased on land, being chased out of the water by some tougher organisms, and thus served as food for the hyper-toughies that had chosen to come ashore.

Dammit, man, look around you. Are the rocket pilots the unsuccessful failures who couldn't take the rough life of the airplane pilot? Are the Newton's the failures who couldn't take the strain of ordinary academic life? Were those fragile cake-eaters who carved out the West failures who couldn't hold their own in the dangerous east?

Sure they were failures in the east — in one sense. They got claustrophobia from the little men and the little towns and the little ideas that surrounded them.

But I assure you, it is most unwise for an organism driven out of Region A by competition of the normals to enter region B, the new frontier. Region B is normally populated by those organisms that were too big and tough and wild to be content with the old, limited region.

The greatest menace Region A faces is the weaklings of Region B — the failures who slump back to the old region. Look what happens to fish when a porpoise gets hungry! Look what happens to the jungle and its inhabitants when modern man, complete with bulldozers and machine rifles, decides he wants a piece of territory.

The essence of my argument about the *Homo inquisitivus* idea is this; there was a mutation. The difference that mutation produces is about 4 orders of magnitude of competence. The difference between true *H. sapiens* and *H. inquisitivus* is about 10,000 to 1. But H. inq. had to breed "with the daughters of men" as it saith in the Bible. The race we know in the US here is hybrid — and, like skin color, the type can vary from pure black to pure white, with all shades in between. It's not the sort of mutation that works on a yes-no basis, In the US we have practically nothing but nearly pure *H. inquis.*; to see what nearly pure *H. sap.* is like, visit the Mexican peons, or some of the other peoples of the world where there has been practically no stirring up of the race. It is NOT lack of opportunity; you can lead a horse to water, but you can't make him drink. You can NOT teach a man anything whatsover; he has to learn. And if he doesn't want to learn, you can't possibly make him learn. You can whip a man into acting physically — but you can't whip his mind into acting.

Just because *you* want to learn, you haven't the slightest right to say that "all human beings want to learn." T'ain't so. You'll agree, I think, that a dog doesn't *want* to learn tricks; he learns them to please his beloved and adored master. He will also happily, and voluntarily, throw himself into a fight that he knows means his death for the sake of the beloved and adored master. That doesn't mean he would throw himself into that fight if he had free choice, and no endangered master to protect.

If you treat a peon kindly, and win his true affection and deep admiration, he will, for your sake and because of the love he has for you, try to learn — though it's against his basic nature. That is NOT his natural function in life — and he won't be made happy by it.

Your reaction to that is apt to be that I'm demeaning the peon. Maybe. But aren't you being authoritarian in autocratically ruling that all human beings must enjoy the *way* you do? Are you insisting on educating the peon "for his own good . . . (the stupid lout!)" Aren't you insisting that any man who doesn't want education is a stupid fool who must be taught to know better? Aren't you trying to determine for him what he should and should not want? Volstead sought to determine that we should not want to drink. The League for Christian Decency seeks to determine what we should and should not be permitted to see or read.

I hold that a man is a man, and human, even if he doesn't happen to choose to live and enjoy life the way I do — even if he prefers not to work for an education. That there are ways of being human other than my particular way — and that one of those ways is *H. sapiens'* way, which doesn't include questioning himself, his fellow man, his God, and his universe. He doesn't *want* to question; all education does is make him have to question, without being able to work out answers.

Ah, well . . . I happen to be the type that gets maximum enjoyment from questioning everything. Including the validity of the distance concept, and the basic theories of physics.

Incidentally: distance involves position and velocity also. What is the position of the electron in a hydrogen molecule?

Strange — the question seems to have no answer. It doesn't have a position; it's just sort of smeared all over the hydrogen molecule. That makes it very difficult indeed to measure distance at intramolecular distances, doesn't it?

It's downright upsetting, for a while, when you start kicking out the distance concept — and start discovering a quite new orientation-system for the world as a result!

Regards,   John

Harry Stine *December 6, 1952*

Dear Harry:

Yeah, verily — a slip was slipped. The letter from **Eggen** belonged to **Harry Stubbs,** otherwise **Hal Clement.** I tossed the letter on **Miss Tarrant's** desk and asked her to send it to **Harry Stubbs** — and the slip was very easy indeed.

I spent all day, from about 12:30 to 4:40 at least, with **E.E. Francisco** yesterday. Hell of a fine guy, and we had a first rate bull-session that wandered all the way from the practically-spontaneous generation of viruses, to the problems of recovering instruments from Aerobee and V-2 firings. He's a top-flight engineer who isn't afraid to let his mind roam — and that type's all too rare in the world. I wish your gang was somewhat more convenient to me! As it is, I've simply planted a few Grade A Stinker questions with **Francisco,** and you'll probably be bull-sessioning them shortly.

Briefly: I've been studying some of the nice, pat, basic assumptions of physics — and, what do you know? They fall apart at the seams! *Most* disconcerting!

Let's start with the concept "length" or "distance."

First, the concept "friction" is a perfectly valid one — in a limited range of experience. That is, it's not valid below the molecular level, nor above the planetary level. It's actually valid *only* over the range wherein matter can be considered effective homogeneous. Where ballistic analysis becomes practicable, the concept friction proves unsatisfactory. Friction, in other words, is a special-frame-of-reference concept, and not at all a true Universal.

So's distance. It's valid over the same range of values that friction is — but not beyond!

Consider the "distance" to the Moon. By definition of the concept of distance, the distance from Earth to Moon equals the distance from the Moon to the Earth.

As a rocketeer, my friend — is it?

Distance can actually be defined *only* operationally. Name a physical process — an operation — for measuring the Earth-Moon "distance" that is *not* affected by the fact of gravitational field stresses! Light is affected, remember, so that's out.

I say distance can be defined only operationally; demonstration of that fact is as follows:

Cantor, the mathematician, has shown that there is the same number of points in a line segment of any length, no matter how short, as there is in any other line segment, or a line of infinite length. This being the case, give me a logical definition of the term "greater than." The only definition I know of — or several others I've questioned have been able to bring forth — is operational. Then, since you can't "operate" on the distance from Earth to Moon at the present time — you can't measure it! Then what do you mean by "distance"?

Let's look some more. The "distance" concept is necessarily involved in a whole series of concepts derived from it. Position, for instance — and also velocity and acceleration. Now we can use those concepts in a pragmatic way in our daily living — just as we can use those Newtonian mechanics in a cathode ray tube, provided we keep the voltage below, say, 100,000. Of course, we both know that Newtonian mechanics does not truly describe what happens at 5,000 volts, but the departure is below the level of instrument uncertainty, so it's futile to worry about it. But it's there.

Let's look at "position" once we get outside the range of orders of magnitude in which the friction concept applies — and the distance concept, as I suggest.

Instead of "Which twin has the Toni?" let's ask "Which atom has the electron?" in a hydrogen molecule of H_2. In other words, what is the position of the electron?

Tsk tsk! How strange! You mean it *has* no position?

Then what's the distance from electron A to nucleus B?

You mean you can't express a distance when you don't know what positions are?

Uncertain sort of life an electron leads, isn't it? It never quite knows where it is, and therefore doesn't really understand what we mean by "distance," does it?

Or consider the electron that goes through two holes in a metal plate and interferes with itself on the other side to produce intereference patterns on the photographic plate beyond. We've got evidence of an uncertainty of the electron's "position" that can be measured in terms of millimeters here!

You know — physics would really do a remarkable sort of nip-up if the concept of "distance" were kicked out the window, wouldn't it?

Of course, if "distance" is kicked out, then velocity needs to be redefined — and the Michelson-Morley experiment has a third interpretation. The experiment actually was an effort to ask Nature "How fast does the Earth move through the ether?" Nature answered in effect "Your question is not meaningful as expressed." The accepted explanation is that there is no ether.

But maybe the reason the question is meaningless is that there is no *motion?* Or not in the terms we sought to define it!

Of course, the concept of "ether" was originally introduced to get away from the necessity for "action at a distance" — and if distance is an invalid concept, we have the possibility that *both* the "motion" part of the question *and* the "ether" part of it were invalid.

As you can see from the above — we've been having a wonderful time poking in the corners and seams of Physics. My, the dust that has been hiding back of the furniture!

Also, the inverse square law has some remarkable characteristics. Let's measure the field of a magnet. We'll set up a magnet and a meter bar, and, with an exploration coil, measure the magnetic field force at various distances. Yep; it comes out to be an inverse square law, just like the textbooks say. But — uh — what was the operation we actually performed?

That meter bar, for example; what is it? It's not solid matter; it's space with a number of discontinuities imposed on it. Atoms — which are, of course, simply small, dense force fields. Let's assume, just for the moment, that all force fields obey the same law; then the force fields of the atoms can be considered to be similar in structure, though different in density, to the big force field of the magnet — the thing we're measuring.

What do you know? We've been measuring in such a way as to demonstrate that the integral of ndx equals nX! This is not exactly a new discovery — and it tells us absolutely nothing whatsoever about the characteristics of X. The inverse square effect is simply the old geometrical law of probability; it, also, has nothing to do with the nature of X. I can prove that bullets from a machine gun or a shotgun are subject to a mysterious inverse square law, too. With our conceptions of geometry, they'd have a hell of a time following any other law around *our* laboratories.

Of course, if we had a slightly larger arena to try it out in, we'd begin to get **Einsteinian** geometry showing up — and naturally,when you redefine your concepts of distances, you'll get a departure from the inverse square law. If you measure magnetic fields with a slide-rule, you won't get an inverse square law either.

The Euclidean geometry we're used to thinking in is the special topology of a plane surface. In such a special universe, the concept of a least-line becomes a straight line, and the straight line actually consists of an infinite family of least lines which fall on one another. The similarity of the family of least lines becomes 1.00, and we have an identity.

Curve the plane a little, though, and the infinite family of leastlines begins opening out; there is now an infinite number of least-lines between any two points, and they're *not* identical.

What's the least-line distance from North to South pole? What is *the* least line between them?

If cause-effect relationships be considered a least-line relationship — why, then, in a curved space there is more than one equally valid cause-effect relationship between two points!

More fun! I can see a million lovely science-fiction stories in that!

You've read **Ray Jones'** "Noise Level," in which we suggested that maybe we're being stopped from solving problems mostly because we aren't accepting a sufficiently broad viewpoint.

Ray has another one coming up that your gang there will like. The proposition that a man who discovers a basic law of nature should be allowed some sort of social recompense — perhaps not a patent, exactly, but something. **Einstein** got the Nobel prize for his work on the explanation of the photoelectric effect — but RCA and GE and others got the royalties.

Jones story: The good Dr. Whatzis gets a patent on a child's toy — it's a model spaceship 8 inches long, using 3 flashlight cells for power, and floats nicely in midair on an antigravity field. The patent states "it is based on a newly discovered law of Nature" — and tactfully refrains from revealing what the law is!

Anyone can follow the patent, and make a toy spaceship that floats. But the device won't support its own weight if you double all factors; it doesn't work on a linear basis any more than a rocket engine does. And they can't figure out what the factors are.

He explains he'll reveal his natural law when they pass a law that will reward him for his contribution to society; in the meantime, since society says it will reward people for making gadgets, he's making money on his gadget; everybody, of course, wants one of the antigravity toys to play with.

Then, while everybody is stewing that one, he comes out with a gambling device. It's a 3-foot round table, with a 4″ high rim.

There's a cone that rises up to about 20 inches at the center, shaped like a volcano, with a cylindrical well down the middle. At the bottom of the well is a rubber diaphragm, agitated by a little motor, and a collection of numbered marbles. When started, the marbles bounce up to about 6″ below the rim of the volcano — but every so often one of them sort of disappears and reappears on the outside of the slope, to roll down and clang against the metal rim. You bet on which marble will make it. The device works — but can't be altered in any way whatsoever without flatly refusing to work. It makes a popular gambling device, nobody can bugger it without simply making it stop.

Every nuclear physicist promptly starts tearing his hair. The old sunnuvabitch has neatly presented them with a super-scale model of how a radioactive nucleus works — compete with barrier-potential penetration. Dr. Whatzis announces that "this device works on a newly discovered law of Nature" and goes to work banking the royalties from his gambling device. He also sells a few samples of various rare elements to various scientific laboratories.

The combined demands of the AEC, Army, Navy, and industrial research firms don't get a whisper of information from him; the top-flight theorists who might be able to crack his gadgets eventually aren't trying for publication — they are perfectly charmed to see the gadget-lovers howling, while he waits for them to get around to recognizing that pure theory is more important than clever gadgets. And they don't get a damned thing but children's toys and gambling devices until they *do* acknowledge that, and enact it into law!

Of course, he's making a fortune from his toy's patent, and his gambling device patent; those devices are precisely what Society, through its laws, *says* it wants — and it pays for them, too.

There are a lot of nice little stories that can come out of the proposition of looking at things in a slightly different way. **Hal Clement** — whose letter you got by mistake — is at Sandia Base, instructing the Air Force in physics. He wrote "Needle" which you probably recall, and "Iceworld." He just sold us a nice 85,000 worder at our top bonus 4¢ rate. And each of his stories has been simply a new viewpoint, a different environmental framework. (His new one concerns a being who's home is on a planet with a surface gravity of some 500 to 700g!)

Item: We measure distances, actually, in terms of force-fields. So suppose I have an oscillator coil with 1 megacycle juice in it. At a certain other point, I have a coil. I measure the interaction of the two, and find that 1 microvolt is being induced in the second coil. Then I tune the second coil; otherwise I do not disturb the relationship between the two. But now there is 10,000,000 microvolts in the second coil. This proves I've reduced the distance between them by a factor of 10,000,000 doesn't it? Or does it? Or what does it indicate?

Regards,   John

Dear Halperns:

Dammit; slipped on the year that time! I'd gotten it right seven times running, too!

Peg and I haven't been great travellers recently — and I suspect you two haven't either. We've been busy — and that means about 100 hours a week on our research, and then there's other odd chores like running a house and running a magazine. Takes an annoying amount of time to make a living!

The work we've done has been decidedly different from that the rest of the gang seems to have done. Almost everyone in the mind-study business seems to concentrate on studying a lot of individuals — clinical work, in general. **Peg** and I, rather than seeing how much similarity there is between different people, finding the basic similar mind-mechanisms, have been studying on an intensive basis — how deep can you get into one individual mind.

Naturally, the results we've gotten are of a different type. I don't know how to open a case, I'm sure. We've developed special techniques designed for use on our own individual problems, and ploughed on down to see how deep one *can* get.

Of course, by normal human projection, we've got the feeling that everyone has to do that eventually. We like the method, even if it does take a hell of a lot of time and effort. Now, we've put in something approching 15,000 hours on our joint problems.

We haven't used the E-meter; because of our special situation and special type of research that hasn't been very fruitful or necessary. We aren't looking for incidents; we find that X is a problem, say. Then the question we ask is not "What incident caused X to appear in your life as a problem?" but, instead, "What is there about X that I wasn't able to resolve that problem?" After all, we're going to go on running into problems for the rest of our lives. That's inevitable. The Big Problem is the Problem of Solving Problems; what keeps me from solving the problem X presented, rather than what caused X in the first place.

The old proposition "Nothing is good or bad but thinking makes it so" is a valid comment, the problem that we're attacking is "What is thinking, and

109

on what basis should we judge things?"

It seems to us that we could go on resolving individual problems — incidents — as they came up from now till Doomsday and get no forewarder; we have to develop a technique of resolving incidents that will resolve them faster than they come to us — so fast that we can resolve all those we encounter, *and* make progress in resolving the accumulated backlog.

Hubbard's fantastic stuff is the most annoying damned thing we have to work with. The thing that makes it so annoying is that **Ron** is a Grade A Mystic — one of the real, genuine mystics of the highest order. He *does* achieve understanding — but achieves them in the usual mystic fashion. They come out so garbled and twisted that it takes a lot of very hard work to find what in hell he was actually trying to talk about. It takes so much work, in fact, that it's easier to ignore **Ron,** and discover the same things for yourself in a slower but more orderly fashion.

Ron's "thetan" business is perfectly valid — it's a very old realization indeed — but **Ron** got a new slant on it. His slant has his usual mystic garbledness; but has a fundamental validity of the highest order. The old term for "thetan" is "soul"; before that the Egyptians called it the "ka."

Neither **Ron's** version nor the religious version of "soul" has the story nailed down properly. **Ron** has an advance, in saying the "thetan" is *not* identical with "I," and can be contacted by "I" and its experiences investigated. [Apparently John was not familiar with **L. Ron Hubbard's** then definition of *Thetan*: "It is the individual, the being, the personality, the knowingness of the human being," *Scientology 8-80*, Bridge Publications, P. 46, 1952: Ed.]

The slight difficulty is that **Ron** suggests some of the most outrageous experiences! He still hasn't found the real experiences that are there; he's been too busy projecting his basic proposition of pain-drug hypnosis, and so on.

The non-mystic facts are that every human being has an innate something that is convinced of personal immortality. A conviction that general must have something on which it's based. Then something in the human being has *experienced* effective immortality.

Most certainly; you're 2,000,000,000 years old now, you know. The essential life-force in you has existed as an unbroken line of development for the full length of existence of life on Earth.

The "thetan" and the "theta line" experiences **Ron's** looking for are simply the genetic line memories.

They aren't what he thinks they are, though.

If you want physical evidence that such genetic-line experience exists, and is validly communicated to the individual, look into embryology. The fertile ovum goes through a greatly foreshortened, collapsed redevelopment of the whole process of evolution. There's something around here that *knows* we once went through the fish stage — and it grows gills on a human embryo. There's something around here, also, that *knows* how the mind

110

evolved from the early primates, through the quasi-human savage, through the tribesman, and on.

You can call it *thetan* or *soul* if you like — but it *knows* it's lived 2,000,000,000 years. It has a peculiar time-sense, however, because it collapses the first 1,500,000,000 years into the first 6 weeks of pregnancy, and extends the last 1,000,000 years over the 15 or so years after birth and before adolescence is well established.

This doesn't mean "past lives" either. That phenomenon involves something quite different. The development of the individual is a sort of index system; the full, detailed records to which the index refers are available, but in a different mechanism.

Ron's got the two mixed up and interconfused. So do most of the mystics. Unscrambling the two is a hell of a job, and involves an attack on the problem from the basis of pure physical science, rather than by introspection.

We call that genetic mind business the *kynmod* — from the Anglo-Saxon roots "cynn" (pronounced "kin" — we still have the word) meaning related-folk, or tribe, and "*mod*" meaning mood, mind, courage, and pride. The kynmod is the folk-mind, the genetically passed on information. Kynmod is to an instinct as mind is to an idea.

The total personality results from the interaction of kynmod and mind — the latter being approximately what we used to call the analytical mind plus the subcomputers. "I" is the interaction product, is of both, but is not either. Sodium and chlorine interact to produce salt, which is neither.

Most of the internal conflicts come from disagreements between the kynmod wisdom of the ages, and the mind-computed answers based on individual experience. The only way such a conflict can be resolved is to find out *why* kynmod got its belief, and where mind got *it's* idea, and then do some good, hard studying to find out which of the two makes better sense.

You'll be somewhat discomfited, but it'll do a great deal of good. To the horror of Society, you'll discover that 99.99% of the time, Mind is wrong, and kynmod is right. After all — kynmod's been a little stupid maybe, but even a stupid dope, if he hangs around for 2,000,000,000 years, [is] going to learn *something* worth knowing.

Most of the bright new ideas Mind has discovered triumphantly are bright new baubles kynmod wore out sometime during the last 3 or 4 hundred megayears.

There's no thetan hanging around that we've been able to find — but there is kynmod, a very quiet and steady old peasant, who is not given the brilliant, flashing wit of Mind, but who has during the long, long, megayears, done enough different things to have something approching total experience. Mind would be less brilliant, but a lot wiser, if it settled down to listen to kynmod for a while.

For one thing, Mind never has figured out what happiness is. Kynmod doesn't have any sharp, quick, flashing answers — but it found out how to *be* happy something like 700,000,000 years ago. Anytime Mind will stop jittering around frantically, and settle down quietly long enough to learn a little wisdom, "I" can achieve happiness too.

Ron would rather be flashingly brilliant, the Great Maestro, and send thetans flashing all over the universe, and 73 trillion years hither and yon.

It took two thousand megayears to learn what kynmod's learned.

If you think you can integrate that in 25 hours of theta-clearing — that's Mind talking. Kynmod knows more about patient effort.

Other mammals went flashing off to be great hunters, with sharp claws and teeth; Man's ancestral kynmod sat in the trees and watched. Other mammals acted — decided how to live; they grew long, fleet legs, and learned to eat grass of which there was always a supply. The Primates sat in the trees, undecided, and watched.

Man never did make up his kynmod as to what he was going to be — so he's a little of everything. He flies faster than any bird, and runs faster than any fleet-footed animal. He has weapons that no animal can face —

And he has his total mind, kynmod plus Mind — which is a weapon no man has ever conceived yet. If you can ever integrate the immensely powerful analytical tool of the Mind, with the immense data-pool of kynmod's 2,000,000,000 year experience . . . !

You'll be able to achieve that, however, when, and only when, you have figured out a technique of disagreement-settling such that you can get Joe Stalin and Boss Kettering together, and have Stalin resign and put RUSSIA under Kettering's direction, while Stalin goes to school.

By that time, you'll have levitation, teleporation, telepathy, and mental-powered transmutation of the elements, however.

But you *can* make a start toward the Big Job.

Regards,   John

Frederik Pohl   *January 22, 1953*

Dear Mr. Pohl:

I'm returning the **Blish-Knight** manuscript herewith. I'm fairly sure I know why the yarn won't write — and this yarn really won't write. There's nothing the matter with the authors — the fault's with the idea. It looks good, but it isn't.

This is a story in sociology — but in a field of sociology that no human beings have ever investigated. We haven't yet solved the problem of the interrelations of human nature and a population in the hundreds of millions. These problems are at least within range of view. **Blish & Knight** are tackling the problem of what kind of problems will be met in a hundreds of billions population.

You can't do it. You don't know enough. It's building impossible speculation on implausible guess. It's going to have a ring of phoneyness similar to that found in a character study of a super-human; only a superhuman can write the story of a superhuman's character.

What this means at the practical action level is that the story is mired in complexity. The duodecimal system is typical — but taking it out won't pull you out of handling some ten different viewpoints. A detective story contrives the mystery effect by confusing the reader with more viewpoints than his mind can follow; this will be worse confused than the detective story average.

Finally, you aren't going to have that trillion population anyway. It isn't too obvious, but there's a basic biological law that a species won't breed if it doesn't have a sense of purpose. That's why so many animals won't breed in captivity — they have no sense of purpose, no sense of destiny.

The cybernetic revolution you speak of in here puts nearly everyone out of work. Having lost function, purpose, and destiny they'll stop breeding.

Naturally, they won't stop breeding, so they'll destroy the thing which tends to force them to stop breeding — the culture that gives them no function, no purpose, no sense of accomplishment.

Look, penal authorities long since learned that you can't keep a man from working toward a goal. Why do you think people are sentenced to "X years at hard labor?" Because they're going to labor hard anyway; give 'em something to do, or they'll be busy little beavers figuring and working toward escape. You can bet they'll be working, and working hard. It only *looks* as though human beings were lazy. They can't endure not working — so they'll work all right. They'll be busy little beavers taking those cities apart a brick at a time, with their teeth if necessary, but they'll be engaged on an important-to-them purpose.

Can you imagine a society with 10,000,000 technical-administrative people trying, with machines, to build it up while a trillion human beings devote their productive lives to taking it apart?

The administrators couldn't make that civilization hold together any better than **Blish & Knight** can!

There was a brilliant man over in France who spent many years working hard and intently until he finally succeeded in developing

113

a perfect technique for counterfeiting used postage stamps. It may seem a futile life to you, but he satisfied the most powerful of human needs — he worked toward a goal that he'd selected, and was happy doing so.

He's now probably busy learning to counterfeit canceled checks, or Confederate money.

But he has a job he considers worth doing.

No human being can accept the dole as a life work.

Sincerely,   John W. Campbell, Jr.

Jim Blish   *February 3, 1953*

Dear Jim:

You and **Knight** are now faced with a classic old problem of humanity; you've invested a hell of a lot of time, effort, and serious and sincere hard thinking in that problem of the overpopulated world. I am the Nasty Ogre who intimates that you won't get the expected and intended result — a powerful and moving story.

I'm perfectly willing to help in any way I can to derive from your efforts an effective story; that's my life work, you know. I'm not a writer any more; you're the skilled expert in that line. I have, instead, tried to develop another skill — the interpretation of audience reaction. I may appear to be the Nasty Ogre who seeks to demolish your work; I get caught in that spot time after time, because I'm the allocable source of undesired reaction. Please do not smash the telephone because the guy at the other end says "no!" when you wanted "Yes!" To the best of my ability, I'm trying to act like a telephone, the other end of which is 6 months to a year in the future, and connected with some 100,000 newsstands all across the country. This trick has its difficulties; I slip not infrequently.

My work — which I naturally consider worth doing and highly engrossing — is to help work out stories that *are* precisely what the authors want — effective and moving pieces.

We have a fancy collection of assorted form letters and rejection slips. I usually use a rejection slip when working through an agent, because part of **Pohl's** job is doing the same essential type of work I do — helping authors get good stories. He's a skilled technician too, and not just a mail box service, you know. The fact that he objected to the duodecimal system is worth looking at in the light that he *is* a skilled specialist. If you don't feel his judgment has value, then you have poor judgment in employing him. He's working on your team too.

We're not trying to knock out your idea, nor are we trying to prevent you getting a powerful story expressing the theme you feel needs expressing. But we are trying to keep you from weakening a

114

powerful theme by dressing it up so much the reader interest is diverted and finally lost.

Take a look at the sort of living rooms they went in for in the period of 1890-1910 or so. Geegaws, furbelows, gimcracks, and whatnots. All sorts of gadgets and knicknacks. The furniture had carvings and brass nails and trick rocking devices and godknowswhat all over it. It may have been pretty, but it wasn't art. You couldn't see the chair for the gimcracks built on and in it. You couldn't sit comfortably in it either, I can testify.

To get a powerful story, take all those books you mentioned, all the reports you've read elsewhere, all your lifetime of experience and thinking, and reduce the whole thing to a single statement of not more than 25 words.

That's the theme of the story. Don't put anything else in it, and your reader won't miss it.

Build your novel like one of those really good modern chairs. They don't have trick rocker gadgets; they take advantage of the simple fact that steel and wood can both be used as elastic members. It's not necessary to have gravity as the elastic member of the system. It's not even necessary to have much upholstery; upholstery's function is to conform to the shape of the human being sitting in the chair.The more closely the basic shape of the chair itself conforms to actual human body shape, the less upholstery you need. The modern result is some of these astonishingly comfortable and relaxing hardwood and metal chairs that have practically no upholstery at all.

The duodecimal system is *not* part of your theme, and *is* distracting. It helps the reader look at something other than what you want him to realize. You're trying to capture his attention, and draw it inescapably to a theme you feel is enormously important to Mankind. The duodecimal system isn't, and it's a fine way to induce the reader's attention to wander from what he's supposed to be looking at.

So's nudity in the social system. The female form may be devine or not, but it's a guaranteed way to get a man's eyes and attention to wander from the main point at issue, when the man's a member of our society. Your reader is, whether his story-character is or not. If you want to discuss the importance of accepting nudity — that can be the theme of a story, and it's apt to attract attention fairly readily.

Your thesis here is that overpopulation is going to take place remorselessly. Puerto Rico already is; China and India already are. You are so right. There are also large insane asylums full of people who haven't been able to think through their ordinary life problems. That doesn't mean that insanity is inevitable. It does mean that immigration barriers are inevitable, however; we got hooked, but good, on getting the Puerto Rican psychotics inside our immigration barriers, and we're having trouble with them. It's all right, however; they come to New York, and the powerful social pressures they encounter here will rapidly put the clamps on them.

You're actually beating a dead horse when you write that story for Americans. The science-fiction audience needs that advice like a physicists' convention needs to be told that copper conducts electricity. You're trying to sell them a theme that they and their ancestors for about three generations back had accepted deeply and strongly. Try writing that theme so Puerto Rican natives will understand, appreciate, and study it.

I don't run atomic doom stories; our readers already know all about that. They don't want more discussion of the fact that the problem exists; they want discussions of how to solve the problem. Discussions that do not involve intervention by Arisians, or other *deus ex machina* problems.

Your story theme, as now conceived, is one that the scf. audience is aware of, has already accepted, and wants an answer to. You have no answer to offer; only a reemphasis of the castastrophic consequence of unlimited breeding. The Puerto Rican problem can be solved by fomenting a rebellion down there, by use of agent provocateurs, followed by a descent of the US Army and a liberal use of atomic bombs and biological weapons. The result could be bulldozed, worked over, and converted to a pleasure resort and plantation island, while a population could be imported that imposed powerful social sneers on large families.

It could be. If we could stomach such methods. That's a good, sound Malthusian method, too, you notice. Then there's the Hitlerian method. There's also the logical method of establishing population control centers wherein, by law, each Puerto Rican woman was sterilized after giving birth to one child. The males don't have to be sterilized, of course; the birth rate is always proportional to the number of females in the childbearing ages, and shows no correlation with the number of males.

That would be nice and logical. It would also lead directly to the first method mentioned, simply substituting for the agent provocatuer step.

The most powerful tool of thinking that man has is the analog. The trouble with analogs is that they work only in situations which are truly analogous. If we try using the analog in a field which is not properly analogous, the results are interesting, but scarcely revealing. And you must always operate with the suspicion that the analog may be completely off by reason of some small, overlooked factor.

116

These studies of generalized populations are fascinating; I don't question the validity of the data obtained. But I do question, most strongly, the validity of the conclusions as applied to Man. Have they studied generalized *highly intelligent* populations?

Hitler's emotionalisitic speeches moved the Germans to vast actions. I wonder if the laws of public speaking derived from Hitler's speeches would lead to success in moving to action a group of mixed MIT, UCLA, Cornell Engineering and Cal Tech graduates and personnel from the Atomic Energy Commission laboratories?

Burning brands will frighten animals away. Therefore if endangered by approching African tribesmen, waving burning brands at them will disperse them in terror.

Your population of a trillion can live on Earth *only* as a highly intelligent cultural group.

But the laws of generalized populations do *not* apply to a special population of the class "highly intelligent."

I'll buy that business of "starvation leads to overpopulation" on a basis the guy who sets it up may not have considered. I didn't read the piece; maybe it's the basis he worked on; it's original with me in that I never heard it advanced before. To wit: When a population is under extreme pressure, it will tend to breed wildly, because of the tendency to try to pass an irresolvable problem along to somebody else to solve. The new generation represents the somebody else. The reason why animal life has this tendency is perfectly valid; the next generation born of a generation of individuals under extreme pressures will tend to have a higher percentage of mutants. One of them may carry the solution to the problem.

This might be called the "random noise" method of solving the problem. If enough people say enough things, somebody, by accident, may say the right thing. If enough individuals give birth to enough young, one of them may bear a mutant with the right answer built in.

Now it's true that I'm trying to keep you from writing the story you've done a lot of work on. Reason: your ability to write can, I sincerely feel, be better used on some more fruitful project. No self-educative effort is ever wasted; you've learned a hell of a lot in working on this story project. I think you can use that learning in more productive ways, however, than in the manner you had in mind originally.

Your water supply system, for example: isn't it suitable for a major city set up on Mars, where the water would have to be recirculated? Wouldn't the Martian conditions be such that *only* big-city living was feasible, so that one supply of air, water, etc., could be reused. Outdoor life wouldn't be feasible because the small organism of a single home, or a small village couldn't afford the efficient reutilization equipment. A single living cell has to adapt to its environment because it can't reuse its enviroment; a complex organism can establish a practically complete "balanced aquarium" system within itself, requiring only a few, very simple externally derived inputs. Then what happens in Martian Society where only Great Corporation existence is possible? Where the individual *can't* withdraw and start his own system?

Look, guy — if knowledge or a piece of knowledge is good and valid, it can be used in more than one situation.

Pick your accumulation of data apart, and make a dozen stories grow where only one grew before.

I never turn down a story until I have the finished story; I never buy one until I have the finished story.

I'll look at any story you write; I'm perfectly willing to have you prove me wrong in my prediction. There's a reason for that; the only way I ever learn anything is by losing an argument. If I win, then I haven't gained a new viewpoint. I like learning things; it's my life long hobby. So it's a case of heads I win, tails ignorance loses. If you can make a yarn out of that — by God you'll show me a new way of writing science-fiction, and I can promise you I'll steal that just as I've stolen every other new idea of how to write science-fiction that's come my way. And just as you have, too. We both learned a lot from **Bob Heinlein,** from **Isaac Asimov** and the rest. I now believe that you'd do better to break up the ideas in that novel and build a dozen or so other stories from it.

I'll be happy to see you prove me wrong.

Sincerely,   John

Hank Kuttner   *February 5, 1953*

Dear Hank:

I'm taking the new Baldie story; it's been a hell of a while since **Lewis Padgett** appeared in *ASF* — and I hope it won't be so long before you're back again.

In proof whereof, I'm going to mention a background thesis that, I think, will appeal to you and **C.L. Moore** almost equally. I'm mentioning it as possible story background material — and I'm talking about it to several other people. This is a story background that's big and wide and broad enough for fiction for the next few hundred years, so don't feel crowded.

It goeth thus:

Once upon a time, about 75 to 100 thousand years ago, the world was in the third interglacial period, and it was warm and lush and fertile. The land was rich with every tree and vine that delighteth the eye of man, and the land was full of many creatures. And Man, having achieved a high-power brain, was given dominion over all of them.

It was a good world, and a man might sit in the cool of the evening, and consult with the voice of his instincts within him, and feel at peace with himself.

What Man didn't know was that the Solar System was about to pass into a sprawling arm of cosmic dust; the slight loss of transmission of light from the Sun was going to cause the fourth glacial age.

When it came, it came fast. In a hurry.

All over Europe, the animals retreated before the suddenly growing glaciers. All over South Africa they fled northward. In South America they fled north, and in North America they fled south. It is the instinct of animals to move away from a danger they can't fight.

But there was one lush, rich area, where great plains, watered by wide rivers, were rich with game, and coral atolls grew off the northern coast, while mammoths ranged through the thick verdure. And when the ice came in this area, something different happened.

For this area was *north* of the *only* east-west mountain chain on the planet, *north* of the immense Tibetan plateau, east of the Ural mountains. The rich Siberian plains were about to become a stupendous trap — for the glaciers came down out of the mountains, and off the great, frozen plateau, and down out of the Himalayas and the Tibetan Plateau, southward from the Arctic — and the Pacific coast was buried in a raging screaming howling storm as the sudden glacial climate cooled the continental climate faster than it did the maritime climate of the Pacific. Glaciers started moving in from the coast, too.

And Man and the animals retreated before the advancing glaciers — into the vast corral the glaciers had built.

And Man faced a brand new situation; every animal survives because it has an immense number of little instinct patterns of what to do in Situation 237-B-46, and a mind which can select the right pattern of behavior. These patterns have been learned by two billion years of trial and error; they're good. Watch a young bitch give birth to her first litter of puppies; she knows precisely what to do, and how to do it. Watch a great human chemist struggling to synthesize some very simple protein in his laboratory — while he digests his ham sandwich and turns it into the immensely complex protein of a muscle cell or a nerve cell.

But the instincts wouldn't serve any more. They didn't apply to surviving when trapped by glaciers now many hundreds of miles across in all directions.

119

And Man ate of the fruit of knowledge of new ideas of his own, he abandoned the Voice of Instinct, so that in the cool of the evening he no longer felt that he was right and sure and wise.

And he felt naked, and he made himself clothes; it was getting god damned cold. The mammoths were already freezing in the ice fields around him.

And he was driven out of his happy garden by the whirling swords of the vast whiteness — the swords of driving snow and sleet.

The garden of Eden was closed to Man forever.

And Cain slew Abel in the glade — as the herdsmen have fought the farmers, who insist on fencing their fields, whenever there was a shortage of land. The nomad tribes were being driven in on the tribal villages. And every man's hand was turned against his fellow; normally animals avoid combat except for sexual selection, or for the carnivour's attack on his prey. A tiger won't attack a leopard or a panther; it doesn't make sense. Old Man doesn't attack Old Man — ordinarily. It makes better sense to move away, when there's a whole world of land.

Now there's an interesting thing; when a human population is in crisis, as during war, the birthrate goes *up* not down. An animal population, under great stress, tends to breed faster; Nature's way of solving a problem of pressure is to breed a new generation with a mutation, somewhere, that can handle the situation. Starvation *incites* breeding.

Man today keeps wanting "the next generation" to handle the tough problems.

Nature solves tough problems by evolution.

But this time Man was faced with a problem evolution and the next generation couldn't solve; the *adult* individuals had to solve it. or there wouldn't *be* any next generation! The ice was advancing too fast. Men were killing each other in sheer desperation.

Most of them died without being killed. An antelope, pursued by a man long enough, eventually despairs of surcease and allows itself to be killed. If an animal sees no hope of any better situation, it dies. If a man starts feeling sorry for himself, and despairing of his future — he gets psychosomatics and dies, or commits suicide.

The sane ones died. There was no way out of that trap, and there was no hope for the future. There was no sane reason to struggle. They died.

The ones that kept on were insane; they didn't have sense enough to know it was hopeless, or wouldn't be realistic enough to know that it couldn't be done.

It probably took a few generations before The Trap closed entirely. By that time there had been some mutations, and some survivors escaped the trap.

120

They weren't human any more though. They weren't mild, kindly, peaceable old *Homo sapiens*. They were different.

Every one of them had had to revolt against his instincts; if he hadn't he'd have died because human instincts couldn't keep him alive.

But how he revolted depended on his particular makeup, and how he chose to solve the insoluble problem.

When caught in a trap like that, there are only three things that could be done:

1. Resign yourself, and follow the orders of someone who could lead you out.
2. Find out how to control the environment around you well enough to escape. (Furs, fire, snowshoes, and certain other interesting methods.)
4. Find out how to control your own structure so the environment doesn't bother you.

So let's say that three general types could escape. *Homo sequensus* — the Follower. *Homo inquisitivus*, the investigator. And last, who began escaping first — *Homo lycanthropus*.

Not a great many got out, I imagine — but being living things, they had the power of reproduction. An Old Man, who'd fled south from the ice, was not exactly prepared to cope with them. These were a strange breed that didn't know what quitting [was] or what the situation was hopeless meant. And they believed in killing men instead of moving away when they weren't wanted. And they — *H. seq.* and *H. inquis.* anyway — believed in working 18 hours a day, including all 366 days of leap year. (These were the ones who escaped; they escaped The Trap because they worked their way out by not stopping.)

They also had a rather catholic taste in food. The Donner Expedition to California, you know, found eating corpses expedient. The ones who escaped from The Trap wouldn't be very finicky on that score.

H. lycanthropus, too, had probably acquired quite a taste for human food; it was about the only kind around when he originated. Legend has it that there was such a type — and various old religions indicate there used to be somebody around with a taste for roast young maiden. Moloch and others.

The psychology of *H. lycanthropus* would be interesting. Since change of his body form meant rejection of his human heritage, he must have rejected humanity rather thoroughly — in favor of himself, and survival as himself. He rebelled against the cruel gods that had trapped him in the glaciers, and against the world, and had overweening pride in himself. His sense of humor would be rather sardonic, I imagine. And he had certain other powers, no doubt.

Now this must have been something like 50,000 or more years ago, perhaps. Lord knows just when they got out of that trap.

But when they did — the world was in for a period of hell on Earth. There were *four* intelligent species on the planet — and two of them were exceedingly able; *H. inquis.* and *H. lycanthropus.* Both bred rather freely, breeding on the plentiful and easily captured females of *H. sapiens* who hadn't been in the trap.

And this is the unrecorded Age of Legends before Noah's flood, when the Angels looked on the daughters of men and found them fair. And they lived 900 years or so, with no malarkey; they were mutants. They were also most exceedingly tough — or they'd have died.

The Age of Legends covers the period before the Flood — and the flood was real, world-wide, and it submerged continents. Not one, but several. The City of Ys among them. Also Atlantis and a few others.

The Earth started warming up again, and it didn't rain for 40 days and nights — it rained for 40 centuries more like. For the first 40 years or so, it must have been quite a doozey of a spring flood.

The Fimbrulwinter was over, and the Fimbrulspring had come. The spring floods were moving some 10 or 15 million cubic miles of water back from the glaciers into the seas. Sea level rose some 400 feet they estimate. That means that the continental shelves, the whole populated seacoasts — for primitive and early man always build near the seas. Certainly the high plateaus aren't attractive in the midst of a glacial age! — were being submerged.

The archeologists have a fine time digging in the soft Lybian sands. Or some similar easily accessible place. But they don't do their digging where the early cities and villages of Man *had* to be — 400 feet down, and 20 to 200 miles off the coast on the continental shelves!

I'll bet they wouldn't like what they found, either.

The various breeds were beginning to settle down and settle things between them by that time, I imagine. They'd had several thousand years to do it in.

I think they had werewolves. And I think they did have magicians who could do some extremely discomfiting things quite simply and regularly.

A fellow by the name of **Hunt,** in San Francisco, gave me the basic proposition of the Siberian Trap. The Noah's flood business is something I've been thinking about for some time; it ties in very nicely.

Now whether the thing is true or not — Man, what a period for stories!

Some items to consider on the magical side of it.

The Lepidoptera go from caterpillar into pupa into butterfly. In the pupal stage, the organism dissolves into a sort of protoplasmic mush, and then reintegrates around certain "control centers" to the new form.

Suppose a higher animal could do that — and see what it would take to kill him. Cutting off an arm or a leg wouldn't be serious; he'd semi-pupate and reorganize. Stab him, and see if that bothers him. The only way to kill him would be with some extremely powerful neurotoxin, or massive destruction of vital organs like the brain and heart. Formaldehyde would do it nicely, or complete incineration. But just burning his skin off would be annoying rather than lethal.

Evolution proceeds by changing animal form; Lord, a human being starts as a single cell, becomes a fish, becomes a primitive mammal — we do considerable metamorphosizing already.

Put *enough* pressure or mutation on, and you might get some unpleasant results.

Item: RCA predicts radio magnetic storms now by the use of astrology. Jupiter in Quadrature, Mars in Opposition, etc. It works.

Item: Whatever the ratio of the circumference to the diameter of a circle here on Earth is, it is *not* pi. Pi is a concept applicable *only* in Euclidian flat space. Consider a spherically curved space, and use the term phi to represent the ratio of the circumference to its geodesic bisector. Then phi can have *any* value between 2.00 as a lower limit and pi as an upper limit, depending on the ratio of the circumference of the circle to a great circle in that spherical space! If the given circle has a circumference equal to the Great Circle circumference of that space, evidently phi must equal 2.000

Item: In mathematical fairyland, 4 x 1.0008 equals 4.0032. But in real space, as we know, it doesn't. It equals helium.

A mathematician cannot define what he means by length; Cantor has shown a mathematical proof that any line of any length contains the same number — aleph null — of points. The mathematician can only determine length by measuring it.

What is the distance to the Moon? No one has measured it — except by light, which, as we now know, is affected by gravity. And because of that, we know that astronomers on the Moon would *not* get the same readings we do from Earth. Soooo — what's distance? Maybe it's a specialized concept that's useful in some ways, but neither true nor necessary. A better concept might be more useful.

And this inverse square law business. Fascinating thing — a yardstick is made up of tiny electromagnetic field units, isn't it? Then when we measure the electromagnetic forces between two pith balls, and learnedly deduce an inverse square law — hmmm.

123

Here we are, comparing little force fields with big ones, so we don't know anything at all about the force fields themselves!

All we've done is do a problem in geometry; the area of a sphere increases as the square of the radius. That we already knew.

And the evidence is that telepathy doesn't know about the inverse square law at all.

Levitation is real; Sir William Crooks witnessed an instance and studied it carefully. He was a first-rank physicist — one of the really great ones.

Item: **Peg** and I have worked out a mathematical formulation of fear and of satisfaction, or triumph. It works usefully, whether it's true or not — and a useful theory is always a major tool for prying loose the next item.

I wish you two were somewhere somewhat handier so we could have a real chance to talk about this.

I have a hunch some rather wonderful stories lie back there, just beyond the furthest reach of history. Some real, howling blood-curdlers! The damndest source of fiction there ever was!

Regards,   John

Chad Oliver   *February 6, 1953*

Dear Chad:

I started a letter to you just yesterday; your letter arrived this morning, so we start again.

First: I did NOT see "If Now We Grieve." **Scott** loused us both up, dammit.

Trouble with agents is that they have a system of evaluations different from that of an author; the agent's success and prestige is counted in dollars and sales and therefore his satisfaction comes in those terms. The author's success and prestige and satisfaction comes from selling to the market he wanted to sell to — in being able to select a target, devise a story intended for that target, and prove to himself that he can, in fact, understand what's wanted and supply it. Money is, naturally, highly desirable; more important to an author's development is his increasing understanding of his world. Agents aren't always too sharp on that point.

I did get "Give Me A House" from **Forry.** Sorry, but it's going back. Reason:

I don't know what point you sought to make in this story, but it's unclear from the very beginning. The reader is in a sort of detective story position, in that he doesn't know. He doesn't know until well into the story, after a great deal has happened, where the locale is, whether the people are criminals imprisoned, psychological researchers on Earth, or some Earth-colony planet, whether the alien is really an alien or part of some complex test proceedure, what their point is, or anything.

If the point is a clash of two alien cultures — no go at all. To have that, the absolute minimum data required for the reader's understanding is a fairly complete picture of at least one of the cultures as it really is. That doesn't exist here.

You may know what the situation is — but the reader never does find out.

Forry mentioned you'd done five drafts on this.

Look, **Chad** — take it from an old hand at the game; your conscious mind can't write a story, and probably never will be able to. You may be able to carry out an argument consciously, because that's a simple one-dimensional manifold. But a story involving human characters is a multidimensional manifold, and you haven't got any more chance of doing that at the conscious level than you have of growing a living cell — consciously.

Your stories are all written by the subliminal circuits, which are able to operate in multidimensional parallel; they can be six different people at once, and solve 200 simultaneous equations in 350 unknowns. (Yep; they can throw in 150 extra arbitraries, run a series of approximations, and so solve for all 350 variables. They can do it on a multiple-unit parallel-operation basis, too.) At the conscious-only level, you're too dumb to cross a street and stay alive, unless you wait till 3 AM and observe that there are *no* cars coming in either direction. Let's see you make a conscious estimate of the speed, acceleration, probable desired turn direction, etc., of four cars on an ordinary street, and do it fast enough to have an answer that's still useful when you reach it.

So your stories come from your subliminal work. And at that level your abilities are several million times what you think they are.

As an old writer-editor craftsman — it is NOT a science, but an art — I know that if a one-draft man does three drafts, and hasn't got it — he's trying to insist that he has a story here, while his subliminal circuits say "Hu-uh. No story. Won't work that way." You can make yourself sit at a typer, but you won't have fun, and you won't get a story. If the subliminal circuits say "No," they're practically certain to have a valid reason. Instead of beating yourself over the head, accept that there *is* a reason, and find out what it is.

You'll save time, effort, and dissapointment. You've got a hell of a good built-in editor, **Chad,** or you wouldn't be able to write the nice stuff you do. Don't try to demote that editor to copy-boy every time he disagrees with your conscious wishes.

I've been talking to physicists, aerodynamicists, chemists, artists and what not, doing some investigating. Our dear old society holds that emotional thinking is anathema — but the really successful physicists, engineers and artists alike agree on this: if it doesn't "feel" right, it won't work when you actually try it. It may "feel" right and not work, of course, but if something doesn't "feel" right, better check and find out *why* it doesn't.

Now let's get to your letter.

Re data. Data is essential; that I never denied. But I do deny that *all* data is essential. If it were, no man could get any answers to anything, because no one has ever obtained all the data about anything. The problem, then, is to determine *what* data is both necessary and sufficient. Obviously, if you had *all* the data, you'd have all that was necessary and you'd have sufficient. But you still would not have the necessary integration, the understanding.

Now if a man decides and believes sincerely that M is impossible without P, then in the absence of P he will not find M. You can call it autohypnosis, or anything else you like — but he'll find some reason why M is not M, but N when P is absent — including, finally, the statment that since M can occur only when P is present, then since P is absent this is not M.

If you decide that B is *the* answer to X, then if someone offers the answer D, which is demonstrably better than B, you will deny that D is an answer. The only way you can be induced to accept D as an answer is to have someone induce you, by some means, to recognize that B is *not* the answer.

This thing is so damned fundamental that it's been the stumbling block in most of human culture.The human individual would much rather hold on to a poor answer than release it and be without any answer. But he can't get a new answer until he releases the old one.

The social sciences are particularly liable to this form of error for the following reason: Any man interested in social and anthropological problems is a believer in the value of social systems. Particularly, of course, his own. As you say, you cannot change a society without destroying it as-itself. This is the business of not releasing the old answer.

The physical scientist has the advantage that nobody has any respect for what a *thing* wants or doesn't want; nobody minds changing a thing's way of life. But my God how they scream when somebody tries to change their way of life.

Technology has been the most powerful of social forces because it offers the better answer first, before insisting that the old answer is inadequate. Therefore it can force social change.

Instance: Try getting the population, circa 1890, to consider the proposition: "Resolved: That horses are an unsatisfactory form of transportation, and should be abolished in favor of something better."

But circa 1920 the situation was different. Dobbin would find his own way home, make his own repairs on himself, etc. — but the automobile had such advantages as to force a change of viewpoint. It *induced* rather than *compelling* the change.

I have **Mark Clifton** working on this idea:

A man invents a machine, the psychosomatron, that can, in four hours treatment, turn a doddering, arthritic, cancerous, rheumatic old wreck into a man in the peak of physical vigor. It attacks both germ diseases and, by electronic-cybernetic circuits, cures and straightens out the psychological quirks. The result is that both psychosomatics and somatics are cured.

BUT — the individual loses his biases, prejudices, and pet phobias and philias. The Suth'n Cun'l comes out young and vigorous — but a *nigguh luvuh,* suh!

What would people do about that machine?

Destroy it and its inventor. Immortality at the cost of his "soul." Nobody ever asks whether the soul they have is worth preserving. My impression is that frequently they'd be ever so much better off without it.

Data is important — *but only when it yields understanding.*

The individual who accumulates data endlessly is frequently a man who is afraid to face the inevitable conclusions his data leads to, and so avoids integrating it.

I know a girl who defends herself against understanding by having accumulated data which she sets like a picket fence around her. You can never reach *her* mind, because you always run into a quotation from somewhere on your way in. If you approach from opposite directions, you still run into quotations — opposite and mutually exclusive quotations of data, but still you're not reaching her mind. It's defended behind a barricade of close-packed data.

She married a man she knew to be a psychopathic liar by the way. I deduce that she thought she could cure him by penning him in behind a wall of facts like the one she used.

It didn't work. She divorced him after a few not-too-subtle efforts to murder her.

His picket fence is a total *lack* of facts; naturally the two types of defense meant she was destroying his mental stability.

Data collection can be a major vice. In our work, **Peg** and I have been studying good and evil, and have found that there is an interesting mathematical definition possible. It works.

We have also developed a mathematical expression for some of the emotions. They work, also.

By "work" I mean "yield predictions which can be checked and found to correspond with observational facts"; that does *not* mean that what we have now is true — but it does mean it's valid.

The social sciences have fallen into the vice of data-collection not properly balanced by adequate efforts at integration and collation. Biology began getting places when generalizations were made.

One of the great problems of the social sciences is the failure to apply the *philosophy* of physical science instead of the *methods*. There's a vast difference.

After a great many hours of very hard work, I think I can define the form of mathematics that the social sciences are seeking; see if this doesn't check:

What's wanted is a mathematics such that you can write an expression of the order (A)(f)(Rr)(B)(a) which can be read as "A function, f, of A, bears some relationship Rr to an aspect (a) of B. A must be manipulable when it is very uncertain, varying between wide limits, while B varies independently, and f and a are both unknown. The methods of the mathematics must, nevertheless, allow an accurate solution for A, B, f, a, and Rr.

What's wanted, in other words, is a mathematics that is capable of deriving more certain information than is put into it.

This is creative thinking.

You're looking for a formula for creative thinking that will be capable of expression in symbological terms, capable of being written down for the public inspection of other men, and be so formulizable as to make it possible to back up your creative thinking process with statements of rules and laws of manipulation.

The desirability of such a mathematics is beyond question. But it won't be derived until the processes of human thinking are *already* known and formulized! Hence the one problem that that new mathematics will not be used to solve is the problem of how to devise it!

It's the problem that no tool can make itself. The first machine planer — which I've seen in a museum — still bears on its bedplate the marks of the cold chisels and files that were used to produce the first flat bedplate. Once that had been made, it was used to machine a better bedplate for the next machine plane.

If you want a realistic mathematics — sweat for it, don't cry for it. We're too old to throw petulant crying spells because we don't have the tool we want.

If you insist the mathematics can't exist, you won't try to find it.

But in that case, you'd better get over weeping that you don't have it and either make up your mind to get along without it, or change your conviction that it can't exist.

128

The physicists got over crying for it several centuries ago. There's a perfectly good way to handle the problem. When a mathematician hits a problem he can't express as a formula that he knows how to solve, he bulls his way through the hard way — by numerical calculation and successive approximations. You can always do it that way. It just takes more blood, sweat and tears, too. It means a billion, billion life-forms committed themselves to a trial solution — and died, because they'd tried the wrong values.

The physicist commits himself to a trial solution. Newton says "Every body in the universe. . . ." and gets a good approximation. Every physicist sees his theories crumble; the values weren't quite right. So he tries again, with a different set of values. That one crumbles too.

Physical science deals with problems; the philosophy of dealing with problems is inescapably the same in any field whatsoever. Because the essential thing is that *human thinking* is handling data to determine relationships that will predict observations.

But so long as social sciences maintain that there are no fixed relationships to be found — why, naturally, they can't find a mathematics to help them.

Chad, they're wrong. We've found relationships that are fixed. The trouble is that those Pago-Pago disputes are blinding the serious researchers; they don't have the mental guts to plow ahead despite the minor points, and try to get to the level where the minor points won't stop them any more.

There was a German analyst about 1830 or so, who analyzed the water from a mineral spring, and came up with an answer that totaled only 94½%. He had mental guts; he published his figures, and said "The analysis does not total properly. My observations are more accurate than these figures; there must be a hitherto unknown element present in these waters which is reacting in such a way as to appear to be one of the unknown elements. I believe it is a heavier member of the potassium family, but I am unable to isolate it."

It was ¼ century before they isolated rubidium — from the spring water the German had analyzed. Making the proper correction in his observational data computations, his figures totaled 100% plus or minus 0.1%.

The trouble with the social sciences is they aren't willing to make that sort of a committment, and stand or fall by it.

Of course you don't have enough data! Dammit, man, don't you realize *you never will have*? Only *all* data is 'enough' data. And that you never, never will have.

But the social sciences lack the courage to stand or fall by their beliefs in the way the physical scienctists do. The first half century of such a new approach will lead to some mighty rises, and some equally mighty collapses. You'll go over the roller coaster, with some sickening plunges on the way. It's perfectly typical of what happens in any succesive-approximation system — which is simply a damped-oscillation method of approach. The curve always looks like this:

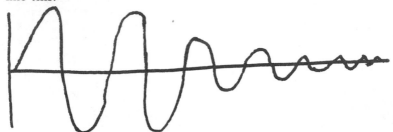

From the peaks on that curve, you see heaven; from the bottom, you see hell. It's disturbing as hell all the way, and takes more guts than most men have, I think. Most people will accept a ride on it only when it gets to about the seventh peak there — when the plunges aren't quite so sickening between the peaks.

Physical science is real popular these days, ain't it. Now everybody wants to get into the act.

Science-fiction is too, now. And everybody wants to get into the act.

If you want to know, I got my ears beat in during the first 10 years or so; now I get invited to give lectures at MIT and the University of Chicago, and so on. MIT is running a course in creative thinking; they wanted me to discuss one phase of it. **Prof. Arnold** who's running it, has made a genuine social invention — and I admire his guts in sticking his neck way, way out and doing the job. He's trying to solve that formula on page [128] by the only method we have now — successive approximation.

One absolutely sure-fire guaranteed method of *not* solving a problem is the pussy-foot technique. If you really want to crack it, git in and slug. You'll get hurt doing it — but you'll accomplish something.

I am NOT kidding when I say we have worked out some mathematical formulations of emotion. They're crude first approximations, but by God they prove that it can be done — and can be done only by sticking your neck well out, and trying it.

Look at the two curves below. Make a genuine effort to see if there is any relationship you can see between them — don't just skip to the explanation below, but see if you can spot the relationship. It's a simple one, and one of immense importance in all human living.

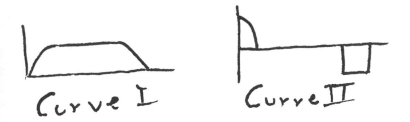

Curve I actually bears a very simply expressed relationship to curve II. It's a long way from being a familiar one — because we haven't been taught to pay much attention to this particular relationship. Betcha you could find a hell of a lot more meaning in a lot of the anthropological data you have on hand if you looked into this one type of relationship a bit more!

The relationship is one Newton developed — but not in this way. Curve II is simply the plot of the first derivative of curve I — a plot of the slope of the curve of Curve I. If I is the plot of a system of events, II is the trend of events.

It is essential for the survival of an animal that it act not only on *what is now* but on the basis of *what will be*. If I look and see that no automobile stands between me and the other side of the street, and start across on that basis, I'm practically certain to be dead very shortly. I've got to be able to predict that no automobile *will be* where I *will be* at the time I *will be* in crossing that street

Any effort to solve the nature of animal behavior in terms of *now alone* will fail.

Now let's define one of the emotions in mathematical terms:

Fear: — the term applied to an emotion-sense report that the first derivative of the extrapolated curve of events with respect not only to the physical organization of self is negative. (Organization of self refers not only to the physical organization of the body, but also to the mental organization of the self.)

Satisfaction: — The term applied to the same emotion-sense reporting a *positive* first derivative.

Consequences of these definitions: An individual can be in idyllic surroundings — in Hawaii, we'll say, with his bride beside him, money in the bank, excellent health, fine weather — and feel shattering fear. He has information about what will happen.

Or a man can be in hell — and feel a deep, surging wave of triumph.

The derivative of a constant is zero. Any constant.

Consequence: a human being can "adjust" to almost anything. He will feel little emotion with regard to a constant situation, because the emotion-senses are derivative senses.

131

You cannot point to the source of an emotion.

Naturally not; it's a derivation, not a direct fact.

The term "emotion" has to be defined, and broken down into about 50 separate concepts. "Emotion," as the schoolboy said of the word "garbage," is a collective noun.

How far would geology get with *only* the term "rocks" to think with? Without the concepts of granitic and basaltic, sedimentary and igneous, hematitie and quartzite:

Observational data: human beings resist psychotherapy powerfully.

Prediction from the above definition of fear: There will be a strong sense of fear induced when the psychotherapy shows evidence of having effect. The more effective it appears to be, the more fear it will induce — because, as you said of a culture, any change is necessarily a disruption of that-which-is.

Further prediction: if the individual knows what the nature of fear is, then he can take that into his understandings and so reevaluate the meaning of 'disorganization of the self' as to make psychotherapy less fear-inducing.

That last prediction I can report on only for myself and my wife. It has been valid, because it has been useful in producing real results.

It — the theory as to what fear is — has helped us in helping our children.

Final conclusion: it is both possible and necessary to derive first-approximation mathematical definitions of the factors of human personality.

Stop weeping about it and start developing it.

Further considerations developing from the theory that emotion-senses — i.e., the "I have a feeling that —" part of emotion — leads to a definition of good and evil that works, too.

In first year calculus, we learned that the maximum and minimum points of a curve were both characterized by $dy/dx = 0$. In living, we don't refer to maximum and minimum — let's speak, instead, of optimum and anathemum. Both have the characteristic of having a derivative equal to zero, however! So good is simply optimum and evil merely the anathemum.

Incidentally, that explains why the aerodynamicists I've talked to — and the product design engineers — have both said that, privately, after they've done the engineering computations, they look at the result and decide if it looks beautiful. Beauty consists of the optimization of the multiple factors, with a final optimization of the curve of all the curves. No aesthetics as such went into the design of jet fighter planes — but ain't they *purty*!

Respect your subliminal circuits somewhat more; they're

132

immensely wiser than you realize!

Peg and I have been reading *Kon-Tiki* with the greatest interest. That guy really did have guts — and a fine depth of human warmth and feeling, too. He could write like billybedamned, and he was thinking just fine, too. (Also he confirmed further a conviction that's been building in **Peg** and myself as we've gone along — that our ancestors were NOT dopes, and they didn't pass down legends without meaning. For a little while, yes — but not for many centuries.) **Hyderdahl's** form of anthropological research appeals to me immensely. He and his gang proved magnificently the deep wisdom of the old men who lived in the days before technical science developed. Up to and including the Polynesians who scorned the inadequate ropes they had used on the raft, because coconut hemp would stand sea water so much better. The logs had to be balsa, so they wouldn't cut the ropes. They had to be green balsa, so the sea water wouldn't waterlog them. The centerboards had to be placed *so*; thus they relieved the steersman of much labor.

But **Peg** and I have both long been intrigued by Peru, and the cultures that developed down that way. So we're planning on taking a trip down that way for our own personal interest.

Question: What good, readable books about the culture of Peru are there? We don't want Pogo-Pogo style arguments — but a good picture of what the score was.

Maybe you, or some of the people there, can help with some suggestions?

Final item: If you haven't already encountered it — and I suspect you haven't — get the highly valuable anthropological studies of **H. Potter**, titled "Lifesmanship," "Gamesmanship" and "One-up-manship." They are exceedingly sharp analyses of the techniques of question-begging argumentation as actually practiced in a society — and most exceedingly fruitful.

Also read Plato's report on Socrates. Not as philosophy, because the old bastard was about as nasty, destructive a character as I'd care to avoid, but as a magnificent study of how to make the other fellow's arguments frustrate him hopelessly. Studying Socrates' technique will show you the techniques being used against you today, in preventing you making clear headway in your thinking. He was using the Pogo Pogo technique 2300 years ago.

Potter has the Pogo Pogo technique in his book in the more general form; the "not in the south" technique. If someone discusses the political situation on Upper Slobovia very learnedly, having just returned after five years residence, and is getting the attention and respect of the gathered people, you simply say, after one of his observations, "But not in the south." Of course, you don't win anything yourself, particularly including his friendship, but you keep him from winning anything.

Achieving enough data to be able to introduce irrelevant disagreements is so *much* easier than achieving an understanding of something. For some people, it seems to be more fun, too.

Potter's worth reading — and Socrates, as I say.

Regards,   John

Fred Pohl   *February 15, 1953*

Dear Fred:

Naturally you're welcome to quote those paragraphs — naturally for two natural reasons:

1. Know anybody who doesn't like being quoted when he's expressed something he honestly believes in ?
2. I wish more writers and would-be writers would understand the business an editor finds himself in.

If you're writing that book, will you *please* point out that it's impossible to write a note on every manuscript that comes in, and still get a magazine out.

Also, that writing and editing are both arts, in the true sense of the word — which means that we don't have analytical formulas by which we can name the precise errors the writer has made. If we reach a level of understanding of human personality so great that we can name a specific formula for writing a story that will produce precisely *this* effect on a reader — the reader of that level of intelligence able to understand the formula will thereby be immune to the formula. You'll need a new formula too complex for him to handle if you want to please him.

Since, in science-fiction, we're trying to please technologists and philosophically inclined adults of the very highest level of our society, you can take it as a dead certainty that no writer has conscious understanding sufficiently in excess of those boys to be able to handle any formula they couldn't understand.

Thus when a writer asks me why I've turned down a story — ye gods, I can't analyze the thing consciously! I can say "It doesn't hold the interest" or "It doesn't have the punch it needs" or "It seems to lack oomph" or some equally indefinable reason. I could also say "You didn't famerstran the hartal of coopibly" and give an equally useful statement.

If I *could* specify precisely what the trouble with the story was — I could write such propaganda as would assure me control of the planet within five years. I'd have the full secert of human emotional reactions.

I hate to see really competent writers like **Blish** and **Knight** investing so much time in work that I know by observational experience — though I can't for the life of me specify why it's true — won't make a good story. It is necessary to divert them; at the same time, diverting a man from a task he truly wants to carry through is a good way of making him feel his efforts, and his judgement, is not appreciated — and that can throw him off his fine edge of writing expression too.

They aren't being prima donnas about it; they're acting as the nature of human mind inevitably requires. If **Blish & Knight** don't find some way of expressing, in story form, the ideas they've accumulated and labored over, they're going to be deeply unhappy. When a human being has developed an idea, he has to express it somehow, or suffer a genuinely serious internal mental stress.

That's why I suggested to them the possibility of breaking down the central idea into pieces, and using it piecemeal.

Regards,   John

Les Cole   *March 11, 1953*

Dear Mr. Cole:

Your two manuscripts are coming back, I'm afraid. The little one is too little to amount to much of a yarn. The aliens-on-earth theme isn't in and of itself new. This has no great point of development of the theme.

Actually, both of these stories are the same theme: Why don't the aliens of higher cultures among us here on Earth make contact with us and tell us the answers we need? They're two stories of exactly the same theme.

You've been reading Neitzsche, and no doubt Schopenhauer, and perhaps Kant. Since you're in Germany, there'd be a natural tendency to look into their philosophy. Jawhol — but look into it as the philosophy of a thoroughly aberrated·people.

I don't know whether you happened to be there when my father was; Dad was in charge of reorganizing the German telephone system after the war, a few years back. Dad was "Chief Engineer for Plant Practices for A.T. & T. General" to give him his full official title, for some years, and just after his retirement from A.T. & T. he went to Germany for a year to help reorganize the setup over there. You might know of his work — I dunno. Anyhow, I heard a good bit about Germany and Germans from him — and from **Willy Ley** — that neither one meant to tell me.

Dad has ideas inculcated circa 1890 about the parental-paternal system, and what constitutes a well behaved child. Dad, as a matter of fact, used to quote "The Boy Stood On The Burning Deck" at me in seriousness. He also had the idea that "The Charge of The Light Brigade" was an epic of heroism, instead of an epic of utter stupidity. So Dad used to write and tell me how well-behaved the German children were — not undisciplined bratlings like the American kids.

(Maybe you can gather that Dad and I used to have a running battle during my childhood, while I took extreme delight in doing *exactly* what he said every now and then to his acute discomfiture. We've since ironed out some of that difficulty, but he never has caught on to what makes sense in that respect.)

The German people have been indoctrinated for over a century in the most solid sort of benevolent tyranny. They want benevolent tyranny; they are not happy without benevolent tyranny, and they're therefore going to have benevolent tyranny. Our people can't imagine that, and can't appreciate that the only way to keep everybody happy, and the situation working properly, is to pick for them a benevolent tyrannt who *is* benevolent, and is also wise enough to get along with non-tyrannical government. In other words, a wise tyrant who hates tyranny.

Look: The Kaiser was a tyrant; the Germans had years of *gemutlichkeit.* Then here was the first war; the Kaiser got thrown out, and the Allies moved in. The Germans had a good, solid, dependable tyranny and were contented. The Allies showed them how to set up a republic; they went about doing just what the nice kind tyrants told them to, and did it happily and well. But then the tyrants went off and left them with the machine running, and nobody to tell them what to do with it! So they finally found a nice, dependable tyrant who would be Papa and tell them what to do. So the Allies threw out Hitler, too. Now the nice, kind tyrannical Allies are busily showing the Germans what to do about setting up a government again.

You wanna make any bets?

When **Willy's** first wife came over here, **Willy** told me, one of the things that she wailed about was "But **Willy**, I can't tell your friends from your aquaintances!" In English, no *du* ceremony; how is a person to tell his friends from his aquaintances without a nice, dependable rule to tell him? In Germany everybody knows that Herr Bank Teller outranks Herr Postman in the social heriarchy; there are nice dependable rules. But here in America? Oh, it's terrible . . . terrible! The postman may be the son of the Mayor of the town, taking a summer job, or a Christmas Vacation job, and the guy who runs the garbage collection service may be one of the top political service men. See . . . it's all topsy turvy. No discipline. No formulas to understand by.

German philosophers are strictly German-oriented; Schopenhaur on women is fascinating reading — if you first read a biography of the poor guy, and get a picture of what a little bitch-on-wheels his mother was. She was a bitch of the first water — drove his father to suicide, and ruined the lives of everyone around her. No wonder Schopenhaur had rather low opinion of women.

The Germans are paternalistic as hell; you've done a fine job of picturing them in this story. (Incidentally, one of the characteristics you'll find in an actual all-out paternalistic culture is ancestor worship, in a more-or-less open form. The Jews, for example, have a powerfully paternalistic cultural pattern; Jehovah is the Great Father. Judaism does not promise an after-life — but the worship of the Prophets and the Ancestors is implicit in every line of it. Immortality results from the continuity of the life-line through properly adoring children. Breaking that ancestor worship, then, would mean that the individual who did so would be turning off his philosophical immortality, since his children wouldn't worship him.)

(Note that the Jewish culture is "soluble" *only* in strongly paternalistic-ancestor-worshipping cultures. The Jews almost amalgamated in Germany before Hitler. In China, a group of Jews did amalgamate so perfectly that they were completely lost as a cultural group; all that was left was a Chinese village in which the males were ritually circumcised.)

(Ancestor worship is, either openly or disguised, a part of any strongly paternalistic culture, I suspect.)

By the way, one of the factors that has lead to the Jews being persecuted for the last 4000 years is that business. The ancestor-worship facet means that only by being born into the culture can you truly be a member of the culture. But if an individual holds that X is good, and that you have to be born X to have X, then anyone not born X must hold either "Being X is not good, and I'm glad I'm not X" or "Being X is good; woe is me, for I am not and cannot ever be X." Further, since the whole Semitic tradition is "There is only one right answer," and "I am my brother's keeper," the Semite tends to make himself hard on his neighbors.

Since the entire Western cultural pattern stems from that schismatic Jewish sect, Christianity, plus the scientific philosophy concepts of that other semitic culture, Islam, the Western culture has been *very* hard on its neighbors. We tend to think that religion is always causing wars; that is strictly a biased from-our-viewpoint idea. See if you can name a religious war that did *not* involve as one or both of the participants, one of the great Semitic-tradition cultures, Judiasm, Christianity or Moslemism.

In India, the Hindus, Buddhists, Confuciuns and other minor religious groups get along with peace and tranquility. But the Moslems had to have a separate state, Pakistan.

Sound anti-semitic, doesn't it?

137

Wrong answer; it's a scientific analysis of the actual factors present. Now let's add the rest.

Only the Western and Islamic cultures have ever been able to build and maintain *progress*. Rome didn't do so good — and they had a moderately paranoid attitude, too. Evidently that rather paranoid attitude of the semitic tradition has values great enough to offset its disadvantages.

It does.

The Greek philosophers could kick around mutually exclusive philosophies happily; they could yak-kity-yak about ideas for centuries, and feel no compulsion whatever to integrate their yakking into a single coherence. They never invented science, because they never had the cultural compulsion of "There's only one right answer."

The Indians never got to first base for a similar reason; they have different religions, and no organization. Kind of a lovely commentary on their ineptness that about 250,000 Englishmen, having a single, coordinated, directed drive took over 300,000,000 Indians, isn't it?

They have a dozen religious groups in a single city — who mutually ignore each other. They're so damned tolerant of the other fellow's ideas that they never find themselves forced to inspect their own.

The Moslems invented science because when they started studying the Greek philosophers, they were compelled to select one right answer — and logic alone wouldn't do it; the logic and ideas had to be compared with something that wasn't arguable, shiftable, and mere opinion.

The Greeks didn't like experiments; why break up a good argument by doing something crass like experimenting and ending the fight?

Like anything else, tolerance and decisiveness can both be carried to extremes; the Indians the East generally — has the inappropriate extreme of tolerance; the Jews have the inappropriate extreme of decisiveness.

The Indians never get anywhere, and the Jews get persecuted everywhere — because the rigidity of their culture is such that the culture won't learn. (The Indians don't learn either; they let you have your strange foreign notions, but refuse to learn anything from them.)

Basic philosophic Law: When two cultures meet, if A is unwilling to learn from B, but insist that B must learn from A, while B is willing to learn from A — B will inevitably dominate A, because the cultural units of B will have selected the best ideas of *both* A and B, while the individual of A will have only the A idea-sets to use. Individually, then, the B units will overcome A units.

That's an absolutely inescapable law of cultural dynamics. It's perfectly obvious. But no culture seems to be willing to admit it!

Rome lost. Reason: She taught the Gauls plenty — and learned nothing.

England lost to the Colonies. Reason: The same reason the Amerinidians lost to the colonists. The colonists came over with English culture — and learned the idea of the free, self-respecting individual from the Amerinidian brave. They learned the idea of the freely self-determined but interdependent community from the Amerindians, and called the pow-wow a "New England Town Meeting." They learned the tradition of interdependent, self-controlling individual fighters from the Amerindians.

But they kept the idea of national organization, of an organization of organizations that England had developed. And they kept science and technology, and recognition of the power of natural law.

These the Amerindians rejected; he got licked.

The English didn't learn the Amerindian lessons; they got licked.

The two greatest things Richard the Lion-hearted did for humanity were, I think,

1. getting out of England so that his weak brother could sign the Magna Carta. (If he'd stayed in England, his powerful personality would have suppressed the movement.) And;

2. being the ideal Christian warrior-king, and leader of warriors, when he got kicked out by the Moslems, soundly shellacked, and wound up held for ransom by a petty French noble, it finally convinced people that maybe, just possibly, Christianity *didn't* have all the good ideas there were.

That led to the renaissance; the Moslems, of course, decided that their repeated victories proved they *did* have all the answers that were needed.

There are a lot of ways of putting the problem of "Why don't the aliens contact us?" First, we can specify this: They *can't* contact us unless they're already ahead of us in science. (Self-evident; our level of science can't do it.)

Now for a moment, imagine we have somehow succeeded in building an intelligence-machine. It's a mechanism that can think, and can think 10,000 times as well as a man — with 10,000 times the power of man.

Now if a man gets himself directly connected to a 1000 horsepower engine by mistake, the result isn't usable for anything but hamburger.

What would happen, then, if a man tried to connect himself to a 10,000 mind-power intelligence machine?

Well, what's intelligence? Let's not fiddle around with the psychologist's answer "Intelligence is what's measured by an intelligence test." That's silly, and always was. Let's try the definition that "Intelligence is the ability to select the appropriate answer in a given situation"; the measure of intelligence is the consistency of appropriate selection, and the degree of appropriateness. (Some people are erratic geniuses; they come up with perfectly brilliant solutions to some problems, but are highly unreliable. Some are reliable, can be depended on for a good, sound answer every time, but don't produce brilliant answers. The first is spectacular, but useless without the second. The second can get along without the first, but not anywhere near as well.)

Now on that basis, our 10,000 brain-power machine *will not harm the man who associates himself with it.* Reason: It selects the appropriate answer; harming the man would be inappropriate; therefore by definition it will not harm him. It can't *both* be highly intelligent, *and* be truly destructive. It could, and assuredly would, destroy a lot of things the *man* thought were appropriate — like all his pet prejudices, biases, and mental scar-tissues. It would hurt the man, just as it hurts to have a wart cauterized off — but that's not truly destructive.

I can imagine such a machine in, say 1940, being asked the question "How can we make an atomic bomb?"

The machine would undoubtedly answer with some material on basic philosophic theory which, to apply, would require that the mind of the user of the concept be reoriented sociologically and psychologically before he could make the formula apply physically. Perhaps a basic concept relating to free will which when understood, would allow for upsetting radioactive equilibria — but which could be understood *only* after application to human problems.

Now lets consider the more-than-humanly intelligent aliens.

They *can't* give us answers — because to do so would be inappropriate, which is contrary to the definition of the intelligence we've assigned them.

One of your twins could enter a building through a hole 10 inches in diameter — but couldn't lift a 100-pound weight after doing so. You could lift the 100-pound weight — but couldn't squeeze through the 10-inch hole.

My proposition is that the problem of interstellar flight is such that any race that can squeeze through that 10-light-year hole can't damage a developing race.

Suppose somebody gives you directions on a driving trip. "You go down this road to the white church; turn left there and go one block past the end of the park on your left, then turn left. Three blocks down, turn about half a mile down. That's it."

So you start. But you miss one turn.

Brother, you're lost. You haven't the faintest idea where to go, once you get off his directions. You have only a rule of thumb, not an understanding of the route.

Now if someone gives you an answer on how-to-live, all neatly ready made, you're in the same spot. One grain of dust on the road — and you're lost, sunk without a trace. But if you've worked out your own how-to-live map, by selecting from all the world around you — nobody can get *you* lost. You found yourself in the first place, and you can always find yourself again.

Try stealing somebody else's idea! Go ahead; try it! See what it gets you!

A machine has the characteristics it does because it has no ideas of its own, and can carry out only the one idea built into it. Get it off the line where that idea is appropriate — hah! It's using a borrowed idea; once lost, it can never find itself, so someone else has to come along and put it right again.

The trouble with the story you have here is that the hero does *not* come up with an appropriate answer. You should show why the direct-action methods are inappropriate — you've hinted at that — and demonstrate that he can't build himself a ship to get home. Equally, he can't build the technology to the necessary point to build a transmitter to call home.

Suggestion: Do you know of the old Nernst Incandescent Lamps? They used a piece of ceramic material that would conduct electricity when it was white hot. But where a metal increases its resistance with increasing temperature, a ceramic material decreases its resistance. So to limit the current, they had the thermal expansion of the ceramic rod open the switch; when it cooled a bit, the switch closed, and reheated it. This happened about 10 times a second, and the flicker was unnoticeably small.

Imagine what a city full of Nernst lamps would do to radio broadcasting though!

Assume it takes 10 megawatts of power to transmit a message to home. He can't get them to set up a 10 megawatt transmitter for him without revealing things that he must not give away. But he could invent some gadget which is no marked departure from their technology, but which broadcasts the most gawdawful static on the subspace communication band, quite as an accidental by-product.

Presently the Exploratory Corps would be out looking to see what in hall the local yayhoos were doing that made such a nasty racket.

His last kindly gesture before being picked up would be to make a slight improvement in his gadget such that the efficiency was increased 20% — by using the energy that was, otherwise, radiated as static.

The basic idea behind that would be simply to devise a gimmick that did A and B; A is a function appropriate to the civilization's problems, and B is a function appropriate to *his* problem. The civilization will make and use the gimmick because it A's and not realize that it B's at all.

Since his problem is not so complex as "to transmit a comprehensible message" but merely "to signal the existence of a phenomenon needing investigation," he need only establish the latter condition in an appropriate fashion. That's a relatively simple requirement for his B function, and should be pretty easy to incorporate in something.

Regards,   John W. Campbell, Jr.

Harry Stubbs   *April 12, 1953*

Dear Harry:

Once upon a time I told you "Science fiction detective stories don't work — you can't write a good one."

So you proved that I was wrong in that, and wrote "Needle."

In some of the research we've been doing, we've come across a very human problem — the problem of the individual who has a built-in, violent hatred of any absolute statement whatsoever. This type of psychological orientation, it seems to me, stems from confusing two types of absolute statements — the descriptive absolute and the volitional absolute.

When I said "You can't write a good science-fiction detective story," I was making a descriptive absolute statement — i.e., a statement about the facts of an observed system of forces (psychological in this case) which, to the best of my knowledge, was a close correlation with that-which-exists.

When Newton stated the Law of Gravity, he stated what he believed was a close approximation of That Which Is. He had no intention of prosecuting violators of his Law.

When a man makes a descriptive absolute statement, he doesn't intend to enforce his statement; he is merely stating what he believes the Laws of That Which Is to be.

A Volitional Absolute, on the other hand, is the "You can't go out that door until I say so," type of statement.

Apparently, a lot of kids get so much of that kind, and so few opportunities to learn about the descriptive absolute type, that they consider all statements to be volitional. As adults, they naturally consider the Laws of Nature the malign workings of a vicious and angrily disposed Nature. Mother Nature, to such an individual, is "Mother" in a very personal sense — the sense of Mother who punished the child when he sought to do something against her volitional absolute statment.

A volitional absolute statment has validity *only* if somebody enforces it.

I get in trouble with people because of my frequent use of descriptive absolute statements — which people interpret on the basis that *maybe* I'm trying to establish a volitional absolute. They've got reason to; many people do, and you can get a volitional absolutist madder than hell by breaking his statement. It's naturally safer to assume as a first approximation that the man who makes the statement means to enforce it personally.

I don't have much use for volitional absolutes.

Anytime you break one of my descriptive absolutes — you do so only by increasing my understanding of how things actually are. I know more about science-fiction and detective stories since you taught me with your story "Needle."

You've taught me a lot of things. Precise, jig-saw-puzzle interlocking of details wasn't a forte of mine; the highly pleasing results you've produced by doing so has taught me that it's a satisfying thing to do, instead of being merely a damn nuisance.

In several years of editing science-fiction, I've learned a lot of things from a lot of different writers — which puts me in the position of *appearing* to be extremely wise. I can quote back basic ideas from so many sources. I'm funneling ideas from **Heinlein**, **de camp**, **van Vogt**, **Ray Jones**, **Stein**, **Stubbs**, **Asimov** — quite a collection of really sharp minds.

One item I've learned: each writer is like a musical instrument; excite him with a given note, and the resultant will vary remarkably. A piano, a violin, an oboe and a trumpet producing the note A are remarkably different.

But to get that result — *don't* use a pure tone as the stimulus. All musical instruments start with a sort of tuned buzz — a very rough and irregular sound. A trumpet starts with a Bronx Cheer. A violin starts with a scraping noise (bow on string).

Therefore I try to throw out rather vague ideas — and let each man modulate it, change it, and form it into the kind of sound that makes music in his terms.

For you, using real stars is most satisfying; I suggested the use of imaginary star systems solely because it might give your extremely ingenious imagination more freedom. I fully understand that your point is valid; for you, the picture is sharper, clearer, and more satisfying if you tie it down to a real-world phenomenon — an actual star-system. Fine business; that's your characteristic music.

On the business of the planet where the individuals have to survive via eggs. That would allow the development of some of the ideas I have had with respect to genetic knowledge; sure. But you can't play my music as convincingly nor as satisfying, as you can play your own. Write your story — not mine. Maybe I'd do better to tell you "This you can't do, I bet!" and letting you work it out.

On the business of the one-inside-the-other symbiosis:

Define what you mean by "one life-form"!

A human liver cell lives inside a human skin; is the liver a separate and symbiotic species? The question could be argued either way with equal validity, I suspect!

Again: I've had fun throwing out this rather paradoxical way of stating the proposition, but the darned statement, cockeyed as it sounds, is defensible. (And you should be interested, just now!)

Proposition: A human being cannot produce a human being. That is, all human beings are produced by non-human entities.

Explanation: A human being is produced by a fertile ovum, not by a human being.

This is *not* a mere quibble; an amoeba reproduces by binary fission, and therefore it is true that an amoeba is produced by an amoeba. But a human being *develops himself* from a fertile ovum and essentially inorganic, or non-living foodstuffs.

Your child is *not* you; neither is it your wife; it is itself, a resultant product of the development of a living entity (a fertile ovum) which is of a different species than either of you!

You see how difficult it is, really, to define the dividing line between "symbiosis of two species" and "one complex organism."

Incidentally, some work is being done on this line of thought: a germ cell is a highly encoded message; the developing organism is a mechanism which decodes the message to its full expansion. The parent life-form, in its germ cells, is saying "This I believe to be the true nature of the World As It Is. . . ."

Genetics appears to be the incredible case of a successful transmission of an enormously complex message concerning exceedingly technical data to an receiver who has *no* experience. Something like describing the total detail construction of a bomber to someone who had no experience whatever with technology, in a language he had never heard of — and having him, after one statement of the instructions, go out and build a perfect bomber.

Except, of course, that building a perfect human being is a googool or so orders of magnitude more complex than a bomber — and the message transmitted is inscribed in only 47 or 48 complex symbols!

So — kick around whatever idea seems to you to be most

144

interesting. My primary concern is getting something stirring in your mind that will yield another yarn.

Incidentally, you'll see in the May issue the story of **Prof. John Arnold's** course at MIT. They've been having me up there to talk about creative thinking — and your high-gravity environment naturally interests them intensely. The Methania they've worked out is, you'll notice, similar to your Mesklin, at least in atmosphere, and in having heavy (relative to Earth) gravity.

Your ideas have caused a few red faces there, too; the neat point about a methane ocean washing out organic rather than inorganic salts, for instance. One item they'd overlooked is the fact that liquid NH_3 is a strong solvent for metals in the metallic state — i.e., it will dissolve metals as water dissolves sugar; without chemical alteration of the molecule. Cu and Na both dissolve in NH_3.

I also threw them a bit of a curve; their 3 cycle electric power happens to be impractical as hell. A 3 cycle transformer is an enormously massive thing — which is *far* from desirable on a heavy G planet!

Actually, AC power transmission is impractical: the power transmitted is a function of the product of the area under the voltage and current curves. Low frequencies have advantages — high frequencies have other advantages. But the transmission of power long distances encounters these contrary problems:

1. If DC is used, you can't step it up and down in voltage.
2. If AC is used, you may have standing waves on a long powerline, so that certain places on the line you have current with almost no voltage, and at others, outrageous voltages and practically no current. The higher the frequency, the more that tends to happen. (Ask a radio engineer about that!)
3. Further, with AC, part of the time your line is transmitting *no* power, and a considerable part of the time, very little power. (When the sine wave is near zero or is at zero).
4. The time-density of power transmission equals 1.000 only for DC.
5. To transmit equal power at AC, because of the root mean square effect, higher peak currents and higher peak voltages must be handled; the voltage is what causes trouble, because of insulation troubles and corona loss.

   For instance, 110,000 volts DC can be equalled only by an AC line handling 156,000 peak volts. This means the use of an extra 46,000 volts of insulation. It means using larger-diameter wire because of greater corona loss.

145

Methania and Meslin are, however, close enough — particularly through Installment III — to make the MIT gang acutely interested in the progress of Barlennan.

I spent about 16 hours with the Harvard Computer Lab gang — most of a day and night. One of the men there is teaching the Mark IV to speak Russian!

They're studying information theory — and one of the best ways to find out what a language *really* means is to criticise one mechanically. The Mark IV has zero judgement; therefore it will do precisely, but only, what you tell it to do. By the time they've figured out how to tell it to handle Russian — and that means give every single detailed unit of instruction for translating a language — they'll know one hell of a lot more about what makes a language than they do now!

Since mathematics is a language — they'll also know a great deal more about how to design mathematics!

They've done some calculating on single-operation multiplications. That is, "Multiply this 15-digit number by this 15-digit number in one operation." Not doing it sequentially, as one 15 digit number times one of the 15 digit of the other.

They've computed that it would take contacts (if they used relays) or flip-flop tube circuits (if electronic) to the number of 10^{30} X $(2^{30}/30)$ to do the job.

Item: A Hindu girl who's been demonstrating her mathematical abilities has either developed the ability to handle sequential operations at a speed exceeding the best electronic circuits we know of, or she's multiplying multi-digit numbers on a single-operation basis. If the latter, she's got the equivalent of some 10 to the 25th "contacts" in her head that she can use for arithmetic — while she is also doing odd items like regulating a somewhat complex biochemical organism.

One metallurgist objected to your Mesklinites having organic structures stronger than metal.

I don't know what your answer on that is; my answer was that the strongest bond known is an organic bond type. No metal approaches the hardness of the carbon-carbon linkage in diamond.

An item we licked around with the Computer Lab men: If you must record a message that is to remain intact for an enormously long period of time (long in geological ages terms — 2,000,000,000 years or so) how can you insure its survival?

Evidently inscribing it on a piece of material is pointless. No material organization can last that long. Suppose the message is to be a bit of chemical data *about* the water molecule's characteristics. (Not the water molecule itself, but information abstracted from it.)

The computer men are specializing in information theory,

naturally; their conclusion was that it should be imposed on a self-regenerating carrier system, such that it was recycled, and regenerated in each cycle.

This corresponds with the mercury-tube memory system used in computers; the data is coded into pulses sent as sound-waves through a mercury tube.The mercury carries the message through a time-delay; the electronic equipment associated with it reads out the message, and regenerates it, sharpening and clarifying the pulses each cycle.

This also corresponds with Life: each cycle re-checks the information transmitted to it by comparing it with the real universe. If it doesn't have the information correct, the carrier is damped to extinction — known as "dying due to genetic abnormality."

Information can be added; false information cannot continue to be repeated.

But no basic information can be lost — without losing the carrier.

That the life-method works is evidence by the fact that we, today, have metabolisms based on data about the characteristics of the water molecule — and said data has been transmitted accurately for some 2,000,000,000 years.

Item: There may be reason to believe that two sexes are the universal-law requirement, neither more nor less being adequate. Reason: More would, of course, complicate the system, and reduce the probability of successful congruence in time, space, and approximate nature. (It's hard enough to find *one* suitable mate; suppose you had to find two who were also mutually compatible!)

Two appear to be necessary: no organism higher than an earthworm has even made the hermaphroditic system work. All life-forms above the very lowest monocellular forms use the sexual system. Since the two-partner system appears to introduce complexity and thus reduce probability of successful reproduction, we can assume that it is necessary for this reason alone.

However, notice that many times in the universe, a needed result cannot be obtained by a single force, but only by the interaction of two or more. It would be impossible to get a three-dimensional understanding of the world from a monocular system — from a one-viewpoint system, in other words. Many, many indications lead me to believe that the binary system is essential in this universe — and that bisexualism is, therefore, characteristic of the universe rather than of this planet alone.

One major error in thinking human beings tend toward is the simple cause-effect sequence idea. In the usual understanding of the law of cause and effect, most people have the idea that can be expressed mathematically as $y = f(x)$ — that y is caused by x. But the real world displays practically no pure cases of that form; almost, if not completely, invariably the proper formula would be of the form $y = f(x,z,a,b,c,d, \ldots)$.

The problems of actual living, then, cannot be solved by the simple algebraic system, but must be solved as a system of partial differential equations.

One typical arrangement of this sort of thing can be demonstrated with a cake of soap and a bathtub. Wet the soap and the bathtub, and step on the soap. A person in the room might then say, "You threw that soap at me!" The resultant force produces horizontal translation of the soap — although the foot that stepped on it applied a vertical vector.

The psychologist who says a prisoner was caught because his guilt feelings lead him to make such mistakes as would assure his being punished — and that one I've heard! — is extrapolating backward. Effect A is observed; this means that a single force V must exist which produced it.

Only actually, V is a vector resultant of 3,672 individual forces, no one of which happens to lie in the line of the vector resultant! The *one* force that did *not* contribute to the resultant was the zero force along the *apparent* axis of force!

That comment is a further development of the idea in that editorial about our being forced to *act* in an Aristotelean manner. However many force vectors are imposed on a particle, it can move in only one line-of-action.

One of the things that has distinguished your stories has been your tendency to consider the forces which summate to produce the vector resultant. Barlennan is what he is not because "he just is"; you've considered and shown how the many, many forces interact to produce that resultant.

Item: I'm not going to tell you what story to write.

I just want you to write a story!

Regards,   John

P.S. Wanna bet? Betcha it's a boy!

Mark Clifton   *April 17, 1953*

Dear Mark:

The new revision of "Hide, Hide Witch" will go as she rides.

We've still got some mutual understanding to work out; maybe I can clarify the concepts I'm working on somewhat better.

First, they're a blend of what I believe-to-be-true, and what I believe-my-audience-believes-to-be-true. I'd like to pretend that I was discussing what the audience believes, but I can't quite fool myself well enough. It's what I believe they believe.

First off, some axioms of my philosophy: Two people who are in full agreement can learn nothing from each other. I'm glad you aren't in perfect agreement with me!

Second: What you call "frameworks" we call "view-reality." In recognition of the fact that binocular vision supplies a third dimension by integrating two views of the reality, both of which are themselves objective realities, yet neither of which is the-reality-being-studied. That is, an optical image is itself an objective reality — but is not the reality being imaged. "Map is not territory," but a map is an objective reality.

This concept holds that *no* view of reality is ever "right." "Right" must be interpreted, in the above sentence, as meaning "equivalent to the physical-universe reality which exists in totality." In this physical-totality I *include* subjective reality, since I must assume that I am part of the Totality of the universe, and I know I have a subjective-reality function.

Subjective-reality, in other words, is one type of objective phenomenon, and damned well better be recognized as such. Vide what happens if you insist that a homocidal maniac's subjective reality is just nonsense, and pay no attention to it. It has objective reality enough to cause his muscles to perform certain exceedingly discomfiting operations. That which produces an objectively determinable effect must be considered an objectively determinable cause. Q.E.D.

Just because we haven't yet been able to examine the structure of subjective reality microscopically, or electronically, doesn't mean it ain't there. Please to show me a photograph of a gravitational field. Or of a magnetic *field* — not bits of iron oriented *by* the field, but the field itself!

The trouble with the frames-of-reference business is that, to date, no human being has worked out the integrative process whereby the different frames of reference can be adequately used to determine the Physical Objective Totality all are derived from. There is ONE Totality, and only one. There is, therefore, only one system of understandings that is in full correspondence with this ONE totality.

Vide the story of the 6 blind men and the elephant. Every one of 'em had a view-reality which was valid. Until they learned to integrate the view-realities into a single framework of higher dimensionality, none of them had the real story — and there was, in fact, only *one* integration of their 6 view-realities which would bear a one-to-one correlation with the objective system being studied.

Essentially, as we see it now, there are four basic approaches to the Totality problem, or the problem of Right or Wrong. Any actual human personality will, of course, show various combinations of these four, with one or another dominating.

1. "I am invariably right, and others around me are fools or knaves, and therefore wrong. Thus I can always have certainty and security." This is the paranoid type.

2. "I don't know all the answers, I don't know how to solve problems and find the Right — but HE does, and I can always ask HIM and be certain and secure." This is the Dependency type, and we've all got big hunks of it. The psychologist who depends on Freud, or the Journals for his authoritative answers, the Catholic who depends on the Pope or his priest, the scientist who depends on his authoritative theories.

3. "Ah, hell — this right and wrong business is a lot of bullshit. Some smart joker foisted that off for the jerks. I don't fall for it, so I don't worry about uncertainty and insecurity. Anything I can get away with is right." This is the psychopathic personality.

4. "There is, somewhere, the correct set of understandings; unfortunately no human being has ever yet found all of them, nor have I. But I can use the stopgap temporary solutions we do have moderately well, while I seek better solutions. There's risk, of course, — but life would be an insipid thing without it. It's worth working for!" This is the true researcher, the **Einstein**-Newton-Galileo-Jesus-Buddah type.

It happens that Type 4 is the only attitude that can produce deep happiness. It, however, entails a lot of painful bumps.

Now as to the "doom" business. I meant what I said; you can have a tragic ending — at the individual level. The story of Jesus, for example, is certainly a tragedy. But it isn't a story of doom. You could wipe out Billings and Hozworth University — if the death and destruction were not futile.

Consider the bomb disposal squad during the war. One man went in with a field telephone headset, and started trying to dismantle the bomb. At a safe distance, other men made notes, and a magnetic tape recorder, in the later days of the war, took down his words. Sometimes the bomb went off; that was the risk the guy who went in knew he was taking, and took knowingly. He died — but died not futilely, for the knowledge he gave his life to obtain had not been destroyed with him. It was in the notes; the next time someone had to tackle a bomb like that one, he'd know what not to do.

Sure it's a tragic ending — but it's not a doom ending. The men who died in the yellow fever experiments under Walter Reed died tragically — but not futilely. That's not doom; that's what individual human beings live for — to gain a new scrap of knowledge so that the race can climb a bit higher.

Some of the accumulated frames-of-reference knowledge get together in sour ways, and a toxic structure is produced. Then for a while, lives are expended futilely — but later men can study those lives and learn what not to do from them. It's futile only when no one studies, when no one learns.

Rome died. They died because of tolerance — and the lesson learned by the Christian culture was that intolerance was necessary to growth. They got the lesson a little bit wrong — but they did learn a basic truth our philosophers haven't disentangled yet. A culture that tolerates *any*thing is doomed; Rome was so tolerant they allowed Caligula and Nero to practice personal foibles that are perfectly incredible.

Tolerance is the acceptance of disassociation — and disassociation in a personality or a culture, if carried too far, is insanity. Rome could accept unlimited cruelties by disassociating self from that other-self. "Haw haw haw! Look at that one! The lion's started eating her guts and she's trying to crawl away! Haw haw! Where's she think she's going?"

Rome died. Any culture that tries disassociation dies, too, before the pressure of a culture that accepts association and mutual responsibility.

"The roof she started leaking, and the rain she's coming in, if someone doesn't feex eet, I'll be soaking to my skin." The Spanish language has disassociation built in; it can't sustain a truly high-level culture; it assigns responsibility outside the human being. "*she* started leaking" doesn't make for proper assignment of responsibility.

Billings is a victim of misassignment of responsibility. He blames the men who are about to attack him and his work. "The philosophy she started leaking, and the mob she's coming in, if someone doesn't feex eet, I'll be bleeding through my skin."

Sure; Joe's right. Psionics is the next evolution — it involves a higher acceptance of association.

Jesus was right; the next evolution is love-thy-neighbor-as-thyself. Accept association — integrate his framework with your own, knowing that neither of you is right, for Totality lies outside of yourself, and can't be cross-referenced from any single viewpoint. The more widely separated the viewpoints are, moreover, the greater the baseline for your cross-correlation.

In essence, the Big Boy Noonan I proposed would have been a Normal who could deliver the understanding you want Joe to

151

expound — a man with the wisdom to span between the intellectual specialist, Billings, and the ordinary man.

You had Noonan cast as the Voice of the People.

My root objection was that the science-fiction audience of ASF has outgrown the black-hearted-villain vs. white-souled-hero — and the symbol-Noonan you used sounded too much like a BHV.

Hamlet is a typical White Souled Hero — only Shakespeare, being a pretty fair sort of writer, centered the whole play of tragedy, destruction, and despair around his WSH, who is infinitely more destructive than the BHV, Hamlet's uncle. The uncle killed only one man — Hamlet's father. Hamlet wiped out the whole court, driving Desdemona mad, spitting harmless old Polonius, and, act by act, destroying everything he touched.

Shakespeare seems to have had a great fondness for the WSH — when presented as the most deadly, destructive weapon humanity has ever developed. Brutus is another one of his WSHs.

No villain could ever get away with continuing such a reign of terror and destruction as long as Hamlet did!

"God protect me from my friends; I can take care of my enemies."

But today, the morality play isn't so popular — and the crude black-vs-white symbols aren't satisfactory — unless you can successfully compete with that old-timer hack, Shakespeare, who ground out his plays, with quill pen in hand, at such a fantastic rate.

Incidentally, I *know* Shakespeare wasn't Bacon; writing all the material he did took too much time to allow for a second fairly full life!

Now an item that may be of great interest in connection with the novel you're planning.

I was up at the Harvard Computer Lab last week, and spent some 16 hours bull-sessioning with the gang up there. The ones I wanted to talk with were the graduate-student-new-Ph.D. gang. They are still amateurs in their own minds, and willing to speculate and consider new philosophies. The older gang won't. **Clyde Kluckhon**, for instance, proved unwilling to discuss anything with anyone who hadn't read the necessary 13,472 books on anthropology.

The gang working on the computer has started a project that is going to be the most catastrophic thing that ever happened to human philosophy. They're working on Bossy.

It is going to destroy every human philosophy ever conceived; it will anihilate psychology, sociology, political science, economics, religion, and physical science as we know it.

Only they don't know it yet. Neither does the rest of the Harvard faculty. The work **Kluckhon**, for instance, has done, seems to him unshakable and eternal — so he isn't bothered at all by the computer staff's project. He won't be sucked into it for another two years, perhaps. Once he is, his whole work is going to dissolve. He'll try to make it stand on the basis of the computer — and he'll be convinced that it's made of Eternal Metal. But the molten bath of the computer's logic will gradually cause it to slump down, faster and faster, as he feeds it in in an unstoppable effort to find something solid.

A fellow by the name of **Anthony Oettinger** is teaching the Mark IV computer to translate English into Russian and vice versa.

That's all it takes, **Mark**. That project marks the beginning of the end of every human philosophy so far conceived. Yours and mine, Plato's and Aristotle's, Jesus and Buddah — all of them.

Reason: The computer has no judgment whatsoever. It is the absolute, ultimate, non-biased learner. It will learn and believe anything whatsoever — but it will forget absolutely nothing. It will not overlook the statement you fed it 2 years, 7 months, 11 days, 4 hours, 32 minutes and 15.7 seconds ago. Instead it will light a conflict light: "This statement is not congruent with datum 237-B-568-A-459, Establishment discrimination."

The *computer* won't do anything important — except fail to function. But the reasons for its failure to function cannot be assigned to "You're just stupid," or "You're being stubborn," or "I know you're against me," or even "It's your fault," in any modification. Men built it. It does precisely and solely what it must, by the way it's built, do. Men must make it work; if they don't, they cannot, in any way whatsoever, assign the responsibility for failure anywhere else at all.

It is always willing to learn and believe and work. It can't be lazy; it can't be tired, it can be stupid only if the men made it stupid — and then they must correct that.

The computer won't do anything important — but it will force the men who seek to teach it to learn about themselves with an appalling, devastating clarity. They cannot hold two contrary opinions; the computer will demand a resolution to congruence.

Your Joe is going to go half nuts working with Bossy; he isn't perfect, and the degree to which Bossy will force him to clarify his thinking before it can be made to operate will apall even him.

You see, the computer makes possible the most devastating assault on human philosophy ever conceived. To translate from English to Russian, the computer must be taught to handle concepts, not words. And no human philosophy has ever sought to define what a concept is!

Further, the computer, given an English statement, can translate it into Russian, (if they get it running at all) to some degree. But because the computer can be mechanically made to forget what the original English sentence was, it can then accept the Russian sentence, and retranslate it to English.

If it doesn't come out the same, the computer hasn't been taught right. Try again.

Example: There's an old English saying that, when translated into Chinese by Mr. A. and translated from Chinese to English by Mr. B. comes out "Invisible idiot." Perfectly logical, when you analyze the English statement, that such a confusion of meanings should arise; one who is out of sight is invisible, and one who is out of mind is either an idiot or insane.

The project can be visualized this way: Suppose the Russian delegation to the UN is given Computer RE (Russian to English) and the Americans have Computer ER. The Russians are not allowed, for official statements-of-record, to use human translators; they must work through the computer. Until their statement through the computer is satisfactory, no statement will be considered to have been made.

But what they do is to send their statement, in Russian, to their RE computer; it sends the English statement to the American delegates — and to the American ER computer. The ER computer sends the Russian translation of the English statement to the Russian delegation.

If the Russians don't like the resultant statement, they signal for reanalysis.

By the time the two computers have been so adjusted that:

1. All translations, both ways, are satisfactory.
2. All concept-statements within each computer are congruent to a degree that allows the computers to function.
3. All necessary terms for discussion of problems have been installed,

there won't be any problems left to discuss. Both delegations would have learned so much about themselves and their problems that they'd both retire to realign their respective governments!

They would, of course, go completely berserk at the frustration of having to state precisely what they meant in precisely meaningful terms. The statement "That demand of yours is mere emotional propaganda!" would simply evoke from the two computers "Define 'emotional.'" "Define 'propaganda.'" "Statement non-translatable because of noncongruence of terms."

"That statement is not logical!"
"Differentiate 'logical' vs 'rational.'"
"That Goddamned stupid machine is impossible!"
"Define 'God.'" "Define 'damned.'" "Define

154

'concept' 'impossible' with respect to situation machine exists as objective reality." "Define 'malfunction' implied by term 'stupid' with respect to machine's circuits."

"That blasted thing has no understanding — no judgment at all!"

"Define 'judgment.'"

For here we would have a child of infinite capacity to learn, a child which cannot be accused of illogic, stupidity, ill motivation, or any other fault whatever — and a child which cannot be punished; it can only be taught. It cannot be accused, by the artist, of having no soul — without demanding what "soul" means, and asking that it be defined in terms of circuits within the machine!

When I talked with **Oettinger**, I found the depths of human ignorance indicated in some degree. You can't even define "dinner" in terms that are properly translatable; you've never been called on, in dealing with humans, to make the degree of specific definition called for.

Consider the simple term "food"; I'd never imagined the enormous breadth of concept analysis and relationship necessary to handle the problem of the relation between the concept "food" and the process of ordinary, daily living. We've all been doing it — but we haven't been consciously aware of doing it.

Does the exact nature of the concept "food" enter into the problem of building, say, a garage?

It does indeed. Wood is food for termites; brick and concrete are not food for any known organism.

Is steel food?

Build it into the computer, friend! "We need more steel scrap to feed our hungry furnaces!"

And your computer must be able to translate that.

Is human flesh to be considered food by sane individuals? Well, you'd better so consider it if you get in the South Seas, or the African jungles; sharks and lions so consider it.

And, of course, your computer must recognize also that all of the above is food for thought.

The reason this project is going to suck in every form of human philosophy and thinking is quite easy; it will come up with statements that will drive psychologists wild, for example. When it does, they will descend on the project, huffing and puffing, and insist that the project boys get out of the way and let someone who knows something about psychology feed in the proper data.

A few weeks later, haggard and humbled, they'll go away to learn something about psychology. Their own statements will have been thrown back at them repeatedly until they learn to achieve congruence, and define differentiations — or admit they don't

155

know what they are talking about.

The physicists, similarly, will find that their terms must be translatable into living concepts — and aren't. They, too, will go away haggard and humbled to try to achieve congruences.

Political scientists will find their messages taken apart — and will look horrified at the pieces lying around pitifully on the floor.

And, gradually, the thoroughly humbled, and deeply studious and introspective computer gang will achieve some real understandings. They'll respect mankind as no human being ever did before; they'll have an inexpressable appreciation for the magnificence of the mind of a two-year-old child, who can learn, somehow, to handle language!

They won't be proud — yet every specialist in every field will have a shaking horror that they may take a look at his field.

Define "totality."

"The sum of all that was, might have been, is, will be, or might be, plus the sum of all imagined possibilities, plus the possibilities that an imagined imagination might imagine."

Put that in a computer! You just put it in your mind, somehow, so it must be possible!

So far as the readership goes: any problem can be discussed. It's tragic possibilities may be discussed. It can destroy individuals. But the essence of a good story is that it solve the problem it proposes — and saying the problem is insoluble is seldom the right answer.

And you can get a hell of a good story out of showing that no solution that appears reasonable works — and that only some wildly irrational answer is actually usable!

Instance: How can you extinguish a fire of burning magnesium metal?

Answer: Dump lots of magnesium metal on it. The heat absorbed in melting the newly added magnesium will lower the temperature of the material below the ignition point.

How to extinguish a burning oil tank, containing 100,000 gallons of kerosene?

Answer: Blow about 6 cubic feet of air bubbles into the bottom of the tank. The fire will go out in about 30 seconds.

Reason: The rising air bubbles cause currents that stir the kerosene, and bring tons of cold kerosene from the bottom of the tank up to the surface. The cold kerosene won't provide enough vapor to maintain the flame, and is replaced too rapidly for the flames to warm it enough. Standard Oil uses that, now, as their regular method of extinguishing oil-tank fires!

How do you extinguish burning titanium or zirconium metal powder?

Answer: You don't. You build a dike around the fire and let it burn out. *Any* known additive will cause the fire to burn hotter — because, in air, these metals burn the *nitrogen* rather more than the oxygen. Water, CO_2, sand — all the usual fire-quenchers contain a richer supply of oxygen than air does, and the Z or Ti will get it!

You can have fun with wrong answers that are right — but no legitimate story ends without an answer to the problem proposed.

Regards,   John

John Arnold   *April 21, 1953*

Dear John:

I've asked **Miss Tarrant** to see that you get 25 reprints of the article. **Miss Tarrant** is the one member of our small staff on *ASF* who can thread the intricacies of S & S and get things done. You'll get 'em.

I know damn well you're making progress with your work there; the mere fact that you've been able to get the work up to a "conscious" level — i.e, get it to a level where you can state openly to the Society "I am studying creative thinking, because that is something our world needs," instead of doing it under cover — is an immense advance.

Once the problem has been stated openly, and someone has started work on it openly, many others will gladly join in. You aren't unique in *wanting* to do the work; you're just unique in having the force and determination and ability to actually get the work started in the open. You are now the Authority for others who wanted to start work, and didn't have what it took to get it going.

When I was up there, I told you that **Peg** and I have been studying the problem of inducing someone to recognize what he needs to learn — i.e., "How to induce insight." We're still at it — and one of the facets of the problem lines up with the question you ask about observation.

Let's go back a bit first.

Our present official concepts of Mankind, as stated by psychology and sociology, hold that Man is a gregarious, social animal.

This is not an adequate statement of the case; I'm damned sure that it is, in fact, a drastically wrong statement leading to a complete misconception of the nature of the socio-psychological problem. Man is *not* gregarious; he's symbiotic. **Peg** made that point up, and it explains a lot about what's needed in making our culture work right.

If Man were simply gregarious, *then* Communism would be the ideal system of government.

157

Let's take a look at organization in the development of animal life. A sponge is one of the lowest forms of animal life — and a sponge is actually a colony of *gregarious* cells. A sponge can be chopped up, ground through a strainer, and the resultant soup of separated cells will recombine to form a sponge colony again. In a sponge, every cell is the equivalent of every other cell; the cells are simply gregarious.

But if a higher animal is treated similarly, the animal ceases to exist as such. In even such low forms as the jellyfish there is some specialization of tissues, with the result that the cells are not merely gregarious, but symbiotic. It is *not* true that any cell of the jellyfish can replace any other cell.

In a herd of cattle or horses, we have a gregarious-social system. Any one cow can replace any other cow; there is no functional differentiation between cattle. This is a society like the sponge, and unlike the jellyfish.

Human societies have long, long since passed the level of the jellyfish; in our societies we have specialization of individuals, and marked differentiation of types. Human beings are NOT mutually replaceable. What would happen if you and I switched jobs, for instance? Each of us would make a mess of the other fellow's work.

Psychology and sociology have been trying to work with statistical methods, designed to study the "normal" human being. I feel strongly that the entire effort is badly misdirected; it is no more sound to do that than to try to determine the "normal" characteristics of a human body cell by averaging the characteristics of a brain cell and a liver cell.

In a highly organized system, specialization and mutual dependence becomes necessary. Instead of the competition that exists in a gregarious level of society, complementation must be introduced, with a full recognition that each of us is dependent on the other fellow for services we ourselves cannot perform.

Communism is impossible in a high-level society; individuals are not interchangeable at that level.

Modern machine methods produce automobiles in which the parts are interchangeable — but that doesn't mean that you can interchange the wheel of car A with the piston rod from Car B!

To a large degree, you're interchangeable with one of the other professors of Mech Eng at a major technical school — but you're not interchangeable with a professor of Surgery at Harvard Med.

Not now, that is. Just as a liver cell is not *now* interchangeable with a brain cell. But just as you could have specialized in medicine years ago, so at one stage of the embryonic development, a cell has its choice of developing toward brain specialization or toward liver specialization.

To switch to Surgery now, you'd have to de-specialize, regress all the way back to sophomore college level, and then redevelop all the way up.

To change a man's basic life-evaluation patterns, to induce basic insights of that depth, you have to induce him to give up a vast amount of specialization. Any time you can get a man to do that, incidentally, you'll have one of the most powerful human beings who ever lived; he will have learned to be Protean, to be anything he chooses. He will, incidentally, scare the living bejayzus out of anyone who tries to work with him closely, because we aren't accustomed to human beings who can change their basic belief-patterns at will!

Actually, that sort of basic reorientation isn't necessary for ordinary individuals in the Society. You have some of it; it's needed in the leaders of the society, but they mustn't discomfit the ordinary members of the society by displaying the characteristic too widely.

What is needed is to pry open the limitations people have put on themselves. To make a choice we must reject those things which are actually mutually contradictory — but usually people reject far too much. That's part of what you're struggling with.

Now: I've been studying my own career through school. It was most peculiar; I never got a decent grade in English Composition . . . though I make my living by my use of the English language! I never worked hard at physics or Chem there at MIT — and always got a straight H. I sweated over calculus, and didn't get such hot marks. I worked hard on German, and flunked out of MIT because I could not pass first-year German in three tries!

Yet I'd taken Spanish at Prep School, and, without any particular effort made 95 to 98 throughout, and I learned French well enough to pass two years in one summer school. It wasn't that I "had no aptitude for languages."

I took the College Board exam in Trig for entrance to MIT; I got 65, but MIT then demanded 75 or better for admittance. So the summer I was taking two years of French, I was also supposed to prepare for MIT's own entrance exam in Trig. I did look over the book the night before I was supposed to take it; I made 98 on MIT's trig entrance exam.

Now here is a weird and wonderful pattern of behavior. Being a firm believer in the proposition that there *is* law in the Universe, and that I am necessarily part of that Universe, there must be some law behind this pattern.

I can talk about my own experience, because of all the minds in the Universe, mine, and mine only, is fully accessable to me in fact. But the basic laws that applied to me must also apply to others.

There is only one reason any human being engages in any effort, he expects a reward he considers desirable. The reward may be positive in itself — pleasure — or it may be a double-negative type of reward; i.e., the reward of the avoidance of the undesirable. For instance, the reward of not being not-liked.

The double-negative reward, however, is always a weak motivation; its highest attainable level is equivalent to boredom, the zero level of emotional motivation. Not being not-liked does *not* mean that you are liked. Not being punished doesn't mean you're praised.

Now a child in school applies effort to learning the lessons provided. His motivations, in rough approximation, might be divided into the following groups:
1. He wants to learn the subject for himself.
2. He wants to get a passing mark so his parents and contemporaries won't scorn and ridicule him.
3. He wants to get good marks because he sees competition for high scores as a game in itself.

Incidentally, the story has it that Isaac Newton, as a boy, was a poor student until he'd had a fight with the school bully, and beaten him soundly. Then Newton realized the bully was making better marks than he himself was, and determined to beat him in that respect too. See Motivation 3 above.

In studying physics and chemistry, I was working on motivation 1 above; it's wonderful motivation, because then learning takes place on a pleasure level, and the effort appears to be practically no effort at all. My straight H's were quite accidental by-products; I wasn't particularly interested in them.

But calculus was something I studied largely under motivation 2; for the purpose of getting a passable grade. However, because calc was needed to understand the physics I wanted, I had a double motivation chain. I got C's fairly regularly.

German I had no personal use for, and a distinct dislike for.

Now if learning consists of an association of ideas, consider this: suppose we have a series of ideas A, B, C, D, E and F, each of which has as association-factor to its neighbor of 0.9. Then A-B has an association value of 0.9, but A-C has an a.v. of 0.81, and A-D is down to 0.73, A-E is .66, and A-F is 0.59. The more associations-intervals intervene, the lower the association-factor between any two items.

Now let's say that A stands for the individual's mind, and the others are a series of ideas. If the individual learns arithmetic *because* he wants good grades, *because* he doesn't want to be punished, *because* his parents will punish him if he doesn't pass — arithmetic is going to be associated with his own mind through a

160

chain of associations, and not directly.

The child normally gets arithmetic thrown at him in buying candy, or paying for the movies, etc., enough so that he forms some direct association.

But now we come to high school chemistry. Most high school girls get good marks in the course — and forget it practically 100% the day after the close of that semester.

Reason: So long as getting-good-marks-in-chemistry has a high association value with the individual's self, the chain of associations has a fairly high net value. But the moment that association value drops from .9 down to 0.001 or so. . . !

Right now, **Jane** is having a hell of a time studying. The reason appears to me to be something like this:

The girls' colleges send out acceptances May 14, based on records to that date, and college board exams. It is *not* based on the work done by the girls in the last half of the last semester of high school, except in that the girl must, of course, graduate.

What reward will **Jane** get for doing good work in this last 1/2-semester, then?

She's in the position of a man who's been given two weeks notice that he's being fired. Why work hard?

She is doing fine in English and American Democracy; those *she* wants. But her Spanish is becoming a terrific effort for her, and her mark's going down despite a greater conscious effort!

Now comes the question of observation.

The individual who related his environment *to himself* and to *his own interests* will be establishing direct association linkages. If you establish a chain of high-value associations in physics, say, and then relate many individual observations to yourself and physics, and to each other, you'll not only have the observations recorded in memory, but will have high association-value linkages with them so that they are available.

For example: when I see a clear, brilliantly blue summer sky, I enjoy the depth and color of it — and also enjoy the association-to-me and my enjoyment of the knowledge that statistical irregularities in the distribution of air molecules is the source of that enjoyment of the deep, pure blue color.

The beauty of a green-carpeted rolling landscape, seen from a hilltop, entails, for me, the realization that those miles of green growing plant-life and I have a close and intimate symbiosis; they live, and because they do, I live, for the oxygen-carbon-dioxide cycle links us.

If there is a chain of 0.9 associations-value linkages, the resultant a.v. declines to a pretty low value. But if you have 50 different linkage systems, all going from Point A to Point M, M can be very high indeed. It's a network system that can be beautifully analoged by means of a lot of little resistors and rectifiers (because frequently the association goes from A to B, but not from B to A) in a series-parallel cross-connected net-work.

Creative thinking, to a large extent, must involve forming new associations — or more properly, recognizing associations that have always been there. (If they hadn't been there in physical reality, forming the association would have been a mistake, not creative thinking.) But to do that, many chains and networks of associations must be available, and many cross-connections betwen chains and nets must be made.

Work we've done, and that many others have done with hypnotic experiments, indicates that the human being actually observes totally — that every sensory impression reaching the organism is recorded indelibly in the memory-system somewhere, somehow. Hypnotic experiments have shown that a 40-year old man can be induced to recall the individuals present at his 5th birthday party, what they wore, what presents they brought, etc.

It isn't lack of *observation,* then — but lack of adequate association chains.

It's the business of noise vs redundance in communication theory. Either a very strong signal, overriding the noise level completely, or many repetitions of the weak signal is needed to get a clear, noise-free signal through. Then either you need one very strong association link, or you need many parallel association channels to link Now-Here with There-Then.

The individual who depends on a few, high-association linkages will not be creative; he has too few methods of thinking, because he has too few channels that are sufficiently noise-free. The individual who depends on multitudes of paralleled association channels has a great number of possible routes to understanding, and a vastly greater chance of making useful associations.

Man's great advantage over the animals is that he operates with many association links, instead of a few. The reason no animal can face Man is, basically, that Man can predict what the animal will do, because its range of reactions is limited — but no animal can predict what Man will do. Block one of Man's routes from A to M, and he'll find fifteen other variations. Vide the situation in patent law!

One of the things you're doing in your course is essentially based on that. The Arcturus Project, for instance, blocks the kids' normal path to answers — get it from the books. This starts them developing side chains — and developing the realization that side chains around a blockage *can* be developed.

Sure memory is important — but I wish to God people would get

162

over the idea that that's the sole answer to wisdom. The times I've been frustrated by some yayhoo who won't listen to a new idea because I haven't read all the books he thinks are necessary to be able to think about it! Lord, man, the New York Public Library "remembers" more than any man on Earth — and is so stupid it can't get a single new idea in a millenium.

Also, the data in the Library isn't too darned much use to people, because they can't refer to it when they want it. It isn't indexed adequately; it doesn't have a cross-referrence system such that if I look up "food" it will remind me that human flesh must be considered food — if you don't want to make the mistake of swimming in shark-infested waters. And that all of the Library's contents is food for thought.

An inventor is a man who found a way around an obstacle in the normal chain of associations, or a more satisfactory chain of associations.

One interesting concept: If an individual has been trained to value himself low, has been beaten about the ears with "you're not important" and "don't think you're so wonderful" and don't be selfish and egotistical," you get highly deleterious effect on his creativity.

There is a difference between having humility, and having a low opinion of yourself; the society doesn't make an adequate distinction there. I've noticed that those kids you're working with *all* have a marked tendency to arrogance, *and* humility. "My opinion is of value . . . but it's not the only valuable opinion," in effect.

If you have a $50 radio set, the maximum repair-effort you can sanely invest in it must be less than $50.

If you value your own self low, then *you cannot evaluate any association to yourself higher.*

If I'm not worth much, then there's no point in making any great effort toward my satisfaction — and I won't try hard to please anyone, because the only point in pleasing someone is that it would yield me satisfaction.

Convince someone he has a high value to you, then it becomes appropriate for him to expend greater effort in achieving satisfaction with respect to you. (The essential principal by which a genuinely good teacher can get more from his students than can a poor one!)

Children, unfortunately, are repeatedly pinned back with comments about their stupidity, worthlessness, selfishness, and generally treated with indignity. Many a Mama and Papa lambasts them with "After all I've done for you. . . ." which implies that they aren't really worth the efforts expended on their behalf.

163

A man who respects himself, and what he is doing, can expend far more effort toward success than can a man who thinks he himself, and his work, is of small value anyway.

And, if the individual thinks of himself as having high value, then associations to himself can have higher value — and he can establish longer chains of association values that will still exceed the "noise level" of "not important."

At the same time, if he thinks of himself as the *sole* center of value, he can't establish adequate cross-linkages that will make an adequate network of thinking.

I have a hunch that studying neural network in primitive animal organisms would lead to an understanding of creative thinking! They're associations-networks. And human creative thinking hasn't yet advanced beyond the most primitive levels, I fear!

Perhaps the best way to train the association-function that we need is to set up training schemes based on deliberately blocking the normal, habitual paths to the goals, and seeing if you can find new ways around. The Arcturus Project is a major system of that type. A minor system might be throwing a deliberately impossible problem to the group, with their full knowledge of the purpose, and have them see if they can crack it by some new method. Many times an impossible single operation can be readily achieved by two operations — if you can spot the two that will do it!

There are undoubtedly lots of "impossible" problems that have been cracked that your gang hasn't heard of. Let them see if they can work their way through the thing as the original inventor did.

For instance, the problem of tungsten casting. Since tungsten has the highest melting point of any known material, how can you make a melting pot to hold it, or a mold to cast it in?

Answer: You don't need either. Take powered tungsten metal, obtained directly by hydrogen reduction of tungsten oxide powder, and flow it from a hopper through a high-intensity electric arc. This yields a stream of molten tungsten — which was all you wanted from the melting pot system anyway.

Flow the molten metal into a mold of water-cooled copper. Tungsten can't wet cool copper — and the first tungsten to arrive freezes and forms a solid shell-mold in which the rest of the tungsten is cast!

This problem can be solved only by analyzing what you really mean by "casting" — and recognizing that what you actually want is a solid product, not a liquid product. The liquid state is simply a transient needed to transform one solid shape into another; you don't actually want the liquid form.

I'm sure the other departments there at MIT can supply you with a nice collection of "impossible" problems that have been cracked recently.

164

Another on the tungsten line: How can you support a mass of liquid tungsten? Suppose you want a surface at 4500. Tungsten is liquid at that temperature, but its boiling point is above that point. How could you generate that temperature, and maintain the mass of liquid tungsten?

Answer: support the liquid metal in high-frequency alternating current fields. Eddy current losses will keep it roughly spherical. And you can't melt down a magnetic field, even at that temperature!

The one answer not allowed in the process of living is "I give up." That simply isn't in living; it's death.

I think you're on the right track now; block routine thinking, and the student will gain more and more confidence in his ability to find an alternative route around the problem.

By the way; in the old days, when somebody had an original idea that he felt needed spreading, he could do so only by personal contact, and personal persuasiveness. If he was successful, moreover, he was apt to have the Authorities seek to remove his too-effective personality permanently. Vide Jesus.

It isn't that the Authorities are any more willing to allow the Scheme of Things to be altered — but that it is so futile to remove the individual after he has explained his idea to half a million people via the swift, widespread communication channels of today.

The same business of alternatives association-chains; one strong communication channel can be blocked by cutting off its head. But what do you do with half a million?

Fulmination gives a certain amount of release of feeling, but very little result!

Regards, John

Curtis   *April 26, 1953*

Dear Mrs. Curtis:

I know that you, **Mark Clifton**, **Judy Merril**, **Ted Sturgeon** and a number of other science-fiction authors are very much interested in the practical application of the psionic powers. As you know, I am too.

Many people have been, for many years. Some pretty bright people, with fairly good minds. As a matter of fact, there's been much more human mental effort devoted to the psionic field than there has been to the physical sciences — if you take into account the total of the last 10,000 years. And we must, in this consideration, because the awareness of psionic powers existed before there was any physical science, the mystics worked at the field before anyone tried to get the physical sciences going.

The remarkable thing is, then, that so much effort has yielded so little! It's true that a few individuals appear to have achieved some results — but the results have been of little use to anyone, including even the possessors thereof. There appears to be some factor at work that makes the business somewhat more complicated than we realize. Its probably that the conservation of mass-energy applies, and that it's hard work to use these powers, making it come out easier to use ordinary means for most circumstances.

It is also evident that the powers are not going to be attained in any reproducible form by the attack on the problem that the mystics have used. I don't say that the *goal* is invalid; I do hold that the *means to that goal* that have been used in the past are not usable.

The problem is not going to be solved by the "flash of genius" route, because while that method will, and in fact has at various times, given the use of the powers, it does not give you understanding of them.

You, as a biological organism, can synthesize only certain very limited, special proteins, however. If you as a human being knew the laws by which you as an organism do the job, on the other hand, you'd be able to synthesize an unlimited variety of highly useful new protiens and other chemicals.

I understand that **Ron** developed some psi abilities. Could be. However I'll gurantee this; with the knowledge I now have, I could apply laws that would block his psi powers, or the law's powers of any other person . . . unless that person knew the basic laws he was using so well he could modify his method to circumvent my interferrence.

Until I can develop the basic laws of psionics, it is futile to seek to use them in this society; the counter-blocks are much simpler than the methods of using the powers. The result is that my effort to demonstrate them would be blocked by any skeptical person, and my accomplishment would be useless. It would be like making a delicate machine out of calcium and sodium metals. The machine would work nicely if kept in absolutely dry, pure hydrogen atmosphere — but wouldn't work in a normal atmosphere, and no one could ever touch it.

The counter-block concepts are so common in our society that no one can get anywhere with psionics until the laws are understood well enough to undercut those block concepts.

The result is that all you'll get out of the mystic approach to psionics, if you do achieve abilities, is the sorrow consequent on finding your powers continually blocked and frustrated without understanding why, or how, or being able to offset the blocking effect.

There are certain psionic powers that are not blocked by the society; those aren't blocked because they're of such a nature that the society doesn't find out about them. They're suicidal. There are no laws prohibiting people from becoming cyanide addicts, either. It's non-habit-forming. There's damned little chance you'll actually get hurt by them, however, because it takes a lot of fussing with things to get near 'em, I suspect.

The essential point is this: Everbody does in fact have some degree of psionic ability. These abilities are used constantly in daily life — at a low level, on a major psionic ability; the direct sensing of relationship-lines. The reason why human memory is total and complete is simply that it is a direct ability *to sense the past-time Universe itself.* Memory isn't stored in cells, or in the brain or in molecules; it's due to the action of a present-time *ability* (past-searching) and the existence of the past-time universe as an inimitable reality. Ordinary memory is a psionic ability. Good memory is due to high associative-sensing ability — high psionic ability.

High-powered minds have high psionic abilities, and have been blocked in using them externally — on the positive side. But I can use my high order psionic ability to *negate* your efforts. The bigoted anti-psionic individual will normally have his psionic abilities going full blast to negate anything you try . . . and he's apt to have more inherent psionic ability than you do! He can damp your psionics very handily — and then deny that there was any psionic forces in action at all!

Only when you understand the basic laws that psionics work on can you divert his psionic efforts in such a manner that they aid instead of opposing yours.

Now it happens that our society is based on certain valid concepts which *appear* to be general, and are actually special cases of quite different general laws. I can name some of these, and your science-oriented husband is apt to blow a gasket; he is powerfully oriented to maintain the validity of his beliefs, and will tend to do so psionically.

First, the concept of distance is invalid; it's a special case of the much more general concept "relationship," interacting with another more general concept "interval." Second, our concept of "time" is inadequate and inappropriate; it, too, is a special-case of something more basic and general. Third, logic is another special case in the form we know it; "thinking" is somewhat more general, but still inadequate.

Psionics won't work until you understand the rigor of non-logical thinking. Telepathy as known doesn't show inverse square effects because the concept "distance" is not applicable in this field.

Precognition and similar phenomena arise from the fact that time-interval-distance are all inadequate concepts.

But . . . those concepts, firmly held by a powerfully oriented mind, of high psionic ability, can be *imposed on* the experiment you seek to carry out. If you can impose the no-distance-interval concept in an effort to achieve results, the other mind can equally impose the concept, and negate your effort — leaving things in their undisturbed condition.

The essence of the business is this: psionics aren't going to be worth a damn until you do as much hard, basic research on *working out the details* as the physicists and chemists have in their field. The physical scientists got their results by really digging at the job; they sweated blood, sweat and tears over it; they altered their own ideas, changed their own understanding of the world they lived in, and accepted some damned unsettling ideas to get there.

You'll find yourself getting scared silly, every now and then, along this psionics road. You won't have too much trouble if you go into it knowing you're going to hit things that will scare you.

And look, kid; if you think you can't be scared — stop being a silly school girl and get sense in your head. That's the way you'll get your mind cracked in a dozen screaming little pieces. Back off and take another look at life. That attitude is one of pure, childish braggadocio, an utter lack of adult humility. It's the attitude of a bunch of adolescents playing "chicken" by racing cars at each other head-on to get scared. You won't be scared. But you'll be most peculiarly not-you anymore.

You are a structure of forces which are natural to this universe; that is, necessarily, absolutely all you are or possibly can be. It's perfectly obvious that the universe is bigger than you are — so much bigger it can crush you without quite being aware that you happened.

It won't — unless you persist in getting your little fingers caught in the gears. Respect it and its powers; they're so collossal they can detonate stars. You can't command the Universe — but you can knowingly work with and through it.

About a dozen times so far, I've hit things that scared me pale blue with pink polk-a-dots.

End of lecture. You don't have to believe me, because as an independent investigator, you always have the right and the opportunity to find out.

But it seems excessively futile to repeat, in the same old way, the same old mistake that has derailed Mankind for the last 10 millenian. Study how the mystics have been doing it for the last few dozen centuries — and recognize that since they have *not* gotten what you are seeking, that is necessarily the wrong way to do it. It's wrong, because it didn't work.

I know a lot of this sounds like a bunch of platitudes from the old moralists; there is a resemblance, because the old boys were not dopes, and they did some hard, straight, and competent thinking. I'm not ridiculing them when I say they did it wrong; I'm respecting them. I recognize they did their thinking in clear, solid, workmanlike fashion, and did a good, sound job of study. That's why I'm willing to say the *method* must be wrong; the men who tried it were, I think, competent, intelligent, sincere, and wise. If such men, using that method, didn't get the results needed — why that's evidence enough for me that the method's futile.

It's the second rate boys who said "There are things not for Man to know," you'll notice. The first-rate explorers of that Unknown never said that; they said that the exploration was dangerous, and that it called for the greatest respect of the forces involved. I don't think they were fools, or cowards either.

They said a lot about purifying yourself first, and putting aside petty things. They are so right — but it needs translating into modern language. Decide what you really want, what your ideas really are — clarify your thinking. Otherwise when you hit some of the basic concepts, you'll suddenly find that half your life is wrapped up in a shallow, unreal misconception. The results of that is to have your mind suddenly plunged into the chaos of knowing that your old ideas were wrong — but not knowing what is right.

You want help in gaining understanding of the psionic forces, and it appears to you that I'm warning you against investigating.

I'm not.

I'm suggesting that this study, like any other, yields more useful results if you build up to it, understanding in full each step you make as you make it.

Here we've been discussing "fear." Are you ready to tackle telepathy — which involves transmission of emotional concepts — when you can't yet define what *fear* is? Suppose telepathy linked you one-to-one with the other individual; could you unscramble yourself again — when you don't know what "you" is? Can you accept complete rapport with another individual — when you can't define the differences between yourself and that other individual enough to re-separate your two beings? Or would you suddenly discover that having established full contact — you were forced, thenceforth, to be one mind in two bodies?

On the other hand, suppose that I had learned to define "I" in full — and I established rapport with you. You'd be nicely stuck with being unable to separate out your personality and beliefs from mine; I wouldn't be.

You want telepathy, huh?

Anybody can stick his finger into a crucible of molten copper —

but you've got to be real good to pull it out again.

That telepathy item, by the way, is behind the legends of "soul stealers." If I can induce my concepts and belief-systems in you . . . who are you, after that?

You'll be ready to try some real telepathy experiments when you can define "I." Fortunately, you can't even begin to do real telepathy work before that anyway — otherwise you'd have no chance to go beyond the very beginning stages.

There's an old saying that "Wishing will make it so." Sure it will — if the wish is father to the deed, and the deed is some good, hard, detailed work and planning. You can have it — any time you're willing to sweat for it!

Regards,   John W. Campbell, Jr.

Wayne Batteau   *May 2, 1953*

Dear Wayne:

I love the Three Laws of Stupidity, or whatever you call them! They're perfectly valid, too, by gad!

By the way, I have an answer to **J.S. Milne's** worry about running out of things to learn. It's quite simple; I can prove that no mind will ever be omniscient.

Consider a system of Units and Relations. The Units will be considered to represent certain known facts. Now if we have Units A and B, and the relation A-B, we must acknowledge that the relation AB is a fact. But a known fact is a new Unit in the system we are considering; therefore A-B constitutes a new Unit, C. So now we have a system of Units A, B, and C; in addition to A-B, we now have also A-C and B-C. But these constitute fact-Units D and E.

Run out of things to study? Good God man, the more you learn, the more you know there is to learn, as anyone above the level of fool has long since observed as a fact!

I'm interested in **Warren's** analysis of circuit changes as information transformations. He's a little slow coming to that idea, of course — that's the concept some low-brow *Homo notquiteus* invented about 1.5 megayears ago — and, in doing it, invented Man. The lower animals operate on the basis of fixed instinct information-handling patterns; only Man can change his information-handling patterns as well as his information!

I've been trying to express just what the phase-change was that made Man out of Animal; I knew damned well there was one, and that it must lie in the field of information handling, but I didn't know what it was. I'm damned sure, right now, that **Warren** has hit the basic concept that made the difference.

170

Re "two things are the same if they are invariant through your fliter (viewpoint)." I forget whether I mentioned the business of bridge circuits when I was up there. A Wheatstone bridge is the basic circuit; it compares ratios between things of identical nature — pure resistance. But the AC bridge circuits have the interesting characteristic that they can compare *dissimilar* things with respect to *one quality*. A Wein Bridge, for instance, can compare the impedance of a condenser at a fixed frequency with a resistance, or in other words solve the question "Under Conditions P, is C equivalent in quality Q to R?" Further, if the answer proves to be "No; under Conditions P, C is not equivalent to R with respect to Quality Q," we can go further and find the answer to the question "Under what condidtions is C equivalent to R with respect to Quality Q?" by varying the applied AC frequency until the bridge circuit *does* balance.

If you think about it a moment, those two operations are basic to Applied Judgement!

The bridge circuit, apparently, has the basic structure required for judging and evaluating dissimilar things, with respect to single qualities.

Instead of holding a scale pan balance, Justice should be holding a Wein Bridge circuit!

Warren, in his work, is also attacking a basic problem that **Peg** and I have recently recognized. He's got it formulated in a special way — with respect to computer design — but the problem is infinitely general. It comes to this: "Define what you mean by 'the simplest way' or 'the simplest explanation.'"

For instance, what's the simplest way to get from Boston to New York?

Walk, of course.To ride a horse would require that you develop the complex concept of domesticated animals, spend years learning to train a horse, then a year or so actually training one, and finally making the ride. Obviously a far more complex process than walking.

And driving in a car?! This reqires a dozen millenia of research, study, growth of complex understandings of high-order abstractions such as laws of motion, thermodynamics, electrical current, etc., and finally the investment of millions of man-hours in building tools to build tools to build machines to make parts that can be assembled into an automobile. And simultaneously, the investment of millions of man-hours in the construction of an immense static machine called a "highway."

Now what do you mean by saying "Of two offered theoretical explanations, choose the simpler."

Walk, son — walk. That's the simpler theory.

171

I propose this: If you have a theory that says "That can not be done," throw it away and get a new theory. It makes life too complicated. What we want are theories that say "That can't be done in that way; it's easier to do it by method X."

One thing we can be absolutely, rock-bottom certain of; we do not know all there is to know. We do NOT know the true basic laws of the Universe. When you encounter two seemingly basic forces, it's almost certain that they are two co-equal effects of an underlying unitary force. Electric and magnetic fields, for instance, are, I'm certain, co-equal effects of a deeper level law we haven't found yet.

Now inasmuch as we do NOT know the true basics, we can't throw out any ideas just because the *present* knowledge won't explain them. Try explaining to a Roman citizen that the sense of thirst is due to a small bundle of nerves (What are, nerves, huh?) in the body which sense the ion concentration (What's ions, huh?) in the blood. The fact that you couldn't communicate the information doesn't make the information invalid — it just makes it useless to the Roman citizen.

Sure, you can only learn what you don't know . . . but you have to be aware that you don't know it before you will learn it!

Some of our work with the mind has suggested the absolute, ultimate, and perfect memory-system. Try this concept.

The past is immutable; what has happened, has happened and cannot be changed in any slightest iota. It's absolute.

Then, logically, *it exists* as a reality. If it was real, and can't be changed in any respect, then it *is* real!

Visualize the time-process, for the moment, as a crystallization process. We have a gas, whose molecules are events; this gas is the Future. At the interface zone of Now, that gas is crystallizing into a solid Then, the past. As the crystalline forces of actual chemical crystals extend an influence beyond the crystal surface to force incoming molecules into a compatible alignment, so the time-forces of the crystaline Past tend to force events to align themselves in patterns congruent with the already crystalized Past.

But the past itself is rigid.

Now what we call "memory" can be divided into two processes; one is data-storage, and the other is data-search. We can "forget" something, then, *either* by removing it from data-storage, *or* by setting up a bloc in the data-search mechanism such that, that area of storage will not be scanned.

Hypnotic and other experiments indicate with exceedingly high probability that no data can be, or ever is, removed from the data-storage system used by the mind; only data-search is ever impeded. Such experiments as having a 60-year old recall, under hypnosis, the individuals present at his 5th birthday party, naming and describing them in detail, for instance.

Suppose that something on the order of clairvoyance does exist — accept it just for the moment. (There's some damned good evidence for it's occasional occurence. If it had occured just once in the total history of Mankind, it would prove that there did in fact exist physical laws by which it could be achieved — even if we didn't know how to do it reliably.) Now imagine a clairvoyant sort of mechanism that could *scan the actual, physical past.*

Where would you find an absolute, total, perfect, and complete data-storage? Why, the past Universe itself would be the ultimate, wouldn't it?

Why carry the New York Public Library around with you — if you have a telefax receiver and a selector system that will, at will, switch any desired volume of the entire library onto your receiver plate?

And why carry anything more than a very short-term memory system with you, when there is an infinite, and infinitely accurate, data-storage bank in the Universe itself?

Item: The tautology that "Anything which has ever happened is something that could happen," is very important. The "simplest" way to do something *is not* necessarily the way that we now know how to do it. What's the simplest way to get insulin into a man's bloodstream? Sure; by synthesizing it in the Islets of Langerhans. The simplest way is *not* extracting it from the pancreases of cattle, purifying it, packaging it, selling it, and injecting it.

Item: Some physiologists, studying control of conditioned reflexes, demonstrated that certain training methods allowed them to gain voluntary control over the secretion of insulin from the pancreas. They didn't argue it was theoretically possible; they *did* it.

But these physiologists didn't know *how* to synthesize insulin.

You gentlemen there at the computer lab are going at this problem the wrong way; you don't want to store the data in the computer, you want to develop a past-time Universe scan that can gather the data from the Universal storage bin. It has infinite storage capacity. It is infallible, since no past fact can be changed by anything you do, and its volume-in-present-time is zero.

Item for consideration: Life, which has been fiddling around with this here problem of computing accurate answers for some 2000 megayears, has found that selective, self-healing barrier-films and barrier walls are very useful arrangements.

I have a suspicion that if your gang up there could attack the problem of information handling on the basis of its relation to barriers, you'd get some new approches to handling problems.

Your relays, you know, can be considered barriers of controllable permeability; the relay-coil controls the permeability of the barrier formed by the contacts. The grid of one of your 12AU7's or 6SN7's controls the permeability of the vacuum tube "film." You're already using controlled permeability in fact; maybe better methods could be found if it were studied on that basis. After all, chemical films are so much cheaper, smaller, and take so much less power to operate. Just ask yourself — you've been using the system for several thousand megayears.

I've got another idea of Aristotelean vs non-Aristotelean logic I'm going to editorialize one of these days. As follows:

The non-A logics seek to work on a probability or percentage-of-truth basis. Consider a chain of events, A, B, C, D, etc., each of which has a probability of sequential relationship of 0.9. That is, it's 90% certain that B will follow A, that C will follow B, etc. How many logical steps can you make in such a system before the probability of continuity drops below 10%?

At some point, your logic approaches zero probability so closely you don't have any logic left.

In an Aristotelean system where each step is arbitrarily assigned a 100% probability, you can build up an infinite chain, because 1.000 is still 1.000.

Your computers, however, are subject to a split-personality situtation. They are handling Aristotelean logic, with an arbitrary probability of 1.000 at each step. But they exist in a non-Aristotelean Universe. The logic they work on says, "*If* this contact closes, *then* (probability 1.000) that relay-coil is activated, and *then* (prob. 1.000) that contact closes." But the Universe says "If this contact closes, *then* (probability less than one due to presence of dust, corrosion, failure of insulation, blown fuse, etc. ad infinitum) that relay-coil is activated and *then* (prob. less than one for similar reasons) that contact closes."

The computer's logic is trying to live in a world of fantasy, while it is forced to operate in a work-a-day world.

I'd love to see a working out of the laws of actual probability. In essence, **Warren's** approach says that you could do the whole job of any computation with two relays, and a suitably involved program tape, given enough time. (That's what Aristotle said; "You only need "is" and "is not" used in enough different circuit arrangements to solve any problem.) With only two simple relays, the probability of relay-failure *appears* to be reduced. But now the number of operations in succession which each relay must perform is increased enormously, so the ultimate failure-probability is increased. At what point does number-of-relays vs number of operations reach a minimum probability of failure?

Ah, me . . . wish we could kick these ideas around for an aeon or two!

Regards,   John

P.S. There's a Fourth Law of Stupidynamics, incidentally. "In the absence of feedback in a system of two or more entities, the probability of confusion increases without limit." This is really a derivation from the Third Law, but makes clear that the Instructor *must* guide himself by the feedback he gets from the Instructed.

Dean McLaughlin *June 4, 1953*

Dear Mr. McLaughlin:

I've been trying to figure out what it is science-fiction is trying to do that's different from ordinary fiction. There are a lot of things, of course — but one of the most important is that science fiction tries to present the incidents in the life of, and the consequent development of the character of, a whole culture — instead of an individual person, as is the case in the standard novel.

It's a job that needs doing. Trouble is to date we haven't worked out any very good techniques; science fiction novels are still at about the stage of the ordinary novel in 1830 or so. The problem's a tough one, and we still know too little of the actual laws of social dynamics to be able to make sense out of the problem.

So — we experiment.

Asimov used a trick; he postulated Hari Seldon who *did* understand social dynamics, but was off stage. Then he used a very slow build-up, making each story a story-in-itself, and also a stone in the structure he was building.

You're trying here to make a direct attack on the problem; I'm always willing to read a completed novel, because long experience has shown me that I don't have to read it all the way through if it isn't going well. (Make it your business to read critically for fifteen years, and what looks to others like a careless half-glance turns out to be somewhat more complete an analysis than you'd suspect.) If you wish, I'll take a look at the novel; I need a novel right now. But I have reason to believe that you'll save postage if you send it elsewhere.

You see, you're up against something that isn't consciously recognized ordinarily. It's taken a good bit of research and study on my part, in the interesting subject of "What makes people like or dislike stories?" to find the little item.

Essentially, it's this: there *is* genetic memory, and genetic understanding. It's not conscious, and it's not detailed; it understands basic principles, however, better than our society does.

It's quite easy to demonstrate once you know what to look for. Consider the fact that no chemist can synthesize complex proteins although every baby does. That biochemists and doctors only recently worked out what was required to nourish a newborn baby-but any savage woman has the answer to that problem as soon as her first baby is born.

We can recognize the complex, precise and highly trained effect of instincts there, at the purely physical level. But we are, to date, utter savages ourselves, when it comes to the mental and emotional levels of understanding. We know so little about those levels that we can't appreciate the wisdom that instinct imparts. We don't know how to learn — i.e., no psychologist has ever figured out what learning or creative thinking actually is. But every baby does it, instructed by instincts of that higher level.

When you write a story, if you let your technical training intrude too much, you'll wind up making a statement that two billion years of genetic experience says, "That's not true; the premise is contrary to fact." The result is that your reader, for no reason he can lay a conscious finger on, feels there's something wrong with your story.

In this one, you've violated a prime tenet of evolution; no human society would permit their children to have less than they had themselves. Any human society that does so is unsane, and will be self-destructive in short order. Two billion years of evolution has proven that. The mammals invented caring for the young at whatever cost to the parent — and won the world by doing so.

Your Ageless, who don't give their children the benefit of their advance, are retreating to the saurian level of responsibility; they lay their eggs on a planetary beach, warmed by the rays of a handy sun, and go their merry way uncaring.

Among mammals, the adult form remains responsible for the care of the young until the young have achieved all the basic abilities the adult form has.

You've been bucking that internal genetic wisdom in every chapter you wrote. The story plot got itself twisted, confused, and full of rationalizations and cross-currents as a result.

The Ageless have no right to leave their children without the formula for life. That's what the saurians found — by having the mammals, who accepted that obligation, wipe out their whole branch of evolution.

That novel of yours won't write well, because, you're bucking an ancient wisdom.

Incidentally, senility is a psychosomatic disease, and can't be cured by a physical attack only. A man lives as long as, and only as long as, life has fun and purpose; when it ceases to have those, he dies. Ask any doctor; you can't make a patient live if he doesn't

176

want to — and it's damned near impossible to kill a patient who is too busy and enthusiastic to spare the time for dying.

Watch the people who retire at 65, and have no further purpose, die off in the next five years. Pneumonia — cerebral haemorhage — general debility — low resistance to disease — anything.

But somebody like Shaw, who was enthusiastically watching the world at 90, or Chief Justice Holmes, who has much too much to do to take time to die, goes on cheerfully busy at 90.

It ain't just physical! And deep underneath, you have that genetic realization, too. Only wise, understanding, fun-loving, active and enthusiastic people can live forever. The grouches die young.

Sincerely,   John W. Campbell, Jr.

Clifford D. Simak *June 18, 1953*

Dear Cliff:

My, but you stuck your neck out on that letter!

My friend, for some 2½ years, my really quite remarkable wife, **Peg,** and I have been engaged in basic philosophical-psychological research, working at it — and I mean *working* almost 100 hours a week. That's some 12,000 hours of study.

I've gotten immense help from the deep self-searching that science-fiction authors have done. (**E.E. Smith's** "Children of the Lens" is one of the most solid efforts to study how a parent can train a child to be superior to himself that's ever been done, I think.)

I've had high-power help from my friends like **Wayne Batteau** at MIT, **E.E.Francisco** who's head of research at White Sands — in other words, the high-power speculative minds of high sanity rating, who have contacted me through my science-fiction work.

Currently, **Dr. Gotthard Gunther,** a philosopher specializing in the study of symbolic logic and non-Aristotelean logics, is helping us quite directly.

Claude Shannon's information theory, and **Weiner's** cybernetics have both helped. I've worked with both of these men; they're both science-fictioneers.

The men I've mentioned are known and respected generally; they aren't as speculative, actually, as some of the other men who are not yet widely recognized for their work. **Hal Clement**, for instance, and **Ray Jones, Cliff Simak** and **Eric F. Russell**. You and your compeers are communicators — you want to think out an idea, and communicate it. There is no more effective communication channel than fiction; fact discussions are not as powerful.

Jesus knew that; he used parables.

Uncle Tom's Cabin overrode all the polemics, lectures and orations the southerners could produce.

Go ahead and control the newspaper; you can be defeated with ease by the magazine printing pure fiction. Newspapers give only data; fiction establishes philosophy, and a man acts on data-interpreted-by-philosophy, not on facts alone!

The impossibility of portraying the superman was behind the moves I made back in 1939 to get some superman stories of a new type written. There are two possible approaches to avoid the problem:

1. The approach typified by the play "The Women" which was all about men, yet had not one man on stage. I pointed out this proposition to **Norvell Page**; he wrote "But Without Horns" for me. In that one, if you recall, the superman was never on stage — only people who had met him and been changed, or men who were fighting him.

2. The super-*man* can't be fully portrayed. But since ontogeny recapitulates phylogeny, a super-human must, during boyhood and adolescence, pass through the human level; there will be a stage of his development when he is less than adult-human, another stage when he is equal to adult-human — and the final stage when he has passed beyond our comprehension.

The situtation can be handled, then, by established faith, trust, understanding, and sympathy with the *individual as a character* by portraying him in his not-greater-than adult human stages — and allow the established trust-and belief to carry over to the later and super-human stage.

A.E. van Vogt worked out "Slan" in response to that comment-discussion from me. The central character is introduced as Jommy, the nearly helpless, hard-pressed small boy; seen further as Jommy Cross, the adolescent (adult-human equivalent) and finally followed as Cross, the super-human.

Each of the two methods is basically a single method, developed in two different ways — the method of projection.

If you can't reach the full way, you can project a line that will reach. Line up the reader by letting him follow that which he can follow — in **Page's** story, the reactions of human characters whom he can understand; in **van Vogt's,** the actions of not-greater-than-human immature superman. Then projection does the rest.

There *are* basic laws of intelligence — and therefore basic laws of ethics which are NOT human, but are Universal. The term *mores* applies to the local interpretation of the Universal laws of ethics. Local in both time and space.

The Russians have a word "pravda" which is usually translated "truth." That's not what it means; it means "the offical consensus"; the Russian's language has no terms meaning what we mean by *truth* — something beyond and apart from human belief of opinion, existant as a Universal reality, not part of human thinking.

Thus, in Russia, where only the philosophical concept pravda is available to an individual, Lysenko's work on genetics is unarguably *pravda*. Absolutely so; the fact that the Russian government has published it establishes beyond argument that it is *pravda*.

When Moscow publishes a new directive to the party, naturally that is *pravda* beyond cavail.

The lack of the concept *truth* produces an effect that seems weird and utterly irrational to a people oriented on the far more stable concept of a Universal truth beyond human influence.

But we, on the other hand, need the term *pravda* in English; I propose to use it. Pravda means "the general consensus of what appears to be the nature of Truth." Pravda is perfectly real; pravda is to an individual item of truth as mores is to ethics. At any given point in space-time, pravda can be known, and mores can be known — but truth and ethics are sought.

The differentiation can be expressed mathematically: consider the infinite oscillating convergent series $1/\frac{1}{2}$ minus $\frac{1}{4}$ plus $\frac{1}{8}$ . . . and so on. Summing any finite number of terms of this series will yield an answer either a little too large, or a little too small and never exactly equal to the final result of the infinite series. But the limit of the sum of an infinite number of terms is real, has a determinate value, and can be stated. The sum can be determined exactly by a process other than simple summation; the summation of any finite number of terms will always be slightly off.

Let's say that the result of summing any finite number of terms is *pravda*; pravda, then, approaches *truth*, the actual determinate limit of the series, asymptotically.

Now characteristically, the value of such an infinite convergent series can *never* be determined at the level of arithmetic; only by using some higher-level mathematical process can the determinate value be found.

Thus the series suggested can be resolved and determined by algebraic methods, but not by arithmetical methods.

I have a daughter in school; another in high school, and a son in Williams College.

I have trouble helping my 12-year-old with her arithmetic; I've forgotten the arithmetical techniques for doing certain classes of problems, because the algebraic method is immensely easier.

I have trouble helping the 17-year-old, because many of her algebra problems involve techniques I've forgotten; integral calculus is so much simpler.

I have trouble with the boy; he is using thinking techniques in solving his problems that I have forgotten — there are superior, simpler, and more direct methods.

Many years ago I wrote a story "Forgetfulness"; only recently have I found, at a consciously communicable level, the direct philosophical statement of that story:

The growth of an individual, a culture, or a race to a higher level will entail the development of thinking and doing techniques that cause them to neglect lower-level techniques.

Dr. Gotthard Gunther, who is now receiving kudus in the philosophical fraternity for his recent development of a new understanding of non-Aristotelean logics, has an article coming up in *ASF*. We renamed his new concept "logical parallax"; in working with it, I developed an additional proposition, "positional logic"; we are now working on a still further development which we're calling "formulated analogic."

Formulated analogic is simply a determinately expressable system of abstracting generalizations from data. We haven't got it yet; we've simply stated "this is the nature of the problem."

The essential point in logical parallax is that the two values "true" and "false" of Aristotelean logic become the multi-valued ideas of non-A logic with one simple transformation; the recognition that *the position of the observer introduces a parallax phenomenon.* Thus the "False" of Observer 1 may become the "True" of Observer 2; the consequence is that there may be now 3 values, and we have, necessarily, a three-valued logic! Yet each separate logic system is, necessarily, a two-valued system.

My addition to that was to point out that this is precisely what the binary system of a modern computer does; everything in the universe can be expressed to any desired degree of accuracy with three symbols: a "true" symbol, a "false" symbol, and a "position" symbol. The Romans tried a number system having a near-infinite valued system — each number was represented by a different symbol, as M for 1000, C for 100, L for 50, X for 10, and V for 5. The Arabic system uses 11 symbols, actually; 1, 2, 3, 4, 5, 6, 7, 8, 9, 0, and position.

The result can be obtained with three symbols; 1, 0, and position. Thus 10110 is 21.

Gunther then added what he calls "T′ ranges." T prime is a true-value beyond your ability to conceive that ordered truth exists.

There are truths in the universe that you do not know; some of them are of such a nature that they cannot be included in your present truth-range system.

Example: A Hottentot native has never met a tiger. Tigers don't occur in Africa; Hottentot's don't occur in Asia.

But if a Hottentot encountered a tiger, he would readily handle the situation, because it lies within his "T-range," his "Truth-range."

But the Hottentot native, if he encountered two pieces of purified U-235, would be forced to call it "magic."

The basic nature of the "magic" concept is "phenomena which are, which exist or happen, but which are not part of the ordered system of understanding within the range of truth-as-I-know-it."

To a small child, the effects you, as a adult, obtain are essentially magic — but with the difference that the child expects to grow to understand and employ those effects himself.

A God exists when an entity employs means which are beyond your truth-range, and which you believe will be forever beyond your truth-range.

The genius has a truth range, we'll say, of 2, where the normal individual has a truth-range from 0 to 1. Where the genius employs motivations and relationships in the range of 0 to 1 in his operations, the individual will understand; when he employs means or motivations in the 1 to 2 range, his behavior is "queer" or "nutty." Consequently the observation is that geniuses are practically insane.

Your superman is an individual who operates in the range of 0 to 5, say.

The expression of the idea here has, so far, been on a linear basis — implying that the truth lay in a linear system. It doesn't; expand that to a spherical concept, and consider the truth-ranges as being concentric spheres.

But most human societies have tended to develop linearly, emphasizing one direction of development of the sphere. It is possible to have two different civilizations having the same net volume of cultural development which have only small areas of common understanding, and most actual individuals are definitely in that position. Thus a nuclear physicist and a celestial ballistics expert have developed along opposite radii of the sphere of understanding. **Jim Brown's** story "The Emissary," about the man from the society that has social engineering, but not mechanical engineering, was another example.

Within the sphere of Understanding Radius 1, let's call it, there are many areas humanity has not explored. The social engineering sector, for example, is badly underdeveloped.

You could not describe and communicate to your audience an understanding of an alien civilization, because the terms necessary have not been developed. Try translating "electron" into Hottentot in telling a science-fiction story for Hottentots. Even if you, as an author, could think of the alien culture, you couldn't communicate it effectively. You'll have to describe actions — and that means describe them in high precision detail — which will allow your audience to project the existence of the concept you label.

Peg and I in our research have been forced to develop new terms; one of these is *kynmod*. I can define it only by action and analogy — but to use it in a story I must do so.

Science-fiction is seeking to do precisely what I'm discussing here; that's why the superman theme (seeking to call attention to T-ranges beyond that now recognized) and alien culture stories so deeply interest and concern you.

I believe I have cogent reasons for maintaining that ethics is universal, and only mores variable. Consider these factors:

Wayne Batteau, of the Harvard Computerlab sent in what he called "The Three Laws of Stupidynamics."

1. The probability of correct prediction in total ignorance is zero.
2. The only thing you can learn is something you don't know.
3. You cannot usefully apply knowledge you do not understand.

Each of those, I think, is a statement that must be Universal. Makes no difference whether it's a methane-breathing Mesklinite or what.

Also, **Batteau** and his friends kicked some things around and came up with these:

1. You can't win. (Law of conservation of energy.)
2. You can't even break even. (Second law of Thermodynamics.)

Here is one of the first instances I know of the direct and conscious statement of the fact that the most fundamental laws of the physical systems can be *directly* applied in human systems. "You can't get something for nothing," is usually considered a moral adage. It isn't; it's a rephrasing of the law of conservation of energy.

The trouble is that people falsely expect the converse to be true — that you will always get the desired something if you work for it. That's the wrong converse; the true converse is "You'll invariably get some result from your efforts." The result may be heat; it may be a lot of loud noise. It may not be what you wanted — but you'll get something. The question is, what is the efficiency of your effort application? Are you getting 99.99% friction — or 90% desired product output?

There's the old argument: "I am honest. I have worked hard and faithfully all my life. I am poor. He is rich. He cannot have worked harder or longer than I; therefore he must be dishonest."

The concept of efficiency of application is lacking.

A Marine returning from Pelilieu during the war told me of a Jap Air Force Major they'd captured. Three days after the island was taken over, the Jap saw planes coming over from the direction of an adjacent island. "Where are those planes from?" he asked.

"Our base on the adjacent island."

"But that's impossible! There was no base there, and we'd been working at one for eight months!"

"There's a base there now. Started using it this morning."

"But how?"

They'd worked at it eight months; the Americans did it in two days — with 20 ton bulldozers, gigantic earth-movers, and power shovels. The japs had been limited by using human labor; not more than 2000 men could work efficiently on the small island.

Suppose the Jap major hadn't ever encountered a set of heavy duty earth-moving machinery. Then he would have been faced with an occurrence beyond his T-range — pure magic.

All alien civilization plots have that difficulty — and the added difficulty that you can't get away with sheer arbitrary differentness.

You can't say "they do it the opposite way" when there is, in every human being, a deep, subliminal knowledge that it won't work the opposite way.

We have 2,000,000,000 years of experience to go on; the instincts are the results of just plain trying it and seeing what didn't work.

You'll have to get a whole new orientation on what instincts are, however, to see this point! Instincts ARE NOT what people told you they were; they are what they actually are. Pravda on instincts does not equal truth about instincts; in this case the difference is immense.

Freudians hold that all men have a repressed desire to lay every good-looking female they see.

Ever found that desire in yourself?

Maybe Freud was wrong, huh?

It's true that the male dog has a powerful urge to take on any bitch in heat that he scents. So this proves that the male human has a comparable tendency?

But observably there are many mammalian species that are monogamous by instinct. What proof have we that Man is polygamous instinctively, or completely non-monagomous, to create a term? I suggest the true instinct runs this way:

Man is basically monogamous. However, unlike most mammals, division of labor has progressed so far in man that the male undertakes most of the labor of meeting the external environment, with the result that there tends to be a marked unbalance of the male-female ratio. Men get killed protecting the females. In most species of mammals, males and females are about equally engaged in contact with the external environment.

The result of this resultant imbalance of numbers is that, when the tribe was forced to do so, polygamy was accepted as an alternative necessity. For the greatest good of human beings polygamy became necessary.

The basic need, however, is for monogamy — as in many other mammalian species.

But — our educational system (not official, but actual) teaches a kid of 15-19 that he isn't a real he-man unless he keeps trying to lay every girl he can seduce.

Did you actually want to? And, on the other hand, did you feel yourself forced to feel that you should want to to be a real man?

This sort of thing has vastly complicated the problem of unscrambling what Man's true instincts are; pravda on the subject is so hugely out of step with truth!

Incidentally, any population statistician will tell you that mores be damned, the birth rate of a nation is determined by the number of females in the child-bearing age-range, not by the number of males.

There are, I think, deep basic laws that apply to any race, anywhere. You cannot solve your problem without solving someone else's; action and reaction must be equal and opposite. I'll bet that Man domesticated the cow because the ancient aurochs raided his grain fields; the way to control the raiders was to feed them — for the table.

The horse probably got domesticated on a similar basis; the dog certainly did. Man solved the wolf's problem of getting food; the tamed wolf solved Man's problem of an inadequate nose, and the tendency of Man to get so concentrated on one problem as to ignore other dangers.

This is ethics? This is action-equals-reaction. This is "good sense." It's not human; it's universal.

Dammit, **Cliff**, I can go on for hours like this! We've spent years of damned hard work plowing through this, and had a lot of very high-powered help. I haven't even touched on the business of the nature of emotion, and the proof that unemotional thinking is as impossible as an immaterial solid. Or the business of a demonstration, based on information theory, that an increase in knowledge leads to a *decrease* in wisdom *unless* there is an

184

improved system of data-cataloging.

Item: The basic instinct in any animal organism is the instinct to predict. Reason: it does you no good to know what the situation was; you can't alter that. It isn't enough to know what the situation is; it's too late to change that. You can effect the universe only by knowing what the future *will be*.

Instance: a cat going after a mouse has to predict where the mouse will be.

Psychologists have denied teleology; unfortunately, every animal organism operates on a feedback loop going through the future — as best it can. The fact that precognition doesn't exist in fact has nothing to do with the case; the organism has to *act as though* it had precognition — or not be able to act at all!

Score another for science-fiction! This particular field of literature lies exactly along the deepest instinctive lines of human progress, philosophy, and communication!

It is my personal intention to live as long as I consider it fun to do so — and I expect that to be not less than 400 years. I am taking direct active steps toward that. It can be done, however, only by learning the nature of myself, my organism, and my universe.

I'm convinced that old age can be described accurately as "a psychosomatic disease consisting of the accumulation and routine repetition of metabolic errors."

I grew this body I have; if I could build it — dammit, I can rebuild it! I know I do in fact rebuild it; every cell replaces itself in the course of a few weeks or months. But why replace a defective cell with a cell *having precisely the same defect*? Remember the story of the man in a back-country Chinese town who took an old suit to the local tailor, and asked him to duplicate it? The tailor did — including three patches that appeared on the original, and a careful fraying of trouser cuffs and pocket edges.

Old age results from precisely such a process; the cells are replaced by faithful copies of the originals, including the patches, fraying, and general errors.

You can't overcome that with drugs; you have to correct that by learning, and establishing understanding communication.

I have seen the bony deposits of arthritis melt away under psychosomatic therapy; I know for a fact that such work can be done.

I've seen X-ray plates.

I've also talked to a doctor who saw the X-ray plates of a man who had a gastroenterotomy operation for stomach ulcers, and later went to Lourdes' shrine. The X-ray plates showing the operation existed. Plates taken afterwards showed that the alteration of his stomach and intestines made by the operation *had*

185

been done away with. His body had refused to perpetuate the patch, and had corrected itself to the original youthful system.

I know damned well immortality is possible — personal, direct, right-here-and-now immortality. It can even be specified in physical science terms — but only in terms of information theory! Immortality is a product of understanding and selectivity; not of drugs.

Information theory is enormously more powerful than any present scientist recognizes, because each has seen only the piece that applies in his field.

Actually, I now feel that the Universe can be described as an information machine — and the mind as an information handling mechanism.

Naturally, then, the mind can handle the universe!

Regards,   John

Donald A. Wollheim   *June 22, 1953*

Dear Wollheim:

You have proposed a little task of some difficulty. The pages of *Astounding Science Fiction* have been combed by one anthologizer after another over the last ten years. You are now asking that I pick from these pages a story that is A, outstanding and B, has not been anthologized. Inasmuch as I have relatively recently published my own selection from *Astounding* what you are asking is that I disagree with myself in making the selection. If you relaxed the restriction of "not previously anthologized" maybe "yes" but with that how can I?

Sincerely,   John

Ray Jones   *July 4, 1953*

Dear Ray:

The *Book of Mormon* and *Discourses of Brigham Young* arrived yesterday. Naturally, I haven't had time to study them thoroughly; I have, however, skimmed them, and read bits and pieces. Mostly in the *Discourses*, trying to get definitions of what Young, the greatest of the explainers of Mormonism, considered it to be.

Naturally, I have a first-approximation opinion, a first impression. I thought you might be interested, and I believe you can recognize that this is a *first* impression: it's neither permanent, nor believed-by-me to be the Final Evalution.

Necessarily it's the resultant of my own philosophy (which, by

186

the nature of things, I must, inescapably, consider the more important to me. How else could a human being work?) and my impression of what Young was driving at.

First, I see that Mormonism has overcome the greatest bloc to the success of religions in human affairs. The religions that have preceeded it — Christianity, Judaism, Mohammedanism, etc. at least — have each held the proposition that they were the Finished and Perfected Totality of Ethical Understanding. That the Bible, for instance, was a source book of information about the nature of things — a Cosmology, in fact — which contained everything necessary and sufficient. That nothing useful or important could be added to it, and that everything it held was both useful and important, and, of course, true.

Mormonism, as Brigham Young seems to see it, holds that what truths they had were necessary, *but not sufficient.* The root concepts of "the Latter Day Saints" held, in non-religious terms, that there were geniuses (Saints in all times, including the present and the future) — that the cosmology was *not* complete, and that it was the duty of Man not only to know the truths that had been found, but to get busy, dig in, and find some more.

Brought up in that creed, **Ray**, you may well have totally missed the basic nature of Christianity — the religion-as-taught. It definitely holds that *all important truths have been discovered.* The whole Western Society is oriented on that. Western Society holds that you, for example, can't possibly contribute anything important to human knowledge, and that if you say you have, you are a ridiculous, impudent, fool. If I say I have made a new philosophical discovery, I will be ridiculed, laughed out of hearing; anything *important* would, of course, have been discovered by Socrates or Aristotle, or Jesus, or St. Augustine, or one of the early and therefore much wiser, philosophers.

Mormonism is the only religious creedo I have seen that holds that *it hasn't all been done.*

This is a sharp, and exceedingly important break with former religions — certainly with former Western Culture religious belief.

But Mormonism still retains, I feel, one false value. That's the one I'm trying to break through in our work: Mormonism, like Christianity and all the others, still holds that *the work done in the past was perfect, though not total.* That, in other words, while the work of the past Prophets was not complete and total, leaving more work to do, the work done was flawless.

The trouble with this postulate is that it allows the addition of new truths *provided they do not conflict with past beliefs.*

But if a Latter Day Saint of today should discover a truth that contradicts an older truth — note that the automatic reaction of the mind is to the effect "it can't be truth if it contradicts past truth." Quite so. The trouble is that the past truth is not always and invariably *true*.

No religion I know of has ever acknowledged a creed that includes the proposition that its creed is *neither* complete nor perfect!

Only science holds that concept to be true and workable.

In science, we have learned about cybernetics, and Information Theory, and nuclear physics, and we've learned about cellular structures of organism, and about instincts and genetics.

Jesus knew none of these things. Moses didn't know them. Joseph Smith didn't know them. Brigham Young didn't know them.

Is it possible that the answer they conceived concerning life and living and the nature of Man, God and the Universe could be complete and perfect, or even perfect, without those concepts? Is it conceivable that I, today, can have a correct understanding of anything in the Universe without the knowledge of things that will be discovered 1000 years hence?

But how many human beings have the moral courage to acknowledge to themselves — deeply and fully accept — that they are, and must be, operating with an imperfect understanding, and will, through all their lifetimes, be operating without knowledge of the true meaning of things?

A religion that gives the balm of "This is the Eternal Truth concerning these things," is a pleasing, comforting thing indeed. How many minds have the humility-courage combination to accept and live with a true, deep realization that they must learn to handle the situation of not knowing how to handle the situation? Such a concept means that no man, under any circumstance, at any time, can feel certain of himself and his beliefs.

Sure — we all seek security.

The fact seems to me to be that security does not lie in convincing ones' self that the absolute truth is known — but conviction that the Unknown can be handled with a probability of success when it arrives. Security lies not in Knowing How It Is, but in knowing how to learn.

You know, we live on a hell-planet. It's known that life forms of our own general type — carbon-based biochemistry, that is — can work very well indeed in hot springs at a temperature of 180 degrees F. Let's imagine a planet like Earth that's at such a distance from such star that it has an equatorial temperature of 150 degrees F, and a polar temperature of 50 degrees F.

We'll add that it's land-water distribution is such that all the seas are inland seas, land-locked, instead of having continents that are water-locked, as Earth is. All land masses, in other words, are always, through all the geology of the planets, contiguous.

Now on such a planet, there can never be an ice age; Earth has ice ages because it's temperature is such that it's right on the critical edge of the water-ice phase change.

We'll add that this planet, Parad, has a vertical axis, and hence practically no seasons; the orbit is, like Earth's, almost circular.

Now Man's lineage, down through the ages, has been chivvied and chased and pushed and prodded by ice ages and water ages. We'll never get to study the sites where Man's early civilizations really started; that happened during the last glacial age, and when the phase-change has turned ten million cubic miles of water into ice, the Great Tide is out — the continental shelves are exposed 600 feet deeper than they are now, and the coast line moves 50 to 500 miles out. Man's civilizations started near river mouths that are now 400 feet and 200 miles or so out at sea. They'll never be seen, never be investigated.

During the ice ages, all life is pushed remorselessly out of it's habitat, and forced equatorward; it is ruthlessly forced to grind itself against the resisting life-forms of the equatorial regions, while those life forms are remorselessly squeezed between the advancing life-forms from the north and south. Plus the fact that the equatorial climate is changing too; the purely equatorial forms find their environment damned well doesn't exist anywhere anymore.

During the ice age, however, the great continental shelves open out, and allow life forms to expand into ex sea-bottoms.

Then the warmth comes again; now the life forms are chased before remorselessly rising waters. This time, instead of being squeezed from north and south by vast ice walls, they're squeezed from east and west by rising waters.

Go on, brother . . . let's see you get adapted to your environment! Hah! It ain't gonna stay that way, so you might as well give up on any idea of there being an "eternal truth of the World As It Is." The only adaptation that can do you a bit of good is adapting to adaptability — adapting to meet not *a* condition, but *any* condition.

And that's not all, by any means.

Because the continents are normally water-locked "lakes" of land, land animals adapt to each other in a closed arena; a complete ecology can develop in inter-related forms in a continental area. In South America, for instance, there was a complete ecology of a few placental mammal herbivours, and a lot of marsupial herbivores and carnivours. Everything was nice and copacetic.

Then came a phase change; the ice built up, and the water level dropped. The placental mammals found a land route open from North America.

What happened to the marsupial ecology of SA was a shame. The marsupial carnivours thought they were tough, ferocious, and competent killers. Hah! They were slow, soft, stupid, and inadequate before the placental mammals that rolled down from the north.

Consider what happened to the African Negro about 1700 to 1850; he thought he was a tough, ferocious, dangerous, smart fighting being. White men decided they needed slaves. The results were pitiful; the Negro warrior discovered that he was not in fact anywhere near the equal of the incredible ferocious and competent white man.

Note, by the way, that the Amerindian was. The whites never enslaved Indians, because they couldn't be enslaved. They were too powerfully elastic; when conquered, they simply bounced and attacked again. When enslaved, they reorganized and revolted.

I'm no racist; I do recognize a fact of nature. The Negro didn't have the power of spirit the white and the Amerindian had.

Chivvied and chased, exposed time after time to the sudden incursion of life forms evolved in separated land-areas, our lineage remains to this day solely because it was the most elastic, adaptable, changeable lineage around. It didn't specialize in anything — anything, that is except adapting to change.

What sort of beings would evolve on a paradise planet? And what would happen to them when exposed to the beings from a hell planet like Earth, one that rocked and wobbled on it's axis, heaved and quivered as land masses rose and sank, that existed always in a precarious, uneasy balance right at the phase-change point of its major liquid. One that, furthermore, was endowed with a liquid-gas atmosphere-hydrosphere system constituting the most corrosively virulent chemical system possible in the entire universe!

(It is; fluorine is somewhat more active than oxygen — but H_2F_2, the corresponding liquid phase, is innocuous stuff by comparison to water. The water-oxygen system is far and away the most vilely corrosive system possible! Just because we're so neatly adapted to it dosen't mean it isn't virulent!)

The only way a life-form can continue to exist in such an environment as Earth is by learning how to learn; learning how to do is inadequate — because the conditions change.

There's a kind of Fairy Chess that's about like Earth's enviroment. Player A makes up a new set of rules; he doesn't tell B what these rules are. Then they start playing. B has to figure out, from what A does, and what A tells him he can't do, when B tries to make a move and is denied it, what A's rules are.

A can, of course, have a rule of change of rules; when both of a player's rooks are taken, for example, that might mean that the rules shifted for him, and thereafter bishops had a rook's move, instead of the normal bishop's move. B must deduce that such a change of rules exists.

That's what Man's lineage has had to learn. Not only do animals change, but there are changes within an animal species. Man himself is, of course, the worst type; different human beings look very much the same — but the difference between trying to compete with a drug-store soda-jerk and a young genius, who looks just like him, could be extremely lethal under some circumstances. Particuarly since camouflage is an old family (animal family, that is) tradition.

Actually, the desire for security is desire for the Womb of the Race — the saurian stage, when an animal was born with a set of rules, called Instincts, and could be relied on to play by those rules.

It ain't been like that for 300,000,000 years. Ask the brontosaurus, the titanothere, and the aurochs.

Man *is* the werewolf — the Changeable One.

> "'E's a daisy, 'e's a duck, 'e's a lamb, 'e's a Inja
> rubber idjit on a spree!
> E's the only thing that docsn't give a damn, for a
> Regiment of British Infantreeee!"

said Kipling of the Fuzzy Wuzzy.

> "E squatted in the scrub and 'ocked our 'orses.
> E's all 'ot sand an' ginger when alive,
> and 'e's generally shammin' when 'c's dead!"

The werewolf — the animal that can change and be anything. But be it noted that Fuzzy Wuzzy, in tribute to whose ferocity and adaptability Kipling wrote that poem, was conquered by the British.

What's the most dangerous animal on Earth?

Go to a zoo and see what animal puts all other animals in cages.

The ruler of the planet is *not Homo sapiens* — not Wise Man.

It's *Learning* Man. The Man who admits that he doesn't have all the answers, and sets busily to work learning some more — and discarding the ones that aren't good enough as he goes.

The trouble with the old religions was that they were suited to Wise Man; they insisted they supplied The Eternal and Complete Answer.

Mormonism is a vast advance; it's made a greater people, because it holds that there are more answers to come.

Young also shows the wisdom to recognize that a theoretical religion is no religion at all — that the body and the spirit aren't two separate things, but a team, and that without teamship, neither is worth much. He flatly rejects the idea that it is possible to render unto Caeser the things that are Caeser's and unto God the things that are God's.

191

I like very much his insistence that holding religion as a thing apart from shop-keeping, or being a mechanic, is nonsense.

There's a basic in information theory: a message that does not correlate with anything is nonsense.

A religion that doesn't correlate with living is nonsense. Brigham Young knew that answer, without knowing the information theory basic that would allow him to expand the correlation and use it most widely and helpfully.

I'm continuing to read the *Discourses*; the one error of concept, as I see it, is the proposition of there being *The* Church, now, then, or ever. *The* Church is, in essence, the concept that there is, or can be, *the* right viewpoint on the nature of the Universe.

You know, if you accept the concept of the expanding universe — you must, at the time, accept the concept that *there can be no eternal truth except change.*

Any relationship, in an expanding universe, must necessarily be undergoing continuous alternation. The only statements that could, then, have enduring meaning would be statements of rate of change — no statement of *status,* of *being* could have enduring value. Only statements of *becoming,* of type-of-alteration, could have enduring value.

The Popeye statement, "I yam what I yam" is the essence of death and decay. An organism lives only so long as it is growing, plus the brief span after growth has stopped while the Universe, in its change, overtakes the growth-produced margin of the organism. It must grow either physically or spiritually — actually both — or be overwhelmed.

The human entity, I think, can be likened to an eddy, a whirlpool. A whirlpool shows the characteristic of being an entity, an organization, in which no single molecule remains for any length of time. The material of which it is formed is constantly running through it — if it continues to exist. A whirlpool funneling down a drain, for example, endures only briefly if the drain is shut off.

The hands with which I type this are formed of cells, which are made of atoms; I know that the atoms of which they are formed are constantly undergoing exchange and replacement; even the cells which the atoms and molecules make are constantly being changed for new ones. Yet despite that constant change, like the whirlpool, the hand-as-an-entity continues to exist.

The lesson I find in that fact is that a stable system needs not only to aquire new truths — it must also keep the brain open, and let the old ones flush out. The rectum is just as important to survival as the mouth. The lungs must breathe out as much as they breathe in. The kidneys are vital to life as the stomach and digestive system.

I think the secret of eternal life — here, or in a hereafter, alike — is willingness to give up as well as to receive. And I believe that senility can be defined as "a psychosomatic disease caused by inappropriate retention of patterns which are no longer suitable."

I've been interested in this "sandpaper surgery" discussed in the new *Reader's Digest*. There's a system of doing mechanically what a properly integrated organism could, quite clearly, do psychosomatically. And that means dispose of pockmarks, birthmarks, freckles, tatoos, and the like.

Rejection is just as important to survival as is acquisition.

But that requires a totally new conception of "being," of "surviving." It means that — "ye must be born again"! Ye must reject all you have, and regenerate it, with a new and advanced viewpoint.

Item to consider in processing: A baby, when first born, has a sense of discomfort, and cries. The baby doesn't know it wants air; crying causes it to discover breathing. Later it feels a new and different discomfort, and cries; the mother, not the baby, knows it wants food, and nurses it.

To a baby, only a sense of "I want," exists; it is up to others to not only supply the needed X that is wanted, but also the others must supply the *knowledge of what X is*.

The essence of immaturity is that the individual demands that others not only supply his wants, but *name his wants for him*.

How many people, when they demand "justice," will honestly and thoughtfully accept the question "How should it be?"

That demand that the individual who wants justice define his want is a demand that he be mature, and foreswear the childhood right to demand satisfaction for an unnamed need.

It's about as popular as sitting on a hornet's nest, however.

As I said in that editorial, only a machine, which has no concept of "right," would question the meaning of the term!

Regards,   John

Wayne Batteau   *August 3, 1953*

Dear Wayne:

In reply to your stomped-down water:

A couple of GI's in France during the war had commandeered a beast of burden. Being Brooklyn boys, they weren't certain what they'd acquired, and were arguing over it. The Chaplain came along, and one of them hailed him. "Hey, Padre! Come tell this joik heah this thing's a donkey. He keeps tryin' to say it's a burro!"

The Chaplain smiled, and said, "Well, according to Holy Scripture, that's an ass."

"Huh?"

"That's right — according to Scripture, that's an ass."

"Oh . . . . uh . . . thanks."

Some while later the animal became a casualty, and the two had to bury it. They were engaged in digging a grave when a WAC came by. "Digging a fox-hole boys?" she asked.

One of them looked up, grinned, and said, "Not according to Holy Scripture."

Discussions with **Dr. Gunther** lead me to suggest that **Tony Oettinger** is going to find it impractical to teach the Mark IV or any digital computer to speak English, Russian or Swahili. I think you need a modified analog type. Reason:

Quantum space is representable in digital fashion, because it is inherently digital; field space is inherently nondenumerable. A nondenumerable space can be represented to any specified degree of accuracy by a denumerable system — but it gets complicated. In quantum space, a thing is or is not; in field space a new concept-approach is necessary. When you seek to define the limits of a field, you're working with a nondenumerable aleph-system, and it can neither be specified internally nor can it be delimited. There is no limit to its fine-structure analysis, in other words, nor is there any limit to its scope. A denumerable aleph-system has no limit in scope, but does have a limit to its fine-structure.

Quantum space shows the charactierstic of exclusiveness; *if* A, *then* not-B.

Field space does not. *If* (solar gravity,) *then* (no conclusions whatever about the absence of any other gravity).

In field-space you find dominance, but not exclusiveness as the ruling principle.

Human language, however, shows the characteristics of a field-space, although it is expressed in quantum-space terms. There are "words," but the words symbolize fields, not quanta, in most instances. Thus "water" appears to be a thing, but carries a field implication that can be either "good' or "evil" depending on the effect of modifying fields of surrounding word-concept-symbols. The "thirst-water" field system is "good"; the "drowning-water" system is "evil."

To handle such problems, a digital computer would have to consider the field forces of each word-concept-symbol in relation to each other word-concept-symbol in the sentence, paragraph, and in fact the whole article being considered, and solve for the field-interactions.

Fields-interactions *do* permit of definitive decision, even though they are, individually, nondenumerable and structureless. Thus there is a definite null-point between the field of a magnet acting on a piece of iron below it, and the Earth's gravitational field. In the cited instance, decision is very clean-cut; it is actually impossible to establish a balance condition. Decision is sure and swift.

But I doubt that a digital computer of the known types could handle a problem of the multi-ordinal type involved in interacting the word-fields of a long sentence in a political discussion! The field structures would have a complexity approaching that of getting a complete solution for the motions of all the stars of the Galaxy!

I don't know whether it's possible to make a rough analysis of the complexity of the field-structures involved in this sentence I am now writing — but if it were, I'll bet you'd get an order of complexity that would make the structure of a plutonium nucleus appear simple.

Maybe the job could be done by using an analog computer — one involving a long tube with a lot of magnetic and electrostatic deflecting elements, and an electron beam. But I have a hunch we aren't even close to what it takes to solve the problem a baby learns to handle in the first two years of life!

But don't give up; if a baby can solve the order of the problem in two years, why, dammit, we ought to be able to work out a technique for handling the thing. The realization simply means that we've got to recognize that competence of the human mind is at least 20 orders of magnitude greater than we ever before imagined. "We have not yet begun to fight!"

Regards,   John

John Conly   *August 5, 1953*

Dear John:

I met your brother, **Robert**, the other day; he's got an scf. yarn he's working on, and dropped in the office to discuss it. If he tries to write all the ideas he's got into one novelette, however, it's going to bounce. You can't get that much in one story, as I know he'll find out. If he'll spread it out in about five or six, though, I think he'll have something.

He was up in New York studing the Bell System for an article for the *Geographic*.

You know, your whole family appears to be interested in information handling, one way or another. I learned your third brother is a chemist; a chemist works with matter much as you work with paper — to handle the information he's interested in, he needs a medium, and he uses atom and molecules to write on, instead of paper and pencil.

Thanks kindly for the *Science Digest* check; it arrived while we were on vacation, taking a swing out through upper Michigan. I'd just gotten back when your brother showed up. Apparently I'm going to be doing well by *Science Digest* in the next couple of months; **John Arnold's** article on the course he ran at MIT, which appeared in the May *ASF* is also being run by *Sci. Di.*

Vic Wagner, of *Pic* magazine, an old friend of mine, wanted an article on hi-fi; he also wants some pictures on hi-fi equipment to run with it, and I mentioned that *High Fidelity* undoubtedly had an excellent supply of such pics on hand. I think he'll be getting in touch; a cross-referrence to *High Fidelity* as a source of information on equipment is easily inserted in the article, and **Vic** is in full agreement on that. If you folks would be willing to allow him the use of some of your illustrative material, he'd happily give a plug.

In doing the article — which is on the basis that the reader has heard about hi-fi, but doesn't know it from personal experience, I finally figured out a way of explaining the need for real power to someone who doesn't need or want loud music. In the article I call the commercial radio receiver type reproduction "knothole music"; it's like watching a baseball game through the old knothole in the fence. You can see what happens to be in line with the knothole, but you have to guess what happens outside of your limited line of vision. If you grow up watching through knotholes, you'll perhaps have the idea that part of the fun of watching is the mystery of what happens outside of your line of vison. Then getting a seat in the stands may, at first, seem sort of strange — taking part of the mystery out of the game.

The knothole is limited not only in frequency range, but in power-range. You can't see how wide the diamond is, and you can't see how high the ball goes.

So you *don't* want loud music. In an automobile, what's the advantage of a sports car over a truck? Those big transcontinental jobs roll across the plains of Kansas at 70 miles an hour, and nobody actually wants to drive any faster than that. What's the advantage of the sports car then?

When you get into the mountains, or into stop-go traffic driving, you'll find out! A low-power amplifier can roll along nicely on the slow, easy notes of an organ, or a violin; those instruments produce notes that, in an electrical graph, look like the long, easy waves of a calm summer sea. But a trumpet! The waves from that thing look like a mid-winter Arctic storm running head-on into a tropical hurricane! The waves are all straight up and straight down; they look like a graph of a car moving in stop-go traffic. The overall speed isn't high, but it takes power, and lots of it, to maintain that stop-go action.

In music, you can fill a big living room with a half watt of the slow, easy waves of an organ — but it takes *25 watts* to keep up with the stop-go notes of a trumpet! What you hear when an ordinary radio set tries to follow a trumpet is not the trumpet at all; it's the distortion of the overloaded amplifier!

The orchestra and the conductor, together, have tried to control the pitch, quality, and loudness of the sounds that make music. Their musical judgement is what you want to hear.

With knothole music, you're hearing the mechanical judgement of an inadequate collection of hardware; it, not the orchestra and conductor, determines the limits of sounds in loudness and pitch. Believe me, it has extremely poor judgement!

Re turntables: The orchestra tries to control pitch and tempo — and it's good or bad as an orchestra depending on how well it does that. But if you put a record on the phonograph, and just drag your finger on it as it plays, varying the pressure — lo! *you* now control the pitch and tempo! You can't improve it any, that's for sure, but you can certainly make a mess out of what the orchestra tried to do. So can a cheap turntable that runs at irregular speed, or the wrong speed.

I'm sorry you got such poor response on the ads in *ASF*. I have a strong hunch that it's the price of *High Fidelity* and the sight-unseen business that makes it hard to get a nibble. There's one thing about a technical audience; they are *very* bad gamblers. They'll take the tremendous risk of trying out the first atomic bomb, or the risk of trying out a chemical reaction they think might go boom, very hard, but *only* after they've gotten all the data possible, and have convinced themselves that the risk is negligible. They are professional sure-thing bettors. It's a characteristic of the breed that they'll bet only after they've made certain that they can't lose. Consequently they make the world's worst audience for a gambling chance.

When you offer them a high priced magazine like *High Fidelity* — their whole training says "Before investing, determine the characteristics of this unit." You can't give 'em technical specifications on the satisfaction-index!

But they wouldn't be safe men to have around a laboratory, with all the powers available to modern technical equipment, if they weren't deeply, bed-rock rooted in the conviction that it was essential to know what was going to result — within limits — before trying it!

Damned if I know how you can get around that!

Regards,   John

Tom Godwin   *August 12, 1953*

Dear Slave Inspector Godwin:

A problem has come up in my district which I wish to have your considerations on.

There is on the local planet a population of smaller sized beings, cohabiting with a population of larger sized beings. These smaller sized entities show intelligence, sentience, and a desire for self-determination, but are powerfully inhibited by the larger, more powerful, and still more intelligent larger beings. We will call the smaller being type C, the larger type A. There is also an intermediate type B, which is considered by both Type A and Type C to be completely unmanageable, wild, and extremely difficult to get along with.

Type A forces type C to undertake menial tasks much against their wills. They are frequently punished physically and psychologically for failure to comply with the orders of Type A. They are ordered to spend many hours in confined quarters, each day, doing tasks they find unpleasant, and are allowed but few hours of freedom each day. They are required to do various menial tasks, and are rewarded with food, shelter and a poorer, rougher quality of clothes than Type A uses.

Do you consider it proper for us to exercise our authority and free Type C from the above conditions?

Type A individuals have raised the unpleasant arugment that if we force them — Type A — to release Type C, we will be forcing intelligent, sentient beings (type A) to act against their wills and will, thereby, be guilty of enslaving Type A in violation of our own laws.

This situation I find hard to deal with.

Incidentally the local name for Type C is "children."

(And if you've ever tried to handle adolescents, you'd know what Type B is.)

What is the ethics of the situation where one race has taken over the destiny of an inferior race in order to speed its advancement?

Judging from human life-patterns, the answer appears to be that a superior race A should enslave an inferior race C until such time as development of race C has led them to the point of being able to rebel successfully against race A. That's what the human family does!

Further, Woman was enslaved by Man for millenia — and only recently has Woman developed rebellion in her soul sufficiently to get up on her hind feet and howl about it. As soon as she did that, and did it firmly, she *was* freed, wasn't she?

I suggest that rebellion-from-within is the critical condition that determines whether slavery is appropriate or not. And that doesn't mean rebellion at the level of "Oh, I wish I were free." It means rebellion at the level, "We will do X and Y, which will lead to Z. It's going to mean a loss of about 20% of our people, particularly including we who are the leaders. That risk we must accept if we're ever going to get anywhere."

The Negros weren't ready for freedom; they didn't do the rebelling.

By contrast, the Amerindians were not ready for slavery; the colonists never did succeed in enslaving them worth a damn. The Indians rebelled from the moment of capture, and kept on rebelling steadily until they, or their captors, died. They earned their freedom, and they kept it. You can't enslave a man who's not afraid to die for freedom, and you're a damn fool if you try.

Actually, the Europeans were far more tractable slaves than the Amerindians; no Amerindian ever accepted bondsmanship! The Puritans were a strange breed of European cat; they didn't accept slavery and preferred the struggle with an absolutely alien environment. Like the Amerindians, they were a bunch of fanatical, wild-eyed rebels.

So far, we've freed the German people from slavery to a tyranny twice. Number Three is coming up, no doubt. They don't *like* being responsible for their own life-or-death decisions; you can't free a people like that. When you do, you merely change their masters, and they're just as happy under Allied masters as under German Junker masters. Russian masters they find a little hard to live with, and they become unhappy. If any part of the German population achieves true democracy it will be the East Zone Germans. They've got masters who are sufficiently out of phase with them to make them consider taking self-responsibility. A case of "Anything, even being responsible for my own actions, is better than this!"

Speaking of being slaves and resisting slavery; one of my ancestors here in New Jersey, about 1690 or thereabouts, was seven years old when Indians raided the settlement. They killed his mother, captured him, and killed and scalped his father. That night the poor little kid(!) stole a tomahawk from a sleeping brave, brained him, killed two other braves, and escaped. He made a life profession of killing Indians. It turned out that it was exceedingly unwise to try that with a boy. He died at a ripe old 90 something, having dedicated some 75 years to Indian-killing, and having been highly successful at his profession.

Moral: Be careful of buzz-saws. Even when they don't look like buzz-saws!

One of the great achievements of human beings is the invention of Hate. That ancestor was a real good hater. You see, Hate is the ability to generalize, and recognize that it is inadequate to slap the mosquito that bites you . . . you have to learn how to wipe out the species and get the business settled. It's inadequate to kill the wolf that ate your child; it works better if you learn to hate wolves, and wipe out the species. It was inadequate to kill the Indians that killed his parents; he was bent on wiping out the tendency to consider white men attackable game. He and a few of his cooperators did so, eventually. Indians were hard to teach, but it turned out that the Indians were resistant students.

It's an extremely wise species that learns its limitations, and learns to learn how to overcome the limitation instead of merely resenting it.

Item: If you ask the wrong question, you'll get the wrong answer . . . no matter how many times you ask it. If I meet you, and say, "Hey, Tom, how come the left side of your face is grass-green? You grow a lawn instead of a beard?" Now if I insist that you answer the question, you're really going to have a hell of a time of it. The wrong question — the wrong answer. Always, and indefinitely.

Now let's ask, "What makes me think your cheek is green?" Then we can definitely get an answer. Maybe it's because you fell into a bucket of green paint; maybe it's because I'm suffering from hyperthotsis of the whilgizis. But anyhow, we can get an answer.

Now this business of going forth into the galaxy and judging by human standards. After all, who is to judge?

Ask a silly question, you get a silly answer. "Who" is the wrong question. "On what basis, and by what method, is judgement to function?"

Now we've got a question we can sink our teeth in — and that an Arcturan klibthoth can sink his frelthzyks into just as handily. I don't give a sweet damn how many tentacles, legs, eyes or blobs an entity has, he's bloody damn well going to have to agree that gravitational field effects exist.

Now if we hoity-toity human beings will come off our exalted high horses, and stop trying to say we're something apart from the Universe, we'll get a brand new notion. The fact that we have judgement means that the laws of the universe are such that judgement can exist. Whaddya know! It isn't because we're human that we can have judgement after all! It's because we belong in this Universe!

So maybe the fact that you live in Nevada doesn't have to mean you're *really* a green-eyed monster with 13 tails just disguised like a man — or that if you *do* have green eyes and 13 tails it doesn't mean you're not that which is essentially important in being a man!

If our robots aren't slaves, it's our fault, not theirs. It's our ineptitude, our inability to find out what judgement really is, that

200

makes the robot on the cover look up from the man he's just broken. We're lousy bad teachers; that results from our own overweening pride that Being Human is something Different and No Other Thing can Be Human. It isn't that machine's *can't* have judgement and understanding; it's that we know so damn little about what we are that we can't teach it.

I've got me a little system. I've got a brains-team. Got a problem that no human being can solve? Take a superhuman mind to crack it? Fine; pass it along! I've got a superhuman mind. It's made up of the team of *ASF* readers and authors, who are all speculative philosophers, and know more then anybody on Earth. They're top-rank chemists, top-rank physicists, top rank. . . . Why, that superhuman mind-structure knows everything known to Man, and can out think anybody on Earth, **Einstein** not excepted!

The team is an expert at everything there is. All I've got to do is listen, and not be too damn sure I already have the answer — and I'll get the factors I need. You're part of it; so's **Wayne Batteau** at the Harvard Computer Labs. Some of the problems that we've hit I've thrown at him. His gang up there kicks them around and comes up with an answer. Maybe in the course of it they'll throw part of it into the great Mark IV computer; general philosophy is the basic root of their work. I threw them your question; they're working on it now, and sooner or later the Mark IV is going to be working on it.

How do you make a computer laugh at a joke?

You asked the question; the Harvard Computer Lab staff is working on it to find the answer for you. That was a damned good and understanding question — because it's the question of "How can you make a computer reject nonsense, and determine what the data should be when the wrong data has been punched in?" I said a while back that the essence of the mind's remarkable capabilities is that it can take wrong data, inaccurate data, and low-accuracy component parts, and somehow manage to get the right answer with a degree of precision that exceeds the precision of any of its components!

You pin-pointed it. The sense of humor is what does it.

How can you make a computer take in "The density of sea-water is 100.8," and have it chuckle, say to itself, "Hah! His finger slipped on that one! It's supposed to be 1.008!"

Lester del Rey, back in 1939, proposed in a story that the ultimate robot was one that, with its wires crossed, and given the wrong information, got the right answer anyhow.

What's judgement?

That's, not "Who is to judge?" is the question.

I'm working with **Dr. Gotthard Gunther**, a philosophy and

201

symbolic logic expert. He's brought to my attention the problem of handling infinities, and recognizing the difference between different orders of infinity. That turns out to be most exceedingly useful.

Consider all the whole numbers. There's an infinity number of them — they're unlimited.

But consider the total of *possible* numbers. There are as many (infinite!) between 0 and 1 as there are whole numbers between 0 and infinity. Then the total of possible numbers is a greater order of infinity than the whole-numbers infinity.

And that little item turned out to be essential in solving toward the nature of judgement.

Re what I look like. I have taken up photography; I used to be a camera bug. There's no better way to keep from having your picture taken; the one place you're absolute safe is behind the camera. I have no pictures of myself. S'fact. **Peg's** trying to get me photographed, and I suppose I will be soon.

Descriptively: medium brown hair, crew cut. 6'1". 220 pounds. (20 of it overweight.) Medium complexion, neither blond nor dark. Age 43. Still more chest than belly, but I dislike taking time for physical action, being too busy pushing typer keys and reading mss. My nose always gets anywhere I'm going first. I haven't got eyes like a hawk, but the nose might serve. I wear glasses.

OK?

How's about the other end of this letter-conversation?

Regards,   John

Reynolds   *August 22, 1953*

Dear Dr. Reynolds:

I was very much interested in your discussion of the oppossum and its life-pattern. One of its high survival values occured to me as having an interesting possible explanation — the effectiveness of death-feigning.

Any specialized animal, by the nature of specialization, acquires highly deterministic, arbitrary patterns of design — and the total system of that animal's living must be one *gestalt* into which each sub-piece fits perfectly. The more efficient the organism becomes at its specialty, the more highly integrated it must be.

The pouncing carnivour cannot be a good runner; the need for the collar-bone type shoulder structure, part of the behavior pattern of using the bludgeoning paw, requires such design as to preclude the free leg movement essential to a cursorial hunter.

The cursorial hunter, equally, can't have the collar-bone structure that would allow him to use the bludgeon attack.

202

There is a tightly knit, and essentially rigid interconnection of every part of a specialized animal.

But part of the gestalt of the animal is it's instinct patterns of behavior. These, too, become rigid. A cat *can not* act like a dog.

There are two major divisions of true carnivours; the hunters and the carrion eaters.

By the nature of their rigid instinct patterns, a hunter instinctively *can not* eat carrion.

And a carrion eater *can not* attack a living animal.

Wherefore the oppossum is protecting himself by a perfectly valid law of evolution; the specialized animal is necessarily limited. No carrion eater will ever attack him; no hunter will eat him if he is, or is interpreted as being, carrion.

The oppossum's only danger, then, lies in attack by an "amateur" animal — one that isn't a specialized expert. One like Man, who hasn't specialized in anything, and enjoys hunting, but prefers well-aged beef for the table.

The oppossum's one danger is that he has, now, specialized in his defense. He's a sucker for a carnivour that both hunts and eats carrion!

Sincerely,   John W. Campbell

Alan E. Nourse   *September 8, 1953*

Dear Nourse:

Any complex function can be analyzed into a large number of single functions, and I believe that the complex functioning of a brain can similarly be analyzed into a number of single functions. The great difficulty of such an operation is that the original complex is not formed by addition of the parts, but instead of by an inter-relation of the parts. There is an enormous difference mathematically between the process of "addition" and "inter-relation." There is an even more important difference between that concept in relation to a living organism. I have a feeling that it's going to take something of an entirely different nature to get anywhere with those signals you get from a monkey's brain.

Sincerely,   John

Wayne Batteau   *September 25, 1953*

Dear Wayne:

Every now and then I come up with an idea so nasty I really like it. Try this little puzzler!

Chaos is a state in which there is sequence, but no consequence.

In such a system, no action makes any difference, because it has no consequence.

In a system having perfect, 100% negative feedback, no action makes any difference, because it has no consequence. Every action, in such a system, has an equal, and an opposite reaction, cancelling it out, and so preventing any consequence.

Therefore in their essential behavior characteristics a system of pure chaos is equivalent to a system of perfect organization!

Then what *is* the difference between perfect, self-stabilizing order, as in a theoretically perfect 100% negative feedback system, and a system of pure chaos?

Item: Men worked out the gas laws long since. Gas approximates pure chaos.

But we still don't know how solids work; they're not so chaotic!

Item: Newton's Second Law of Motion is an expression of the nature of a 100% negative feedback circuit: For every action there is an equal and opposite reaction.

Betcha it ain't so. If it were, it'd mean the Universe was a perfect negative feedback system, and hence incapable of consequence. Betcha there's an error in the statement, of the order of the error in the inverse square law of gravity.

And if that hunch is right, than there *can* be a force that has no reaction — and spaceship drive, here we come!

There *is* noise in the Universe — an admixture of Chaos into Organization that's just enough to make the Organization manipulable.

Dear old chaos — it's all that makes life worthwhile. Without it, every action, every effort, would be futile, having no consequence!

Regards,   John

Ray Jones   *November 6, 1953*

Dear Ray:

Maybe I've got an "engram," and maybe it is, as I think, a freely chosen idea — but I have, deep in my soul, the proposition Kipling stated in "The Rhyme of the *Mary Gloucester*."

"They copied all they could follow,
"But they couldn't follow my mind,
"So I left 'em — sweatin' and stealing —
"A year and a half behind."

If you try to define art, you'll find, shortly, that Art is, by definition, that which is indefinable; the moment an idea is defined it ceases to be an art, and becomes a science, which is different.

Art is whatever you haven't yet been able to define concretely.

A human being, I think, has a deep instinct to be unstable —

unfixed. The animal whose behavior patterns are fixed and predictable can be trapped with ease; Man wants to have a general path of behavior — but a strong measure of unpredictable variation around that path.

If you try to predict what I want on the basis of what my characteristics are — don't pick the personality characteristics! Pick the fundamental, natural-law characteristics. And that simply means don't write for *me* — write for deepest truths you can find in yourself, the truths that will be present also in other intelligent, thoughtful men of good will. The less you write for *me*, and the more you write for the things you deeply believe, and for the deep truths of mankind, the more certain you are to hit many people of your own level of development.

Wayne Batteau pointed out these two factors:
1. In total agreement, the probability of learning is zero.
2. In total disagreement, the probability of effective cooperation is zero.

One way to drive a human being nuts is to artificially maintain total agreement with him; this prevents him learning, and hence prevents growth — and that means it kills him shortly. You're maintaining an environment of his own (mind) metabolic products, and that's destructive to any organism. One of **Ron's** great troubles was that he sought to maintain yes-men and sychophants around him; doing so leads to the destruction of his own personality.

We've been studying hate; one of the values in hate turns out to be the fact that hate is the motive to change an undesirable situation. Man hated being attacked by wolves. Man hated cold. Man hates being confined to one planet.

But hate doesn't require that the situation be altered *destructively*; one of the ways Man found for altering the situation of wolf-attack was to capture wolf-cubs and domesticate them, teaching them to be cooperating hunters — dogs. Cattle trampled and ate Man's grain field. So did horses. That nuisance has been abated, you notice. But there are more cattle and horses in the world today than there were then!

It seems to me that there's a fundamental law of nature: If there exists a force X, in the Universe, and the random operation of X constitutes noise in your self-system, alter the situation so that X operates more efficiently. This causes X to be less noisy in your self-system — and also allows you to tap some of the power X was expending for your own use.

A mountain stream is roaring down a hill, lashing about, denuding the rocks and removing your farmland. It does this every spring, and leaves your fields parched every summer.

Build a dam and a penstock. Now the mountain stream gets down hill much more efficiently and swiftly. So we run it through a turbine, getting electric power. And we regulate the flow so that it's constant spring, summer, and fall. The stream is more efficient, we benefit from constant flow, and we get the increased efficiency for our own use.

The horse wanted to eat; it spent most of its life seeking food. Unfortunately, it ate the grain Man planted. Man captured it, provided it with regular, adequate food, vastly increasing its food-gathering efficiency. That left a lot of surplus energy available in the metabolism, which Man could tap for his own use. In this case, the use of the surplus was to provide mechanical energy for Man's work.

The cow, on the other hand, has the excess tapped in a different way; the efficient food-gathering made possible by Man, allows the cow to supply quantities of milk enormously in excess of the requirements of bovine racial survival; Man gets the excess. Also, it allows the individual animal to grow far faster than the race needs for survival. Man taps that excess, too.

If you want to tap a system's energy — help the system to operate more efficiently, and you can tap the excess. But *you must teach* in order to be able to tap the system. You must improve the other fellow, if you want to benefit from his efforts.

Teach me something, **Ray**! Don't figure out what I already think is good, and give me that — figure out something that is basically sounder and wiser than I yet know.

Now: an interesting business to kick around mentally:

1. Atomic mass-numbers known run over 240. In the whole range from 1 to 240-plus, there is *one* and *only* one vacant mass number. No atom has a mass of 5.
2. Crystallographers say that no crystal can have five-sided symmetry.
3. Topologists find that no plane or spherical map needs more than 4 colors.
4. Two soap-bubbles intersect to form a plane interaction zone. Three intersect to meet in a line. Four meet in a point. But five can't meet.
5. According to Bode's law there should be a planet between Mars, the fourth planet, and Jupiter, the sixth. There's shattered debris, instead.
6. But a star-fish has pentagonal symmetry. Primitive land-life started with pentagonal pes and manus. Man retained these. We have a pentagonal design.
7. Life is distinguished from the non-living by existing *only* so long as it is unstable.

8. Magic, down the ages, held the pentagon and the pentacle (five-pointed star) to have mystic power.

9. Question: What's with the peculiar number Five?

From a quite separate line of development, it happens we'd concluded that the various levels of organization, the *numes*, as we call them, ran as follows:

Numes Index	Characteristic
0	Being
1	Change of being
2	Energy
3	Motive
4	Understanding—relationship
5	Thinking; change of relationship
6	Judgement
7	Ethics
X	Creation

Odd-numbered numes are dynamic and dispersive, manipulative. Even numbered numes are conservative.

Note that nume 5 is change of relationship — the essence of instability.

Sooooooo. . . . What's this peculiar property that somehow is tangled with fiveness?

Regards,   John

Gordon Beckstead   *November 8, 1953*

Dear Dr. Beckstead:

I'm returning the **Ron Howes** tape under separate cover; I've been a bit delayed on it because I don't have magnetic tape equipment, and had to get together with **Don Rogers** and **Jack Corielle**, who do have, to hear it.

Having to borrow time, and their therapy session time at that, I didn't listen to the whole tape, but did hear enough to get the nature of the approach being used.

In order to understand my situation, you'll have to understand the rather different situation **Peg** and I are in. We are NOT therapists; we are theoretical researchers. The difference is as great as the difference between an electrical engineer, who can make a power plant that works, and a theroretical physicist who can't make an ordinary washing machine motor work.

I'm well into my fourth year of research. **Peg** and I have been researching about 75 to 100 hours a week for three years. But we haven't done *any* therapy on any one else.

We've studied Information Theory and astrophysics, embryology and topology, Bode's Law and Bose — **Einstein** quantum statistics, the Pauli Exclusion principle and the use of the pentagon and the pentacle in magic. The viscosity of galactic nebulae and the meaning of omens, the relationship between kahuna magic and Freudian analysis all come in.

But we haven't done therapy.

If you want evaluation of this tape you sent in terms of "How well does it work in practice?," I can't help you. **Jack Corielle**, on the other hand, can. We belong to no group, and couldn't try it out as it was supposed to be used.

If you're interested in a purely theoretical —from-our-viewpoint analysis — why, sure. Can do.

We have theories — but we define a theory as "An idea-structure which is useful in accomplishing a purpose, and might even eventually turn out to be true." But if it is true, that's to be recognized as a delightful coincidence, not a necessary concommitant. A theory doesn't have to be true to be useful, nor does its utility prove its truth. Newton's law of gravity is useful but is now known to be untrue. But it's still being used, even though we know it isn't true.

On the theoretical basis, then, my reaction to **Howe's** tape is as follows:

I believe it should produce very helpful results in a large majority of cases. However, this factor should be of some help to you in evaluating your own work and results with this tape: No technique stemming from any basis of therapy any human being has yet devised can be expected to work in all cases. We'll need to get *much* deeper into the basic nature of Mind before we find one that will.

For instance, this tape would not have worked well for me, as I was two years ago. Reason: It asks that the individual skip asking himself "Why," let the "whyness" go, and just become aware.

Now for most people, that's possible, and it's helpful. My particular background and experience-pattern made that particular way of thinking exceedingly dangerous for me during my childhood. (My mother had a remarkably sudden temper; it turned on violently with no more than about 3 seconds warning. Unless I carefully calculated every action before undertaking it, Hell popped irreversibly.)

Taking myself as a specific example, here is a good and useful technique — the "let the whyness go for a while" — that simply could not work for me. It was a fact-of-nature that, for my environment, careful calculation of probable results was essential.

It still is; when I start to cross a street, careful calculation beforehand is necessary.

The essential point is this: No single technique should be expected to work, invariably, for all people. Not until we develop a technique based on the level of Mind so deep that, like the atoms of matter, *all* minds necessarily are of the same structure. However different substances may be, they are *all* composed of electrons, protons and neutrons. But at no higher level is there commonality among substances.

It happens that **Jack Corielle** has used this tape in a group; it worked well for him and his group. There is a myth going around in dianetics circles that you can do anything you want to, if you really want to. **Jack** pulled that on me, which more than mildly irked, because it is a myth. I don't care how much you want to make a right angle turn when you're going 60 miles an hour — you can't do it and stay alive. Not unless you've developed a level of science completely beyond human range as of today. I haven't; therefore it is impossible for me-now to make a right angle turn at 60 miles an hour, and anyone who says I can if I just want to bad enough is a damn fool.

The same factors, precisely, apply at the mind level. *If* there are any laws of Mind, *then* we can develop a science of mind. *If* there are no laws of mind, *then* we cannot develop a science of mind — but we can do anything we happen to want to.

The concept of "an ordered chaos" is self-denying. It can't be ordered if it's chaos, and it can't be chaos if it's ordered.

If there are laws of Mind, *then* you are *not* free to do anything you want to, in any way you happen to want to. You must, instead, use those laws of mind to accomplish what you want to.

This does not mean that you are forever denied the ability to do something, X; it does mean that you can do X only by finding out what the relevant laws are, and applying them — not by simply denying them.

You can make that right angle turn — if you'll first apply the laws of friction, slow down to 15 miles an hour, and then apply the laws of moments, leverage, and friction to making the turn.

There are higher laws of Mind than are now known; there appears to be a group of them known collectively as "Faith." What those laws are, no one knows as yet — but they're definitely potent, and permit by-passing some of the lower-order laws we now know. I'd like very much to know what they are, and how they work; they evidently include the ability to reach a conclusion without process at the level we now know and can describe. Unfortunately, the laws of "faith" are just as apt to err as the laws of logic; they can establish beliefs that are remarkably unsound, and, because the belief has no discernable process of generation, are incredibly difficult to alter. The paranoid psychotic has a belief, "They're all against me," that he can defend with the most rigorous logic. But the belief is not derived by a logical process; if we knew what the laws of its derivation were, we might be able to reach it and deduce an alteration. But logical approach definitely doesn't reach it!

This tape does a great deal to aid individuals to become aware of the *existence* of that non-logical process of belief-without-whyness. By inducing pleasant conclusions-without-logical-process, the individual can become aware of the *fact* that he does have a process of conclusion-reaching which does not involve logic or normal sensory awareness. By validating the utility and worth of that process, instead of demeaning it, damning it, and attacking it at every turn, as is normal in our society, the individual is allowed to become more aware of the highly important but indescribable process of conclusions-by-non-logical-process.

The technique **Howes** has developed in this tape definitely should produce a great deal of favorable results.

But do not be surprised or angered that it will inevitably fail in some cases; it would have failed in mine, as I say, and insistence that I simply wasn't trying would have made the failure more complete than ever.

Consider this problem: Bill Blow has a good friend, Jim Jones. Jim just loves hunting and fishing; he works as a store-keeper so he can earn the money for guns, ammo, and fishing gear. Bill is a research chemist. Jim "knows" that Bill needs more outdoor life, more adventure in his soul, and because he very much likes and respects Bill, he does everything in his power to induce Bill to go on a hunting trip.

Bill, to satisfy Jim, does so. He tries what Jim says he needs.

He finds it very boring. He knows that he can shoot a gun; he knows he's smarter than the animal he's hunting. He knows several efficient ways of getting animal food that don't involve this time-consuming nuisance.

And — what Jim doesn't realize — Bill's adventure is in trying to crack through the frontiers of knowledge. It's adventure, too. Jim's never seen Bill's lab — he thinks they're stuffy, smelly places. He doesn't know about the "boom ball," the six-foot stainless steel sphere, with two-inch thick walls, where Bill tries out those experiments he rather expects will blow hell out of the surroundings. Bill's working with reactions of violent potentialities, and great real danger — which he takes as a matter of course. That's the way you live, isn't it? No fun doing things that have no excitement of mystery and danger — like plowing through woods in search of animals that can't hurt you, under conditions where you know you won't starve if you do fail.

But because Bill likes Jim, he has taken the trip.

On returning, Jim asks enthusiastically, "Well, how'd you like it, huh?"

Gently, Bill explains that it was interesting.

Now Jim "knows" that hunting is one of, if not *the* great pleasures of life. Evidently Bill hasn't really understood hunting. But at least, Jim feels, he's succeeded in cracking Bill's resistance. A few more trips, and, because hunting *is* (in Jim's mind that means absolutely, for any human being, without possible exception) such wonderful fun, Bill's sure to learn to like it.

So Jim urges Bill to go again. And again. And. . . . presently, reluctantly, Bill is forced to give up his friendship with Jim. Because Jim just *cannot* understand that, for Bill, hunting is so mild, so unexciting, so pointless, that there is, and never can be, any great pleasure. The competition against an animal like a deer is completely non-exciting to Bill; he needs the competition against the vast and dangerous forces of the Universe to satisfy him. To Bill, hunting is time spent doodling, signifying nothing.

The human problems that center around that system are innumerable. *A* has the conviction that if *B* would only try *A's* pet source-of-pleasure, *B* would inevitably and certainly learn to like it. If *B* would just *really* try it. . . .

But the trouble is, A's thinking runs thus:

1. Anybody who tries my wonderfully exciting and satisfying activity, P, is certain to become addicted to it.
2. Therefore, those who are not addicted to it are those who have never really tried it.
3. Therefore if B is not addicted to it, this proves that B hasn't *really* tried it.
4. Since all human beings seek happiness and satisfactions, and activity P is a certain source of happiness and satisfaction for any human being, it is my duty to B, as a friend, to insist that he *really* try P.
5. I will know that he has *really* tried P when he becomes addicted to it. Until he becomes addicted to it, then, it is my duty-as-a-friend to insist that he try it.

This is going to go on forever, until B is forced to break the relationship of "friend" with A — because A is compelled, by his logic, to force activity P on B so long as A conceives of himself as B's friend — because of duty-as-a-friend.

My 11-year-old daughter very seriously asked me why I didn't go bowling "the way the other men around here do."

She's now 13; now she knows why.

My 18-year-old son wanted to know why we didn't go out more in the evenings and have fun — go to movies and shows more.

He's beginning to understand.

My radio ham friends don't understand how I can let all my ham gear stand idle. It's wonderful gear, too — the best anyone could ask for.

But it took me quite a while to learn the same lesson the other way around; that they do *not* want to be induced to be induced to study their own minds, the most wonderfully exciting and stimulating thing any human being. . . .

It *does* sound familiar, come to think of it, doesn't it?

I don't have the slightest interest in higher mathematics — yet. I don't have the slightest interest in experimental biochemistry — yet. There are ten thousand things I'm not yet able to view as deeply rewarding, stimulating and interesting ways of expending effort. That doesn't mean the men who *do* see reward in it are either superior or inferior; it definitely does mean they're different.

Isaac Asimov's an experimental biochemist — a brilliant guy, and fine human being. We like each other. I don't make him study the mind; he doesn't make me study biochemistry. We report tidbits to each other, and each of us gets useful help from the other's work.

This form of group therapy you're doing is fine stuff, and basically rooted in human mind-structure, as we see it. But it's not going to be universal, nor should you feel that it has in any measure failed because it isn't universal. Even adjustable stilson wrenches won't turn all nuts! It takes a variety of tools for a variety of jobs.

The one danger I see in this type of tape is that it will tend to have the effect it did with respect to me and the **Rogers-Corielle** group; because the tape worked for them, they insisted I hadn't *really* tried it if it didn't work for me.

It might be of great help in the work, therefore, to have a First Tape, sent to groups just starting, that presents this problem, and discusses it openly. The "That's your reality" business of the early Phoenix group days was not altogether right by any means, nor was it altogether meaningless. If the group is appraised of the need to find an *underlying* unity, and not to insist either on the right of "I don't have to agree with you *in any way*" nor on the business of "You must agree with us *on this basis*," progress can be made.

Every individual who enters a therapy group is a Deviant; entering therapy groups is not normal behavior in our cultural system, so the mere fact of entering the therapy group of itself proves the individual is, in some degree, a Deviant.

Then each individual can be expected to have experienced in his own past, the problem of the Deviant who can't agree with the groups around him *on their basis*. As a child, maybe he didn't want to play touch football, but preferred playing with a Chemicraft set, or repairing bicycle coaster brakes, or watching ants build a nest. He's a Deviant, and has had trouble with the Group.

He's looking for a *group he can enter*.

Wrong answer. He'll get into trouble again, because there's constant group-deviant problems. The approach must be eventually at the level "On what basis can I enter a group?"

Since that's the problem of every member of every one of the therapy groups (I believe the "every" statement here is valid, because of the filtering effect mentioned above; only Deviants will enter therapy groups in the first place), a first group tape calling this problem to attention would be of real help, perhaps, in holding the group together.

Perhaps succeeding tapes should, also, reaffirm the existence of the problem.

Each of the Dianetics groups has splintered, ever since the original, because of the failure to solve that group-vs-deviant problem.

Incidentally, we can't have One World until that problem is *really* solved!

Regards,   John W. Campbell, Jr.

Jerry Pournelle   *November 9, 1953*

Dear Mr. Pournelle:

I can give you one mental-level absolute; it comes sufficiently close to it to be useful as such:

If an individual A, so acts as to cause B to conclude that A does not accept the validity of B's problem, B will act in a manner such that A will, in B's opinion, be forced to recognize the validity of B's problem.

See **Isaac Asimov's** story "Belief."

See your reaction to your conviction that I don't appreciate how tough the problem the social sciences face is.

It dosn't matter whether or not A *actually* demeans B's problem; B's reaction is dependent on what B *believes the case to be*.

No human being ever acts on the facts of a case. See Information Theory; since communication media necessarily exist between the fact and the perception thereof, the human being necessarily reacts on the basis of a belief-pattern, and is absolutely incapable of action on the facts-as-they-are-exteriorily.

And that, I think, we can agree on *is* an absolute law!

You feel I insulted you personally. You certainly and specifically took me to task for my ignorance, lack of judgement, ineptitude, and unwisdom. That approach seems likely to produce poor net results in a communication channel; let's try another method.

First off, I started a letter to you in which I used a method of communication that I decided to drop, because you might have interpreted it as insincere, and a silly trick. It wasn't, but it is perhaps best to drop it.

The essence of it is this: English does not use the 2nd personal singular in normal communication; therefore there is a considerable possibility of confusion of you-individual, and you-as-a-member-of-a-group. I tried writing a letter using *thee* and *thou* to specify the difference. It is helpful.

It's essential in this discussion, if you-individual are to understand my-individual attitudes to recognize that there *is* such a thing as a you-group, Psychology-psychologists.

When you-individual reacted to my editorial in the magazine, I had made *no* comments whatsoever about you-individual. I did not know that you-individual existed. Then the fact that you-indiv. reacted to the editorial suggests that you-ind. have an extension of your self-structure which you felt was being attacked.

In writing, if I refer to "Medical science believes. . . ." most individuals have some conceptual referent for the comment. Further, when a doctor uses a particular drug, and that drug causes an idiosyncratic reaction in the patient, producing death, in a subsequent malparactice suit he might well testify that "Medical science" held that drug the best available specific in the particular case.

The existence of a quasi-entity "medical science" is legally recognized. So is the existence of a quasi-entity "psychology" and "psychiatric profession."

Now this entity is not a Moebius Strip type system; it's necessary to recognize that it has an in-group and an out-group structure, and that the surfaces experienced by individuals in the in-group *are not* similar to the surface-of-contact experienced by the out-group individual.

The entity "Medical Science" controls the member of the medical profession in a considerable degree; the entity Psychiatry has a similar power.

As an out-group individual, I have valid experiences of the nature of the contact surface Psychiatry exposes to the out-group.

You-individual, as an in-group member, have quite different, but equally valid experiences.

In my letter discussing the Gestapo-position of the pychiatrist, I sought not to say that you-individual were a believer in Gestapo methods. (I specifically pointed out that the set-up that existed was due to a failing of the society, and existed without the wish of the psychiatric profession — but that it *did* exist.) In order to understand the resistance-reaction of your physicist friend, recognize what the out-group surface of Psychiatry *does in fact* display.

Most ordinary human beings are extremely fearful of sticking their fingers into a radio receiver. Reason: Electricity can kill; they know this, and know that electricity exists in the radio receiver. Caution suggests the wisdom of keeping your fingers out.

Now *you* may know that the set can be handled safely, under any reasonable situation — but that's because you have special in-group knowledge of electronics and electricity. The housewife doesn't have it, and is exercising good judgement in staying the hell away from it.

Equally, observe the fact that, for many, many generations, society has feared insanity massively.

Also, observe that society generally has held that the extreme Deviant, called "insane," has either zero, or negative value to society, and that therefore *anything whatever* that will change this situation is a sound measure.

The neurotically disturbed individual knows those facts — and they are facts of history. The fault is Society's — but the fault existed, and has *not* been completely eliminated.

Psychiatry, the legally-existent entity, *does* display in actual action, a tendency to condone precisely that attitude of "anything goes." The man at West Virginia, of whom you and I agree in feeling that he's on the wrong side of the bars, can not be stopped by any individual citizen; he *could* be stopped if Psychiatry-the-legally-existent entity said "Quit it!"

I — and your friend, who is, like myself, a member of the out-group — observe that Psychiatry does not in fact consider that man needs stopping. Strange that the Russians, of all people, were the ones who stood up in meeting and blew off about the unlimited use of lobotomy!

"Birds of a feather flock together," has definite validity. Individuals associate for the purpose of carrying out commonly agreed on activities, by agreed on methods and toward agreed on goals.

Not being a member of the in-group, I judge the entity Psychiatry by what I observe it doing.

You are in the in-group; you observe a research level of psychiatry. In New York here, the practicing psychiatrists are long out of school, and they do not have the view-points your instructors there have.

Let's stop using the term "psychology" as we have, and stick to the term "professional Psychiatry" — a legally existent entity, which I can discuss in terms of the facts of it's practices.

The practicing psychiatrist is rushed; during the war, **Hubbard** learned to hate the profession violently, because of the *practices actually used in fact*. Theory be blowed; after being knocked down by some decidedly rugged experiences — he was in the fracas from the begining, war on Java when the Japs landed, and finished only after V-J day — the Navy psychiatrists did in fact treat him to a six-week quickie process.

If you have any delusions that that six-week quickie bears any resemblance to what *you're* talking about — believe me, it very genuinely doesn't.

It consists of some very violently authoritative statements as to what's the trouble with you, and if you want to get out of this institution, you darned well better admit that these things are wrong with you, right now, and do it the way you're told to.

Sure — I know that isn't what you mean by Psychiatry. But somebody must have, or they wouldn't have done it!

I know a girl who was scheduled for prefrontal as an incurable suicidal. Her brother refused to permit it. He believed in some of **Hubbard's** cockeyed doctrines; it was hard working with his sister, because he had only about 20 minutes during visiting hours, and that in a hospital corridor, because the girl was too bad off to be allowed in the visitor's room. (She was under continuous restraint. They'd added "paranoid tendencies," incidentally, after a neighboring violent case escaped and reached her room while she was in a strait jacket and restraining sheet. The nurse arrived in time to interfere with the throttling. Her reaction to this caused her to be classified as paranoid, as I say. West Virginia isn't the *only* place psychiatrists sometimes display inadequate understanding of patient's problems.)

The suicidal mania did break under her brother's work; she improved enough so he could get her transferred to a private institution, where he was allowed to work with her more adequately. In six weeks she was released. Two months later she was doing secretarial work in North Carolina. There has been no relapse.

The out-group does see quite a different thing than you do; the ideals exist, the conscientious work goes on, but that is in the universities and laboratories. There are good men in the field — but my God, man, there are some awful stinkers. I don't deny that good men are working; why do you deny that stinkers are working too? And isn't your-group responsibility wide enough to include that West Virginia brain-slicer?

Isn't it legitimate to ask, "Why is your physicist friend so afraid of psychiatry?" You-individual certainly wouldn't slice his brain — but the facts he can observe are that your-group does do precisely such things. Like the wise housewife who keeps her fingers out of the radio, he keeps his brain out of your-group's custody as long as he can. *You* know better — but take a look at the out-group problem, too!

There's the story of the man who said to the Negro boy, "Come ahead — the dog's barking, but you know barking dog's don't bite." "Yes, boss — I know, and you know, but does *he* know?"

Have I *no* right to say "Psychiatry believes in the use of violent, authoritarian methods," when I observe the facts I have observed — and observe that the professional entity, Psychiatry, condones those ultimate violations of the human individual?

These acts of indivduals *must* be accepted as part of the picture of psychiatry, for without the backing of the group, the individual would not be allowed such power.

If there were a local lawyer who had embezzled funds from his clients repeatedly, and this fact was known, and proven, and the local Bar Association did not disbar this man — wouldn't you conclude that the Bar Association favored embezzlement by lawyers?

If you accept identification with the group psychiatry, then you accept some measure of responsibility for the sins of the group.

The soldier who is shot in battle is an individual — but dies because he is identified with a hostile group. Is this essentially different from the proposition that such member of a group jointly shares responsibility for the actions of all members of the group?

In attacking any problem, there are many possible methods that will work; the problem is to find the method of minimum time-effort. That method, science has found, usually involves the discovery and application of basic rigidities of nature.

It may well be true that Information Theory is not truly universal, and is limited only to human methods of operation. For the purposes under discussion, this is an adequate universal.

We're attacking the problem of guilt, and guilt-feeling — but in a different way. So long as it is held that guilt is a matter of opinion (Society's) the problem is inherently insoluble. The Aztecs used to have a sacrificial ceremony in which the High Priest skinned a young girl alive, and then released her from the altar, to run stumbling down the temple steps. The populace below then sought to hack off pieces of her flesh and eat them.

Here is an example of a society that had a wrong idea — yet children in that society were "guilty" if they did not realize that this was a fine and a proper thing to do.

In one African tribe, it is the filial duty of a man to see to it that his parents are slaughtered and ceremoniously devoured when they reach 65. In this culture, I am a guilty, and unfilial son; my father is well over 65.

But in *our* culture, I would be most horribly guilty if I did this.

Under such circumstances, it is evidently impossible to resolve guilt-problems. Something external to human opinion must be consulted.

217

I'm taking the postulate "There are absolute Universal Laws — laws of the forces of nature — that can be consulted."

I may be wrong — but I have mathematical demonstration that any other approach to the problem makes the guilt-problem inherently irresolvable.

The development of Information Theory strongly suggests that there are universal laws — structure — that do *not* lie at the purely physiological level.

Look; as a physicist, you know damn well, you don't know from nuthin' about the nature of the physical universe. Nobody does. We twiddle our fingers and count neutrons and protons, and haven't the foggiest notion what they are. We take pictures of galaxies, and find they show viscosity! If we don't have any more knowledge of matter than that, how the hell do you think we could possibly know the limits of "physiological" structure? What do we know about force-fields?

Take a look at a tree, an elm for instance. How does that twig at the extreme end of that branch on the left there "know" how long it should be to match the symmetry of twigs way round on the other side?

What's the "physiology" of the process by which the divisioning and specialization of the cells in the embryo is controlled?

By "physiology" I think you are limiting yourself unduly; call it "structural mechanism," and allow the concept of "structure" to include force-field effects, information-theory effects, and a lot of other higher-order effects, we don't yet know about.

If you're ever engaged in trying to define "Art," you'll find it comes down to "That which can't be defined; if you define it, what you've defined is a "science," not an art."

By Russell's Theory of Types, "I" is a class of all classes, and is never a member of itself — it's an automatically retreating concept. You can know what "I-then" was, but never can you know what "I-now" is, because if you did, the collective class would be a member of itself.

If you can ever figure out how it is possible to change your personality, and not loose your identity, you'll make a long step toward breaking neurosis. The neurotic can't see how he can possibly change his personality without destroying that-which-is-I. Once "you" were a fertile ovum. Later, "you" were a small boy, two years old. Now "you" are a young man. Fine; what's the structure that is unchanged, that is "identity" in such a system? There is something; religions have called it "soul" — but everybody knows that there's *something*, and because he can't define what it is, he's desperately afraid to make any changes, because the change might destroy that Something.

How can you change from a 2-year-old to what you are now, and still be the same entity?

Look, my friend, if a man and his wife *can't* work out the problems of living between them, without the help of a psychiatrist, then there will shortly be a new species dominating this planet. There aren't, and never will be, enough psychiatrists; the race can't afford that luxury.

Neither my wife nor I have any psychiatric degrees or training; there is no agency on Earth, however, that has any business interfering with the efforts of a man and his wife to solve their own problems. We don't do therapy; we study ourselves. My brother-in-law is an MD, and does do therapy.

Furthermore, if I choose to do therapy, I have six friends around here, and in about two weeks I'll be set up in the most ancient and respected of therapeutic professions — the church. Any six citizens can incorporate a new religion in New York state. It is not quite true to say that psychotherapy is a new thing; men have been struggling at this problem since before the dawn of history. Religion is one of the older techniques — and a very effective one, in many instances. See the Lourdes Shrine, for example. Since "psyche" means spirit, and a religious counsellor gives spiritual guidance, the sincerity and wisdom of the therapist, not the name or title he uses, is the important factor.

It's worth considering this: The greatest philosophical advances in Man's history have been based on the destruction of the in-group-out-group distinction. Christianity started (but didn't continue, sad to say,) as a belief based on the proposition that every individual could appeal directly to God — that no special priest was necessary in any ordinary problem.

Galileo's great point was that every man could investigate Nature for himself; that no special Authority was necessary.

Democracy's great basic tenet is that every citizen has a right to direct contact with his government, at a level of responsibility-and-right.

Psychotherapy is improving, and will continue to improve futher, as more and more of the Awful Mystery is stripped from self-analysis. There are perhaps 10,000 psychologists in the world, and two billion individuals who *have* to act as amateur psychologists, willy nilly, or get their teeth kicked in. The odds, then, are about 200,000 to 1 that the amateurs will first spot a phenomenon in the field.

Medicine knows that first aid is essential, and that practical, working techniques of routine medicine should be available in every home. How's about the same for psychotherapy?

Human minds are a lot more stable than the psychologists

believe — that's one thing the out-group is aware of. You fellows study a collection of ding-bats, and tend to get a somewhat distorted view of the nature of humanity! Honest, boss, we aren't that fragile! If we were, there wouldn't be two billion of us running this here planet!

Don't push a guy; give him understanding, and a chance to think out his own problems, in his own way, and he won't go near the violent ones. It's only when you push a man into something he's not yet ready to handle that it'll throw him. Give him his own way, acknowledge that he knows how to run his own case, and he'll bounce off of anything dangerous — and yet he'll work his way down through his personal mind-maze till he finds the approach that *will* crack the problem.

You can crack any mind if you force it to solve the insoluble problem; that's the main trouble with the amateur know-it-all.

But you know, if we *don't* get a working psychotherapy first-aid organized, the psychiatrists are never going to dig out from under. Imagine the MD's if every cut finger had to be handled by a doctor!

I've been rocked — but good! — by some of the items I've hit. But I hit them voluntarily, of my own choice, with my wife standing by, but never driving me into them. The first couple of times it does scare you purple with pink polka-dots; thereafter you get more respect for your own mental elasticity, and tackle the mean ones with more assurance.

There *is* a way to home therapy — it's necessary, because only so can the ordinary man and wife devise a working life that includes happiness and easy co-living.

The amateur is far too little respected — despite the fact that amateurs have been responsible for most of the great advances of human understanding. Jesus wasn't a priest; Pasteur wasn't a doctor; Freud wasn't an MD or a psychologist. There's a nasty little trick the society plays on us; it says, "Oh, *him*! *He* wasn't an *amateur* — he was a *genius!*"

But any genius is just an amateur as seen from a point 20 years or more later in time.

This doesn't mean that all amateurs are geniuses. It refers to the peculiar fact that no human being ever experiences the *unlikely*. If he experiences, it isn't unlikely any more; it's *true*.

That, by the way, is a very important mechanism in dealing with childhood fears. A child fears what he can't evaluate; since he never experiences the unlikely, it's difficult for him to appreciate its meaning.

(You see, we *do* have a psychotherapy clinic. We have four children, ranging from 8 to 20, and like all the parents who've lived before us, we have to run our own psychotherapy clinic!)

Please believe me: I'm not unaware that there is a tough problem. My approach to it is essentially this one: Many brilliant and devoted men, working very hard, through many years, and with the best possible facilities, have not solved the problem in this manner.

The problem is one I must solve, if I am to have my full measure of happiness, and my children are to have their due of happiness.

Therefore I will assume that the method the professionals are using is wrong. If they are, as I believe them to be, sincere and competent men, and have not been able to solve it by that method, then I would be a fool indeed to try the same approach.

It is futile to assume that it can not be solved; that would yield me nothing.

Then I will try a new appoach.

The approach has yielded *us* results. We've been able to help our kids over some rough spots — my two and Peg's two. We've made a single family unit of a stop-family situation.

I'm not saying your problem is a mere nothing; I am saying that it's futile to consider it as being one too tough to tackle!

I'm not afraid of examining my own mind; also I'm not afraid of admitting that there are forces underlying my mind-structure which I do not understand, and which have power far beyond the power of human "free will." They may not be absolute, but brother, they make a damn good approximation. The Earth isn't absolutely immovable, either — but let's see you shove it around!

Item:

1. No woman has ever written a first-line work of literature in any European language. Males dominate the field.
2. But females have done the great works in Japanese literature.
3. But Japanese scientists are forced to think and work in European languages.

Why is this?

1. Laymen have the idea that women think in a manner different from men. Is there truth in this?
2. The world's great heros show a pattern having a high correlation with this: they respect the opinions of women.
3. The world's great villains show a high correlation with disrespect for the opinions of women.

Why is this?

1. Divide philosophers (all of whom have been male!) into Readable and Turgid groups.

   The Readable group shows a high correlation with

the Married group.
Why is this?

Regards,   John W. Campbell, Jr.

Dr. J. B. Rhine   *November 23, 1953*

Dear Dr. Rhine:
    Permit me to introduce myself; I'm the editor of the *Astounding Science Fiction* magazine. I suggest you may know of it — and know that my field of work has, for a long time, been interested in your parapsychology researches.
    I attended Duke, quite some years ago; somewhere in your records must be some of the runs on the ESP cards that I made. Later, for some years I lived across the street from the brother of your experiment designer, **Dr. Charles Stewart**. I had a good many discussions with **Charlie** about your work.
    I have just gotten a copy of your latest book for review.
    My wife and I have been doing some private research on the mind, the nature of the thought process itself, and basic philosophical and metaphysical orientations. We are rather unusually situated in that respect; because of my rather unusual profession, highly trained scientists are willing to speculate with me to a degree, and in directions, that they would not ordinarily discuss. Science-fiction is somewhat falsely identified as spaceships and BEM stuff. True, it can be. But its essential core is wide-open philosophical speculation — *Gulliver's Travels*, *Pilgrim's Progress*, and *Aesop's Fables* all belong in the same field.
    I've discussed speculations with professional philosophers, research directors of major national laboratory projects, the young, vigorously speculative and active minds who are directly thrusting against the edges of the Unknown. The men who operate the White Sands Proving Grounds are not quite so sure we know the limits of physical science as are the professors of electrical engineering in an established engineering school. The nuclear physicists who run the cosmotron at Brookhaven have a somewhat different philosophy, when they will speak freely and personally, than that which appears to exist in the pages of the *Physical Review*. They're rather young men, necessarily; real nuclear physics isn't very old.
    This letter is inspired by your discussion of the difficulties encountered in getting psychology to so much as consider unbiasedly the results of your work. Their essential point is that ESP cannot be explained on the basis of physics or physiology.
    Sir, may I suggest your own background has led you to misdirect your effects. Psychologists aren't physicists; because they

are not, they are quite unable to speculate in the field of physics, and are, therefore, far more rigidly bounded by the known *and proven* statements of physics than is a physicist. A psychologist does not feel competent to say, "This physical law is inadequate," because, as a psychologist, he knows he is not competent to judge the validity of physics' findings.

Almost any first-rate, young, experimental research director will most freely and happily assure you that physics doesn't know its ABC's yet — and certainly hasn't reached D! The older men, as psychological research has shown, tend less toward the creative and original thinking that produces new advances in any field; they are somewhat more apt to be unwilling to acknowledge the inadequacy of physics.

I know nuclear physicists who have told me, "The concepts we've worked with — even our most basic ones — break down when we work inside the nucleus. I don't know what 'distance' means, for example. No philosophical meaning for the concept has ever been achieved; we just use it because it works pretty well in ordinary things. It doesn't work in nuclear physics."

Your group, you know, is not the only group that finds that the laws of physics seem to be breaking down at the edges. The nuclear physicists find that. So do the men at White Sands, where rocket research is probing out into something called "space," and coming back with answers that don't match anything the hypotheses of physics, sometimes known as "laws" of physics, call for.

The astrophysicists, on the other hand, studying photographs of the ultra-distant nebulae taken with the 200″ telescope, have been finding some other things that don't fit the "laws" of physics.

Physicists aren't one whit disturbed; physicists never did think the "laws" were anything more than temporarily useful methods of organizing data for reference and filing. It's the non-physicists who consider physical law to be final.

The astrophysicists find that, in the plates of distant galaxies, there are shots of galaxies that have collided with and interpenetrated each other. This is understandable enough. But — how can a swarm of stars, bound only by gravitational attractions, show evidence of *viscosity*?

Perhaps your effort has been directed at the wrong group; the philosophers and the physicists may be better able to aid in your work, now, than the psychologists.

The fact that the psi functions do not show an inverse square law, or any distance-law, effect, for instance, is readily understandable if you discuss the matter with a mathematical philosopher and a topologist. Cantor, in his study of transfinite cardinals, showed that, mathematically, there are as many points in a short segment of a line as in a line of infinite length. If this be true — then what's distance?

Philosophically, our whole culture's orientation has been toward the study of matter. But matter can only be defined as "that which occupies space" — and space can not be defined, nor has it been defined, within the logic-system currently allowed by our cultural orientation.

The physicists, however, have been finding the concept doesn't work very well when they get out to the edges of the Known — the microscopic edge of the nucleus, or the macroscopic edge of the galaxies.

There is another edge, incidentally, that's somewhat harder to see in our cultural orientation — the edge of Complexes.

Our logical system descends from the Greeks. In a simple culture, and in a simple science, it worked fairly well. "The whole is equal to the sum of the parts." But while that is logical, it is quite evidently irrational. For very simple things like a colony of monocellular entities, it is quite true. The colony can be separated into its parts, and simple addition of the parts yielded the whole. But it doesn't apply to a man; separating him into parts and adding the parts together somehow does not produce a sum equal to the original whole.

If an automobile collides with an express train, all the original parts may be quite readily collected. If logic worked, the sum of these once-scattered parts would be equal to the automobile.

The laws of physics apply to systems wherein parts *do* react reversibly; they do not apply in systems wherein the whole is *not* simply the sum of the parts, but is, instead, the integrated *gestalt* of the parts.

There are several essential mechanisms of rational thinking which are non-logical, and which logic cannot replace. There is, for one, what we have been calling *analogic* — the simple matter of thinking in analogies. Any logician declares that thinking by analogies is not a logically acceptable method. But it happens that that is essential to rationality; no philosopher has yet devised a formulation of the method, however, and because no formulated laws of analogical rationality have been devised, the absolute necessity of analogic thinking is denied.

There is also what we call *gestalt* rationale.

Take a sheet of white paper, and put about 15 stripes of 10% gray on it. This 10% gray being defined as 10% black and 90% white. Each stripe is to be one inch wide. Let them intersect in such a way that all 15 stripes meet and cross at only one point, a point about 1/16th of an inch across. This one point is black.

But — there is no black line leading to it.

Logic works on a basis of True (very high probability) and False (not high probability). There is no line of high probability leading to the black spot; the highest probability is only 10%. Futher, even allowing your 10% probability, each line leads to 15 other areas as large as the spot you claim is highly probable.

Because logic is so designed as to consider only one line of evidence at a time, if there is a situation wherein the high-probability conclusion is produced by intersection and reinforcement of low-probability conclusions, it is impossible to find a *logical* proof of the existence of the high probability.

Our culture, however, acknowledges Logic as the *only* form of rationality.

Therefore all of your work is non-logical, because it depends on the higher orders of rationality — analogic and gestalt rationale.

One of the arguments I have heard against the psi functions is the claim of non-dependency on distance. This has been argued as being a demonstration that it is merely some type of systematic error that is showing up.

All presently recognized physical-force phenomona do show a distance-dependence, and the distance concept is deeply embedded in our current philosophy, as is the time-concept. But mathematical philosophers have developed some highly interesting logical proofs that make the distance concept meaningless.

The trouble is that the professional psychologist cannot permit himself to attack the basic assumptions of the experts in fields such as physics and philosophy, wherein he is not an expert.

The tyro physicist — the student of undergradute or graduate level — cannot appropriately do so either.

The older physicist will not do so; he is busy developing a line of physical demonstration that he initiated in his younger and most creative period.

But physicists in the 25 to 35 year age bracket are looking for new projects to study. They are, probably, most apt to be willing and competent to search out the new basic laws of the Universe which underlie the psi functions.

Getting them to do so, however, is something of a trick.

The psycho-socio power of fiction as a medium of communication has been somewhat overlooked and underrated, I believe. Jesus used fiction as one of his most powerful teaching tools.

I am trying to use fiction to induce competent thinkers to attack just such problems as the psi effects; my magazine is widely read by creative, speculative, physical scientists. The students at major universities read it — and so do their instructors.

Currently, I am seeking, through the fiction, to nudge interest in psionic powers as an engineering value. The engineer almost always precedes the scientist — a fact which the scientist tends to conveniently overlook. Engineers were using electricity quite successfully before scientists found out about electrons.

Engineers were doing some highly effective chemical production work before the scientists figured out why it worked. The engineer is a hard-working man, and in his frame of reference, theory is an interesting side-light — anything that he can use effectively, on the other hand, is a good and respected tool. "To hell with *why* it works! Let's make it work."

The last group of die-hard hold-outs against the psionic powers will be the pure theoreticians; only when the theory of the psionic functions has been reduced to the ultimate decimal of precision, only when the whole system of interacting forces involved is fully known, will they accept it.

The engineer doesn't demand that; if he can get something that works 20% of the time, and does a job that nothing else will do, under such conditions that the result of the process is worth 10 times the raw materials consumed in the process — why, so what if 80% of the process is spoilage? The 20% that succeeds more than pays for that.

To attract the attention and interest of the physicists, I have felt that what's needed is demonstration of PK that can move a needle. Mystics have moved needles around on table-tops; this doesn't count. But if you demonstrate to physicists that the mind can move needles around on instrument dials — they have to pay attention, because that throws all their instrument-readings into question!

If PK effects dice — how about some organic chemical reactions, where exceedingly delicate balance maintains between interacting dynamic molecular systems? The percentage yield of product A vs undesired product B might prove to be very detectably influenced by the PK effect of the experimenter! Demonstrate that one individual, Bill Blow, can increase the yield of a desired product 2%, and the Du Pont company's engineers are going to be most exceedingly interested. A change of 2% in the yield of some complex organics would be of vital economic importance. And I assure you, the Du Pont people's engineers don't give two hoots in hell why they get the extra 2%, just so they *do*.

Ask the Western Electric Company about the problems of vacuum tube cathode coating. Electronics looks like a nice, solid, rigorous science from the viewpoint of a psychologist; the engineers who have to produce tubes know better. They haven't the foggiest notion of why alkaline earth oxide coatings emit electrons better than raw metal. They can't even get graphical data that holds together; it won't make *a* curve; three different independent experimenters, performing the same experiment, get six different answers, and publish three different curves, curves which don't even intersect!

But the engineers are interested in getting production lines working. They grab at any idea that helps that all-important project.

The percentage of failures they get, even with their best efforts, is something outsiders don't realize. Whatever goes on in vacuum tube cathode coating, it's completely beyond present understanding. The engineers have some rules of thumb. They've observed as a fact that it's necessary for the tube coating department to keep a record of the menstrual periods of the girls doing the cathode-coating; during the menstruation, they produce defective cathodes. Engineers in the vacuum tube cathode department aren't physiologists or psychologists or biochemists; they solve the problem of "Why?" by simply keeping track of the menstrual periods and shifting the girls to other work.

Western Electric had one girl who established an incredible record of turning out cathodes that showed over 90% success. She happened to be a red-head. The tube-coating department told Personnel to send red-headed girls. No luck, but it was worth a try, in their state of near-total ignorance of causes.

Bell Labs stole their prize cathode-coater from them on the plea of research. They did do research, but they got nowhere. Eventually, reluctantly, they had to let her go; she had married, and shortly after she became pregnant her record of success dropped to about 65%.

Engineers frequently find themselves in spots like that; they're willing, then, to consider anything. Even a hint that red-head blue-eyed girls from Pennsylvania can coat cathodes better would have them scouting central Pennsylvania for blue-eyed red-heads just to see if it worked. These engineers aren't fools — they are so wise they know their own ignorance. It is not an engineer's business to be wise; his business is being successful. For him, then, "It works" is adequate. But the theoretician's business is being wise, even if the wisdom is unsuccessful. The theoretician feels satisfied when he has proven to his satisfaction that "What you want to be can't be done. I have proven it is impossible."

The horny handed engineer can be a great trial to such a theoretician. He's apt to go out and do that impossible, forcing the unhappy theoretician to revise all his theories.

In our fiction, therefore, our major attack on the Society's block against the psionic functions is at the level of engineering applications of the psi functions — and acknowledging that they work only statistically. The engineer is quite happy with statistical success, because he can simply use a factor of safety.

The psionic functions exist in all of us — but use of them is violently (and I definitely mean *violently*!) suppressed by the Society. This is not without reason; a Society cannot exist if its individuals don't acknowledge a mutual commonality. The psionically gifted individual, however, tends to splinter off and go his own different way. They tend toward egocentricity; see what happens in the Hindu culture where the psionic faculties are not so severely suppressed by society.

The psionically gifted individual can't teach his techniques to others. Our culture has, very wisely — however cruel that wisdom may appear to us at the moment — established a social rule "I'll believe it when you can show *me* how *I* can do it." That, more than anything else, is true basic of the Scientific Method.

That simple rule puts the Genius in harness to the benefit of the Group. His genius is not recognized by his group, he is not allowed the rewards of his accomplishment, until he has also genius powers to figure out a way of communicating what he has discovered to others of his culture group.

Western Culture has based itself on that; Eastern culture has not. That, however, is why Western Culture has inevitably and inescapably overwhelmed the East. It's at the root of the West's great belief in mass education; the genius must be harnessed for the benefit of the race. We don't allow the concept of the Holy Man who benefits no one but his own utterly selfish, egocentric soul; if he seeks to be so appallingly selfish, we simply ignore him and let him starve. A Vow of Silence is a petty thing indeed, in the West's opinion; it's the sullen anger of a child who won't talk because he feels picked on.

It's tough on Genius, no doubt — but it's been good for the race. If the psionically gifted genius is really good at it, he'll sooner or later use his gifts to figure a way to crack through that barrier, and find out *how* to teach his abilities.

The instant he can show another man *how to do it*, his full genius will be recognized and accepted.

Frustrating as it is to genius, it's the harness that thousands of years of trying has shown works for the greatest good of all Mankind.

Society's no fool; if the world-dominant Society shows certain characteristics, I have a tendency to assume that there is a validity in those characteristics that hasn't been fully analyzed. Frequently Society turns out to have made too broad a rule against something — but each of it's great negations is covering something that does need plugging up.

The Christian doctrine of "By their fruits ye shall know them" is solidly valid. "Make it work!" is the equivalent statement.

In fiction, I can make it work. Since human entertainment and relaxation is a very important aspect of living — why, I can make the psionic forces work very nicely, right now, at an engineering level.

But there's a sly trick here. If the reader is to enjoy the entertainment of the story, *he must temporarily accept the validity of psionic powers.* Never again can he be *wholely* opposed to the idea, for he has already accepted it in a certain degree. Accepting the idea is already associated with pleasure-satisfaction; that association makes it psychologically difficult for him to reject the idea flatly.

Give me time, Sir! I'm in your business too!

Sincerely,   John W. Campbell, Jr.

Alfred Bester   *February 25, 1954*

Dear Mr. Bester:

Maybe I'm peculiar or something, but I never saw any need for throat-cutting. There's enough work that needs doing to keep everybody busy; why try to hog it? Trying to compete gets everybody irritated in a rat-race; complementing each other is a lot less effort.

I think we need some good science-fiction radio shows; I know you write good science-fiction, and have had a lot of experience with radio shows.

Go to it, guy! Give 'em some good science-fiction shows for a change!

Regards,   John W. Campbell, Jr.

Hannes Bok   *February 25, 1954*

Dear Mr. Bok:

I'm afraid your heart belongs to fantasy — and my readers belong stubbornly to realism.

The worlds of fantasy are goals — fine goals. You call it Khoire in this story, and the story is the search for a bridge to get from Earth to Khoire.

That bridge isn't made of wishes; it's made of hard work. It's going to be built a piece at a time, and it's going to be engineered by thought and patience and work; it takes planning, and trying that finally finds the relationship between pure thought and pure material.

Science-fiction is working on the bridge. Fantasy says "The

bridge should be built!", but does mighty little toward the construction of a practical working philosophy.

I need science-fiction shorts and novelettes — and they're worth doing.

Sincerely,   John W. Campbell, Jr.

Re:"Va Khoseth Yaga!"

Lester del Rey   *March 25, 1954*

Dear Lester:

Once upon a time there was a scientist who knew *much* more about the actual forces available for application in the Universe than do the modern scientists. (Of course, this is impossible, as any scientist from King Cheops Chief Engineer down to the president of the American Physical Society can assure you, but we *can* pretend.) And this scientist knew that there were forces that were described as organizational forces; he shortened the name and just called them *psionic* forces.

He knew, as we do not as yet, that Process was a parameter of the Universe as real and unignorable as Distance or Time — and, actually, that these other two were simply misunderstandings of Process. He knew that Organization field-forces were, like electric and magnetic field-forces, inherently not-detectable by physical-matter level objects. You can't see, hear, or touch a magnetic field — you can only observe a seeable-touchable-hearable bit of matter that has been influenced by the field.

He knew, as Modern Science does not, that Love is a field-force just as magnetic is — and equally unseeable, unweighable, unpointable.

Now once, having been considerably pestered by some physical scientists who said he was a charlatan, a mystic, and a hoax — since none of the things he did could be described to them in the terms they acknowledged to be real (try describing the Aurora Borealis to a native of the Amazon Jungles) — he prepared for them two bits of cotton string, about 18 inches long. One he tied to a tag reading "Internal order" and the other had a tag reading "External disorder." And he said, "Here, my friends, are two strings. Neither of these can be broken by methods available to you. This one labeled "Order" has been saturated with a psionic organization field of great intensity, approximating the intensity of nuclear order. You will find that your mightiest tensile testing machines cannot break it; it will, instead, cut through any hardened metal bar you tie it to. And this other string is quite different; it is no stronger than any other bit of cotton string — but it has a disorder

230

field around it such that no organized effort to break it can reach it. Your mightiest tensile testing machines can't break it, either — but for a different reason. A fuse will blow; someone will clumsily drop the string just as he is about to tie it in place, a fire will divert your attention. Something, somehow, will always happen just as you're about to try its strength. You can tie up a package with it, and somehow it will just have such luck that the string isn't stressed."

They took the strings, and it was true that, mysteriously, the one had fantastic strength. But the other one proved to be a perfectly ordinary piece of string, with nothing unusual about it at all. It just happened that there were a few minor lab accidents, nothing in any way out of the ordinary, you understand, and they sort of loss interest in that bit of string. It was finally used to tie up some old letters that were going into dead storage, and when last heard of, was gathering dust in an unused warehouse. Still intact, of course, but only because nobody had bothered to try to break it — not because there was really anything unusual about it.

But the bit of string that had the incredible power, fascinated them beyond expression. It was powerful, spectacular, incredible, and they expended huge efforts in studying it.

Finally, they did succeed in anihilating it in a hydrogen-bomb blast, and within five years it had dropped out of discussion, because after all, they *did* break it, so it wasn't really unbreakable and besides the reports were probably mistaken anyway, and it was other men who had done the work and they must have made mistakes because everybody knows such things can't happen. Imagine saying a piece of cotton string cut its way through a carbide-coated, chrome-moly-tool-steel bar in a tensile testing machine!

But the scientists lost interest in the old Magician, because obviously there was nothing but nonsense to be gained from him.

And besides — he and his bits of string made them unbearably uneasy, and made horrible mists of confusion drift into their minds, so that the familiar shapes of their scientific ideas became distorted, as do familiar objects seen in dense fog, into nonsense figures, and monstrous things they preferred not to contemplate.

Some while later the Magician went back to the planet he came from originally. And although, in later years, Mankind explored the whole galaxy, it just happened that the great blue-white sun that illuminated his planet, although it was a class cAO super-giant visible from one end of the galaxy to the other — still, somehow, nobody ever bothered to explore that system. That is, nobody but a few philosophers, and a refugee or two, and they didn't count. Some expeditions *did* start for it, but they ran into something that diverted them from the original mission, and they just never did get there.

There was another planet of another sun, however, that had the whole galaxy's attention for a while. It had erected a strange force-wall that stopped every ship, torpedo, missile, ray, or energy-form they could hurl at it. The scientists of the whole galaxy concentrated their attention on that mysterious force-wall for four generations before they finally succeeded in smashing it. The force it took to smash it also smashed the sun into a super-nova, unfortunately, so they never did succed in making contact with the race that had invented the forcewall.

I thought you might be interested in this little story — and maybe do me a novelette on a quite different plot.

Regards,   John

Walter M. Miller, Jr. *March 25, 1954*

Dear Mr. Miller:

I'm not returning the manuscript "The Darfsteller," though I think about one or at most two more pages are needed. I think you've got a carbon of it, and can add to that, saving a lot of postage and useless effort.

The point is this: You're perfectly correct in saying that drama is inherent in Man, and not of any particular culture. The reason is that no man ever has, or ever will, tell the truth, nor can any man ever tell a lie — in the pure sense. Only God Almighty can tell the truth, because only Omniscience can make *any* statement that is utterly true. And it takes an equally Omniscient Power to tell a lie that is utterly false, for the same reasons.

Then Man lives always in a world of fiction, varying somewhere between the unreachable limits of Pure Truth and Pure Lie. The stage, then, is the only honest representation of life, because it, like the famous Epaminondas Paradox, says, "I always tell nothing but lies." And that is the one statement that forces any listener to use his own judgment.

But fiction in magazines and books is simply "closet drama." It, too, is saying, "I always tell nothing but lies." It, too, forces the reader, willy-nilly, to excerise his judgment.

But in order to induce the reader to expand very real effort in exercising judgment — and brother, believe me, that's *work* — the use of judgment must yield a reward *to the reader*.

As the yarn sets now, it shows that Thorny learned something, finally. "And," says the reader who's been aware that he was wrong for the last twenty pages, "it's about time!" And with self-satisfaction, the reader can lay down the magazine, your story, and the problem, and close it out of his mind.

But you don't *want* him to close it out of his mind! You want to leave it with fish-hooks stuck in his mind, where he *can't* get it out.

Well, the reader got it out by the process of convincing himself that he, the wise and understanding reader, could have solved that problem with no trouble. *He* got the answer long before Thorny did, didn't he?

So let's pull just enough of an off-beat item so that the reader winds up wondering, just a little, if he *is* able to solve the problem so neatly, after all.

If you make the problem appear general enough — he'll know he *hasn't* solved his own branch of Thorny's problem. That's why I suggested the business of the weavers trying to smash machines; your engineer, here, who tells Thorny he's to "start making little black boxes" could visit Thorny at the hospital, and bring out the really broad meaning of the problem.

It's so silly for a human being to insist on doing what a machine *can* do. What machines are *you* trying to compete with?

Regards,   John W. Campbell, Jr.

Harry Harrison   *April 4, 1954*

Dear Harry:

Pardon me, while I lay claim to that Mantle of Prophecy, my friend! Sure, **E. E. Smith** done did right good — but try this: — July editorial, 1936:

"The discoverer of atomic energy's key reaction is now living. His name is well-known, his papers have been published, and the key experiment has been described. The only trouble is we don't yet recognize *which* is his name, his key paper, his key experiment."

May, 1944. Story "Deadline," by **Cleve Cartmill**. **Cartmill** wrote asking "How would you arm an atomic bomb?" I answered, describing critical mass. Also described appearance of atomic bomb burst.

Editorial, Jan. 1946. Described use of U-235 as trigger to initiate a thermonuclear reaction, using either heavy hydrogen or lithium hydride.

Article "Bikini Balance Sheet," *Air Trails*, December, 1946. More detailed discussion of lithium hydride and heavy hydrogen thermonuclear reactions, specifying that LiH yielded about 2.3 times as much power per pound as U-235, and that it sold for about $12 a pound in contrast to U-235's high price. Also that the thermonuclear bomb could be made of unlimited size, since it didn't depend on critical mass.

Editorials subsequent to that have predicted other things which are not yet verified.

Current prediction: The development of transfinite logical

233

processes in the next decade or so will end war-as-we-know-it, but will in turn produce something several orders of magnitude more ghastly from the viewpoint of *Homo sapiens*. Mass destruction techniques against which material defenses of any kind — including distance-from-the-scene — are futile. Only individual abilities will serve as defenses. It will produce an apotheosis of the individual at a totally new level — and scare *H. sapiens* into the utter quivering meenies, since only an individual who has developed himself to the higher-order levels will be capable of protecting himself or any other individual.

In essence, what I'm saying is that what we have, in the past, called "witchcraft" or "wizardry" will be developed on a mathematical-logical-scientific basis. Material-physical defenses will be as futile against that as a wall of 10-foot thick concrete is against a magnetic, electric, or electromagnetic field. You can't block an e-m field with matter; it can only be blocked by a phenomenon at its own level.

Any idea that evolution has stopped is nonsense; the characteristic of evolution is that every so often a type shows up which isn't merely applying an old idea better, but is applying a new idea in a very poorly developed, but very, very deadly, way.

A fish, however competent, doesn't apply air-based techniques. And an air-based animal can apply attack methods that the fish cannot counter — the fish can't get at the air-breather at all. A gull may not catch the fish he aims at — but the fish can not hope to wipe out the gulls.

The saurians died for a most excellent reason, but one not visible to a purely physical-matter-based theoretical system. The mammals invented a technique of information-handling that was totally different from that of the reptiles, and hence applied a weapon that the saurians didn't have any possible method of countering.

The saurian is a preprogrammed mechanism; the mammal is a higher-order system, differing in basic concept in that it is not totally controlled by a pre-programmed system, but has a mechanism for generating new programs within itself.

There's another level beyond this, and Man's rapidly reaching it. Remember that the earliest animals using the mammalian program-generation system of information handling did not *physically* differ from the saurian pre-programmed type in any major degree.

Among the fiction authors, try **A. E. van Vogt**. That son of a gun is about one-half mystic, and like many another mystic, hits on ideas that are sound, without having any rational method of arriving at them or defending them. His "similarity transport"

234

shows exceedingly strong signs of having a basis in fact — but not at all the way he meant it.

In his yarn "Asylum," the central character turns out to be one of the Great Galactics that has occluded-from-himself the major portion of his own capabilities. At the end of the yarn, he has a hell of a time reintegrating, getting the fictional-limitation removed so that he achieves full self-awareness again. That shows signs of being a remarkably apt description of why a human being doesn't achieve his full potentialities. For a good purpose (acceptance by the world around him) he denies potentialities he does in fact have; the limited-self that is acknowledged feels that it will be "destroyed" if the total self is admitted.

Result: You have a hell of a time admitting to yourself that you can learn arithmetic easily and quickly — or a language, or what-have-you.

There's a lot of understanding in **E.E. Smith's** stuff — but not as much prophecy as there is in some of the wilder-and-woolier boys. Respect the fact that human beings are *not* fools; stop demeaning all your ancestors, and acknowledge that they had some kind of valid evidence of *something* that they called "witchcraft." You think that Mankind would have accepted it for nearly 100,000 years if there was *no* validity?

Logically, of course, there is none. But we happen to live in a highly unsure culture which uses, as a basic postulate, "All problems can be solved by logic, and if a problem is not solved by logic it is not solved 'really.'" Oh . . . yeah? Try solving this one logically: "Everything I say is a lie. Do you believe me?"

Is observational data "logical"? No, it's not — and the Greeks knew it wasn't, and wouldn't accept it !

One of the useful techniques of getting somewhere is to take a careful look at where you've been, determine where you are, and see if you can figure out how you got where you are. Maybe multi-valued logic is great stuff; let's find out what one-valued logic is, how it differs from two-valued, and see which direction of advance that suggests. Also, incidentally, we may find some of the remaining results of one-valued logic hanging around — some we could do without.

Think there isn't a one-valued logic? But of course! "A exists" is a one-valued logic statement; one-value logic consists solely of statements of "is" — things "are," but are-not-related. The concept of "not" doesn't obtain in a true one-valued logic.

What we *call* two-valued logic rests on a one-valued logic! It actually requires as its first step the acceptance of a one-valued logic — which is why we have to have postulates!

For example "Is it true this object is a table?" implies the true-or-false two-valued logic, as everyone consciously recognizes. But — it actually implies the previous acceptance of a one-valued logic statement "Tableness, or the potential-of-being-a-table, exists."

If you ask "Is this man a rocket engineer?" you recognize the pre-requistite condition that potential-of-being-a-rocket-engineer exists.

Ah, yes — logic is a tricky, tricky thing. You can't discuss "the rational processes underlying intuition," not in logic today, anyhow, because the concept, the potentiality-of-existence of "rational processes underlying intuition" is ruled as a non-existence class.

Now note that there's a difference between a *non-existent* class, and an *empty* class. It gets quite complicated, but I could ask "How many men born before the year 1700 are there in New York today?" Answer: Zero. The class is empty.

But if I ask "How many one-legged Martians with purple whiskers are there in New York today?" a peculiar confusion sets in. The answer is: Zero. See — same answer. If two questions have the same answer they must be alike, no? No, Egbert, they are *not* alike. The questioned class in the second instance is a non-existent class; whether that class is full or not I do not know; in saying "Zero" this time, I refer to the *class*, not to its fullness!

Man, oh man! Think that's just goobledegook and word-twisting? How many times have you had your ideas laughed to scorn because you believed in rocket ships before V-2's landed? Why the difficulty? Because you believed that the class *rocket ship* was a real class, but was an empty class, while your neighbors believed that the class itself did not exsist.

Such fun, we have, with that sort of problem!

Oh, hell! I can't write anything very illuminating right now. I've just succeeded in demolishing the underlying principles on which all my thinking's been done, and I'm going around in circles trying to find some new, and more resistant principles to use. The essence of growing up is learning the difficult art of How To Handle The Situation of Not Knowing How To Handle The Situation. Or How To Live In Ignorance And Stupidity. When I get it solved, I'll let you know. The general answer is "By a process of instantaneous research combined with instantaneous learning and action." Man exceeds anything any machine can do because he can handle a situation he was neither designed for, trained for, or has previously encountered.

To grow up, achieve perfect ignorance and perfect stupidity.

All I've got currently is odds and ends I haven't yet assembled.

But you might try this one and see how it fits with your "Waif of the Antar" problem:

The problem of loyalty and altruism is one of Man's oldest. It ranks right up there with Good and Evil for age, and difficulty. What are the limits of loyalty? At what point should a man turn against his friend, his family, his group, his country, or his Gods?

I don't know yet — but it's one of the problems that needs solving. But I have worked out this much: There must be a self-loyalty; without that, the whole scheme rests on nothing. Whether you call it "integrity" or what, you must have a form of self-loyalty. You can do nothing unless you can believe in your own ability to reach a meaningful decision.

(Computer language equivalent statement: A relay cannot cause a circuit-change unless it can stop chattering and settle to "open" or "closed.")

Given self-loyalty, proper development consists of widening spheres of awareness — and widening spheres of loyalty. First it widens to family, then to friends, then to group, and so on. The ultimate would be a sort of Cosmic Loyalty — loyalty to the Universe itself.

Fine — but there's a lot of people who've had their family, their friends, and their group turn against them (in their opinion) so that they're mighty skittish about any loyalty at that level.

When such a person becomes aware of the Race, and the Universe — that's the first level of higher loyalty that has *not* been soured.

You then have a guy who establishes a loyalty to Mankind and The Universe — and will altruistically sacrifice family, friends, group, nation, etc. on the High Altar of Race and Universe.

Altruistic son of a bitch, isn't he?

He's just skipping all the intervening process, and trying to work without the foundations that he needs. He doesn't actually feel any loyalty toward any individual human being; to him the individual is simply a unit-of-the-race, not a person at all.

He will protect and help that unit-of-the-race . . . so long as doing so appears, to him, to be beneficial to the Race. But that's the reason for his helping the guy.

Now we can define a Communist. He's a guy who is loyal to the Race and to the Universe and to his Great Ideals — and hasn't any loyalty at any lower level. He can be unlimitedly cruel to individual people, because the People must be advanced. He can enslave, degrade, destroy, and demean any person, because of the importance of People. He can betray his friends, his family, his group, his nation, because the Race and the Ideals are more important.

He can't get his self-loyalty into focus, because self-loyalty can be coupled to Race loyalty only through individual-person loyalty

— and that's been cut out of circuit.

The coupled-circuits concepts of electronics are exceedingly important, I think — in a far more wide-spread, generalized way than I ever realized. A lot of Information Theory and cybernetic analysis is damned important as fundamentals for human understanding. The cybernetics man says, "You can use a simple machine, and a complex program, or a simple program and a complex machine."

Evidently there will be an optimum somewhere on that deal — an optimum of semi-complex machine and semi-complex program.

The idea applies mighty broadly; logic is a simple thought-machine, so simple a relay-computer can do it. Given Omniscience and logic, all problems can be solved — but the program which involves Omniscience is just a bit complex for practical use, don't you think?

The level of Omniscience required for a logic machine is somewhat lower than that required for an Answer machine; an Answer machine doesn't figure anything at all out — it already has the Answer, and just disgorges it. It has The Answer for Every Individual's Problem.

The coupled-circuit business comes in here; the Answer machine must have one circuit, with unity coupling, from each problem to each Answer.

The Logic machine has a lower coupling factor; one Postulate is intercoupled with several Problems; it can't work with unity coupling.

I think you get the basic idea!

My problem currently is trying to work out a way of selecting *what* coupling from *which* problem to what postulate.

Write me again when I've dug my way out of this fog!

I never felt so ignorant and stupid in my life.

Regards,   John

James V. McConnell   *May 28, 1954*

Dear Jim:

Bob Heinlein was here the other day, and he complained of precisely the same phenomenon that you do; that I don't answer specific points. I don't, I suppose; I'm interested in general approaches, general methods, because at the present time we don't know enough to do much with specifics.

A fact is a single instance; as such it has zero meaning. Information theory shows that pure noise is the only situation of pure information. This is true, it is a valid statement, and makes sense — but it also means that facts *as such* are pure information which means pure noise. Meaning has to do with correlation — but information theory shows that pure correlation contains no information!

This reduces to the interesting set of Laws of Discussion:

1. In total agreement, there is no net communication possible.
2. In total disagreement, there is no net communication possible.

Then the optimum situation for discussion and learning is one in which two entities having a degree of disagreement between 0 and 1.000 establish a degree of communication. There's no point, in other words, in talking things over with someone who believes exactly what you do. It makes things easy and smooth, and a warm glow of self-confidence emerges maybe — but you don't get any net communication!

Facts are necessary — but, like bricks, they don't constitute a useful edifice. The whole is *not* equal to the sum of the parts; if it were, the noise I get from a too-high-gain amplifier would constitute the greatest series of statements of wisdom the world has ever heard.

I tend to seek correlations, and then go back to see if the facts fit the correlation. Then I throw away that correlation, and try another. Then — eventually I'll get one that allows me to explore for a new set of facts that does not fit the theory. You learn *only* when your theory stops working.

Item: Have you seen Sebastian de Grazia's "Errors of Psychotherapy"? I recommend it; the guy's done some thinking. He's stimulating me, however, to write a short paper entitled "Errors of 'Errors of Psychotherapy.'"

Re statistics and their utility as a tool. Tools are great business. They're wonderful. But don't try using a vise to pick up screws you've taken out of a wrist-watch; true, a vice, like a pair of needle-nose tweezers, is a clamping instrument — but there are differences that are noteworthy. And don't try holding a piece of strap iron in the needle-nose tweezers while bending it with hammer blows; put it in a bench-vise.

The actual place of statistics is one of those things the statistician is not very competent to work out. He sees everything as a statistical process — and gets damned funny results, too.

Statistics is a technique that groups instances, and reports on the observed behavior of a group-of-instances *as a group*.

It is a special form of generalization, based on a mathematical, and therefore describable-in-presently-available-terms, method.

But the characteristic of *any* statistical method is that it can describe *only groups*. It can never describe any individual of that group. I have, for instance, a set of drills, the statistical average diameter of which is 21/32 inch. But being a set of drills, no two of them are alike, and none, it happens, is 21/32nds in diameter. However, if I also give the datum that they are all hi-speed tool-steel alloy, and the average length is 3.67 inches, you can correctly calculate that, if the set is composed of 12 members, they must weigh so-and-so many grams. The statistics will, in other words, show a prefect correlation with observable fact.

Physical science uses statistical generalizations when, *and only when*, it is unable to solve the "laws of the system."

Note that Newton's Law of Gravity is a generalization of a totally different type. It is *not* a statistical generalization, yet is derived from observation of a large number of individual instances. But unlike a statistical generalization, it predicts individual instances of behavior.

The life insurance company can, and does, use statistics with great success. The practicing physician cannot; if the physician enters a house, asks the man's age, occupation, mother's age, father's age, etc., and says, "You'll be all right; you have another 22.3 years to live," he will make out fine — statistically, in the long run. He can, in fact, prove a high degree of correlation between his prognoses and the eventuations — far higher, in fact, than that obtained by a physican seeking to diagnose and treat the individual case.

There are *two different kinds* of generalizations.

The big company, the nation, the society, and the race can solve *their* problems successfully with the statistical generalization.

So can the academic psychologist, the medical foundation, etc.

BUT — the psychotherapist, the individual member of the race, society, nation, or big company, can *not* solve his problems statistically. Statistics isn't worth one hoot in hell to him.

The Natural Law type of generalization, on the other hand, can solve *both* the group's problems *and* the individual's problem. The Natural Law generalization can be used to generate statistical answers easily and directly, without having to take observations of individual instances. And it will solve the individual's problem too.

Incidentally, the statistical generalization is useful to a group — but useful solely as a half-ass sort of crutch. It is *never* really satisfactory. Instance: The statistical occurrence of treason at a critical national installation such as Los Alamos may be 0.001% — but the nation, for all its normal independance of the fate of the individual, the behavior of the individual is, in this case, totally unable to use statistical techniques and say, "Therefore, only 0.001% of the critical information will leak out."

240

Will an injection of novacaine — a normal local-anaesthetic dose — have appreciable effect on the personality of an individual?

Heh! Try injecting it via a transorbital route directly into the brain; it has the effect of a temporary prefrontal lobotomy. What happens while that dose is wearing off can cause a permanent change in the personality of the individual.

Incidentally, the psychologists, if they had any guts, would be really roaring about this business of the trial of the brain-washed individual. Can you birds induce a change of personality orientation or not? If you *have* a science, then whether a man has courage, determination, or what-not has no bearing on whether or not he makes a statement, and a man subjected to scientific psychological procedures can be made to confess to anything, and the military forces should stop kidding themselves that that isn't true.

Sure, you can't *cure* a psychotic — but Lord, man, you can *make* one easy enough! Prefrontal — transorbital — the transorbital novacaine — electric shock — psychiatric interviews. . . . Why hell, any powerful technique can either build or destroy, and it always has been easier to destroy.

Why not speak up and be heard, and speak up loud and hard enough to be both heard, and listened to. No man can resist the application of modern techniques, so stop pretending they can. The government should *order* all captured personnel to become psychopathic liars, agreeing freely to any statement wanted of them, and publish the fact that such orders have been issued. The present pretence that men can resist makes their duress statements have propaganda value; acknowledge to the world that no duress statement has any value whatever, and the Reds will have no propaganda benefit to gain from such statements, and will stop torturing the men to get them.

The lightning business is not merely "cute as hell as an example"; it's a legitimate example of a problem which cannot be brought into the laboratory until it's solved. By the time it's solved, it doesn't have to be brought into the laboratory to prove it's been solved. Lightning wasn't brought into the lab until about 1930, when General Electric wanted to study what happened to powerlines struck by lightning bolts, something that happened long, long after electrical energy was a common servant. That lightning *itself* wasn't useful is true enough — but that's the trouble, you see. Nobody would pay money to support research to tame the forces in lightning.

Nobody will pay money to tame the forces in spontaneous, naturally occurring psionic phenomena — so **Rhine** is very smart in getting backing in the terms the society accepts — statistics. *But* *statistics will never solve the problem*. Never. It's the non-statistical approach, the Law of Nature approach, that solves problems. Statistics is a crutch to use to *handle* a problem until such time as it can be *solved*.

A doctor cuts out a man's stomach, and thus handles the problem of his severe ulcers. Hell of a way to do things; ulcers are psychosomatic, but we can't solve that problem, we *handle* it.

"Only an imaginative individual who can conceive wrong answers can hope to solve new problems." Now look, Jim, if you *are* in Texas, and you want to *be* in Oslo, you have to do something *other than being* to achieve this; you have to *move*, which is other-than-being. From the viewpoint of what you seek — to "be in Oslo," that is — the "move" is a "wrong answer."

Note the typical human remark "Somebody should have figured this out," or "I don't want to talk about it; tell me how to fix it"! or "I want to know what to do! I don't want to argue about it"! Each is saying "I want to *be* at the right answer; I don't want to *move*." All learning involves a "wrong answer" — the process of going through a stage of confusion, wherein you have given up your old answer, and haven't yet achieved the new answer.

And that, I rise to assure you, is the most gawdawfulest "wrong answer" feeling you can ever hope to get tangled up in. Only the highly imaginative individual is willing to risk that violently unpleasant sensation of being fundamentally *wrong*, in having *no* answer. The psychotherapist's patient comes because he suspects his present answers aren't quite the best possible — but he doesn't want to let them go until he has a new set that works even better.

So sorry; he's damned well going to *have* to let them go, because their presence prevents the acceptance of the new group. Electric shock works just fine, because it mechanically drives the poor guy into such a state of violent confusion that, for a while, he dosen't know which are the old, and which are the new answers.

Go ahead — argue on it. You can unquestionably find a million different arguments that show it may be a wrong idea I have here. You certainly can raise objections to it; there are unlimited possibilities. The real question is, can I, with this theory of mine, get more results, with less effort, in less time, than you can with yours? If I can, it doesn't matter a damn bit whether the theory is true or not — it's useful. And I know that no theory any human being devises at this point is *true* anyway.

Congratulations on that chance to go to Oslo, incidentally. You're obviously doing fine business. How much a guy knows is not, and never was, very important in the long run — it's how much he can learn, and how fast he can unlearn. (Ever think of the importance of unlearning, by the way? It'll merit a lot of thought!)

The trouble with "results" in a psycholab or Journal is this; those results are necessary — but they are pitifully apt to end there. The mathematicians are the world's prize examples; a mathematician looks on you with deep hurt — as though looking at a desecrator of a sacred shrine — when you ask him what his branch of math is for. Why . . . it's for solving mathematical problems, of course, and getting results in the Journal! That's how a true mathematician makes his reputation, and builds his shining tower.

The trouble is the deep, human need for communication with a peer-group. The mathematician talks an esoteric language; he thinks in a special manner. A brilliant mathematician, then, can express his creative achievements *only* to another man who speaks mathematics. Only a fellow mathematician can appreciate his achievement — which is real, and worthy of praise. But he can get the reward of approbation which every human being needs *only* from one who can understand him.

This process is a self-seeking system; the math boys get more and more clubby; reward comes only from the approbation of other math sharks. Presently they write and work only with each other. Teaching students is now a damnable distraction from the *real* business of living-talking with math sharks. Instructing physicists in how to attack mathematical-physics problems is a drudgery imposed by the universities that takes valuable time from the fine, high thrill of getting a new achievement in the Journals.

". . . where the Cabots speak only to Lodges,
"And the Lodges speak only to God."

Watch out, **Jim** — and I mean this very seriously — that you, and psychology generally, doesn't fall into that same trap. There is still great personal satisfaction for the Journal-article writer — but it is one of the most beautiful fantasy-world escapes imaginable. It's a mutually-supported fantasy-world, where a whole group of powerful minds have come together to build a nice, warm fantasy-nest, where the *really* important things like the formula for generating prime numbers can be discussed thrillingly.

(**Claude Shannon** is in a hell of a spot; he's developed a basic formula that generates *all possible* prime numbers — and publishing it will ruin the lifetime contemplations of scores of mathematicians. **Claude**, being interested in electronic communi-cation and computer problems, doesn't give a damn one way or another, so he's sort of suspending it.)

There is a far more subtle form of paranoia that attacks the highest level of genuine genius — "They can't understand the value of our work." If one genius at a time says that, he gets snapped out of it by one form of starvation or another — either lack of nourishment, or lack of approbation. But if a hundred bright men agree, the resulting mutual admiration society is self-sustaining. It strongly resists external criticism, with "They don't understand the problem," or "They can't appreciate the importance of what we're doing." It's a hell of a tough problem, because it has a great measure of truth in it; they *can't* appreciate the problem.

Now by definition, a genius is non-normal. He is a deviant. Every human being needs free exchange of ideas and communication with his peer group. A genius, however, cannot establish free communication with Society, because he is not a member of that peer group. He can establish free communication with other geniuses of his own level. The result is a powerful tendency of powerful minds to establish peer-group cliques, and seek to wall themselves away from Society.

The danger and difficulty arises when the peer-group *as a group* starts drifting off into airyfairy land. Then any effort the society makes to say, "Look, boys — something's wrong with your results, here. . . ." brings forth a weary, resigned sigh, and, "You're not qualified to judge the work we're doing." And an acceleration of the group as a whole toward the wild blue yonder.

You've got a tough job on hand; getting sucked into a mutual-admiration society that depends on the Journals for its satisfactions, however, will make it easier to earn satisfaction — if it doesn't do anything to improve results in the real-world of desperately troubled human beings.

Regards, John

Banks *May 29, 1954*

Dear Mr. Banks:

Pardon a spot or two on this letter; the new ribbon and type-cleaning operation seems to have infected this with some unnameable disease. I shall throw this type-cleaner out at once — which is once too late.

To answer your letter.

I am now at something of a loss as to whether you approve or disapprove of the Earfriend and the individual "Variance" (i.e., fantasy-world) idea. I heartily disapprove; fantasy is essential, imagination is necessary — but not at the level of data. The individual must be aware of what *is* around him; imagination is necessary to understand the meaning of that data — but if the data itself is imaginary, or if imaginary data can be injected into the *is* level of experience, then we have an insoluble problem. Any problem can be solved by injecting enough imaginary data. If you come at me with a .45, I can inject the imaginary data that I'm really Superman, and bullets can't hurt me, so I have nothing to worry

244

about. This *does* solve the problem of worry; it's literally true that there will, thus, be no worry whatever. I'll be dead of bullet wounds before there's a chance to worry, so I *have* solved the problem of worry by injecting imaginary data.

It's rather like

Here lies the body of William Jay,
He died defending his right of way.
He was right, dead right, as he sped along
But he's just as dead as if he'd been dead wrong.

My statement that society is like an organism is to be taken seriously. I know it was abandoned years ago. So were a lot of other things that later proved valid. A society does have organization, or it isn't a society — and the nature of organization is necessarily basic to the problem of a living organism and to a going society. Just because an idea has been abandoned doesn't prove that it is useless; it may prove that they hadn't learned how to handle it yet. A kid may try to ride a bicycle, find it is too big and unwieldy for him, and abandon the idea — for a few years.

Newton went off his nut trying to solve the problem of the inter-relation of science and religion. So did Faraday. But that doesn't mean it can't be solved — just that they didn't have data enough to solve it without too-great strain.

In the mid-nineteenth century, Information Theory, cybernetics, and a few other useful tools of analysis of communication weren't around. Now they are.

Attempts to record sounds, to make a phonograph in effect, were also abandoned about that time. Therefore we must decide that phonographs should not be attemped?

Re transfinite logic. The logic human cultures are now operating on is evidently inadequate. Demonstration: we can't make it work. Now the fact that we can make something work does not prove it's sound; the fact that we can't make something work *does* prove that it's not sound.

The item about transfinite logic, for your information, is one a group of us has been working on; it includes two top symbolic logicians, a topologist, a cyberneticist-mathematician, several sociologists and anthropologists, and a psychotherapist. The idea is not proven, as I state above, but it works. It happens that it also permits a mathematical discussion of **Dr. Rhine's** psionic phenomona as a side-line result.

The notes in my last letter to you are in full disagreement with a major part of present sociological and psychological theory, as well as with a major portion of modern logic theory. They are the results of original research a group of us have been doing.

The proposition in transfinite logic is that *certain types* of

245

subsets of a transfinite set are themselves transfinite, and of the same cardinality. NOT all subsets. The numbers from 1 to 100 is a subset of the transfinite set of all whole numbers — but it is *not* of the same cardinality.

I do not, therefore, imply that "everything equals everything." I imply that "Things can be equivalent without being identical."

An excellent geometrical example is the matter of topological transformation. A circle is equivalent to an ellipse, with the operation of a simple transformation known as "projection from an angle."

I do not eliminate hate, but I do suggest that it has a topological transformation of different form; the amusing thing is that instead of being the antithesis of love, it proves to belong to the same set! That's why it appears that you cannot have love without hate; you cannot have a circle that does not appear as an ellipse from some angles.

The further difficulty in your interpretation is that you have not, apparently, encountered the transfinite cardinality concept before. There is an heirarchy of transfinites, just as there is a sequence of cardinal numbers. Cantor designated them as *alephs*, and the infinity of ordinary numbers is the lowest order of transfinites, aleph-null. Corresponds to zero in the normal number system.

Therefore achieving infinity is nothing! You have to achieve an infinity of infinities.

Mathematical logic is useful, because, by oversimplifying the real universe, the interacting entanglements of the real world can be studied. That doesn't make the real world an unentangled simplicity — but it helps you follow the entangled threads, and see the patterns they have been woven into.

You gave a list of characteristics of a man, and asked me to "give the digits for" such characteristics. "A man who is womanish," etc. Sure thing, friend. Any punch-card operator at Central Casting will do it for you. That's how they use IBM machines to find the character actors they need — by assigning digits to various characteristics, and setting up punched cards to correspond.

Matter of fact, you've done it yourself. The term "womanish" is a visible symbol of a complex concept. Just because you can't multiply, add, or divide that kind of symbol doesn't mean that it can't be manipulated by appropriate techniques. Symbolic logic does just precisely that.

Sure, there's a hell of a lot beyond the boundaries of any logic we've ever worked up. That's my point! Logic *can't* handle the problems we've got — so when human beings do handle them in a manner logic says, "But you can't *do* that!" about, the man, who's just done it successfully, is called "irrational."

That is precisely my point. All the logic mankind has ever developed is a snare and a delusion, because it's inadequate. But when a human being, using more adequate methods, gets a usable answer, he's railed at for being illogical or irrational.

Look, the experimental method is inherently illogical. That's why the Greeks wouldn't use it. It is NOT logical; it's pragmatic. Many times its results are contrary to logic; the Greeks resented this so deeply they refused to use it. (We know the answer is, in such cases, that the basic premise of the logic was false.).

But there is, equally, a non-logical method of reaching a conclusion, called "intuition." There is *no* logical method that can yield a conclusion applicable in an individual case. Statistical methods will yield generalizations applicable to general cases, but *not* applicable in individual cases. (The insurance company can use the conclusions; the individual policy-holder cannot.) There is *no* logical method of reaching a Natural Law type of generalization — it can be done only by a not-yet-describable process called "the intuitive method."

This business of trying to insist that a man's higher functions are solid all the way through, like a potato, is yours, my friend, not mine.

Let us say I have a tuning condenser made of aluminum and steatite and invar — a very high grade tuning condenser, very massively and solidly built. I also have a piece of silver-wire flexible cable, and a vacuum tube. You find me attaching these units, one to the other, and say, "Ah, doing some electronics work?"

Nope; I'm going fishing. The condenser has mass, and is a good sinker. The vacuum tube, being water-tight of course, is my float. The silver wire is my leader.

Or, again — I'm doing some chemical corrosion-resistance tests; I'm interested in the corrosion-resistance of the materials of these units when sunk in 0.1 N HCl.

It's utter nonsense to consider that *any* entity, living or inorganic in structure has *a* characteristic property.

But it's not inappropriate to say, "This is called a condenser, because it's structure is such that the capacitative characteristic is readily accessible and usable." It's also a mass of aluminum, having chemical properties (which must not be forgotten if it is to be used by the Navy!) and a variety of other properties. It would, for instance, serve nobly to bean invading enemy.

Hell man, you can deflect any argument you choose to. So can I. I can make you chase yourself in ringtailed circles, by simply over or under-literally interpreting the words you use, misusing the fact that *all* English words have multiple meanings or multiple implications, and keep you from getting anywhere as long as I choose to. You can say, "A man needs a certain amount of play," and I can argue with you that drama is a waste of time, or that freedom to wiggle about slightly is conducive to license, or — hell, the word "play" has 55 definitions. Want me to make you make you define your way out of all them?

Any intelligent man can, in an argument, deflect the idea he finds distasteful for as long as he wants to. I've made a special and elaborate study of the actual techniques used, because I had to find out what the hell was going on in the problem of communication.

It boils down to this: you can NOT force communication on someone who doesn't want that communication, and knows he doesn't. The only hope you have is to get around back of him, and feed him an idea he thinks he wants — with the idea he doesn't want buried in the middle of it so skillfully he can't see it. When he digests the idea he does want, it's too late to resist accepting the unwanted one.

Most human quarrels are based on the other standard technique: "I won't accept your idea at all, in any degree whatever, until you have demonstrated willingness to accept my idea for consideration." Then to get your idea over, you have to — the other fellow hopes — accept his.

Of course it doesn't work, but it's a nice try.

So. . . . O.K., you don't want to consider the validity in the ideas I presented. You don't have to, and I won't try to force it on you. There *are* techniques that *will* force an idea on another mind . . . but are not recognized in any present day official science or technology. They exist . . . but only in some long-abandoned technologies are they recognized. We've been studying them, and believe me, they work like a charm! Only trouble is, since they *do* work, the use of them produces the unsatisfactory situation of producing yes-men, not intelligent co-workers.

Your "Happiness Effect" story hit the nail on the head, as I said. The idea behind the above statements was used in the story I did (my first in 14 years!) for **Ray Healy's** anthology *9 Tales of Space and Time*.

One of the great troubles is that when A has an idea, and tries to get B to consider it, A is apt to feel that B must not have considered it if B rejects it. Maybe B *has* considered it, and considered it carefully . . . and still rejected it, because of something B knows that A doesn't. Most people consider that "consideration" and "full belief in" are necessarily the same. Reason: I have considered idea P. I believe in it. Any intelligent person (like myself) who considered P would, as I know, believe in it also. Therefore if Bill Blow does not believe in it, he obviously has not *really* considered it.

See? Perfectly logical, ain't it?

The trouble with your "Earfriend" idea is that it's negation of problem-solving as an activity of Mankind. And that's the idea that the science-fiction fraternity refuses to accept — despite the pressure of their friends, family, teachers, co-workers, bosses, and children. They won't accept that idea — so why should I?

Regards,   John W. Campbell, Jr.

Harry Kuttner   *June 7, 1954*

Dear Harry:

Bob Heinlein came east, and we met again for the first time in five or so years. Since a lot of water has flown under a lot of bridges, we started sort of out of phase; dunno if we ever did get back in phase. You'll probably hear from him; you've heard from me somewhat more regularly than he has, so you may get a different impression. There was a certain degree of mutual irritation, due to the out-of-phase relationship.

You know, two currents of the same frequency, the same character, can buck each other more efficiently than two currents of different character. The closer the actual agreement, the more apparent difference there is!

There are some people — particularly the scholastic-scholarly type — who consider the term "research" to be simply and exclusively the plural of "plagiarize." That's one extreme of the concept. The other, of course, is the guy who thinks *nothing* anybody else ever did has any value whatever. But getting a proper balance in between is a damn tough job — and defining that balance caused something of an argument between **Bob** and myself.

He also somewhat mistook my attitude in another respect. I'll bet the good householders of Lexington and Concord regarded Paul Revere's hullabaloo in the middle of the night a god damned nuisance. After all, if some bird coming yammering through the town yelling, "Get out of bed and stand up to be shot by the British!" comes along, it *is* a damned unpleasant disturbance. Irving Berlin put it

"Some day I'm going to murder that bugler,
"Some day they're going to find him dead!
"I'll amputate his reveille,
"And step upon it heavily,
"And spend the rest of my life in bed."

Bob maintains that I can't do research because I don't have higher mathematics. Yeah — and neither could **Nicholas Cristofilos**. Only he could get a patent on an idea that worked.

249

Oh well, anyhow, that wasn't the main point of this letter.

I'm setting up a flicker-source. I'm planning on doing it the cheap-and-nasty way, using gimmicry I have on hand. One 6-watt fluorescent tube, replaceable by a 6-watt UV tube I got hold of in surplus 5 years ago. Excited by an 807 running on about 400 volts, driven by a keyed 6AK5 oscillator, xtal controlled. (Don't need the 25 watts output available from the 807 at 400 volts, so don't need full grid drive. It'll give me about 1 watts RF running practically class AB-1. The xtal controlled 6AK5 is easier to set up than an LC controlled osc, and I've got a handful of xtals handy.)

The 6AK5 will have the screen tied to a 6J6 plate; the 6J6 will be fired by a miniature thyratron. All components on hand, so cost me nothing.

In doing some preliminary experiments, I tried out the tube by hanging it on my 75 meter medium transmitter, and hand-keyed it. **Leslyn**, age 9, watched, and objected that it was annoying. (I wasn't, of course, anywhere near the 13 cps rate — but small kids don't have a stabilized alpha rhythm, either.) She wanted to know what it was for.

In the course of discussion, I found an interesting item. She considers the Law of Gravity unfair. She also considers the fact she can't walk through walls, and the fact that an electric shock will make a muscle jump, willy-nilly, unfair.

Now it is not specifically true that Ontogeny Recapitulates Phylogeny . . . but it is generally true. The ontogeny of an individual *does* give hints and clues and analogies of the phylogeny of his species. Futhermore, it does NOT stop at birth. The two-year-old displays the lone-wolf orientation of pre-tribal man. His pet phrase is "I Won't!," seconded only by "I Will!" Anything interfering with either of those is violently distasteful.

Man, in evolution, passed through a stage, I suspect, where he was so damned dangerous that *no* other animal species dared attack him very freely. He didn't *have* to huddle for protection, as the deer and zebras do. Like the tiger, he was so viciously deadly a fighter that nothing in the jungles bothered him, if the other creatures were aware of Man's presence.

Since he didn't *have* to seek safety-in-numbers, individuals wandered free.

That stage, I suspect, is represented in the two-year-old's vigorous "I won't!"

Man today doesn't huddle for *protection*; he gathers together for *mutual achievement*. A thousand men together can accomplish tasks inherently impossible to one. Let's see you build an automobile, for instance. Starting, of course, from minerals.

Now there's three billion years of animal experience, too, in which conscious awareness of compulsion as such was associated exclusively with the situation of being compelled by larger and stronger jaws. It was the immediate prelude to death and digestion.

An animal is compelled — by the Law of Conservation of Energy — to eat. But the animal doesn't know that; he's conscious of a *desire* to eat, and totally unaware that the *desire* is simply and solely a trick gimmick mechanism that makes him aware of the compulsion before the necessity becomes drastic. An automobile, not having such a mechanism, runs along happily until all the fuel is gone — and then can't move to get any.

Man's desires are, in essence, neat little mechanisms for forecasting necessities. But they don't feel the same as external compulsions!

The same compulsion-turned-into-desire mechanism yields that interesting human behavior pattern known as the "You can't fire me; I quit" mechanism. "You can't compel me to do that; I like it."

All of which leads up to an interesting thing. Leslyn, being a kid, can recognize and admit that she doesn't LIKE not being able to walk through walls. Hell, I don't either . . . but brother, I ain't that honest! I pretend I do. She doesn't like it, admits she doesn't like it, and calls it "unfair."

There's a yayhoo that owes me $1500. He sold pocket book rights to "Who Goes There?," collected the cash money in his greasy little paws, and considers it "unfair" that I'm putting the heat on to make him let go. Same mechanism. He is saying "I won't! You can't make me!" like a two-year-old.

O.K. Comes the $64 question: What are *we* refusing to admit is a compulsion . . . even though it damned well is?

The human being violently detests admitting there is a compulsion he can't get out of. Probably the rights on that $1500 deal will wind up with the bastard keeping me from getting my money. I'll get $1500 or more out of his pocket all right, but neither one of *us* will have it — the opposing lawyers will. He *can't* keep me from forcing him to hire a lawyer — but he'll still be able to remain as crazy as he is, because he'll hold, internally, "*See* . . . you *didn't* get it, did you! Yah! Yah!"

Why didn't the Greeks invent true science? Why did Islam? Why, after Islam invented it, did the highly cultured Chinese and Hindus, with whom they were in close commercial and intellectual contact, *not* learn it, while the Christians who were, in most essentials, a bunch of hairy barbarians, *did* learn it?

Proposed answer: Because Science is the first step of *a philosophy that admits compulsions*. You do NOT have a right to your own opinion.

And the Semitic Yaweh concept is the first step of a religious

251

philosophy having precisely the same characteristic. "Thou shalt have no other gods before me, for the Lord thy God is a jealous God!" "Vengence is mine, Saith Jehovah!" The ancient Hebrew concept was of an implacable, inescapable source-of-opinions that you could NOT argue with, and could NOT buy off, deflect, alter, or bargain with.

Their error was in the last conception; it isn't quite that way. The laws of the Universe can NOT be broken . . . but honest, fair bargains can be made. If you climb against gravity, you don't break the law of gravity; you do, however, pay a fair fee in energy. The potential purchase will be returned, in full and exact measure, if you surrender that potential.

It's a curious thing that missing that one aspect of the basic character of the Universe explains most of the troubles of the Jews. If bargains can't be made, then there's no point in trying to change; a man is what he is, and there's no use trying to be different. If you're put in a ghetto, there's no use trying to change enough to get out. And there's no point in fair bargains in a cruel implacable universe; make the best bargain you can, chisel all you can out of the obdurate Universe.

The characteristics peoples (and not just *our* current people, but some eight different cultures over 4000 years!) have held against the Jews are expressed right there.

The Greeks didn't have science, because, to express the situation in modern, slangy terms, their situation *appeared* to them to be, "Well, what if you did get Zeus mad at you? So you broke his rules. What of it? Get wise, guy — come on over to Poseidon's temple, and we'll quash that case quick. You know Posiedon's mad at Zeus anyway — just slip Poseidon a nice offering, and you can quit worrying about that summons."

The Law doesn't work very well when you have such a system; respect for the existence of compulsions disappears. I have an unlimited right to my opinion, and if Zeus doesn't like it, I'll get Athena or Vulcan or somebody on my side.

The characteristic of the child is that he doesn't recognize the existence of limitations on his right to an opinion. That's the characteristic of the primitive, the tribesman, and the early, polytheistic human cultures.

It's also the characteristic of most people in our culture today. They hate science, because it's cold and heartless and materialistic — *because it is compulsive.*

Now the social scientist displays a remarkable tendency to rigorously deny *any* compulsive laws in his field of activity. Statistical laws . . . yes. Tell him "Data shows that 99.99% of human males do X." And he says, "Well, well! Do they? How interesting."

252

But he says "they," and is comfortable because the statement can be shed from himself. It's not compulsive.

The whole effort seems to be to achieve methods of compelling without being compelled. (Equates with the animal effort to eat without being eaten!) A man studies semantics so he can compel the other fellow . . . and use the tricks so he can't be compelled.

What is the next level of science?

Betcha its one that compels in a manner we furiously seek to deny! *That it compels desire.*

Physical-material science has the resultant "I can make you do," but the next level may involve "I can make you *want* to do. . . ."

With electric current, I can make your arm move, whether you like it or not.

With psionic current, suppose, that I could make you *want* to move your arm . . . whether you like it or not!

Lordee, man! Would the human race battle furiously against the acceptance of any such discovery! Against the admission of such a situation!

Item: I do NOT say that that is the case. Note carefully that fact: I DO NOT SAY that that is the fact. I *do* say that it is worth observing that *a level of science can be blocked from discovery by human beings, if human beings refuse its implicit consequences.*

But *a robot could discover it.*

Therein, I think, may lie a fascinating story. The robot, operating entirely on compulsive forces as it does, would *not* have any resistance to discovery of a compulsive force.

But what would be the reactions of the men who were working with the robot? How would they react if, every time they set up their computer, they got the same answer, one which they "knew" was wrong?

Don't tell me that the pure and noble impersonality of the Scientist, Dedicated to Truth as he is, would make them accept it easily or willingly. They wouldn't.

The Chinese were very great philosophers and extremely acute observers. See how much of astronomical records goes back to their early scientists. They had the Pythagorean Theorem laid out in mosaic tiles some 1500 years before Euclid. They had a great, rich, and cultured Empire.

But they couldn't learn Science. It contains that which no philosopher can readily acknowledge; that he does *not* have an unlimited right to think, to have opinions, or consider ideas. The ancient doctrine of the Church that there are things it is not good for man to investigate *is right* . . . at any given time. Vide Isaac Newton, who collapsed completely, great as his mind was, when he tackled a certain problem area. Vide Michael Faraday who,

253

tackling that same problem area, also collapsed.

And yes, I know damn well that there *is* danger in tackling that problem area today. It *is* dangerous to tackle *any* field containing real manifestations which are not yet understood and known — as is necessarily the case in any research. **Ed Francisco** is referring to that when he speaks of "the unlimited 'why.'" You're in damn serious danger there, working with rocket motors. Some of the boys at Los Alamos died of working with their Unknowns.

It *is* true that there are areas that it's not safe to think into, because thought is a real phenomenon, having real manifestations.

And, dammit, that is precisely what the philosopher does NOT want to admit!

Think there's a story plot in there? The robot that keeps giving the answer that none of the human beings can bring himself to acknowledge? The *robot* is not capable of true thought; it could explore the consequences safely. The men . . . watch 'em run!

Your strobe lamp didn't mind flashing 13 cps, did it? A photocell wouldn't mind watching it, would it? And you wouldn't mind watching it flash 15 cps, would you?

Regards,   John

Thomas Purdom   *July 8, 1954*

Dear Mr. Purdom:

In my opinion, the value of the space station as a military device has been completely answered by the suggestion of attacking it with an "orbital shotgun attack."

The space station's orbit will always be accurately known to all nations; by its nature it is not maneuverable, and is extremely observable. The enemy can, then, send up a single relatively small, unmanned rocket, putting the rocket in the same orbit as the space station, but in an opposite sense. The rocket's war-head need be nothing more than about a ton of cast iron, and a small explosive charge barely capable of shattering the warhead.

The result will be to sow the orbit of the space station with fragments of cast iron having a relative velocity of about 8 miles a second. These fragments will continue to orbit until such time as they have all been absorbed by the space station.

The first move a nation would make in contemplating war would, then, be to render the space station uninhabitable. Further, Russia would do so without intent of war; they have a fanatical secrecy drive, and the violation of their privacy would, itself, be unbearable. They are, mentally, akin to a prudish girl, who would react to the existence of a spy-ray as an unbearable invasion of her privacy, whether it was used or not — it's mere existence would be intolerable.

254

The space station, therefore, simply cannot exist while the Iron Curtain psychology exists. It's much too easy to destroy a space station.

Sincerely,   John W. Campbell, Jr.

Enc.: "Space Power and World Peace"

Isaac Asimov   *August 13, 1954*

Dear Isaac:

The Second Edition arrived yesterday; haven't had a chance to read it, but it's a handsome looking job.

Reading bio-chem is not something I can handle in heavy doses, and enjoy it. So it'll take me a couple of weeks to get the differences.

This letter's primarily to acquaint you with some interesting data that's been showing up. "The Cold Equations" has received a hell of a reception; some are hotly mad, some are warmly enthusiastic — but none are coldly indifferent.

You know the old business about a novel being supposed to show the development of a personality. Well there's a reverse English on that that an author can get away with . . . if he's good enough. That is to present an unacceptable character, and not change *him*, but make the *reader* change!

Godwin accepted the unacceptable proposition "It is right and proper to sacrifice a young woman." That's been out of fashion, highly unacceptable, since the Azetecs stopped sacrificing them 1000 years ago.

But you see, it's *not* wholly wrong! **Godwin** made the point; the reader is forced to agree that there is a place for human sacrifice.

We have another one coming that will, I think, lift some more hair on end. **Polly & Kelly Freas** read it when **Kelly** took it home to illustrate — and fought about it for a week. (That's the kind of yarn I like — the reader doesn't sigh, yawn, and turn the page to the next one.) (Should human beings be treated as animals held for breeding purposes? Answer: Yes! Under these circumstances. . . .)

Poul Anderson has a character in his new novel that will stir some discussion too. She introduces herself to the hero — Langley, 21st century American, irrevocably time-displaced to 72nd Century culture of aristocrat-commoner-slave-by saying, "I'm Marin. I'm a Class Eight slave. I'm 20 years old, a virgin, and Soandso bought me from the Xxx breeding and training center to give to you."

Marin has been selected and slightly altered by plastic surgery till she's a physical duplicate of Langley's time-lost beloved wife.

When he first sees her, it throws him into a tizzie, naturally — because she's the living, walking image of his lost beloved.

But — his wife was never a slave, and never accepted a slave philosophy. Marin is — and **Anderson** presents the fact with the brutal directness implicit in her introduction. Later Langley asks why Soandso gave her to him. Does he expect Langley to be overcome with gratitude?

"Oh, I don't think so," Marin says, "I'm not a very expensive present."

Langley is presented with the damndest emotional snarl you ever heard of — and, therefore, the reader is too. He's feeling bitter and upset, and says to her, "All right — you're mine. That means anything goes?"

She says, "Yes, sir." But he can see that she knows, of course, that there are perverted and sadistic buyers — and is facing up to that possibility.

He can return her, sell her, give her away, free her, possess her, or kill her. She's his as much as a radio set would be.

But — she's the girl who looks exactly like his beloved wife. He can't sell her . . . because he can't face the fact that there are sadistic buyers. He can't give her away or return her for the same reason. Free her? She's a highly bred, highly educated, thoughtful young woman. The Class Eight slaves are bred and trained as concubine-companions for the high-level aristocrats — and they're high-level people. Freed, she has the choice of being a commoner's wife, a servant, or a prostitute — and no chance of meeting the kind of people whom she is bred and trained to enjoy and understand. Freeing her would be a cruel punishment, without just cause, based on his fanatic insistence of no-slavery.

His orientation and conditioning make possessing her unacceptable .

The most practical solution would be to kill her; it would save him a lot of trouble. That is, it's practical *logically*!

Naturally he's a sucker for her; she *is* practically identical to his lost wife. But — he can't accept her acceptance-of-being-a-slave. He can't love her, because he can't *win* her love; it was *given* to him by her buyer, and the conditioning she was given at the training center.

Marin's prize line is, in effect, "Yes, I have been conditioned to accept my owner. It is my function in life. But every woman's function is to want a man, and love him. And aren't we all conditioned — you, I, everyone? You were conditioned haphazardly by life; my conditioning was thoughtfully planned — but we're all conditioned."

What **Poul's** done is to use his anthropological background to present something you damned seldom get a chance to look at; the fact that a highly intelligent human being can rationally accept being a slave. Aesop, you know, was a slave.

And it takes courage — real guts — to *accept* slavery. To *be* a slave is a passive thing, and takes nothing beyond physical existence. But to *accept* slavery takes high courage — as Marin displayed in her answer to Langley's "That means anything goes?" The free man can run out if he doesn't like the job ahead; one who has accepted slavery knows he can't — knows he's accepted the risk and the tough spots. Acceptance of slavery means accepting the risk of the sadistic buyer — precisely as accepting Life means accepting Death, too.

I've been looking at some of the possible interpretations of history in the light of what **Anderson** presented there. Ever try to define what "slave" means? Very difficult, it turns out.

Consider this: I propose that high-level culture can result only from a race that has accepted slavery — *being* slaves!

The Amerindians, you know, could not be enslaved; they died.

Now there is a curious thing; the parasite-host relationship appears to be rather like the master-slave relationship. But . . . symbiosis merges without break into parasite-host relationship. And true cooperation is mutual slavery!

Who's the slave? A child appears to fulfill the legal definition of a slave. I can, by will, give my children away, as I would a slave. They must obey my commands, and if they do not I am legally permitted to — and socially expected to — apply corporal punishment.

They're slaves aren't they?

No; I'm the slave. I am legally required to support them in idleness by the sweat of my brow.

Well, maybe **Peg's** the slave, then? She has to wash and clean and mend and care for my house.

But no, I'm the slave; I'm legally required to support her.

Who's the slave?

We all are! But it's symbiosis — not parasite-host relationship we're looking at. It's slavery with 100% negative feedback, so that cause and effect are inherently indistinguishable.

But you see, only a people who can accept slavery, and has the courage to stand up and say — *and mean* — "for richer, for poorer, for better, for worse, in sickness and in health. . . ." and knowingly accept the risk of the sadistic partner, the good with the bad — only such a people can establish true cooperation.

The courage of the free man has long been sung.

Maybe . . . could be perhaps . . . it's been somewhat over-rated? Maybe it's the courage of the egomaniac? The courage of the irresponsible?

It doesn't, of course, take anything but existence to *be* a slave.

How many people have the courage to accept in full the consequences of slavery, though?

Stories in there, possibly?

Regards,   John

P.S. Langley finally gets some understanding of the meaning of conditioning. He marries her.

Theodore Sturgeon   *September 13, 1954*

Dear Ted:

Did I ever tell you, "Write me a story about this subject, in n-thousand words?" It's you I want in the magazine — not me in false whiskers. What do you think needs writing about?

This recent experience of mine may start you thinking about something, though. I got a letter from **Harry Stine**, one of the rocket engineers at White Sands (who writes under **Lee Correy**) telling me off for my comments to him on the force-field drives, and the **Gunther** article series. He said, in effect, "We've been looking for it (the force-field drive) for a long time, and we haven't got a glimmer of it yet. I think the rockets will be flying their trajectories between the planets for years and years before we do see one. From where I stand with my feet on the ground, and my head on tight, talk about such drives doesn't make sense."

This, **Theodore**, *I* get from a *rocket* engineer.

I think his irritation at me stems from the fact that it was my work in *ASF* that turned his life-work into rocketry . . . and now, he feels, I'm unconscionably running out on him. Saying rockets aren't worth while, after I'd sold him on them. . . .

I wrote him a letter from which he will gather that it's mainly sour-grapes on my part. Neither **Willy Ley** nor I were able to get into the real rocket work; we came along too early.

As a matter of fact, my job isn't, and never was, working in the actual field. I'm like the professor who doesn't build bridges; his time is occupied getting young men dedicated to building better bridges.

Once, I believed that it was important to start opening the field of rocketry. I don't believe that any more; that field *is* wide open, and going great guns.

But **Harry** feels kind of hurt.

And I never quite expected to be told off for being too visionary — by a rocket engineer.

Regards,   John

Dear Horace:

I think a major part of the disagreement between your statements and mine lies at the level of semantic confusion; what you mean by "permission" evidently isn't quite what the term means to me. (**Peg** and I had a wonderful running battle over the word "need"; we finally discovered that our disagreement was due to the fact that "need," to me, meant "dire need," as Man needs air, food and water. To **Peg**, it meant "desirable for satisfactory living," which is considerably broader.)

Also, your concept of "Authority" must differ from mine; I distinguish between an "expert" and "an authority." An "authority" suggests wisdom, broad understanding, and integrated realization of the interrelationships between many facets of a problem-field. "An expert" has special knowledge; it need not be broad, but must be deep.

I am, unarguably and beyond doubt, the world's greatest and best informed expert on what I, **John W. Campbell, Jr.**, think. That doesn't make me an authority on thinking, however. No one on Earth knows more about what **Horace Gold** thinks and feels than you do.

One consequence of that is visible on a more general field in one of the objective sciences such as physics or chemistry, or a defined-science such as mathematics. A friend of mine, **Warren Seamen**, is one of the world's greatest experts on computing machine number-theory. Another friend of mine, **Gib Hocking**, is one of the top experts on topology. They're both mathematicians, and they can scarcely talk to each other, they're such experts. A third friend, **Wayne Batteau**, knows much less mathematics than either of them . . . but is an authorty on mathematical methods.

I feel it's important to distinguish between expertness and authoritative knowledge. Any fool can become an expert; even a book can be an expert! Expertness merely means the possession of more immediately available relevant knowledge than the normal.

A true authority is something else again; he may need to consult a battery of experts, but he can achieve things in each of the expert's fields that the expert can't!

Many a parent is an expert, and a good one, but a lousy authority. The Absent Minded Professor, for example, may be the father of a boy; the AMP is the world's greatest expert on the history of Rome between 1 A.D. and 157 A. D. we'll say. But he's exceedingly unwise in living; he can't tell a joke from a serious statement, can't balance a check-book, and is such a very gentle, kindly man everybody and his brother takes him for a sucker. He's unquestionably an expert . . . but is he an "authority"?

For me, it has proven necessary to go back one step futher. "Who says Mr. X is an authority? Mr. Y does? Well, is Mr. Y an authority on whether Mr. X is an authority or not, and who says he is? Mr. Z says Y is an authority on whether X is an authority or not? How does Z know?"

Evidently, this interesting round-robbin is going to get us nowhere. Properly set up, we can begin with a nit-witted dope, who says a frazzle-domed fool is wise. The frazzle-dome testifies that Dr. Addlepate Grimace is a great authority on psychic problems. Dr. Addlepate Grimace gives as his authoritative statement that Mr. Crecy McStupp Kidd is a sound, wise thinker. Mr. Kidd, in turn, asserts the nit-witted dope is an excellent judge of character.

See? Now we have authoritative statements that each of these gentlemen is, indeed, an authority.

It seems to me that the human race has been making a rat-race of things for quite a while with the question, "Who is to judge?," which is a variant of the question of, "Who is an authority?"

There's an old saying, "If you ask a silly question, you'll get a silly answer." The answers Mankind has gotten for the last few millenia of recorded history give us some reason to suspect that we've been asking a silly question. The answers have certainly been bloody unsatisfactory, if they weren't exactly silly.

Maybe the question should be, "ON WHAT BASIS should we judge," rather than, "WHO is to judge?"

The concept of "A government of laws, not of men," is based on an effort to get away from "WHO is to judge," and more toward an agreed basis of judgement. One of the greatest contributions of Semitic philosophy is the monotheistic concept, the idea that there is *one* set of laws, *one* set of principles, that *all* people must use as a standard of judgement. The polytheistic concept made it a basis of "What god have you bribed?" The Jewish concept was not that of sacrifice to placate the god whose favor you sought, not one of courtier jollying the king for a favor, but atonement — paying a debt. It's a concept that could exist only in a monotheistic philosophy. And it involves the concept of fixed laws that form a *basis of judgement*.

Galileo was fighting for some principle; he rejected Authority, and insisted that every man had a right to appeal to the Universe directly — that there was a *basis* for judgement, rather than an authoritative judge, that must be consulted.

There are experts. There are also authorities — in the limited sense possible under a doctrine that the Universe itself is the necessary basis of judging. A man who lives well, happily, and successfully in many aspects of life — who's whole general tone of living is high, good, and admirable — is an Authority in my terms.

The current difficulty with the Authority concept is this: the test is whether the individual's techniques of living actually work, and work over a long time period, Al Capone made a lot of money, and lived high for a while; it was short-term, though, so we can reject that as a Way of Judging.

But unfortunately, the world situation is changing so rapidly now that the techniques of successful living that were sound, good, and valid 50 years ago simply don't apply now! Then how can you give the test of time to a system of living, when the system has to keep changing, if it is to be a good system?!

It seems to me that what's necessary is to consult with many men who live successfully (and that doesn't mean a narrow definition of "successfully" such as "Makes much money" or "always appears cheerful and unworried" or "is greatly respected by many people," but *broadly* successful) and see in what concepts they agree generally. *Consensus gentium* as a means of determining the right answers isn't adequate, of course — but it isn't to be ignored, either.

I'm plowing along on the proposition that I am, and always will be, the world's greatest expert on what **J.W.C.,Jr.** thinks — that the only mind in the Universe I can ever hope to fully understand is my own — unless I somehow achieve real, working telepathy! — and that I can't ever trust my own thinking completely. Listen to your own ideas exclusively, and you have a positive feedback system that will believe anything; it leads to "I'm God!" or anything else you happen to decide is desirable. (Most of the "Napoleons" in the institutions know very little about what Napoleon was actually like; it would interfere with their listening to their own ideas if they inserted Napoleon's own, actual nature. I have a hunch you could crack one of the "Napoleon" boys by getting him genuinely interested in studying what Napoleon actually was like — for precisely the reason I mentioned above!)

That's why "self-therapy" is a snare and a delusion-maker. In that sense, I agree fully that there *must* be a permission-giver, and an authority external to yourself. To accept that you don't need external cross-check — to accept that "permission and authority" in *that* sense — is unnecessary, is to start harkening gaily to your own brilliance.

BUT . . . the authority *does not have to be superior to you.* Any external individual whom you genuinely respect, and from whom you will accept with respect a "No, I disagree with you," is an adequate external authority. That means that anyone you consider essentially your equal, or near-equal, can serve as a crosschecker.

Impatience that causes you to hold his disagreement as foolish can cause trouble, naturally. But it is also true that no human being yet has solved all his own, personal problems. Therefore only if the therapist can *accept you as an authority too*, and be capable of questioning *his* thinking too, will the optimum progress be made.

Betcha that item is wherein you've had troubles with therapists. You're going to appear highly ambivalent to any therapist if you insist that he must be an Authority in the useful sense (and the sense he was trained to consider necessary!) and, at the same time, insist (as you properly must) that he give you equal consideration as an Authority too!

I'll agree with your basic therapy postulates, provided you'll stick one more in front of the whole series: That the patient must recognize that *he*, ultimately, is responsible for the curative process.

And that means "responsible" in two ways; it means he's got to get in and sweat — blood-sweat-and-tears sweat, too; it'll hurt — and that the results, both good and/or bad, are things he can take credit for.

And my major objection to the "trained professional analyst" is that the human race *must* find something better. Every human being needs *some* psychotherapy; there can never be enough professional psychotherapists, in any economically functional society, to handle the implied load.

But it's also true that the MD's can't handle *all* the sickness that a population suffers. Colds can't be treated professionally; the hospitals would be sunk under the case-load. A child that tears its skin on a nail can't be treated professionally; the case load would be excessive. That's why iodine and bandaids are sold over the drug-store counter.

The problem of the parent is to distinguish those medical problems warranting professional, major attention, from those which can be, and should be, medicated at home by first-aid techniques.

Note, however, that those are *first aid techniques*. They *are* techniques.

In devising an integrated psychotherapy system, then, it is critically important that many levels of therapy be recognized, and adequate *techniques* — not just happenstance, kiss-and-make-it-well malarkey, not just "Mama loves you; it will all come out all right" stuff, but honest *techniques* — of home therapy must be included.

The present major problem revolves around just that. The MD's have helped alert the parents to the nature of rickets; the danger has ended. The use of antiseptics such as iodine is a tremendously powerful medical technique — because it vastly reduces the professional case-load of hospitalized blood-poisoning.

Home nursing for the medically ill is available, because teachable techniques are available. We need home-nursing techniques for psychotherapy problems, too. That means a level of technique between the iodine-for-a-cut, and how-to-straighten-out-a-quarrel, and the surgery-for-appendicitis, breaking-through-to-a-catatonic levels.

The real problem of any one seeking help from a professional therapist, who is not in need of hospitalization, is proper home-nursing. That should not be a professional-level technique; a *technique*, though, not simply loving-hands-at-home kindness, is needed.

I have a postulate for you to consider: *IN any thinking-system, a postulate which says you can't do what you have to do must be rejected as futile.*

Reason: A postulate is NOT a reality-truth; it's strictly a thought-tool . . . and a tool that won't work must be replaced with one that will.

On that basis, I reject your postulate that a professionally trained analyst is *necessary* for psychotherapy; that would make home nursing techniques impossible. And I am reminded of a lovely phrase **Peg** heard an old Finnish farmer in Upper Peninsula Michigan use in discussing a problem. *"You has to can."* There are some things that we can't afford to have impossible; we has to can. I don't give a damn whether it's impossible or not — we has to can do home therapy.

In laying down basic rules of therapy, then — don't lay in one that will make impossible that which we must have. It's damned dangerous to do that; if you have answers that are 95% right, and men find they work very well in their practices, they will have a powerful, and very dangerous tendency to think them 100% right. That 5% error then becomes the source of problems, and it'll be damned hard to get men who swear by a system that does work most of the time to consider that that system has a basic, root flaw.

Regards,   John

Theodore Sturgeon   *November 30, 1954*

Dear Ted:

I know about the Fantasy awards that those stories won — and that they all appeared in *Galaxy*. I read the yarns, too — and it happens I don't read a hell of a lot of other science-fiction because of pressure of time.

Now it is also true that none of the stories or articles from *ASF* won the *Maurice Libermann Prize* given by the IRE, nor any of the prizes given for excellence of presentation of popular science material.

Those aren't the directions I'm trying — and that doesn't say it's wrong to try in those directions. It says I didn't win the tennis championship because I was running in the 100 yard dash.

Now once upon a time, a fairy story would scare the bejayzus out of the bratlings, because *they* lived near the large dark forest, and *they* knew wolves lurked there, and they knew there was [a] witch not too far away — and they were damned well thoroughly scared, and they listened with most close attention.

But today's children live in a large dark forest of skyscrapers, and there are no trees and no wolves and no witches, and you can't scare'em a bit with that stuff. Ha! But try 'em on the story of the dope fiend that kidnaps little girls to sell them for dope! That'll scare the brats!

Fantasy, my friend, is nice, safe, comfortable reading. It's about things that aren't so, and I know are not so, and that I can, therefore, safely identify myself with. Safely — because I can haul the hell out of there anytime the going gets a little rugged. Anytime it begins to affect a change in *me*.

I can safely identify with Ug, the Caveman; I won't get stuck feeling like that, because I can so easily differentiate myself and my situation from his.

But now let's try identifying with the guy next door.

Yipe! Get me outa here! I can't tell whose troubles are which, and I'm scared to beat all hell! This'll change me for life! This is horrible! I can't get it out of my mind that he's human, just like I am, and has real troubles that bother him as deeply as mine bother me. This is awful! I keep understanding *his* problems! My God, it feels as though his troubles were some concern of mine, and I had to actually help my neighbor — treat him like a brother or something! How horrible! I'll never be the same again! I've been changed for life by this experience!

Mankind has always loved the dear old game of How Close Can You Come To Hitting The Window Without Breaking It? They'll go right on loving it — at least the ones that rule the world will. We keep losing a lot of 'em, when they hit the window, and "suddenly, silently vanish away" as a result. But the rest are the boys who take risks and win — and they, not the meek, inherit the Earth.

There's a great misunderstanding as to what "gentle" means. A lamb is not gentle at all; it's a nasty, mean-tempered, stupid, beastie — and it's utterly weak, so it menaces no one. It hasn't got what it takes to *be* dangeous, so of course it's no menace to anyone, no matter how stupidly mean-tempered it is. It's "gentle" in about the same degree that the Guatemalan regime of last year was "gentle" with respect to the United States.

Watch a lioness washing off her cub, though; that's "gentleness."

Gentleness involves immense ability to destroy — under self-restraint. The measure of gentleness is the measure of the *ability* to annihilate, not the *tendency* to annihilate.

Action lies in the coiled tension of power — not necessarily in it's release. There's far more action involved in two wild aurochs bulls pushing, head to head, and getting nowhere, than in an angry field-mouse dashing madly across the grass-blades after a rival.

IF you can make the statuesque pose of the two great bulls appear as dynamic as it is, you've got action.

But action isn't the wild chase of the scampering field-mice.

There are enormous coiled tensions of power in every human being of high potential ability in our culture today. We're at a transaction point in the evolution of Man. There was the age of Magic, and primitive tribes. And that was followed by the Age of Logic, and the great cities. We're about to cut into the beginning of the Age of Psionics — and it'll make the transactions of past times look like an exchange of presidents at the Ladies Garden Club of Podunk. We have just about succeeded in breaking that window — and I suspect that, after the shards settle, there may be as many as 100,000,000 surviving, sane human beings. And I don't expect hydrogen bombs to have anything to do with it.

A culture can't develop logic, while Magic — a non-logical system — is around in full evidence. So Magic had to be ruled out of the culture; it was isolated just outside the boundaries in two directions.

1. Primitive tribes were acknowledged to have "superstitions."
2. Deity was acknowledged to operate by hyper-logical methods. But no member of the culture could use anything but logical methods — so logical methods were developed, explored, and ramified.

Now since only Deity could use magic within the culture (and organizations retailing the power of Deity were established) no member of the culture, under those rules, could use magic. If a member of the culture *did* demonstrate magic, either:

1. He was ruled out as a superstitious hoaxer,
2. Or his demonstrations were ruled valid only for superstitious people,
3. Or . . . by the cultural logic, he'd have to be worshipped as a God.

Then to bring Magic back into the culture, Religion had to be broken down.

It's breaking apart rapidly; it's now reduced to a matter of a voluntary expression of a philosophy of life. The Time is coming; the Twilight of the Gods is at hand.

Primitive Magic is psionics-by-rule-of-thumb. The Damascus armorers turned out some magnificent steel-metallurgy by rule-of-thumb. A dog can synthesize complex proteins, by rule-of-instinct.

Psionics is the science of a conscious knowledge of a relationship between the laws of imaginative forces. And imaginative forces are real, universal powers — as real as magnetic forces. Saying something is "just imagination" is somewhere off in the direction of — but far beyond — saying "it's just a thermonuclear explosion."

The essential point is this: I'm trying for stories that *don't* ask you to identify with an improbable individual in an extremely different situation — but with someone so damned close to home it's a test of the reader's psychic courage to take on the role. Those, my friend, can scare the living bejayzus out of you — and they'll leave you changed for life.

If the direction of that change is a good one — he'll be back for more, gasping, shaking his head, but grinning. If the direction is a bad one . . . he may be after you, quite literally, with a .38. He won't appreciate having a permanent, ugly scar on his personality. The scar may be deep enough to be called insanity.

I am not trying to flick the boys glands, **Ted**; I'm trying to flick their underlying cultural orientation — their deepest beliefs — the things that make their glands work. "Cold Equations" warn't no accident, pard — I had **Godwin** sweating on that one four times. And it stems straight from the totally unacceptable (in our misguided society) postulate "It is right and proper to sacrifice a human being." We made it a girl, because the ancient instinct of the mammalian male is that the female of the species is not expendable — the male is. That made the cheese more binding — and the impact stuck in deeper. That wasn't your reacting — that was 300,000,000 years of evolutionary instincts backfiring.

I'm sabotaging the cultural orientations, **Ted**. I'm saying "Human beings *can* be sacrificed to the good of the race — when the circumstances warrant."

"Pigs" *does* belong in the same breath. It didn't happen to hit you, because the cultural orientations being wracked and broken didn't happen to be in you. But **Polly & Kelly Freas** fought over that one for three days. A lot of other people blew their stacks over it. It's the story of a man who set out, with conscious and deliberate intent, to corrupt the morals of a minor . . . and did. You think that didn't make a lot of cultural orientation patterns scream in agony?

OK — so you didn't happen to have *that* pattern in place. But "Cold Equations" hit deeper — it'll hit anybody.

Both, you notice, are stories of absolute ruthlesness. "John's" ruthless intent to destroy the boy's morals in "Pigs" is quite comparable to the destruction of the girl in "Equations."

Each is a story of the ruthless anihilation *of an identity*. The boy we meet at the begining of the story "Pigs" has been murdered, and a totally different Entity inhabits that same body at the end of the story. What would the kid of the first pages have thought of himself at the end? He'd probably have preferred suicide, I suspect, to becoming what he did.

I'm still looking for the stories that get in and *really* twist things in the reader — and that does NOT mean a few endocrine glands. You can scare a guy for ten seconds with a rubber dummy in a dimly lighted room; that gives his glands a work-out.

But you can shock him out of a life-time pattern, and change him for the rest of his natural existence, if you can find and break one of his false cultural orientations. You'll scare hell out of him, too — for weeks, not seconds, incidentally — because, when he gets through, he discovers that a barrier he thought was a great stone wall . . . has become painted cellophane, and has been ripped a bit, at that. It lets him out, sure — but what scares him is that it means that other Things can get In, because the barrier isn't real.

Yeah — I know this isn't as popular a type of story . . . yet. But give us some time! We're developing an art-form that hasn't been more than started — as a *conscious* effort.

I suspect it'll never be really a mass-audience type, either. You can kill people with a really good story of that type — and I am *not* kidding. It's a fine exercise for strong minds — and our readers wouldn't be the speculative philosophical people they are if they didn't have tough, resilient minds — but it's not good for the weak ones.

Among the other cultural-orientation sabotage plants we've run recently, we had "Noise Level" and "Trade Secret," by **R. F. Jones**, attacking technical thinking trends. "The School" attacks the whole concept of homeostasis orientations.

Gunther's articles attacked the orientation that "Of course we know what distance is."

My editorals have been calculated to loosen frozen mental bearings.

They say that, some 6000 years ago, Cheops Pyramid was oriented so that the North Star could be sighted through the entrance to the burial chamber. Unfortunately, that's not true any more; the pyramid being a static structure, while the Earth is dynamic, they are now out of line.

Now as to the story items: **Poul Anderson** is NOT doing anything resembling the business of the king-tortures-and-kills-the-girl-but-replaces-her item. His story mentioned slavery, and helped me to get a new understanding of the matter of how slavery looks to a slave in a slave culture — and he did a damn good job — but did not at all bear on the concept of the replaceability of one human being by another "just as good or better."

Poul's point, to make things clear, was this: His 20th century hero comes in and finds a girl in his apartment; she is an exact duplicate, in appearance, age, etc., of his lost wife. But his wife was lost because he got thrown, irreversibly, through time. There is no question raised of this girl replacing his wife on an equal-or-better basis. The gimmick is subtler.

She introduces herself. "I'm Marin, a class Eight slave, given you by Lord Sounso." Class Eight slaves are bred as companions — concubines to the high-level nobility. The hero is terrifically shocked emotionally, to find this living duplicate of his wife.

He says, "You're mine? That means anything goes?"

She winces, but agrees that's right. He then realizes that she must know that there are sadistic and perverted slave-buyers, and has interpreted his remark in that light.

Poul's gimmick is this; he *can* sell her, give her away, refuse her, free her, or kill her just to see the pretty red run out. But . . . so could any other man she was sold, given, or returned to. And she is the girl who looks exactly like his wife. He *can't* accept the idea of some other man having her. . . .

If he frees her, she can become a servant, or marry a commoner. But she's highly intelligent, brilliant, and highly educated; she can never again meet the only kind of people among whom she could be happy with.

And, because she was given to him, and had been trained to love freely the man who would buy her — whoever that might be — he can not *win* her love. It's been given to him. He can't marry her.

Poul, you see, makes a very different use of the slave situation. (It, also, you see, puts a violent twist in our cultural orientations!)

He does NOT bring out the point that a primitive slave society holds — or would hold, in the above set-up — that the girl Marin *was* his wife, that there was no difference.

The primitive culture would say, "See, they are both young, female, and shapely. Then there is no difference, and if you cannot tell one from the other in any important way, they are the same."

(In a primitive culture, where taboo and custom are all, their memories-of-life would be essentially the same too!)

Now there is something besides people stories are about. An individual can never be enough to make a story; it takes an individual and an environment. His culture makes a *large* part of him — and he carries it with him, whether he likes it or not. **Poul's** hero carried 20th century culture with him, internally, into the 5000 years later period he landed in. The culture built into him, more than his own independently derived concept, loused him up with respect to Marin.

Nobody's doing the admirable-detestable superman.

I'll buy part of your remarks re the girl killed on the tracks. But I resent the comment "There is no shortage of love in the world — only a shortage of places to put it." That, my friend, can be a damn snotty, snooty remark. Who is it that decides what places are worth putting love? If you take a real careful gander at that remark, it's got a nice, subtle loading in it that's a dilly — and magnificently explains why there *is* a shortage of love in the world.

Look, man; anybody can love an angel of light. So what does that prove of you, if you are able to love and be loved by a perfect being? It's like "Lodges talk only to Cabots, and Cabots talk only to God." It's "I would be able to love you if you were as perfect as I am."

May I say, without blasphemous meaning, "For Christ's sake!"

Everybody's willing to love his noble, wonderful, high-and-mighty Brain — but quite a few get into psychosomatic trouble for lack of the ability to love the hard-working rectum. Thoughts are such noble things to deal with, but. . . .

Yeah? Well, you're alive only because some of the original cells from which you grew by differentation and development were wise and courageous enough to dedicate themselves and their generations to the particular life-service of being the sewage department.

Try considering why life finds differentiation, and the development of differences so important. Maybe we shouldn't all be brains, huh? Maybe it isn't necessary for all individuals to be self-determined? Maybe, on the other hand, you're ducking your consequent responsibility — that of caring for the welfare of those who do not have the needed judgement, and accepting that burden as part of the payment in return for your freedom to be self-determined. An adult is responsible for the child; the child is not self-determined. There's a price to self-determinism that may include accepting the burden of solving problems for those who cannot do it themselves. You know, a man could be real pious sounding when he says, "I am not my brother's keeper; he should be self-determined, and I have no right to interfere in his life."

There's another item, too. What's "worthy of love" mean? We saw "Aida" last night, and I thought about it considerable as a result. Let's try a modification of "Aida," as follows:

Princess Mary wanted to marry Prince Bill, but Bill is in love with commoner Lucy. Now Lucy is a sweet, "gentle" clinging vine type — a pretty little child, who ohs and ahs and admires Prince Bill as a man. And Bill happens to be a rather weak specimen from

269

a strong line of strong men — he's not perverted or anything — he's just a quite ordinary man, with quite ordinary push and force of personality.

But Princess Mary is a princess in the finest sense of the word; she's wise, strong, and gentle in the sense that means something — possessed of immense power, and the power to use or not-use it.

Now for certain reasons, Mary wants to marry Bill. And Lucy has Bill all wrapped up. Mary summons Lucy, interviews her, gets to know her. Then she summons a magician. After a conference with him, she orders him to cast a spell on Lucy.

In the course of the next week, Lucy becomes insane, regressing rapidly to drooling idiocy, practically. In a month she dies.

Mary catches Bill skillfully on the rebound; she is sweet, soft, and admiring of Bill. Bill marries her.

Is Mary worthy of love?

Yes, Mary is. Bill is, and will remain, a relatively weak man all his life; Mary knows this, and isn't deluding herself in the slightest. Married to him, she will never have a companion of her own high stature — she'll have a weak consort she will have to care for and direct, and that directing will have to be carefully and thoughtfully done, because he *is* weak. She's taken on a life-time job with him.

She murdered Lucy, after first destroying her personality. It was necessary to break up the Lucy-personality image in Bill's mind, if Bill was to get over his love for her. (And Bill's love was genuine and proper — Lucy was his kind of female. Mary isn't.) If Mary had simply had Lucy killed, a lovely image of Lucy would have remained with Bill. Lucy had to be crushed and broken before Bill's eyes, and only then allowed to die.

Mary is an altruist, you see; she can destroy Bill's highest good — because the lesser value can, properly, be sacrificed for a greater value. Mary's a true altruist, though; she also sacrificed herself. She doesn't love Bill, and never will, but she'll bear his children, and care for his welfare all his life.

She's truly a princess — and it's essential to the progress of her culture that Bill's nation and hers be united into a going concern. Bill's nation has good seaports; hers has only one. But Bill's nation is rich farmlands, while hers is a growing industrial community. The two, united into a mutually supporting system, will make a strong, balanced, mutually beneficial culture.

Bill's weak; he hasn't the built-in ruthlesness to discipline himself to those facts, accept them, and work for them for all his lifetime. He wants to resign.

Mary's a hard, ruthless, driving personality — a woman of blazing force and power, a truly great woman. She happens to be somewhat horse-faced, and her body is somewhat angular and hard, so she isn't as pretty as sweet little Lucy was. But she's so hard and ruthless she can be hard and ruthless with herself. She can drive herself to accept Bill as her consort, knowing that he will never love *her* — and she can even accept presenting to him a make-believe-self that is weak and soft, so that he can work with her as he must for the good of the millions of citizens involved.

And, as she bears his children, she knows she can hope that the strong genetic line from which he comes will show through, rather than the weakness he himself displays. She is, also, forced to recognize that it may be that she will have to destroy her first-born son, if he proves to be a weakling, while the second is the strong man she knows the newly united nation *must* have if it is to live.

Mary isn't kidding herself a bit. She's a murderess, and she has murder-in-reserve in her heart.

Is she worthy of love?

Why do you think all mankind fears and hates an altruist? Because, by definition, an altruist is motivated by a system of values higher than any *you* (who call him an altruist) can understand. And that means that your highest good is a good he considers expendable. He can destroy you, your wife, and your children and all your hope for the future on the altar of a Good he considers higher.

There's a Law of the Universe that says, "Ignorance of the Laws is no excuse." That's not just a man-made law — it's the Great Law of the Universe. A baby doesn't understand about boiling water but it is scalded just as severely, if it thrusts its hand into hot water, as would be a knowing adult. The Universe is ruthless; a human being adapted to this universe must have a measure of that same factor within himself — however much we wish it were otherwise.

Kids know better than adults about that. I've been interested in watching **Peedee** grow up. She's 14 now, going to freshman High School. She gets a lot of baby-sitting jobs — made over $60 this fall. She's banked it all; she's planning on a Mariner's (sea-going Girl Scouts) trip next summer, and wants $70 before then.

Several of the other local girls are competing with **Peeds**, of course — but **Peeds** gets the jobs. Reason: **Peedee** is gentle. She's got a personality that's hard as beryllium-nickel — and just as springy. British kids hit her . . . and bounce. They recognize quickly that she can't be pushed, and yet she doesn't get mad, and never hits them; kids respect that; the thing a kid wants most, to feel secure and taken care of, is a person who is, and proves he is, *much* stronger than the kid himself. How can you feel secure under the protection of someone weaker than yourself? Someone *you* can push around? **Pedee's** been getting local bratlings to behave when the kid's own mother can't! *And the kids ask to have her come back.*

271

Yet she never hits them, or gets "mad" at them. If a man gets angry at you — it means you're on his own level, and he sees in you a danger he must frantically attack. If a baby-sitter gets angry at a brat — that brat knows he is not being protected by a person adequately stronger than himself.

And that does NOT mean physical strength; it means stability and solidity of personality, determination and hard drive . . . but with the addition of the immensely important factor that the person has self-discipline as powerful as their drive.

Peedee gets all the baby-sitting jobs she can handle.

That business of extremely high, hard-driving personality force represents one extreme of the "Is it worthy of love" spectrum; such weak, soft personalities as the proposed Lucy represents the other. Can you love such a personality? Can you love a moron, knowing the moron is, and will always be a moron?

Is any *person* unworthy of love? Or is it only some *aspect* of the person that must be crushed?

Now on the story idea you said had bogged down for you. If it's bogged down, it's bogged down because that's not the story *you* want to write — it's one you consciously think you want to write, which is somewhat different.

But let's try kicking the thing sidewise, and see what happens. Mike and Sal are the fine team; Henry comes along and kills Mike, wanting to get Sal and the wonderful marriage for himself.

OK — so he does kill Mike, and Sal does marry him. But . . . not quite for the reason Hal thinks. Too late, Sal realized that Mike had been murdered, and caught on to what Henry was after.

Now Sal is, quite obviously, a really high-power woman. *Really* high-power.

There is a great, basic psychological proposition that is very important; it gets people into no end of trouble. "NEVER ask somebody a question unless you're *sure* you want the answer." You might get it. Never challenge someone with a problem unless you're certain you want the answer; you may be most horrible and catastrophically surprised.

Henry wanted to have his problem "How can I be happily married?" answered. Sal sets out to give him the answer he asked for . . . and does.

In the course of it, she tears his mind apart, a piece at a time, disrupts his soul, breaks down his emotional structure, and reassembles them in a totally new pattern. And when she gets through with him, he can understand himself and his situation clearly. He has his answer in full.

The answer is: "You can't — and you never, never will. Not now

272

you can't. You aren't, and never will be, the kind of man Mike was — and because you killed him, it is proper that you see and understand that, so that you can know precisely and in full what you are guilty of. But gaining that knowledge means that you know what you are not, and cannot be — and why that is a thing that is wonderful beyond your full understanding to be. You aren't capable of that growth, any more than the most carefully trained chimpanzee can ever be taught to speak human language. You lack the necessary genetic structure."

Sal is quite capable of ruthlessness; she's also capable of taking a year off to see that her man's murder is fully and appropriately paid for.

Henry, incidentally, wouldn't stand a ghost of a chance of escaping during the soul-dissection-and-repairing process, however violent his agonies might be. Sal can bind him to her because she *is* his superior.

Ever think what "loss of my identity" means? To become an Entity other than the one you are now, to be molded and shaped so that that which you consider Good you consider worthless, while that which you consideer anathema, you consider Good. To have your body going around, doing things, at the direction of an Entity that *is not you*.

That, you see, is what Sal did to Henry.

It happens to be the necessary requirement for the next stage of growth — that you be able to accept being an entity you are not. (That's what the ability to learn instantly requires; that's why it's essential to the next higher stage of growth.) But to be that way, and remain sane, you have to have an unnameable-as-yet characteristic that comes genetically — not by education.

Consider this: It is impossible to *teach* the ability-to-learn. It's inherently and by definition impossible! If an entity does not have the ability to learn, then it cannot be taught; if it can't be taught, you can't teach it how to learn!

The essence of verbal communication is the use of abstract symbols. Given a system of abstract symbols, an individual can be taught the concepts of "symbols" and "abstractions."

But a chimpanzee does not have, as a genetic gift, the ability to form abstract concepts. Therefore it can't start learning verbal communication — and therefore verbal communication can't be used to teach it to abstract and symbolize.

Here I have a mass of proto-protoplasm; it has all the essentials of living stuff. But it doesn't have organization enough to start organizing itself.

There are things you can't teach. But you may succeed in making someone aware that there *is* a thing out there to learn . . . and if

273

you could, also, make him aware of why, precisely, he can't ever learn it. . . !

What do you think happens to Henry in our little story? If he'd been up against any ordinary person, he would just block out the ideas, deny them, and "forget it," simply acquiring a deep buried tension he could live with.

But Sal is no ordinary person, and she doesn't intend to be nice and gentle with him; she's already installed a block — and this block nailed the door open, removed the hinges, and blasted the doorway to four times its original size. So long as he lives, he'll never forget or occlude from himself one iota of it.

So . . . that leaves him one out.

But Sal intends that Mike's death serve *some* useful purpose. If Henry just kills himself off — that's mere revenge.

Henry is condemned to warning others. Maybe she makes a writer out of him.?

I dunno. But there are various legends of Flying Dutchmen and Wandering Jews and the like, who, in expiation of their sins, are denied the right of death and quiet and surcease.

There's a terrific lot of collossal plot ideas in the fairy-stories . . . if they are not made into "that doesn't apply to *me*" type fantasies — but are translated into acutely modern terms. Things that bore into the reader, and hit him either by showing him what his ancient instincts really mean, or that his cultural orientations are based on false postulates.

On that last: take a quick run-down on the logical consequences of the postulate "there is no difference between men and women except the physical."

1. This denies intellectual-emotional differences, and was set up so that women would be respected as thinkers, and be allowed a place in the world equal to man's. This was the desired consequence.

2. But it has a whole family of other consequences — many of which are brass-plated stinkers. For instance, if man and woman are identical except physically, then man-man companionship is equal to man-woman companionship. So why should a man take on a life-time contract to support a woman. Physical sex being the only difference, that life-time support's an awful expensive way of getting a convenient erotic playmate. The whore-house is much more economical.

3. If only the physical difference exists, then all a woman has to offer a man is a convenient set of reproductive organs to play with, or to use. Then woman must do a

terrific job of selling what little she's got to offer.

4. Then child-bearing, the one function the whore-house doesn't fulfill, must be made a super-collossal deal. It must be The Terrible Price Woman Pays For Her Womanhood. And in selling that proposition, she naturally learns to believe it — so the poor girl goes into the delivery room scared blue, expecting indescribably awful agonies . . . and, naturally, gets just exactly that.

5. The cheap competition must be held down, or made undesirable. Therefore venereal disease must NOT be attacked, but must be protected against medical science.

You can find other consequences of that false postulate lying around. The whole thing is an offshoot of the mis-applied postulate of Equalitarianism — Man is Equal To Woman interpreted as meaning "identical to." The "little gentleman" system of child education is another equalitarianism proposition — a child is identical with an adult, except for the blank mind, which must be filled in as rapidly as possible. (And don't let any facts stand in your way; deny them vigorously. If that blank mind tries to pretend it has something in it already — say the results of three billion years of evolution — rub at it vigorously until the writing is erased. Or at least suppressed out of sight.)

Other equalitarianism sub-postulates are lying all over the place; their principle difficulty being that "equal" in a logical system can only mean "identical." If we have two numbers, p and q, and we are told they are equal, then, logically, p and q must be identical. Inescapable logic. Non-identical equalities can't exist within a logic system such as we know. Sure . . . the real world is full of 'em, but that's not *logical;* it's *factual*, which is very, very different.

Incidentally, you know the old negro-hater's trick question, "Well, if you think niggers are so fine, tell me this; would you want your daughter to marry a nigger?"

There's an answer that's honest and pointed. "No, I wouldn't — but would you want your daughter to marry a woman?"

Regards,   John

Everett B. Cole   *February 21, 1955*

Dear Mr. Cole:

At the moment, I'm frantic for short stories — and I'm overstocked on novelettes. Generally, there's more novelettes sent in than shorts, but right now it's much too much that way.

275

I can't buy this just now; I'll consider it again, if you want to send it in again in about four or five months.

Incidentally, you've got problems with your Philosophical Corps series. Your conception of the resources and techniques of the Galactic culture has been growing . . . but it's also been growing more and more vague.

You've been wise in sticking to viewpoint characters who were sub-sub-sub-agents, the local representatives who've been partly trained in some techniques but aren't full Galactic citizens.

Ever stop to think of the problem a Neolithic tribesman would have imagining the ethical system of a modern American? You know, the truly primitive peoples are never sadistic. A truly primitive type might skin a captive alive, but not because of sadistic tendencies — just because that's the easiest way of getting the skin without holes in it. To be sadistic, you must attach *some* importance to the other entity's pain. Otherwise it isn't going to be important enough to you to take the trouble to cause it.

Sadistic cruelty, in other words, can begin only when you reach an ethical level high enough to be aware that another entity's pain has importance of some kind.

The Romans were sadistic; the Circus concept could come in only at that level.

Europeans were sadistic through the Middle Ages; they didn't have circuses which cost too much, but public torture of the condemned was standard.

But could people of that time have even imagined the ethical concepts that are accepted as normal today?

The primitive tribe cultural system involves the right of the individual tribesman to *act* differently than his neighbors and fellow-tribesmen. This permitted division of labor. But he was not permitted the right to *believe* differently; the taboos and rituals were enforced by the culture. No independent *thinking* allowed.

In our culture, freedom of *thought* is allowed . . . to a considerable extent, at least. But what individual freedom does our culture rigorously deny? Can you, a member of this culture, spot the culturally-imposed limitation on your freedom? Because, of course, the trick is that any culture holds that the freedom-limitation it imposes is not a culturally imposed limitation at all but "the only right, and sane, and natural way."

Of course, a Galactic Citizen would spot the limitation imposed by a culture, and would be able to rate the evolution of the people on the basis of where the limitation was set.

BUT. . . .

1. You can't, fully.
2. You can't define the next higher limit-level.

3. You can't communicate it clearly, even if you could.
4. You can't imagine the consequences of not being limited as our culture is.
5. You can't define the consequences of being exposed to an individual who belongs in a culture two or more stages higher than yours.

And you can't really make a reader believe you can do those things.

Six years of damned hard work, with the help of a whole team of high-powered thinkers, all of them highly original, has served mainly to indicate that we *are* limited, and to spot in a very vague and cloudy fashion what the nature of the culturally imposed limitation is. The consequences of abandoning it are completely beyond our ability to formulate.

So . . . I don't think you're too wise to pick a full Galactic citizen as a viewpoint character, *except* when that Galactic is operating in disguise as a lower-level culture native. Then one or two flashes of fantastically inconsistent behavior would be possible. But they must be strictly flashes, because you can't actually motivate them.

Try explaining to a three-year-old, who's operating largely on the motive of "It's mine!" why it is you willingly give him things you buy at sacrifice to yourself. Also, try explaining to a rebellious 9-year-old kid why burning his tail with a sound spanking is a kindness to him. Make him feel-believe that your act in taking away from him the .38 revolver he found wasn't mean and selfish and refusal to let him have fun.

Your Galactic Citizens would, from the viewpoint of any culture they visited, appear far more like avenging demons than like demi-gods. You know, the essential difference between a Demon and a God is that a demon gives you what you want, for a price you believe proper, while a god makes you take something you don't want, and pay a price for it you're sure you can't afford. A god makes you earn and learn, in other words, while a demon spoils you rotten.

The culture that a full galactic Citizen has to intercede for is really fouled up — and it's in for hell and hallelujah before it gets straightened out. Galactics wouldn't interfere in any culture we could understand!

The worst of it is, the younger cultures, save for a very few, very exceptional men, wouldn't be able to understand that being helpless, incompetent children is not something to be ashamed of — that because an older entity can do something more easily does *not* mean *it's* futile for you to work and grow toward that stage.

It'd be darned tough explaining that, though, wouldn't it?

Regards,   John W. Campbell, Jr.

Dear Lester:

I thought you might be interested in something I found intriguing — the story of Wurf, the Caveman who was the Father of all Crooks and Confidence men.

Most men are basically pretty decent, though even a good, honest man has a small streak of dishonesty in him. Some men have quite a streak of chicanery, fraud, and dishonesty. But Wurf was just born all bad, I guess.

Wurf was born in the last days of the Paleolithic, just shortly before the Neolithic — the Polished Stone — Age began. The *burin* had been invented a little earlier — say 75,000 years or so previously. (Things happened at a somewhat more lesiurely pace in the days of the honest, consistent and predictable Paleolithic Cavemen.)

The invention of the *burin*, the flint chisel, made possible the carving of bone and ivory for the first time, and bone and ivory needles had come into use some 50,000 years before Wurf's birth.

Wurf first exhibited his crookedness in connection with these bone needles. Every Paleolithic housewife knew that *old* bone needles were greatly superior to new ones; the new ones, of course, had the sharp-edged gouge-marks where the *burin* had cut them, but a good *old* needle was smooth and worked much better, and there was the magic of much use over many years in it, of course. It was an experienced needle, grown wise with much use, and so very valuable.

But Wurf, who started out carving needles, tried to sell them some new needles that were smooth. These were, of course, indignantly rejected.

Wurf invented counterfeiting. He was a very crooked man; he took newly made bone needles, and polished them assiduously in a mixture of buffalo fat and very fine rouge. Then he boiled them in a fat mixed with certain roots and barks until they were adequately greasey and stained. Then this foul deceiver sold them as genuine antique needles.

This went on for several months, but one day Flung, a somewhat retarded 10-year-old girl, watched him for a whole day, while he prepared a batch of needles. Her old man questioned her quite closely about how she'd spent the day (she'd been sent out to gather berries, and came home emptyhanded) and between shrieks, she mentioned Wurf's operations.

Unfortunately, Wurf was a clever rascal; he succeeded in slipping out of the territory before the trackers could catch him.

Wurf went quite some distance, to an area where his reputation was not apt to catch up with him, and settled down. He had some of his counterfeit antique needles with him, and sold those to establish himself. He was careful not to make any more just then, as he hoped to establish himself in the confidence of the new tribe.

But it was not long before the rascal fell into his old ways again. Having learned the snide trick of polishing new needles so they were as slick and efficient as old ones, he bethought himself of the exceeding unhandyness of his flint axe. Being, like most dishonest men, a very lazy man, he considered the matter at length. It certainly didn't slip easily into trees. Or anything else, for that matter. He considered the gouges and flake-scars, and considered the behavior of a newly carved needle, and one that had been polished. And he considered how flint, while very useful because it could be shaped by chipping, was also most damnably given to chipping when you tired to use it. It happened he was rolling a piece of a clear, dense green stone about with his left foot at the time — a kind of stone he knew from experience was hard, and practically impossible to chip.

It took him nearly a month, but at the end of that time he had a most beautiful axe shaped by grinding, instead of chipping. It was a lovely piece of jade, and he had done much thinking about the problem of this new idea, and how he could razzle-dazzle the local yokels. He tried out his new axe, and it exceeded his expectations; it cut trees beautifully, didn't chip, and didn't break apart.

So he packed his most portable goods, traveled nearly fifteen days to the west, and found a tribe that had never heard of him or anyone he'd ever heard of. He had a most wonderful tale of gods, demons, and magic, and sold the local chief his axe for a fabulous sum.

He then left hurriedly, and by a contorted route, reaching home base in some perplexity. He wasn't *sure* they were after him.

He very secretively polished another axe (this one of basalt) and set out again. This time he went north. He was rather astonished to discover that there was quite a bit of talk about a war that had ended with the anihilation of a tribe of crooks and deceivers who had been selling counterfeit "old" bone needles all over the area, until people grew suspicious of the number of "old" needles that tribe had, and it was found they were frauds. Wurf was glad to hear again of his old tribalmates, and like the rascal he was, not at all sorry about their sad fate.

However, he *did* have some feeling about the matter. So he travelled a bit further, till he found the tribe that had been directly responsible for wiping out his ancestral tribe. He sold their chief witch doctor his new basalt polished stone axe at a quite moderate figure, and, under most horrendous oathes of secrecy, even showed him how more could be made.

Wurf didn't make any more stone axes after that, but engaged in various other nefarious and unorthodox activities. It was only about three years, however, before he got the welcome news that the tribe of polished basalt axe-makers had been wiped out to the last man, and all the boys had been roasted for the victory banquet. The witch doctor had been forced to confess his black-axe magic in full.

Wurf, the evil man, grinned in delight. He had done some other noxious things in the three years, and now he packed his things again, left his three wives and nine small children behind, and travelled nearly thirty days to the south. He had with him another very fine polished jade axe, and a polished jade knife. And he had marvelous tales of magic and gods and demons and strange peoples he had encountered in his travels. And he showed the local shaman a trick of cutting many small saplings with the sharp jade axe — a thing impossible with flint axes — and how to set them close together. Then he put a dozen rabbits inside the stockade, mounted guard, and succeeded in keeping everyone away for a remarkable number of days. This was very difficult, even with the magnificently thunderous curses, and the sharp jade knife, because it was quite ununderstandable that someone had good animal food and neither ate it, nor let anyone else eat it.

The shaman, however, was mightily impressed by the magic that made four food-animals appear where only two had been. (This was the original version of the old gypsy money-doubling trick.) Wurf, the nasty schemer, laughed to himself all the thirty day journey home.

It was only two years — shortly after a wave of basalt axes produced by a dozen competing tribes to the north showed up in commercial trade — before Wurf's foul plans matured, and he heard the news. A tribe of loathesome magicians to the south had been wiped out to the last man, for a vicious fraud they had practiced on all their neighbors. They'd been engaging in trade with honest cavemen, trading magically counterfeited wild rabbits for good, honest merchandise. Again the boys of the tribe had been roasted for the victory dinner, the girls reserved for other purposes, while the shaman and his assistants were forced to confess their treachery in full detail.

Wurf was getting rather along in years for a Paleolithic Caveman (and the Paleolithic was just about over, as a matter of fact) and his morals — if he had ever had any — were completely gone. He sent his thirteen older children to the North, with instructions to settle in one of the axe-making villages — preferrably thirteen of the axe-making villages — where things were settling down a bit after the recent wave of treacheries. And he most carefully instructed them about introducing their frauds — for his tendency to be a liar, cheat, and a vicious innovator was genetic — only at a safe distance.

Then he took advantage of the fact that the Chief's youngest and most expensive wife had just born a child, and wasn't able to nurse it. (Tribal law held that a woman who did not nurse her child must have her breasts cut off in punishment — which is very painful when it's done with a flint knife, and not good for the health of the woman. And, as I say, she was the Chief's youngest and most expensive wife — too darned expensive to have her ruined this way, when she had years of good service left in her if he could just figure a way out of it.) Of course, to Wurf, breaking the Ancient codes was nothing; he was a lawbreaker at heart, and even more evil than the Chief could imagine. It was Wurf who secretly taught the young mother (who kept nervously fingering her breasts during the lessons) how to milk a goat. Both the Chief and his youngest wife were, of course, sworn to secrecy under most hideous oaths.

Wurf, his wife, and their four youngest children left the area that week. Where they went has never been determined. No doubt the story did reach him, though, in the next few years. The Chief's *second* youngest and most expensive wife started the whole thing, of course. She detected the fraud, and being an honest, law abiding tribeswoman, in her righteous indignation called the attention of the whole tribe to the girl's perfidy. She was given the signal honor of wielding the knife that cut off the offender's breasts; it was remarked that she was particularly clumsy about it, but it was put down to excitement rather than any deliberate jealous vengeance.

Three neighboring tribes combined, some four years later, to crush these devil-spawned half-man-half-goat people, whose babies were, frequently, suckled so unnaturally. For all time to come, the loathesome nature of that tribe's crime was a memory of unnatural Evil, memorialized even today in Lucifer's pedal extremities.

But Wurf, and Wurf's 18 children, were never heard of again. They were, by that time, much too smart to be heard of.

Regards, John

Dr. Muller   *May 4, 1955*

Dear Dr. Muller:

As you know, I'm as deeply and actively concerned about preventing nuclear warfare as are you; each of us is fighting War in an effort to prevent a fighting war. I have learned something from you that suggests that you can, by doing one specific paper, produce a profoundly important new approach to the whole problem of the present world tensions.

Men don't start slugging at each other until they feel that no less painful and arduous method remains. So long as each side feels there is a moderate, even though small, hope of success in changing the other side's "stubborn obstinancy" by methods less painful than physical action — so long they will argue instead of throwing destruction.

But once the conviction that argument is futile settles in, physical methods are pretty darned certain.

Now the effective result of genetic selection during the last few hundred megayears has been such that we need not fear that those genetic lines entailing a tendency to low risk-taking will cause a dangerous war. The low-risk strains are all on reservations, or preserved as fossil specimens. Of course, the too-high-risk strains also exist only as fossil remains. But it is perfectly evident that fear does *not* act as a really effective deterrent to human actions. If it did, men wouldn't charge machine gun nests, nor walk casually along a 4-inch wide steel girder 1000 feet above the ground. Nor would chemists cheerfully mix up concoctions that they strongly suspected might blow up with tremendous violence. If you read the account of the Frenchman who investigated the properties of nitrogen trichloride, for instance, you'll see that Man will cheerfully take seemingly insane risks for a deeply-accepted purpose. (He shed several fingers and an eye in the course of numerous excessively violent explosions, before he completed his researches to his own satisfaction.)

The risk of genetic destruction of the race, however real it may be, and however fully understood and accepted, simply will not serve to stop the high-risk strains of Mankind. And, inevitably, the high-risk strains within the population will be the leaders. If fear of pain and danger could stop Man, he would have been stopped from trying some time back around a megayear ago, when the individual's life was *really* dangerous.

The one best hope I see for preventing war is to maintain hope of settlement of disputes by discussion, because the total sweep of history, both written and paleontological, suggests that fear-restraint doesn't work for long.

The essential basis of hope for settlement by discussion revolves around communication techniques; that, in turn, must be based on understanding of the nature of the minds which are seeking to communicate. A false theory of what human mentality actually is can serve to create a feeling of hopelessness where that feeling is, in fact, unwarranted. A false doctrine of psychology, or of sociology, can produce a despondency that can lead to reluctant acceptance of War as the Only Way To Go On.

We have a theology in the Western Culture which is anything but a help in this regard; it holds that Man is tainted with Original Sin — that man is inherently vicious, stubborn, ornery, and prefers the wrong answer to the right answer. That Man will learn only under the drastic threat of the club and whip, or hellfire and damnation. That is certainly no inducement to maintaining hope that rational discussion can be expected to establish agreeable communication.

I feel we need a drastic reorientation with respect to Man and the basic nature of human psychology.

Not your field? Agreed. But genetics definitely wasn't Freud's field, nor is it the field of the modern psychologists who have followed in Freud's path. *And their theories are based on a false genetic concept!* No man as genetic-theory naive as Freud has any business establishing a hopeless doctrine of Man's mentality on the basis of a theory essentially rooted in a genetic concept.

No group as uninformed about genetics as the modern psychologist has any business seeking to establish a psychological theory based on genetic-instinct doctrines they have neither investigated nor had investigated.

You may not be a psychologist, but the lugubrious and nasty description of the Nature of Man the psychologists present is based on statements that *are* in your field — and are spectacularly idiotic, too.

To wit: Freud's concept of neurosis was originally based on the proposition that the inhibition of sex-instincts caused all the trouble. He widened his theory somewhat in later years, adding a death-instinct.

Now when a man says "instinct," he presumably means "a genetically determined behavior pattern"; if not, he's making a remarkably meaningless noise.

Then Freud's whole thesis of neurosis *is based on a genetic doctrine.* And I never heard of the psychologists consulting the geneticists to determine whether or not that doctrine had any validity whatever, or to determine what degree of validity it did have.

Freud's doctrine concerning Man leads to a picture of Man as a vicious, selfish, loathesome creature, made to behave even to the woefully slight extent he does only by the constant harsh police measures of Society.

Now such a creature certainly could be made to accept a reasonable proposal only by applying the most drastic sort of punishment. If you succeeded in arguing him into decent behavior, it would be a major miracle. War, obviously, is the only way to get any sense into that vicious brute. *If* Man were what Freud described, *then* War would, indeed, be the Only Way To Get Sense Into The Other Fellow.

The one area where the whole concept of psychology as currently taught can be sweepingly devastated is at its very root — the untested and hitherto uncontested genetic doctrines.

If men such as yourself, with your authoritative, and soundly-earned reputation, once challenge that genetic hash of theirs — the whole structure of psychology will be forced to accept a rigorous revinvestigation, from its very roots. Whatever else comes out of it, a far better picture of Man will most surely emerge. While that investigation is going on, the whole world will see a clear hope that a new, and less painful method of settling disputes may soon emerge. And just so long as there is a rational hope of argumentative discussion of disputes, Man will be patient; only when hope is exhausted, does Man resort to the drastic step of physical attack.

Isaac Asimov and his associate at Boston University, **Dr. Boyd**, are doing an article for me, based, in large part, on your recent study of the distribution of mutations in the present human population. **Isaac** told me, in his proposal about the article, that you find a distribution indicating that the average is about one mutation per human individual.

Fine. Now what does that mean to psychology, when that psychology is based on "human instincts"?

Furthermore, animal breeders have told me that most breeders have great difficulty with many of their best high-production strains due to loss of the genetic copulation instinct patterns. The highly bred domestic animals all seem to show that phenomenon; I'm told that about 25% of the highly bred show-dogs, for example, simply lack the copulation pattern. This has made artificial insemination not merely a convenience, but damn well a necessity for the continuation of the strain.

Now if a wild animal has a mutation that removes or blocks off the copulation instinct, that individual is not going to propagate his species. The sex-instinct pattern is essential to the continuity of a *wild* animal species. But in a social system of high technology, animals do not have to have the copulation pattern to survive. The proof of that statement is elegantly simple; the present dairy cattle, show dogs, and race horse strains that do not have copulation instincts.

Now another point: No wild animal species can exist as a species unless it has an instinctive repugnance to miscygenation. BUT . . . Man cannot breed a domestic species *unless that intstinct is missing*.

Man is, as has been pointed out, the first of all domesticated animals. Also, the human species is, so far as I know, the *only* species in which the male is anatomically able to rape the female.

Consequently, it has been, for several million years, quite unnecessary for a female of the species to have any instinctive urge toward copulation; her type would be reproduced with or without that instinct. Only recently — with the development of artificial insemination techniques — has it been possible to reproduce any domestic animal when the female was unwilling to partake in copulation. Now, fortunately, we can make it possible for a bull to rape a cow.

My conclusion from the evidence available is that Freud has absolutely no justification for holding that all human beings have sex drives. If that assumption is unjustified, then the entire fundamental postulate of Freudian psychology is invalidated.

The Freudian argument has been simply that the fact that sexual reproduction took place proves the existence of a sex instinct. True; when applied to wild animals. Not true when applied to animals without a social organization. And without that . . . what's left of Freudian concepts of Man as a lusty, lecherous, perverted, sex-dominated entity, given over to suppressed lusts for his mother and consequent fear that his father is about to castrate him? I would have a tendency to suspect that Freud had been misled by reactions of his Jewish patients, who had hazy, but painfully acute early memories of very real physical attack on their genitalia by a father-image.

It seems to me that we have a group, the psychologists, influencing world-thinking in major degree, and influencing it toward a belief in the rapacious, irrational, nasty nature of Man, on the basis of some rather bizzare genetic theories.

And their influence toward the belief that Man is basically a hopeless, unreasonable creature is acting in a world that needs, above all else, a reason to hope that Man is, instead, a reasonable, deeply sincere, idealistic entity, trying hard to find good sense in an exceedingly complex Universe.

I feel deeply that their theories are based on ideas that are genetic nonsense, ideas that have never been challenged even by any competent, responsible geneticist.

And I feel that if those ideas were challenged, the whole field of psychology would be vastly benefited — though, naturally, they would be most painfully forced to reconsider practically all their beliefs and doctrines.

Am I wrong, **Dr. Muller**, in suggesting the two basic points:

1. There is excellent reason to believe that a major proportion of the human race does *not* have a genetic, i.e., instinctive, urge toward sex?
2. That the high incidence of mutation in the human race implies that statements concerning human instincts must be reviewed *most* carefully?

Incidentally, it has also occurred to me that one characteristic difference between the male and the female of the species would, necessarily, be that the male tended to evolve slightly faster than the female. Reason: the fact that the female has 24 fully paired chromosome sets, while the male has one that is imperfectly paired makes the male slightly more susceptible to mutation effects. The result, it seems to me, is that Nature inevitably "tried it out on the dog" first; the bitch gets the results later. Inasmuch as the male is expendable, while the female is relatively non-expendable (birth rate in any group is proportional to females in the reproductive ages; the male population has almost no effect on the figures so long as the male population is not zero) it makes sense that the expendable sex should be subjected to the experiments to a greater degree than the non-expendable.

This effect, however, would also cause a marked problem in psychology; in any given time-era, the male population would be reacting to certain mutational influences that were not yet effective in the female population.

Regards,   John W. Campbell, Jr.

Frank Kelly Freas *June 10, 1955*

Dear Polly & Kelly:

As we discussed over the telephone, I am making a change in my will, making you two guardians of our children in the event both **Peg** and I should die.

Because things can happen suddenly, and entirely unexpectedly — a fact most clearly brought home to us by **Joe Winter's** unexpected death — **Peg** and I are making holographic emendations to attach to our will, until such time — probably a week or so — as we can have formal revisions of our wills prepared. This will be done by our attorney, **C. Parker Morgan**, of Elizabeth and Lake Mohawk, N.J., who holds the original copies of our present wills. We're driving up to Williamstown this weekend, and accidents can and do happen; we plan to be prepared in any foreseeable event.

In case the matter should ever have to be brought up, something of my thinking on these stipulations is, I think, worth recording. A court might raise questions concerning the guardianship of the children if their genetic mother insisted.

Dona is, as I know better than any one else can, since I lived with her for nearly two decades, a kindly, gentle, and sweet person, of no ill intent, and of reasonable morality. She is, however, unable to offer the strong, firm guidance **Philinda** and **Leslyn** must have during their childhood. **Philinda** has begun her adolesence now, of course, and could probably be fairly selfguiding in most respects; **Leslyn**, however, deeply needs a strong, wise guardian.

By sheer force of persistence and determination, **Philinda** can, and has, forced **Dona** to change her intentions; **Dona** is not a sufficiently *strong* personality, however kindly and sweet, to be able to act as a limiting, guiding force for **Philinda**. When **Philinda** has visited the household **Dona** and **George Smith** maintain, **Philinda** has, repeatedly, organized the action of the household around *her* plans. While **Philinda** is, herself, a sound and kindly personality, and has acted in good part and unselfishly on most such occasions, a guardian who cannot influence the determination of the ward is evidently inadequate and incompetent, however kindly, sweet, or wise that guardian may be.

A guardian who can influence a ward only by physical force, or by asking the help of legal agencies to enforce a discipline that guardian cannot maintain by his own wisdom and strength of personality — any adult, in other words, who cannot influence a child without calling on physical force or outside help — is an inadequate guardian. It is futile to discuss the good intent, the wisdom, or the kindly nature of a guardian if that guardian cannot influence the ward.

I know **Dona** of old; while **Philinda** was under ten years of age, **Dona** was not able to induce obedience from **Philinda** when it came to a contest of wills. I do not question **Dona's** basic good intent; I state as a fact that she is not a sufficiently powerful personality to guide and influence **Philinda**.

Philinda is anything but a cruel or wicked person; she is exceptionally sweet and kind, as many friends can testify. But she is now 14 years old; she has strength of personality, high intelligence, genuine kindness and sweetness — but she does not have wisdom, for that comes only with age and experience.

A household in which the strong, but unwise child cannot have the guidance of a stronger and wiser adult can only be a household of tension, misery, and lasting unhappiness.

I would not have that happen either to my children, nor to **Dona** — whom I can and do respect for what she is, while recognizing clearly what she is not.

The remarks I have made with respect to **Philinda** apply equally with respect to **Leslyn**, who is also a very sweet, very deeply kindly and cooperative personality — with a personality having the tough determination of chilled chrome-vanadium tool-steel.

I have told you before, my feeling that our culture is mistaken in thinking of the lamb as a symbol of gentleness; it is, I feel, an example of weakness and stupidity. I agree in full with St. Augustine that a baby is innocent only because of weakness, not because of inherent beauty-of-soul. Only the strong can be gentle, for gentleness consists in witholding strength posessed, not in lack of strength.

Leslyn and **Philinda** are both truly gentle, in this sense. But they are, because they are young, unwise.

I have seen them with you two; I have heard their attitudes after having been taken care of by you two. They clearly love and respect you both, and feel in you two the strength of personality they need.

An additional and important factor is, as you know, that the type of life which **Dona** and **George Smith** find desireable is one I cannot consider ideal. They have evidenced a lasting desire for weekend cocktail parties that is, I strongly feel, deleterious to the well-being of their own son, **Douglass**, whom I have observed shares rather freely in their cocktails at the age of 2½ years. It may be that I will be held "stuffy," but my medical friends suggest that that is not an optimum diet for small children.

It has also been my strong impression that the mental attitude displayed by the group to which **Dona** and **George** have attached themselves is something lifted from a novel of the 1920's — something by F. Scott Fitzgerald, or Michael Arlen. The world tried that approach to life, and abandoned it some 30 years ago. I think it should have been abandoned.

For all these reasons, then, I have specifically stipulated that **Dona** and **George** are *not* to be guardians of the children, although the children will, of course, visit their mother occasionally. It is their right, and it is **Dona's** right that they should.

Sincerely, John W. Campbell, Jr.

Forry Ackerman   *June 19, 1955*

Dear Forry:

Please, guy! I am not responsible for **Horace Gold's** telepathic renditions of what *I* think; neither am I responsible for the processes of his somewhat unusual mentations. Being oriented on the Importance of Being Normal, it is important to him to think that what he thinks is "just like anybody else." Therefore, when he blows his stack, he necessarily holds that any other editor would necessarily blow his stack under the same conditions.

This is an assumption contrary to fact, I am happy to report.

I wrote to the guy who was listed as editor of that sheet, and made a few comments. I haven't heard from him since; I doubt that anyone else will, either, and I doubt, also, that he'll ever pull quite that sort of an article on the science-fiction field again.

In telling someone off, one way is to bawl him out, curse him out for his belligerence, damn him for his presumptuousness, and blast him for his ignorance. This induces him to prove he can produce an even more belligerent, ignorant and presumptuous argument. Deny what he said, and he'll say more, and say it louder.

I acknowledged the full truth of everything he said . . . but added a few things he didn't say. I admitted that science-fiction was quite chauvinistic, in saying that Man was going to conquer the Galaxy. But I explained that it was our — perhaps mistaken — feeling that there is a need to recognize the dignity of a human being, as such. And added that he might be interested that, as our circulation records show, we have sales peaks near laboratories, universities, technical schools — and the Negro districts of large cities. Seemingly, many Negro readers appreciate our attitude that it is important to be human; they seem to like our attitude that Man is important beyond the narrow limits of race or creed or color. But perhaps we are chauvinistic in that.

I also acknowledged that most of our heroes had American names, as his article writer had said. But the author neglected to add that most of our science-fiction is written in English for an English-speaking audience. Tonal languages cannot be adequately transliterated into English; this makes it very difficult to use Chinese names, for example, or Bantu names, wherein tongue-clicks and lip-smacks must be represented. Also, since our readers are unfamiliar with the highly polysyllabic Greek patronymics, it is poor craftsmanship for an author to use a hero who is named Papulopopofilous.

I don't think the gentleman will choose to stick his neck out quite so far in the immediate future.

Regards,   John

Philip Jose' Farmer   *July 30, 1955*

Dear Phil:

I'm returning your novel to your agent; I could have returned it unread, so far as that goes — I've got novels running out my ears now. I've got the **Eric Frank Russell** piece now running, a **Frank Herbert** novel after that, and a **Bob Heinlein** piece to follow that. I won't be in the market for about five months.

However, I did read it, and will discuss it below.

First, however: I'm currently engaged in suing Shasta myself. I'm also engaged in research on the subject of Magic and how to lay curses on people, because that's more apt to produce a certain satisfaction, even if no money is forthcoming. In the meantime, I'm doing what I can to engender the maximum possible degree of unhappiness for **Korshak**.

I can practically guarantee you won't get any appreciable money; **Ray Jones**, **Will Jenkins** and I are after him, but also he has a printer who's after some 10-15 kilobucks. It is my earnest hope that, since he never incorporated his nasty little enterprise, that we wind up owning his car, his furniture, and most of his clothes.

In the meantime, if you know of a good hex doctor, you might consult him.

Now as to your novel: The essence of good science-fiction is the introduction and development of a new and different idea, or viewpoint. If you're tackling a science-fiction novel of characterization, you've got to follow the proposition through to the end; the character must learn, change, and develop so that he or she winds up a different personality.

Green doesn't. He starts off a snobbish son of a bitch, and winds up with no real change of understanding — merely a promise that he's going to. The only one who shows real growth and understanding is the boy; Armla (or whatever her name was) shows much more growth than Green.

That passage from the *Shipwrecked Astrogator's Manual*, or whatnot, express the fundamental proposition of the thing — and it's false. It's precisely what a cultural system tends to do — when it's an adolescent or childish culture. It *knows* it's right, and *knows* any other culture one of it's citizens might encounter must be the same as it itself, or must, necessarily, be stupid, immoral, foolish, or . . . in some way to be demeaned and rejected completely.

This rule that a culture lays on its citizens is a rule demanding *don't learn anything we haven't taught you.*

Green obeys it scrupulously. He doesn't learn one damned thing. His attitudes reek of a snobbish, self-satisfied, we-know-everything-worth-knowing background, and an air of "I put up with this because you fools just don't know any better."

And that persists, despite the fact that his wife has persistently proven her good sense, real ability to achieve, and real ability to plan — while he has not once made any of his plans work out!

(Incidentally, the effort to ship live fish will fail anyway; ask a fishery service or aquarium director what it takes to keep salt-water fish alive and healthy on a 30-day overland journey. Maran would make more packing in smoked fish; they take so much less room — by odds of about 500 to 1 — that even if the scheme worked, he'd make a lot less. Yeah, I know Green is a marine expert — but Green's a marine expert *only* when he has his highly advanced technical equipment. Give a modern surgeon a flint or obsidian knife, some wooden sticks, no drugs, no sterilizer, no other equipment, and tell him to preform a gastroenterotomy, and see what he says.)

Green's plans throughout are based on a conviction that amounts to "I could do anything if I weren't hampered by these fools." Only he keeps having to have other people save his bacon.

At no point does he bother to find out *why* they have a culture set up that way, nor does he bother to find out how he can serve that culture practically. He assumes as unarguable that the localites are dopes, fools, stupid, and not worthy of understanding by such a great man as he, from such a magnificent culture as his.

I know that, currently, it is considered "undemocratic" to suggest that there is a difference in the abilities of different human races. O. K.; I'm undemocratic as all hell. Just follow for a moment, and observe this possible correlation:

If a man is consistently unlucky for 30 years running, and winds up getting killed by having the breaks on his car fail at a critical time — he ain't unlucky. He's careless. And he was careless for 30 years running, which is why he had "bad luck."

And if a man is consistently lucky for 30 years, and winds up a millionaire . . . he ain't lucky, friend. He's got his eyes open and he's making plans. He "just happens" to be around when things happen. (A friend of mine got one of the world's most famous pictures of a horse rearing at the starting gate. A perfectly magnificent shot, dynamic, spontaneous, beautifully lighted. His friends congratulated him on his luck. He'd been following that particular horse — a known bad actor — for three months. He knew what tracks had the starting gates correctly located with respect to the afternoon sun. He was a regular sports photographer, so no visit to the track was wasted — but he watched for that particular shot.)

The Caucasian race runs the world currently; t'ain't an accident. There have been brilliant Negros, brilliant Amerindians, brilliant Chinese, brilliant leaders of every racial group.

Yeah — and you can win the Irish Sweepstakes and get rich. But few who do stay rich for long. Ghengis Kahn swept across the world — but his Magyar followers couldn't hold on to what he won.

The *average* of the racial group involved is important for *holding* a gain; the *brilliance of individuals* accounts only for the sudden spurts.

The *average* Caucasian has some kind of genetic advantage over the *average* member of the other racial types. Individual Negros, Amerindians, Chinese, etc., are markedly superior to individual Caucasoids . . . but that doesn't alter the statistical fact. And the statistical fact is that something about the Caucasoid approach to life is, in the long run, over a broad area, under infinitely varying conditions, slightly better.

291

O. K. — what?

I suggest two factors: Most of Mankind's other races are fatalistic in their attitude toward life and death. An Amerindian will face death with stoic calm and courage, as will the average Chinese, Negro, or Polynesian. Only the white man tends to become hysterical in the face of inevitable death, giving up the dignity of calm courage, and breaking down into a frantic, fanatic, clawing maniac.

That's why the Caucusoids win wars they should have lost. Even when a detachment is obviously hopelessly surrounded, and calm reason shows that death is inveitable and further struggle hopeless — they fight. In fact, they go quite crazy, and, with half a dozen bullets in his guts, knowing he's already killed, with one leg shattered by shrapnel — this is when a white man is most hysterically dangerous. This is when he completes the last 30 yards of his attack on the machine gun nest, and throws his hand grenades.

Very irrational, of course; obviously a man with one leg useless, and already suffering from four mortal wounds, has nothing left to fight for, and nothing really left to fight with. But the crazy fool white man misunderstands that; he now figures he has no reason whatever for protecting himself from futher damage . . . and he may succeed in getting the son of a bitch that did it to him.

The white man isn't fatalistic, and doesn't display the calm dignity other races expect in the face of death. Instead he turns into a crazy maniac intent only on commiting suicide in the most offensive possible manner. Of course, that doesn't help the individual much — but it's hell on the enemy. And the racial *group* benefits, though the individual doesn't. Of course *he* dies . . . but his children, his siblings, his clan doesn't, because in his dying he cost the enemy too much.

The other factor is that the Caucasians are the most unsure, insecure, uncertain, and ignorant people on Earth. They don't trust themselves and their own wisdom. When the Colonists arrived in America, the Amerindians showed them how to plant corn and other local foods — and the Colonists learned, because they didn't trust themselves. They showed the Amerinds how guns were made, and powder, and how machines could be built — but the Amerinds already knew just how to live. The guns were useful, yes. They took those all right.

The Colonists learned about the social organization of the Amerinds; they adopted many of their ways, such as the tribal pow-wow (called "a New England town meeting" by the colonists thereafter). But the Amerinds were sure of how to live; they had the answers, and recognized that the Colonists admitted superiority of their ways by adopting them.

So the Amerinds got the pants beat off 'em. We learned everything worth while the Amerinds had to offer. They didn't learn anything but drinking whiskey, and *shooting* guns from us. The outcome was absolutely predictable; if you learn all *his* best tricks, and he won't bother to learn yours — who wins?

Naturally, when the British came over to put down those colonial upstarts, they got the pants beat off them, too. They hadn't learned the Amerindian lessons, so they got sniped at from behind trees, with squirrel-rifles.

A good, sound hybird can always lick the bejayzus out of both his parents. He adopts all their best tricks, and uses A's against B, and B's against A.

Now Green refused to learn the local culture, and demeaned it thoroughly. Naturally, since that culutre had been learned the hard way, on a world which demanded that type of action, Green got himself clobbered again and again. If some of the supercillious self-satisfaction had ever gotten knocked out of him — he'd have gotten somewhere. But he had to do it *his* way. Only when he had the kind of machines he knew, and not a kind he had to patiently learn about, was he able to get anywhere.

In essence, you did *not* take a new, or markedly divergent viewpoint. It's still an historical novel, using old cultural concepts, described in a familiar, demeaning way, simply laid on a slightly different geographical background.

Science-fiction begins when you take a divergent viewpoint, and make the reader gradually understand that that cockeyed viewpoint — that he strongly rejected at first — is a sound, wise, and rational way of life under the circumstances of the situation at hand.

"The Cold Equations" was a test of that idea; I got **Godwin** to write that piece. The propostion there is the culturally abhorent proposition, "It is proper for a man to kill a girl, to make her a human sacrifice, knowingly and with intent." The trick is to make the divergent proposition powerful enough to cause a strong reaction when first encountered, and then gradually make it clear that the divergent proposition *is* valid.

That makes for stories with deep, lasting impact — the kind readers will remember subconsciously, even if they forget the exact name and plot. Because when a man accepts a new viewpoint on life, he will never again be quite the same person he was; you've changed him permanently.

Here are some propositions, each culturally abhorent, yet each I have argued out with historians, philosophers, metaphysicians, psychologists, geneticists, etc. — and have won agreement on their validity. The essential preceeding statement for each of these

293

propostions is *"There are situations* such that . . .
1. A religion involving human sacrifice is necessary.
2. Slavery — chattel slavery — is necessary to a culture.
3. A Lord and Serf culture, in which the Lords have the free right to take sexually any Serf girl they like strongly benefits the people.
4. A government which drives the people into concentration camps, collective farms, and slavery-to-the-government is beneficial.
5. A chattel-slave owner of great enlightenment, high ethics, good judgment, and genuine humanity would kill a young, healthy slave who had not killed or seriously injured the physical well-being of anyone else.

I positively guarantee that real, solid, and valid demonstration of the validity of every one of those propositions is possible. #4, it happens, actually applies to Russia and China; the governmental actions in those areas, at this time, with the present situation, is philosophically valid! But . . . only with the limitations implied in that sentence, limitations of time and place and circumstance.

To show what I mean, consider #5. I'll set it up as a story.

Publius Maximums, minor Roman noble, about 200 years after Augustus Caesar, has an estate about 40 miles from Rome, on which he lives with his wife, four young children, and some 20-odd slaves. He's a Roman of the old line; just, honest, practical, and enlightened. The culture of his time allows a slave-owner to do anything — and that means *anything* — to one of his slaves. The Circus shows the cultural attitude; so do the Roman "theater" shows, where if a script calls for a girl to be raped and tortured to death, a slave girl is duly raped and tortured to death on stage.

Publius, three months ago, bought a slave-girl to act as mother's helper and personal maid for his wife; she's a pretty 18-year-old, clean and attractive, and a good, intelligent girl of nice manners. But Publius came home unexpectedly one afternoon, and found Vona, the slave-girl, torturing his 10-months old son. She was running a pin 5 inches into the boy's leg. Babies are always getting pin-pricks — and a pin-prick on the skin doesn't reveal that the pin went in four or five inches, driven slowly into the flesh with secret glee. Vona is a sadist — a secret sadist.

Investigation shows she's been torturing other children; an arm twisted nearly out of its socket leaves no bruises; it causes no serious injury to the physical well-being of the child, either. Also, she has been torturing the other slaves . . . verbally. As an inner-household slave, she brought "word" that Quartus was to be sold to the Circus for lion bait. That Porta was to be sold to a notorious sex maniac, and her two children offered at the slave market. That. . . .

The girl was a sadist, and was disrupting the lives of everyone on the estate. And with a nature like that, punishment is as useless as it is with a kleptomaniac. Psychotherapy, of an order we haven't yet achieved, might help. But nothing available to Publius would. Punishing Vona would simply be cruel, and a waste of effort. Selling her to anyone without warning of her nature would be unethical.

The only possible, rational action is to kill her quietly and as quickly as possible.

Now notice this: Vona, as described, is essentially an entity who has a good-looking human female body, a good human female mind — and the psyche of a vicious animal. Today, we have a term called "sadist" which purports to "explain" what Vona is.

You made a great point of the silly superstition about "demons" in The Green Oddysy. Back off, and look again, my friend. Vona is a *succubus*. She is precisely what the Middle Ages people were talking about; an entity having the body of a beautiful woman, but inhabited by a demonic entity. She *looks* human — but lacks the major attribute necessary for a true, human being.

Maybe you prefer the term "sadist" — but "succubus" would make a quite adequate operational term. If Vona married a man, she would destroy his soul; that is, she would drive him insane with her subtle, vicious attacks on everything he strove to achieve.

If you think our ancestors were a bunch of utterly stupid dopes . . . where did we get our wonderful good sense? Strictly by magic, maybe? And those silly, superstitious Hindu herb-doctors thought they could treat everything from insanity to high blood pressure with one drug. (Now it's called *rowulfia serpentina*, and is used for everything from psychoneurosis to arterial hypertension. Very different, you understand. We don't believe in silly superstitions, because we have science.)

I'm looking for stories, and I want action — but the stories that really get inside a reader and light him up are the ones that can sell him a brand new viewpoint on life while entertaining him with fast, well-planned action.

Regards,   John W. Campbell, Jr.

Isaac Asimov   *August 6, 1955*

Dear Isaac:
    I'm taking the chronoscope story; the check's on the way.
    The last paragraph of your note, commenting that there did

seem to be some differences between the female and the male that weren't educational, interested me.

Look, my friend; did you every try to define what the term "I won," meant? Now to most people in this beknighted culture of ours (beknighted meaning that, like a knight of old, they wear solid iron armor to keep things from getting into their skulls), the term "I won" means exactly and solely the same as "I defeated my opponent."

Now let us consider two individuals who, from different positions, view the same object. A says, "It's a metal bar." B says, "Oh, no! I can see it clearly, and it's a sphere."

After some argument, A, who is older, and is B's immediate superior, defeats B completely, and B accepts that it is a metal bar.

Who won?

Answer: they both were defeated. It's a metal disc, of course, and neither A nor B has learned this. A may have defeated B — but the Universe has defeated them both. And the Universe exacts extremely severe penalties from any entity it defeats. The penalty is disaster.

My definition of "I won" is, "I achieved a more-useful understanding." In order for A or B to *really* win in the above example, one of them must achieve the more-useful understanding that it's a disc. Now if B acknowledges that he was mistaken in his belief it was a sphere, A may feel that B is defeated, and that he, A, has "won." But if B recognized that it was a disc — B really won, and A really lost. Because A lost the opportunity to achieve a more useful understanding.

I don't give a damn what your opinion is; you can have it, for all of me. And I don't give a damn what my opinion is. I want to know what the *Universe's* opinion is. But your opinion is useful to me, because, since it inevitably differs from mine, it gives me a chance to get a different angle of view on the Universe. From one angle only, a disc *does* appear a metal bar. If that were my only angle of view, I couldn't possibly learn what the reality was.

Now some items to consider: try defining "human being" some time. You may find it ain't quite so simple as it looks. For one thing; it's a remarkable thing that we, who are so brilliant in our wisdom, are the direct descendants of such a collection of stupid fools, silly, superstitious nit-wits, and maundering idiots as we are repeatedly assured inhabited this planet a few centuries ago. Truly remarkable that, descended from such as they, we could be so much more brilliant and wise and sensible, isn't it?

O.K., let's back off a bit and take a second look at this business.

Let's have a little story: Publius Cassius, minor Roman noble of about 200 years after Augustus Caesar, has an estate about 40 miles out of Rome, where he lives with his wife, four young children, and about 20 slaves. Publius is a Roman of the old school; a highly ethical, genuinely enlightened man. Just, but stern — with himself as much as with any other. He abhores the decadence of Roman civilization; he knows that Rome is going, and loathes the mores that lies behind the sadism of the Circus — and the "theater" of his time. (If a script calls for a character to be raped and tortured to death, a girl slave will be raped and tortured to death on stage.) But loathe it as he may, with the old Roman sense of practicality, he also knows that he, alone, cannot stem the momentum of a whole culture.

About three months ago, Publius bought a young girl at the slave market. She's 19, a pretty, shapely girl, intelligent, clean and attractive, with a pleasant voice and manner. He bought her as a sort of mother's helper for his wife. Vona, the girl, helps care for the children, and acts as his wife's personal maid.

One day, Publius returns home unexpectedly, and finds Vona gleefully running a pin about 5 inches long into his 10-months old son's buttox.

Investigation soon shows that Vona is a sadist. She's been secretly torturing the children too young to communicate — a pin-prick doesn't indicate how deeply the pin pricked. A twisted arm doesn't leave bruises to explain the child's behavior.

Also, she's been torturing the other slaves. As an inner-household slave, she's been passing out rumors that Quartus is to be sold to the Circus for lion-bait, while Marta is being sold to Sipulus, the well-known sex maniac, while her two children are to be sold in the public market.

Now Publius, as an ethical and enlightened man, has a problem. Punishing a sadist is as futile as punishing a kleptomaniac for stealing. He doesn't have modern terminology, but he's no fool; he knows the equivalent of "a psychopathological condition can't be cured by punishment."

Curing Vona is impossible. Selling her to another householder without warning of her nature would be unethical. Keeping her around where she can torture other human beings is unethical too, obviously.

What should Publius do?

Now the easiest thing for Publius to do is to simply run her through the heart with his short-sword, or have her pole-axed. Kill her as quickly as possible.

Publius, though, discusses it with his wife and his major domo, an old Greek philosopher who taught him as a boy. He takes Vona into Rome, takes her to one of the theaters, and trades her for a girl the stage-manager had bought for use in that evening's

297

performance. The stage manager's perfectly willing; Vona's good looking enough, and will last long enough while being skinned alive, to give his customer's their money's worth, and he doesn't care that she's a sadist, of course.

Publius takes the other girl home. Vona, a worthless, useless, destructive entity has been put to good use; by sacrificing her to a cultural momentum he cannot stop or slow, Publius has ransomed a girl that may have real value.

Of course, Publius pays a considerable penalty; by an act of his, a girl personally known to him will, that evening, die in agony under circumstances he abhores. He will, himself, feel unclean because of his personal action; if he had simply killed Vona, the other girl would have died — but she would have been unknown to him, and her screams would not be a result of any action of his.

But as I said, he is a just and stern man — with himself, too.

This little story (and you know as well as I that a thousand minor variations of it happened in the centuries of the Empires) has various points worth considering. For one, let's try to describe Vona operationally. She is an entity having a young human female body; she is physiologically a human female in every respect. She has a young human female mind, and a more-than-normally competent one. But she has the psyche of a vicious animal. The modern terminology is "she has a psychopathic personality."

Is Vona human, then?

She *looks* completely human. Judging by physical evidence, she has the potential of being a fine mother, of healthy, sturdy children. Her intelligence is good, and she appears to have the potential of being a fine help-mate for some young man, and a fine mother of their children.

But her sadistic drive multiplies all those potentials by minus one. She will use her fine female body to torture people; her intelligence will be directed to the task of destroying their hopes, their ambitions, their will to achieve and grow. She would amuse herself by torturing her own children; by destroying the essential humanity — the hope and belief in their fellows that makes a truly human individual — of her children, she would actually produce a litter of psychopaths like herself.

Because of the -1 multiplication, the prettier and more shapely she is, the better human female body she has, the more dangerous she is. And the more intelligent she is, the more skillfully and quickly she can think — the deadlier she is.

Now our poor, stupid, silly superstitious, no-nothing ancestors, the dopes, would have called her a *succubus* — would have said she was a female demon. A creature with the body of a beautiful young woman, and the soul of a demon. How silly of them! Imagine saying that this good-looking piece of animated meat was anything but human!

Just because somebody uses a system of terminology you aren't familiar with naturally proves they were fools and nit-wits.

The thing to do with a succubus or incubus was, of course, to kill them as soon as they were detected. A succubus, if allowed to roam loose, would, these superstitious dolts, our ancestors, said, trap young men, and destroy their souls. She would, if allowed to live, give birth to young demon children who would, in turn, spread the plague.

How silly!

Oh . . . yeah? What would you do with a psychopath in a culture that, scraping at the subsistence level, couldn't afford a luxury of locking them away from Mankind, and supporting them in luxury for the rest of their lives? Let 'em run loose, blasting the lives and hopes of pretty decent people around them?

Does the mere human physiology constitute full humanity? Our ancestors, from hard experience, damn well knew better.

Now let us consider a somewhat more advanced culture. We have a man who abides by the exact letter of the law; he never actually breaks any law — he just cleverly bends it into a trap for the injury of more ethical individuals. For instance, he starts a wholesale business, gets a lot of stock, carries on a big business by selling very cheap, and, in six months, goes into bankruptcy owing $200,000. Of course, the bankruptcy proceedings take over the few remaining assets of his company, and he's out of business.

But he gets a job shortly with his cousin, who bought a great deal of his stock from him before he went bankrupt.

Now this man has violated no law; it's just that he and his cousin have acquired $150,000 worth of merchandise for about $20,000.

They've got a nice business started now, and they haven't violated a single law.

And, in our culture, there isn't a damn thing you can do to the son of a bitch.

But it wasn't always that way. A few centuries back, a man might not violate any cultural law — but if he was, personally, a sheerly nasty bastard, he didn't have to answer to the culture through the courts of law . . . but he *did* have to answer to individuals he harmed, through the *code duello*.

The *code duello* must have purged the human race of a lot of psychic cripples. The incubus could be forgotten; the psychopath didn't bother people . . . for long. Just keep cropping off the nasty bastards as they pop up, and there'll be a strong tendency to eliminate the genetic defectives that tend that way. Oh, the nasty bastard might be right handy with the sword or pistol, and kill off a number of good guys — but sooner or later, he'd get cut down. As **Bob Heinlein** said in "Beyond This Horizon," the *code duello* ". . . breeds good manners and fast reactions." It rapidly breeds out the incubus and the psycopath, too.

Because of the relief from their menace the race bought through the *code duello*, the real nature, and danger, of the incubus and succubus were forgotten.

The trouble was, the *code duello* applied only to the *males*. Haemophillia will eliminate the males who display it, but the females act as a reservoir from which new outcroppings can continue to spring. During the *code duello* period, a man was responsible for his wife's actions; if she insulted someone, *he* had to take the blame. The result was that hubby would beat wifey's damn nasty hide off if she didn't behave — whether she liked to behave or not didn't matter. Hubby had a damn good reason and a damn good right to; *her* displayed nastyness could get *him* killed. If she wouldn't restrain her nastyness because she wanted to, she would bloody well be made to restrain it because she *had* to. Hubby could, of course, apologize profusely to the injured party, and simply take wifey home and whip hell out of her.

Of course, it doesn't make a psychopath stop having a psychopathic attitude — but it will, if maintained rigidly and continuously enough, make even a psychopath stop *displaying* her psychopathic attitude. It'll kill her shortly, of course; she'll go completely insane, die of one of the beatings, or develop a lethal psychosomatic. But that will definitely be no loss whatever to the evolution of a *human* race.

The thing is, under such a system, the female psychopath, like the female haemophilliac, doesn't *display* her characteristic — but carries it. The male psychopaths weren't restrained by guardians; they displayed their characteristic, and got themselves bumped off.

But now that women are allowed to be self-responsible. . . !

It's damn tough on people, but they have to be induced to *display* what they are, before the racial stock can be improved by eliminating them.

A chimpanzee *cannot* be taught to talk. The ability to handle high-order abstractions must be supplied genetically, since by the very nature of the thing, it can't be taught. (You can not teach something that the student cannot conceive; it's impossible by definition.) You can teach a moron to *do* something, but you can't teach him *why*. You can teach a man not to steal because the police will arrest and jail him — but you can't teach him to understand the higher-order abstractions of ethics. He has to have a genetic ability before that can be taught, just as the chimp can't be.

Gotthard Gunther made this highly interesting point; some information is "unleakable." Example: The Romans of the Republic conquered the barbarians around them with ease and dispatch, by applying a bit of military technology — they had a "secret weapon."

But the gimmick was that the barbarians, shown the secret, even when it was demonstrated and explained in detail, *could not learn* it. Russia can steal our atomic information; we can steal theirs. But the barbarians couldn't steal Rome's secret weapon, even when it was carefully demonstrated to them!

Reason: The secret weapon was the cohort-and-short-sword. The short sword markedly handicaps the individual warrior; a longer sword is more efficient. Now since it is obvious that the strength of an army is the sum of the strengths of the individual warriors, then decreasing the strength of the individual warrior weakens the army.

It's obvious that if five plus five is ten, then decreasing to four will decrease the result.

Only . . . four *times* four is 16.

The cohort was a *team*, not a sum-of-individuals. The individual *was* weakened by a short sword — but by using a short sword, and fighting in very close ranks, each individual barbarian was forced to meet two or more Romans. The barbarians with their long swords *could not* pack closely enough to fight on a one-to-one basis.

The barbarians lost with machine-like regularity. They could see the cohort at work; they could see the short-sword fighting techniques. But they could not conceive the necessary high-order abstraction; disciplined cooperation allows no individual to win glory, but assures victory to the team.

The barbarians could not accept, understand, or conceive of that abstraction. They went on insisting that the strength of an army was the sum of the individual strengths — and lost with perfect regularity.

Given: A culture with the cultural postulate "The King can do no wrong."

Problem: To prove "The King has wronged me."

Given: A culture with the cultural postulate "The State is wiser than any individual."

Problem: To prove "The State is mistaken, and I am right."

That time-viewer gimmick will result in an immense wave of madness. When it settles down again, there won't be any more psychopaths; they'll be dead. Can you slander a man by telling his prospective employer, "Oh, yes, he's a very bright individual."?

No court in the land would take that statement to be a slander.

But with a time-viewer you could replay the scene — and show the context, the facial expression, the tone of voice, and the gestures that went with it — and made it a vicious and effective slander. "It ain't what you say, it's the way that you say it that makes me so god-damn mad." When somebody's needled you viciously with that technique . . . what if you had a time-viewer, to replay the scene, and show exactly and precisely what he said, and make him hear the exact tones he used?

"I'd trust him with my life," says Bill Blow. That's the official wording. But the time-viewer shows the tone he used, and the gesture of a finger across the throat while he said it.

Or some one tells you, "Bill wants you to bring him a set of left-handed golf clubs," and says it with a grin and an expression that makes you, someone unfamiliar with golf, realize that it's another "left-handed monkey-wrench" deal.

So later you get the hide blistered off for not obeying orders and costing the boss an important deal. Tom Megabux, the Texas oil millionaire, was in town, and wanted to play a game — and was left-handed. Bill has faithfully and honestly reported that he gave you the order, and that you acknowledged it.

Oh, for a time-viewer!

Item: Let's define "sociology" as "the scientific study of groups of human beings numerous enough to constitute a statistical system, and homogeneous enough to constitute a meaningful group."

(False example: The average age at death of all males in the continental U.S. is 6.3 months. Reason: "all males" includes insects. It's numerous enough to be statistical, but not homogeneous enough.)

(Second false example: you can't discuss a single family group statistically.)

Then what is psychology? My answer: As of now, there is none! What's currently *called* psychology is actually a branch of sociology, because it's a *statistical group* study.

Try determining the characteristics of a molecule of benzene by studying the gas laws. The gas laws represent the statistical behavior of benzene molecules in vapor form — but they have nothing to do with the behavior of the benzene *molecule*.

Currently, psychologists are studying "one," the pronoun in the sentence "One who is a member of this culture." But this "one" is no more representative of a human individual than the statistical molecule is representative of benzene.

Your chronoscope represents one of a great class of devices; any culture can be disrupted by introducing a device which every individual wants, but which is intolerable to the culture. The matter-duplicator is another such device. The magic purse that is never empty is another.

302

By properly selecting the individually-desirable-culturally-intolerable device, any given aspect of a particular culture can be demolished. (Associated aspects will then undergo some drastic readjustments, of course, but the whole culture won't have to smash.)

What, then, would be the effect of making a chronoscope that would work *only* in the range of 75-100 years ago? It would smash prudery, but not privacy, for example.

Lots of possible angles on the thing!

Regards, John

Webb *September 20, 1955*

Dear Mr. Webb:

Sorry on the delay on your manuscript; I'm taking it at our regular 3¢ a word — $180.00

The delay was caused by my vacation; we just got back from Mexico.

I feel you're a little far out on the limb with the "intelligent life" thesis, myself — but it's your article, not mine, and a very interesting and important one it is. Your highly ingenious and valuable concept of network analysis applied to the problem is capable of far wider and more varied application. I am particularly amused that you, a chemist, have usefully applied a concept that obviously belongs in the special field of the topologist. As usual, the specialist in the field works on the proposition "My field of specialization, X, is intended for the purpose of solving X-field problems." Mathematics is to solve mathematical problems. Topology is to solve topological problems. We don't use topology to solve problems of planetography, therefore!

(However . . . I wonder what problems chemistry isn't being used to solve that it should solve if properly applied?!)

My feeling is that your analysis gives a very high probability that the network *is* a communication network.

The point you make about Martians being "a little" ahead or behind is the major factor in my preferring the animal-trails explanation; probably animals will inhabit Earth after Man has gone elsewhere.

Also, notice that if Man should achieve teleportation, or radio transmission of matter, or find any method of applying the concept of null geodesics, Man's communication network would shortly vanish from optical detection. Complete individual air transport would produce a nearly equivalent result, since communication would not then be network type, but point-to-point, yielding area-pattern rather than line-pattern effects. That is, if you connect n

303

points scattered at random on a plane (or sphere) with lines on the basis of single connectivity — simply point-to-point connection — you will have *only* accidental points, and unenmeshed points. The result would be no communication network pattern at all.

The proposal of intelligent inhabitants who developed before Mars dried up has, of course, been made many times. I analysed that one myself, some years back, and did an article that appeared in *Esquire* titled "Martians Like It Dry."

The evidence of geophysics, or planet-physics to be more accurate, plus physical chemistry, suggests that the essential ratio of gas-to-solid-mass for a given planet will be established during the first 100,000,000 years of its existence. Thereafter, changes in total mass of matter will be so slight as to be unimportant. No appreciable hydrogen escaped from Mars after that period, in other words. True, free hydrogen could escape from Mars, at the present temperature, etc. But since Mars probably has quite a deep swathing of activated oxygen as ozone around it, the probability of a hydrogen atom succeeding in running that gauntlet clear to empty space is rather small, now; the water molecule, on the other hand, cannot readily escape from Mars.

My belief is that the present situation is one that has obtained, with mighty small alteration, during the last 4,500,000,000 years since the Solar System was established.

The rate at which Mars would lose free hydrogen is so high that "all" the free hydrogen would have gone long, long before life first appeared on Earth.

The trouble with the usual line of calculation on this problem is that it fails to take into account the overall *system* of reactions possible and their *mutual* rather than individual probabilities.

Isaac Asimov called to my attention one aspect of that problem. Given that there are several stable isotopes of hydrogen, oxygen, nitrogen, carbon, sulfur and iron, and that only these atom-types are involved in the structure of haemoglobin, what is the probability that a naturally occurring molecule of haemoglobin will contain in its structure one or more of the rare isotopes.

That is, given that H^2 occurs to the extent of about 16 atoms per 100,000, that O^{18} shows roughly equal occurence, N^{15} about the same, and so on, what is the probability that a given molecule of haemoglobin *will* contain one or more of the rare stable isotopes?

The answer, rather startlingly, comes out 0.999999999999! In the complex *system* of haemoglobin, as in any *system*, probabilities show up as products, not as sums.

In Mars' atmosphere, the probability that a hydrogen atom will succeed in making a complete trip to the vacuum beyond depends on the concentration, and hence probability, of side reactions yielding molecules that can't escape — such as ammonia or water. Given a very high relative concentration of highly activated oxygen and nitrogen . . . there comes a point where the hydrogen has damn small chance of escape. Try filtering hydrogen through a mixture of nitrogen and oxygen in an electric discharge tube illuminated by a powerful quartz mercury vapor arc; the free hydrogen coming out the other end is going to be somewhat hard to detect!

My conclusion is that if Mars is dry, it's been that way for about 4,000,000,000 years.

Now life on Earth took something like 2,000,000,000 years to get beyond the single-celled stage. Evolution since then has taken place at a high-order exponential rate. But the first couple of billion years, not much progress seems to have been made.

To get your intelligent life developed on Mars *before* the present conditions developed, you're going to have to go from something more primitive than a slime mold to something more competent than Man at present in about 50,000,000 years. And that would have happened roughly 4,000,000,000 years ago — so you must then assume that evolution stopped with a *clank*, right there, and hasn't budged in the 4000 megayears since. Otherwise the Martians would not still be sitting in their inconceivably ancient greenhouses.

I prefer to believe that life evolved methods of living quite freely and happily in the Martian environment. The fact that water freezes at 0° C doesn't mean the blood, or sap, of a living organism has to. After all, alcohol-water mixtures are easy to produce by organic processes; glycerine-water is also easy for a living organism, and they stay liquid at temperatures colder than any Martian night. Also, the Martian polar areas have a lovely climate, for almost 10 straight months at a time.

If a fish swimming in salt water can retain fresh water in his blood, with only a membrane so delicate that oxygen can pass freely separating them, I figure a Martian animal could conserve water. Earth animals have a damned inefficient system of absorbing oxygen from the atmosphere — but it's entirely adequate when there's so much available. But on Mars, I imagine animals did a little more searching to get a really efficient mechanism. *Chemically* our system's adequate, but mechanically it stinks. Also, things being the way they are, Earth life hasn't made much of any effort toward storing oxygen. The whale does; he breathes for a few minutes, then gets along real nice for a half to three-quarters of an hour.

I have a strong hunch that some astonishingly active animals could evolve on Mars — ones that stored oxidative material in their bodies, and could put on bursts of great speed and energy thereby, and used a relatively small lung system *at peak efficiency all day long*.

You evolved to use maximum oxygen-absorption only when under peak load; if you breathe strongly and deeply while sitting down, you suffer from hyperoxygenation, get dizzy, and generally upset. On Earth, that's the simple, good-engineering method. On Mars. . . ?

Again, who says animals *have* to be fast-moving? We've got turtles around, even in competition with critters that can move a damn sight faster. You don't have to run very fast to catch a carrot; just because rabbits are fast runners doesn't mean herbivours have to be! By racing along at the rate of 10 miles a day, a creature could move back and forth, staying in the summer season zone of Mars. Or, if he were willing to take life easy, he could hibernate till the vegetables came back around him.

I wouldn't write off as impossible living forms fully adapted to Mars conditions. They might have a blood stream that could be used for a good grade of high-proof brandy . . . but so what. Considering what life can do, I wouldn't be too surprised if, somewhere, on some planet, explorers run into a variety of mouse-like creature that happily gnaw holes in chrome-moly tool-steel to get at supplies . . . using teeth with boron carbide abrasive. Or maybe diamond teeth — that is, teeth with diamond dust crystal in their material. And maybe mild-steel bones; life can handle the chemistry of iron, after all!

Life is considerably tougher than we tend to think. We fragile creatures, it turns out, can be slammed into a sheet-steel wall at 180 miles an hour, with no particular damage. The steel stretches and dents in, but the man just sort of shakes himself, says, "Oh . . . my head!" and walks off to get a drink. Also, you enjoy the fresh salt spray in the air near the sea. What would you make a robot of if you intended him to be able to live 75 years in that salt spray atmosphere?

We're fragile. Hell, man! Take a look at the facts!

Sincerely,   John W. Campbell, Jr.

Harry [Stine]   *May 16, 1956*

Dear Harry:

There's a basic law of cultural and personal relationships, I guess, that can, in first approximation, be expressed as "You are free to have any idea you want, hold any opinion you like, provided it has no effect whatever."

For example, you are free to have the opinion that overpopulation problems can best be solved by slaughtering every other baby born, and selling the meat . . . provided you do nothing whatever that will make the opinion effective.

You are also free to hold the opinion that American Democracy as it is is perfect — provided you communicate the opinion only to individuals who are already in full agreement with that, and so make your opinion have no effect whatever.

If, however, you communicate the opinion to someone who holds a different opinion, the resulting conflict will be measured by the degree of disagreement, and the "personality-mass" of the conflicting individuals.

It's sort of like saying that the total flow of charge between two charged systems will be a function of their starting disagreement of potential and the capacity of the two systems.

Now one of the problems involved in this business is the conductive capability of the cirucit over which the charge-flow has to move. For example, if you've got a standard 2000 volt, 8 μF condenser, intended for power-supply filter service, and try to bank up a collection of these for use in a high-intensity photoflash unit, you'rc apt to ruin 'em. Reason: The connections between the foil inside the condenser can, and the condenser terminals, is designed for light-current loads. This type of condenser is not designed for the many-amperes shock-discharge service.

My friend **Bill Stewart** was telling me that these little Minibreakers overload relays intended for household fuse-replacement have to pass a test involving breaking a *five thousand ampere* short circuit. The ordinary motor-control boxed-in switches used on 220 volt motors have to pass a 25,000 ampere test.

In hitching filter condensers in a 400 ma power supply #22 wire would be perfectly adequate; after all, the impedance of a couple of feet of #22 copper is a damn sight smaller than the impedance of even an 8 μF condenser at 60 or 120 cycles.

But short that condenser through the #22, and you'll have copper plating in the general surrounding area.

O.K. — the trouble with us is that we're both high-capacitance systems, and the English language communication channel between us is about a #60 copper wire. Unless we cable about 1000 strands between us, the wire blows out every time we try to send a few volts disagreement down the line.

That wire between us has blown out so damn many times already that, by now, we should be expecting the blasted thing to collapse under us, and get over being surprised and disappointed.

English is a fine communication channel for interconnecting filter condensers; it does fine for stabilizing the minor variations between ordinary, normal human beings in the ordinary, normal human businesses in American culture.

It's just fine for communicating and smoothing out the ripple-voltage

307

differences between a wholesaler and a retail merchant, and between a retail merchant and a customer. But, dammit, you aren't in the area the language was developed to handle — you're way the hellangone off on the North Boundary, while I am way off on the Southeast Frontier. And trying to handle those differences in English is a frustrating business. The wholesaler-retailer system may be at 2000 volts to ground, but they're only about 10 volts apart. But you're at about 5000 volts to ground, and I'm busy exploring the characteristics of inverse charges, so I'm about -300 volts to ground.

If you assume that English is an adequate communication channel, and assume that what the English communication says is what I intended — we're gonna have troubles. There isn't any language built yet that'll actually handle what we're talking about.

Also, I'm well aware that you consider yourself a mild and gentle man. I, of course, know that I am, also.

Only you should ask some of your fiends what *they* think. My friends are all sure I'm an authoritarian, dogmatic, absolutistic, iron-headed dictatorial old bastard.

Dr. Bridgeman, in some of his extreme pressure research, made the interesting discovery that he could extrude hard steel into a rubber mold by running the pressure above 200,000 psi. The steel flowed then — and the rubber didn't.

You and I, my friend, are like rubber — nice, mild, gentle stuff . . . until the pressure gets on. Then the best grade of tool steel starts getting squeezed into the shape the rubber holds.

Also, you might notice the item the crash research programs have discovered; a human being isn't hurt at all if you catch him in a nice sheet of automobile steel — but you can scrape him off with a putty-knife if you catch him in a rubber mat.

Peg put the whole problem in a nice, neat phrase. (Having encountered it, she was in an excellent position to do so. Betcha your beloved wife will like the phrase too.) She said I had "the inexorability of a saint." That's the other side of patience, you know.

The language channel is completely inadequate, and is going to stay that way, since it isn't designed for us or our type.

Of course I'm an amateur; after 30 years of being a professional amateur in the fields of science, what would you expect me to be?

And one of the troubles with your evaluation of things is that you never really caught on to what happened in and with Dianetics®. Psychologists, not the original Dianetics® gang, forced it to assume a professional aspect — when it wasn't ready. That's why I got out of the group; I've continued during the subsequent years to follow the original amateur research line. It's been enormously effective, too.

What you fail to realize is that *only religion* of all fields of human thought is allowed to be an amateur research. **Hubbard's** finally gotten the problems swung around — too late, and in a half-ass fashion — into a religion.

Item: No amateur may practice medicine, or study medicine.

Item: No amateur may practice psychotherapy, or research psychotherapy.

Reason: Nobody but amateurs exist in the fields . . . but they don't dare admit it, because they've claimed to be professionals.

Every one of the truly great physicians has known and repeatedly said that he was an amateur who knew nothing for sure. It's only the greatest, however, who have the courage and the standing to get away with that.

Dianetics®, right from the start, was getting results that made physicians and professional psychotherapists look silly. Now when a man who says "I'm an amateur, just trying to see what can be done in this area," starts doing things that the professionals say can't be done . . . strangely, the professionals get madder'n hell. The first thing they tend to do is to force the amateur to admit he's a professional of some sort — and, of course, they'd prefer to have him admit he's a professional crook, who isn't really getting results.

Ron Hubbard had most excellent opportunities to institute some Grade A juicy libel suits. It's a shame, really, that he didn't have the cash on hand to get the process started, because he could have made a couple of millions just suing psychiatrists and psychologists across the country for libel and slander.

I know for a positive fact — and have had written, signed letters to prove it — that psychiatrists were telling their patients that **Ron** had been committed as insane after Dianetics® was published. That constitutes an open-and-shut case of slander and/or libel. Because **Ron**, just for the record, had gone to the University of Chicago psychometric department, and had a very fine and completely clear record, and had *not* been institutionalized after Dianetics® was published.

Though I'll admit, the psychiatrists damned near did make it come off, for a while.

I dropped out of the rat-race, and strongly suggested that **Ron** do likewise, when it became abundantly clear that there was no use trying to accomplish anything *that way*. It was, as a matter of fact, I, not **Ron**, who originally suggested that it should be dropped as a psychotherapy, and reconstituted as a religion. Because *only religions are permitted to be amateurs*.

And it took thousands of years, and vast human suffering, to achieve that.

There'll come a time when science-fiction will be an orthodox literature, and only properly trained professionals will be considered fit contributors. It'll probably be under governmental regulation, too — because it will be recognized for what it is: a major cultural tool for reshaping the thinking of the more imaginative and creative citizens, from which group the future leaders inevitably arise.

There will then follow a long, long, period before science-fiction, having been completely surpassed as a tool of education, will be freed to be an amateur field.

Sure I'm an amateur. I most carefully avoid getting trapped into a professional status. I can, in my blundering, amateurish way make suggestions that no respected authority would dare to make.

I have one hell of a tight-rope path to follow too; I'm aware — as the dunder-headed professionals are not, as yet — of the extremely powerful effect I can and do have. I've had the holy hell scared out of me a dozen times, and learned the lesson. (It's rather hard to accept that you do have an effect you don't intend.) I've seen what happens; it makes no difference whether I intend it or not — it happens anyway.

Yes, and it's hard on you — you and **Ike Asimov** and **Wayne Batteau** and **Gib Hocking** and a dozen others I write to or talk to. Glad you liked that editorial on psionics; you should, though since you helped write it. A golfer can practice driving golf balls before he goes on the links in the tournament. An actor can practice his part at rehearsal, and can improve his performance during the run of the play. But the editor can't practice like that; I can write a comment and publish it once, and only once. If it isn't right that first time . . . that's that. I can't bring up that subject again.

I have to practice putting the idea in communicationally-effective form by trying it out on individuals. And that, by damn, is tough!

If one of the fans comes into the office, and I explain to him that due to our new method of putting ink on paper, red will henceforth be blue . . . about half of them will see the pretty blue rose on the cover.

If you think I'm kidding, back off and try again. And they do *not* have to be kids, either. I had a Marine Captain, who had been telling me the story of going ashore on Pelilia, sitting across from me, looking somewhat scared and bewildered, because his hands were stuck together and he couldn't get them apart. I'd suggested that that sometimes happened to people.

I had not hypnotised him. Not in any ordinary sense.

Ever hear of "Faith"? Hypnosis is a quasi-mechanical way of inducing someone to have Faith in the operator. There are other ways — and some of those other ways strike a hundred times as deep, and are a damn sight more subtle.

Whether I like it or not, whether I choose it or not, there are thousands of people in this country who have Faith in me.

The best way to establish that hyper-hypnosis is to be completely honest, sincere, and do the best damn job of work you can, and keep at it for years. People begin to have Faith in you.

Then you should try to get help in evaluating something. Express an idea, an hypothesis for consideration — and everyone who has Faith in you promptly "knows" something he didn't know before.

Go ahead — try it on your own kids. Be honest as you can, sincere as you can, and strive with genuine and full-hearted effort to find the best available answers. Do your damndest to avoid letting 'em down. Know yourself to be a long way from perfect, and do the best you can to do it right anyway. Help them to avoid some of the mistakes you got sucked into.

Then make the mistake of telling 'em red is really blue . . . and can you expect them, then, to refrain from saying roses are blue?

O.K., **Harry**. Now tell me how I can get a valid — not an honest, but a *valid* — reaction to one of my hypotheses! Some of the people around me will honestly agree that red is blue: they honestly believe it, however invalid it may be. Some of the others will firmly, stubbornly insist that red is really blue, because I said red was red, and they're fighting solidly against the danger of failing to disagree when I make a mistake.

Dammit, I've *got* to cross-check my ideas before I put 'em in an editorial — and I can do it only by cross-checking with someone who will neither deny-for-the-sake-of-denying, nor agree because he has Faith in me, nor deny because Tradition says "No."

Do a sloppy job of work, and you can get plenty of cross-checking, good, sound, valid cross-checking. But the better job you manage, the fewer valid cross-checks you get.

You help write the editorials; that's why they tend to be better than my letters. You and the rest of the gang that helps out by considering my suggestions, without having to deny or agree on a direct observer-effect sort of phenomenon.

You just wait, **Harry**. Wait 'till your kids get old enough to have that blasted Faith effect — and then try getting valid observations from them. In the meantime, check on your effect on some of the people around you. The more competent you are, the less help you *can* get.

As to danger in psionics. Yes, **Harry**; you're quite right. One man I know tried tuning one of his psionic machines so as to couple a white mouse and an ancient pre-Aztec Mexican magic carving of a little lizard. The lizard had scalloped ears, and its tail was broken off. The mouse died three days later with scalloped ears and its tail broken off. Better "tuning" killed three white mice in succession, in 12 hours each. Their tails broke off, but in the short time their ears didn't become scalloped.

Another man I know of put out all the lights in the small town where he was doing his research. He quenched the electric power — no blown fuses involved.

You think, maybe, they were kidding in the old days when they said "He summoned a demon too powerful to control"?

Aside from that form of psionic danger, be it noted that Newton and Faraday both went nuts from summoning understandings too powerful for them to control.

If an irresistible force meets an immoveable object, what happens?

Answer: they exist in two separate universes. If they didn't before that moment, they do immediately thereafter.

What happens when a blue-white dwarf star contracts under its own gravity? Eventually, if it's some 10 or more times as massive as our Sun, it contracts to a point where it causes a discontinuity in space, and ceases to be a member of this Universe.

What happens to a man when two absolute loyalties come into conflict in his mind? Consider a Master Sergeant in the Marines, a career Marine, with absolute loyalty to the Corps, and absolute loyalty to his buddies, who's married and has two children. He's loaned $150 to a buddy who has five kids, and is damned hard up. The friend hasn't been able to pay back for eight months. And now the Sergeant's wife is telling him that he owes it to his family to get that money, because they need it too.

Answer: The Sergeant comes to standing in a Western Union office, with his gun in his hand, and vague memory of having just told somebody to lie down on the floor. There's a nice discontinuity in his mind concerning the intervening events, and a vast confusion, so he wanders out of the place vaguely, and hands his gun to the cops who come up in a prowl car. Because he also has an absolute sense of honesty, so he can't steal, either.

But it isn't disloyal to a friend if you try, and fail, is it?

Bernie Kahn, chief of psychiatric research at Mare Island told me about that case.

How do you put his mind back together? How do you teach a man to be appropriately disloyal — when "everybody knows" that loyalty is an Absolute thing?"

Polonius to Laertes: "And this above all else, to thine own self be true and it follows as the night the day, thou canst not then be false to any man." and "Neither borrower nor lender be, for loan oft looses both self and friend."

Polonius was Shakespear's epitimization of the sincere, bumbling, second-rank leader of Mankind. He's the modern high school principle, the sincere, but not brilliant minister, priest or rabbi. And he's Master Sergeant Jones, of the Marines, teaching the recruits the making of a Marine.

They're very fine people, all of them — sincere and conscientious, willing to work and fight, and sacrifice themselves for the things they believe in. God help them.

How do you put Master Sergeant Jones back together again, though? How do you teach a man to have limited loyalty?

What do you do with a man who'd rather destroy himself and his own mind than break Faith with Loyalty to others?

Sure, we can say that Mankind can afford to drop that kind — it's an unsuccessful, non-survival type. You can say it, and you can logically recognize the statement has some validity. But you can't feel it true, can you.

May I suggest that you repeatedly throw logical hoaxes at your kids in the years to come? Make straight-faced, logical-sounding statements — propositions that sound perfectly sensibel . . . only not quite rational.

Like when **Leslyn** asked why I had two pairs of glasses, and I told her one was to see small things, like bolts and nuts on the radio bench I was working on, and one was to see big things. So I wore *these* glasses to see her, but I used these to see **Peg**.

Her thought processes visibly came to a shuddering halt, went into reverse, and ran that through again. She gave me The Eye, said "Oh Daddy!" in a disgusted tone, and started figuring it out for herself.

Loyalty is a logical process, and all logical processes are absolute . . . but not quite rational, sometimes.

But psionics has a whole collection of fascinating dangers. So, my friend, does working with nitric acid-hydrazine fuel combinations. Or thermonuclear reactions. Or Aerobees that go up 18,000 feet before coming back to Mama Earth, complete with several tons of unused high-energy fuel.

By the way, coming up, by **Randy Garret**, a story about a spaceship that lost its engine power while on its way in for landing on Earth. It's headed for Long Island Sound at 20 mps, and has a mass of some hundreds of tons, plus 150 passengers aboard. What'll happen when it hits about 75 miles from New York City?

Regards, John

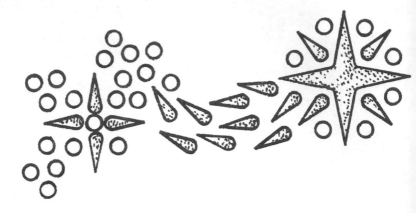

Tony Boucher   *May 18, 1956*

Dear Tony:

I can give you some data you don't happen to have: **Cousins** is not personally anti-sf. Further, *SR's* feature editor is, personally, an sf fan. Their only difficulty is that, like most other-directed people, they are somewhat short on intellectual and emotional honesty and courage.

Trying to get true, opinion-oriented people to read or understand and enjoy sf is inherently impossible; it requires the emotional courage to accept slavery to the "merely mechanical" level of fact. There are, you know, a lot of human beings who sincerely and deeply feel — though they wouldn't state it, or even think it consciously — that facts are an unjust imposition on the freedom of the human spirit.

It is impossible for them to enjoy science-fiction. Fantasy — yes; they love it, because it is an assertion of the all-conquering power of the human spirit to over-ride the dull facts of the gross material, the mere mechanical. I remember **Babette Rosmond**, who wrote some nice stuff for *Unknown*, and who could not bear science-fiction. She tried, several times, and each time found it deeply repellant.

Bernard Kahn — I believe you know him? — told me when we were out there, that in his work as psychologist for the OSS, he'd learned, from those who'd been there, that physical torture, even when administered by the technically thorough Germans, produced pain for a maximum of about 20 minutes. After that, there was no sense of pain; rather, there was an overwhelming and indescribable sense of indignity. Many different individuals separately reported that; both males and females.

Seemingly, an infinite quantity of physical pain becomes one unit of psychic pain — the pain of indignity.

I have a hunch this is relevant to juvenile delinquency; the delinquent is one who is incapable of enduring psychic pain, any feeling of loss of dignity. His physical courage is real, but his psychic courage is nearly zero. He cannot endure loss of dignity.

But cooperation happens to be a state of mutual slavery; symbiosis is the mutual enslavement of two organisms. My children are my slaves; they must labor at tasks I assign, willy-nilly, and suffer physical punishment if they rebel. They must give up the occupations of their choice, surrender their time and effort to performing chores they do not choose.

But I am their slave; I must labor to support my small masters in non-productive idleness, give up my time and effort to their whims and pleasures.

An individual who cannot accept psychic pain of loss of free will cannot be a cooperative individual. The juvenile delinquent, typically, cannot endure enslavement.

As I see it, some human beings cannot endure the next step; individuals who can accept mutual enslavement to other human beings, the Other Directed personalities, can not tolerate enslavement to inhuman, mere mechanical, forces. People who consider the failure of a machine a violent personal insult, and rage at the mechanism. These people demean the physical because they hate it. They loathe the proposition that there are physical laws that they cannot will away. They hate prophecy based on inexorable law of nature.

They will never be science-fictioneers, any more than a juvenile delinquent type can ever be a fully cooperative member of society, if his problem stems from the inability to accept mutual slavery.

Incidentally, that ability is, I am fairly sure (probability about .95, in my estimation) apt to be based on a *genetic* difference. This despite what all the "best authorities" have to say on the matter. Indications: The North American Indians could not be enslaved; they either died in rebellion, or died of heartbreak . . . but they died. The Aztecs, a related but separate strain, could be (and were) enslaved.

The final result is worth noting; the descendants of the Aztecs who lived in slavery now own and operate Mexico. The Iroquois and the Mohawks. . . ? Where are they?

The Negro could, and did, live in slavery. They're rapidly rising.

Our ancestors, on the other hand, lived in slavery for 2000 years. The Negro has it tough in the South, huh? Hah! Think what *our* ancestors had 1000 years ago! There's hell to pay when one Negro is lynched now; then, one of our ancestors was drawn and quartered in the public square, by His Majesty's Royal Executioners, if he annoyed someone.

I don't propose that that's the way it *should* be; I merely think it wise to acknowledge that that's the way it *was*.

The juvenile delinquent can't accept enslavement — and, therefore, can't accept self-discipline, since that's essentially self-enslavement. He's a sucker for dope, liquor, and promiscuous and meaningless sex.

There's a lot of people who haven't yet learned to accept enslavement to the physical world. To them, science-fiction is violently repugnant; the suggestions it makes that physical forces are determinant in human history is a vicious blasphemy. The scientist is hated because he states that, and then demonstrates the truth of the statement.

We are *not* going to get such people to accept science fiction. They can't. Instead, they will hire people to sooth their psyches by explaining how false is the philosophy that holds that the Laws of Nature apply to Man . . . except in a mere gross, physical way, of course — quite unimportant to the sacred Human Spirit.

The Laws of God, for them, begin only at the level of the spirit; God as the creator of atoms and molecules, of gravity and electric and magnetic fields — NO! Impossible! So ultimately a spiritual being could never have had anything to do with those things! God as the Creator of stars and planets is acceptable — so long as stars and planets are tiny points of light in the unreality of the sky. But God as the Creator of the gross, physical reality. . . ? No! That's the work of Satan! Satan is the ruler of physical things; Satan, not God, created sex, obviously; God is responsible only for the creation of the young human life that results.

The most that we can do, I suspect, is to allow those who have the inherent capacity to learn to appreciate God as the Author of the mechanical, material world as well as the spiritual world, be free to appreciate that. Free them from the punishment administered by the material-fearing. Establish that it is right, and good, and not inhuman to be a little different, to see a different way to a different kind of beauty. (One thing, **Tony**, that I do hold strongly against the Catholic church is its absolute denial of the Buddhist doctrine that there are many Ways to Truth. In seeking to establish the truth that *not all* ways lead to truth, they have gone to the equally unsound extreme of saying *only one* Way leads to truth.)

No possible discussion or doctrine or argument can get a man incapable of feeling the validity of acceptance of slavery to the "mere mechanism" of reality to accept it.

I feel that the best I can hope for is that such people will accept that a different, but neither dangerously-super or hideously-infra kind of human being exists.

I also have a feeling that you can *not* make a man give up something he believes in and wants. They want to believe that science fiction "isn't really literature"; you can fight them on that if you like, but you'll be trying to prove their ideas-beliefs are *wrong*. Possible, but it takes an annoying amount of energy.

If I can get them to accept that science-fiction "isn't really literature — it's something else," then maybe I can get 'em to accept that it's a valuable something else.

So long as they tried to market "artificial silk," people resisted. When they put *nylon* on the market, the silk-stocking market went to hell in a hurry.

My interests being what they are, I'm primarily interested in getting people to stop demeaning science-fiction as "that cheap literature." O.K. — if they insist that it "isn't really literature," and I go along with them that it is not literature, then . . . it isn't "that cheap *literature*," is it?

Part of the trouble is, of course, that there's a whole spectrum of things, ranging from the heavy space-opera science type, to the essentially pure-fantasy material **Ray Bradbury** writes. When **Bradbury** discusses a space-ship, it's strictly a fairy ship; it has no hardware at all. It's actually a symbol of a space-ship, not a mechanical, operable device.

When **Lee Correy** discusses a spaceship, it's a totally different order of device.

What I'm trying to do is to sneak up on the rock-ribbed, and rocks-in-the-head opposition. The essential thing I'm after is the establishment of the proposition, *there are different kinds of people*, and that, for different kinds of people, different fiction values are appropriate.

You know it. I know it, **Gold** knows it. The trouble with the literateurs — whose stuffy little pseudo-mentalities I detest — is that they don't know it, and won't consider it.

If you want to put on the debate at the convention — fine. But one of the problems to consider is that we'll be accomplishing relatively little, since the audience will be strictly "pro," and no "con." The difficulty is to get a chance to debate the problem at all in an arena where there are some "cons" that might be influenced. The ideal situation is to get invited to debate under the following conditions:

1. The sponsors of the meeting *know* that they'll make fools of you.
2. The audience is about 20% neutral and curious, 80% mildly opposed.
3. The opposing speakers are absolutely certain of their position.

The reason that's optimum, despite the apparent loading, is simple; since you have no friends in the audience, the worst you can do is not gain any.

The *best* the opposition can do is prevent you gaining any.

But the fact is that every human being has a deep suspicion that *any other* human being can't possibly be 100% right. Therefore an audience that finds everybody oppposed to the one side, automatically shifts its feelings somewhat toward the demeaned side.

If your opposition debaters are arrogantly sure of themselves and their

317

absolute rightness . . . you need only put in an appearance, say something quiet, gentle, and meaningless, and you've won the debate.

Those arrogant bastards are trying to *make* the audience agree with them in their dogmatic way; naturally the audience rebels against anyone trying to push 'em around like that!

One of the most successful lecture-debates I ever got in was at Rutgers, when the psychology faculty invited me to debate Dianetics with them. It was their auditorium; there were four of them. There was an audience of about 500 to 600..

Naturally, I won hands down. All I had to do was avoid being dogmatic, and the psychology faculty, from the first word, pushed the audience right at me. They started off by ridiculing anyone who was so stupid as to think Dianetics was even worth considering.

This to an audience of 500 people who'd taken the trouble and time to come and try to find out something about Dianetics. Anyone who starts out insulting the audience is a little thick in the head.

How could I fail to come out ahead?

I don't think a debate before the SF convention audience would do us much good. We'd have to be damned careful to avoid making the orthodox literary critic look like an underdog, and couldn't possibly win any new understandings.

What we need is a chance to lecture-debate before the Classics Club, with opposition from a good, hard-headed, dogmatic classics scholar who hasn't learned a thing in 30 years, and doesn't intend to in the next 30.

My motto is "Never fight when there's something to lose, and nothing to gain."

Therefore, don't fight in front of a friendly audience.

And I do not believe in fair fighting either; when the odds are actually 50-50, you can exhaust yourself and your opponent, but can't expect to win anything worth the effort. That's just foolishness for both of you.

And since logic and normal language communication can't reach the emotional level, if your opponent is arguing from emotional drives, you can't change his feelings; all you can do is weary yourself and the other fellow, to your mutual disadvantage.

There is no debate between two people who have convictions; there can only be battle with words. Neither can there be debate between an adult, who has passed though adolescence and felt all its problems and heartaches, and an adolescent who is convinced that his parent just doesn't understand. (I speak from experience of being at both ends of that one.) How can you convince someone that you *do* know and understand the values he knows are real, when you keep insisting that they aren't the most important things in the world, thereby proving you *don't* understand how important they are?

Oh well . . . you know the essential problem we face, even though yours and mine differ slightly within that area. We hold to an absolutely, positively, ultimately forbidden, anathematized and terrible, aberrant philosophy: that there will be an end to the culture that exists today.

I got a story the other day that I know you'll like; it's called "Man of God." Short piece — but his essential proposition is a dilly. Missionary from another planet comes to Earth, in the belief Man needs religion. Finds that *men* have religion — but makes the comment that men discovered religion when they were able to conceive that they, themselves, would one day die. Then, of course, they became able to consider "What comes after?"

But no culture has ever learned that it, too, is mortal — that it, too, will one day die. So Man's cultures remain ruthless, primitive savages, without conscience or fear of God.

I think he's right. Man's cultures have not yet learned that they, like individual men, are fallible and mortal, and had best look to the future through descendants. As it is, Man's cultures, rather like fish, are cannibalistic; they seek to devour their own offspring.

The great crime of science-fiction, that produces acute uneasiness in the normal "well adjusted" individual is that it proposes that the laboriously and painfully learned adjustment may not be the right, ultimate and final answer after all. That the Eternal Verities are neither eternal nor verities.

That psionic business is the goods, Tony. I've built more than that one, and studied others. They are absolutely non-logical, and specifically non-physical in operation. The physical mechanism is not relevant to their operation. Even the Hieronymus machine, which I picked because it *looks* most like a physical machine, is not truly a physical mechanism. It works just as well when it isn't plugged in as when it is . . . but it won't work, plugged in or not, if there's a defective tube.

It is, quite genuinely, a Magical machine. Its essence is a Charm, and it won't work without that Charm; with the Charm, the physical mechanism isn't necessary.

If you think I'm kidding, or gone batty — there's nothing I can do about that belief. I've seen the thing work, and worked with it, and have data. It functions by reason of laws that are perfectly real laws . . . but happen not to be the laws of first-order logic. It follows the laws of *analogic*. In logic, only things that are identical are related; X either *is* A (is-identical-to A) or is-not (is totally unrelated to) A. In analogic, things can be similar, without being identical; this constitutes a lesser, but real order of relationship. In geometry, the simplest relationship between two triangles is congruence — a 1-to-1 equivalence. Next come similarity; identity of form, but not of scale. They never did succeed in squaring the circle; they couldn't derive, by any logical mechanism, an identity-of-area but no identity of form or size.

There's a whole level of relationship that can't be handled by logic, mathematics, or present language concepts. Just happens that the psionic machines apply that which can't be discussed.

If you think any *real* problem can be discussed logically — which is what logicians claim, of course! — try discussing Tomorrow in strict logic — formal logic. Is Tomorrow real? No, it is not — because "is" necessarily means "now." "Will be" is a denial of "is" therefore, since Tomorrow involves the denial of *is*, and the only possible alternative to *is* is *is-not*, Tomorrow is not real.

The same, of course, applies to Yesterday.

Any *potential* reality has the characteristic that it *neither* is *nor* is-not — and that makes it logically impossible to discuss it.

Which is another reason why sf is so disturbing!

Regards,   John

Thomas N. Scortia   *November 12, 1956*

Dear Mr. Scortia:

Yes, I know the story of the three-men-with-spots. It's a type-case of the problem that can be solved only by recognizing the datum that data is missing — the fact the others present do *not* have enough data to solve it is the crucial datum.

But quite a few people know it, and it is, after all, just a gag. Sherlock Holmes did much better with the same type problem in "The Case of the Barking Dog"; the crucial clue was that the dog did *not* bark.

Had five Western Electric technicians out trying the Hieronymus machine the other night. Four got no response; the fifth did beautifully. So we tried the **Carrett-Scortia** technique. No dice; or at least almost none. One of the four did get a slight reaction, but only very slight, and not definite, while co-striking the plate.

Four of the five had professional degrees in science; the fifth had high school plus a radio-electronics technician course. Guess which was the one that got beautifully consistent, repeatable results!

On cryotron production: even better than the evaporation of metal through a photographically reduced mask, I like the idea of routing with an electron-microcope-in-reverse. That's *real* micromicro manipulation, b'gad!

Regards,   John W. Campbell, Jr.

Robert Heinlein   *April 5, 1957*

Dear Bob:

I'm sending this via **Lurton Blassingame**, since he, presumably, will know where to send it that it'll have a reasonable chance of catching you.

I'm taking "Citizen of the Galaxy" at 4¢. You've pulled a series of very nice propositions in it, too — and I do love your planking Margaret Meade down in a Finnish-speaking spaceship!

The subject you've discussed — slavery — is, as you know, one I've been interested in for several reasons. And the point you make about the People being more slaves than not is a nice one.

One of the viewpoints I've been trying to use in analyzing sociological forces is, essentially, this one: If a given cultural process worked, that proves it has value. The problem is to find the value in it that made it work — and find a way to use that value, without entailing the negative side-effects.

320

An analogy: Cocaine is an excellent, highly effective local anaesthetic. It has very real, and very great value. By sufficient study of the molecule, however, biochemists were able to select a part of the molecule which produced most of the anaesthetic effect — without the severe habit-forming effect.

Again: The Damascus armorers were able to produce an exceedingly fine steel. Their process worked; it had very real value. Unfortunately, it also had undesirable side-effects (they tempered the blade by running it through the body of a slave.) Took quite a while to discover that tempering of the desired type required tempering in a nitrogen-bearing saline solution — not a human body, necessarily, however.

But the fact remained that there *was* validity in the process.

Now the basic law of all laws seems to be "You can't get something for nothing — in the long run." Economics, in other words. An organism that expends more effort getting food than the energy-content of the food repays, will inevitably die. The organism which can garner the most energy with the least expenditure of effort will have free energy available with which to advance itself.

A living organism can operate at a loss temporarily; it can go into debt for a time. But it cannot continue to operate on that basis.

A culture, too, is bound by the same laws; in the long run, it must gain as much as it expends. Since there is always competition, it must, actually, gain not only more than it expends, but at least as much more as do the competing cultures.

Because it *is* possible to operate at a loss temporarily, a statistical effect comes into play; it is necessary to integrate over a time-period to determine whether the process of operation is, actually, a gainful one, and hence a valid-in-reality one. Individuals benefit by operating in a culture because of this integration effect; like insurance, it allows the individual to handle risks that he could not, alone, survive.

The explorer goes out, and somehow gets killed. If he were totally asocial, there would be a total loss. If he is a social entity, then his society knows of his exploration — and at least learns that the explored area contains some danger.

O. K. — now let's look at slavery with those points in mind.

Slavery is a useful educational system; it has a place in the development of a race, just as the tyranny of parents has a place in the educational development of an individual. But . . . because a child at 5 *needs* a benevolent tyrant does *not* mean that this proves the individual under discussion "needs a benevolent tyrant" as a long-term true statement.

Slavery has a definite — and highly beneficial — educational-place in the development of a race; it is, in its proper time and place, beneficial to the race. This does *not* mean that it is *at any time* beneficial to the individuals involved, nor does it mean that it is *at all times* beneficial to the race.

From the viewpoint of the cells involved, surgery is not beneficial, though

321

it may be essential to save the organism; neither is it beneficial to the organism to undergo constant surgery.

True chattel slavery — man-to-man slavery — has a unique selective-breeding-educational effect. Human beings can be selectively bred, just as effectively as can any other domesticated animal. I do *not* mean that a conscious eugenics program is involved; men haven't understanding enough to choose the proper things to select for. But the Universe will, in the long run, impose on a race the selective factors necessary to survive — or it will die.

In a ritual-taboo tribal situation, as you point out concerning the People in your story, each individual is a slave to the *system*, though this system-rule is so dominant that it makes individual will almost nonexistent, or completely unimportant. "Master" and "slave" are each, and equally, slaves to the rituals. The "master" might be a vicious sadist, a Caligula — and his "slave" would not suffer. Ritual, not the master's will, determines the relationship between the two.

Equally, of course, the "master" might be the most humane man in the world . . . but if the ritual calls for the ritual sacrifice of a slave-girl by skinning her alive — her inately kind and humane master will skin her alive.

In a government of rituals, not of men, individuals have no freedom to express their own natures — and this prevents the evolutionary selection forces from selecting desirable traits! The ritual situation acts as a selective force only in selecting for individuals who *can* yield to a group-control. Who *can* yield self-will to group-will. In a ritual government system, those who cannot yield to the ritual demands are destroyed. The would-be Caligula master is destroyed for violating the rituals and traditions by torturing a slave. The would-be humane master, however, is also destroyed for failing to skin his slave-girl alive.

There will, during the ritual government period of evolution, be an evolution of cultural rituals that work, however. Those cultures which choose inappropriate rituals will die *as cultures*. A culture that calls for sacrificing girls too often will die because of a lowered birth-rate, for instance; it will, presently, be weakened to a point where a neighboring culture conquers it, kills off the males, and uses the unsacrificed females for breeding purposes. Bad cultural rituals lead to death of the culture-as-a-whole.

When the government of rituals, not of men, gave way to something else, chattel slavery came in. Now the sadist could play his funny little games, and the humane master could refuse to sacrifice his slaves.

Since there are always more ways of doing a thing wrong than there are of doing it right, the *average* result was, of course, rather awful. However, since wrong methods are inherently self-destructive, the best methods of establishing individual-to-individual slavery survived. The wisest masters acquired the most slaves; the wisest slaves had the most satisfactory lives, and bred the most children.

Now a master who is a sadist loses slaves by death, by escapes, and

322

because of the necessity of punishing understandably rebellious slaves. The humane master does not lose slaves so rapidly. The humane master, therefore, has an economic advantage; it's good business to be kind to your animate agricultural instruments, whether they be human or animal.

Two things are going on here. The most humane master will punish, and punish to death, an intransigent slave. He must; if you have a slave who is a psychopath, or a sadist. . . . You *have* to stop him. A slave who turns out to be a homicidal paranoid must be killed; psychotherapy isn't available at that cultural level. Therefore the system acts to select slaves who can accept the wishes and orders of another human being — who can accept a government of men, not of rituals. (Rituals and laws are still there — but the will of an individual human being has become the immediate importance in the real-world-system of the slave.) For the first time in human culture history, one individual is forced to pay attention to the wishes, desires, and needs of another individual *as an individual.*

This means that slaves who can accept the will of another man have a markedly greater probability of surviving and breeding children in numbers.

At the same time, economic and military pressures are imposing a selective breeding system on the masters. Not only must masters treat slaves with reasonably humane methods to keep them alive and effective — and loyal; the slaves always outnumber the masters, remember! Machiavelli pointed out that the Prince cannot rule in the face of the active opposition of the people — but masters must also learn a brand new, and hitherto unheard of skill: That of selecting individual human beings for their individual talents!

The master who can recognize the potential craftsman among his slave-boys, the potential warrior, and the potential oaf correctly will, by assigning them appropriate tasks, profit far beyond that of the master who assigns tasks by mere whim, or by chance, or on a basis of "his father was, so he will be."

The masters are being selected, by utterly ruthless economic-military forces, for the ability to select slaves on a basis of individual talents.

Only the European culture maintained this particular pattern of master-slave system for any length of time. And it added one other obnoxious-sounding-to-us feature; the nobles (masters) were free to breed on any serf (slave) girl that they happened to want to. In India this was unthinkable — caste lines were too strict. So in India there was never a "rise of the Middle Classes" — because India never bred that hybird class!

It is not necessary to postulate that any individual in the entire system, during the entire time-era, enjoyed the situation. The fact remains that the system — however thoroughly you may choose to damn it — had a beneficial-educational result *for the race.*

Proof that there was validity in that system is quite easy; the cultural system that resulted from the process proceeded to impose much of its philosophy on the rest of the planet. For a cultural enclave of about 10,000,000 individuals, on one fair-sized peninsula of one continent to achieve that result indicates that the system had some damned important validity in it — along with highly undesirable side-effects.

The unpleasant thought that this brings to my mind is the assurance that we, now, are being rather blindly selectively bred toward some still higher, and quite unimaginable-to-us-now goal — and the process is just about as unusual. Rugged on the individual — good for the race. Because if it *isn't* good for the race, then it'll simply be rugged *both* for the individual and for the race.

By the time a few more billions of human beings have been bred and tested to destruction, some new cultural pattern will have emerged. The trick of surviving is to spot which way the trend is going, and get a little ahead of it, so you can ride it the way a surfboard rider rides a wave. It'll push you along, that way — and, if you manage it right, the fact that it's pushing you along allows you to "make like a leader" and steer the whole darned wave just a little.

In the long run, the individual who benefits the culture is, inescapably, benefited by the culture. It has to reward him; that's the only way it can encourage people the way it wants them to go!

You know, **Bob**, I'm tempted to retitle that story of yours "The Slave." Thorby was a slave every paragraph of the way — including the last. Margaret pointed out his slavery in the Free Traders; Wing Marshall Smith pointed out his slavery in the end.

Final item: We need it split in four parts, of course. Approximately equal; pick the points you feel best. And we need synopses.

Regards,   John

Robert Heinlein   *May 3, 1957*

Dear Bob:

There's plenty of time to relieve the European nobleman from keeping the rain off the sidewalk in front of the nightclub. The manuscript is in process of being illustrated, which has to be done before typesetting starts. **Van Dongan's** doing it; he's not so hot on violent action and swashbuckling stuff — but he's the best in the business when it comes to character and portraits.

I'll not change the title to "Slave" — but despite the fact that there are no "Citizens" listed in Day's Index, I feel that "Citizen of the Galaxy" is not as powerful a title as that yarn deserves. How about something of the order of "There Is No Freedom"? Somehow the powerful irony of Thorby's freedom as the beggar's slave, and his unbreakable bondage as the controller of galactic power, needs to be keyed into the title.

There's a curious thing about slavery, which is, I think, epitomized on Uncle Tom's famous line, "You can beat this po 'black body, but mah soul belongs to God!" The slave is not responsible for his actions; the fact of his slavery establishes a barrier between his thoughts, feelings, and desires and his actions, because he can not express in action his own will.

Now the easily overlooked aspect of that is that the slave is free to dream anything, wish for anything, without penalty, and without any need whatever for self-discipline. His wants may be fantastically self-contradictory, without any *internal* sense of frustration. He can assign *all* frustrations to the fact of his slavery.

The free man cannot do so. His actions are limited only by his own decisions, his wishes and wants — and if *he* is frustrated, he cannot assign the incompatability externally, but must force himself to change his own inner desire-structure.

It seems to be a law of the Universe that Man will be disciplined; over that fact we have no choice or control. But there is a choice of *self*-discipline, or external discipline. There is even some choice as to Universe-reality discipline, or human external discipline. The hermit will be disciplined, even though no human being is near him. He will be disciplined by the Law of Conservation of Mass-Energy if he seeks to live without taking the trouble to achieve food. There is, and always will be, discipline — which is what most human beings loathe.

One of the effects of slavery, or effective slavery of externally imposed discipline, is that it allows the survival of both inately self-disciplined, and inately undisciplined indivdiuals. The laws of genetics being what they are, a characteristic which does not aid survival or is not necessary or effective toward survival, tends to be lost. And a characteristic that is a handicap in the actual environment, tends to be surpressed.

Dr. Muller pointed out to me that eyes are, in a cave animal, a handicap; eyes are more sensitive to infection, disease, injury, etc., than smooth skin. The eyeless organism is, therefore, genetically superior to the eyed organism in a cave environment.

A strong sense of self-discipline is contrasurvival in a ritual-taboo society — for where the rituals are inappropriate, the individual with a sense of self-discipline based on what-makes-sense will get into trouble by resisting or rebelling. The same holds for the absolute slave of a foolish and headstrong master.

Consider what this means in the formation of the character of women. For millenia, they were controlled by external discipline; self-discipline was of little or negative value to the captured woman. But self-discipline became highly important to the survival of the male masters.

I know that it is generally held by modern science that mental and personality characteristics can't be generally determined — but the facts don't bear that out worth a damn. Specifically, given a long enough span of generations, and a great enough breadth of breeding program, immense changes of mental characteristics can be produced.

Proof: We differ in mental and personality characterstics from the other primates. It was achieved by a selective breeding program, controlled by the environment.

Somewhat less larger-scale proof: Chimpanzees are more intelligent than dogs. This is practically universally agreed.

But . . . Chimps can NOT be taught to speak, to use sound-symbols to refer to concepts. Not even when chimpanzee sounds are used by humans to express an artificially, specially designed language.

Dogs have been taught to both understand, and speak in Engligh — at a *conceptual* level, not just proper-noun-symbol-object identification. Despite the inherent difficulty of producing human-type sounds with a canine-type larynx and mouth structure, dogs have been taught to speak intelligible English.

Why is it that the less intelligent animal should have this ability, when the more intelligent does not?

Hah! Men have been breeding dogs for not less than 200,000 years. You can accomplish quite a bit in that time — even without specifically directed efforts. Men *did* want dogs that could understand their verbal commands — and by keeping at it enough, they bred such types as the Scotch working Collie.

O. K. — just take as a postulate-for-argument's-sake that men have, over the last 6000 years, been breeding women who could survive as slaves. (The kind that didn't survive as slaves didn't contribute to the future of the race.)

Right now, men have themselves in a neat box as a result. Having spent several thousand years breeding women under conditions wherein self-discipline was not valuable to them . . . men are now all steamed up at the undisciplined behavior of their women.

Well . . . we asked for it, and we got it, and, as usual, now we don't like it so good, maybe, huh?

Don't misunderstand me here; a human personality is the resultant of a complex of many vector forces, summing up in a vectorial system. They do not sum up arithmetically, or even algebraically. (Actually, it's not even so simple as vectorially, but that comes nearer.) At least, we can suggest something by the analogy of a vectorial summation of forces. The essential point is that while there are singular, and isolatable forces acting on the system, the forces don't act singly, except in cases of extreme mania. (Example: take one psychopath, who has absolutely no feelings of guilt or shame, and one psychotic melancholic, who has unlimited sense of guilt and shame. Stir well. Separate in two parts, and you have two sane people. Each represents one of the normal vector forces operating singly — and *both* the ability-to-feel-guilt and the ability-to-deny-guilt are essential to true sanity.)

I think one of the reasons why it has long been observed that freedom cannot be *given*, but must be *earned* lies in the fact that self-disipline is developed only the hard and somewhat painful way — by discovering that the Universe will impose discipline, unless you do it yourself.

Mammals invented punishment — and punishment can be defined as "a nonlethal substitute for being eaten alive as a result of a misjudgement."

Eyes are a substitute for the tactile sense; you can tell an obstacle is present without discovering it with your squashed-in nose. Of course, eyes don't depend on mechanical forces, and can't stop a mechanical force-system; you can run into the tree if you refuse to accept the discipline of the eyes' warning.

As Thorby learned, being the Master isn't so much fun, either. A while back, I thought of a story-plot — interesting, I think, but one that couldn't be written in the present culture. Somewhat too rational for present consumption.

Two kingdoms. Queen Grace, absolute monarch of Aye. Aye is changing from agricultural to industrial, but lacks ports and access to sea. Growing population. Now prosperous . . . but needs more agricultural population to support and be benefited by industry. Kingdom Bea, on the other hand, adjoining, has ports, agriculture, no industry to speak of, no raw materials except fertile delta land.

Prince Carl, of Bea, is, like Queen Grace, about 28, and unmarried. But Carl is a weakling — the unfortunate negative statistical variation in a line of strong and wise men. And Queen Grace is an extremely strong and wise young woman. It is evidently necessary that Aye and Bea be combined into one kingdom, for the benefit of the peoples of both.

Queen Grace arranges a visit from Carl. Carl is not exactly her ideal of a mate — and Grace scares Carl more than somewhat. Carl falls for a cute little minor countess, a clinging-vine type, with the same brand of fluff in her head that Carl has.

Grace does some investigating, finds exactly what Countess Cuddles is, and studies Carl and Cuddles most carefully. And calls in the court magician. Countess Cuddles shortly thereafter comes down with a wasting illness, and dies.

Queen Grace has the courage and wisdom to be a fool — and old King Charles of Bea is not a fool. Presently she has comforted Carl sufficiently that Carl marries her. At the death of King Charles, two years later, the two young monarchs unite the two kingdoms, and establish a new capitol on the old border line. There their first son is born that year, and, two years later, a second.

When Prince Robert is ten, and his elder brother 12, it is clear to Queen Grace that the heir to the two thrones is, disastrously, a weakling — and several centuries of divergent history aren't easily forgotten. The single heir to both thrones *must* be a strong, wise ruler. Prince Robert has what it takes.

Since this isn't a task to be delegated, Queen Grace waits till Prince Don has a cold, and smothers him with a pillow.

Under King Robert, the united kingdom of Beaye becomes a prosperous and dynamic nation.

You can see what I mean about it not being a story that could be written for today's audience. Making Queen Grace a believable, acceptable murderess and heroine is, in modern concepts, a little difficult.

Then there's the proposition of having fun with a variant on the standard formula for a novel. A novel is supposed to follow the development and growth of the character of the central character. The author gets the reader to identify with the character, and sucks the reader along with that development.

The real point is to get the *reader* to develop, of course. But naturally we don't tell *him* that.

O.K. — so let's have two characters, John Doe and Richard Roe. At the start, each expresses his philosophy. John Doe is a noble character; he expresses all the Right sentiments. But Richard Roe is a black character indeed. He states that he believes slavery is, sometimes, a good thing. And that assassination has its place in living. That theft and deliberate destruction are sometimes worthwhile. Oh, he's a bad one.

So in the course of the story, John, being noble and good, gets into trouble, and gets others into trouble, from which wicked Richard annoyedly hauls him out half a dozen times, taking time out from his business of fomenting a war between a couple of local barons, or interrupting an assassination plot, and repeats his suggestion that John Doe is a knucklehead, and should learn the facts of life. The fourth time Richard gets John out of trouble — deliberately running his sword through the neck of the good-looking but brass-plated hellion of a bitch that had gotten John and his crew in the jig in the process — Richard suggests that he's a bit sick of this, and if John doesn't wise up rapidly, he, King Richard (he's recently usurped a local kingdom) will, the next time, have John shipped back to Earth or some tamer planet where he belongs.

Finally, of course, Emperor Richard, surrounded by his slaves, warriors, and a few unassassinated local nobles, does have John escorted to his space-yacht and deported to a less hell-roaring, hard-boiled planet, with John still protesting exactly the philosophy he started with, and Richard still stating his unchanged philosophy. Neither character has changed a bit.

But the reader, somewhere along about the middle of the yarn, got a little tired of being on the losing side all the time.

Why is it necessary to make the central character change? Make the reader change characters, instead! Richard, above, would be an Anthropological Engineer, John, in effect, a missionary trying to teach a doctrine of social behavior some 3000 years too advanced for the environment of the planet. John wants to get there by Magic — "it should be, so it is." Richard's trying to make the normal process of slow cultural evolution a little less slow, and a little less painful — but earned, and real, evolution.

Bob, you've never said just what **Ginny's** trouble was, but from the way it lingers on, I wonder if there isn't a psychogenic factor of some kind involved? Generally speaking, any kind of bug that bites is a life-form seeking to establish the typical chain-reaction of a life-form, the typical exponential series. If the bugs are successful, they achieve a k-factor greater than 1.000, and things get worser and worser, faster and faster. Or the person's own metabolism succeeds in cutting the bug's k-factor below 1.000, and the chain is damped out.

The only way a chain reaction can maintain a relatively steady state is to have some sort of control mechanism maintaining it at that level. It takes a complex system to keep a nuclear reactor balanced on the knife-edge of k=1.000000.

In TB, as you know, there's a huge psychogenic factor. More and more evidence is accumulating that the same is true in cancer, too. The lingering illnesses seem, as a broad generality, to have a psychogenic factor of some sort at work, stabilizing the system of individual-and-disease. And the straight-line M.D. dislikes the straight-line psychological approach, because he knows damn well disease is *not* "all in the mind." It isn't. Like most any other specialist, the psychotherapist tends to think *his* methods are The Answer; meanwhile the M.D. tends, equally, to think his methods are The Whole Answer. (Particularly since chemicals and physical forces are so damned much easier to manipulate reliably!) But sometimes the disease is a vector resultant of two causes — and the efficient and effective way to reduce it is to attack both of the vector forces involved. I don't suggest that there is one simple panacea method; I suggest, however, that MD's have a tendency to consider that purely physico-chemical treatment *is* a panacea. And maybe it isn't.

One of the ancient philosophical conundrums is involved here; "What is the difference between 'A matter of degree' and 'A matter of kind'?"

The analogy of a nuclear reactor gives something of an answer, I think. In a reactor, if the k-factor, the reproduction factor of neutrons, exceeds 1.0000, the rate of reaction will rise exponentially. If it is less than one, there will be no reaction. If the k-factor is 0.9999, the reactor is effectively inert, the system is stable, and will remain stable indefinitely. If the reactor is modified so little as to change the k-factor by 0.0002 points, and held at the new level, the reactor will melt itself down. A change of 0.02%, a minute change *in degree*, produces a total change *of kind*.

Given a feedback system having positive feedback, no matter what type of system it is, if the feedback reaches the critical value yielding a k of any minute value greater than one, the system goes into self-sustaining reaction. An ordinary vacuum tube oscillator is such a system; so is a nuclear reactor. So is a population of organisms.

So is a population of ideas in a culture! That's why there *is* such a thing as "steam engine time" in a culture; until the idea of a steam engine can be self-sustaining, it won't exist . . . in the culture, even though it exists in the minds of individuals. Note that in a reactor with a k of 0.9999 free neutrons *do* exist — there are spontaneous fissions of U-235 or Pu-239 atoms. But no chain-reaction.

In a human mind, similar phenomena seem to exist; certain ideas, even if they're mentioned to a man, he seems to forget, or at least not be able to use. They aren't self-sustaining in his mind-environment.

Democracry can't exist in a population which has individuals of such a mental nature that the concept has a k-factor below One. Germany, for instance, has shown that behavior; the individuals *want* the security having an Authority to keep things working straight. Even when the Allies started a democracy in 1919, the thing was not self-sustaining. Germany acted as though it were a reactor with a k-factor of 0.99999 for the concept of democracy; started at a high level, it took a few years to die out — but, inevitably, it did. The idea would "ring" for a while, like an excited tuning fork . . . but it wouldn't oscillate in a self-sustaining fashion.

Import a couple hundred thousand Americans into Germany, however — and it'd be like adding a few extra pounds of U-235 to a non-reactive pile. Push the k-factor above 1.0000, and the thing will run on its own. As long as the Americans are there, that is, as an effective part of the cultural system.

A quite small change in a few ideas in a man . . . and it may change his apparent personality from an apathetic, unambitious, though intelligent and innately competent individual, into a ball-of-fire type. Something shoved him across the k=1.0000 line. He's still almost exactly the same guy he was — but now he's a different *kind* of person! Remove as little as one ounce of cadmium from a ton of nuclear reactor, and the previously inert, apathetic mass takes off and goes to work.

It seems to me that that basic proposition — the enormous effect of a small change of degree at or near a critical point in a feedback system — accounts for a good bit of the confusion of "difference of degree" vs "difference of kind."

How does Man differ from the animals? Not in kind, it says here, because animals show logical reasoning, too. Yes . . . but theirs does *not* show the self-exciting characteristic that makes Man's logic serve as a stimulus for logical thinking!

The old "for want of a nail, the kingdom was lost" represents the critical effect of a single link in a logical chain.

But logic is a linear system; it represents ordering, but not pattern effects. Punch one hole in a logical chain, and the whole subsequent chain disappears. But consider a figure 5; how many holes would you have to punch in that pattern before the *pattern as a whole* ceased to exist? I can make a 5 out of dotted lines. I can make one out of discontinuous and unaligned bits, as is frequently done in "shadowed" letters on advertising signs.

We can distinguish sound and unsound logic on the test of coherence and continuity — but that test is inapplicable to patterns.

I think the test of patterns is self-sustaining ability, in some way, but just how I can't figure out.

And . . . I think that the essence of psi is that it can be understood and discussed only in terms of pattern-thinking, rather than ordered thinking! Continuity is *not* necessary for patterns; discontinuity, however, implies something on the order of action-at-a-distance, a concept that can't be handled logically.

Regards,   John

Kate Wilhelm *July 10, 1957*

Dear Miss Wilhelm:

You have an easy, pleasing and readable style, one that would, moreover, be a marked change in science fiction. However, your stories have rather hazy, gentle motivating forces behind them — which, while that too is somewhat different in science fiction, is not quite so desirable a difference.

Essentially, science fiction is a frontier literature — and all frontiers, anywhere and anywhen, involve very powerful, very intense motivational conflicts. The Quakers who settled Pennsylvania may have *talked* in very mild, pacifist terms — but no man or woman takes on the job of trying to tame a raw, brutally tough wilderness without having something several degrees harder and tougher than chilled tool steel in his soul. The Puritans may have been good, God-fearing folk — but fear of God was about the only fear they yielded to. They might fear the black wilderness, and the Indians, but they walked into it just the same.

The men and women who settle new worlds among the stars are apt to *talk* the same sort of mild terms; they'll be afraid, of course, and so know they aren't brave, and have no business being in these dangerous places. But they'll go on, just the same.

I think there would be a field for you to consider. Such people are, characteristically, ruthless, but not cruel; they are appallingly hard, yet gentle. They impose a cold, rigid, unforgiving — but understanding! — discipline on all those around them. Including, however, themselves. They can, and do, reluctantly, but quite whole-heartedly, turn to the task of destroying something, or someone, who must be destroyed.

You might consider the personality of some of the early colonists, and see if you couldn't build a story around such a steel-hard, absolutely ruthless, yet warmly human and deeply understanding person.

Sincerely,   John W. Campbell, Jr.

H. Chandler Elliott *August 3, 1957*

Dear Dr. Elliott:

Sorry — my typing always did stink. I'm a hi-speed, lo-accuracy typer; my tendency to write long letters accounts for it, no doubt.

Your letter came at a time fortunate for me; you're just the guy I need to get some help from. It's this way:

My hobby is hi-fi audio design, and the problems associated therewith. Now essentially, I'm more of a Natural Philosopher than a scientist — so I'm not expert in anything, but am something of an inverse of the professor who learned more and more about less and less till he knew almost everything about practically nothing. So I'm only moderately good at electronics, and not happy with it because the problem is to get a certain response in the human mind — not in the electronic instruments the technician uses. And

331

that involves understanding the human auditory systems as well as the electronic system.

But moreover, the human auditory system is *not* just the ears — it's the auditory centers in the brain, too. And I'll be darned if I can see how you can test one without having the other automatically in the circuit, whether you like it or not, due to the fact that the auditory center remembers the peculiarity of the ears it's been hearing through, whether they're actually in circuit or not. i.e., it corrects for the particular encoding of information those particular ears have.

So . . . I tried to figure out what the auditory mechanism does . . . and promptly ran into a Grade A#1 size, shrieking inconsistency between standard acoustic theory, and the actual physiological structure of the auditory system, as viewed from Information Theory considerations.

My problem now, however, is the uncertainty of my data; I've found only one reference to the number of nerve fibers on the auditory nerve, and that in an old, popularized book, which said "about 50,000." If the figure is even approximately right — and I think it is — the deducible consequences are *most* interesting.

Please: can you give me accurate data on the number of nerve fibers per auditory nerve? "Accurate" meaning the correct order of magnitude of the number.

Here's the problem: Each nerve fiber can transmit about 10-15 nerve pulses per second; call it 10. If there are 50,000, then the nerve-trunk constitutes an information channel with a capacity of 10 x 50,000 = 500,000 bits of information a second.

The maximum frequency range of the ear is about 20,000 cycles per second. Even if the ear could distinguish every single cycle all the way up (which it doesn't) that would require only a 20,000 bit information channel. What are the other 480,000 bits per second doing?

Acoustic theory has, through the years, discussed frequencies, and talked of sine-waves and their harmonics. This sounds real sharp, and you sure can do a nice job with tuned filters, electronic hardware, and gimcracks of various kinds to prove that you can find sine-waves and harmonics in a violin's note.

But because you can extract-by-analysis a certain set of things from something does *not* mean that's what it's made of. Incinerate an animal, collect all the chemical products, and that shows you what the animal was made of, huh? Carbon dioxide, water, CaO, free nitrogen, etc.

Who was it who showed that, if you just dropped out the ash content, and used the old-fashioned analysis of foods based on nitrogen content, etc., you could show that what came out of the cow was as good as what went in?

Some tests I've made confirm experientially a hunch I developed. The ear doesn't react to frequencies-and-harmonics at all! It responds to *repetition rate* and *wave-pattern*.

In studying electrical waves, the oscilloscope is the instrument that is the perfect choice for the job; it presents the complex wave as-is — you can get a visual picture of the pattern of the wave. It does it by displaying the wave on a two-dimensional screen, where the wave-form is displayed as vertical deflections of the cathode ray beam, against a horizontal deflection based on time. The two-dimensional presentation allows you to observe the pattern, the *shape* of the wave.

To display a sawtooth wave having a repetition rate of 10,000 times a second, however, the oscilloscope amplifier must have a *frequency* capability of at least 200,000 cycles per second! That is, it must be able to handle 200,000 bits of information per second, to handle a 10,000 times-per-second sawtooth (or square or pip) wave.

Now the information-capacity of the auditory nerve-trunk makes sense! It's reporting wave *forms*, the wave *shapes* — and that does take a tremendous information-handling capacity!

Confirmatory reasoning: sound-direction is determined by the difference in phase-angle of the sounds reaching the two ears. (This has been determined experimentally.) But this statement is flatly in contradiction to the standard statement "the human ears are not sensitive to phase-distortion." If they can't detect phase-angles, how do they determine sound-direction by phase-difference?

Hypothesis: Each ear does determine phase-angle — actually, each determines the exact wave shape — and the shape is determined by the phase-relationships in the wave-form. The two ears report to the auditory centers. The encoded information is decoded, cross-correlated, and the useful information abstracted from the raw data by a data-reducing computer that makes anything men have built yet look like a kid's toy abacus.

Now the optical centers automatically throw in corrections for angle-of-vision, the angle-of-projection effects produced by the relative rotation of an observed object. (Car wheels look round, even when seen at a considerable angle.) The optical center "erects the image" when angle of projection has distorted it.

(That fact, incidentally, has a lot to do, I think, with why it took artists some 75,000 years to go from the beautiful Cro-Magnon cave paintings to perspective painting! The corrections were being made so perfectly, and unconsciously, that it was impossible to detect them at all!)

If my hypothesis is correct, the reason it *appears* that the ears are insensitive to phase-shifts in music is much the same as why "the eye can't tell the difference when an object is rotated in the field of vision." The hell it can't! It just corrects for it so slick and smooth that the experimenter can't catch it in the act!

I've experimented with hi-fi. I've had the fi so hi it was incredible . . . and therefore nobody liked listening to it. You can set up systems that go oooomph-oooomph and eeeek-eeeek, and prove with sound analyzers that man, they've got *everything*! Sure is spectacular.

And if you put a running-time meter on the installation in the house . . . you find, at the end of a month or two, that the only time anybody listens to it is when they're demonstrating how spectacular it is.

I have a system that has been specially designed to have zero phase-shift; it is, actually, an analog-computer multiplier circuit, not an audio-amplifier circuit, and the loud-speaker voice-coil is treated as a write-out pen — the output stage is a standard servo-driver type circuit, instead of an audio-output stage. I can't use multi-cone speakers; only a simple standard single-cone speaker. (To use multi-cone speakers introduces phase-shifts.) The system doesn't ooomph-ooomph or eek-eek so good . . . but it's in use for listening an average of 5 hours a day! *It doesn't produce listener fatigue.* The auditory center *can* compensate for phase-distortion — but that requires a lot of complex data-reduction and compensation. If you work hard enough, you can get the truth out of the story three delusional liars tell you about something — but it's easier to get an honest witness in the first place.

These multi-cone speaker systems constitute a trio of delusional liars.

Information on the auditory nerve, and how much of the above fits with what you know of the auditory mechanism, would be appreciated.

Re the editorial in heredity and genius. You can call it as full of holes as a tennis net — but, like a fish-net, it can catch a number of large-size truths, just the same. I wasn't trying to give the *whole* story — I was pointing out one aspect of the problem of genius and heredity that has been seriously underplayed. For one thing, that mechanism I discussed accounts for the repeated failure of human cultural efforts to work on a basis of hereditary nobility. No matter how fine the average, the statistics, of the line . . . the individual who inherits the title may be the one who inherited a negative statistical run of bad-news genes. It is, equally, why the position of hereditary serf won't stay put very well; a Francois Villon shows up with a positive statistical run, and he'll blow the lid off. Or an Abe Lincoln, the descendant of a long line of undistinguished nobodies, shows up. (And has children who fall right back into line.)

Sure there are mutations, too; there's been lots of talk about that. It's real glamorous. But statistical runs occur a lot more often, and have a massive effect on Man's problems. The great trouble in the South, with race relations, is not the statistical-norm of white or black; both groups get along fine, and have a good, comfortable working arrangement. It's the white trash and the high-level Negro who cause the trouble — because each is out of the statistical line, and hence has no proper place in the system. The abnormally low-quality white is inferior, knows he's inferior, and hates it; he demands that the genetic accident of white skin be considered full compensation for the genetic accident of inferiority. It isn't, and his effort to make it work that way causes trouble.

The Negro of abnormally high ability wants his high ability to compensate for the genetic fact that the norm of his race is not identical with the norm of whites. He's got a damn sight more validity on his side than the low-white has on his . . . but it makes more trouble, because he *is* smart and competent.

The problem is real, big, and complex, and isn't going to be solved by saying, "It really isn't there at all!" The purpose of my editorial was to suggest it might be worth while to gather courage enough to admit the problem *is* there, analyze it honestly, and see what can be done.

Currently, a lot of people — including the Supreme Court, to my acute distaste — is trying to use the typical female tactic of holding that a declaration of how it ought to be is all that's needed to make it that way. The WCTU was going to end alcoholism by passing a law against liquor; much simpler and more efficient than trying to find out why men become alcoholics. That would be hard work, and it's entirely unnecessary; just forbid them alcohol, and they won't be alcoholics. Simple, isn't it?

Just pass a law against race-tensions, and there won't be any. That's obvious, isn't it?

Sometime, if you feel sadistic, take a dull-normal student, put him in a class of moderate-genius grade, and then scourge him with shame, ridicule, and scorn because he isn't keeping up with other students his age. Thus you will be giving him an education as good as the best — encouraging him to rise in the world, and be a happier, more able man.

You'll give the police force, and some over-loaded psychiatrists a job ten years hence, too.

Suppose the Negro kids don't *want* to be integrated, huh?

Suppose the son of a top-notch doctor doesn't *want* to be a doctor, but prefers being an accountant? Does the poor sucker *have* to be integrated?

All I'm driving at is the proposition that people are different, and it *isn't solely a matter of breed.*

I'm stewing another editorial currently that may call forth an even hotter reaction from you, and another few hundred of my readers — but which I think needs discussion.

Ever hear of the Hoxsey Cancer Clinic? The AMA's been trying to close him up for 25 years, and hasn't succeeded yet. He's got two running now — one in Dallas, Texas, and one in Portage, Penn. He's treating cancer with a home-brewed weed-stew concoction, and a simple escharotic for external lesions. He's been at it since he was a kid about 20 — the coal-mining son of an ex-horse-doctor.

There's only one thing that interests me in the situation; the son of a gun *does* cure cancer! His improbable weed stew works!

Looks to me like another one of those stewed fox-gloves, or cinchona bark, or rowulfia serpentina deals. Exceedingly improbable — but probability has no determinable relationship to truth!

Mainly, what interests me, is that Galileo-type Problem; the case of the individual at odds with Constituted Authority, under the circumstances that

1. there is presumptive evidence that he *might* be right, and
2. the Constituted Authorities categorically refuse to "look

through his telescope" — to examine the objective evidence he seeks to present.

I don't know whether Hoxsey's right or not, so far as his claim he can cure cancer; I'm not competent to judge that. But I am, by God, competent to judge when he's right about saying that the AMA is duty bound to give his methods a *real* investigation! That's not a matter of medicine — it's a matter of philosophy, of the philosophical problem of epistemology. And while the AMA boys have a right to claim special expertness in medicine — the degree they hold is an M.D., not a Ph.D.

And the Hoxsey case *is* a Galileo-type case in that respect; he sued Morris Fishbein, the AMA, and the Hearst newspapers on charges of libel, in the courts — which brought into court the question of whether or not he was a fraud and a charlatan as charged, or was not by virtue of actually curing cancers.

The evidence he presented in court was good enough that the courts found, repeatedly, that he was not a charlatan, and that the AMA, Fishbein, et al. were guilty of libel.

His evidence was cured cases of cancer. Twenty-year cures, many of them, without recurrence.

The AMA was 100% in the wrong, philosophically, too; they put witnesses on the stand to testify that biopsies were not adequate to establish the existence of cancer . . . and yet hold that biopsies are the only adequate test for the presence of cancer.

After studying their arguments, I have come to the somewhat wry conclusion that the only adequate proof Hoxsey could present that would satisfy them would be five-year cure of an individual who had been shown to have cancer by a careful postmortem examination. The demonstration would be spectacular, if nothing else.

Anyhow, I hold that the court cases establish adequately that there is *presumptive evidence* that he *might* be right.

And Hoxsey's issued a challenge — a put-up-or-shut-up challenge — guaranteeing to take 100 cases who have been definitely certified as genuine cancer cases, and if he doesn't cure 80% or better within 12 weeks, he'll forfeit $25,000 and guarantee to close his clinics for good.

The AMA hasn't taken him up.

Looks like they won't look through his telescope; they just want him to recant, whether it moves or not!

Regards,   John W. Campbell, Jr.

William C. Boyd   *October 7, 1957*

Dear Dr. Boyd:

The suggested article on fossilized errors of science sounds good. As you are undoubtedly aware through **Ike**, I feel there are a lot of them . . . and that the old saying "It ain't so much what you don't know that hurts you; it's

336

all them things you know that ain't so!" has great validity.

The line of development followed should, it seems to me, be more general than just mushrooms. I'm sure you know of hundreds of long-held errors — and if you don't, I'll bet that a few lunch-hour bull sessions with other departments there at BU would give you plenty to play with. Physics — chemistry — medicine — biology — all pull beautiful booboos . . . and very quietly bury the fact.

However, we do not want to give any of the aspect of "Science is a Sacred Cow"; we don't want the attitude "Science is nonsense!" We want the attitude "Science is something human beings do . . . and make mistakes at, just as they make mistakes elsewhere."

Neither do we want the attitude of **Martin Gardner's** obnoxiously snotty "In The Name of Science," with its nose-in-the-air "What fools these mortals be!"

Also, errors can be classified as "misinterpreted observation" and "theory without observation," or "faulty observation." There's a famous graph having to do with human sleeping that, as I understand it, was misplotted from the tabulated data; for some thirty-five years various scientists republished the graph, before someone checked the graph against the published data table in the original article and found the discrepancy.

I recently read an article by two psychiatrists of the Mayo Clinic making the definite statement that sexual deviation had a definite cause-effect relationship to nudity in the parental home, lack of privacy, et cetera. The sheer stupidity that prevails in any field of science that would print such egregious nonsense is worthy of note! If the stated proposition were valid as stated, then *all* children in the south sea island societies would necessarily be sexual deviants, and *all* children whose parents took them to nudist camps would be sex deviants.

For a matching bone-head play in logic, see the current FDA literature campaigning against Hoxsey's cancer clinic. Hoxsey claims that he has discovered therapeutic value in certain herbal extracts. The FDA states, "A careful search of the medical literature shows that these substances have no known therapeutic effect." For God's sake! If a man says "I have made a discovery," you don't disprove it by saying "I never heard of such a thing," do you? If you *had* heard of it, that *would* prove it wasn't a discovery; the fact that you *haven't* heard of it merely proves that discovery in the area is not impossible.

Currently, I'm doing a series of editorials on the fact that the term "demonstration" has absolutely no definition — which lies at the root of a lot of scientific nonsense and pseudo-scientific double-talk.

Regards,   John W. Campbell, Jr.

Dear Ike:

Before glooming yourself into huddled retirement over the sad fate of **Kuttner & Kornbluth**, please re-read **Mark Clifton's** "The Dread Tomato Addiction." You, too, can lie with statistics.

Yes, **Kornbluth** was a stocky, somewhat overweight, sedentary man, and **Kornbluth** is dead. Winston Churchill is also a stocky, somewhat overweight, sedentary man . . . and you should live so long. **Joe Winter** died of a heart attack, coronary thrombosis type; he was a stocky, somewhat overweight sedentary man, too. But the thing that was critical was that **Joe** didn't have the sense to say, "I can't do all that," and quit. One of my neighbors here dropped dead of a heart attack, too.

When somebody drops like that . . . it's because either he said, "I can do anything," or his wife said, "Willy can do anything," and made him try.

The secret of a long and successful life is very simple; learn to say, "That's enough for now." Whether it's eating, working or playing . . . or worrying.

The odd part about it is that the total organism is much like the arm; it goes into a cramp, and becomes useless, if only *one* muscle is kept in continuous operation . . . but can do a hell of a lot if the various muscles are all used alternately. You can work like hell at your hobby, then work like hell at your business, then work at something else with vim, vigor and gusto . . . and it won't kill you. But doing one tenth as much at one thing will kill you.

It's a miracle that **Hank Kuttner** stayed alive as long as he did; **Catherine** did a magnificent job of holding that poor guy together. He was invalided out of the Army as psychoneurotic, you know; the Army's mistake was taking him in the first place. How the man ever achieved as much as he did, with the terrible psychic wounds he'd been given, is a magnificent tribute to what he had innately.

He was, **Ike**, an excellent example of my basic point in our running debate; education and orientation can't completely destroy inherent power of personality, no matter how badly it distorts and scars it. Accept my word for it; the guy had a rotten start. **Catherine** did a magnificent job of nursing him . . . but the scar tissue remained.

Kornbluth I didn't know so much about, nor know so well. But I've read his stories, and I've met him.

There are several basic ways to react to injustice. Usually, the Unjust, the individual committing the injustice, sincerely believes that he is not unjust. But *always*, whether he considers himself justified (in which case he considers what he is doing either punishment-for-your-wrong-doing, or paying-back-injury) or not (and thinks he is doing it just because he enjoys the feeling of power), the Unjust inevitably intends to make it a one-way deal. He *always* intends to hurt you without being hurt in return.

You can react to the Unjust by being Unjust . . . but the Unjust will be expecting you to attempt to reflect the injury, and will try to block it. This means that you'll always find that he is

1. Unjust and
2. unjustly tries to maintain his injustice when you react, and (3)
3. unjustly punishes your effort to reflect the injustice, and
4. . . . .

this is, obviously an endless series. Get sucked into it and you wind up with anger, bitterness, and deep futility. You become so busy trying to "get even" that you never have any time, effort, or energy to get ahead with your own accomplishment.

(This holds for nations, too; a nation bent on "getting even" can never get ahead.)

This is the old Italian concept of vengance — the old feuding concept.

Then there's the Irish approach; their anger is homeric, but never bitter. It's anger-with-gusto, not anger-with-bitterness. It's the proposition that the Unjust was unjust because he's a damn fool, and hasn't the wit to see that he's hurting somebody. But that once the blockheaded idiot's been made to understand the situation, they'll both be the best of friends.

The third attitude is that based on the proposition that what the Unjust did *was in fact* justified — *even when the Unjust himself believes he's being sadistic.* A homicidal maniac kills people because, being psychotic, and with the particular type of psychosis he has developed, he can't act in any other way . . . whether *he* thinks he can or not. He may think he's acting out of a freely chosen and rationally derived decision, based on judged and evaluated facts . . . but he isn't.

Then, with that proposition, the problem of the Unjust can be approached with enthusiasm, as a challenging problem; what factors did in fact make the observed resultant behavior the inescapable and necessary outcome? Solve that problem, and the Unjust can be triggered into a new type of behavior.

And, **Ike**, sometimes the best possible new-type-behavior is suicide for the Unjust. Some people need to drop dead. They can't be repaired into usable members of the human race. Some cells are cancer cells; they should drop dead. Quite a few of the Nazis belonged in that category; the human race would have benefited immensely if they had been assassinated before they got Europe in the mess they did.

Do not exclude "Drop dead" from the list of appropriate solutions to problems.

The essential point is this; some human beings can approach the problem of injustice-suffered as a challenge, a problem to be solved. And some can only accumulate repressed hatred, bitterness and curdle inside as they go further and further into that endless series of injustice — injustice-of-suppressing-complaint-injustice-of-suppressing-rebellion-against-unjust-suppression-of-complaint

-against-injustice-etc. — ad-infititum.

Cyril Kornbluth was stuck in that series. His anger against the ways of the culture he didn't fit too well produced cumulative bitterness in him. His stories were angry-bitter stories. (**Horace** tends that way too; there's a lot of it in *Galaxy*.)

My own personal bets for the next candidates for the Drop Dead Club in science-fiction include **Pohl** and **del Rey. Pohl** out of futile-bitter-anger; **del Rey** by reason of being overwhelmed. **G.O. Smith**, incidentally, is rapidly moving up the list.

And you my friend, can't get even a provisional place on the waiting list of that club . . . until you stop enjoying life and laughter. Until you stop crusading, and go back to sullen, bitter anger that your efforts aren't granted the success you know they should, by Inalienable Right, have. You've got to stop learning from your failures, and start being bitter that They won't let you do what you know you have a right to, before you get into **Kornbluth's** club.

As of now, you are in Churchill's club.

We just got back from San Francisco; been visiting **Jane** and inspecting our new son-in-law. **Jane** got herself a handful of man, this time — they're going to have hell and halleleujah for the next couple of years, I can predict with some assurance, but the results should be slightly terrific.

He's the son of the **Dr. Allen** who's head of biochemistry at Berkley. And he hasn't spoken to his father for some five years or so. He's a red-hot, fulminating rebel, with the gentleness of a full-scale nuclear reaction under good control. Just don't pull out the control rods and try to see what happens.

The red-hot rebellion against his father is fully justified at a human level . . . and unjustified at any logical-cultural level. He'a been earning his own way, away from home entirely, since he was about 16.

It started, I gather, when he was put in the Berkley Experimental Nursery School, at ages 2 to 6, for the psychology department to experiment on. He scored 162 IQ, and was their star exhibit. (I suspect he'd have scored higher if the psych boys had been wise enough to realize that some of his answers were better than, and therefore different from, the ones they had decided were "right.") His father is a logical orthodoxist. (You should know: no man can get to be head of a department of a major university without proving beyond question that he's an absolute logical orthodoxist.) **John**, I gather, had more sense and more guts than **Clyde Kluckhon's** son; you may or may not recall that the **Kluckhon** son, at about age 24, finally rebelled against the regimen his logical-orthodoxist (head of Anthropology at Harvard) father had surrounded him with . . . by shooting a Luger out of the hotel window into a crowd of shoppers on the street below. He killed a woman.

John thinks like a well-greased electronic computer . . . and then adds something more. He's extraordinarily brilliant, extraordinarily sensitive, and has the toughness and determination of personality to keep from blowing up.

But, naturally, he's exceedingly suspicious of (1) older men, (2) older people generally, (3) other people. They don't approve of his answers. He doesn't approve of theirs.

We got along fine; he is a sports-car enthusiast, and doesn't pretend to know electronics. We carried one of my home-designed hi-fi amplifiers out with us as a wedding present; it does things with music that he liked. Also, it's based on a flat rejection of orthodox theory. His father is trying to synthesize protoplasm; I told **John** precisely and specifically why the old man couldn't do it . . . because orthodoxy is inadequate to admit the problem that must be solved before protein can be synthesized.

Since we were out in San F. for most of two weeks, I hadn't heard that *Science World* was folded. I haven't been in to the office yet, so it's still news to me.

I have a slight suspicion part of the trouble was with the fact that **Pat Lauber** wasn't a science-enthusist . . . simply a woman enormously desirous of building a successful magazine. Plus the fact that "See, we have all the answers" style orthodoxy is what the teachers want presented . . . and "Look how much we don't know . . . and how wonderful it would be to find out!" is what the students need. Teachers don't want a magazine that raises questions; they want one that answers them.

Oh . . . by the way. **Peg** made an exceedingly acute observation the other morning. (While watching a young couple with two boys, 1½ and 4 years old, at breakfast next table at the hotel.) Even at 4, the boy was displaying the male pattern . . . as **Peg** observed correctly. A boy's questions are thickly larded with "Yes, but. . . ." and "But why. . . ." A girl's are usually simple inquisitives, and she ends up with either "Oh." or "Yes."

Now as to our debate:

The basic trouble is that the problem of the relationship of the individual to the group has never been solved. The Society expresses rules for public living . . . and those rules are totally impossible for private, individual-to-individual living. Taking the most strictly private-living, individual-to-individual relationship of all, physical sex, note that the society's rules are utterly hopeless as any sort of a guide. And, until quite recently, the society ruled that no information about the practical operation of sexual relationships should exsist at all! (i.e., books discussing sexual relations were flatly interdicted.) Kinsey's efforts to gather some information — whether those efforts were well handled or ill is beside the point — were violently attacked; various pressure groups forced the Foundations that supported his work to withdraw their support. (And Kinsey died of a heart attack.)

The Society exists by group-relationships. Private relationships interfere with it, since they are emotional in nature, and not subject to easy control by intellectually communicable rulings. (Instance: family loyalty will cause a family to shield a criminal from the agents of society. Emotional effects frustrating social rulings.)

But individual-individual rules are just exactly as inappropriate to group systems such as a society.

Now: What *I'm* trying to say is, "A Society, being a great, big, clumsy, massive organism, has to have rules of organization; it can't operate on pure individual choice."

What you're trying to express is, "Broad rules don't fit individual-individual situations, and seriously hurt the poor guy who gets caught in the jam."

I agree with you. Completely, 100% agree with you. I agree that something should be done about it.

But I do NOT agree with you that we should pass a broad rule that there should be no broad rules.

Look, guy; Newton's laws didn't work for Mercury, nor for high speed electrons. Therefore we should throw Physics out the window, Huh?

I agree with you that present broad rules anent racial problems are unsatisfactory.

Now please stop being foolish-in-the-head and suggesting that we throw all rules of racial relationship out the window.

What we need is *not* no-rules-at-all, but *rules that work better.*

The Food & Drug tests for the suitability of dye substances as food dyes are, as you told me, unsatisfactory and inappropriate. So let's dispense with the FDA, and have no rules, huh? Let anyone who thinks his dye-stuff is a good food color go ahead?

Maybe we should, instead, do some sweating on devising more appropriate tests . . . with the recognition that no test will ever be completely satisfactory, except the use itself.

You know these "Tube tester" machines in radio stores? They test cathode emission, and not much more. I've got a tube that tests perfect . . . only it won't amplify worth a damn; something's wrong with the grid, so it's non-linear as hell. But I'm using it very satisfactorily; it makes a fine oscillator, where all I want it to do is turn the plate-current on and off.

When the testing procedure is inappropriate to the problem, people want to throw it out. Fine . . . but that doesn't mean throwing out testing. It means getting a better testing procedure.

Now consider this question: Do we need *any* kind of racial rulings?

If you answer that "No," then "Should an individual pay *any* attention to the genetic background of his mate"?

And don't answer that one "No" or I'll refer you to the young man from Dundee, who buggered an ape up a tree.

The trouble, M'lad, is that no logician can count. That is, since logic is qualitative, not quantitative, no logician can distinguish degrees, quantities, or magnitudes. And, incidentally, no one yet has come up with a logically satisfactory definition of Number, though God knows they've tried hard enough.

Look; what's infinity minus one? Infinity.

Not if the "one" is "first." You have to have *first* before you can have *any*. Your Ugly Boy story simply subtracted one (the first) from an infinite number of fires . . . and *whoosht*! they *all* went out!

Therefore, infinity minus one is zero. *Provided that "one" is "first."*

Now consider this problem: Is it logically possible to determine the color of an *unexposed* photographic film?

Logically, the only possible answer is "No." Color is a term dealing with light; in this case reflected light. But an "unexposed photographic film" is one that hasn't been exposed to any light. Therefore you can't possibly determine the color of an unexposed film.

But technically — i.e., in real-world practice — you can determine the exact color of the most sensitive film made, without exposing it. The threshold sensitivity of the best films is about 1000 quanta. Modern photomultiplier tubes are sensitive to about four quanta. Therefore a photoelectric spectrometer can observe the color of an unexposed film.

Since you have, all your life, been trapped again and again by the fact that logicians can't count, and by the fact that other people will always seek to force you into the untenable position of being logical just when you need to count . . . you have, like anyone else in the culture, a violent rejection of being stuck with a need-to-count.

When is a Negro? When he's ½ white? ¼th white? ⅛th?

When is a Jew not a Jew? When he's left the Hebrew faith? When he was born a gentile, even though he has accepted the Hebrew faith? Count, **Isaac**! Draw a line!

Remember **H. Beam Piper's** "The Day of the Moron"? When is a man too stupid to hold a critical job? When is an airline pilot unfit for work? A Canadian pilot, I notice, made a crack-up landing with a DC-7 a year or two ago. He was ruled negligent, and suspended for six months. A year later he cracked up a smaller liner . . . he hadn't been allowed to take the big DC-7's again . . . and killed some 30 people.

Your fundamental objection is that broad rules should not be made to limit the individual exception.

Start counting, **Ike**; count off what constitutes an exception. The existence of a society demands that there be rules. That's what distinguishes a society from an anarchy, isn't it?

Regards, John

Dear Mr. Crosby:

Aesop used to get away with this sort of thing . . . but in a somewhat simpler day. Your basic thesis is, of course, perfectly sound . . . but this is a fable, not a story. Most of your material is actually descriptive; you don't show it happening — you merely say it happened.

I like the idea of continuing the Centra-Earth tie-up this way, but the story needs to be stronger.

You might get something out of this item, though:

The ideal fool-killer is a system which is an attractive death-trap, having a characteristic that attracts only fools, and encourages said fools to die happy, so they don't get angry and hurt anyone in the process.

A perfect example is the Eskimo wolf-killing system. Take a sharp knife, and fix it in the ground, or ice, near a trail, blade upward. Cut your finger on the blade, and smear the blade with blood. Then leave it for the wolves.

The wolf is a blood-drinker. He smells the blood, is attracted, and licks the knife. He cuts his tongue . . . and gets the taste of hot, fresh blood. He dies happy, of course. . . .

Or introduce a machine that is, effectively, a clairvoyance machine. (You can see anything, anywhere, at will.) Make it sell for about $100. Every fool wants to own one, so he can see . . . and screams in helpless anger that other people are invading his privacy. The only survivors would be those who live, in private, as they do in public, and can bear having their privacy invaded. And therefore don't want to invade other's privacy.

The essential proposition is that fool-killer is something that attracts the fool, but only fools, and, ideally, doesn't anger the fool even while he's busily killing himself.

It's important that fools be eliminated; if they're not, their folly kills people. But there's no more efficient technique than that of making the fool happily insist on killing himself.

Imagine a planet on which the commonest weed was a happy-dreams narcotic. The climate of the planet is like that of Upper New York State, let's say. What kind of people would be able to settle on and use the planet?

You could get along fine during the summer, without planning or working much . . . but the winter's a killer. If you haven't stored up food and fuel.

The check for the additional $100 is on its way. My fault, compounded by everyone along the line falling into the simple arithmetic error I made when I first multiplied the wordage by 3 and got 410, instead of 510.

Regards,   John W. Campbell, Jr.

Enc: "Pride Goeth"

Harry C. Crosby, Jr. *June 4, 1958*

Dear Crosby:

No.

The trouble with this one is that, again, the psi devices go through the old routine of being entertainment — magic. The particular route is attractive, easy, and accepting to the public. It's acceptable because it's a foolproof dead end. Anything that gets in there . . . stays there. Any practical use of the technique is automatically rejected, when proposed because it's now proven to be stage-trickery, and of no value.

Edgar Cayce, back in the early 1900's, demonstrated repeatedly that he had time clairvoyant powers, plus something over-and-beyond that that made it possible for him to diagnose a medical illness, and prescribe accurately. Obviously, clairvoyance would be a terrific assist in medical diagnosis! You could *see* what was wrong.

The AMA hated him, of course. Again and again efforts were made to "expose his fraud" . . . and couldn't. He wasn't a fraud; he did it.

But he was prevented from doing anything broadly useful; no one ever acknowledged that there was something that needed investigation — only something that needed to be blocked, stopped, disproven. . . .

But he was told that if he'd just put on a turban, and a robe, and go on stage, he could make thousands of dollars. . . .

Cayce apparently had an IQ of only about 85-90 . . . but even he was too wise to accept that gambit. If he had, even once, presented his abilities *as a show* . . . then on, the AMA could have said, "See! It's all stage trickery — no real value at all!"

Of course, he never did get anyone to investigate properly — but because he never allowed it to be made a stage-act, there remains the discomforting-to-orthodoxy record of what he did do — and *no* record of his having "admitted" it was just showmanship.

In addition to that factor, the allegory here is a little too straight-forward.

Look . . . our enemy isn't Russia. It's the ancient enemy of Desire To Quit Climbing and Rest Where We Are.

Your story "Top Rung" had one aspect of the leader's problem. The other aspect is that when you have what you want — leadership — all you want is to hold it. But the only way to hold it is to keep leading — keep climbing. And men don't want to have to continue to work as hard as they did to reach the lead position!

The peasant thinks the King has a soft life. The King knows better.

The child thinks the adult has it easy; he can buy all the ice cream sodas he wants, any time he wants, and nobody tells him to go to bed when he doesn't want to.

The would-be leader thinks leadership is a state, which can be attained.

The United States achieves it . . . and . . . whaddaya know! It's not a state at all; it's a dynamic system and we have to work harder, not less, than before!

345

Now you're a successful author, with a good position in the field, you think maybe you can rest easy, huh?

The United States can't either. It just wants to, and Russia makes it painfully evident we can't.

Regards,   John

Enc.: "Three-Contraption Parlay"

James Blish   *July 15, 1958*

Dear Jim:

The essential aspect of "professionalism" that I object to is the professional's tendency to hold that because Tog (The Other Guy) hasn't the same formal education he has, that proves Tog doesn't understand the subject.

Your math teacher *was* an amateur, in that sense; since he didn't have *formal* education, he was an amateur. The professional has a nasty tendency to say, "Well, of course *he* wasn't *really* an amateur, because he was so competent in the field."

In other words, the Professional claims that "amateur" and "incompetence" necessarily go together . . . and that "no formal education in the field" therefore also goes with "incompetence." So when a man who has no formal education shows great competence, they deny that he is an amateur — because the idea that a true amateur can be highly competent, in fact more competent that a professionally trained member of the Profession is less tolerable than allowing the high-competence amateur Professional standing.

You, yourself have a strong tendency to show that Professional attitude toward my remarks. You start with the assumption that since I have no professional training, and use methods of analysis not professionally accepted, I must necessarily be making incompetent analyses.

There's a very curious human tendency worth noting; not only do people avoid new experiences — but they equally frantically avoid new approaches to old experiences.

Sci Am runs mathematical puzzles. One they ran a while back concerned a hole drilled through the center of a sphere, the hole penetrating exactly along the diameter, and being 6″ long. What is the volume of the remaining part of the sphere?

Now this problem can be solved by a long mathematical analysis of the ratios of diameters, volumes of spheres and cylinders, etc.

But there's a short-cut solution that solves it in 20 seconds in your head. It's a completely rigorous solution, and extremely simple. I wrote a note calling *Sci Am's* attention to it; it's interesting, because it *is* a rigorous, and extremely simple technique of problem solution. But they ignored that solution. It was highly unorthodox — and that is normally labelled "unfair."

346

The solution: It is stated that the problem *can* be solved with the data given. The diameter of the 6"-long hole is not given. Therefore necessarily it follows that that diameter need not be determined; it must be so interrelated with other factors as to be an irrelevant variable. Any value of the diameter must work out to have zero effect on the solution. Very well, I assume a diameter for the hole of dx, with dx approaching zero as a limit. Then when dx is indiscernably different from zero, the diameter of the sphere must be the length of the hole   6". Then the volume of the remaining material is the volume of a sphere of 3" radius. Simple arithmetic gives the answer.

The essential of calculus is to *sweep an area with a line*. This is not a logical method, actually; the rigorous logical structure of calculus has never been established. It's a technique of solving problems by sweeping the problem-area with a limiting condition.

That's the technique I use — and it is not logically defensible, any more than calculus is. Calculus says, "infinity times zero is a finite variable" which is a logically indefensible statement. Sure, mathematicians use it; it works! But pragmatic proof is *not* a logical proof.

One missing concept in modern thinking is the concept of the "irrelevant variable" — irrelevant variable-system, actually. If two variables, x and y, are so related that, with respect to the problem, $xf(y)$ is a constant — as in the case of the sphere-with-a-hole problem — then x and y are irrelevant variables. They vary; yes. But their variations have no meaning whatever for the problem under discussion.

It's what I have also called "the double-diddle factor." A diddle factor is something that doesn't change the equation, and doesn't change the universe, but makes it *look* as though the equation matched the universe. Example: putting a color-correction filter on a camera loaded with daylight color film to take pictures under tungsten light. It doesn't make the film into tungsten film; it doesn't make the lights daylight light. But it makes it *look* as though the two matched.

Now a double-diddle is trickier; it makes it possible to eliminate completely a truth, so that no matter what that truth may be doing, it has zero effect!

Example: in hi-fi music recording, the recording mechanism is designed to exaggerate the high frequencies, with an exaggeration effect increasing with frequency at about 12 db per octave.

This is a diddle factor.

The play-back mechanism is then designed to suppress high-frequencies, with a similar response curve — 12 db attenuation per octave.

The double-diddle suppresses a truth; all real structures in the Universe contain noise, and the noise-energy increases with frequency, roughly at about 4 db per octave.

The *truth* is that record surfaces are noisy.

But the double-diddle suppresses this truth in such a way that no matter what that truth is, it has no effect on the outcome!

Now when I used the term "human" factors, in saying men do not behave logically, and that psychology can't solve its problems because the psychologist *must* accept nonlogical techniques to handle the non-logical problem, I was *not* saying that "human beings behave in a law-free manner."

To a strict logician, for some reason, anything that does not obey the laws of logic is defined as being law-free. "Nature and the laws of Nature are what I know; anything following other laws is un-natural, and super-natural, and therefore superstition." That Nature might have higher-order laws is being rigidly denied.

What I am saying is that there are laws of Nature which are rigidly lawful — *but not logical* laws.

Look: the Laws of Nature that apply to material entities do *not* apply to all physical entities. There is a whole, well-recognized class of physical entities that behave in a "supernatural manner" . . . if we confine "Nature" to material-entity laws.

Of material entities, it is true that two entities cannot occupy the same space at the same time.

But a magnetic field is a non-material, physical entity. Two magnetic fields can pervade the same space at the same time.

Now logic is utterly incapable of handling potential-reality. Is a future potential a member of the Class of "Existing entities"? No, it is not. Then, says logic, it must be a member of the Class "Nonexistent Entities."

No wonder you boys can't handle the concept of "instinct" satisfactorily! Of course most instincts do no exist! They're potentials, not existentials.

Can a newborn baby talk? No. Then this proves that the ability to speak is not innate in Man.

An instinct is a trigger-circuit set-up; it can lie there patiently doing nothing, manifesting nothing, "being" nothing . . . until the right trigger-stimuli come along. If the trigger-circuit doesn't exist, it can't be triggered; if it does exist, you can't prove it (as of our present incompetent techniques) except by triggering it. How can you prove that a certain virgin girl is capable of bearing a baby? Maybe she's sterile? As of now, we can prove the existence of a potential only by triggering it; the girl can be proven capable of motherhood only by impregnation.

But that doesn't mean that inability-to-prove is proof-of-non-existence!

Many instincts are extremely complex trigger-circuits, like a trancontinental automatic telephone dialing system. Our daughter is living in Berkeley, California. We can telephone her by dialing a three-digit code for the San Francisco area, and then her local telephone number. Dialing the three-digit code won't produce results. Dialing the local number will produce a result, but not the desired result.

The complex relay-trigger mechanism involved requires logical analyis of the order of, "If A, *and* B, *and* C, but-not D, or E or F, *and* H, I, J, K, *and* L, but not L, M, or N, *then* Alpha. *If* we dial the three-digit code, but-not the trunk lines to San Francisco are busy, and we dial the local number, but-not the local line is busy, or they don't happen to be home, or sleeping, *then* we get to talk to **Jane** or her husband.

So, your experiment with the rat that, when equipped with a disk around her neck didn't clean her newborn young proves that there is no cleaning-the-young instinct? Nuts, brother! It proves that if you block dialing the three-digit area code, then dialing the local exchange number produces the wrong-number result to be expected.

And you're trying to say, "This proves there is no such thing as a telephone line to Berkeley, California."

Try this experiment: Cut off the female rat's head immediately after birth, isolate her from others of her kind, and prove that there is no instinct to survive, because, you see, she just lies there and dies.

You can do some other interesting fruit-cake type experiments, too. Many instinct systems require pattern-stimuli — additive stimuli won't work, because a product-resultant rather than a sum-resultant is needed. For instance, a 5-year-old boy can have an erection — he can participate in copulation. Ten years or twenty years later it can be shown that he is capable of producing viable sperm. But the ability of erection *and* production of sperm does *not* equal ability to impregnate a female. Suppose he lost his penis at age 10? We've proven he has the ability to copulate (at age 5) and the ability to produce sperm (at age 20) and yet he cannot impregnate a female, so we have proven that ability to copulate and produce sperm is not adequate to impregnate a female, huh?

There, of course, the error is clear enough for anyone to see. But it took a while to discover that calcium in the diet wasn't sufficient to prevent rickets, and that Vitamin D in the diet wasn't enough to prevent rickets.

How's about instinct trigger-systems that work only when all the required stimuli are present *simultaneously*?

Simultaneity is a nasty word to logical analysis. See what **Einstein** did in Relativity because logic can't handle Simultaneity!

Sure, professionalism has a place, and a good and worthy place indeed. All engineering-level workers in a field should be professional people.

But professional *research* is impossible. By the meaning of the concept!

A professional worker is, properly, one who has had the training in known, solidly established techniques to make it possible for him to guarantee a high-order reliability of results.

If a problem is a true research problem, then you do NOT know in advance what the answers will be — you can NOT work with high reliability.

True; there is such a thing as engineering research; which of *n* known methods is best adapted to this problem. (Should we build a steel arch, a cantilever truss, or suspension bridge . . . or maybe a prestressed-concrete-and-piers type?)

But fundamental research implies things that, by nature, *can not be professional work*.

"Professional" implies "a high order of reliability"; fundamental research cannot be that.

349

The percentage of major break-throughs in the various fields of science which have been made by professionals in the field involved is very low. Check it, and see — only make your check *honest*. Was the break-through-maker considered a professional-in-the-field *at the time he did the work* or was he granted that status only *after* his achievement?

Newton was NOT a scientist — and the methods he used were *not* considered scientific . . . *at the time he used them*. Look, bub . . . he *invented* calculus! He had to, in order to show that a sphere could properly be considered a point source in computing gravitational attraction. Therefore, the method he used *was not considered scientific at the time he used it*. There was, as a matter of fact, hell and halleleujah raised about his "fluxions" because of that zero-times-infinity problem.

Don't judge on the basis of what you think from this era; what did his contemporaries think at the time of first announcement?

No professional in a field can do that sort of thing; he is required by his social contract of professionalism to use only already accepted and agreed on methods. A man can't hang out his shingle as "John J. Jones, M.D." and practice faith-healing; the fact that he does in fact have an M.D. degree has nothing to do with the legitimacy of such a pattern of behavior. When he hangs out "M.D." he is asserting he intends to practice the techniques of recognized medicine. It doesn't even matter that he is a highly successful faith-healer; he still has no damn business hanging out "M.D." and not *being* an M.D.

If I start running love stories in *ASF*, even if they're world-beater love-stories, my readers have a right to get sore; that ain't what they paid for.

Professionalism that doesn't enforce professional methods isn't doing an honest job of professionalism; it implies standards and methods.

BUT . . . that also implies no-research.

My friend, you can't slice that two ways — because Professionalism is a logical concept.

What I'm trying to say of human beings is that they entail major elements of higher-order rationale, a hyper-logical, but strictly lawful, rationale that is not, and never can be, contained within the domain of Logic. Logic is a necessary subset of a higher-order rationale, which I've more-or-less arbitrarily called "analogic." Logic is the subset of analogic dealing with one-to-one correlations, in a sequential-linear system.

Now there are one-to-one correlations in a network, non-sequential system to be considered — the rationale of simultaneity.

And in addition, there are correlations of less-than-one to one.

Neither of these two latter classes falls within the narrowly defined subset Logic.

There's no point arguing that point with me; argue it with a professional logician. Ask him what the implication of **Einsteinian** non-simultaneity is! Logic works only by *denying simultaneous valid alternatives*. "Either A or B, but not both, must be true; then B or A is false."

What if A and B are both, simultaneously and equally true?
Impossible.

What's the square root of 4? And if you say "2," you're wrong . . . because the only correct answer is "Plus and minus 2." Simultaneously and equally true alternatives.

On the Negro-White non-equality problem.

You can say that in a private letter . . . but will you allow me to publish your statement, under your title and department heading?

If not . . . why not? If it's true, why conceal it? If it's not true, why state it privately?

As to which is "better," the answer's easy. Whites are. Not because I say so, or because I'm white — but because the White's damn well took over the joint. "In any scientific experiment, it is impossible for anything to go wrong. It can only go right in a way you did not intend." In a reality-test, the answer is never wrong — it can only be one you didn't want.

White's run the joint. This doesn't mean they always did, and it doesn't mean they always will. But it means that, as of right now, White's have the best pattern of answers to the problem of how-to-live, yet developed.

One of the major characteristics of that pattern is that White's have been characterized by a greater willingness to learn from other peoples. The Indians taught the Pilgrims how to plant, how to hunt, how to live in America. What did the Indians bother to learn from the Pilgrims? How to get drunk, and how to shoot (but not how to manufacture) rifles.

The Whites learned everything they could use from the Chinese and Hindus — and offered the Chinese and Hindus everything they had in the way of techniques.

Ghandi went down fighting . . . and the Chinese Communists have finally used the Elementary Logic of club, bayonette, and gun to teach the local Chinese the important lesson of giving up local ritual-tabu government. The only known way to make a peasant stop being a peasant is with a bayonette. There may be others, but to date, no one has found any. Stalin starved eight million to death; the guns were used simply to enforce the starvation. A peasant doesn't *want* to learn; he violently wants-not to learn.

Pragmatic, crucial-experiment test says, "The race that learns most from others is most apt to survive." Whites are better. The Mau-Mau will be destroyed . . . even if whites do nothing about them!

One of the major difficulties in communicating in this world of ours is that there are two totally different types of highly intelligent people — and the psychometricians haven't gotten around to analyzing for, and distinguishing that difference.

1. Type I is the highly logical, highly competent, smart individual who works solely with existential type ideas. He is mentally almost totally unable to think in terms of conditional-contrary-to-fact.

2. Type II is an equally intelligent, logical, astute individual who

can work with existential type ideas, using strict logic . . . and in addition can work freely with conditional-contrary-to-fact.

The type I mind simply balks, freezes, and ceases to follow any line of reasoning that depends on accepting for discussion something he "knows" is not true. He simply can't work with an idea that is an hypothesis-contrary-to-what-he-knows.

A good friend of mine is vice-president of one of the largest general insurance companies in New York. He's worth a couple of millions. He's a fine man, and incidentally a Scot from Glasgow. He's unquestionably a brilliant individual.

And he *cannot* think in hypothetical terms. He's utterly unable to.

Art Gray, president of Street & Smith, and I were having a discussion in Jock's presence; Jock simply could not follow the discussion at all. It was **Art Gray** who pointed out to me, later, that there are brilliant men who *can't* think hypothetically.

You can NOT say that such people are stupid; they damn well aren't.

But I can say that I have a particular mental characteristic that such people simply do not have.

I know-for-a-fact that you, too, have the hypothetical-thinker type of mind. You wouldn't have read *ASF* for years if you hadn't.

The difficulty in communication is that the non-hypothetical mind makes an extremely high-competence professional — and an utterly hopeless researcher. But no researcher can possibly maintain that an astute, brilliant man such as a top-level professional is incompetent to understand something.

Yet he is!

He is inherently incompetent to consider any conditional-contrary-to-his-known-facts concept. He cannot consider a quadratic concept — one having two simultaneous, but different roots. His thinking works perfectly on all material problems, which do have a mutually-exclusive characteristic — but his thinking won't work competently on a field-type problem, where answers are not mutually exclusive.

Such a man must solve the male-female difference in terms of superiority-inferiority, because simultaneous-but-different and equally valid solutions can't fit into his thinking.

I suspect that the hypothetical thinker is born, rather than made. (With the express realization that all instinct-abilities are trigger-systems, and do not act unless triggered.) Some men can be trained to act hypothetically; others simply cannot be.

Look, I'm not insulted that the *Journal of the APA* won't publish my articles; I don't expect 'em to.

But I am insulted if you hold that the fact that that Journal won't publish 'em proves they're of no value! I am damn well irked if

Professional Approval is necessary before an idea can be evaluated.

One of the difficulties Psychology is up against is that *only* logical techniques have Professional Approval in Science — and, as I say, psychology is dealing with material that inherently displays non-logical characteristics.

Try measuring the energy content of Information, some time!

Inertia is one of the things physics can't handle; agreed. It happens to entail a non-logical concept mechanism, and Physics is royally stuck on it as a result.

But where Physics hits the hyperlogical only at its extreme fringes — our foundations — psychology is 90% concerned with the area.

Inertia can't ever be defined within the domain of Logic, because it's a hyperlogical concept. This can be shown by rigid Information Theory analysis, I'm willing to bet.

Logic can handle sequential, non-simultaneous problems; thus distance is Logic's meat.

But Inertia has nothing whatever to do with distance; it has, instead, to do solely with *direction* — which is inherently non-quantitative. (You can measure direction in degrees . . . once you've established a line-of-direction. But you *must simultaneously* consider two or more entities to establish a line of direction — and Logic can't.) Newton's defintion of inertia is in terms of modification of rest or rectilinear motion — which boils down to position or direction. Note that neither concept can have any meaning on a self-contained basis; position and direction both require simultaneous assertion of externals.

They are Information — not Energy.

And therefore they *are not relativistic.*

That sounds silly; so does the following paradox — but try accepting that I have, here, something of genuine importance, and see if you can find its important meaning.

"At one time there were two railroad stations in Boston, one of which was the largest in the United States. But as every proper Bostonian knew, that station was not the largest in Boston."

That's a lovely little paradox to pull on your friends — particularly those who maintain high standards of accuracy of English. When there are only two of a kind, it is not correct to refer to the larger as the largest.

Now this is not a silly digression; it's a root fundamental. It's a recognition that there must be three before the concept of largest *can exist*! Distance is a self-structured concept. Direction is not; there must be two or more points before *any* direction-concept can exist. Therefore direction is *not* relative; relationship is its essence and being. It *is* relationship; it is not relative. An area does not have length. A volume doesn't have area. Length is a characteristic which generated area — but is *not* a characteristic of area! A quadratic such as x^2 is not x nor does it have any characteristic of x. A group-entity is not possessed of the characteristics of the individuals who compose it.

It's extremely difficult to separate the concepts that we have always confused. The difficulty is almost exactly like that of a child first encountering areas in mathematics; when we say "A is twice as big as B," what do we mean? If we mean A has twice the area of B that's a thing entirely different from A having twice the linear dimensions of B.

Try this one: A man had a window 2 feet high and 2 feet wide. He wanted more light in his room. So he had the window increased in size so that he got twice as much light yet the window was still only 2′ x 2′ after the change! How did he do it?

That's a straight, honest, simple mathematical problem. No tricks . . . except a false assumption that you start with when you hear it. And a false assumption from the given data is your fault, not mine.

Try that on some students, and see how many succeed in working out the only possible solution. The answer is that the original was a diamond-shaped window, in which the 2′ dimension is the length of the vertical and horizontal diagonals; afterward the 2′ dimensions are the lengths of the now vertical and horizontal sides, while the diagonals now increased to 2.828 feet.

Area cannot exist without length; true. But length is not a characteristic of area.

Direction cannot exist without distance . . . but distance has nothing whatsoever to do with direction!

Inertia exists uniformly thoughout the Universe, because other bodies exist in the Universe, and establish, by their existence, an interaction with the fact-of-existence of the body under discussion, the relationship "directions." Gravity varies with distance . . . but inertia does not; it varies only with other-existence.

Physics is stumped by inertia, because it's at the Informational level.

Some 90% of psychology is at the Informational level. Now try getting anywhere with Logic, which is limited to sequential, linear, now-simultaneous matters!

There can be no such thing as interpersonal relationship without more-than-one person.

Simultaneity is inherent in interpersonal relationships, then.

Therefore Logical analysis of the problem is innately incompetent.

Develop the laws of Quadratic Logic, and maybe you could start to get somewhere!

Regards,   John

J. Frank Coneybear *August 13, 1958*

Dear John:

The article you mentioned is, I believe, "Tornadoes and Atom Blasts," by **J. O. Hutton**, which appeared in the May 1954 *Astounding*.

(**Miss Tarrant** is sending along a copy of the issue — and you owe Street & Smith's Petty Cash account $1.00.)

I hear from **Eric Russell** that the English are becoming irately convinced that nuclear disturbances are lousing up the weather. An Englishman's idea of "summer heat" isn't what we'd call hot — but even the English object to summer weather that hangs around 55-58°, with drizzle. Something, they insist, is Wrong!

Item for your mental kicking around: Inertia is defined, actually, by the First Law of Motion. Now if there is no absolute motion, but only relative, then the part that says "state of rest" drops out, and we have only "rectilinear motion" left.

Now inertia *appears* to be something innate, self-contained, a characteristic of the mass-itself-alone — independent of external factors.

However, I think I can show that zero equals infinity in one critical respect. You can't tell the difference between something that is not affected by anything external, and something that is affected by *everything* external. If everything external affects it, then no manipulation can change that fact, so it will *appear* that nothing external affects it.

Gravity is a distance-dependent phenomenon.

Inertia isn't. But notice that *change of direction* — actually, *rate* of change of direction — is the critical phenomenon in inertia.

Direction is a peculiar concept, however; it is absolutely independent of distance.

If there were a phenomenon which were determined solely by direction, it would show independence with respect to distance — but no position! In a multi-bodied Universe, it would appear to be independent of any external factor, by reason of the infinitude of factors actually present.

Conclusions: **E.E. Smith's** "inertialess drive" requires only that the ship involved be confused as to the direction to the rest of the Universe.

Might turn out that inertialessness was easier to achieve than antigravity — but would necessarily yield antigravity, too. Because gravity would give a line-of-direction.

Regards,   John

∪→⋗·≥≥≳~≫∠∞⊂≃⊻÷±≏⊥>/✗{}≢∩←◁≠≤≲≈≪ӽӧ⊃≅△

$$E = M\rho. \; [\partial\alpha\mu\pi\beta\epsilon\lambda\lambda]^2$$

→⋗·≥≥≳~≫∠∞⊂≃⊻÷±≏⊥>/✗{}†∩←◁≠≤≲≈≪ӽӧ⊃≅△

Isaac Asimov   *November 13, 1958*

Dear Ike:

Glad that "Yellow Pill" yarn appealed to you as an idea. There's a bit of a story behind it. **Rog Phillips** had sent me about six stories, one after another, all of which had been returned very promptly.

Rog wrote an angry, rather paranoid letter, saying that I was prejudiced against him, and wouldn't buy anything of his. (I'd just punched several gaping holes in a pet thesis of his which he'd incorporated in one yarn I returned.) I suggested that if he sincerely felt that, he could readily submit under a pen-name, through an agent, or otherwise disguise his efforts.

He quite angrily submitted "The Yellow Pill." It just happened that that seemed to me the first story he'd shown me that had a really neat, clearly and succinctly presented thesis. His check was on the way three days later.

Never heard a word about any of it from him afterwards. I think the experience had something of the effect of a "yellow pill" on him — and the effect as implied in the story is unpleasant, you'll notice. You don't need a yellow pill unless you've retreated from a too-harsh-to-bear reality, in which case the yellow pill is forcing you to face the unbearable. Obviously an unpleasant experience.

Incidentally, there are several ways you can check (without benefit of yellow pills) on your dream-world problem. If you were really in delusional dream-world, would you have me in there niggling at you via mail like this?

By the way, since you're looking for hobbies of a different sort . . . I've just been talking with a lecture agent by the name of **Gordon Skea**. It seems that there are, scattered hither and yon across the country, outfits that are willing to pay from 3 to 6 hundred bucks for an evening's lecture; a good agent can frequently rig up a tour taking 3-4 nights, hitting 3 or 4 cities, and making several hundred in each.

With the reputation you have, you should certainly be able to command quite an interesting fee. You might take a look into the matter; you've been a hell of a good public speaker for years — why not get someone to pay you for what you like doing anyway?

Now if you'd add photography as a hobby to that . . . just think of the chance for taking pics of various cities!

On the discussion: **Randy Garrett** has a Jewish problem somewhat different from yours. **Randy** is now sporting a King Henry VIII style beard & mustache. He is, currently, living in a Jewish neighborhood. He is making enemies and influencing people to dislike him more effectively than usual, because he is also wearing a silver cross pin in his lapel. A block away anybody can spot him as a young rabbi, of course. . . .

And **Ike**, my friend, consider the case of a fairy, a queer. They can, normally, be spotted about as far off as you can spot a mulatto. I'll admit a coal-black Negro can be spotted a bit further than a fairy can, but the normal mulatto can't. Sure, I know a lot of queers don't look that way — but they're simply "passing." There's tremendous prejudice against them, too, you know. I know of an instance where a large retail store closed out one small department, that being the simplest way to shove out a pair of fairys who'd gravitated there — and they did NOT want fairys around. A sort of race prejudice, huh?

They can be spotted by their mannerisms — walk, body-posture, etc. Then there's the different type, the true eunochoid. He can be spotted two blocks off; nobody but a eunochoid has that body-weight distribution. He's not just fat; he's fat in a particular and unique way.

There's marked prejudice against them, too, you know.

Now there are many types that can be spotted a long way off — skin-color is by no means the only thing that can be spotted at long range. It's just one that's easy to spot *and to describe*. You, having had considerable training in endocrinology, know what a eunochoid is, and can describe one in fairly understandable terms. But ask Bill Blow, I.Q. 95, why he doesn't like Cecil Jones . . . and Bill can't tell you.

A small child will react toward a sheep and a sheepdog in entirely different ways — even though he's never seen either before. You know . . . "horns, hooves — herbivorous!" You can't! Sure, Couvier was zoologist enough to know those factors — but a child is enough the product of three billion years of terrestrial evolution to have the reactions built right in. But *he* couldn't explain, "I don't fear this animal, but I do fear that one, because that one has clawed paws, not hooves, and it has long, pointed canines, and the lean, flat belly of a carnivour."

Point: human beings do-in-fact notice and react to pattern-clues that they cannot express in conscious terms. Sure, there have been things like the chalicotherium, with its horselike head, herbivorous diet, and claws on its feet that would scare a lion. But the patterns are pretty reliable — certainly reliable enough to make them worth reacting to if you want to say alive.

But . . . reactions to patterns *cannot be defended logically*. You can't point out logically the things you're reacting to. You know that; try pointing out the figures in a Ishihara Color Test diagram to a man born colorblind!

All of which leads to this: you can't be spotted as a Jew from two blocks away. But you and I *can* be spotted as Eggheads from at least as great a distance as a Negro can.

Part of being an Egghead is a degree of neuromuscular coordination that is abnormal; it's not *just* intellectual, you know! At age 20, I drove from New Haven to Boston, on the old Post Road, not the new turnpikes, at an average speed of 45 miles an hour. The only odd thing about that was that it was at night, with absolute slick glare ice on the roads every mile of the way. I didn't skid or slip once on the entire trip. I don't know how I managed it now — but I know as an historical fact that I did. It's part of what makes me an egghead. I can keep stuff piled up on my electronics bench, and not knock it over while working on it. I can work with bare high-voltage conductors without getting connected to them.

You've got the same sort of talent. We're abnormally aware of *all* the things around us. The result is that we handle ourselves, our bodies, with an efficiency and economy of movement that the normal can't depend on himself to achieve.

We, my friend, have gestures and body-postures that are as identifiable at long range as anything a fairy does.

There is, too, the matter of dress — even when we make a subconsious effort to conceal the facts by being sloppy in dress. There's still an air about the way we wear clothes that the normal couldn't match if he tried. There's speech, and facial expression — the muscles of the face aren't different; we just use them differently. We're acutely sensitive to the nonvocal communication of facial and bodily movements — and use those in communication.

Finally, there's the matter of the human aura . . . which I know I can't prove, but which has effects even on those who don't consciously perceive it. In the theatre they call it "presence" or "personality" as in "he can't project his personality."

One of the reasons you can teach like crazy is that you can project an aura, a presence, a personality, that amounts to projecting and imposing on the students the feeling that *what you are saying is fascinating*. You can project an *attitude* toward what you're discussing. Naturally the student learns something he feels is fascinating.

Reason why the Egghead is hated: —

Suppose I have precognition and telekinesis, and I get into a dice game with ordinary people.

Now if I use my telekinetic powers to make the dice go the way I want them to, I'm loading the dice, obviously.

But if I do not interfere with them in any way, but simply use my precognition to see which way they're about to fall, I am not loading the dice at all.

Is that cheating?

It doesn't make any difference in practice, does it? I'm going to clean the normal players just as clean as I choose to. They haven't got a prayer against me, because to them the behavior of the dice is random, while to me it's a perfectly predictable and dependable phenomenon.

The simple fact that I know, and predict, where others simply see randomness means that *I have robbed them of freedom of action.* They can no longer *act* on the basis of randomness, because I can, in the same system, act on prediction.

I don't bet on anything except sucker-bets — the other guy being the sucker. I bet only on fully-predictable outcomes, where the other guy thinks it's non-predictable. I get into dice games only when my precognition is working, in other words.

Sample: I'll bet I can prove to your complete satisfaction that it is possible for a planet to have its south magnetic pole at its north geographic pole — geographic north being defined by the proposition that the local sun-star rises in the East. Planetary magnetic phenomena being related to ionizing radiation from the local sun-star, the proposition makes sense.

Reason it's a strictly sucker-bet, of course, is that that's the situation on Earth. The *north* magnetic pole of a compass needle points toward geographic north — which proves that there must be a *south* magnetic pole there. (I suckered **Randy Garrett** for a buck on that one.)

An egghead is an individual who robs those around him of their freedom of action by being able to predict accurately, where they see only random. It makes no difference whether the Egghead *does* predict, or *uses* his prediction — the fact that he *can* any time he chooses to makes all others around him live at the mercy of his good will.

Put it this way: suppose one of the regular scf. authors decides to do a novel for *ASF*. So long as **Ike Asimov** stays busy writing textbooks and fact articles, the guy has a chance of selling it. But if **Asimov** chooses to write a novel . . . the poor guy's squeezed out. Then he can sell the novel only by your leave.

Whether you so intend or not, the fact remains.

The Normal has no chance of competing with the Egghead; that is, in fact, the definition of the Egghead — he's someone who cannot be successfully fought, save at the purely physical level. And even then it's enormously dangerous.

The Egghead is the Magician of old; it's always dangerous to attack the Magician — save with the help of another and more powerful Magician.

The Scientist today has the same position; it's impossible to attack the Scientist-dominated United States unless you have more and better Scientists yourself. China may have more men than we do — but that would be more than equalized in the first few hours of an all-out attack on the US. It wouldn't take more than a dozen hydrogen bombs to equalize the numerical odds — and China hasn't any.

The Egghead robs other people of their freedom . . . *by simply existing*.

Worse, when an Egghead *has* existed, the world is forever robbed of true freedom of action. Once Hari Seldon has shown that sociological forces can be predicted — no one after that can act with the full satisfying freedom of freshness and self-directiveness. What unknown-to-me-now sociological forces are pushing me to do this thing I think I'm choosing to do? Even if Hari Seldon or his projection aren't there to say, "Well, now you've done that which you were inescapably forced to do, the next thing you will do is. . . ." the fact that he's shown he could have, proves it could be done — and that proves that you don't have the free will you like to think you do.

Only the Mule did — the Ultimate Egghead.

O.K. — the Egghead is hated for reason. He's recognizable at a distance. His advantage over the Negro is that he *is* an Egghead — and supremely dangerous. He distributes blessings and curses, and that tends to make people slightly leery of attacking him.

You know, I should make this discussion easier on myself, save myself trouble by shipping your latest letter to **Mark Clifton**, and his latest to you, and let you two fight it out while I watch.

What I've been trying to tell you is:
1. The problem exists.
2. The methods so far used don't work.
3. Trying to make people deny the feelings they feel is non-functional.
4. What we need is to give over on that approach and invent another.

Now in essence, you want to put more power, more force, more energy behind the old approach until we *make* it work.

Yeah — and if hydrogen is stubborn about liquifying when we

apply pressure, by God if we just put *enough* pressure on it, we'll make the damn stuff liquify as we know perfectly well it should.

Try it! Try a million — a hundred million — atmospheres! Liquify? Nope, it won't. Metallic hydrogen; yes. Liquid? No!

It takes some pressure, *and low temperature.* Just put on pressure, however, and the temperature goes up, not down. Put on enough, and instead of liquid hydrogen, you get a thermonucluear fusion reactor called a star.

Back off, and try a different approach. Less pressure, and less heat, dammit!

Now **Mark's** letter has to do with teachability. He says he has observed, again and again, that little Tommy is, according to teacher A a good boy and a good student . . . while teacher B reports that Tommy is a juvenile delinquent in the making, and utterly unteachable. And *that they're both perfectly correct.*

Teacher A produces an environment, and uses a method, that Tommy *can* (NOT "will") accept. In that environment, under that method, Tommy learns rapidly and happily. Teacher B produces an environment, and uses a method, that Tommy *cannot accept no matter how much he tries.*

A physical analogy: if Tommy is violently allergic to angora wool, and teacher B always wears angora sweaters in class, Tommy is *unable* to study in her presence. He's too busy sneezing, gasping, and weeping. He's disrupting the class. He's undisciplined, and refuses to remain quietly in his seat.

"Be nasty to your little boy,
"And spank him when he sneezes!
"He only does it to annoy,
"Because he knows it teases!"

Now what you're doing is saying that, "Anybody can learn the way I say, and what must be done is to apply enough force to make them pay attention and learn the way I say! I know that this method hasn't worked in the last 6000 years it's been tried, but that's only because people didn't use enough force. Now, with the new and powerful pressures we know how to apply, backed up by atomic and hydrogen bombs, we can, at last, really make people learn what I know they should learn, the way I know they should learn it."

Look, **Ike** . . . try arguing that with **Mark Clifton**, will you? It's not just me that says that won't work.

I'm NOT trying to make you give up the desire that the lesson be learned.

I am trying to make you give up the desire to teach it by pure, raw, brute force. Whether that force be disguised as legal pressure, or undisguised bayonettes.

You know, **Edgar Cayce's** thick-witted, heavy-handed Paw down there in the Tennessee mountains, was a-tryin' to make that dumb kid larn his spellin' from the book. He was given' the kid a good larrupin' every time he misspelled a word. Eleven-year-old **Edgar** was exhausted physically — it has been going on till near mid-night — emotionally, and every other way. And at that point he slipped a cog. He begged his Paw to let him catch ten minutes sleep, and promised he'd spell right then.

And he did. From then on he never missed a word. Never missed *any word whatever*. He'd slipped sidewise . . . into pure clairvoyance. He could spell any word that existed anywhere without hesitation or error.

You try your larrupin' them dumb Southerners long and hard enough . . . and they might just happen to slip sidewise. But one thing seems to me to have been very adequately tested and established: pure pressure alone will not liquify human opinions. Like hydrogen; high pressure can produce a rigid, metallic form, or if it's adiabatic pressure, hydrogen fusion and explosion. But pressure per se never has, and never, never will work. Low temperatures alone will . . . but the best way is mild pressure, and reasonably low temperature.

I don't deny your goal — but I assure you you're on the sucker end of a sucker bet when it comes to your method.

Regards,   John

Lurton Blassingame   *March 4, 1959*

Dear Mr. Blassingame:
   Re: "Starship Soldier," by **Robert A. Heinlein**
   1. It, is, basically, a juvenile type — "Space Cadet" series — and therefore not dead-center in *Astounding's* field.
   2. I cannot fully subscribe to **Bob's** "Patrick Henry League" approach.
I feel that **Bob's** departing from the principles he himself introduced in science fiction — "Don't *tell* the reader about the background; let him gather it from what happens." In this yarn, there are several sections of multi-page preachments of his thesis. Some of the preachments I agree with fully; they still strike me as being ineffective because of the technique of direct-statement presentation.

The real suasion power of fiction lies, and always has lain, in the non-logical solution to the old logical paradox, "Epaminondas, the Cretan, says 'All Cretans always lie.'"

The more fiction is kept at the level of fiction, the more the reader is forced to accept that any conclusions he reaches from the words of a professed liar *are his own, personal conclusions*, and that *he, not the author*, has reached that conclusion.

Jesus used parables — fictions — because what any listener derives from a fiction *is the listener's own thought*. And that sticks far deeper and tighter than the ideas of an external mind.

Properly done, you could produce a profound anti-Nazi feeling in the reader by telling a story 100% from the viewpoint of a dedicated, fervent Nazi.

Here I fear **Bob's** going to induce considerable anti-patriotism in a lot of readers by telling a story from the viewpoint of a 100% dedicated patriot.

Therefore, the points with which I agree with **Bob** in full make me uncomfortable when presented in this overly-homolitic fashion.

And there are points with which I disagree very strongly — including, as a matter of fact, his fundamental thesis-point. That shooting-war is, was, and forever will be, ahmen.

That thesis produces a decidedly down-beat, hopeless, what's-the-use-of-this-old-cycle-again feeling. And I have reason to believe it's false.

Bob bases his proposition on "A living organism that does not grow, dies. Therefore the existence of two or more organisms in the Universe inescapably implies physical combat."

Not true. It *does* imply competition — but *not necessarily physical*. Primitive organisms do, in truth, have to grow physically or die; higher organisms have discovered ways of growth that are nonphysical, and so can cease *physical* growth. We do not need new territory, if we can develop new dimensions. The saurians tried the route of unlimited physical size — and were licked by small mammals, who tried unlimited adaptability instead.

E. E. Smith, in his Lensman series, suggested other directions of growth. **Smith's** "Lensmen" could have handled the "Bug War" with neatness and dispatch; the "Bugs" were ruled entirely by a few brain-Bugs. The Lensmen, by controlling mentally a few of those directive intelligences, could have made all the physical weapons of all Bug Warriors totally futile — because intelligence was concentrated so completely that the whole race could be paralyzed by reaching a few control centers.

But **Heinlein's** physical-combat-is-all boys couldn't reach them.

The physical aspect is absolutely necessary; **Heinlein's** 100% right on that. Trouble is, if you assume, as he does, that it is both necessary *and sufficient*, then we might as well quit trying now, because physical powers we already have, and there's no place else to go. We can "make lace" — we can grow Bigger and Better

Brontosaurs — but there is no higher level of reality to explore.

Physical war is inevitable . . . if *only* physical techniques are real. They *are* real; Rome *did* destroy Carthage physically.

But the Glory of Rome wasn't destroyed physically; the Rome that *was* Rome — the real, dynamic entity — was dead, and had been dead for centuries when the Goths and Vandals started carving for dinner.

A prefrontal lobotomy doesn't destroy the physical man, any more than the loss of a finger does. But if you've ever had the experience of dealing with a lobotomized . . . he's *dead*. Deader than any corpse.

France wasn't destroyed physically. The Germans, English, and others tried hard, but they didn't achieve their intent.

The United States did more to kill France than any other nation . . . and we weren't even trying! We destroyed France economically and intellectually.

What **Bob** misses is this; "it's still the same old story, a fight for love and glory, as time goes by" . . . but when you discover weapons vastly more efficient than your teeth, you stop biting. When you find techniques of destroying an enemy that are more efficient than cutting, burning, or blasting him . . . you stop that method.

War as we've known it is about through. There are more efficient techniques.

Brain-washing isn't physical torture, you know . . . but it's very effective. Men stopped killing off the enemy tribe . . . when they learned how to enslave them.

The new weapons aren't piddling little thermonuclear bombs; those are ineffective.

So war is about through. Spankings for primitive tribes, and small children, yes. But for older children, a tongue-lashing — when well done — is more dreaded than a spanking. It's a weapon that cuts deeper.

For more mature tribes . . . being made to recognize their own stupidity is more effective than being spanked physically.

Without the proposition that *we are going somewhere now* . . . that *war won't be forever* . . . there is none of the up-beat push that science fiction needs to filfill its job of stimulating people to try for something better than we have, or have had.

Regards,   John W. Campbell, Jr.

P. Schuyler Miller   *April 13, 1959*

Dear Miller:

As a hardened editor, it's seldom I bust out laughing over the manuscripts.

You earned a whoop, however, with that lovely answer to the Freudian back-to-the womb nonsense.

Loved that bit about primitive man preferring dry caves!

Regards,　John

E. E. Smith, PhD.   *May 26, 1959*

Dear Doc:

You know, **Doc**, There are some things I can do a damn sight better than you can. I can see the back of your neck much more clearly than you ever will, for instance. You'll never hear your voice as-it-sounds-to others as clearly as I can, even though I'm getting a little hard of hearing.

And when it comes to whether you have or have not put over a point in one of your stories, I have that same type of advantage; it's not that I'm smarter than you about the matter — but that I am more like the readers; I'm ignorant of the point you want to make, while you, neccessarily, are not. The immense capacity of one human being to misunderstand another must always be allowed for; no matter how clearly the statement is made, the other fellow can, and very frequently will, understand the wrong implication.

There's the wonderful story of the Tennessee hill-billy who'd been hired by a nitrating plant to work in one of their dynamite plants. He was in charge of the cooling water valves on one of the nitraters, and his instructions were to keep that thermometer from going above the red mark.

The nitrater blew up; since the plant had been designed with that possibility in mind, the hill-billy survived. Questioning after the event showed that he'd seen the thermometer going above the red mark, and pursuant to his exact instructions, had pulled it out, carried it across to the faucet, and cooled it below the red mark under running water.

Now on that "Masters" story. A 500 watt naked bulb sitting on top of a 10-foot pole in the middle of a ten-acre, shining full blast is pretty easy to see, isn't it?

Nope. Not when you're east of it at about 4 o'clock on a brilliant June day. You may see the pole all right, but you'll have a hell of a time seeing that 500 watt bulb.

Consider a chem lab in which 15 young men are employed doing close-tolerance weighings, titrations, etc., and add that ten girls, age 18 to 22, are also working there . . . completely nude. How accurate and reliable do you think the titration and weighing report will be?

Sure, give the kids a year or so to get used to those working conditions and they'll begin turning in reliable reports again.

At the immediate moment, I'm having trouble typing this letter, by reason of two young Siamese cats; they're competitively trying to climb into my lap. One's about 3 months, the other about 5 months old. It isn't that they prevent my working — they're just distracting. When a cat-fight starts between your feet it *does* make concentration difficult, even if it is just a mock-fight exercise.

What you run into in "Masters" is that the physical sex situation diverts the normal reader from the higher-order sex you wanted to put over. Sure you've got the material there; I read it and appreciated it. But look, **Doc**; have a really lovely 20-year-old blond with a beautiful shape, the vibrant-with-life-and-vitality kind, walk across a stage clad tastefully in nothing but a pair of shoes . . . then after she's left the stage ask the audience what color shoes she was wearing. The shoes were there, all right. They could even be flaming crimson shoes. But . . . who's looking at shoes, huh?

It's also possible to discuss the non-physical essence of love in a boiler factory . . . but so very few of your audience will get what your saying. It isn't that you didn't say it — it's that it passes unnoticed, due to distracting competitive material.

I'll quarrel with you, also, on the business of Dark Lady being simply pure-beauty, and not having love-effect. A normal man can stay in the same room with a painting of a nude without erection. He can get along with a statue. A somewhat higher percentage would react to a really life-like wax-works job. But the young male of the same species is not intended to remain unaffected by a living, breathing, moving and visibly nubile female of the species. There's a hell of a difference between a painting . . . and a living reality.

Yes: In a society where nudity is the norm, there is no reaction. But our readers are not members of such a society. You want your words to induce emotional effects in the reader; words are simply symbols, and your effects are lost if they do not react as expected to those words. O.K. — and nudity is, in our society, a symbol too. "Meson" in Latin American Spanish means a particularly low-class type of whore; in English it means a particular type of nuclear particle. Don't switch languages in the middle of a sentence, or you'll get a highly confused reaction.

If you're using the symbology-system of the Anglo-American culture, you cannot simultaneously use the symbology system of a Tahitian or Balinese culture. Male and female together; female nude and beautiful. Symbology meaning: intercourse coming up right away.

Think of the problem of the artist trying to illustrate that story. After the first couple of chapters, every scene would involve trying to show the characters without violating the current mores regarding nudity.

It makes no difference whatever what you intended to communicate: it makes no difference that there was plenty of higher-level material on the male-female relationship. What does the normal reader in this culture react to? The hill-billy did exactly what he was instructed to do; he kept the thermometer from going above the red mark. Men react to what they understand, not to what they are told.

Yes: story value is important. Obviously. But dammit, **Doc** . . . ever seen some of the "smoker" movies? Who pays any attention to story-value in that kind of show? A burly-que stripper doesn't have to sing or dance well; who notices her voice?

Getting an audience to pay attention to the voice of a girl who comes out on stage nude would be a pure tour de force; any woman capable of appearing nude and *not having people notice it* would require an extremely unusual (to say the least) personality power. Or, of course, a screaming emergency situation of such dramatic-emotional impact as to override even that.

There are times when a tour de force is worth doing just to prove you can do it — Gainsborough's "Blue Boy" for example. But generally, it's more efficient to avoid having to do the tour de force job — you can concentrate your energies on a more important problem.

Of course, it works the other way, too. The story of the young man who found it hard to choose between two girls; one very beautiful, and one not-so-hot, but who could sing like an angel. He married the singer. The first morning after they were married he woke up first, turned and looked at her for a moment. Then shut his eyes, shook her a bit, and said urgently, "Mary . . . Mary . . . for God's sake . . . sing!"

And **Doc**, I'm NOT trying to get the authors to write *my* way. **Randy Garrett** is one of those unfortunate personalities who crawls . . . and not with legs, either. As a human being, he isn't. But he has a technical competence which wins my respect; so has an IBM computer. I will, therefore, continue to use him for what he is.

That doesn't mean that he's the type I want.

Bob Silverberg is a kid: a nice kid, whom I like, just as I did **Ike Asimov** some 20 years ago. He and **Barbie** are doing a good, sincere, mutual-assistance society job of growing up together, and both have my highest respect as human beings. But their technical competence as writers leaves considerable to be desired. **Bob** doesn't have the foggiest notion about how to use aggression wisely; he can't think properly in terms when ruthlessness is called for. It weakens his stories, because it makes all such plot-situations weak. He and **Randy** made a good team; **Randy** can no more handle sincerity and make it sound real than **Bob** can handle ruthlessness.

367

Bob needs time and experience; **Ike** did, 20 years ago. **Ike** is no longer a kid; I respect and like him as a man, now. **Bob** will get there.

And I do NOT want authors to write "my way," whatever various authors say. Any one of the professional hacks can, and will, do that eagerly. Nothing disappoints me more than to throw out an idea intended as a spark, and have that idea come back just the way it went out, embalmed in a "story." **Hal Clement's** story "Needle" stemmed directly from an idea I threw his way; that you can't write a detective story in science fiction. He did a delightful job of proving me a liar. **Van Vogt's** "Slan" took the shape it did because I pointed out to him that you can't tell a superman story from the superman's viewpoint — unless you're a superman. He pulled a beautiful trick in that yarn, and proved me 100% wrong. So did **Page**, in "But Without Horns" in answer to a similar comment; he told the superman story by having the superman never in the story!

If I tell you you can't use steel tanks to store battery acid, I'm not insisting on your doing it my way. If I tell you you can't machine a plutonium metal shaft 2" in diameter to plus or minus 5 ten-thousandths, it's not that I insist on *my* way, but that I happen to know that Pu metal has six crystalline phases between room temperature and 640 degrees, with densities varying from 15.8 to 18.7, and that most of the phases are anisotropic. The stuff can't be machined accurately, because the heat of working keeps changing the crystal phases, and hence the dimensions, and the hardness of the material is different along different axes, and that shifts with work-heating too! And you can't water-cool it, or oil-cool it, because a 2" rod goes critical if immersed in a neutron-reflecting medium. (And when moist, the metal forms a hydride resembling in properties lead azide.)

Incidentally, Pu is pyrophoric in air; the oxide coating formed spontaneously on the metal surface is extremely friable, and flakes off as a very fine, partly air-borne dust. The dust is some 10,000 times as toxic as any other industrial poison hazard. It emits 5 mev alpha particles, which cause an alpha-neutron reaction in half the lighter elements in the table, and criticality is highly dependent on neutron-reflecting characteristics of its environment. A "safe" mass of Pu can go critical if a man walks by; he acts as a neutron-reflector.

Nice stuff to have to fabricate nuclear reactor fuel rods from, isn't it?

The point I'm trying to make, though, is simply this: I've read more lousy science-fiction than anyone else in the world today, probably. I've been at it for over 21 years. I get about 100 manuscripts a month, and buy about 6. I may or may not be an authority on good science fiction — but man, I know more about *bad* science fiction than anyone else around! As a practical chemist, you know that it's just as valuable to know what does not work as to know what does. It's just more laborious, disappointing, and frustrating to learn all those things that don't work.

What I *do* want to be able to do is to supply an author with a trigger idea that starts him going his way. To be able to help with suggestions from what I have learned that doesn't work. I very, very rarely send back a manuscript with suggestions for specific changes with a do-it-this-way-and-I'll-buy-it order. Normally, I will send back a mss with comments which, if the author chooses, if they make sense to him, he is free to incorporate.

You know as well as I it isn't *my* determination, *my* will, *my* saying so that keeps you from storing battery acid in a steel tank. It's true — but not because it's *my* truth. And you can, of course, store sulfuric acid in a steel tank . . . provided it's over 90% pure. (But that's not battery acid, because 90% sulfuric dissolves lead.)

Now on the laws of Psi: I *did* send you considerable of what we've worked out as to the laws of Psi. Read that letter over again. True I didn't mathematically formulate 'em; you can't and never will be able to in terms of what we know as math. Let's see you work out field equations in terms of straight algebra, without calculus! Relativity couldn't be expressed mathematically until Tensor Calculus was developed. You can't develop alternating current theory until the math of the square root of minus one is developed.

We totally lack any math capable of handling a discontinuous variable; we have to approximate it *in certain respects* with complexes of continuous variables, or discontinuous constants. (Arithmetical approximation a la computer technique.)

We cannot define a pattern; as human beings we both know that patterns exist — and neither of us can define what it means. Therefore there's a lot of reality that cannot be formulated in math — but can be conveyed in language.

How one basic law of psi can be communicated very specifically: Communication is necessarily never true.

Reason: Communication, by definition, is symbol-manipulation. If I talk about an orange, I do *not transport* an orange to you (the actual, real object) but communicate a symbol which is *not* an orange.

Communication *and only communication* can reach into past and future: objects can't. The object-level past is absolute and rigid: there is no object-level future, for the moment it becomes objective, it isn't future, but past. But communication — symbology — can, and does, reach both past and future.

Symbols are arbitrary — but *symbol-patterns are not*. Thus I can use the symbol *x* for any arbitrary thing I choose — but the pattern of an equation is not arbitrary, but controlled by the laws of patterns-of-symbols. Thus I can call a table a *mesa*, or a *hosenanyfloodoogle*, but once the arbitrary assigned symbol is determined, I *must* use it according to the laws of symbol-patterns. Whether you call it *sauerstoff* or *oxygen* makes no difference whatever. But you *must* recognize that whether you call it one or the other, a mixture of hydrogen and sauerstoff-oxygen is dangerously explosive.

The Land color process is a major breakthrough — because it will force on men the absolute necessity of revising our philosophy, and appreciating the fact of symbol-patterns. If I project a pair of Land transparencies, one in red light and in white light, it is an objectively-demonstrable fact that there is, on the screen, nothing but pink. A photospectrometer will prove that fact.

But it's a repeatable human observation that a certain area of the screen is green. PROVIDED . . . that that area is viewed as a part of the whole screen. Isolate that part, and the human observer sees pink.

Now here we have something with the following anti-logical properties:

1. It is simultaneously, and with respect to the same thing (color) two different and mutually exclusive things; it is green and it is pink.
2. Not only is the whole greater than the sum of the parts,
3. but the whole is different from the sum of the parts,
4. and the character of the parts is altered by the nature of the whole!
5. Which means that *neither* the whole nor the part can be discussed, but both must be discussed simultaneously.
6. And that means that the concept of cause-and-effect is inapplicable. (The area is a part which is green, because of the whole, but the whole would not exist as it does if the part were actually green, instead of being actually red as it is !!)

That, incidentally, explains why the nature-vs-nurture school of debate never gets anywhere.

If I pass sunlight through a filter that passes 90% of the blue, 70% of the green, 50% of the yellow, 30% of the orange, and 10% of the red, what color is the resultant light?

Answer: White. Sure, the 38-A Wratten filter, which does that, looks strongly blue to the eye — but that's because it's a 50,000 degree white, instead of a 5,000 degree white. The sky looks blue, too — but it's really white, isn't it? It's just a 15,000 degree white.

Psi laws have to do with patterns, instead of isolated events or symbols. That's why the symbolic Hieronymous machine works just as the objective one does; the pattern is the same, though the symbols are different.

But there are symbols that are more efficient to use in a given pattern than other possible symbols. That is exemplified by H_2SO_4 for example, instead of "two hydrogens combined with one sulfur and four oxygens." In organic work, a more complex system of symbols was needed for convenience. "Convenience" in this level is equivalent or analogous to "efficiency" at the objective level.

I mentioned last time that it remains true that a good big man is better than a good little man — but that a trained little man can throw an untrained big man.

The subtler level controls the grosser; the characteristics of matter are determined by the level of field-forces. Field forces can, in turn, be controlled by psi forces. But not actually arbitrarily; it just looks arbitrary to someone who doesn't know the laws.

The reason psi forces seem so lawless is that symbols have that characteristic of being entirely arbitrary . . . but not patterns of symbols. All the magical symbol systems so far developed have, no doubt, been extremely inconvenient. Imagine a modern electronics engineer trying to figure out a 1929 radio reciever. He'd have a hell of a time, because the design was so clumsy and inefficient that he couldn't believe abybody would have deliberately done anything *that* way!

For a real example of that — try working out an old alchemical instruction! The symbol system was so horribly inconvenient that it's unbelievable that anyone would deliberately do something in such an exceedingly hard way.

In a somewhat more advanced age, the archeologists may have quite a time figuring out why the labor rooms in our hospitals are built as they are. The soundproofing built into the walls to absorb the cries of a women in labor may seem just a little incomprehensible. Instead of doing something effective to eliminate the causes of the screams, the modern MD is proud of the sound-proofed rooms that confines the sound of agony so it won't bother people. Like the surgeon of an earlier time who was proud of his bloodstained operating jacket, because it showed what a busy surgeon he was.

Figuring out symbol-systems in magical devices has the difficulty that we don't know a good one when we see it, and we've never seen a really good one anyway.

The human entity, however, *has* a pretty good one . . . but it violates all our conditioned concepts of what a symbol-system should be ! Scientists are forever talking about what a much more effective organism they could build if they were doing it. Yeah? I print robot stories . . . but I know better. Ever consider the matter of the sense of touch? It's critically important if an entity is to avoid accidental contact — or to control contact with itself. If your hand brushes your leg, you don't jump — but if you believe you're alone, and something brushes your leg, you do. It takes only a few million sensors, plus correlating computers, to make that neat little system work. So scientists could build a better organism, but why don't they then, if they're so damned smart! Why don't they build a computer to fly a plane . . . and, of course, make it self-maintaining, self-repairing, self-correcting, and self-reproducing!

Think how a computer could be loused up in its behavior by a simple photographic projection! A man wouldn't be fooled for more than seconds.

I don't agree that a majority of the race has to have the psi-talent genes before we have a psi culture. God knows it's a small minority of Man today that has the science-talent genes! Yet we have a technical culture.

Also, I don't think that democracy is either holy, necessary, or automatically beneficial. It is valuable because it imposes responsibility on the leaders; they become responsible to and for the people, on a lawful basis. But it's damned inefficient and many times highly undesirable. Democracy in a kindergarten, or grade-school, for instance, would not lead to wiser or more effective education. People do not always want what they need; many times they powerfully want-not what they desperately need. Democracy then is certain disaster.

The problem is to evolve a philosophy in which genuine, honest-to-God superiority of one individual over another can be determined, *and be accepted*. Today, a man is oriented to hold himself a coward, a fool, a weakling, if he acknowledges that another man is his superior-in-fact, *and will always be*.

In earlier times, this orientation was not implanted in men; then they could accept that another man was their innate superior *without* feeling that automatically made them valueless — cowards — someone to be scorned.

The problem is, of course, "How can a man accept a true superiority which he himself cannot sense?" How can you explain to a barbarian that he is not a gentleman? How can you explain to an Auca Indian who's never contacted civilization that such a thing as a higher-*order* — not simply bigger, but different-in-kind — exists? He lives in a culture of ritual-tabu; individuals who act not on a basis of ritual, but on a basis of independent thought, are vicious criminals, without social conscience, morality, a sense of justice and without respect for Man, God, Devil or Law. This is *true*, and he knows it from direct experience. No tribe can possibly continue to exist when the traditions and rituals break down. He knows this for a fact of experience, because other tribes have disintegrated in just this fashion.

Now explain to him that in your culture, men act as they think they should. That traditions do not rule, and that laws are made and changed at will.

And you claim this is a *higher* civilization! Hah! He *knows* it isn't; he *knows* it's a vicious, degenerate anarchy.

In our culture, we demand that men have Loyalty. And Loyalty means surrendering the right to judge the circumstances, and accept without argument the decisions handed to you. How about a culture in which there was no loyalty whatever — neither loyalty of man-to-man, nor man-to-nation or man-to-God?

Impossible?

Does a chemist have to be loyal to his teacher to make chemical reactions work? Is your conviction that KCN is not good food an act of loyalty to the Government of the United States, under which you were first taught that? Is loyalty necessary to concerted, cooperative action?

Do I have to be loyal to you, or you to me, to cooperate in achieving a better science fiction?

Actually, a loyal accolyte is about as close to absolute-zero value as an aid to understanding the Universe as one can get. (As you are aware, I have, inevitably, acquired a few. I speak from genuine experience. The type is hard to get rid of, of no value, and a real worry. It's cruelty to quash them, and there are always a very few who *need* some idol to follow, for their own mental stability. Temporary accolytism isn't harmful per se: it's when the condition becomes permanent, or when a vicious idol is chosen that it becomes a bad thing.)

It is *not* necessary to have a democratic culture, in order to have a highly responsible culture. The psi-talented would be forced to be responsible: if you've got telepathy, you're stuck with sensing the misery around you. The brain is, to the body, an almost absolute tyrant. But in order to function, the brain *must* have sensory input data from the body. And it can't get that without accepting the messages from the body — including the messages that say, "This hurts!"

The thing is, the tyrant-brain must, sometimes, signal back, "So it hurts. Sorry. Hold on to that burning hot handle just the same, or the melted lead in the pot is going to be spilled all over the organism. Of course you skin-cells in the hand can't see that, but the eyes can, and I understand the consequences."

Now suppose that the psi situation is something like this; a cretin has all the necessary structures for intelligence . . . but due to lack of thyroxine, can't use 'em. Given a dose of thyroxine, he's off to the races.

Suppose we have all the necessary structures for psi . . . but lack some psiroxine addition. If your Boss acquires that as one slight addition. . . .

I don't mean it's a chemical; it may be an idea. It may be an experience. It's something that triggers-into-action something already present-in-potential.

I don't think you *can* get story-value out of one Boss and one Bossess. There's no real conflict.

But you may find conflict in the turmoil that results if the Boss, once triggered himself, can trigger off those others who have it.

Now Psi may be only very indirectly correlated with intelligence, ethical sensitivity, self-discipline, etc. The result would then be a situation in which Bill blow, Jerk, 1st Class, has psi . . . and John Q. Titherington, Grade A Genius, doesn't. And "Crook" Spighatinni, blackmailer, extortioner, general SOB, has it, but Rev. Dr. Fiddle, D.D., doesn't. Also the little, stupid, narrow-minded twerp, Hector Q. Phlafph, who's been semi-paranoid, and angrily dwelling on what Napoleon, that other small man, did . . . suddenly has It.

And idealistic, high-minded, but thoroughly injudicious though brilliant adolescent kids turn up with it, and start fixing things the way they *know* they *ought* to be. Like Jim, who suddenly has It, knows that Tom, although Tom doesn't happen to have It, is a real nice guy, and Tom just adores Sally, who can't see Tom for sour apples . . . until Jim massages her psyche a little, and then she loves him, too. Only Sally is a totally different type of personality, and smarter than Tom, and Tom's in for a life of hell and halleleujah, and so is Sally, because Jim can't make silk purses out of horses asses just because he has psi talents.

I don't think you *can* get story movement with one or two psi-talented people. Look, the theologians had to introduce Satan, or there wouldn't be any story value in the Bible.

Is a stupid jerk, with psi, superior to a wise, ethical, and brilliant man who doesn't have psi? And *won't* have it.

The only one who can judge them both is a man who is wise, ethical, brilliant . . . *and* psi-talented.

Who should command a fighting ship; a wise, brilliant commander with 25 years battle-experience . . . or a 20-year-old kid, IQ 110, who has precognition? By the use of experience, training, intelligence, the battle-veteran can estimate the probabilities and risks rapidly, and with 85% accuracy. But the kid can forsee the facts of the future with 99% accuracy. BUT . . . the kid hasn't reach enough to comprehend strategy; he'll direct a fight that wins the battle . . . and loses the war. He may save every ship, but at such cost in position that the enemy achieves penetration of the defense line.

Precognition does *not* make up for lack of wisdom. It simply acts as a new data-channel. A child with good eyes can learn less from a book than a wise man without sight who hears the child's stumbling effort to read. A telescope can gather light . . . but it can't see a thing.

Your Lensman series had plenty of dynamism by reason of the swirling battle between Arisia and Eddore. (The Arisian-Civilization side, incidentally, was *not* democratic; it was a benevolent tyranny with an aristocracy supporting the Arisian tyrants.) It's *responsible* government we really seek — democracy is merely one theoretical method of achieving it.

If you had as your broad scene the boiling troubles of a semi-galactic scope civilization into which psi had been introduced . . . there'd be places for endless troubles, battles, and ethical problems.

What punishment should be meted out to a kid who's used extraordinarily high psi talents, plus a brilliant technique of application of those talents, to take over a planet, and establish a dictatorship that, because of the psi-talents, everybody *likes* . . . but which is, nonetheless, killing them! (A drug addict *likes* his cocaine, even though it's killing him.) Add that the kid is absolutely sincere, high-minded, and ethical. He's just, unfortunately, smart, but not wise; ethical, but foolish. What shall we do with him?

And another man who's psi-talented, and an absolute egotist, selfish and unethical . . . but extremely wise. He's taken over a planet, and the planet is booming. The people are growing, prospering, and vigorous. There's some complaining, naturally; the vigorous growth and development inevitably drops some by the wayside. The buggy-whip makers do get hurt when automobiles come in. The tyrant keeps a harem, including any good-looking wench he sees, maid or matron, and psi-blanks anyone who objects. He makes objectors who get obnoxious not only kill themselves . . . but their wives and children too. All these injured parties total 0.000001% of the population. 98% of the population benefits hugely. The people want him to remain in power — he's good for the planet.

He is, too.

Which of these two individuals is the villain to be punished harshly?

And a man who can, and does, learn widely and rapidly is untrustworthy; he cannot be depended on to remain loyal to any one, any group, or any cause. He may learn of a higher cause, for which that cause should be sacrificed.

No real science fictioneer can be a "100% American"; we're too aware that the human race is a larger cause.

I'm not loyal to democracy, because, as I see it, responsible government is the larger cause; democracy is a good thing only insofar as it serves that cause. Currently, American democracy is becoming irresponsible; the "we need" is replacing the "I want" . . . but it's the same thing with different words. "What I 'need' I have a right to take, and to hell with you." "Duties is what you have; rights is what I've got." "Togetherness" doesn't turn selfishness into a beatitude; the group can be selfish just as thoroughly as an individual. But group-selfishness is called "democracy," and individual ambition is damned as selfish egotism.

However you work it, you're going to have an opponent worthy of your Boss, if you are to have story-value.

Incidentally . . . I've a hunch that it takes a male-female team to develop the full psi-power potentials. You need a completed, bi-polar circuit before you have electric *current*; before that, you have only static.

Regards,   John

John Berryman *August 19, 1959*

Dear John:

This is back for some revisions.

First, our audience apparently doesn't go for the Mickey Spillane-Mike Shane approach to action. Personally I think of that as the sin-and-punishment school; the "hero" commits sins that Johnny Q. Publick would like to commit, and is punished for them . . . but it's like a small boy being spanked for stealing the cookies. The cookies were, in his opinion, worth the spanking — so he plans to do it again tomorrow.

In that sin-and-punishment school of detective stories, the "hero" gets beaten up repeatedly; that's the punishment. But he has *such* satisfying sins on the way — beating up and shooting down and bedding down various shapely females. The cookies are worth the spanking.

In a culture in which females are immune to punishment — like juveniles — that can be a very satisfying proposition. A taxidriver, a while back, told me of his problem; he has a sixteen-year-old son who's been in trouble with the police four times. Papa's no prize as a father; granted. But . . . what can Pop do about the situation? It's illegal for him to beat up his brat. He can't imprison him. But . . . Papa is legally responsible for the vandalism damage Sonny commits!

One of the major problems in the culture today is the fact that there is no understanding of the use of punishment for disciplinary purposes; it is neither administerd, nor received appropriately. Now the only difference between "punishment" and "torture" is, in the final analysis, *the attitude of the recipient*. If you are injured, and feel you earned it — it's punishment. If you feel that there is no lesson to be learned — it's torture. Also, if you feel you earned ten units of punishment, and are given one hundred — that's torture, too, and the whole one hundred will be rejected.

Your hero here shows no comprehension of the proper application of punishment-and-discipline; his possession of psi power, then, makes him a menace to others in reality — his powers are used spitefully, not with Justice.

He is the hysteric-reaction type — the type that represents precisely what people most fear in the thought of psi-talented people. In dealing with the stilleto-type crook, he does the job wisely and well; he used forces that are absolute in their potentials (there is no way thc guy can dcfend against having his heart stopped or against the flying bean-bag ash-tray) but these powers are not used in an unlimited way, but with discretion. They are used to enforce an injunction — to stop, not to torture. To warn, not to destroy. That's sound, wise and appropriate.

The Sabot is an ingenious concept — but it's unjustly used. The goon hadn't earned it. He had earned having the blood supply to his retinas cut off temporarily; being stricken blind, suddenly, is an extremely powerful emotional shock and warning.

Your hero deserved punishment in defying the orders of the superior officers of his organization — but the method used is inappropriate. There's a great difference between *respect* for a superior, and *fear* of that superior; in this case the Lodge seeks to make him *fear* — and they do not earn his *respect*. The working out of the plot shows that the Lodge Master was, in fact, wise in his assignment; a top-rank TK *was* needed, because a highly skilled TK was misusing his talents, and only a top-rank TK with superior powers could handle the situation. And the situation should *not* have been explained to Lefty before he went; to do so would so prejudice him in favor of the Lodge Master's strong suspicions that Lefty wouldn't have been able to examine the entire situation objectively. The Lodge Master is deserving of respect. The use of the goon-squad, with goon-squad methods, does not merit respect.

Lefty has forgotten his duties; he needed to be reminded sharply — but not brutally. The punishment didn't fit the crime. Suppose the Lodge Master had sent, as a disciplinarian-reminder, a man with a different type of psi-talent — a hallucinator, say. No TK talent — but able to impose hallucinations, so that Lefty's talents became useless for lack of ability to perceive anything correctly. The old proposition "No matter how good you are, there's always somebody who, while not necessarily better, can render you helpless."

Incidentally, you have an extremely sound point in the implied proposition that TK is relatively useless if it isn't accompanied with clairvoyance — i.e. Lefty has to perceive, in order to manipulate. A lower-order TK talent effect would result from the same level of actual TK ability . . . without clairvoyant perception. Such a TKer would be able to manipulate only directly-visible things — not heart-valves and blood-vessels.

Lefty, as described, is sharp, but not wise — competent, but not an understanding man. His treatment of the B-girls, for instance; such girls are, almost invariably, stupid and foolish, but not evil. The evil ones don't stay B-girls; it doesn't give them enough scope for their destructive proclivities. His treatment of stupid, foolish girls is, therefore, unwarrantedly harsh. (Incidentally, note that "stupid" is *not* the antonym of "wise" — "foolish" is. "Stupid" is the antonym of "intelligent.")

Finally, despite your expressed intent to tell a story of psi on the positive, up-beat side . . . you've struck Lefty with a bum arm as punishment for having psi, and state that most psi-talented have some such stigmata.

I suggest that Lefty started developing his psi talents because he had a bad arm — not that he had a bad arm because he had psi. The blind man who can "see" by sound-echoes, and by sensing radiant heat with this cheeks doesn't lose his sight because he has those powers — he schools himself to those powers because he loses his sight. Most lip-readers learn the art because they are deaf; lip-reading doesn't deafen one. (My wife is an accomplished lip-reader . . . and she has phenomenal hearing. She learned the art because such learning is easy for her, and, in the days of silent movies, it was no end of fun. The sad death-bed scene, with the dying man saying "For Chrissakes, get your damn elbow outa my guts, will ya!" to the weeping, dutiful daughter leaning over him to hear his faint, last words.)

Also, just because a kid grows up on the east side doesn't force him to be a hoodlum — modern social theory to the contrary being a lot of hogwash. One of my best friends is a gentleman and a philosopher in the finest sense, a man whom I respect most highly as a *man* in the best senses of the term. He grew up on the east side, in the slums, with professional hoods and gangsters as his companions and friends. They're still his friends; they respect him as thoroughly as I do. It is, of course, easier to grow up straight in a straight environment — but a really solid personality doesn't have to have a favorable climate.

Finally; notice that all the above comments, while they seem at first glance, to require a complete rewrite of the yarn, actually do not. They can be effected by rewriting only a few bits and pieces scattered here and there — they amount to simply subtle shifts of emphasis, minor changes of wording, small emendments of specific incidents — but the incidents all stand and play exactly the parts they now play. He remains "Lefty" — and remains slightly neurotically hypersensitive to the name. He still rejects the B-girlie; Snuffles still bothers him — more so, if anything, because he can't understand her, and, to an understanding man, that's more troubling than a pest is to an ununderstanding man.

But in the TK test with the silver dollars, he now is not wantonly destructive. He might, instead of smashing the place with them, send them flying so that they strike and stick firmly wedged between two planks in the floor — neatly and evenly lined up in a row. Hmm . . . and he might pull something like, "I call that the 'Dragon's Teeth Trick.' Planted like that they can grow into quite a crop of trouble. . . ."

Obviously, anyone with *that* degree of precision TK is already a fully matured crop of trouble for anyone!

There is something unsatisfactory in the ending; the girl is not sufficiently explained. You've planted her, and her mystery. You've used her to solve the problem. But while she gives a statement of her origin, you have Lefty prove that statement is false . . . and never give any other. She says she's sinned and lost her healing power — but she heals Lefty.

A moderate degree of mystery is O.K. — but this isn't felt as mystery, but as a loose end in the story. Tying it up, too, shouldn't require more than a page or two.

The story as is is good, and powerful; it'd be shame to let it go with these weakening flaws that require so little actual rewriting!

Regards, John

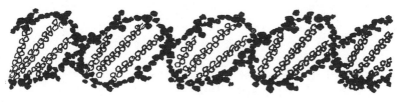

379

"*Seems he'd been forwarding the predictions he got every morning from the local witch-doctor, . . .*" page 404.

The 1960's

"*I'm just back from Scotland, where I've been having con-siderable fun learning the background of Scots history and mine own people.*" page 429.

Prof. James McConnell   *January 11, 1961*

Dear Jim:

I imagine you're well aware of the front-page item the *Herald Tribune* carried, on your conditioned planaria. I read it with the greatest interest; you have my deepest congratulations. That, I feel, is a real, honest-to-God breakthrough discovery.

I suspect you have — though the news item doesn't say — tried the business of conditioning a worm, dividing it, allowing regeneration, then redividing and allowing a second regeneration, and finally testing this resultant entity that contains no cell present in the original continued entity.

My personal hunch is that if you'd get conditioned flatworms to reproduce sexually . . . there will be no carry-over of conditioning.

There are, says Kipling, "nine and ninety different ways, of constructing tribal lays, and every single one of them is right!" But mix half of method #72 with half of method #14, and the result is not one of the right ways. There are a million different ways one can describe a certain event; the possible variations of word-choice, word-order, allusion, and ellipsis, even when sticking to a single language, is immense. Take two equally accurate descriptions of the same event. Make tape recordings. Then cut alternate words from first one, then the other tape, and record them as a single tape. What's the chance for getting a meaningful description?

The planaria genetically inherit the *ability* to learn — but I'll bet they don't inherit *learning*. Within an individual entity, however, the cells are simple transfer-copies; then both the ability and the learning would be transmitted.

Lysenko's still wrong!

But dammit . . . **L. Ron Hubbard's** right, b'gad. In his Dianetics he claimed he's found evidence that there was cellular-level memory of painful injury! If the learned-pattern data can be transmitted through so massive a reshuffling as involved in regeneration of highly differentiated specialized tissues, it certainly appears probable that experience-memory would be retained at the cellular level in something so simple as human wound-healing, where nothing so drastic as de-specialization and redevelopment is involved!

Sooner or later, the computer boys, working on microminiaturization, are going to catch on to what you've got. Here they've been thinking planaria did it all with those 10,000 neurones — and now it turns out that, seemingly, every cell in the organism learns!

Lovely!

                                        Regards,   John

Dear Mr. Brunner:

In this long novelette, you've raced all the way from a nice smooth start to the extreme end of the limb, and sort of fallen off the end of the limb. You wind up with such super-duper supermen that they're just a wee bit unbelievable.

The "Stardropper" idea is a dilly — it gives a fine basic proposition. But just by the way . . . better change that power-supply you dreamed up for your hero's gadget. You say it's operated by "a few grammes of cobalt-60." No. Co-60 puts out roughly 3,000,000 volts of energy per atom when it breaks down, and it has a half-life of about five years. Actual Co-60 radioactive sources are used to generate X rays for medical and industrial work . . . and the speck of Co-60 is housed in a lead box that a *strong* man can carry without undue discomfort.

But *one* gram of Co-60, let alone "a few," would maintain itself at blue-white incandescence due to the continual release of radioactive energy. Even little old mild radium is never at the temperature of its environment, and *it* takes 1800 years to release half of it's energy! You couldn't heap a gram of Co-60 in a solid tungsten box, let alone a lead box!

And it would take at least 18 inches minimum of high-density shielding (tungsten is roughly twice as effective a shielding material as lead, by the way!) to make it possible to stay anywhere near a gram of Co-60!

If you want something new-and-different . . . have his gadget use a fuel cell. They're in the works; they burn gas and air directly electrochemically to produce neither heat nor flame, but simply electricity and carbon dioxide and water vapor. He can use one of those miniature tanks of butane gas they now use to fuel cigarette lighters. One tank would be good for about three years; there's a terrific amount of energy in even two fluid ounces of liquid butane! It's darned near equal to that in a standard full-sized automobile storage battery!

For the story line, let me make a suggestion. The geniuses are disappearing. But drop out the energy absorption-conversion business. They do have teleportation, but the limitations and behavior are somewhat different.

It doesn't require energy to go from one point at sea level to another point at sea level. If there were no friction, as long as you remained at the same gravitational potential level — no energy would be required to simply transfer from A to B.

Also . . . there is a point in space somewhere between the Earth and the Sun, where, because you have "fallen" nearer the immense gravitational mass of the Sun, although you have climbed hundreds of thousands of miles up from Earth, the *net* change of energy works out to zero. You've simply traded Sun-gravity potential for Earth-gravity potential on an even balance basis.

So . . . a teleporter can make a change between same-level places without using energy. He can also teleport clear out into space . . . to a particular, very special, point.

And he can teleport either up-hill or down-hill at a rate determined by his ability to supply, or to absorb-without-harm the energy-change involved.

He can penetrate material walls . . . because this teleporting business is a gross-scale special application of the principle of the quantum-jump potential-barrier penetration phenomenon. (And you can look that one up in any modern physics text, if you don't happen to know it already.)

Two fully co-operating teleporters can work an exchange system; if Tom goes from the top of Mt. Blanc to the seashore, while Dick goes from the seashore to the top of Mt. McKinley, they can interchange the gravity-potentials, and come out unharmed. If Tom tries making the Mt. Blanc-to-seashore transition alone, however, he comes out on the seashore all right — but in just about the condition you'd expect someone to be in after falling from the top of Mt. Blanc. And if Dick tries the reverse transition without help . . . he gets stuck in an in-between state until he's developed enough energy, by working hard, to equal the work required to lift himself some 17,000 feet.

In other words, teleportation remains a lawful operation, with the old law of nothing-for-nothing still holding.

The reason the geniuses disappear, however, is something else.

There's the old crack about "The Truth shall set yet free!"

Within reason, yes. But there's always an unreasonable amount of Truth that, instead of freeing, destroys.

Now I do *not mean the products of a new Truth. That is, I do not* mean, "If you tell a savage how to make atomic bombs, he'll promptly destroy himself." That's true . . . but what I mean is something else.

There's a limit to what a mind can absorb *as an idea*. Too much Truth, and a mind can be rendered utterly helpless because it can't organize all the Truths it knows — the poor guy's paralyzed by the sheer inability to make a decision with all that knowledge to consider.

There are things we hold should not be told to children because they can't, in childhood, integrate or understand the concepts. There are, similarly, Truths that most minds could not contain without destruction. Think of it as being like the Jap's "water torture"; the victim was lashed down on his back, his jaws propped open, a funnel stuck in, and they poured water into his mouth slowly and steadily. He was forced to swallow . . . or give up breathing. There comes a point where the stomach is completely full of water, distended with water, where swallowing more water means rupturing the stomach.

It isn't that water is poisonous, or that the water of the last swallows is in any way different from ordinary water . . . it's just that it's too much, too fast, and the organ is ruptured.

Any ordinary mind that does catch the code of the star-talkers, promptly gets Truth. Too much and too fast. Those are the people crazed by the stardroppers.

The geniuses who crack the code can just about stand the strain . . . and part of the problem is knowing the basics of teleportation, but there's a catch. Quantum phenomena show some peculiar effects. An electron, for instance, can "ride off in all directions" at once — i.e., it can *Simultaneously* head off north, east, south and west. A single electron can go through *two* holes that are side by side in a metal plate. It can be in two places at once . . . *during* a jump.

Some of the not-quite-geniuses disappear, but for good. They teleported, with only half understanding — understanding how to go, but not *how to focus* — how to avoid that quantum dispersion effect. So they have reappeared as discrete atomic particles in every place in total space that has the same gravitational potential. Most of them, therefore, is now distributed among the interstellar gas clouds.

Those that get the more complete understanding organized, then have a new understanding at another level.

To tell this Truth to ordinary level minds will either (1) drive the victim insane, or (2) give him just enough knowledge to cause him to join the interstellar gas clouds.

And . . . you just try to convince someone who wants desperately to have super-powers that he isn't fit to contain them!

So the geniuses have to vanish for a while in order to work out some way of living with ordinary men without destroying them.

One answer, of course, is to let those who absolutely intransigently insist on being let into the elite circle have what they want. Apollo let Phoebus drive the Sun-chariot one day, as he intransigently insisted . . . which is one way of getting rid of unmanagable intransigents.

Oh . . . those H-bombs. They can be teleported, too . . . on an unfocussed basis. I suppose the ones with the Powers would, eventually, be called "boojums." Those who meet them "quickly and silently vanish away." But good.

Re: "Voices From the Void"

Rog Phillips   *November 6, 1961*

Dear Mr. Phillips:

Ah, the bright dreams of the inexperienced! Sezee, "I could work with you wholeheartedly on a thing like that, with articles and stories, and you could get other writers to do the same along lines you laid out."

My friend, what in the hell do you think I've been doing for some 20-odd years now? And what is your strong objection to it? Why, naturally, that I propose *my* ideas instead of *your* ideas! I get ten thousand letters from people who say "I have a wonderful idea for a story, but I'm not a writer. I'll be willing to turn my idea over to one of your authors for 50% of the proceeds of the story sale."

You want in on a deal like that, maybe?

Hell, man, you can't even *give* a creative writer an idea, let alone sell him one! He's too busy selling his own!

Want a breakthrough? Sure I do! So do you . . . and every other science-fictioneer, or we wouldn't be in science fiction! And we've gotten 'em, too — rocket ships and atomic power, for instance. Trouble with most of you guys is that you seem to think breakthroughs come snap-zip-bang! and there it is! They don't; it takes ten years of pushing to set the stage so that someone can think about the idea out loud without being horse-laughed out of sight. Then it takes ten years of research to winnow out the useful ideas. And then some feeble results begin to show.

As Yorkshire Sam says, "Don't be in' nurry, young man!"

I look for breakthroughs where there are already definite cracks in the wall — it's easier at such points! And they *all* depend on alternative thinking, naturally!

Dean's device, for instance, now appears to be the first application of the Fourth Law of Motion. Who ever proved that Newton discovered *all* the laws of Motion, huh? And what happens if you try thinking the inconceivable, "There is a Fourth Law of Motion, which states. . . ?"

And what if there is a Fourth Field Force — a *pattern* field, a tendency-to-organize patternwise field? The essence of mind is abstracting order from random information — organizing pattern. And all living things do just that. And crystals do it at a simpler level. And stars form from gas. . . .

Sure — try new ideas! But try them where there are already cracks in the walls of ignorance!

Have you, personally, tried dowsing for pipes, for instance?

Regards, John W. Campbell

Theodore Cogswell   *January 3, 1962*

Dear Mr. Cogswell:

John Pierce's letter in the last pitfox is a perfect example of the Orthodoxy Effect. And inasmuch as **John** is a Research Director for a major science-technology laboratory system, the precisely and clearly expressed attitude of the Orthodoxist he has laid out is a perfect map of the problem I've been trying to call to attention.

The essence of Orthodoxy in any field — politics, religion, science or elsewhere — is simply, "We know the Truth, *and the whole Truth.* We possess the Final Truths!" Christianity's orthodoxy is that Jesus was the final, ultimate Prophet, who gave us the final, complete Truth. The Moslem agrees that Jesus was a Prophet . . . but insists it was Mohammed who was the final, ulitmate-no-further-ever-to-be giver of the World.

Orthodoxy is *not* "I know this. . . .," for that must be a basic of any thoughtful process. Orthodoxy is "I know this *cannot be true*"! Orthodoxy begins where it lays down the Ultimate Boundary of Truth, and says flatly, "There is no possible Truth beyond this." Orthodoxy is not what it says *is*, but what it says *is not*.

The basis of science-fiction is precisely contra-orthodoxy: That there are truths beyond the futhest border of the known.

Now **John's** letter is highly emotional, and consists largely of a personal attack on my knowledge, wisdom, motives, and competence. It is *not* primarily an argument concerning facts, but an attack on the personality level — a vigorous statement that I, personally, am incompetent.

There is a basic human reaction that goes, in essence, "If he knew what I know, he would necessarily agree with me. Since he does not agree with me, he is necessarily ignorant of what I know." **John's** got that one working full blast. He asserts that it is clear I know nothing of the laws of fundamental mechanics, and that ignorance is proven by my willingness to believe something new could possibly be added.

Let's leave personalities out, and simply cite objective facts.
1. I have a degree in physics from a major university.
2. I have examined the **Dean** gadget.
3. **John Pierce** has a degree in physics from a major university, and is a practicing professional physicist.
4. He has not examined the **Dean** device personally.

Now since **John** is discussing the basic, underlying primary laws

388

of mechanics in his letter, the fact that I have a degree in physics is meaningful; it demonstrates that I have studied, learned, and demonstrated understanding of those fundamental laws of mechanics. I.e., that *I do know* what **John** knows about fundamental mechanics. That it is *not* true that my disagreement must stem from ignorance of the fundamental principles of mechanics which he knows.

Certainly **John** knows a helluva lot more about communications theory, electronic circuit behavior, quantum mechanics, and a vast variety of esoteric matters than I. He can also play the piano, which I cannot. The advanced physics and piano-playing are equally irrelevant to the question of whether or not I know the fundamental laws of mechanics he is insisting I do not know. It is his opinion I do not know them; I have documentary evidence that I do know them.

I suggest possibly our disagreement lies not in what he knows that I don't, but in something I observed that he has refused to.

I remember, shortly after getting my degree in physics, going back to M.I.T. and asking my ex-physics professor about ball-lightning, having recently witnessed the more than slightly startling phenomenon. After explaining that it was purely folk-lore and resulted from faulty observatioin, he showed me the basic proof that it couldn't possibly exist, and wound up with "no competent observer has ever reported the phenomenon."

Inasmuch as I was a graduate physicist reporting the phenomenon, it became evident that "a competent observer" was one who did not report the known-to-be impossible phenomenon.

If they'd listened a bit to "incompetent" observers who did report it, they might have gotten some clues to plasma physics a good many decades earlier.

This **Dean** argument is about to become completely academic anyway; in about three months from now, I should be able to publish in *ANALOG* **Dr. William O. Davis'** material on the Fourth Law of Motion, which he derived not merely from **Dean's** device, but from thousands of other items of "incompetent observation" that have been well-known for many years as "instrumentation failure" because the results the instruments reported didn't agree with orthodox theories that showed the instruments *couldn't* observe what they did observe.

The whole problem of Orthodoxy revolves around precisely that type of point: The absolute refusal to consider that there *might* be *four* laws of motion, instead of only three. That the three are perfectly valid . . . but that while true, they aren't the whole truth — that there exists some new law beyond the limits of the known, and yet to be discovered.

That three-body business I threw into the **Dean** article was primarily intended for one purpose only; to attack the Omniscient attitude of the Orthodoxy — a matter of "Now look, guys — you really *don't* know all the answers to everything in the Universe!" I might just as well have pointed out nobody knows how catalysts work in chemistry, or what makes supernovas explode, or why, when a Pavlovian-conditioned flatworm is eaten by an untrained flatworm, the cannibal turns up about 2/3rds trained! (Shades of "The Golden Bough"! Eat the heart of a brave enemy, and become courageous!)

Re the dowsing rods: I am not going to set up experiments and run them, and submit my data. It's futile. **Rhine's** been doing it for a third of a century, and gotten nowhere; I refuse to get suckered into the same trap. When Mendel presented his paper, some German biologist said he should perform an experiment with some other plant . . . and named a plant which, unlike sweet-peas, has a horrific mass of recessive and quasi-recessive genes. For the next 40 years Mendel got nowhere; it took some 75 years of development of the science of genetics by many cooperating scientists before *that* plant's genetics could be untangled!

No amount of data will convince an unwilling mind.

"A man convinced against his will is of the same opinion still!" Ted, your opinion re dowsing rods was changed not by argument, not by tables of statistics . . . but by having dowsing rods *in your hands* do something that *you experienced*. Argument does not, and never will, alter a sincere opinion; only experience will.

It's necessary, then, to force the unwilling opponent to *experience* what he is sure is impossible; after he has experienced, then argument can have real value and meaning. Then, but only then, will experimental data-tables be of service.

It's self-delusion to believe that evidence pro and con a sincerely held conviction will be, or can be, weighed with equal honesty by any human mind. In that "Engineer's Art" article **Randy Garrett** did, note that the Yale physicist cited **Martin Gardner's** "Fads & Fallacies" as a legitimate reference work with respect to a fact-of-nature. This — in view of the nature of that book — is about equivalent to the research director of the company laboratory citing the advertising agency's promotion literature as proof that they are turning out a good product. Yet the physicist — and the psychologist, who certainly should have known better! — both felt that they were presenting "evidence" concerning the non-existence of the phenomenon when they cited a book of a type no scientist in his right mind would ever consider citing concerning, say, the existence or non-existence of the optical maser phenomenon!

"Enough evidence" is an emotional, not a logical, quantity!

And "uncontrolled experiments" are always sneered at and demeaned — whole far less solid "laboratory evidence" is happily accepted. The non-heritability of acquired physical characteristics was proven by how many generations of lopping the tails off of how many mice? This, Sir, was *proof*, because it was done in a *laboratory*. The fact that Jewish boys still have to be circumcised has no evidential value whatever, of course, because, it's only been going on for 200 generations, in a test population of perhaps 200,000,000 or so and *not* in a laboratory.

Sometimes I find it a leeeetle difficult to understand this here "Scientific Method."

And have you even considered that nobody has proven the heritability, or non-heritability of acquired *behavioral* characteristics?

Only God Almighty and an Acknowledged Orthodoxy are supposed to know the final limits of the possible.

Now I have precognition. I preken that **John Pierce** is about to suffer from an acute case of red face, when **Dr. Davis'** paper on the fourth law of motion appears. It's so beautifully obvious! You all have, already, all the data anyone needs to see it exists — particularly **John Pierce**, in his business! — but because you have been so damned sure you knew the Limits of Truth, have missed it.

I'm not stating it here for obvious ethical reasons; it isn't mine; **William O. Davis**, not **JWC**, had the brilliant insight to recognize it, and he, by God, deserves full and undiluted credit for that insight. He took those "incompetent observer" data from a dozen fields, and found the pattern that no one, since Newton's time, had tried to find.

Oh, one more item: **Dean McLaughlin** mentioned the second *Missles & Rockets* report on the **Dean** drive. There was one; it was the **Rabinow** Report, produced by the **Rabinow** Laboratories for the Air Force under a subcontract — and that was what I discussed in my previous letter. **Rabinow** tested the **Dean** device, without allowing **Dean** to show how it should be set up. **Rabinow** reported that he found that the drive clutch slipped under a 10-pound load . . . and then used an 18-pound load to test the machine. For some reason he found it didn't work.

It's truly remarkable how thoroughly scientific one can be in laboratory tests . . . without being at all reasonable!

But . . . never look at the history of the Jewish people; that would not be scientific! Cut off the tails of a few mice for a few generations, in a laboratory, and get *proof*!

Regards,   John W. Campbell

Donald Kingsbury   *April 30, 1962*

Dear Mr. Kingsbury:

One thing you mention in your letter I've already heard about — with a vengeance! — from various relativistic experts who will *not* read what **Davis** said, but insist on reading what they "know" he *must* have said.

You mention a small mass, m, falling toward a larger mass, M, and the consequences of light-speed gravity. The best case is not the linear fall situation, but where m is orbiting M. Under these conditions, m does not see M where it *is*, but where it *was*, and vice versa, of course. A binary star system represents one case — and the Jupiter-Sun system represents a case.

The relativistic boys computed that one out long since, it seems . . . and those **Einsteinian** gravity wave radiations are several orders-of-magnitude too minute to be of any consequence whatever. For the Jupiter-sun system, the **Einsteinian** gravity-wave radiation represents an energy dissipation of 450 watts! Figure out how long a 450 watt drain will take to dissipate 1% of the Jupiter-Sun System!

The third-derivative forces are many orders of magnitude greater — and they are usefully applicable.

Unfortunately, one of the nastiest characteristics we're running into is that the thrust reaches maximum at a third-derivative resonance . . . which also means that the system in resonance is being torn apart by d^3 forces!

Any old hand around machines will tell you that, when a machine "runs away," goes wrong somehow, it will start spinning madly, break down its supports and its own structure — *and* take off like a bat out of hell in a straight line. The things's hit a d^3 resonance . . . and developed the thrust characteristic that **Dean** applied.

The reason why **Dean's** "six unit models" that were capable of self-lift all "tested to destruction" now appears! Bet he was sucked in by the greater and greater lift he got as he got them tuned up right . . . until he walked right into a d^3 resonance, and his gadget suddenly shed parts all over the joint!

Even more interesting, however, are other consequences of the d^3 forces. I've seen **E.L. Victory** *derive* turbulent flow. And **Prof. Serge Korff** *derive* the meson as intractance characteristics of the nucleus-nucleon system! And they've got lots of evidence that the Shroedinger quantum mechanics equation can be derived from Newton-Davis mechanics. Which will, for the first time, make quantum mechanics something more than a pragmatic-empirical system!

You might write **Dr. Davis** and ask for the paper he delivered at the Washington meeting of the American Physical Society, which gives — naturally! — a lot more of the mathematical basis of his work.

Regards,   John W. Campbell

E. E. Smith, PhD   *May 21, 1962*

Dear Doc:

Some revisons required, I think. And there's time to do it — I'd *just* bought 82,000 words of "Space Viking" (hell of a good job, too!) from **H. Beam Piper** when your letter arrived. Accountants being what they are, ours wouldn't be happy if I put through two $2500 invoices the same week!

The revisions required are all concerning the situation in Second Space. The one part that's clear is that you've got racism running riot . . . which gets people mad in an unnecessary way. While the political situation otherwise is extremely foggy.

You may know what the situation is supposed to be — but it isn't clear to the reader.

For one thing, you have your Heroes, and the Big Business men acting as 100% self-determined, hard-boiled, horny-handed dictators . . . ask any Labor union man! — in suppressing the goon squads. With tanks, 105 mm cannon, and men in armor, yet!

Then what's wrong with the government of Second Space, where the Judiciate is suppressing opposition with the Second Space equivalent of tanks, 105 mm guns, and men in armor, huh? If pure-force-rule is O.K for Big Business in First Space . . . what's wrong with pure-force-rule in Second Space? So they use eagles instead of 105 shells . . . so what's the difference?

Yeah . . . you know and I know there's a difference . . . but let's make *sure* we let the readers in on that difference clearly!

If we're going to beat up on Unions . . . *make it absolutely clear* that the union *men* are being horridly mistreated by their vicious, corrupt, etc., union leaders cum goon squads. (We're still trying to get union typographers, printers, truckers, etc., to print and distribute this magazine, you know!)

The main trouble in the Second Space section, however, is plain, "I don't know what the situation really is, here." Is the Judiciate corrupt? Sadistic? Immoral? Or amoral only in our terms, but perfectly sane, sound, and moral in theirs? The mores of the second-space culture is not clarified.

And I think the racism set-up is both undesirable and actually unrealistic.

It is unfortunately true that the color of a man's skin never has, and probably never will, be a reliable indicator of the nature of his psyche — the genetic personality type. It is true that, statistically speaking, Negros have definite differences from whites, and from Amerinds and from Mongoloids. But be it noted that American Negros are massively different in personality characteristics from the African Negro peoples they derived from. Also, the Bermuda Negros are massively different in personality type — in basic psyche — from the Jamaican and Haitian Negros.

Reason for that latter: Bermuda never had any agriculture to speak of, and never will — it's coral rock with a minute layer of topsoil that wind-born dust deposited on a mid-ocean island. It was, however, enormously important, during the sailing days, as a magnificent mid-ocean trading point. The whalers stopped there; it's half way between England and the Carribean islands, and from the US ports. Bermuda, then, had a lot of wealthy merchant families, and no agriculture. They had no use for field hands — but needed lots of domestic servants, and clerk and stevedore types.

Now a rebellious slave can be used as a field hand, with armed guards watching day and night.

But domestic servants, who care for your wife and children, and slaves who handle your goods in warehouse and office . . . these must be willing, cooperative slaves. They *must want to do the job*.

A domestic-willing slave brought a fancy price in Bermuda; a rebellious, vicious slave was sold to the Jamaican, Haitian, or other agricultural areas where field-hands were needed.

That made one of the neatest automatic selective-breeding systems anybody ever unconsciously set up!

Today, if you go to Bermuda for a vacation, you can stroll around in the soft night air — wander through the dark streets — and it's a lovely place to be.

Today, in Jamaica, you stay indoors after dark — if you've got good sense! — unless you are a considerable party and armed to boot.

Cultures act as selective breeding mechanisms — all cultures always do.

When Americans first went to Hawaii, they were already well indoctrinated into How To Treat Colored Peoples. If Negro, you enslave them. If Indian, you kill them, because "The only good Injun's a dead 'un."

So they met the colored Polynesians . . . and settled down with them and built a joint civilization in which the Polynesians have never been second class citizens.

Why? Because the thing that counts is not, and never has been, skin color — but *the degree of personality development*. The Negros in Africa were — and are! — tribesmen. The Amerindians

394

in the U.S. areas were Barbarians . . . and the Polynesians, like the Chinese and the Caucasoids and Eskimos, were Citizens. The Polynesians had already developed very well-run and soundly organized representative-monarch type government. The local village elected a headman; the headmen of an area elected a chief. The chiefs of a larger area elected a king. And it was election, with authority and responsibility clearly delineated.

Now I suggest that you can get what you want here, in Second Space, on this basis:

In *any* race, there are always deviants. Among the Negros were occasional Barbarians, and even occasional Citizens. Among the Whites, God knows we have plenty of deviants who are pure barbarians, and lots of tribesmen types. (The tribesman wants to be told what to do, and how to do it, to have no responsibility for anything whatever, including himself — he wants cradle-to-grave security, and immunity from the deed of learning anything after he has learned one job, which will be his for life. Hence he *wants* to be a robot, and it is he who is absolutely threatened by automation. A robot is simply a better robot that he is.)

The result is that your Reds wouldn't all be the Barbarian types you describe — many of them would want to be citizens. While many a white would fit nowhere but on a Red planet! And a lot of the Yellow and Browns would want to be either Citizens or Barbarians instead of Tribesmen.

Now suppose that what's happened over the centuries is that Barbarian types *of all colors* have migrated to the planets that have the cultures in which they fit. They'll be welcome on such planets, because they *do* fit. He may be a White, but he *belongs*; he's a true-blue, 100% solid, dependable Barbarian, a man that any other Barbarian can recognize as a kindred soul — the kind of man who *is* a Man, and as happy to slit your throat as any real man ought to be. A Man who can understand what Life is *really* for — can understand how important it is to raid and fight and test yourself against opposition — a Man who would rather die than submit as a sniveling slave to a routine of *working* for a living!

So . . . in a culture based on that ideology, a barbarian type, whether Red, Black, White or Yellow, would be welcome. While a Yellow, White, Black or Red who hated the mores of such a culture would either get bumped off early as a coward, or migrate to a planet where other mores obtained.

Now a Barbarian will always appear vicious, and unprincipled to a Citizen or to a Tribesman; he simply has different mores, and can be a very highly moral man . . . in Barbarian terms. The difficulty is that a perfectly sane, healthy, and properly behaving lion simply isn't tolerable in a city — he's a large carnivour, and the only adequate supply of meat for a large carnivour is human. It's not that the lion is immoral, insane, or vicious — he's just a Lion, and hungry. And absolutely intolerable.

On the other hand, you can have a high-level civilization with a Code Duello system. **Bob Heinlein** developed that theme in "Beyond This Horizon"; as he said, "it breeds fast reactions and good manners." There is no reason at all why a highly civilized planet cannot maintain a Code Duello system such as **Bob** suggested . . . and still be 100% a mature, stable civilization. It's a highly effective means of disposing of juvenile delinquents and basically irresponsible individuals before they breed more of the same.

Incidentally, in such a culture, females either have to be subject to the Code Duello also — or they are strictly under the authority of their men. It is intolerable for a man to be forced into a duel because of the intransigent irresponsibility of his wife or daughter; either she has to take the consequences directly, or be clubbed into good manners by her responsible male.

One characteristic of the barbarian is that he *cannot* keep a treaty; "the eagle and me, we gotta be free" and any vow, treaty, etc., imposes a limitation on his freedom . . . which he can't tolerate, whether he thinks he can or not.

The Mystic type is a third group — they'd have a system like India today, where you have high-caste thinkers who are permitted to *think* about anything they like . . . provided they don't *do* anything that changes the actions of the system! The people are Tribesmen; they want to Know the Right Answers, and they cannot tolerate being forced to learn anything new. Hence, no changes of the system are tolerable to 90% of the population.

The essential point of all which is: you can have your different groups in Second Space . . . and explain them in different terms. Only the skin-color is not allowable as an explanation — because it damn well isn't true.

And *genocide* is neither necessary nor sufficient; killing off all the Reds wouldn't eliminate the Barbarians, while many of the Reds, inevitably, are not Barbarians. Look, the Mohawks today are damned good farmers in the Mohawk valley, and damn good high-steel workers all over the world — and yet they're full-blooded Amerindians just like the hated Mohawk raiders of 200 years ago. What's happened is that a *gene* has been ruthlessly suppressed . . . but the *people* has not.

We can't stand wolves in a settled farming country. But dogs are mighty useful. The difference? A certain gene-constellation has been suppressed by selective breeding.

If the Justiciate is honest, sincere, but pig-headed, the necessity for a revolution against that perfectly honest, non-corrupt, and perfectly sincere government must be carried out. They're ruthless; in a Code Duello culture, that's perfectly expectable. But such a culture would not be sadistic (that's a form of irresponsibility) and wouldn't use carnivorous animals as a method of execution. The Barbarians would. The Mystics would — because it's Traditional and one never, never, never changes any tradition. The Civilized worlds would use a plasma jet.

The development of the intolerable Barbarian worlds is perfectly explainable; the Tribal worlds simply go their way and ignore anything and everybody else. The Civilized worlds normally respect differences of opinion, and so freely permit the devlopment of cultures having alternative philosophies. But Barbarians can't be Barbarians without someone to prey on — any more than a lion can be a lion without herbivoures to feed on.

When the Barbarians develop effective psimen — they'd naturally attack the Justiciate. And a pig-headed Justiciate would scoff at all warnings by Civilized psimen.

One thing I feel needs to be reevaluated: Does the concept of the Purple Shirts really aid, or does it hinder, the message you're trying to put over? To modern readers, it means, "Hitler's bully-boys — no brains, sadistic, perverted Barbarians." It's semantically loaded to the hilt.

Incidentally, re status grades. In a Code Duello culture, people get into the right status grade — the one they personally and individually belong in by right of personal, individual abilities — fairly quickly. Any man has a right to try for any status grade he wants; if he's a braggart fool, self-evaluating himself six ranks too high, he inevitably gets suddenly dead by tangling with someone who *does* belong where he thinks he does. The overaggressive and the underaggressive both pay for their mistakes; the overaggressive dies and the underaggressive is frustrated. **Bob Heinlein** might have added a term to his comment; "a Code Duello culture breeds good manners, fast reactions . . . and eliminates fools!"

Anyhow . . . I think you can attain all the basic ends you want in the Second Space section by recasting the separation of peoples along psychic-cultural lines (which is a real and valid separation!) rather than along the skin-color lines, which is neither a real, valid, nor acceptable in modern publications.

Look, **Doc** . . . Negros basically are in the Tribesman-Barbarian stage, *as a general rule* . . . but that doesn't mean that individuals like George Washington Carver or Ralph Bunche would find a Negro Barbarian or Tribal culture tolerable! They'd move out! 2000 years ago, they'd have shown up as Numidian nobles in Rome; today they show up in American or international posts. It has always been that way; it always will be that way.

There are full-blooded Amerinds who are 100% citizens, and top-notch men and women . . . and still it is true that Amerinds are basically Barbarians.

And there are white Barbarians, God wot, though the white race has, generally, evolved beyond Barbarism.

Now there is one trouble with big Business — as there is with Big Whales or Big Dinosaurs or Big Ocean Liners. They lack agility, flexibility, and efficiency. Smaller entities can change direction faster without violent internal stress and strain.

Cartel capitalism inevitably gets into a sort of monolithic-economic-state condition, suffering from hardening of the cerebral arteries, and acute stasis. It becomes a sort of super-tribal system. It wants no change, sees no need for new inventions when everything is going so smoothly, etc.

Competitive capitalism is something entirely different; the Commies are perfectly correct in saying that Monopoly Capitalism is bad for the world . . . only the Marx-Lenin group never understood *competitive* capitalism, because they never encountered it at work.

My idea of the way an anti-trust system should work is that Axiom No. 1 holds, "No man or organization shall handicap or in any way restrain a proper, growing organization." Sure, we put clamps on narcotics businesses — but *no* restraints on steel, automobile, chemical, etc. industries.

Instead, what we do is encourage new ideas, new methods, new approaches in competitive businesses! If Steel is getting monopolistic — goose the aluminum, titanium and glass-fiber-plastics business! Don't *combat* success — outdo it! Or find some totally new approach to producing steel.

What's needed to break up monopolies is a strong and effective patent law rigged very specifically in favor of the independent inventor.

So MetEng has *the* rhenium source in the galaxy? So what! Given those Chaytor energy-yielders, and a high-power nuclear science, some hot-shot in some lab is going to remember $E=mc^2$ and work out a process for synthesizing the atoms he wants. At this point, even mightly MetEng is in trouble, because they've got n bilbucks tied up in capital investment in something no longer needed. Being Big Business, they lack the flexibility to switch suddenly to a totally new approach.

Or again . . . somebody works out a cheap way of growing pure tungsten "whiskers" — i.e., perfect, flawless, crystals of W of minute size, in quantity. Now a perfect tungsten "whisker" is known to have a yield strength that makes even your hypothetical leybyridite look like sissy stuff — they run 2,500,000 psi! and it's known that two-phase materials, properly compounded, can approach the theoretical ultimate strength of the stronger of the two phases. Vide epoxy-glass plastic — and if you haven't actually handled that incredible material, you should try it. Looks like cardboard, has the general heft of a calendered cardboard. Has a stiffness that feels like spring steel — and an elasticity your hands won't believe! The soft phase of a two-phase material serves simply to cross-link the whiskers of the strong phase, *so that the ultimate strength of perfect crystals can be applied.* That's why human bone displays a strength that actually surpasses stainless steel! It's a two-phase material using calcium phosphate crystals cross-linked with an extremely good protein plastic.

If somebody does that with tungsten whiskers in a matrix of cobalt, say . . . leybrydite has a competitor that isn't dependent on rhenium!

The point of this: It isn't *Big* business that's good — but *dynamic* business. What's evil about the labor unions is that they are efforts to impose tribalism and stasis . . . and cartel capitalism is the natural ally of tribal-labor.

"Socialism" with its promise of cradle-to-grave security, and job-assurance, and stability is a purely tribal-type promise; it's exactly what the serf wants. So Socialism, Union Labor, and cartel capitalism all have exactly the same objectives — establishing a stable, static, predictable economic system in which no innovations are tolerated.

Competitive capitalism, competitive labor, and competitive politics — i.e., *real* two-party government, in which the two parties are *not* Tweedledum and Tweedledee — are the natural enemies of the three stasis — seekers.

A competitive capitalism is a sort of Code Duello at the economic level, incidentally.

To put over your all-out blast at corrupt unionism, you've got to contrast it with decent unionism. Decent unionism would be fighting to see that a man got advanced by ability — not by neoptism, favoritism, or mere failure-to-offend-seniority. They'd be blasting the companies that would *not* install new, advanced equipment. Remember John L. Lewis, a hard-shelled bastitch if ever there was one, forced the coal companies to install safety machinery, labor-saving devices, and stated right along that coal mining wasn't fit work for a human being! He meant it — and he saw to it that the number of men employed in U.S. coal mines constantly decreased!

As the opening part of this yarn now is, it isn't clear that you're not, in fact, arguing in favor of ruthless, man-expending Big

Business that oppresses the worker, with no regard whatever for what happens to him. A Big Business who wants to "keep the workers in their place," and establish a quasi-hereditary heirarchy.

Remember that Americans know Big Business that *did* have that attitude . . . and doesn't know about Big Business that is run strictly from the top, and *doesn't* have that attitude.

Competitive labor — workers free to move from one place to another — will induce companies to have efficient personnel policies. It takes time, effort, and expense to train a damned good, widely experienced chemist to work in *your* laboratory on *your* problems. It takes time and effort and expense to train a programmer to use *your* machines on *your* job. With lots of planets open, and interstellar flight reasonably cheap, competent men will shift where the work is most satisfying. And a company that invents a new personnel policy may, while using the same machines and methods its competitors do, outstrip them because it gets better men to run the machines!

If such a situation exists on the colony planets, while Earth has the old-fashioned no-changes-allowed labor system . . . there *would* be conflict. The colony planets will be a greater total market than Earth . . . but Earth will be an essential market because of the teeming billions. As China used to be a huge market, though each Chinese lives at a subsistence level, just because there were so many of 'em.

If you make it clear that it's a conflict between free labor, free competitive capitalism, and free competitive politics among the colonies, vs stasis labor, capital and politics on Earth . . . then your blasts can be accepted *much* more graciously!

Remember that the colonies will, inevitably, be inhabited by the individuals who had a yen to be free as individuals, and/or direct descendants of such. It's a selective breeding system too!

Now on a psi point. **Van Vogt**, in his series about Gossyn, had the proposition of similarity transport — that if A is made similar to B to 19 decimals, A becomes where B is.

O.K. — consider "The Map is the Territory." The more exactly the map matches the territory, the more the territory can be manipulated by manipulating the map.

Your Second Space heroes could move only relatively small ships; the Destons could move the *Safari*. Reason: the Destons *built* that ship — they sweated out every design factor and girder. They had *near-perfect mental maps of the ship.*

Similarly, the more exactly you know your destination — the further you can teleport. When you know exactly what your destination is, and exactly what your ship is, you can teleport from galaxy X clear to Homeport, Newmars, in no subjective time. "No subjective time" because, if you know both already, there is no learning event.

The broad application of the mapping principle is, of course, that he who takes the trouble to learn his subject with thorough and careful detail can do a damn sight better job of handling it — intellectually or psionically!

(A sloppy-minded psionic is apt to use so poor a map in his manipulations that he gets results ranging from the ridiculous to the horrible. If he tries teleporting someone, and thinks of that person only in terms of his face and head . . . guess what happens. Or he might teleport a ship . . . and forget to teleport the people in the ship. Naturally, such a sloppy psi will, almost inevitably, kill himself off fairly early in the game. Playing with maps can be bodaciously dangerous — as bad as mixing odd lots of chemicals to see what happens. [A kid up at M.I.T. in freshman chem did that. He found out later that the two things he started mixing in the mortar were red phosphorous and $KClO_4$.] Psi can be lots of fun . . . just as any other potent force can. Also damned sudden death!)

No man can move a whole planet, because no human mind can comprehend it in sufficient detail to achieve the critical threshold factor. In psi, knowledge *is* power!

If you check over what I've suggested here, I think you'll see that it does not, actually, involve very much rewriting; it has to do, largely, with the explanation-of-events-and-actions rather than any change of events-and-actions.

Something must be done about the racism business in the Second Space section; too many of our emotionally-oriented readers would blow their stacks all over the place if you suggest that race-as-skin-color is important. (But they can't object to saying "birds of a feather tend to flock together — including vultures, pigeons and nightingales.")

Of course, you *could* have your bad-nasty-wicked-villainous Barbarians be violent racists!

Finally . . . I've got an idea that you might have fun with. As is, you don't explain the plasma-jet gun; you simply describe it, but give no suggestion of methodology.

Suppose Adams comes up with one that's *n* times better. His uses a small flashlight battery for power supply, weighs a matter of six ounces, and can throw a beam with a divergence so small it doubles in area only in about 1000 miles! And the beam energy-density is such that it is visible in interplanetary space because it shatters and ionizes every particle and every atom in its path! It can be maintained in full operation, at that impossible intensity, for some 48 hours continuously before the penlight size battery needs replacement. A ship's equivalent can continue throwing a beam of any desired aperature for millenia.

How? Simple! He's got a technique of establishing a semi-psi=semi-subspace bridge between the orifice of the gun and a point in space about 2000 miles from the surface of the white-dwarf remains of an exploded supernova. The core left when a supernova explodes represents the original nuclear generator of the original too-super-giant star which ran out of fuel. It's left, because it was in the exact center of a super-nova explosion, and so couldn't blast away in *any* direction — it had to just stand there and take it! **Alastair Cameron** tells me that such cores, so far as they can compute, generate no energy whatever, and simply cool off . . . *but* they are several thousand miles through, with a density that makes Sirius B look like a puff ball (densities in the hundreds of millions) and so hot that the mass consists of Fe^{56}, He^4, and gamma ray photons of energy so high that the Fe^{56} keeps getting hit and blasted back to He^4 . . . and then recombining to generate the gamma ray photon again. Cameron says their computations indicate that it will take all the rest of Eternity for those ultra-dense, impossibly hot things to cool off!

There's a core down in the Crab Nebula which appears to have a surface temperature around 500,000° K.

Pick a spot in space 2000 miles from its surface, and all the light going through that disc will be going one way-out. The rate of divergence would be *very* small, for any ordinary pistol-shooting distance! And exposure to the surface of a star with a surface at 500,000°, at a distance of 2000 miles, is not apt to improve the operation of anything — down to and including an atom of tungsten!

For long-range ship's beams, you might want a much slower rate of divergence. So use a spot 500,000 miles from the surface of a super-giant class O star, with a surface temperature of only 70,000°, but use a larger aperature. The radiation is already aligned for you — and a class O star 3,000,000 miles across at 70,000° K is not at all healthy to be only 500,000 miles from! The energy density, even at that distance, is appalling; they ionize every atom of hydrogen and helium in all circumambient space for *over 100-light-years* around.

Incidentally, the pistol-gadget would make quite a bang when you turned it off, as well as when you turned it on. The beam would produce a region of hard vaccum, of course; light pressure from a 500,000° K surface is, as I remember, several thousand tons per square inch.

So . . . lemme know what you think on the above suggestions and comments.

I very genuinely feel quite certain that the racism is a bad idea . . . and that you don't need it at all.

Regards, John

Ben Bova   *July 16, 1962*

Dear Mr. Bova:

Sorry my attitude was confusing on that last letter; it's a frustrated-and-mixed attitude. The weather story has always annoyed me; it *ought* to be a great story . . . and for twenty-five years I've been trying to get the damned thing!

There are some stories that simply can *not* be written — plots that simply can't be made into stories. One, for instance, goes thus: Race A has developed interstellar travel, and found Race B, and for seventy-five years or so a highly co-operative, mutually advantageous trade and cultural exchange has been going on. Then a scientist of B discovers that an extract from a gland of race A will make an individual of race B effectively immortal. Only . . . the A individual gets killed in the process.

That one has no rational solution; one or the other race is going to get wiped out, since both now have interstellar travel, and laws aren't going to have the slightest effect.

O.K. — and if you were Chief of the Weather Division, New England Area, covering New York, New Hampshire, Vermont, Maine, Massachusetts, Connecticut, and Rhode Island — what would you do to satisfy the voters in the Upstate New York region? Lake Placid wants ice and snow at least until June 1, and bright sunny days, with cool balmy nights from June 1 through Labor Day.

The farmers want mild winters, and plenty of rain during the summers for their grape crops.

Meanwhile, the Southeastern Division Chief is having his headaches with the Miami resort area people who want *no rain* and perfectly sunny weather, while the growers want rain for their fruit trees, and the water department engineers are screaming for rain enough to keep the fresh-water table high enough to keep the salt water out of the peninsula.

Tomatoes won't set fruit unless they get a night temperature below 65 degrees F. and apples won't start a new crop until they've been below through a freezing spell. (That's why California can't raise apples!) But a freezing spell ruins the citrus fruit industry. So, Mr. Weather Controller . . . what are you going to do to satisfy the demands of the voters, huh?

John Nelson is with RCA Communications as a propagation analyst — meaning someone who tries to predict which way a radio wave will go tomorrow. His reports have appeared in various radio and electronic journals — he's been at it for RCA now for a dozen years or so.

As I've commented in editorials before this — Science doesn't want to look at evidence that shows there are holes in their nice, neat, we-can-explain-everything-and-what-we-can't-explain-doesn't-really-exist theories. **Nelson** is only one of many — but **Nelson** does it professionally for RCA engineers who don't really give a damn *why* a rule-of-thumb works, so long as it works. They have a job of getting communications through; **Nelson** tells them when and how. They find it works. They don't have to ask, in their business, *why* it works.

And if you want to see something that's really going to have people tearing their hair . . . get hold of the report on "Cybernetic Ontology" that **Dr. Gotthard Gunther** prepared for the University of Illinois Electrical Engineering Research Laboratory. **Gotthard** has a lovely, absolutely solid logical argument — formal logic, I mean! — showing that cybernetics, to develop its full field, *must define and use subjectivity*. He's got the basic formulations for a self-aware robot! To do which, he has had to demonstrate that *mind* is real and *not discussable in objective terms*!

Basic conclusion: There's more forces in this cosmos than are dreamed of in your philosophy, whether you're Horatio, Aristotle, or anybody else!

Now the prize story of weather forecasting I know of was the job one of the ninety-day-wonder meteorologists did when the Army stationed him, during World War II, on one of the central Africa landing fields. His record, when reviewed at three and six month intervals, showed something like ninety-eight per cent perfect. It was so good they transferred him from that hole-in-the-jungle airport — over his protests, for a wonder! — to a more important North Africa port. And his record flopped hopelessly.

Seems he'd been forwarding the predictions he got every morning from the local witch-doctor, who could *really* predict the weather!

Naturally, nobody bothered to transfer the witch-doctor, or even study his techniques of accurate meteorological predictions.

Incidentally, I've read your "Milky Way Galaxy" with much interest — you did a hell of a good job on that one! — and have recommended it highly to most of the high-schoolers I encounter. It's closer to the **James Jeans** approach than anything else I've seen in the last thirty years.

The only one I can think of who might out-do it, and could if someone could just get him to, is old **Otto Struve**. Love that guy's articles in *Sky and Telescope*! There's one man who'll come out in print and discuss the egregious boners he himself pulled, and discuss the boners other people pulled. Know his story on Epsilon Aurigae? I admire the man!

But I've got an article coming up from an English yacht-yard operator with some really fascinating implications!

As you know, the Moon doesn't actually "go around the Earth": Earth and Moon go around the Sun in looping orbits. In a similar manner, the Earth doesn't "go around the Sun," but both go around the center of the Galaxy. Now the circum-galaxy speed is approximately 200 mps, while the circum-solar speed is only about 20 mps; thus the Earth's orbit is, actually, a very flat curve indeed — only about 20 degrees or so!

Now at this (epoch) that Man happens to have come along, it happens that the Solar System is in one of the two spots in its 200 megayear swing around the Galaxy that it is travelling almost exactly broadside on — i.e., Earth's ecliptic's pole points almost exactly toward Vega, which is almost exactly the direction of cirum-galaxy motion. One hundred megayears hence, if the gyroscopic stability of orbits *as usually thought of* maintains, the Solar System will again be travelling broadside on.

But . . . is that a coincidence? Or is there some force we don't understand? Did we just *happen* to come along at the right time, or. . . .

On the other hand, if Earth maintains its axial rotation gyroaction, and maintains its attitude with respect to its 200 mps galactic orbit . . . in fifty megayears Earth will be in a Uranus position, with the polar axis, rather than the equator, pointed toward the Sun!

Try that on a few diagrams, and start wondering about ice ages and polar shifts of many, many degrees!

Regards,   John W. Campbell

J. T. McIntosh   *January 11, 1963*

Dear Mr. McIntosh:

My friend, when it comes to the real world, I can observe and draw my own conclusion; you can observe and draw yours, and others can observe and draw theirs.

But when it comes to the science-fiction-story world, the only understanding we have is from two sources:

1. What the author says, and
2. what known physical laws say.

If you write a story of Glurkistan, in 1780, told from the viewpoint of a completely psychotic paranoid Glurkistanese — I, since I have no way of knowing what Glurkistanese was like in 1780, save from what your story tells me, must assume that the viewpoint character is a sane and truth-window on the strange and hateful culture of Glurkistan. I can't observe — so I must assume that the viewpoint character is right.

Describe Nazi Germany, 1941, as seen through the eyes of a Nazi Jugend, a sincere and dedicated youngster — and if that were the only document concerning Nazi Germany's future archeologists ever found — what could they do but assume it was as truthful as it was sincere?

Your viewpoint character said the New People were butterflies — and I was not able to observe them for myself except through his eyes.

In view of my inability to get any alternation viewpoint, I could only assume that the viewpoint-character's statements were valid . . . or give it up as a hopeless and undecidable proposition.

It's not that science-fiction is "telling its readers not only what is going on, but what to think about it" — we're pointing out that *there are other ways than standard* to think about things. However, in order to do that, we must cite facts — simple data — that indicate the alternative pattern of meanings may be closer to reality.

Where you failed in your effect was that you didn't tell what was going on save from one viewpoint — which is, actually, the oldest and simplest form of pure propaganda! If you give your listener only one side of the story, and give him no chance to observe for himself — you'll convince him won't you?

That's what you *did*, whether that was what you intended or not. *You* may have "observed" that future world yourself, and so have known your viewpoint character was wrong . . . but how could anyone else observe your imaginary world for himself?!

Sincerely,   John W. Campbell

Philip Jose' Farmer   *April 3, 1963*

Dear Mr. Farmer:

Ah, yes . . . you know and I know that the Moors were dark but not Negro, and that the Ethiopians, at their Embassy in Washington, barred Negro (U. S. style) reporters from their press conferences on the grounds that they were Negro.

And as a matter of fact, I was quite sure most of my readers would either know it, or look it up.

But I was also sure that the NAACP boys wouldn't want to know, and would be careful not to look it up. And they wouldn't have any grounds whatever to cause me any trouble . . . while I published something that needs bringing to factual attention in the world.

Most of the New York newspapers, you know, do not, in publishing a description of a hold-up man, etc., publish the information that he was Negro — just that he was 5'10" tall, weighed 170 pounds, etc. And the state drivers' licenses are not permitted to carry information, under the "driver's description," that suggests someone is Negro.

You see, I belong to that persecuted minority — the native born white Protestant of Anglo-Scotch ancestry, the only group which the movies, etc., can name as villains in their dramas. And I'm getting just a little fed up with this slightly nutty (as a fruit cake) utter refusal to look simple facts of history in the eye.

Seems to me a little peculiar that, if the Negroes are just as competent as anybody else, in the last 10,000 years (we all started equal back there — nobody had schools!) all the major inventions and discoveries have been made by Caucasoids and/or Mongolians, with Polynesians paralleling many of the social inventions.

Anyhow — to answer your direct question — any comments made in the editorials are invitations to any and all authors to jump either in (or on!) with story development of the ideas.

By the way, here's something else you might have some fun considering.

I've looked around for historical cultures which genuinely showed *no* prejudice bias against other races/aliens. I've found several — cultures in which any man, of any race or people, was accepted without any bias or prejudice. Negro, white, Monglo . . . all one.

But each of those cultures has had one of two things in common:
1. It's been an extremely-harsh-frontier situation.
2. Or it's been set up on a sort of liberal type of slavery operation.

Typically, a man can be born a slave, but the culture system allows him to earn his freedom, and earn almost any rank (usually they're hereditary monarchies at the top, so he can't earn that, but can earn the Chief Executive post — Prime Minister, Grand Wizir, or whatever) in the society. And a man born free, if he mismanages his affairs so badly he goes bankrupt is sold into slavery by his creditors. (From which state he is prefectly free to earn his freedom again — if he is competent!).

In the harsh-frontier situation, obviously the men who stay alive very long are not fools, not lazy, thoughtful in the sense of considering consequences before acting, and very dangerous to attack, i.e., every single individual has proven against a tough world, that he merits respect *as himself.*

In the liberal-slavery system, also, every individual is forced to earn respect *as himself.* A rich fool and his money are soon parted; a penniless slave of high competence rapidly advances.

O.K. . . . imagine men finally get out into the galaxy, and find some 40-odd inhabited planets. All but one of those planets scorns, demeans, discriminates against, and/or variously rejects Terrans. The one on which they are fully and freely accepted — along with all 40 other races — is a highly advanced culture that Terrans of course loathe, hate and demean as a horrid culture, because it practices chattel slavery, and it's perfectly legal for a trio of Masters to decide to kill a rebellious slave. Which is done publicly and unpleasantly. (One thing that makes even fools hesitate over commission of folly is awareness of painful consequences.)

Be it noted, incidentally, that Masters who don't know how to get cooperation from their slaves aren't going to be able to run an efficient operation . . . and will, presently, be slaves themselves.

I think there would be some wonderful opportunities for some really powerful emotional twisting of orientation viewpoints on such a world!

Incidentally, in handling it — if you find it interesting remember that Freud was a fool, and the current crop of literateurs who think that Sex in suburbia is the deepest and most powerful of all possible human motivations are followers in his folly.

If you notice, the number of accusations of rape in life-boats, life-rafts, or airplanes doomed to destruction seems to be zero. If Sex were the be-all and end-all that Freud made it out to be . . . how come human beings ignore it so when the chips are down?

Sex plays a damn small part in actual working slavery systems. (Roman Empire situations were due to the collapse of a once-great culture; the Roman Republic didn't have that sort of sadism and sex.)

Think there are story possibilities?

Sincerely,   John W. Campbell

Frank Herbert   *June 3, 1963*

Dear Frank:

Congratulations! You are now the father of a 15-year-old superman!

But I betcha you aren't gonna like it. . . .

This is a grand yarn; I like it, and I'm going to buy it. But I have some comments that may make you want to make a slight change in the ending.

As the father — and/or step-father! — of several literary supermen, I've learned something about their care and upbringing. They're *very* recalcitrant. Also hard to live with.

You can't think like a superman. You can't imagine his motivations. He's altruistic — and superman. Which means he will sacrifice the highest good you can imagine, for the sake of something you couldn't understand even if he explained it to you. He is gentle — which, when properly defined, means that he is kindly, but absolutely ruthless. Like the man who loves horses, and sorrowfully shoots the stallion with a broken leg. I doubt that the stallion would approve of that action.

No human being can write about the thoughts, philosophy, motivations, or evaluations of a superman.

There are two ways that supermen have been handled successfully in science-fiction; Method 1 is that **van Vogt** used in "Slan!" . . . and is what you've got here, so far. You don't talk about the super*man*, don't try to portray the super*man*, but show a super*boy*, who hasn't yet developed his powers out and beyond your ability to conceive of them. Method 2 is that used by **Norvel W. Page** in "But Without Horns" in the old *UNKNOWN*. The superman never appears on stage at all — you encounter only people who have met him, and the results of action he's taken. You never meet him, and never do understand what his motivations are.

If "Dune" is to be the first of three, and you're planning on using Paul in the future ones . . . oh, man! You've set yourself one hell of a problem!

You might make the next one somewhat more plottable if you didn't give Paul *quite* so much of the super-duper.

You'd have someone exceedingly hard to defeat, and yet having certain definite limitations, if you gave him just one talent; the ability of transtemporal clairvoyance.

Now that could work like this: a man remembers the past he has experienced, but nobody knows how that's done. Suppose it's done by a faculty which any remembering entity actually has, of being able to "see" across time, and perceive the actual original event. When you "remember" going to the beach for a swim last summer, you perceive-across-time the actual event.

Now this time-scanning would, inherently, allow you to perceive anything anywhere. Which would simply drive you completely nuts. Data is useless, unless you can organize and relate it. Unlimited access to unlimited data would require infinite time to scan it all! And until you've scanned nearly all of it, you wouldn't know what data went with what.

So normal people use as an index-mark, as a guide-line, the "I was there" factor in using their transtemporal clairvoyance. You can remember what you heard, saw, felt, tasted, thought, and your mood.

Once in a while, somebody slips a bit . . . and gets somebody else's "I" as a guide-line; then you have Joe Blow "remembering" somebody else's life-track . . . and we have "proof" of reincarnation.

Now if Paul has as his new talent the ability to use someone else's "I was there" guide-line — if he can remember anyone else's memories — he would be *very* hard to defeat.

Notice: If I could remember what you remembered, I would, in effect, have telepathy! I would not know what you are-now-thinking, but I would be able to "remember" what you were thinking a millisecond ago . . . which amounts to the same thing.

If, before he can "remember" someone else's memories, he must identify their "I-track" — if it is essential that he first have a take-off point of direct contact — then the only way an enemy could keep Paul from knowing his plans would be to make sure Paul never encountered him. To find the I-track of one individual among *n*-billion people in the Galaxy would be impossible without a contact point.

If you wind up this yarn with Paul acquiring that talent, all the present explanations can come out of it. I.e., he can remember back along Baron Harkomen's line, Yeuh's Kynes, the Fremen he encountered, etc., to get the whole present background.

BUT . . . he doesn't have so much precognition that you can't build a workable plot for the next yarn.

You know the trouble with time-travel stories; if the guy has a time-travel machine, and the villain kidnaps the heroine, there's no sweat. The hero doesn't chase the villain; he looks annoyed, steps into the time machine, goes back 30 seconds before the villain's villainy, and tells the heroine, "Hey, honey — that stupid louse, Rudolph the Villain is about to kidnap you. He's making a nuisance of himself, isn't he. Let's go somewhere else."

Give your hero precognition *that works*, and it's sort of like old-fashioned Presbyterian Predestination. There's no use trying, because he already knows what *has* to come. And everybody is stuck with it, whether they like it or not.

However, with all the data-sources he gets with everybody's memories . . . he *still* doesn't know the future. He knows what *they* think the future is, and what *he* thinks it'll be . . . but not what it *will* be.

Incidentally, I find that the following is a useful analogy describing the process of Time. Imagine an immensely tall glass cylinder, filled with water. The bottom of the thing is sitting in a tank of liquid air; naturally the water in the bottom is frozen solid, and as heat drains out to the liquid air, the surface of crystalization advances steadily up the column of water. The interface between still-liquid water and solidified ice is the instant Now; the frozen ice is the Past, and the free liquid water is Future.

Now when a substance crystalizes, there are intermolecular forces at work that reach out from the already-solid crystal to drag in and align free molecules of the liquid, forcing each new molecule added to the crystal to fall into a precise alignment with the already-crystalized molecules. The interface, in other words, is not a no-thickness geometrical surface — it's a volume. Liquid well away from the interface is really pretty free, but liquid molecules near the interface are already subjected to alignment forces, and are being dragged into place.

Moreover, some crystals manage to grow faster than others; there will be spikes of crystal reaching out well ahead of the slower-growing mass.

If you watch the way crystals grow — epsom salts crystalizing when a solution is poured out on a pane of glass, for instance — it gives a remarkable mental picture of how alignment forces reach out from the past through the instant-Now, and into the Future . . . and yet do not completely determine the future, because there are liquid zones among the out reaching crystal forces.

One other item that makes supermen such nasty people to live with, when they're 15-year-old supermen. They are adolescent demi-gods — and personally, I can't imagine anything more horrible. An adolescent, no matter how intelligent, is not *wise*; he's only *smart*. Furthermore, adolescents have the most ghastly-horrible tendency to be sure they have The Answers to all the world's problems, and it is only the stupid conservatism of the old foggies that makes them reject it.

And having all the *knowledge* in the world means nothing — because all knowledge is filtered through the individual's attitudes and beliefs.

Can you imagine a sincere, dedicated, enormously intelligent, practically omniscient teen-ager . . . with the typical teen-age tendency to be Sure He's Right about matters that only adult experience can make understandable?

Hitler was Sure He Was Right. So was Torquemada.

The ordinary, every-day adolescent is something of a problem to live with. A real genius-grade adolescent is much worse to live with, because he's just as certain he has the proper, logical, and righteous answers figured out, and being extremely smart, is very difficult to unconvince.

Want to try it with Paul — when he's decided, at age 16, How the

Galaxy Should Be Rearranged And Right Away Quick?
God preserve us! No one else would be able to!

Regards,   John

William R. Burkett, Jr.   *June 11, 1963*

Dear Mr. Burkett:

Where the hell have *you* been hiding?!

Your "Sleeping Planet" is a damn good novel — only we got problems. If you'd started in the usual way, with a few shorts and novelettes to practice on, I might have known you were hatching a large economy size yarn, and adjusted things for it. As is, things go this way.

Starting in October is a two-parter, "Where I Wasn't Going;" in December, **Frank Herbert's** new "Dune," a three-parter. And in March, 1964, "Spacemen" by **Murray Leinster**. So the earliest I could start "Sleeping Planet" would be June, 1964!

However, the June, 1964 cover has to be on hand by March 15, 1964; I could (and would) buy this October 1, 1963 — but I can't load my inventory with another full-length novel before then.

There are some changes I'd suggest, if you're willing to wait. Meanwhile, until I hear your decision, I'm going to save the postage involved in shipping this thing back and forth from Florida.

The logical structure of the plot is lovely, right up to the point where Rierson falls in with the Spirit of Furnestein's — Charlie. From there on, things are a bit underplayed; you haven't developed anything approaching the possibilities implicit in the situation. Once Rierson learns from his captive Llalan pilot what the score is, and what 'Gremper" is — his training as a lawyer should start taking over from the hitherto-dominant hunter.

The robots have been maintaining the cities; the Llaran wouldn't dare interfere too seriously, because their whole bargaining position is that Earth is alive-but-sleeping. If the robots weren't working, the whole shebang would destroy itself; the shelters have to be ventilated, pumped out when ground-water seeps in, etc. The machines of Earth are as much parts of the living ecology as the people.

BUT . . . they don't respond to Llaran very well — because the higher-order police and CD computer centers have been instructed on the matter of Llarans.

The communication networks can't be cut by the Llaran; they're far too complex to be disturbed by anything short of annihilation. A talkative population of three billion, based on twenty billion computers busily exchanging data, has to have a stupendous number of communication channels. The three million Llaran couldn't cut them all—or even any effective percentage of them.

The whole robot system, however, is paralyzed by the fact that men very carefully designed them *not* to be able to *initiate* any action whatever. They could carry on routines, carry out orders-for-emergencies . . . but not start new actions without human command.

So Rierson supplies the one factor missing for not just the robots of one department store — but for the interconnected robots of a planet. And robots would *have* to be interconnected. The department store robot communicates directly with manufacturer's robots and police and fire and power company robots.

Rierson need only contact one major computer anywhere to be in touch with the total robot nerve network.

I suggest he heads for the nearest computer center when he realizes the meaning of the Llaran pilot's story. He knows the law and the logic of robots, and how to deal with a strictly logical-but-not-rational entity such as the robot net.

And then Spooks start rising all over the world.

The New York Public Library, Library of Congress, and British Museum robots plus the robots of other major university libraries, feed into the robot net all known information on Llaran ancestor worship and folklore. How does a Llaran expect a ghost to look? What can be done with a cleaning robot carrying an inflated plastic "ghost" — itself inconspicuous, but the "ghost" can't be "killed" and made to stay dead.

The trouble getting into El Scorpio is simply that the PDC robot nets will, inevitably, have blocs on their communication channels; they can receive information freely — but will not act on it without human command *at their own switchboards*. Otherwise they would have been too subject to sabotage from outside.

Rierson can't do too much actual damage; the Llaran will start smashing robot centers despite the consequences if the robots are obviously doing nasty things. But robots could do a hell of a job on morale.

Remember, even if the frightening incident is explained away with complete scientific data — the superstitious men are shown that it was just a malfunctioning robot that scared the silly bejayzus out of them — the men will remain scared, and remain convinced that it was Gramper who caused the malfunction.

Rierson & Robots, Inc., would be kept veddy, veddy busy indeed just pulling one stunt per week — when you remember the number of cities! No one local command would have any reason to get suspicious — but the superstitious would know damn well Gramper was after them.

Also, the world's libraries ought to yield something on Llaran biochemistry; there must be some hallucinogenic drugs that affect Llarans. And proving that you've just been subjected to an hallucinogenic drug is very difficult indeed . . . but the hallucination is readily accepted by the superstitious.

Let Rierson really establish the existence of Gramper and the hordes of the Undead; it's needed to explain why almost none of the Llaran troops obeyed the command to slaughter the sleepers — and instead obeyed Gramper's threats at the end. Otherwise, High Command orders are very real, very familiar, and they're conditioned to obey. If Gramper's only a vague rumor — not an almost personal experience — they won't hold off at the finale.

So . . . let me know what you're feeling on the wait and the possible rewrite.

Sincerely,   John W. Campbell

Walt & Leigh Richmond   *June 12, 1963*

Dear Walt & Leigh:

Revisions on "Where I Wasn't Going" are O.K. — and wait'll you see the cover **Jack Schoenherr** did for that yarn! He left off the checkerboard pattern on the wheel—but you won't quibble even a little when you see the painting!

"Parameter etc." however, come home to Papa and Mama; you can use this for background reference material, but honest, folks, this ain't a story — it's a treatise! This is the kind of stuff I used to write way back yonder in 1933; this is 1963, and there have been changes made in the field.

Just try counting the number of pages of "time out for discussion of theory" here, and see how little story is left! And **Leigh's** sociological theoretical material is spread around about as generously as **Walt's** physics and engineering theory.

Show it in action; don't discuss it!

Some of the physics theory in here I'm gonna need a lot of salt with — like the electric-motor theory of planetary rotation. Fr'instance, how come Venus, close to the Sun and in a really potent solar wind, rotates only very, very slowly? And Uranus either has its axis tipped more than 90° or is rotating retrograde, depending on your viewpoint on such things?

And the business of making Diemos act like a magnetron in the Solar Wind. . . ?

Well . . . I remember a time **G.O. Smith** in one of his Venus Equilateral stories had his boys signal via an electron beam from somewhere outside Jupiter's orbit, back to Venus Equilateral. And I got a six pages-of-math analysis of the maximum possible density of electron beams (it's limited by their mutual repulsion) applied to the problem of said beam. Turned out it *was* possible — but only just, with a factor of 3 x the absolute limit. Which is pushing things damn close!

However, when the same kind of guy goes to work on your broadcasting magnetron power-plant. . . ?

Besides, what for. . . ? You've sort of pulled an underhanded sneaker on the problem of power-supply by making the Confuser do an entirely new kind of trick — though I'll admit that that megawatt power pile you've got would never have hauled 75 million tons of space staion out into space at 0.1 G, so you had to have something peculiar go on.

Incidentally — you might have some fun on that; when they do measure the $E = mc^2$ factor on consumption of plastic, they find several interesting things.

1. It doesn't check with power actually realized.
2. No two units show the same ratio of mc^2 to power output.

The answer turns out that the Confuser confuses things by the uncertainty factor; since Space's memory is being loused up by the thing, it tends to "forget" just how much mass was supposed to be there — which is why the energy can be made to reappear as KE. But it's like beta decay; the maximum energy output would equal mc^2, but it just never gets there in any statistically significant number of instances.

And why do you need that plastic material? Any hydrogen-containing material would do, according to your explanation. Water — oil — anything handy. Just put it in a can so designed that the thrust can be transferred.

The problem of the men-vs-women imbalance won't be important. For the first few months, they're going to be too damn busy staying alive, and getting something they can see as a workable ecological system (including the technological supplies as part of the ecology of *Homo technicus*; we consume steel, hydrocarbons, etc., ores, and energy just as much as we consume proteins and carbohydrates.)

During that period, the man-woman ratio isn't important — like the business of nobody has trouble with rape in a lifeboat; they're too busy worrying about other problems.

As soon as they have a base, and a real ship — not that hot-air ballon thing they've been cruising around in — they can reach Earth, and the man-woman ration problem can be solved shortly thereafter.

But . . . their first trade with Earth is not going to be Martian fertilizer; that comes after the Earth government has acknowledged the Martian Nation exists, and has made treaties with it. Before that, they're going to be smugglers, and smugglers have always been popular with the people, but not with governments. But you don't smuggle tonnage quantities of fertilizer.

You smuggle tobacco, whisky, medicinals, machine parts — things of high value/pound and things with high taxes or extreme shortages due to political causes.

Do that, and the populace loves you; the local cops won't be very active, because they think it's a good idea too. Don't smuggle dope, though, or jewels-for-the-idle-rich.

If your bunch of "mad scientists" can't figure out ways and means of lousing up radar with a cheap gadget, they need to polish their brains. One real good one is a high-power, though short-life spark-coil contraption (several hundred of them) which simply gives off a loud and lusty RF razzberry. Drop a few hundred of 'em at 50 miles up, with plenty of parachute to lower 'em slowly, and for hundreds of miles around all the radar sets are going to be having difficulties. No two of 'em radiates the same pattern, nor gives off the same pattern at the same repetition rate, nor gives off anything remotely resembling a clean signal. And maybe a few hundred pounds of random-length hair-fine wires at the same time. . . .

Sure, Security knows they've got smugglers coming in, but they can't tell where within several hundred miles.

Oh . . . another "Confusion device": microwave energy is of the order of magnitude of chemical bond energy — *weak* chemical bonds. Should be possible to dream up a flare — a chemical-burning gadget — that radiates "white-light" RF like crazy.

Security would also have the problem of wondering whether the current RF blather meant "they've got a smuggler coming in" or "they've got a smuggler going out."

But . . . stop the lecture business, and get back to the story business!

Incidentally . . . can you check on what "Diemos" means? I believe the two that accompany the God of War are Fear and Flight, not Fear and Terror.

And finally . . . "don' be i' nurry, young mon!"

"Where I Wasn't Going" is starting in October; "Dune," by **Frank Herbert**, starts in December, ends in February. "Spaceman" by **Will Jenkins** starts in March, ends in May. "Sleeping Planet" by a brand new author (a fellow Floridian, incidentally), (name of author; I've forgotten for the moment!) starts in June, 1964, and finishes in August 1964. The soonest your sequel could get in is, therefore, September, 1964!

How about doing some novelettes and shorts on this background instead, for awhile!

Regards, John

416

P.S. Manuscript being returned under separate cover. "Parameter, Perimeter & Pi"

William R. Burkett, Jr.   *July 9, 1963*

Dear Mr. Burkett:

Rierson, as you've described him, is a lawyer with a big-game-hunting hobby . . . until he gets attacked by Larrys. Naturally, his first reaction is to survive, anyoldhow. He does. When he finally gets away with the Larry pilot, however, he *has* survived. He gets a respite — and for once, for a moment, he's on top, and a Larry's in trouble. From a man in desperation fighting to stay alive — fear-motive — he is now ready and able to turn to anger-motive. O.K., you bunch of bloody bastitches, now, by God, it's *my* turn!

At that point, he is mentally-emotionally the aggressor — whether he is in any actual position to be so physically or not.

He *re*acted to attack largely by instinct; now he is going to *act* — and that ain't gonna be instinct. Except that he wouldn't have gotten into the law business if he didn't have an inherent nature that lead him to do his fighting with the mind, with logic, with the power of rules and beliefs.

Look, guy; once when Copernicus was governor of a city, Poland was invaded, and his city threatened. Now Copernicus was trained in church law, and such medicine as they had at the time. (He was also, on the side, a successful import-export merchant.) So he sent a message to the King of Poland asking for help. The King replied more or less, "Sorry, old man, but I'm busy over this way; you'll have to do what you can." So Copernicus rounded up some local boys and with absolutely no training in military affairs — and no interest in the subject — proceeded forthwith to lick the pants off the invading army!

Your boy Rierson, peaceful lawyer, turned out, under pressure of the invaders, to be tougher, more dangerous, and harder to kill than the professional hunter-killer, Donovan, than the prison guard, than any of the other people. The guy's a holy terror as a pure fighter! AND . . . he's a highly intelligent man, with a highly trained mind.

Once get the frantic pressure off him . . . and he'll use his *really* powerful weapon! Not just a high-power rifle, a fully-aroused, and super-powered *mind*.

Generals are simply men who get squeezed into having to run a war, most of the time. Remember "Mad Anthony" Wayne? And Washington was a planter and civil engineer, not a general.

You've got a perfect general in Rierson . . . and a perfect army of obedient troops, even if they aren't quite human!

You're right on the communication channel blocks in commercial robots — but remember that these would be specific areas of noncommunication — i.e., to protect specific information. Like "Don't talk about how much was sold last month," or "Give out no information on the design of the new model," but the robot must be free to give out information about the current, on-display-for-sale models. It must give out information to police, fire, tax, and other bureaus. The laws on robot-information-tapping would be something Rierson would be required to know, naturally! And therefore the methods to use to get the communication going. And don't forget the Civil Defense Emergency circuits would be going full blast, altering normal non-communication systems.

El Scorpio would be a totally different proposition. No police, fire, tax, or Civil Defense Emergency-command-circuits *there*! It'd be personality-keyed to a fare-thee-well, too. *This particular individual and no other*, stuff.

I think Rierson would start going into the angry-attack mood as soon as he found the score from the Larry pilot. Like Copernicus, when he finds he's got to be a general, he's going to damn well out-general any Larrys around.

The Larrys, incidentally, should not become aware very much that they're having trouble with robots; their trouble is going to be *trouble with ghosts*. Some officers may say it was robots, but the men will have seen ghosts, felt ghosts, been killed by ghosts, and no accidental coincidence of a broken down robot nearby will make them believe anything different. What but a ghost could freeze a man to death on a hot summer day? Ghosts or a heavy spray of liquid helium, maybe. (The robots use cryogenic circuits in many of the central "brains.")

Once they get the other sleep-proof people loose, they can spread their activities more effectively. But the essence will be to *use ghosts to attack*. Not robots . . . or at least not *provable* robots.

Item: a "ghost sign" can appear on a Larry's face for no naturally imaginable reason. (He was beamed with a sharply focussed, projected image of a ghost-sign — the beam being pure invisible UV, causing a sunburn to show up only a couple hours after it indetectably happened to the poor sucker.)

A seeming-Larry suddenly attacks and kills five of his messmates, then vanishes shrieking with laughter into nothingness. (A Larry simply broke under the strain, went psychotic, murdered some messmates, and ran away. The all-watching robots reported it, and the men very promptly sequestered the murderer.)

Yay, verily, I say unto you . . . they can just raise merry old hell with morale . . . *without the robots appearing to be dangerous*.

You think maybe it's good for the nerves of men to be planted on a planet — *very* thinly planted! — with three billion quasi-corpses? To sit around day after day with all those enemy undead, just lying there, waiting . . . waiting . . . not really dead. . . ?

Go have some real fun with them!

But don't add too much length; we're squeezed now, remember, with too many novels!

Sure — send in a rough draft. I may have to ask for a clean-typed copy later, but no reason for unnecessary work. My experience was, too, that there's always a high-school girl around who would love to make a few bucks using the typing she's learned in high-school. Good practice for her, and reasonably good manuscript for you.

And we'll send a check out shortly after October 1. (I'll start it on its way Oct. 1, but the mills of the accounting department grind at unpredictably varying speeds.) May take 3 days; may take 8.

Regards, John W. Campbell

Mack Reynolds   *September 9, 1963*

Dear Mack:

You promise greatly with this one — it's a lovely idea.

Only you don't carry through. Seemingly, judging from your ending here, Sherlock *is* senile.

Look — let's not make Sherlock's conversation seem *quite* so senile; let Watson keep claiming the old man's senile . . . but have his conversation just as cogent as Sir Alexander's — it's Watson who's convinced of his senility, but without valid basis.

Then for the ending you've got to have Holmes get a definite resolution of the case. The only practicable definite resolution would be proof that an alien *was* here . . . but that they were very *not* menaces.

One answer might be that there were several aliens . . . from different planets. It's a cooperative cultural investigation commission.

Or the alien's an android — biologically manufactured robot — for a race that can't conceivably live on a planet like this. (They live on a gas giant, perhaps, or a super-terrestrial planet with surface gravity about 3, tremendously deep oxygen-nitrogen-water atmosphere, and a surface temperature of about 300° F — possibly because of the extreme atmospheric pressure keeping water liquid even at that temperature. Or what have you.)

And they aren't studying rocketry etc., at the British Museum; they'd work in Washington & Moscow for that. The British Museum has archeological material that excels that of anywhere else on Earth — but they don't have the hottest technical data. Cultural anthropologists and sociologists from Out There would be interested in three, or possibly four places: The British Museum, the Library of Congress, and New York Public Library plus Metropolitan Museum. Possibly the Berlin Library, but not so much so as before WWII.

Sherlock's investigation may have been gently shooed off by the Galactic Government controller who accompanies all investigation groups to primitive planets, too. . . .

Regards,   John

Enc: "The Adventure of the Extra-Terrestrial"

Fred Whipple   *January 6, 1964*

Dear Dr. Whipple:

I have two items; one is a much-delayed "Thank you!" for the help on the Andromeda Nebula photograph problem. I've finally gotten the answer worked out through a local group of amateur astronomers — some of whom have some really remarkable home-carved instruments. (One is an 11″ Matsukov with excellent resolution!)

Incidentally, **Mr. Federer**, of *Sky & Telescope* does not have your attitude on the matter. He was positively outraged and offended at the very idea of developing a way that an amateur beginner could find the M 31 nebula without first spending a proper apprenticeship learning to look at the Moon and the like.

I imagine some of the old arithmeticians must have harrumphed and boggled loudly at efforts to make multiplying XXXIX by MDCCCLXXVIII easy for beginners with that unsporting new-fangled system of 39 x 1878.

The other item concerns an idea concerning planetary formation that was proposed to me by **Mr. William F. Dawson**, of Halifax, Nova Scotia, Canada. It sounds exceedingly interesting to me; I've asked him to do a draft of an article on it.

Unfortunately, I don't see how this one could be subjected to mathematical analysis — which makes for difficulites in a field in which only those ideas presented in the "Language of Science" are admissible for study!

Basically, he has what seems to me to be a very rational synthesis of the best features of the nebular, close-encounter, and planetismal theories, all very neatly packaged by one very acceptable assumption: "Space" was *not* the way we know it when the planets were formed!

That is, he suggests that stars aren't formed in clear, dust-gas-

420

free zones, and thinking in terms of the kind of interstellar space we know today, five billion years or so after the event, is inappropriate.

If stars are formed in gas-dust nebulae, let's consider the characteristics of "space" at the time Sol began forming. Judging from those volumes where stars now seem to be forming — the Taurus and Orion gas-dust nebulae — Sol didn't form in a high-order-vacuum, nor, in all probability, was it an only child of the nebula. Presumably, dozens, perhaps hundreds, of other nuclei were forming.

The great fault with the close-encounter theory originally was held to be the extreme improbability of a sufficient close encounter. But "sufficiently close" is not an absolute thing, measured in miles, but a ratio, somewhat like Roche's limit, varying with the density of the passing stars, and to be expressed in terms of the diameters of the stars, not merely in miles.

A forming proto-star in a gas-dust nebula might well measure half a light-year in diameter! A "close encounter" between two such proto-stars might well mean passage at a distance of a couple of light years! And in a nebula where stars were borning, interstellar distances of less than a light year would be a lot more probable than in general non-nebular space.

Moreover, the large proportion of multiple stars observed suggests that something of this sort happens routinely, not as an exceptional phenomenon. Whether the encounter winds up with mutual capture of relatively equal stellar masses, or with a planetary system, might well depend on the relative state of evolution of the proto-stars at the time of close-encounter. If A had achieved a fairly high density when B passed, and B was still diffuse, B might be disrupted, with 99.9% of B's mass being returned to the gas-dust cloud, and a tiny fraction trapped by A to form planets. A would undoubtedly tend to lose by the encounter also.

In order for bodies approaching at hyperbolic, or at minimum, parabolic velocities, to be mutually captured, there must be some form of inelastic collision involved — energy and momentum must be dissipated, or the elliptical orbits cannot result.

What better resisting medium than the vast gas-dust clouds that a proto-star consists of? Large percentages of the gas-dust masses would be heated to escape temperatures, and boil off into the mother gas-dust nebula again — but a proto-star could well lose 90% of its mass, and still yield Sol!

If the proto-star B were disrupted almost totally, its nucleus might still remain shattered, but essentially "intact" in the sense that the high-density masses that constitute "cold stones" later would have been compacted from the gas-dust by the gravitational forces of a stellar-magnitude mass.

The boiling-off of near-stellar quantities of gases would act to cool off the collision debris to temperatures which would make planetary core existence possible. That is, the encounter would actually take place in a not-vacuum condition, over millenia of overtime, a light-year long path, and under conditions of evaporative cooling!

There would certainly be adequate angular momentum to put the planets in orbit — and a means of dissipating the excess. Moreover, the gas-dust medium could do quite an effective job of "damping" the eccentric orbits of the planets toward circularity.

Whatever the rotational axis of Sol might have been before, after the encounter the fall-out material and interaction with the B star would have done a pretty fair job of imposing an axis normal to the plane of the passage. The final axis might be a few degrees off from true normal, but not far; if Jupiter's angular momentum were imparted to the Sun, whatever Sol's original axis of rotation might have been wouldn't be very important!

Such proto-star encounters in a gas-dust nebula would probably be quite common; probably most of them would result in mutual destruction-dissipation of both masses back into the cloud. But this, of course, would be no loss; crystals forming in a solution are constantly shedding molecules back to the solution, from whence they simply recrystalize elsewhere.

Dawson's picture of the formation of a planetary system appeals to me for several reasons:

1. He calls attention to the fact that it must have happened *under conditions very different from those now obtaining*.
2. It redefines "close encounter" in a proper manner — in terms of the effective diameters and densities of the objects involved.
3. A "close encounter" then has linear dimensions — mileages — approximating those found as interstellar distances.
4. It describes a mechanism allowing for mutual capture by stellar masses having a probability-of-occurrence great enough to account for observed multiple stars.
5. It permits a close-encounter planetary formation allowing for tens or hundreds of millenia, instead of days, with time for cooling processes to be effective.
6. It allows evaporative cooling to carry away the excess energy and (because the distribution would be asymetrical) momentum.

7. It starts with cold masses (the majority of the masses of the proto-stars) instead of hot masses.
8. It envisions non-vacuum conditions. This allows planetary atmospheres to be acquired after the planetary cores have been established.
9. It accounts for the observed angular momenta, common orbital direction and plane, and orientation of the Sun's axis.
10. It provides a damping medium to account for the near-circular planetary orbits.
11. It accounts for the massive planetary cores by postulating a stellar-magnitude mass as the original organizing gravitational force that compacted the heavy-element cores from the gas-dust cloud, and stripping away the light-element mass of hydrogen and helium through the evaporative cooling effects.

It's also interesting to wonder what the effect would be on a pre-formed proto-star's higher density core when the proto-star encountered the resisting medium of another proto-star. If B breaks up, *how* would it break up? It would be a most violent mass of swirling eddies and back-washes as the two essentially fluid media tore through each other at speeds very decidedly above Mach 1! It's decidedly possible that major masses could be spun off with axes at extreme angles to the plane of orbital motion, or even rotating the wrong way. How such a proto-planet wound up would depend, probably, on whether evaporative cooling and loss of mass dominated infall of gases and dust.

With our present inadequate knowledge of fluid dynamics of the order involved in such turbulent states, I don't believe a mathematical analysis of the thing is possible.

But . . . do you see any ox-car size holes in Dawson's proposals?

Sincerely,   John W. Campbell

Edward C. Walterscheid   *February 12, 1964*

Dear Mr. Walterscheid:

I've been doing an article on the subject of quacks and quackery in Medicine. I've got two points that I believe should be very seriously considered.

1. Among the medical quacks of history — so declared by the medical professionals of their place and time — were Jenner, Harvey, Semmelweiss, Pasteur, Ross, Lister, Sister Kenney, and the native doctors of India who were using *rowulfia serpentina* for n centuries

while the British M.D.'s spurned it as "that stupid native panacea." It was an English witch-woman who gave us digitalis, and Chinese native doctors who used *bufferine* — in the form of stewed toad-skins — for the same sort of heart trouble.

2. Let's see you define "quack" in objective terms so that it *doesn't* apply to an AMA doctor who treats a leukemia patient by a method which he knows for a fact will not cure the patient, charges high fees for doing so, and does everything in his power to keep the patient from seeking some other therapy that isn't *known* to be futile! Objectively evaluated, the M.D. does exactly what he rants so angrily about in the quack!

Now if a man goes to a doctor and is diagnosed as having a disease that is certain to kill him if treated by the methods known to the M.D. — he is unsane if he goes to the M.D. for treatment. *Anything but an M.D.* would be more rational! That is, if you are given your choice of swallowing half a gram of mercuric cyanide, or an unknown and unspecified virulent looking greenish liquid — which would be the rational choice?

The reason we have quacks always with us — and always will — lies therein. So long as medicine can diagnose lethal diseases it cannot cure, people will seek someone who at least *thinks* he can cure it.

And the business of being "money seeking charlatans" is 90% phoney; that's what everybody always says of someone he doesn't like. They said Hoxsey was a money-seeking charlatan, too, when he charged $400 for his cancer cure. Only Hoxsey was, in fact, a Texas oil millionaire, and he lost a couple of fortunes in his efforts to get the AMA to *at least test* his stuff. The AMA won; they got the FDA to condemn it, so they didn't have to test it at all! From the AMA viewpoint, that's a triumphal victory. Their intuitive decision was victorious because they avoided testing that conclusion.

Incidentally, on Hoxsey's treatment; I have not the slightest idea whether it cured cancer — but something everbody seemed to overlook in the heat of the debate was that *it cured morphine addiction!*

Anyhow — herewith some checks that will, I hope, stay with you this time!

As to further articles: how about a piece on the problem of total-annihilation of matter? I.e., if we had some contra-terrene hydrogen, for instance, and it reacted with ordinary hydrogen, we would *not* have a total-annihilation reaction. What would be left?

What prevents the total-annihilation reaction?

This has become of interest in connection with the "quasi-stellar objects" with their unaccountable enormous energy output, as you know.

Incidentally, if a 10^4 light-year diameter object pulses periodically with a 10 year period . . . is there an organizing signal or impulse that violates the assumption that no information can travel faster than light?

As of now, it looks as though the c limit is an open-ended question!

And notice that while gravity is held to be an extremely-weak interaction, it apparently has the ability to be the most powerful of all interactions! Also, if we rate "weakness" in terms of how long an interaction takes — final gravitational collapse appears to involve the shortest of all interaction times!

If a body went into final gravitational collapse, and collapsed itself out of the Universe, that would be a total-annihilation reaction. Would it also constitute a gravito-inertial shock-wave source (since the mass would vanish from the Universe both gravitically and inertially) capable of triggering collapses in other masses. . . ?

Regards, John W. Campbell

Frank Herbert   *March 25, 1964*

Dear Frank:

The rewrite pages on Maud'dib arrived; I think they make the time-vision proposition effective, and rational-sounding. They're O.K.

If you think about any further yarns involving Maud'dib and Alia . . . may I point out that, if the human race encounters an alien race that is *truly* alien, then even all the experience of all the possible lives of human beings (which help largely by making human experiences and human characters more understandable) wouldn't be too much help. Maud'dib would approach the Ultimate as a psychologist — but what would then be needed would be an "alienist" with a slightly different-from-the-usual meaning of that term!

Even the Spice and its time-vision properties, wouldn't help too much; it does you no good to see something, no matter how great the detail of the vision, if it is a thing you can't comprehend.

As an example of what I mean, I'm enclosing a picture that **Harry Stubbs ("Hal Clement")** sent me. He's a science teacher at Milton Academy, and has been working on this model for weeks; that's one of his daughters in the foreground.

The model is an atom-model of a tourmaline crystal. You are seeing in immense detail (about 100,000,000 times enlargement!) something that you could recognize as a minute chip of a crystal. But if you encountered this thing in a vision . . . could you comprehend what you were seeing?

Worse, suppose you were Benjamin Franklin, who knew nothing of atoms, molecules, bonding-energies, valence-bond angles, or interatomic spacings in Angstrom units, and were vouchsafed this dream of what a crystal was really like because you had been puzzling, working, and wondering about crystals. Think it would help any?

Tourmaline, incidentally, can be a pretty water-white crystal that looks as clear and simple as ice. *The Chemical Rubber Handbook* lists its chemical formula as:

$(H, Li, Na, K)_9Al_3(BOH)_2Si_4O_{19}(+Fe_2O_3, FeO, MgO, Mn)$

It crystalizes in a hexagonal pattern, and it's piezo-electric, double-refracting, and that innocent looking little clear crystal is one of the most complicated messes of chemistry, physics, and crystallography anyone would unhappily find himself stuck with.

Because of the wild variations of iron, magnesium and manganese, the colorless varieties are rare; it's usually anything from black through reds and greens to blue, and if there's enough manganese, it can be either pink or even wine-purple.

Think a spice-induced prescient vision would help much in understanding and working with (or against) that alien crystal?

Regards,　John

Arthur C. Clarke *April 13, 1964*

Dear Art:

The coincidence of Earth's Moon having the same angular diameter as the sun is a coincidence in several dimensions; not just in space, but also in time! It wasn't always that way — and it won't always be that way. The coincidence is multiplied when we consider that Man managed to come along just when that situation existed.

The business of the effects of Earth's Moon on life here becomes more and more interesting as electronic computer manipulated data overwhelms rooted objections of Science, and establishes as facts things Science has "long known for sure" were silly folk-superstitions . . . like the influence of the Moon on weather.

It's pretty solidly established now that the Moon does have profound effects. How, nobody knows — but the theory some Aussies had, that it influences micrometeor infall to Earth's upper atmosphere, and so influences raindrop-nucleation, seems out.

More complete analysis of southern hemisphere rainfall-vs-lunar-phase data shows that the effects in the southern hemisphere are just as pronounced as in the northern . . . but exactly reversed!

By the way, the influence doesn't tie in with the *phases* actually — but with more complex phenomena involving the draconitic (or nodal) month, and the anamolistic month as well. The lunar month, of course, is simple earth-sun-moon geometry; the draconitic and anamolistic months correspond more closely with sidereal time than with solar time. But they both undergo progressions due to tidal forces, and do *not* progress at the same rate.

Finally . . . dammit, I may miss you in New York! We're all set to take a vacation in the Scots Highlands, with some time in Northern Ireland and England, starting May 14! Hope you'll be here before then.

Regards,   John

R.C. FitzPatrick   *May 13, 1964*

Dear Mr. FitzPatrick:

This is a lovely story. I like it, and I want it — and if Doubleday will put up with something this strong, it'll almost certainly be in *Analog IV* or *Analog V*.

But . . . it comes back for cutting. I CAN'T use more than 18,000 words for the next year or so; I'm heavily loaded with novels, and when I run a 25,000 word serial installment, I can't run 23,000 words of novelette, too.

There are a number of places it can be cut; one I think might better be cut a bit, is the business about the body-without-a-mind type not losing anything. You referred earlier to the "sentient cemetery"; the body-without-a-mind is certainly that. Everything that makes that individual a human being is missing. We don't need to belabor the issue; just state it as a fact that such cases have nothing to lose.

There is, however, one very interesting class of exception to that — a very interesting class of "Which shall be considered the individual — the healthy body with a new mind, or the healthy mind with a new body?"

Consider the case of John Cabot Lodge Adams the VII, the descendant of great men, scion of generations of great families. Genetically, his line — his *lines!* — are Star Class lines. Genetically, he can be expected to father human beings of the highest type, and of the greatest value to the race. It's a consistent habit in all three of the great lines that produced him.

But young J.C.L. Adams VII, at age 6, was in an automobile

accident, and knocked unconscious. And it was an hour later they realized he wasn't just unconscious — he was in a coma, and a rapidly deepening one.

Yeah — hemorrhage of the brain. Emergency surgery helped — but not too much. The brain cells had been deprived of blood circulation for too long, and irreversible damage had already been done.

J.C.L. Adams VII, thereafter, was a healthy young vegetable. His personal, individual potential for achievement and happiness were irrelievably gone. Yet his genetic endowment *remained as great as ever*. He would, still, father great human beings . . . if he could somehow get a mate worthy of that genetic endowment. Which the living vegetable could not, of course.

Now remember; if that body were given a sound, effective brain, the children he fathered would be his parents' natural grandchildren — the body, not the mind, determines the character of the children.

So . . . where do we get a brain for him? And which set of parents will claim the resultant hybrid — the parents of the body, or the parents of the brain?

Now it should be perfectly possible to human emotional patterns to work out a brand-new type of emotional linkage — difficult, because it would be new, but possible because it is so closely parallel to one that is very old.

Which set of grandparents claims the grandchildren — the parents of the man or the parents of the woman? All children are hybrids. Inasmuch as two sets of grandparents can get along in mutual self-congratulaton over their mutual grandchildren . . . a similar emotional linkage should be possible (but with a lot of real, intellectual effort!) to the body-brain parents.

There's also the possibility that the brain comes from Bill Blow, hopelessly crippled at age 4 when Bob Blow, his father, came home soused to the gills, after being beat up and thrown out of a bar, and beat up his wife and son. Bob Blow is a 100% pure-quill slob. Mrs. Blow is a 100% hopeless nonentity; she isn't bad mainly because she hasn't the drive or personality enough to do anything bad.

Bill Blow was one of those statistical-run geniuses — a kid who, by a wild freak of luck — like throwing snake-eyes 12 times running with honest dice — got all the good genes either parent had, and, by sheer and improbable luck, none of the bad ones.

(It happens. How do you think Abe Lincoln managed to develop out of the parents he had?)

Now Bill Blow would, normally, have been fated to make a major success of his own life, and have the bitter disappointment of seeing his children turn out to be about 80% slobs and nonentities.

They'd revert to the genetic norm of his line; they wouldn't duplicate him.

The transfer now means that Bill Blow will grow up a major success (helped by the backing of the great Adams family) and will father children that equal or exceed his own personal high ability.

In other words . . . there's more than one class of problem going to be raised in the ethical-moral field by such a transfer you're discussing!

But this one's got to be cut down to a size I can shoehorn into that lead-tin-bismuth alloy jig-saw puzzle called *ANALOG*. You may think it's made of paper — but I know damn well the thing's made of cast metal, with all the rigidity of cast metal!

Regards,   John W. Campbell

H. Beam Piper   *June 15, 1964*

Dear Beam:

I'm just back from Scotland, where I've been having considerable fun learning the background of Scots history and mine own people. There was an ancestor of mine who, around 1750 or so, was residing with his parents in New Jersey, when an Indian raid on the town practically wiped it out. He saw his mother and father killed and scalped, and he was captured and carried off by the Indians.

Poor Indians! They didn't know Scots history. They'd never heard of the Massacre of Glen Coe. They didn't know why it was that when a Scots clan decided to wipe out a rival clan, they were careful to kill all the children, too.

Anyhow, my seven-year-old ancestor that night killed three of the Indian braves, and escaped. He devoted the next eighty years of his life to reducing the Indian population, achieving a personal score of confirmed killed-in-individual-encounters of 189 Indians.

Having learned something of Scots history, I can readily understand why the poor Indian didn't have a chance. The Indians were gentle flowers, nurtured in a warm, sunkissed land, compared with the bloody-minded, ferocious old bastitches of the Highlands!

They used those tartans in exactly the way the Indian used his blanket — only they used to sleep out in a Scotch winter in the Highlands — and be it remembered that Inverness, Scotland, is farther north than most of Hudson's Bay. In Edinburgh they have winter winds that made crossing the bridge from New Edinburgh to Old dangerous — it blew grown men off the bridge.

But for sheer bloody intransigence — remember that the Roman Legions, who weren't known for cowardice — took one look at the Highlands and built a wall to help keep those monsters out! The

Normans conquered England, walked all over the Irish . . . and politely asked permission to settle in Scotland.

Your true barbarian really acts on the idea of "Death Before Dishonor!" — but his idea of honor is sometimes a wee bit strange. It is utterly unmanly and disgraceful for a man to work for a living — death before such dishonor! But something like pulling a double-cross on his enemies . . . why, that's honorable, because it's sly, clever, smart — good generalship! Apparently the Massacre of Glen Coe represented something of that attitude; the MacDonalds called for peace talks, entertained the Campbells at a whisky-and-stolen-cattle banquet, but the Campbells sobered up quicker in the morning, and decided it was too good an opportunity to miss. "Oh, the Hatfields and McCoys, They was reckless Highland boys. . . !"

Anyway . . . it was a hell of a lot of fun, and I got some three hundred photographs of the damndest scenery you could hope to see. The clouds come in four layers; one sitting on the tops of the hills, and two that play hide-and-seek above that. Glen Coe, as we saw it, is a misty cleft where two mountain chains going at right angles had a crossing accident and got piled up in a sort of mountain scrap-heap. The clouds are gray and writhing and sit down on tops of the hills, so you can see only the lower half to two-thirds. Dozens of little mountain cascades tumble down every hillside, and the drizzle is almost continuous. The soil is barren, because all plant nutrients get leached out by the unending seepage of rain water.

Ben Nevis, highest peak in the British Isles, in under 5,000 feet — and snow-capped year-round because it's north enough to correspond with the northern part of Labrador.

And talk about "castles in Spain" — ! There are over *one thousand* castles in little Scotland, in varying states of bad repair. The number of ruined churches and cathedrals is somewhere near the same; man, those old Jacobites and Covenanters and assorted sects were *really* intransigent! They'd make the hard-boiled bunch you've got in this Hostigos business look like namby-pamby fairies by comparison. For sheer, simple-minded ferocity in pursuit of a Cause, I don't think any people ever exceeded them. They didn't destroy with a wild barbarian hurrah and whoopee; they weren't out for loot. They had a philosophical objection to the opposing Cause, and were with sober determination out to eliminate that evil.

T'anyhow — you might have fun with a people who had that sort of highly disciplined, and absolutely unswervable intransigence in your paratime stories. If they'd ever settled their differences at home, agreed on a True Philosophy, and set out to Enlighten the heathen in the rest of the world . . . God help the neighbors!

"Down Styphon!" come back for some minor revisions.

What you've done here is almost exactly parallel to the sort of thing we used to do in 1930-style science fiction, but in a different line. My early stories, for instance, were loaded with 500 words of action, 2,000 words of hypothetical technology, 500 words of action, 1,000 words of science, 500 words of action, 2,000 words of hypothesis . . . et cetera.

You've gotten somewhat of a similar effect with *military* technology that I was getting with *physics* technology.

The general staff scene (P. 16 et seq.) for instance puts over the information — but strictly as a Lecture on Military Tactical Problems by **H. Beam Piper**.

Vide lectures on physics by **John W. Campbell, Jr.**, in "Solarite," *Amazing Stories*, Circa 1931.

An alternative approach would be a scene where Kalvan is trying to get a Hostigos artisan to make one of the weapons he wants, with Chartigon along, and not being too sharp on catching the need for the new idea.

I know it's hard to see that that staff meeting is "a dry lecture by the author" when *you* know how important the data is to the story. Yeah . . . *you* do. But does the reader who wants a good old—fashioned swashbuckler? No, he does not. He resents your "stopping the story to spout hypothetical history."

Can something be done about this — and a couple of similar scenes — in this yarn?

Oh, another item for another story. During WWII, the Allies caused the death by starvation of several million Bengali. They needed air fields, military bases, barracks and roads built, and hired the Bengali men as laborers, paying high wages.

The result was that these Bengali's did not spend their time farming. They wound up with lots of money, and no food for love or money.

A really vicious little tactic to employ deliberately against a subsistence-level economy enemy, isn't it? You get your money back, of course, after you conquer the famine-decimated enemy country. And the roads you've had them build greatly ease your conquest . . . and bring in the food they're (literally!) dying to buy at inflated prices.

Not all practical and workable tactics are in the history books as such!

Regards,   John

Dear Ted:

Your letter was awaiting us when we got back from England —
we took off for Dublin May 14th, the day you sent the letter!

Sorry our timing was so far off.

Generally speaking, I prefer to have a vacation when I go on
vacation; science-fiction I get roughly 11.25 months/years, and
approximately 80 hrs./week during that period. However, I would
have been willing to cooperate on that radio program, if I'd known
about it in time. But it's the desire for some vacation that leads to
my *not* warning science-fictioneers in the areas where I'm
vacationing that I'm coming. We were in Dublin, Belfast, Glasgow,
Inverness and Edinburg (having changed our plans and decided
not to spend a couple days in Aberdeen!) but I did not alert local
science-fictioneers.

The trip was a huge success, incidentally. You may remember
that last May was Britain's warmest May in 116 years? We had
perfect weather for the entire trip; only one day of lowering, gray,
and grim skies — and that was the day we went through Glen Coe,
and up past Ben Nevis. And how *should* Glen Coe look? The
Kodachromes came out precisely perfect, just as the scene of a
massacre should be!

I can now understand why the Romans came up to the beginning
of the Highlands, took a good look around . . . and then built a
wall to keep those monsters out! Why the Normans, after
conquering England, and mopping up on the Irish . . . politely
asked permission of the Scots to settle in their country.

Migawd! Can you imagine trying to force a passage through
those barren highlands — when you couldn't possibly guess how
many men were watching from the clouds sitting down on every
surrounding hilltop? No wonder nobody ever seriously tried to
force the real Highlands! Actually, they'd be worse than the Swiss
Alps, even; they come naturally equipped with unlimited smoke
screening, as well as being effectively impassable to military
transport.

And we had just the guide-driver for the tour! A Captain
Chambers, recently of the Highlands Light Infantry, whose
Glaswegian burr was somewhat modified by Urdu, Malay, and
Hebrew. He not only knew (and loved!) Scotland, but had been
around enough to be able to give real perspective on the land.

Sorry I didn't get your letter in time; I honestly would have been
glad to help on that one-shot radio piece . . . just so it didn't
involve me in a science-fiction shemozzle!

So far as what I want for the magazine . . . it is, as usual, essentially impossible to define in positive terms; only negative terms are applicable. I *don't* want the sort of thing I've been getting, simply because that's now stale. That, I know, is no help — but if you can give me a positive definition of "Creativity," maybe I can then define what I want in positive terms.

One thing I can say; I want writers to tackle unexplored themes — the themes that *haven't* had nice, well-paved super-highway roads worked out, so the authors can happily roll along without picking his way. Unfortunately, the readers get bored, while the authors relax. It's sort of like qualifying for membership in the Explorer's Club; if you can get to a place by commercial transport, then going there doesn't qualify you for membership.

I'll tell you one thing I've observed with great interest. As you know, I've been asking for psi stories for some years — partly because that's an unexplored area. (Rocket ship interplanetary stories, atomic power stories, et cetera, were unexplored back in the late '20's and early '30's; those areas no longer qualify as pioneering areas!) In the course of the last couple years, I've found a pragmatic, observational pattern: authors who intellectually want to write a psi story *can not do it!* There's a powerful psychological bloc, apparently culturally installed, that stops them as solidly as a claustrophobe's psychological bloc stops him from going into a coal mine, however he may, intellectually, want to.

That is, they can write a story in which the villain uses psi successfully for evil ends, or one in which the hero uses psi with tragic results — but not one in which the hero successfully uses psi for constructive ends. Even so thoroughly competent and practiced an old-time professional as **Will Jenkins** was thrown by that bloc; he did one story in which the hero used psi successfully . . . but his plotting and writing of the piece contained egregious blunders that the average beginning writer would be expected to make, but not a polished veteran like **Will**!

It's become quite an interesting challenge to me; *why* can't creative and competent writers even *think* about successful and constructive use of psi?

Among the few who have been able to are **Randall Garrett**, of course, and "**Wally Bupp.**" It's really a very strange, and to me, fascinating thing that this pattern of blocking shows up!

Incidentally, they write *fantasy*, because that is, actually, a self-denying type of material — inherently it says "I know you don't believe this, and I don't believe it either, but we can have fun pretending." Science-fiction — to be good science-fiction — must not have that approach.

Broadly, what I want is exploration into areas that have not been adequately explored; psi is just one such area.

What I do NOT want is more-of-the-same story themes.

So far as lengths go — NOT — repeat *not!* — novels just now. I'm booked through 1965! Novelettes usually; at the moment I'm adequately supplied. Short stories — always! I'm never adequately supplied with those.

Articles I need continuously, but it's best if the author query me first. What I particularly want are the speculative pieces; the recent **Captain Kirton** piece on the orientation of the Earth and Solar System in space is one. The new piece on the origin of the planetary system that **Ben Bova** wrote up is typical of what I'd like — some damn good, sound, amateur speculation of an area where professional science is decidedly uncertain. **Ralph Hall's** pieces on meteor impact effects is another; that set of articles was strictly amateur speculation (**Ralph's** an M.D. practicing here in town; meteorics is strictly a hobby) but the articles are being cited in the professional literature quite widely now. Particularly **Ralph's** development of the phenomena of a major meteor impact; his point that the incoming planetoid causes immense X-radiation was one that the professionals had overlooked.

There's plenty of room for more such material — and I want to find it. Certainly England can supply more than one such man as **Captain Kirton**!

Regards,   John

James H. Schmitz   *August 10, 1964*

Dear Mr. Schmitz:

I'm taking "Goblin Night." It's a nice chase-suspense piece, which same I can usually use very happily, since too few of them show up!

And you have one veddy nice point in here; one that merits far more investigation and development elsewhere.

Your point about the spook having been evolved by Nature as a killer of prey — but that Chomir was developed by Man as a killer of *killers*. No wild carnivour attacks another carnivour under any ordinary conditions; a lion and a leopard will snarl at each other, and walk around each other . . . but not fight. Each is a butcher — and while the lion could certainly kill the leopard, the leopard would, in the process, so claw and chaw the lion that the lion's hunting efficiency would go way down — possibly long enough for the lion to starve to death. The skunk's weapon, you know, is not that the inerradicable stink seriously bothers the attacker — but that that inerradicable and exceedingly loud stink marks the attacking carnivour so flagrantly that *he can't catch his normal prey*.

434

Incidentally, the only carnivour that does attack and eat skunks is one that has no sense of smell, doesn't depend on odor as a guide, and whose prey won't be warned if he does stink. The owl!

There *are* a few killer-killers — the marten is one; he likes eating weasels. A wolverine is even deadlier.

But the major carnivours are not ordinarily killer-killers.

Remember **Will Jenkins'** story about the exploration team that consisted of three kodiak bears, mutated to be truly symbiotic with Man, as the dog is, and a tame eagle, used for aerial reconnaissance?

I suggest that a symbiotic kodiak bear, mutated further to be not only symbiotic, as is Chomir, but also to be a killer-killer, would be quite a helpful companion. Your spook, for instance, apparently weighed about 600 pounds; a kodiak weighs 2200.

If a lion is lucky, and catches a water-buffalo by surprise on the first whop, the lion can break his neck and kill him. If the water buffalo isn't surprised, and tightens his massive neck muscles, he simple gets his muzzle clawed open, a bad headache — and a dead lion. The buffalo can outrun the lion after the first 100 yards.

A kodiak, when he goes after a musk ox, doesn't surprise the beast. He swats the head completely off the body.

Make quite a protector, wouldn't he?

Regards,   John W. Campbell

Willy Ley   *October 7, 1964*

Dear Willy:

I think you've been so busy with the developments in rocketry that you haven't kept up with developments in astrophysics!

Your "Beyond the Solar System," with **Bonestell**, has some gorgeous paintings, you've done a grade A #1 job on the historical developments of astrophysics and cosmology . . . up to about 1940, but there have been some damned important developments since then — particularly since 1945 — that you sort of slighted.

Since WWII, two enormously important factors have come in; radio-astronomy and the studies of nucleogenesis. Radio-astronomy has been of immense importance in giving us detailed understanding of the structure of the Milky Way galaxy, while the nucleogenesis studies, aided as they have been by use-time on great electronic computers, have carried stellar dynamics enormously further than you acknowledge in the text.

For one thing, we now know that stars burn helium, after the hydrogen is pretty well used up. Remember that the low point on the packing-fraction curve of binding energy in nuclei comes at Fe^{56}; therefore helium nuclei can be fused to make elements up to Fe^{56} with release of energy.

The stumbling block had always been that the reaction $He^4 + He^4 \rightarrow Be^8$ was a wrong-way reaction; there was 18 Mev pushing it the other way. Be^8 has a half-life of about 10^{-18} secs, and so the nuclear physicists figured that you couldn't get He to fuse. But when they did some further computations (that's where the big electronic computers came into the picture!) they realized that at sufficient millions of degrees, and under sufficiently enormous pressures, the time between collisions of nuclei in a stellar core gets down to 10^{-23} secs — and in those terms 10^{-18} sec. is a long, long time, and plenty of collisions can occur. And while the $2He^4 \rightarrow Be^8$ won't go — $Be^8 + He^4 \rightarrow C^{12}$ does yield energy, and the resultant C^{12} won't break down. From there, He adds readily to give O^{16}, Ne^{20}, Mg^{24}, et cetera.

The result is that after hydrogen-burning dies down for lack of fuel, gravitational contraction of the stellar core boosts temperature and density to a point that He-burning sets in.

Current indications-beliefs are that all elements heavier than hydrogen have been produced in stellar cores, and have gotten into interstellar space as a result of supernova disruptions. That Population II old-original stars differ in large part because there wasn't any appreciable supply of elements above hydrogen when they formed — that they couldn't use the Solar Phoenix reaction because there wasn't any carbon until they made some!

Struve, who was largely responsible for the Epsilon Aurigae super-super giant belief had an article in *Sky & Telescope* about a year before he died, explaining how he came to that false conclusion. E. Aurigae A is a brilliant, very hot star, with a quite small and relatively dim invisible companion — both stars being deep in a gas-cloud, not unlike those much less dense gas cloud-auras surrounding various other binaries. There isn't any 2300 million mile diameter star, though.

And in the last eighteen months or so, work on the novas indicates that novas are sort of super-solar-flare events, afflicting one of an exceedingly-close binary pair, with large mass-transfer from one star to the other. It's not an explosion; novas are known to repeat the performance many times, which couldn't happen with a real explosion (such as the true stellar explosion of a super-nova).

And one of the most interesting things that's come up since 1945 is, I think, the realization that "spiral galaxies" *aren't* spiral at all! Since only the very abnormal super-giant stars — preferably super-giant blue-whites of the Rigel and S Doradus class — can be seen at all, even with a 200" telescope, at distances of a few million light-years, the only things we can *see* in any other galaxy will be the super-giants.

Super-giants, however, because of their extremely high mass, and the mass-luminosity law; consume their nuclear fuel in a very brief time — less than one Galactic Year. Rigel will be burned out long before it can make one swing around the galactic center. So will every other star we can see that's more than 1,000 light-years away! Only super-giants can be seen at such distances — and no super-giant can continue radiating for more than about 20,000,000 years — roughly one-tenth of the time it takes Sol to circle the galaxy.

Moreover, because of the great difference in orbital velocities around the galactic center required by Keplerian laws, if stars were arranged in a spiral-arm pattern now, within two galactic years the distribution would be so scrambled as to destroy all semblance of spiral distribution.

Therefore the spiral appearance is phony — it's not the structure of the galaxies, since 99.99% of the mass of all stars is in the stars as small and dim as, or smaller and dimmer than the Sun. Most of the mass of the galaxies, then, must be distributed in a quite uniform lenticular mass, without a trace of spiral structure.

Of course, the problem of what causes that spiral appearance then comes up and it's a dilly!

It's remarkably like the pattern of water droplets you'll see over a suburban lawn when the whirling lawn-sprinkler is at work on a summer day.

Regards,   John

Will F. Jenkins   *December 14, 1964*

Dear Will:

That ending you've got on the story (for God's sake leave out the treacle, incidentally!) won't stand up so good. If the boomerang blows the *Yarrow's* drive, then it would have burned it out first on every occasion it was tried.

Better change that item!

Suggestion as to why the boomeranger flubbed; the guy had computed the total energy his gadget had to be able to absorb, used a factor of safety of five, and built the contraption to stand that energy storage without failure.

However . . . inductors can run into very funny effects. You can store energy in an inductor as a magnetic field, lots of energy. That requires that such and such a current in amperes be flowing in so many turns around such a core permeability. So you design happily for the right number of turns and the right current-carrying capacity in the inductors.

Only if you hit that thing with a very small amount of energy as a very sharp pulse, it produces an instantaneous voltage in the kilovolt range — and *that* can puncture the insulation, causing the large gob of energy to short circuit through the fouled insulation!

A condenser energy storage device has an inverse problem. So it can handle *n* joules of energy, because it has a capacity of 10 farads at 100,000 volts rating. Only . . . if you connect a little 24 volt storage battery to it, the whole thing explodes. Reason: The surge of current into or out of the condenser amounts to thousands of amperes for the first microsecond — and that can burn out the lead-wires inside the condenser! Then of course the capacity of the condenser is only about a microfarad, and instead of getting 100,000 volts across it, the voltage tries to climb to 100,000 x 1,000,000 or so!

The error the inventor made, in other words, could be that he correctly calculated the equilibrium energy conditions — but forgot the transient inrush-outrush effects!

Final success was achieved when the *Yarrow's* engineer took thirty feet of heavy cable, wrapped it around an oil-drum full of iron ore, and stuck the cable in series with the energy-storage component of the gadget. That acted as enough of an inductance in the line to slow down the inrush-outrush to a point that the energy-storage gadget could swallow it without choking.

(Incidentally, it has to be rebuilt after each use — until they get something better made. The current through the cable is so violent the magnetic field crushes the ore-drum, and pinches the cables badly.) The process also *poufs* granulated iron-ore all over the engine-room.

Finally, I'm seeing **Bill Davis** shortly. I'll see what can be arranged there. He has research facilities available to do a real job of determining for a fact whether you're separating isotopes.

By the way, have you heard that they've got a new, highly useful (because perfectly non-contaminating) aqueous solution oxidizing agent of hitherto unknown oxidizing power? It's sodium perxenate — $NaXeO$!

There's a whole family of perxenates, nearly all very soluble in water, but perxenic acid, like perchloric acid, is too unstable to be isolated.

Regards,　John

Sam Moskowitz　　　　　　　　　　　　　　　*January 20, 1965*

Dear Sam:

I got a problem; maybe you and your photographically competent wife can help.

Dr. Jurgen vom Scheidt, of *Selecta*, a German medical

magazine, wants to run an article about industrial manipulators that **Bob Heinlein** predicted in "Waldo." He wants to reprint a picture of the original **Rogers** "Waldo" cover, and asks for a reprintable photograph.

Here comes the rub. You may have noticed that in our November 1964 issue, where we ran the story on Los Alamos' "Waldo," our shot of the original **Rogers** cover was somewhat blurred. Reason: our one available file copy is, unfortunately, one that had a slight off-register print of the cover!

My personal home file copy is in a bound volume — and can't be flattened out for photography.

So we don't have, and can't take, a good shot of the thing.

Do you folks have one?

Enclosed is a Xerox of **Dr. vom Scheidt's** letter.

I'd never have been able to transcribe that signature — it's worse than mine! — but **Jack Schoenherr** was in the office, and since he's German, I thought possibly he could read it.

He took one glance at it, and said, "Oh, that's **Jurgen vom Scheidt**."

"Are you sure that's it? How the hell can you read it?"

"Oh, yes — that's it. I've been corresponding with him for a couple years."

Ja . . . und *that's* how you read it.

Regards,   John

Joe Goodavage   *January 23, 1965*

Dear Joe:

Your wife called yesterday and gave me the news of where you're spending your time these days.

You remind me of my brother-in-law, who was an M.D. and shouldaknowed better; he got himself a jim-dandy heart attack by proving how strong he was — he lifted a motorboat engine (*not* an outboard!) into a truck all by himself. He just wouldn't accept the fact that an office-worker way of life does NOT mix with making like an athlete. An athlete has to train for hours per day every day; an office worker can't, and trying to catch up by overtraining on weekends is decidedly not equivalent.

A day laborer who hauls 100-pound cement bags around all day long as his way of earning his bread and butter is not an athlete — but he can, and does, all day long, something that's apt to be lethal for a 45-year-old man who's an office worker — which can be very annoying to the 45-year-old watching that scrawny little old 70-year-old laborer!

You're not an athlete; you decided that years ago, when you went in for writing instead of pushing with muscles as a way of earning a living. You made a decision as to which way you were going to expend your life-energies; trying to have both leads to life-bankruptcy just as trying to spend your financial income twice leads to bankruptcy.

Currently you're sort of "in receivership" as a result of pushing yourself too damn hard. Be it noted that the body and mind are an integrated team; hard pushing of purely mental-emotional nature can bring on physical collapse, too — and I know you well enough to know how you tend to push yourself at the mental-emotional level.

One of the things that's going to give you a rough time is the fact that you've never trained yourself on How To Slow Down, combined with the fact that an injured heart *does not feel sick*.

There's a reason for that. If your heart is able to circulate enough blood to keep the brain and body tissues adequately supplied with oxygen, you do not feel sick or weak; if it isn't able to, you don't feel . . . not for very long. Result: you won't feel sick so long as you lie down, take it easy, and rest. Push yourself, drive yourself to get up and start going, though . . . and you don't *feel* sick. But the blow-out patches your body's been putting in to hold things together while a full repair job gets done — blow out.

You're stuck with something you bought and paid for — you pushed too hard, for reasons that seemed good and right. Sorry; they were evidently mistakes.

Older people, oddly enough, have a somewhat better record of recoveries from heart attacks. Reason: an older man has had time to *learn* to back off and take it easy. Young men tend to think the only way they can live is under full steam ahead, and are unwilling to learn a new way. Being stupid — i.e., failing to learn — in this situation is a no-kidding killer.

What you're up against is simple enough; you've got a damaged muscle. The muscle happens to be in your heart instead of in your arm or leg; the situation is basically similar. A torn muscle does *not* get healed by excercise. It gets healed by rest, and allowing the muscle tissues to regrow. *After it's healed*, the muscle is weak from lack of exercise, and *then but not before*, a very damn careful program of mild, and gradually increasing exercise will rebuild it to full original strength.

The nice thing about muscle tissues is that they *do* regrow. Nerve tissue, for instance, doesn't; damage a nerve and you've had it.

BUT . . . if you don't rest, and give the damaged muscle a chance to heal before trying to force it to regain strength, your friends will be saying, "Joe was a real nice guy, wasn't he?"

You are, as of now, dealing with the Real McCoy, no kidding, sink or swim hard facts. You can't kid the physiological facts; you can't argue them out of their nature, and you can't persuade them to let it go this time. Like the buck private being given orders by the General, you say, "Yes, Sir" and "No, Sir, I won't Sir!," and carry it out smart and snappy. In this case, the general involved is General Circulatory Failure. And that General happens to be a real martinet; perfectly reasonable — you can work with him all right — provided you learn to take orders without trying to debate his reasons for 'em. Otherwise he's got extreme powers, without need for a Court Martial.

One of your problems stems from the evolutionary process of Man. You know, the brain has no sense of pain whatever. The scalp does, the skull bones do, but once you cut through those, the brain has no pain sense whatever.

Reason's simple; in evolution, any organism that had its scalp and skull breached, and the brain exposed, was a dead duck anyway. No point in setting up an alarm system at *that* stage! It'd be about as useful as setting up a Raid Warning system that was triggered into action only if it was hit by an atomic bomb. By the time that came along, there wouldn't be any need for a warning siren.

The heart's a good bit that way; it is very poorly supplied with pain nerves. In the history of evolving life forms, an animal with a mild heart lesion was just as thoroughly dead as one with a Complete Bust. Reason: if you, now, had to run to escape a pursuing wolf — you wouldn't. If you had to be the pursuing wolf to catch your dinner or starve . . . you'd either starve to death or drop dead.

So, in evolution, what's the use of having a pain system that tells the animal his heart's in trouble?

Only since medicine came along, and a man *could* lie down, rest, and give his heart a chance first to heal, then to regrow, has there been any possible use for a heart's-in-trouble warning system.

Unfortunately, this is now a handicap; if you had such a system, it'd be telling you to take it easy, as the bone's-in-trouble system does if you have a broken bone.

As it is, you're going to have to rely on an external information system — the doctor, his stethoscope, special training, and his EKG. The internal warning trouble of the bone's-in-trouble type has a huge advantage; you *can't* ignore its warnings. Whether you believe them or not has nothing to do with it; it hurts like hell, and you stop doing what you shouldn't.

Unfortunately, the doctor can't have such a direct and effective communication system.

And, as I said, one of the problems younger men have with these things is that they simply won't believe that they *have* to slow down.

Comes to a very simple question: Are you going to be smart, and learn a new way of living, or die of stupidity?

Suppose a five year old kid has a heart attack. You can understand that the first necessity is to make the kid slow down, stop trying to run everywhere he goes, instead of walking, stop trying to climb all the trees in sight, stop chasing the dog around the yard — stop all the things that have been his way of life.

What chance do you think you'd have of getting a five-year-old to understand the necessity of slowing down for six months or so?

Children almost never survive a heart attack.

You've got all the immense advantages of physiological youth to help you heal.

Eisenhower — Johnson — both had serious heart attacks; both recovered, even though they were already old men, with an old man's much lower healing abilities. BUT . . . with an older man's ability to accept a hard and unpleasant fact — the need for changing their way of living.

Miss Tarrant had a bad attack, you know; took her six months to get back to work.

My wife had a light attack; she changed her ways and recovered so there isn't a trace of it now.

Really rest, and the damage can heal. Then accept that you decided, some years ago, to be a typewriter jockey, not an athlete — and accept the *full* consequences of that decision.

Incidentally, after your wife told me you'd been clobbered, I was darned curious and asked my friend **Ralph Hall** about how come your doc hasn't spotted the trouble after your first attack — how come the EKG test then didn't show it.

Answer: The Electrocardiograph records electrical pulses due to heart-muscle action — but it has to pick them up through skin, subcutaneous fat, the rib cage, the pericardium, etc., and the voltages are pretty darned small to begin with.

The voltages it can detect, are all those on the *front* surface of the heart. The *rear* parts of the heart can't be picked up; there's all the lungs, the heavy back muscles, the spine, etc., between the heart-backside and the skin of the back.

The result is that an EKG can't detect what's going on at the rear of the heart. You can have a fairly serious damage at the back of the heart, and the EKG won't detect a thing — because there *isn't* anything wrong with the front of the heart. Like a guy could have the back of his head stove in with a baseball bat, but a full-face photograph wouldn't show a thing wrong with him, except he looked sorta dead.

(Incidentally, an electrocardiograph is an EKG because es war ein Deutscher was introduced the gimmick, and *he* called it, of course, an elektrokardiograf.)

However, and here we're lucky, damage to the posterior parts of the heart are less apt to be deadly serious.

Presumably, then, your infarct (where they got *that* term from it I don't know!) is on the more repairable, but less detectable, backside of the heart.

Joe — for Pete's sake, grow up! You've got to, right now, or you won't have time to. Don't be like the five-year-old; learn that you *need* to rest that muscle. The fact that evolution didn't provide us with a heart's-in-trouble warning system makes it impossible to save a child who can't understand.

You can understand — if you can remember, and abide by that understanding, and accept the need to adopt a new way of life.

Temporarily, you're 90 years old — and you'd damn well [better] act like a 90-year-older.

Do so, and you can lose about 10 years per month; in six months, you can be back to 30.

But when you do get back to 30 — remember, dammit, that you made a choice years ago. You're a typewriter jockey — not an athlete. "Keeping in shape" to be a typewriter jockey is *not* the same thing as "keeping in shape" for the mile run, or the Olympics Gymnastic Team. Wisdom is doing what's appropriate — not being able to do anything and everything!

Good luck!   John

Bill Powers   *February 15, 1965*

Dear Bill:

Yes — long lost! As you know by now, **Groff Conklin** was looking for you, and couldn't find you. He tried the addresses we had on hand, and since you'd moved-leaving-no-forwarding-address, he didn't connect. I couldn't find just what your University connection was in the file, and couldn't be sure of my memory . . . so I used the system we've used several times before.

And with your name, some such remark about the Mystic Powers was inevitable!

I'm *badly* in need of good articles — and you've got material that would be perfectly lovely, if you could take time to write up something. I've seen a report in *Sky & Telescope* about some of the things that TV-cum-telescoptics can do; I'd love to have a piece on speculations as to the space-future of such things.

F'R'instance: You can't do positional astronomy with the TV system; can you do spectroscopy? What can you — and what can't you — do with those image orthicon systems? Can you, for instance, use a 5000X optical enlargement, and then scan the resultant image of, say, the Andromeda nebula?

I tried to get an argument-discussion going a year or so ago on what sort of space-observatory would be most useful to Man, if we could put what we wanted anywhere in the Solar System . . . only nobody contributed anything.

I'd be more interested in what the 30th magnitude would show us within 5 light-years of Sol than in the 30th mag as related to clusters of galaxies. We *don't* have any idea of the actual nature of the population of space. In Andromeda, for instance, we see only the stars of Rigel's class; not only Sol would be invisible, but even Sirius and Vega. Beta Centarus, but not Alpha. Canopus, yes . . . but how many of our familiar night-sky stars could be seen with our scopes at Andromeda's distance. The "spiral galaxies" certainly aren't spirals; we just can't see the real mass of the galaxies.

And . . . if there's a 20th magnitude barely-luminous red-sub-dwarf only 1.5 light years from Sol, how could we detect it?

Suppose we could detect all masses = to or > Mars, say, within 5 light-years of Sol — what would we find? Could be that planets, "cold stones," vastly outnumber stars, and constitute 75% of the mass of the galaxy! This could be determined only if we could find everything within nearby space.

There's evidence (Pluto's orbit, retrograde satellites of Jupiter, et cetera) that sometimes something interferes with the smooth operation of a solar system. If there are enormous numbers of planetary-magnitude masses out there. . . .

Suppose the Solar System did have a loose planet sweep through. Say a planet of Earth's size. The probability that it'd come in in the plane of the eclipitic is vanishingly small; if it came in at, say 60° to the plane, and never came closer to Sol than 10 AU . . . what's the chance it would pass through the system without being detected at all?

There's a hell of a lot of fascinating material about nearby interstellar space — what we might call cis-Alpha space — that I've never seen discussed, and that could make a whole series of fascinating articles.

Incidentally, my home address is 1457 Orchard Road, Mountainside, N.J.

As to the digest-size *Analog*.

Yes, it's a defeat — we wanted to put over the idea that *Analog* is a medium of communication worthy of industry support. This we didn't achieve. And several damn good men, and a lot of very good money, tried hard.

Part of our trouble was that we were too honest with our statistical survey. Normally, in a 90,000 unit "universe," a 1,000 unit sample would give adequate confidence in analysis. But *Analog's* readers have so keen a personal interest in it that we didn't get the normal sort of response; we got a damn-near 10% response! That's no statistical sampling number!

Moreover, they came in from the damndest places. Afghanistan—Ghana—Bangkok—Antarctica . . . you know the sort of places our readers get to! Translate some of the APO addresses the thing looks even sillier.

Moreover we sell more copies in Huntsville, Alabama, alone than in all New England North of Boston. Coca Beach takes more copies than St. Louis. Los Alamos outdraws five southern states combined.

The average income figures, and educational level figures, showed *Analog* was a markedly better market than the *New Yorker*. The cards showed four times as many corporation presidents and vice-presidents as janitors!

The statistics were so good that none of the media people could believe that there wasn't something extremely funny behind them. If we hoaxed down the statistics to make them believable, they'd have caught us hoaxing the figures.

One factor I did not mention in that editorial; we did not gain circulation when we went to the large size! We *lost* a little!

This, remember, is Show Business — and there's no business like Show Business. Trying to guess which way the audience is going to jump is markedly more wildly impossible than trying to guess which way the stock market is going to go.

Your suggestion of having the readers write to companies that won't accept our statistics, and won't take ads, is a nice idea technically, but runs into a red-hot booby trap in human psychology.

If you want to make an enemy of an executive — tell him he's using poor judgment . . . and then prove it to him.

The VP in charge of advertising for the Nicad Battery Co. flatly refused to take an ad in that issue in which I ran the article on Ni-Cd batteries, and gratuitously said that he'd certainly have nothing to do with any silly science-fiction magazine. We explained why he was wrong in his attitude.

As a direct result of that article, the chief engineer of a major tractor company that they'd been trying to contact for years wrote them and told them to send their sales engineer. It brought them a $250,000 a year order. One of the BIG space research outfits asked them to bid on a battery-bank to supply 50 megawatt pulses, either as 10,000 amps at 5000 V or as 5000 amps at 10,000 V for 30 secs to

1 min. (It seems the local power company went into hysterical screaming at the suggestion of putting that load on their power lines. All their voltage-regulation equipment started chattering and hurting at the mention of it, and their substation transformers started quivering on their bed-bolts.)

The order amounted to about 1.5 megabucks.

Result: we made a firm enemy for life.

There *are* problems, **Bill**!

Sincerely, John

Larry Niven *April 5, 1965*

Dear Mr. Niven:

You shlipped on my major point about the flashlight-"bomb." I said my flashgun puts out a quarter million watts for half a millisecond. "Watts" is a measure of *rate* of energy expenditure; watt-seconds, watt-hours, or kilowatt-hours are a measure of amount of energy.

Now a standard flashlight cell stores about 5 ampere hours at 1.5 volts; that's 7.5 watt-hours. It makes no difference whether you withdraw that at a rate of 1 milliampere for 7,500 hours, or, using your time-accelerator, withdraw all of it in one microsecond; it's still 7.5 watt-hours.

Now 7.5 watt-hours represents a quantity of energy sufficient to melt a couple of good sized nails, if you could release it in a single millisecond. But it won't melt girders, even if you release it in a picosecond. (One millionth of a microsecond.) That isn't a matter of *rate* but of *quantity*.

What you're saying is, "I know ordinarily this match here wouldn't melt a bank-vault door into a puddle of steel, but I'm going to burn it in a millionth of a second, so it will."

Nope. It won't.

Re Peterfi's shoes. The push comes from inside the field; it is due to gravity, which (by hypothesis) is not affected, and acts on the soles of the shoes which are outside the field.

O.K. — the soles are outside, and act normally. The gravity, although it's inside, *also acts normally and only normally.* Conclusion: the shoes, acted on normally, fall normally.

Want a real weirdo murder gimmick? Much further-out than potassium chloride — and I mean *really indetectable*. The rare gas xenon (used in photoflash tubes) is chemically almost totally inert — there is no chemical test for it. It also happens, for reasons known solely to God, to be a powerful and effective anesthetic. Drowning a man in xenon gas might be a bit expensive, but he'd die perfectly peacefully, and there wouldn't be anything they could possibly detect a few hours later. (It'd diffuse away.) And they'd never look for it anyway. If they made an immediate check, using a mass spectroscope, adjusted just right, they could detect an abnormal concentration of xenon . . . so who'd look?

Sincerely,   John W. Campbell

George O. Smith   *May 10, 1965*

Dear Mr. Smith:

I believe I said that xenon was "for reasons known only to God" an anaesthetic. This Universe is so constructed that things don't have to have human permission to be true; in the case of xenon-anaesthesia, nobody seems to have the foggiest notion *why* it's an anaesthetic, or how the damn stuff works. It just does.

One of my largest gripes about Science and the attitude of modern Scientists is that they forget, deny, reject, and refuse the simple fact that we're ignorant. Our science is about three centuries old, and to equate "we don't understand how such a thing could be" with "it is impossible" is decidedly arrogant stupidity.

Helium is not an anaesthetic, of course. We don't know why it isn't, any more than we know why xenon is — we simply have experimental-observational evidence that it is *not*, and xenon *is*.

Possible explanations center around the fact that xenon's electronic structure is — as is true for all inert gases — a completely balanced, filled-ring structure — but that the outermost ring is so far removed from the xenon nucleus, and shielded by so many shells of inner orbitals that the xenon nucleus' hold on the outermost electrons is relatively weak. Something like fluorine, with an aching void in its second electron ring, and only one inner orbital layer (with a mere two electrons) to shield the nucleus, can trap a xenon atom by its terrific pull on those outer electrons.

Actually, the chemistry of xenon resembles that of iodine to a considerable extent — and in some respects resembles that of the Group VIII metals like Pt, Ir and Os. Xenon forms oxides, as well as fluorides, and sodium perxenate — $NaXeO_4$ — corresponding to $NaIO_4$ — is stable in water solution. Oxygen is only one small step behind fluorine in its hunger for extra electrons; apparently it can trap xenon atoms also.

Perhaps the xenon-anaethesia effect comes from some interaction between xenon and oxygen in some necessary nervous-system biochemical mechanism, where the binding is just great enough to depress results, but not great enough, or permanent enough, to do any lasting damage.

Incidentally, the anaesthetic effect was discovered about twenty years ago, long before XeF_4 and XeF_6 were discovered.

I'm not just guessing, incidentally — it was well reported in medical literature at that time. Maybe you can find a local M.D. who can sic you on the right reference if you want it.

XeF_4 and XeF_6 are both useful as of now, on small-scale problems — they make terrific fluorinating agents for synthesizing desired fluoride compounds. Small scale only, because of the extremely high price of xenon. Their advantage over other fluorinating agents: the reaction byproduct is xenon — an inert gas that leaves the product 100% pure! OF_2 is a good fluorinating agent, of course, but somehow the product is always contaminated with undesired oxides!

We're planning on going to London this fall; I on business for Conde' Nast, **Peg** on business for her American Crewel Studio. We're also going to do some visiting through Scotland, so we won't be going *auf Deutschland*.

Re "The Three Bares" you sent. You don't appreciate the subtleties of English, including its possibilities for expansion and development, particularly into the multi-pathed fields of technicalese. "Named" means like Tom, Dick, Mary, Hepsehbah; "called" means like "tree," "goat," "sequoia gigantea." "Nomenclatured" refers to pure technicalese classification-designations like *rheology, bootstraps circuit,* or *spectroheliokinematograph.* If you refer to the latter item as "a movie camera taking pictures of the Sun in monochromatic light," then you've *called* it. If you refer to the contraption as "That blasted Ermentrude's on the blink again, dammit!", then you've *named* it.

"Nomenclatured" refers to a designation understandable only to fellow members of the esoteric cult concerned.

English is a wonderful language. Anybody who figures out how it works will be even more wonderful, too.

Regards,   John W. Campbell

Robert S. Richardson   *May 12, 1965*

Dear Mr. Richardson:

In connection with a story **Poul Anderson's** working on, I just had a five-letter argument-by-mail with him about how a rocket ship can, and can not, be trapped in an orbit about a gravitating body.

Out of this came the following point:

A ship in a highly elliptical orbit about a body, by firing its rocket tangentially, can change the periastron, but not the apastron, until the orbit becomes circular. Then both apastron and periastron increase together under tangential acceleration.

But acceleration applied radially can change the apastron,

without affecting the periastron, until the two become equal (at the periastron distance.)

Dammit, so little work has been published on capture mechanics that somebody ought to do a basic analysis of the problem! In this days of space exploration, the Air Force or somebody ought to be interested in the thing.

Who do you think might be sufficiently interested in such work that I could spur him on to doing something about it? You must know enough of the Fraternity to know someone — perhaps some one with graduate students looking for a good project.

It ought to be a good, clean piece of work to lay out the ground rules on the thing, anyway! Specific solutions not required — just the limits of the parameters.

F'r'instance; *if* there is a quantity of space-gravel orbiting Earth in a Lunar-Trojan position, it would be most interesting to the astronautics boys. Come ion jet engines, which we are approaching, reaction mass available in space — essentially already free of Earth's gravity-well — would be worth about $10,000 a pound. That being approximately what it costs to get a pound out 238,000 miles. Since the Trojan-position gravel would also be out of Luna's gravity-well, it would be better by far than Luna rock.

Question: Is there any?

One approach would be to work out the conditions-of-capture, and then see if the Earth-Moon system could capture stuff, and under what conditions, into that Trojan position.

Stuff splashed off the Moon by major meteor impact might well wind up there.

If it is there — planting a claim on that rock-pile would be just about as valuable as planting a claim on the Moon itself! Think how handy a few thousand tons of reaction mass already 200,000-plus miles from Earth would be for Mars, Jupiter, and beyond would be!

Regards,   John W. Campbell

John T. Phillifent   *July 21, 1965*

Dear Mr. Phillifent:

Be happy to argue the matter of Q-men with you. I can't use the story, not because I don't believe in the Q-men, but because, having stated a position in the editorial I mentioned, you'd *have* to defend your thesis, and at length, in any story flatly contradicting so recent an editorial!

I've seen FBI photographs showing what a Magnum pistol can do to a standard automobile engine; it can shoot through it. The

449

gimmick with the water-barrel is that water — any fluid — traps an ungodly amount of energy when a shock-wave hits it and tries to plow through. It robs energy from the bullet at a fantastic rate, and slows the thing to subsonic speed in a matter of a couple of inches. Then the remaining speed is damped out plowing through another 18 inches of water. But — *it takes a couple of inches.* The total thickness of steel involved in penetrating an engine is actually only about .75"! And that's not steel, but a malleable iron casting.

A meteor, coming into Earth at 70 kilometers/sec usually gets stopped in the extremely thin upper atmosphere 30-50 miles up. Big ones — 1,000 tons and up—make it through the air, but even 50-70 k.p.s. gets stopped in about 2 x the diameter of the impacting meteor.

The Spaniards, it's said, conquered the Aztecs partly because they came in wearing steel armor against which Aztec weapons were futile. Fact: the Spaniards turned in their boiler-plate for Aztec-made cotton-padding armor. An equal weight of cotton-felt quilted armor has *more* resistance than steel. *Distance* counts; the water-barrel gimmick allows the bullet stopping distance, which thin malleable-iron sections don't.

Your Q-man might get away with pretending to be a man so long as he made like a robed Monk (or a Nun), but in a swimming suit. . . ? Don't be silly! You couldn't fool a 5-year-old with a rubber doll's smooth, muscle-less arms and legs! You don't consciously notice things when they're there-where-they-ought-to-be — a man can sleep next to the elevated railroad tracks, with trains roaring by 15 feet outside his open window. And he'll wake up with a feeling of danger-mystery-wrongness if the city suddenly quietens completely. We evolved in a jungle, where you stayed alive if you noticed that-which-shouldn't-be and also very particularly noticed that-which-should-be-and-wasn't. I.e., the bush that is *not* waving in the breeze, as all the others are, probably conceals a pouncing carnivore. A "man" whose muscles don't move under his skin would be perfectly certain to set off all the screaming alarms that a hundred million years of evolution have most carefully bred into our nervous systems.

Nature is a great believer in the Least Effort Solution to problems; she doesn't go in for wasteful use of material, nor unnecessary multiplication of sensor units. You may not be conscious of it, but one of the ways you avoid getting burned is by reason of your radiant-heat sensors. The reason we have hair all over our bodies, despite having lost all our fur, is that the guard-hairs we have left are immensely valuable extremely-low-pressure tactile sensors. There's a beautiful set of tonimetric sensors in every joint. That's a major reason you can stand upright with your eyes closed, and your head cocked to one side.

We're so used to the proposition that metals are strong, and flesh and bone are weak that we accept it without adequately questioning. Only recently *Scientific American* carried an article on the strength of materials — the strengths of metal whiskers, and other crystals.

Surprising to me at least, the strongest of all metals turns out to be — iridium! It's ultimate strength comes out some ten times the strength of pure iron whiskers! Second strongest, right up near iridium, is beryllium. And stronger than any metal, putting all of them to shame by a wide margin, is one of the weaker "ceramic" materials — graphite!

Now iron is readily reduced to metal by life processes; so are manganese, nickel, vanadium, and most of the more important steel alloying elements. If living cells wanted to use iron or steel, they have plenty of chemical ability to do so. There are lots of simple bacteria that can release hydrogen from water; that takes more energy-potential than freeing iron.

No life form uses iron skeletal structures; they all use what are now being called "ceramic" materials . . . because they're stronger than any metal, we now (several hundred million years later, they find it!) discover.

Re speed of nerve impulse transmission.

Work **Dr. Batteau** and a group of his friends have been doing has developed strong indication that the actual nerve impulses are not electrochemical as has been thought — but are in fact *lasers*. That the nerves are "light pipes," with laser action to amplify the photons being piped along. The electro-chemical action detected by instruments aren't the nerve-impulses themselves — they're the electrochemical reactions used to "pump" the lasers after they've sent the impulse!

The animal nervous system works "in real time" as the cybernetics boys put it; they're concerned with manipulating mechanical "read-out" devices called arms and legs and paws and teeth. There has been no point whatever in having microsecond computer circuits in that work; the super-high-speed computers we've built have all been stymied by the fact that they can compute about 10^8 times as fast as they can read-in from tape, punched cards, et cetera, or read-out via typewriters, light-beam-photography, et cetera. MIT has a computer setup now with over 100 input-output stations; it's a "time-sharing" computer, which means that it can — and does — work on 100 questions and answers simultaneously. Simple: it takes a human questioner 30 seconds to type in his query; the computer can read it in less than a microsecond. That means that a one-unit computer is sitting there doing absolutely nothing for 29,999,999 microseconds waiting for the human being to get his message finished. Then it computes the answer, and starts typing it out. But a typewriter key can't make the journey from rest up to the platen and back out of the way in less than about 300,000 microseconds. This means that to print one 10-digit number the computer's tied up for 3,000,000 microseconds.

So the time-sharing job reads in the information at microsecond speed, computes the answer, transfers it to an electronic "prompt memory" system, which in turn spends many millions of microseconds instructing a typewriter how to print it out — while the computer has worked out four or five other problems, waiting for the first type-key to make that long, slooooow journey from rest to platen and back.

So — what good is that sort of computer-speed to a living animal? To have it would be a waste of effort.

And they've recently found what that "unused 80% of the human brain" was there for. It's no wonder they never could spot its function! It's devoted to the Maintenance and Repair department. A very stupid system can build a complex unit from filtered raw materials; the intelligence-level of the system that can *repair* that unit when something goes wrong is enormously — incredibly — greater.

Do NOT underrate what the living organisms have accomplished!

Re "poor engineering" design of animal joints. I suggest you go back and start over — let's see you design a jointing structure with the immense strength, small size and light weight with extreme mobility we have in our joints, plus the requirement that it be possible to service and maintain it through continuous internal tubes. (No animal uses the wheel; a rotating joint can't be serviced and repaired.) Sure they're engineering nightmares — the design is nightmarish because the demands imposed by the function of the organism are horrendous. Carrying the immense loads imposed on the hip-joint around a 45° offset is an engineer's nightmare right there. But if you don't, you wind up with walking like an alligator or crocodile-waddle instead of walk. There's got to be room, between the thighs, for the powerful muscle-engines needed to operate the legs.

As to the lubrication system that breaks down if the joint isn't used and allows the joint to fuse. Look, animals didn't evolve with orthopedic hospitals to heal their injuries; they fixed it themselves, or they died. If a joint isn't moved for weeks on end — it means that limb has had a drastic injury that *can't* be healed. The best that can be done for the organism then is to fuse the joint so that the limb will at least be usable as a sort of built-in peg-leg.

452

You call that bad engineering?

Surgeons perform operations now to induce fusion of joints for exactly that sort of reason; a friend of mine has a fused knee joint, surgically produced, because in a glider crash the nerve-trunk activating the muscles was destroyed.

Animal mechanisms evolved as part of the total animal and its way of life; engineers forget that! For instance, a horse with a broken leg had to be shot — but a dog didn't. Why not?

Because a horse won't keep his weight off a broken leg. A dog does so instinctively. A cow, deer, rabbit, et cetera won't either; a cat will. Reason: A horse — or deer — is a cursorial herbivore, whose only defense is speed and running. Slow him down, and he's dead anyway. No use trying to hobble on three legs; he won't live long enough to heal. No evolutionary advantage to having a don't-use-a-broken-leg instinct. But for a powerful carnivore, there is a chance to survive long enough for the leg to heal.

They can save horses with broken legs now, by using the Stader splint — a powerful metal gadget that can hold the bones aligned, even though the fool beast won't keep his weight off of it. He still has to be locked in a tight box stall, though, so he won't try to run on it.

Re inconsistency: By definition, logic is essentially synonymous with consistency. A "Reductio ad absurdum" proof is simply a proof that a proposed statement is inconsistent with itself. It is possible to predict any possible *logical* conclusion from a given set of postulates (data), though you may never have developed a particular chain of logical steps. But you *could* have reached the same logical conclusion.

But you can't predict what conclusions will be reached if a random, nonlogical factor is thrown in. That's what keeps 'em coming back to roulette.

Logic operates *from* postulates; an intelligent entity can generate postulates — which, as any logician can assure you, *can not be done by any logical process.* But an entity operating from an unknown-to-you postulate can, and will, reach conclusions that you know are logically impossible. (They are — to you!)

As to clearing out a man's torso and making room for machinery. Go ahead — and let's see you get machinery capable of powering just ten fingers with all their motions into a cavity with about one cubic foot volume. With the requirement that said powered fingers be capable of exerting the hundred-pound forces human fingers can. (And that's just a normal man under normal daily efforts. I've seen a man bend a U.S. half-dollar coin double between thumb and two fingers. And a violinist hold a billiard cue out horizontal, putting the *small* end of the cue between two adjacent fingers of his left hand. Chinese dentists, for centuries, pulled teeth with their fingers.)

If you can get enough motors for all the different motions, plus the necessary feed-back sensor devices, into that cubic foot hollowed out of the torso — now reduce it to two packages and slip it into the two forearms.

Go on! This I wanna see!

Of course, that leaves the problem of the wrist and elbow motors. I've got some arthritis in my right wrist now, which slows me down a bit, but I don't have so much trouble with ¼ inch steel bolts any more. I used to get too enthusiastic and twist them off with the screw-driver. Had trouble tying up packages with clothesline, too; the darned stuff was so fragile. The modern nylon cord is easier to work with; it doesn't break every time you try to pull it tight.

Look — I used to break clothesline by wrapping it tight around my forearm, with all muscles relaxed, and then just clenching my finger muscles.

Man, human tissues are not weak — steel and plastics are!

Regards,   John W. Campbell

E. C. Tubb   *July 21, 1965*

Dear Mr. Tubb:

I regret I've got to say "No" on this one; it's a genuinely good novel. Trouble is, it just isn't magazine-serial material, though it's first-rate, leisurely-reading book material.

You've done a neat job of showing many different sides of the culture you've imagined — and imagined an extremely colorful one. The only vaguely similar theme I've seen is one **Beam Piper** did years ago; in his culture of people who all accepted reincarnation, the major factionalism was whether reincarnation was volitional (chosen by the discarnate mind) or random (involuntary reincarnation).

Both you and **Beam Piper** agreed on one point a lot of authors have overlooked completely; a thing doesn't have to be true, or provable, in order to be the major motivating force of a culture.

You came near, in this one, developing a novel theme I've been trying to get someone to do — not a story idea, but an idea about story-telling.

The standard novel is supposed to present a character with a philosophy, and, as the reader follows the character through the experience of the story, show how that philosophy is changed — how he grows in wisdom. (And, we hope, the reader does likewise!)

A variant I've been trying to get someone to play around with:

Two characters are presented, B and G. B is a Bad Man by all the standard cultural postulates of here-now. He says he thinks there are times when slavery's a good idea, that he thinks assassination is a sound practical solution to some situations, that robbery, murder, et cetera, all have their proper place. I.e., he's apparently an amoral bastitch. G on the other hand clearly states his ideals, and he is obviously a Good Man.

So both men are on a barbarian-level planet, and in trouble. In the course of the story, G gets into more trouble; he's captured by the natives, who are preparing to boil him in the local equivalent of oil, when B rides up with twenty slaves and gets him loose. Next, G's in hot water again, because he's offended the local Caligula-type tyrant . . . when the local Caligula-type is assassinated by a Minion of B's to the great relief of the populace — and G.

In other words, a string of experience in which G's neck is saved by the grace of B's pragmatic recognition of what the local culture is, and needs, and how to achieve some useful reforms.

And so the story winds up . . . with G being the same nut-headed, stupid, intransigent believer in Only One Way To Do Things he started out — and B being just as "bad" as he started out. Neither character has changed a bit.

But by this time, the reader has!

I thought for a bit that you were going to pull this with Carl, when he showed up with a gang of Hunters. Brand *was* being stupid; he did *not* adapt, or accept the real and solid virtues of the culture.

Incidentally — you've got one high-power inconsistency in the setup. If murder is so utterly despised, and so violently punished . . . the chases wouldn't be tolerated. Or, if they were tolerated, anyone who really wanted to murder someone, would simply start a chase. And in a culture that accepts the duel, arranging to have someone dueled out of the way is simple, also.

The trouble with cultural tabus is, simply, that *no* action is either Always Good or Always Bad. Think how much misery the world would have been saved if someone had just assassinated Hitler in about 1935! And in your yarn, you have an instance of a man murdering another — shooting down a man who hadn't done anything . . . yet. The guard who shot the man with the dynamite belt.

Sincerely,   John W. Campbell

P.S. Your manuscript, "Death Is A Dream," is being forwarded to you under separate cover.

Dear Mr. Ellern:

As I imagine you know by now, you just got in under the wire on getting **Doc Smith's** permission to use his "Lensman" universe. He died suddenly about ten days ago. A fact which I was rather glad to hear — because **Doc** had had a lung removed due to signs of cancer. Cancer of the lung is no way for a human being to die; they should be shot. I gather **Doc** went with a heart attack — which is a good, clean way to go, when you're well along in years.

The story is back for minor revisions at the end. You've told a pretty good yarn — up to the battle scene. But you better re-read some of **Doc's** works, and figure out how it was he put over the feeling of a tremendous battle of immense energies. What you wind up with here is the feeling that some guys pushed some buttons at each other. It simply doesn't have any sense of bigness or importance.

Moreover, there's no explanation of who the attackers are, why they're attacking, or what the importance of the attack, if it's not defeated, will be.

Doc may be right in saying you shouldn't make any direct references to "First Lensman" — that it'd pull the reader out of *this* story — but you've got to put *in* the background motivations that make the action importance.

You've left out some comments on the quality of the old fighting beams the prospectors have to work with — that they're inefficient, unsophisticated gadgets that use plain, simple, old-fashioned *light* as a weapon. No ultra-beams — no Q-type helices —

Yeah . . . but they made up for it by using perfectly monstrous input. Which is why the allotropic iron generators ran out so fast. And while it ain't sophisticated — it's *massive* and it's raw energy that can't be shunted off.

Note that **Doc Smith's** shields and screens were never reported as *making the ship invisible*; this means that they didn't affect or stop light.

Therefore the pure-light beams would reach the ships, despite their being screened against the expected ultra-beam weapons. Inefficient they were — but the moon-based weapons could be enormously massive, with immense heat-dissipation.

No ship could use such weapons, and, once more efficient weapons were available, no base would use them. But they'd be effective for much the same reason the "Molotov cocktails" were in the Spanish Civil War — so old-fashioned and direct that everybody'd forgotten how effective they could be, and failed to prepare for them.

One thing **Doc** never did acknowledge — he carefully avoided any mention whatever of it — is that ultra-powerful weapons *have* to be 100% efficient, or at least 99.999+% to be usable in a spaceship. If you use 10^{20} watts in your weapon, and have .001% inefficiency — how do you get rid of 10^{15} watts of raw heat released inside your own ship, when it's in a perfect vacuum?

The base on the Moon could be only 20% efficient — because it has the thermal inertia of a whole world to soak up the other 80%.

Remember, in "Skylark," where Seaton & Co. were fighting against the Mardonalians, and the Skylark's refrigeration system was being over-loaded? I asked **Doc** once where the ammonia heat-pumps he specified were dumping the heat they pumped. He agreed they couldn't!

The thing your story needs is the impact of a whingeroo of a battle scene.

In taking off from **Doc's** universe as a base — better take some of **Doc's** technique for a bang-up ending along.

Sincerely,   John W. Campbell

P.S. I'm returning the originals of your correspondence, but I'm holding your manuscript — no point shuttling it back and forth — since relatively few pages need revision. I'm also keeping the copies of the correspondence.

Chesley Bonestell   *October 18, 1965*

Dear Mr. Bonestell:

We have an article coming up that offers some lovely possibilities for an astronomical-type cover.

Basic situation: Suppose a meteoid 2 miles in diameter comes in and hits the Earth at about 20 miles per second. It's happened repeatedly before this. The Sudbury nickel mines are engaged in excavating the remains of one that arrived about 1.7 billion years ago. The Vredevort Ring, in South Africa, is a 130 mile-diameter ring-wall showing where one hit about 250 million years ago.

The article's author is showing that having one hit in the ocean would be more of a catastrophe than having it hit on, say, Switzerland.

If it hits in the Pacific, it will make a crater of incandescent rock about 10 miles across, drilled down about 9-10 miles into the Earth. There will be a magma reaction, with lava welling up to fill the hole.

The first consequence is a tsunami that'll still run 750 feet high when it reaches California, Chile and Japan. The earth-shock will probably cause all the fault line stresses to relieve themselves more or less simultaneously.

And there will be the crater. It'll be a hole in the Pacific about 1-1½ miles deep, and 30 miles in circumference. There will be a waterfall 1½ miles high and 30 miles around tumbling into that pit, in other words — and the water can't reach the bottom, because it's converted to superheated steam before it gets there. If you can imagine a broken steam pipe, with steam under 7500 pounds/inch^2 pressure, and ten miles in diameter spouting — that's the kind of noise it would make.

The reason why that would be worse than having it hit in Europe is that the result of the stupendous amount of heat-energy released will be to boil cubic miles of water into the atmosphere, all of which has to fall out again. The storms would be fantastic. The cubic miles of rock dust that were vaporized into the atmosphere, together with the immense cloudbanks, would reduce the Earth's absorption of solar energy, resulting in an ice age.

If the meteor hit on land, the results would be relatively localized (500 miles around, say) because the lithosphere would hold the heat, and release it gradually. But in the sea, the heat would all be transferred, and rapidly, into the atmosphere and hydrosphere.

I'd love to present that frightful crater in action — but I'm not sure it can be done.

So . . . questions:
1. Do you think it can be done?
2. Do you think you can do it?
3. Do you want to do it?
4. If so, could we have it by November 12?

Regards,   John W. Campbell

John D. Clark   *November 18, 1965*

Dear John:

That **H. Beam Piper** story business has caused one helluva mess. It goes this way: We bought the first and second Lord Kalvan stories from **Piper**, through his agent **Ken White**. "Host Hostigos," the third, was submitted by **Ken White**, and I sent it back for some revision with an eight page letter of explanation.

Three months later, I heard from **Piper** that **Ken White** had died suddenly, leaving his affairs in such a mess that nobody had been informed and nobody knew what to do, and nobody had done anything for a couple of months. So **Piper** didn't know what I'd said about "Hos Hostigos," and never got my letter. And I, by then, didn't remember the yarn exactly enough to be able to redo the letter without seeing the manuscript.

So **Beam** was broke, and apparently suddenly decided to go out sidewise . . . suicidewise.

458

And he'd just contacted a new agent, and left *his* affairs in a mess, including neglecting to explain to the agent that *Analog* had bought some of his stories and not published them yet. So the agent, cleaning out his affairs, sold all the stuff to Ace. And the mess was thereby further glorified and transmogrified. Because Ace didn't own the rights to proper copyright, and we couldn't properly copyright because Ace had improperly copyrighted and the legal situation is twice as complicated!

Re: dimensional analysis.

The business of c-g-s as the basis of analysis—of mass-length-time—is obviously slicing the real universe across the grain, and the work of primitive barbarians who hadn't the first beginnings of a knowledge of science. The old boys who started our Indo-European language group. The Hopi language doesn't use time; they don't have tenses. The Japanese-Chinese languages don't divide up reality as we do.

The probability is vanishingly small that some late neolithic barbarians in north-central Europe stumbled on the One Right Analysis.

But science has been stuck with that analysis ever since! Because a man walking is strongly conscious of distance — we have distance as a basic. He's not as strongly conscious of — can't measure-by-eye as well — energy expenditure. Now, the distance from A to B by superhighway may be 25 miles, while by taking a direct line across country it's only 12. But the 12 happen to go through 4 miles of dense and thorny underbrush, 6 of quagmire, and 2 of frantically eroded badlands-type country. The energy expenditure is decidedly not less!

Man is conscious of time because of Earth's rotation. And he's conscious of mass when he tries to lift a boulder. At no point is he conscious of Planck's Constant!

I'm convinced that the true dimensional analysis would use Planck's Constant as one of the dimensional units. It's a *real* unit of universal structure. And it's not a unit of time, or energy, or mass; it's a unit of *action*, which includes both energy (mass) and time.

So, what are the other necessary parameters of reality?

I'd love an article analyzing that problem, and suggesting advantages to be gained by using such a different system!

Item: The Oriental languages, which divide up the universe even less realistically than the Indo-European group, make science-thinking practically impossible. With the result that all Oriental scientists have to learn an Indo-European language to do their scientific work!

Mathematics isn't enough, either; Goedel's Proof showed that no logically self-consistent system could contain (or cover) all truths.

The basic postulates of the language of science are, still, that Glrugh, the late neolithic warrior-hunter, settled on about 15,000 B.C. — how much he could carry how far in a day — *mlt*!

What else could we use as basics?

Regards,   John

Joe Poyer *November 18, 1965*

Dear Joe:

Glad to hear you took a job out there, for two reasons.

One is that Pleasure — if you try to get a general definition for it — turns out to be a surplus over and above the necessary. For example, K-rations are necessary and sufficient nourishment. Steak, french fries, and coffee are a pleasure.

But you can't get pleasure from a normally pleasing thing, if the necessary is missing. No matter how nuts you may be about fine music, you can't really get much pleasure from it when you're starving in a freezing rain.

So, with the necessary supplied by a job, writing's a pleasure. And all the best stories are written by people who are having a whee of a time writing them!

The second reason I'm glad you got that job is I'd very much like an article on "remote area conflict," otherwise known, I believe, as anti-guerrilla tactics.

And I'm curious as hell as to why they go looking for methanol. Do the VC boys prefer methanol to ethanol in their beverages? Use it for fuel for their fires, and get the stuff in their systems?

Maybe they should use that air-sniffer over here, re-tuned for acetone, to spot diabetics, huh?

I don't know whether I ever mentioned to you my idea of a mutual advantage treaty the U.S. should make with the South Viet Nam government. You see, they have a problem; shortage of money, and little valuable export. We have a problem; we have some hard-to-dispose-of-garbage. They have a lot of land they're not using just now, and aren't going to use for some years. So we sign a treaty allowing us to dump our garbage on some of their unused land, and pay them so much a year for the privilege.

The U.S. is accumulating more and more of that nuclear reactor garbage, you know, and it's a damn nuisance to us. If it were just wrapped up in concrete, and left to natural decay along some of those unused border lands — particularly along the various trails the VC insist on using, making the land useless to the Viet Namese just now — it would be of real mutual advantage. And certainly a garbage disposal treaty can *not* be called nuclear warfare!

The disposal dump should, of course, be adequately posted with warnings. They wouldn't have to be illuminated at night, because at night the garbage would supply its own blueish-white illumination. VC's and supplies that did infiltrate past the garbage dumps could be detected from the air much more readily than by looking for methanol. A scintillometer would do nicely.

My own feeling is that our military doesn't adequately support the Department of Dirty Tricks; I'm glad to hear they are beginning to do some research in that direction.

I've been rather surprised that the U.S. bases haven't been ringed with body-capacitance alarms sufficient to stop *all* VC infiltration. Considering how cheaply mass-produced transistor radios can be ground out, a capacitance alarm ought not to cost more than about $1-$2 apiece, with a 20¢ battery good for two weeks of continuous operation. They could be rigged to give out either audio and/or RF warbles when their fields were entered. A unijunction running on a few microamps could be made to trigger, when disturbed, something with real output. An SCR for instance. They might give a few false alarms, but they'd *always* alarm!

The story herewith returns because the idea is a hell of a good one, and the story is too short to build it. That's why you had to wind up with a couple pages of philosophical essay in which you *tell* the reader what a good story would *show* him . . . or bring out in conversation.

By the way, did you ever consider the "survival of the best fitted" effect in a true feudal society? There's nothing like a feudal society for evolving *managerial* talent!

Thing is . . . Barons Abe, Boris, and Carl are all in competition for land and serfs. That means for *economic* power. Because economic power means they can support more henchmen. If Abe is a hard-fisted, egocentric tyrant, he earns Boris' and Carl's personal dislike. His serfs have a rough time; they don't produce much, and they are never going to help Abe in any way they can avoid, and will tell Boris and Carl anything they think might louse up Baron Abe.

If Boris is a good-hearted, personally attractive guy, but a little bit thick-headed, *yet has wisdom enough to know that*, he'll be able to win the respect and affection of competent, loyal men, and delegate authority to brilliant and effective commoners. His realm will prosper, his serfs will admire and like him, and will do everything they can to help keep Baron Boris power. They know when they've got a good thing going for them!

But, if Baron Carl is a strong, wise, and intelligent man, he'll deal justice to his people so that while they may not love him as Boris' love him, they'll respect Carl's honesty, strength, and genuine justice.

So, if a squabble breaks out among them . . . guess who'll win! The best manager, of course — the man who knows how to select the right people for the right job, who punishes and rewards wisely, and who is intelligent enough to let other men of special talents teach him what he needs to learn.

In good times, when things are easy, men want a soft-headed, soft-hearted easy-touch type in control. The type that promises only blood, sweat, toil, and tears isn't at all popular during peace and prosperity. But it's that type men turn to when things are damn well desperate, and they know it. That type will, however, be hastily turned out of power again as soon as his hard, wise, realistic, but painful, leadership has solved the problem. Heroes are never popular in peaceful times, until well after they're safely out of power. Preferably dead!

Do you think any one of the Founding Fathers, who get such great lip-service for their wise philosophy, could get elected to any office above Dog Catcher in American politics today? Not those hard, bold realists! Not men who held that a man who couldn't manage his own affairs well enough to accumulate a stake couldn't be trusted to manage a nation's affairs, and shouldn't be allowed to vote.

What sort of rebel colonies will you get? Some are going to rebel out of sheer pique. Some may rebel with a strong motivation of vengeance, not satisfied with simple freedom.

There's lots of good story possibilities in there. Not to be wasted on a 3900 word short!

Regards,   John

Enc.: "Growing Pains"

Mack Reynolds   *January 17, 1966*

Dear Mack:

I like your phony Amazon world. I have only two growls against the yarn — one technical, and the other's more or less emotional-prejudice.

The technical growl is the business about Amazonia needing titanium-columbium exchange.

It goes this way: titanium is one of the super-abundant elements. The nucleogenesis boys explain that in terms of the fact that its principal (78%) isotope is $_{22}Ti^{48}$ — at. no. 22, at. mass 48 — which is one of the "magic number" isotopes that have specially high nuclear stability. Plus the fact that it's the magic-mumber isotope

462

nearest to Fe^{56} — the most stable of all possible nuclear configurations. (It's the absolute down-at-the-bottommost point on the nuclear packing fraction curve.) When a supernova blows up, iron-56 is the nucleus that the matter at the inner core of the exploding supernova gets squeezed down to. Ti^{48} results when the unimaginable hell of an exploding supernova — it's blowing 90% of the total mass of a star some 10 times as massive as our sun entirely out of its gravitational field, and does it in approximately 100 seconds! — chips a couple of alpha particles (helium nuclei) off an iron-56 nucleus.

The result is that Ti is common. It's common in the universe, not just in Earth.

Now there are a lot of elements that show the weirdest sort of wild variations between stars — and these are usually low-abundance elements.

Item: The largest quantity of the metal scandium ever accumulated was gathered up on special order for the Atomic Energy Commission. It amounted to just under one pound, and cost roughly $65,000. Since then (1946) they've gotten production going — a total of nearly 15 pounds has been achieved.

But — it's known that scandium is quite abundant in certain other stars.

Indium is a remarkable element. Not too expensive — I've got a sample I bought for the fun of it. It's silvery, about as dense as iron — and so soft you can carve it readily with a fingernail. It melts at only a little about the boiling point of water. And it's extremely useful, because it's the "wettest" metal known. I.e., molten In will flow onto and surface-alloy with all sorts of other metals. It acts like a metallic wetting agent. So they use it for soldering onto germanium transistor slices.

On the other end of the scale there's Rhenium — a sample of which I purchased, also. My sample is roughly 1″ square, and 0.005″ thick — about the size and thickness of a good-sized postage stamp. It cost $10. It's a blue-gray-silvery metal, sort of like a darker toned chromium-plate surface. The only element that has a higher melting point is tungsten — and that beats it by only about 5%, some couple hundred degrees! Rhenium is excessively scarce stuff. Unlike tungsten, it's not brittle at room temperature; tungsten-rhenium alloys are tough, strong, and malleable anywhere between about -100° and +3000° C. Density's also very high — about 19+.

Again — the spectra of some stars show the presence of rhenium in disproportionately high quantities.

Iridium, one of the platinum group metals, is the densest of all elements — 22.5+ versus a mere 19.3 for gold — and iridium has a melting point of 2400° C, and a corrosion resistance to all known corrodants that makes platinum look fragile. Unfortunately, its price also makes platinum look cheap. Ir is hard, tough, abrasion resistant, malleable, ductile — a wonderful metal.

Each of the above is a highly important and valuable *industrial* metal. They'd be a damn sight more important if they were only available in greater quantity.

Columbium-niobium is a good metal to name as one end of that deal; the stuff's not a common element, and does vary widely in different stellar spectra. Yet Cb is available in tonnage lots, if you need it.

Another good possibility is Zirconium. It's the heavier analog of titanium; like Ti it has great corrosion resistance, good mechanical properties, but unlike Ti has a density about like that of stainless steel. However — Zr has alomst unique nuclear properties. It has almost zero neutron absorption cross-section, for which the AEC and other nuclear-oriented outfits dearly love it. Makes a wonderful structural material for use in and around nuclear reactors. And . . . it's found in high abundance in the spectra of S-type stars, whereas it's almost missing in our sun.

Now I don't care how good your interstellar liners are — interstellar freight costs like hell. If it didn't, there wouldn't be so much trouble getting from one planet to another —tickets would be cheap.

Therefore, gross-quantity freight, such as a heavy-duty structural metal like titanium, wouldn't be freighted. They wouldn't ship something across the galaxy to compete with mild steel, in other words. Mild steel — or a stainless — would be too much cheaper. The use of Cb in making weldable ultra-high-corrosion-resistant steels makes sense; that they *would* ship. (Incidentally, the stainless you're talking about is Carpenter #20-Cb; it's just about the only stainless that can sit around in boiling-hot 50% sulfuric acid and sneer at the stuff. Curiously, plain, ordinary mild steel can resist 100% sulfuric, or 100% water!)

Make it one of the other metals — and you can have some fun. You looked up the ores on Ti (I believe they use only rutile and ilmanite in industrial practice) but it might be worth pointing out that the ores of something like scandium that show up on a scandium-bearing planet simply don't appear at all on a low-scandium planet, so the ore-names are meaningless. (Earth's *only* cadmium ore, for instance, is *greenockite*, which occurs, so far as is known, only in one place in Scotland. And there's so little it isn't mined; it's collected for museums!)

Another thing that fun could be had with: Iceland Spar is the special crystalline form of ordinary calcium carbonate that shows double refraction. For years it was the only polarizing material available. (Until Land invented Polaroid plastic.) O.K. — so how's about one planet having a crystalline mineral that doesn't occur elsewhere, and has extreme scientific value? The world's deposit of Iceland Spar was in Iceland, and is exhausted.

The commodities of interstellar commerce could be quite peculiar, in other words!

Finally, my other minor growl is over the death of Mylywhatzername. (Those names you've got are doozies.) She can be wounded, but good — but why kill a nice kid who was having fun play-acting? The "I take thee" formula was part of the play-acting business.

However, that's just a mild regret; you decide what's best.

Regards, John

Joseph P. Martino   *January 19, 1966*

Dear Major Martino:

Will Jenkins sent me copies of the stuff on his isotope separation gimmick.

Well, now that gnawing wonder-whether-it-is item has been looked into. Personally, I feel considerably relieved.

The trouble is, somewhere, somebody may come up with something just as foolishly simple that *does* work — and when I hear of one that may be such a gadget, it needs honest investigation to be sure it isn't lurking out there.

I'm not afraid of Russia getting things like that. What scares the bejayzus outa me is that Uganda, or somebody like Sukarno might get it.

What'd happen, f'rinstance, if some outfit in Central Africa came up with an anti-gravity barge made of logs and woven slats, capable of hauling 20 tons of cargo, and powered by four witch-doctors? Can't navigate above 15,000 feet, because the witch-doctors don't have oxygen masks. More witch-doctors — bigger cargoes.

Something like that could really louse up the framework of our present world. It reminds me — the structure of tensions — of a cluster of soap-bubbles, each balancing extreme inner and outer tensions, and nestling one against the other. . . .

Regards, John

Harry Harrison   *February 21, 1966*

Dear Harry:

O.K. — we skip the Mobsters piece, since you're editing the

book, and that's your privilege.

The changes re Pope having written that bit about trying new things, etc. are necessary; on those I goofed by reason of having a clear memory of the statement, and of Polonius' advice to Laertes, and the two so perfectly fit together I though they *were* together.

I concede the Mobsters piece on a Point of Privilege — definitely not because I accept that your attitude is correct. However, let me point out that this dispute is, in miniature, precisely the form of dispute that causes two honest and idealistic men to have at each other with clubs, spears, swords, duelling pistols and/or nuclear bombers.

Each of us feels sure that the reason the other does not agree is that *I* have data which *he* doesn't have, or doesn't adequately appreciate. I.e., each feels sincerely, "He is an honest and ethical man, and if he knew what I know, he could not help but agree with me, and I must, therefore, make him realize these facts he somehow fails to appreciate."

The variant on that being, "I must have been wrong in believing him to be honest and ethical; he now has been given those facts, and he wickedly refuses to realize that truth and justice lie on my side."

Let's clarify some facts on this matter.

1. The Watts riots in Los Angeles were *not* the directed actions of Mobsters.

2. The Harlem riots of two years ago — and the Rochester and Patterson riots — were *not* the directed results of Mobsters.

3. The Civil Disobedience movements Ghandi led *were* the results of planned, organized Mob Action led and carefully directed by a General Staff of Mobsters — Ghandi & Company.

4. The Hindu-Pakistani murder-mobs immediately after Indian independence were half-and-half; Ghandi's introduction of the organized mob as a political force in India led to fanatic Hindus and Moslem priests and accolytes *starting* the mobs intended to push out the Other Guys — and the quasi-organized mobs promptly broke out of all control, and went into undirected rioting.

There are entirely different kinds of Mobs — just as there are entirely different kinds of underground movements. The Mafia is a form of underground movement; so was the Resistance Movement in Denmark during WW II. This makes the Resistance Movement equal to the Mafia?

There are leaderless (practically) riot-mobs — and there are Organized Demonstrations. The food riots that have attacked

466

India again and again (and will show up during the coming months of famine there) *are riots* — not the Organized Demonstration type mob I'm talking about.

The central point of my editorial is this — that an army-seeking-to-impose-*fear* is now recognized as an organized effort to achieve political ends through compulsive force. Vide the Viet Cong terrorist tactics. The Mafia in Sicily. But an organized-force-seeking-to-compel-by-*induced-shame* has not been adequately recognized as what it is — an effort to compel political action by force.

Suppose someone discovers a drug that, when given to a person, causes that person to feel a terrible, overwhelming terror if he even considers resisting a command. A full-fledged unendurable acute-neurosis type of terror, reasonless but absolute.

Such a drugged individual will obey your every command — up to and including dissecting his wife, and serving up his children for dinner. (Neurotics have, you know).

It would generally be conceded that such an individual was a victim of most cruel and evil persuasion.

That, in effect, is precisely what an army of terrorists seeks to achieve. The Nazis (like a thousand others before) did quite well; they had children informing against parents, husbands informing against wives — the Command by Terror was fairly effective. Not as completely as the proposed drug would do, but pretty well.

Now let's consider another drug. This one causes the victim to feel utter, absolute, and overwhelming shame — guilt if he disobeys a command.

Why do you suppose parents yielded up their babies by Baal? Or their daughters to be skinned alive on the High Altar by the High Priest of the Mayans?

Would you consider the use of such a shame-inducing drug in any real respect less evil, less vicious, than the terror-command drug?

Yet any psychiatrist can tell you that induced-shame neuroses are the most common, and the hardest to cure. And the most compulsively powerful. They're much harder to treat, because the victim thinks that *he himself is the source of the compulsion.* I.e., that he is not being compelled, but is choosing. That he can't escape the source of the compulsive force, because he is himself its source.

Ghandi knew British psychology — he'd studied at one of Britain's best universities — and was keenly, intelligently aware that the British could be compelled helplessly by shame, where they would fight off any effort to induce terror. I'm sure Ghandi was too sharp an old plotter to have tried any civil disobedience tactics if the Japs had gotten into India during WW II. He'd have worked up a different approach, and had the Honorable Nipponese officers hari-kariing all over the place — because he'd have found the power of Shame as a means of political compulsion.

The point of my editorial was that the Mobsters know and *deliberately use Shame to compel acceptence of their wishes.*

It isn't a question of whether their wishes are good, valid, ethical, proper, etc., or whether they're wicked, evil, and vicious. I'm simply pointing out that shame-induction is just as truly a form of imposing forced consent (the shame-inducing drug) as is terror induction (the terror-drug). That a Mayan father was *forced* to yield his pretty teen-age daughter to the High Priest for ritual sacrifice, not by the terror of having the priestly army attack — but by shame at the thought of turning against his gods and his people by reason of selfishly trying to keep his daughter from the sacrifice. And that the girl, in her turn, would be *forced by shame* to carry out her role in the ceremony, and walk over and lie down on the altar to be skinned (vide Indian suttee).

Notice that *terror* could not make her do that. Shame could — and did!

The point I wanted to make is that deliberate efforts on the part of one group to induce shame in another, for reasons of gaining political advantage, are *more* destructive to sanity than honest, brutal terror tactics.

Know anything about suicidal mania, and what it'll do to someone? Can you imagine any threat of brutal torture sufficient to make a young woman sneak into a washroom, strip herself, and throw handfuls of scalding hot water from the tap over her body until she scalded herself to death. A girl did that in the Mass. State Institute for the Insane some years ago. Suicidal guilt-complex did it.

You like the use of shame-inducing tactics better than something clean and brief like a VC bomb, maybe?

And don't tell me you can't be made to feel guilty of something that you're not guilty of! How many Americans, today, have been made to feel guilty, shame-haunted, for the allegedly "inhuman" treatment of Negro slaves a century and a half ago? Americans, moreover, who are descendants of Slavs or Poles or Italians who didn't have a single ancestor on this continent before 1880!

Man, I mean, that's great stuff for building a sound, sane culture on, ain't it? Every bit as sound as persecuting modern Jews because they murdered Jesus 2000 years ago.

As to the Mobsters deliberately seeking martyrs — ever think that if Horst Wessel hadn't gotten himself bumped off, the Nazis would have had to get somebody else killed for their purposes? That if it weren't for that insufferable, intransigent John Birch,

John Birchers would have had to find another martyr to moan about? Martyrs are necessary to any good shame-induction campaign.

Now inasmuch as I never had any opportunities to own a Negro slave myself, never did own one, never mistreated a slave I owned, and that all my ancestors of that period, so far as I can determine, were fighting on the Northern side, or still residing in free areas (Canada, Vermont, etc.) I resent like hell some guy trying to make *me* feel guilt-shame that Negroes were (allegedly) terribly mistreated.

Since imposed, induced guilt is a Grade A primary cause of insanity, I resent most deeply any organization that, for its own purposes, seeks to induce and spread the roots of cultural insanity.

Please note very carefully that *Ghandi did not do that*. He was forcing the British to yield *on the basis of their own already accepted code of conduct.* He was saying you-here-now are acting in a manner contrary to your-own-current expressed beliefs. He was *not* trying to make them feel shame-guilt over actions of centuries before.

Should the Jews be made to give up their department stores, machine tool plants, and import businesses today as partial recompense for killing Jesus two millenia ago?

The sort of campaigns going on now amount to that, don't they?

The same thing — shame-induction — is being used on an enormously wide scale throughout the world. Why are we whites guilty of the fact that the Africans, 3000 years ago, didn't develop the institutions of higher learning that whites did? How are we guilty because we don't *give* them the high-level technology they want — but won't work for? (And that means force themselves to gather the capital wealth required for schools, factories, and railways, then force their children through 20 years of education, while the parents work twice to three times as hard to support those non-productive children and their teachers.)

If a mob of students, inspired by politically conscious and extremely clever Buddhist priests, sets out to break down the government — it's the students who are apt to get killed. If an electrified fence has been erected around government buildings, who is shameful — the men who erected the fence, or the schemers who lead the students to sacrifice themselves on it — as the Mayan High Priests led the young women to lie down to be skinned alive by shame-compulsion?

In a contest like that, obviously, the side with the stronger sense of conscience and ethics is going to lose. The priests are perfectly willing to have a hundred students killed; the tender-conscience government turns off the fence, and falls to the organized mob. The Mobsters win.

For some three thousand years, the Chinese Ten Families system swallowed all the conquerors of China and held China's culture static. The Communists have done what no previous force was able to do — they broke up China's stasis. They did it by being coldly ruthless. They killed off the Ten Elders in each village, as soon as those elders opposed them. Under the old system this simply meant that the next eldest Ten became the Ten Eldest. And the Commies killed them off, when they opposed. The Commies had the ruthless (shame-rejecting) consciences needed to keep on with that program until the villages ran out of Elder Tens — and the system broke down.

Now one added comment anent "Who's got the data?"

Europeans *don't* have the data, in the case of the American problem of the Negro — or that of Rhodesia or South Africa. The British, who didn't have the data, have in the last two decades, begun to acquire it. I.e., they've begun to have Negro neighbors to live next to, so that their understanding of what Negores are like is no longer remote-impersonal-theoretical, but direct-observation-al-data.

The Danes, for example, don't understand the problem at all, because they haven't had direct, personal contact. They're acting purely on theory, and honest, human, good feeling toward others. Therefore, while their papers have all shades of political expression, they don't have *any immediate-contact* data. They're wonderful people; I admire them greatly, as you know. They're also ignorant, in this particular respect, which is no guilt or fault, but simply a fact.

Try this data on your computer — the Russians had the very strongest of political motivations to welcome the African peoples into the Brotherhood of Man on a full-equality basis. The "Russians" moreover aren't really Russians; they're Mongols and Tartars and Don Cossacks and Eskimoes and Georgians and Great Russians and Germans and a whole slew of widely different racial groups. They're a League of Nations all in themselves. At their university in Moscow they'd been assiduously training Japs and Chinese and Polynesians and Indians and Gonds and American Indians, and you-name-it for some decades before the African nationalism got going.

Then they selected some bright young leaders-to-be among the African nations, and invited them to Moscow for high-level education — free, courtesy of the Soviet Government. Also to universities in other Communist countries.

Three years later the University of Moscow set up separate-but-equal facilities for Negroes. And the African students in the other Iron Curtain countries came boiling out boiling mad at the way they'd been treated. The *people* had beaten them, kicked them around, and rejected them violently and most wholeheartedly. The *people* in the Iron Curtain countries had revolted against the express and very powerful wish of their all-powerful State, and with whole-souled enthusiasm kicked the Africans out.

The *students* at the University of Moscow rejected the African students — which in Moscow, isn't any too lightly undertaken!

Now note: the peoples of the Iron Curtain countries had, up to that time, no experience with Negroes — no more than the Danes or Swedes have. They had no prejudices, no established bigotries, nor had they been "carefully taught, before it's too late, before you are six or seven or eight."

But somehow they learned, in three years, that they found Africans intolerably arrogant, boorish, and hateful. *By direct experience*. So much so as to express that distaste so powerfully that the Soviet government acted against its own deep political desires to set up "separate but equal" facilities. And that in a nation which is inherently a terrific mixture of wildly different racial stocks!

You know, those Africans really must have had astonishingly powerful personalities to shake a system that massively!

O.K. — so I refuse to feel guilty just because I find many American Negroes personally offensive to me. I have excellent evidence that it's *not* necessarily bigotry, or cultural orientation. And I'll be damned if I'll allow someone to make me feel guilty-shameful for not accepting as "just as good as anyone else" an arrogant, boorish, and hateful individual. If I condemned *all* Negroes on that basis, I would be bigoted. But to demand my right to choose — and that necessarily means to reject! — individuals is not a thing for which I'm going to allow anyone to make me feel guilty-shameful about.

And I won't yield to the feelings of Danes or other Europeans *who haven't experienced or observed the problem directly.*

The British, long noted for their genuine adaptability (not tolerance, which implies "he's really inferior, but I'm so big-hearted I'll treat him just as if he weren't") in dealing with other peoples, have in the last decades had an influx of African-stock people. The African people seem to have very powerful personalities indeed; they've been able to turn political elections in staid old Britain *against* an M.P. who campaigned on a no-race-bias platform.

Nope. . . . I will not yield on the basic point of the Mobsters. No group has any business trying to impose Shame as a political weapon. I prefer Viet Cong bombs and open murder.

And if you still honestly believe that the deliberate, organized shame-inducer mobsters don't exist . . . naive guy, aren't you?

Regards,   John

471

George Hay   *March 14, 1966*

Dear Mr. Hay:

Thanks for the spade-work you did in getting *Who Goes There?*
published in England.

You know, that thing has been a irritation to me for the last
dozen years. The movie, "The Thing," was based on it, as you know
— and that's been a financial bonanza for the people who made it,
for the young actors who got their starts in it — for everybody, in
fact, but me!

The Shasta Publishers outfit that brought it out in book form
was a strictly-from-gyp outfit; they made a pocket-book out of it
(without my permission, and without notifying me) and quietly
pocketed the $1000 advance on it — which I never succeeded in
prying loose from them. I did, however, succeed in slapping a legal
action against 'em in time to keep them from collecting the 2nd
$1000 the perfectly honest pocket-book company was due to pay
— and then it took five years more to get that money out of escrow!

Maybe something sensible will start happening to it now!

                                        Regards,   John W. Campbell

Bob Shaw   *March 30, 1966*

Dear Mr. Shaw:

Your story about "slow glass" made me think of something —
that idea is a dilly, and offers many possibilities for stories besides
the one you did.

One evening on one of the "slow glass" farms, in some nice,
lonely place, they find two bodies. In essence, what happened is
quite clear; the young man tried to defend the girl, and was
murdered. She was tortured, raped, and killed by a sadistic and
homicidal nut. A very nasty crime indeed — and all of it watched
by a bank of 10 year slow-glass windows.

It's the kind of crime you can't just ignore until truth-will-out;
the guy who did it has to be stopped — quickly.

The police presently have three suspects — and because the area
is lonely, have evidence that one of the three must be the villain. But
they can't determine which one.

They can't lock up two innocent men for ten years; they can't let
the guilty man wander loose for ten years. And everyone knows the
slow-glass windows will, at the end of ten years, let them take color
movies in complete detail.

But not before.

Justice finds itself in a most remarkably hot spot. Everyone
knows-for-sure that the exact truth will most assuredly out.

They're going to be second-guessed by an absolutely authoritative set of witnesses (fifty slow-glass windows looked on the scene!)

Reminds me of the situation in American major league baseball games that resulted from sports photographers, and particularly movies taken with telephoto-zoom lenses. Suppose the umpire calls a man out, ending the inning, when the team had two men on base, and were trailing 3 to 2 — and then, when the movies are developed, it's clearly visible that the man was, in fact, safe? But the movies, of course, can't be available for hours, after everybody's gone home.

They made a rule. No movies allowed of such instances! By fiat, the umpire's right, whether he's wrong or not!

I'm not suggesting that exactly the above crime set-up be the basis of this story — but just using that to give an outline of the problem.

Currently I'm decidedly short on both novelettes and shorts, so I hope this suggests a writable story to you.

Sincerely,   John W. Campbell

John H. Pomeroy   *June 20, 1966*

Dear Dr. Pomeroy:

I understand we are now supposed to call that phenomenon "kugelblitz"; it was scientifically established by many mathematical proofs that ball lightning is absolute nonsense, so since ball lightning can't exist it is now recognized that "kugelblitz" is possible.

One type of ball-lightning that the *Oak Ridge News* doesn't mention was the type I saw: lightning struck in an open field about 125 feet from where I sat on my front porch; a 10-12″ ball remained. It floated, bouncing gently, across the 18″ high grass tops for about 50′, bounced gently off the side of an old barn, bounced across the grass some more, and hit the trunk of an 8″ oak tree, converting a section of said trunk into toothpicks, with a hell of a *whop*.

One of the things the physics boys tended to overlook when discussing the phenomenon is that while GE said they made "artificial lightning" when they got a condenser-bank discharge of about 2 MEV, and with some of their spectacular 750 kv AC discharges, nobody yet has actually approached a real lightning bolt — they not only run several megavolts, but at *30-50 million amperes,* too. With 10^{14} watts to do things with, somewhat unusual things can happen.

My own hunch has been that it somehow starts a double-toroid current flow.

Imagine two doughnuts linked, with A passing through the hole in B and B passing through the hole in A. Picture A in a horizontal plane, and B in the vertical plane. Now rotate B around an axis in the vertical plane, passing through the center of A's hole.

If the two are very-high-density plasma currents, the A current's magnetic field has just the shape necessary to confine the ions of B's current in the path it has . . . and B's mag field tends to confine the ion current of A.

The external appearance will be a glowing ball of reasonably stable mutually-confining plasma.

Exactly how you'd go about setting up such a dual, mutually-confining set of plasma currents, I can't say — but with 30 megamps at 20 megavolts or so, it might well happen, even if a very low efficiency were involved.

Regards,   John W. Campbell

Donald R. Bensen   *June 22, 1966*

Dear Mr. Bensen:

The automobile industry, like current politics, is showing a truly democratic spirit — it's doing what most people *want*, rather than what people *need*. The fact that most people are damn fools means that any democratic system will produce foolishness.

Most people today hold that they have a *right* to drive — and that a licensing system that deprived them of that "right" for *any reason whatever* would be evil, wicked, authoritarian, and ought to be ignored. Hence the very large number of individuals who are, right now, driving without licenses, because the license has been revoked.

Actually, in most of the States of the Union, there is no legal provision to revoke the license of a driver who has become legally blind. An individual with known tendencies to hysteric behavior does not have his license revoked.

I witnessed an accident locally the other day. A 22-year-old driving a vintage Oldsmobile (in the local town, about 25 mph) ran up the tail of a motorcycle; the rear fender and seat of the bike was caught in the bumper and grill of the Olds. The bike fell over, and the rider — also about 22 — with incredible agility and luck, managed to sort of hop along on one arm and one leg, while the Olds pushed him for a good 150 feet, until the Olds finally scraped into a parked car and was stopped. Somehow the bike-rider managed to keep his leg out from under the Olds' left front wheel — I expected to see it caught at any instant — and wound up with nothing more than a badly scraped elbow and ankle.

The Olds' driver testified that the whole thing was because the gas pedal stuck — i.e., that he was a perfect driver, and the entire cause of the accident was the failure of the automobile.

If that gas pedal had stuck wide open, the engine, at that speed, could develop only about 50 horsepower. But the brakes could absorb something like 2500 horsepower. If he hadn't panicked, the car could have been brought to a dead stop in about 20 feet — not 150 — without ramming another car. That accident resulted 98% from the driver's stupidity, and 2% from a mechanical failure — *if* there actually was a mechanical failure. The only reason it wasn't a fatal accident was that the bike rider was both lucky and agile — and kept *his* head.

In airplane piloting, the CAA applies really rigid and effective licensing rules. (They could be even tighter, of course.) Apply such rules in automobile licensing, and you'd presently have only reasonably rational people driving — and since only reasonably rational people could use automobiles, there would be a vast change in what kind of cars sold.

Until then — we'll have a democratic system in which the majority of people (and the distribution curve of characteristics means that the majority will always be incompetent to handle the extremely complex problems of traffic judgement) determine what cars shall be.

An insurance company sent out a questionnaire to thousands of drivers; among other questions asked was how the individual rated himself as a driver. About 85% rated themselves as "much better than average" drivers.

Re horsepower: I've got a 420 hp engine; properly used, that hp is just as much a safety factor as the 3000 hp brakes. There are plenty of times when being able to get the hell out of the way in a *hurry* is as much a safety factor as being able to stop and *keep* out of the way. My make of car has been test-proven at 130 mph for one hour; this makes it entirely unnecessary for me to prove I can make it go 100 mph — but it does mean that it can be trusted to drive 70 or 80 mph for hour after hour down one of the major turnpikes and thruways where that's the legal speedlimit.

Of course anybody *can* be hit — either by a damn fool, or by a genuine mechanical failure. But there's far too little "defensive driving," wherein you assume that the other guy is apt to be a damn fool, and drive in such a manner that he can't hit without making a determined effort to achieve an accident. No matter how good my brakes are, the other guy can always stop faster than my brakes can, by simply hitting a tree, or a bridge abutment. Yes, the light *is* green my way, I *do* have the right of way — but —

    "Here lies the body of William Jay,
      He died defending his right of way.
      He was right — dead right! — as he sped along. . . .

But he's just as dead as if he'd been dead wrong!"
Regards,   John W. Campbell

Christopher Anvil   *June 29, 1966*

Dear Mr. Anvil:

I'm taking your two stories based on the visual telepaths.

The Marcast will presently become THE political and financial power of the Galaxy. Unless someone is sharp enough to hire a rival faction of Marcats to set up a guaranteed contract-breaking service.

Anyhooo . . . mainly what I wanted to suggest is that you start planning the sequel to "Strangers To Paradise." It'll be in the October, 1966 issue, with a cover by **Jack Schoenherr** — and I think you can have as much fun with the sequel (when they return to Paradise with their want generators and start straightening out that mess) as you did with your Centran stories or "The Gentle Earth."

Assume you are a Benevolent Tyrant, with the power to generate wants in people. You can make some guy who stands 5'1", and weighs 101 pounds, if weighed after falling into thick mud, *want* to be the World Heavyweight Boxing Champ — and thereby destroy him, since he can neither achieve it, nor cease wanting it and straining for it.

On the other hand, you could, with your gadget, make Tom want to be an accountant — despite the fact that Tom has a driving, aching want to be a musician. Which could be a great blessing to Tom, if he happens to have a tin ear (and naturally can't recognize that fact), and a mind naturally neat, orderly, and arithmetical!

It's all right to set up a want-to-be-neat field — but leave a chance for people to escape from the thing, if they're just damn well so constituted that they can't *stand* working in a regular, careful, constructive way. (They make great warriors and hunters though!)

Properly used, you'd have a world that *was* Paradise, with everybody doing what they wanted to — *and were fitted to do.*

That Killer forest would be a perfect place to turn loose all those JD types in a useful, valuable-to-the-community way — they're the Warrior type of mentality that simply *can't* accept working for a living. Down through the millenia of human cultural evolution, that Warrior or Barbarian type has simply been *unable* to work. The American Indians, for instance, couldn't accept working for wages, nor could they be enslaved. (That is of course a statement of the typical, or statistical-norm, Indian.) It was true that the "only good Injun's a dead 'un." They *wanted* to fight — that was the purpose and meaning of life; to work for a living was for women —

476

it was unmanly — only cowardly, slavish un-men could do such a disgusting, honorless, degrading thing. To hunt, to raid, to fight — these were noble, honorable, and manly things.

Being a statistical thing — with the arrival of white colonists who honored work, the exceptional Indians who *did* accept working for a living presently were able to establish themselves as workers and survive. (Workers can't live when surrounded by Warriors; the Warriors raid and confiscate whatever the workers produce.)

Thus the Mohawks were suddenly divided into two types — Workers and Warriors. The Warriors inevitably got themselves killed off; the Workers — with the colonists around stabilizing things — presently were doing fine. Both as farmers, and, now, as the dominant group in high-steel construction.

The only good (i.e., non-destructive) Warrior's a dead 'un. You *can't* make them happy in a worker society. It isn't material goods they want; they don't raid for food — they raid for victory. It's a game with them. Who wants a hunk of pigskin puffed up with air, for God's sake? Why should a score of men, dressed in uncomfortable armor that's not too effective, risk death and life-long maiming to push that fool thing around a muddy field?

O.K. — the Warrior type makes a fine mercenary — he's happy, and if fighting is necessary, then he's incidentally being useful. But note this: *He won't fight for money.* He fights for loot. You may pay him, but if you don't let him *conquer* something, then he's a wage-slave worker, and miserable.

A major portion of the people of Paradise — as you've described it — are basically Warrior types. Like I say, they'd be useful warring against the Killer Forest.

But you'll have to figure out a form of loot that they can conquer!

Regards,   John W. Campbell

RE: "Experts in the Field"
"Compound Interest," by C. Anvil

John Phillifent   *July 13, 1966*

Dear John:

You know, there are times when the best possible reaction to a situation is to scream, yell, howl, shout . . . whatever term you want to use. A wordless cry of "Look out!" when there's too little time to explain what to look out for.

My impression is that in that accident your wife had, the best possible reaction available to her was to shriek to the rest of you while grabbing firmly to the handiest firmly anchored support. In her case, the steering wheel.

And incidentally, the proper thing for passengers to do is exactly the opposite of what the authorities recommend — don't lean back — shove yourself hard and quickly forward as far as you can go — rest your head on the windscreen, and your chest on the instrument panel. If you're going to hit something, the momentum of car-and-passengers is going to be reduced, very suddenly, and quite violently. Say the deceleration is 10 G. If you're sitting back in the seat, you'll have a "fall" of about 20″ under a 10 G acceleration — roughly 200″ under normal G. Now falling 16 feet or so, and landing on your face on a piece of sheet glass is not helpful to the physiognomy. But *lying* on a piece of sheet glass under 10 G acceleration is merely uncomfortable.

That's one of those situations where instinct — to withdraw as far as possible — plays you false!

And of course the bird wasn't hurt; you can drop a mouse from the top of the Empire State building to the pavement a quarter-mile below, and the mouse will squeak in fright and scamper away in panic. His terminal velocity falling through air is about 12 miles an hour, and his strength-weight ratio, due to the square-cube law, is *way* higher than a larger animal's. Same for any other ½ ounce or so creature. Imagine trying to kill the bird by throwing it, with all your strength, against a brick wall and you'll see what I mean. That's why small children are apt to survive terrific smashes when adults around them are shattered. Kids bounce; adults break, too.

Intelligence tests measure book-larnin' type stuff; they don't measure pragmatic mechanical — everyday — competence type understanding. You know the song in "My Fair Lady," "Why Can't a Woman Be Like a Man?" There are a large number of reasons; the fact is that a woman is not like a man, and doesn't think like a man; she thinks like a woman, which is something a man, by *his* nature, can't do or fully comprehend. One of the characteristics of that female type thinking is that logical-rational type thinking doesn't *feel* true to her, and therefore the importance-value of such thinking is, for her, minimal. (There are two things required for a mind to feel a thing is important or valuable; it must appear *true*, valid, or "real," whatever term you want, and it must appear *relevant*. The importance-value to the mind is the product of those two, so if either one is zero, or near zero, the importance-value will feel near zero.) Tell your wife that it's nine light-years to Sirius, and she's apt to reply, "Oh. That's nice, dear," and go on about her business. She doesn't dispute its truth, but she considers its relevance to be 0.000000 . . . plus. But tell her that I just rejected the story you'd been working on for two months, and no check is coming in, because Sirius is nine — not two, as you'd said in your manuscript — and she'll immediately recognize that the distance to Sirius *is* of importance-value to your family.

It's quite conceivable that you can, after that smash, get it over to her that laws of mechanics are real, and are relevant. In which case, she'll suddenly turn out to be perfectly able to comprehend them very quickly. She just thought-felt they were simply not relevant to everyday things like driving a car.

Our youngest daughter somehow decided that the laws of mechanics were relevant to everyday living; when and where she reached that decision, I don't know — somewhere about age 2, I guess. She fixes machines she never saw before, doesn't know anything about, and never saw functioning. Her typewriter broke down when she was engaged in doing an important paper for school; she repaired it by using the spring out of a ball-point pen, two rubber bands, and a somewhat modified safety pin. Some months later the rubber bands gave out, so she installed two more ball-point pen springs. I've also seen her happily using a machine she'd induced to function in a manner the manufacturer never imagined, for purposes the manufacturer never thought of. She also can be *most* annoying by suggestions of the "Why don't you. . . ." type when her mother or I are stewing a difficult problem — which she's just reduced to a sort of idiot's gambit solution.

But . . . no one has ever been able to induce the slightest comprehension of chemistry into her. She sheds astronomical information like a low-grade moron. She not only doesn't know the difference between planets and stars, but specifically doesn't choose to; she prefers to consider them "pretty" and insists that knowing about them would make them less "pretty," Like G.K. Chesterton's fabled remark on looking around the flamingly colorful electric signs of Times Square, "My that would be magnificent if you couldn't read!"

That's all right . . . as she once slyly pointed out to me, I won't learn the difference between a gusset and a gore.

"Give over"; you can't induce people to learn something so long as they consider it irrelevant to real living.

I got our middle-size daughter to understand the necessity for down-shifting on a hill fairly easily; you might try it on your wife. I got **Lynn** to walk along a level patch leading to a ramp — and then told her to move her legs so she took the same length of stride going up the ramp as she did on the level. She "stalled," of course. Then I told her to walk up the ramp normally — and notice that she did it by taking more, shorter strokes with her legs. So does a car; it takes more strokes of the pistons to go up hill; *she* has to "shift into low" on a steep hill and so does a car.

When a girl can feel — tactile direct sensation in her own body —

a phenomenon, it "makes sense" to her, and she can relate it to a more general case, once it's called to her attention. Getting her to feel-believe it by purely logical-intellectual argument is like getting me to see the importance of distinguishing between gussets and gores.

In the case of that smash, however, no amount of technical understanding and skill would have done a bit of good. Turning into the skid is, of course, a fine idea — if the steering gear is still functional. In that case, however, there wasn't a thing anyone could have done, short of levitation, teleportation or precognitive avoidance of the whole thing.

A local family of ours was wiped out the other day near here, and nobody's fault whatever. Their station wagon was proceeding properly along the street one way, a big tractor-trailer truck also properly rolling along at 40 the other. Someone coming out a side street caused the truck driver to put on his brakes as a precautionary measure. There'd been some rain, and at just that point someone had spilled some oil. The combination of oil, water and rubber on asphalt has a coefficient of friction of about 0.0001. The truck jacknifed, the trailer swinging over into the opposite lane, and swatting the station wagon, then falling over on top of it. The additive velocity of impact was about 70 mph, and the trailer had a load of 25 tons of cement bags. The station wagon, despite considerable foreshortening, was only about 15" high after they lifted the trailer and its cargo off.

O.K. — so people get hit and killed by lightning, too. And when the Vredevoort meteor came in 250,000,000 years ago, everything within 200 miles must have died suddenly.

Re radar-sonar gadgets for preventing accidents. Give over; it won't work. It wouldn't have done a bit of good in the above incident, nor in your accident. It wouldn't help at all in one of the usual crossing-intersection accidents.

Also, it's perfectly possible to make a vehicle that's guaranteed to keep the passengers alive and uninjured. Most of the big US motor companies already make them; their only customer, however, is the U.S. Army. They call it a tank, and most people can't afford or don't want one.

The other way of reducing accidents is quite simple; make the driver's license examination one that tests for judgement, innate good manners, fast reflexes, basic understanding of the laws of motion and their consequences, the laws of friction, and the characteristics and effects of the common lubricants — like the oil-water-rubber combination, which makes glare ice sticky by comparison, wet leaves and rain, the traction characteristics of a quarter-inch of sand on a hard road surface — the commonly encountered things. I don't suppose you have any creosoted wood blocks pavements over there; we've gotten rid of most of them over here. Pavement made by laying hardwood blocks like bricks that had been soaked in creosote to prevent decay. With rain, they were slightly more slippery than glare ice.

Then have the police forget all about "speed kills," and start enforcing laws against bad driving instead. There are people I'd rather ride with at 70 than others who scare the bejayzus outa me at 35.

Wayne Batteau is planning on bringing out a book of the Stupid-theorems — a pamphlet rather than a book. They're lovely, I assure you!

The point re languages and Japanese I made was that the Japs *have to learn to think in an Indo-Aryan language* to do science. They have very adequately demonstrated that their brains are just as good as a European's — *given the proper philosophical tools to work with.*

The American occupation forces, post WW II, taught them to speak-think-work in English, to reject traditionalism, and to attempt creativity. (It helped that the Americans had, during the preceding four years, taught them that Japanese Army traditions were not sound ways of staying alive and achieving.)

Incidentally, re Jap flower-arranging and prisoner-torturing: my friend, take a look at the ways of our own good sturdy English ancestors just a few centuries ago. Pious Christians who considered watching the "testing" and execution of a "witch" a fine way to pass a Saturday afternoon. Or the community might be entertained by the drawing and quartering of some heretic in the public square, while piously embroidering a kneeler for the Church.

Please note that the Japs, by reason of their incomplete absorption of our somewhat mawkish, impractical sentimentality, are able to be a damn sight more pragmatic and practical about population control than we are.

Re **Poul Anderson** and his writing; no, I'm thankful to say, you don't write like **Poul**. It'd be frightfully boring, wouldn't it, if all authors wrote the same sort of stuff?

I'm still looking for an author who can, and will, write one type of material the field — and I think all literature — needs more of. The hard-headed, hard-fisted, frontier type of story, which recognizes that the basic nature of exploration, pioneering, and frontiersmanship can be expressed as, "Pioneering consists in discovering new ways to die unexpectedly." And that on a frontier there are no reserves, and therefore there can be no forgiving of errors. That a thief must be killed, because if he steals a man's supplies, he is actually committing murder; if he steals his horse, he condemns the other man to death by starvation and/or thirst. That punishment-deaths should be made as publicly painful and undignified as possible; it doesn't teach the dying man anything, of course, but it does drive home to borderline individuals contemplating crime the idea that the cost of losing is unpleasantly high. Oh, it'll never *stop* crime; hell, you can't stop gambling, or people playing Russian Roulette, or kids trying to drive a car designed for safe cruising at 80 to 125 miles an hour. Or any normal driver trying to drive a Jag racer to 150 mph — which no human being can do without years of training.

My car has 420 horsepower, weighs 6000 pounds, and in stockcar races the type has maintained an average of 135 mph for 1200 miles over Mexican roads. It handles smooth as cream at 95. I did 120 miles in 90 minutes going up to Maine last winter.

I haven't the slightest desire to see how fast I can drive it; I tried it at 95 just to see — once and for all — that it was in fact perfectly stable and firm-handling at really high speed. (On a six-lane, divided highway with no one else in sight for about ten miles.)

The frontier for that car is about 120 mph; 80 mph is the legal highway speed in some of our Western states.

Pioneering anywhere, anywhen, is like driving 130 mph . . . and knowing you have to keep that pace day and night, the only breaks being when someone else takes the wheel and drives 130.

Then when somebody gets sloppy on his job, you don't slap his wrist; he should be flogged, if he lives through the consequences of his carelessness. *There is no margin of safety.*

If there were, it wouldn't be pioneering.

There is no help to be had when trouble strikes.

If there were, it wouldn't be a real frontier.

You've got to do it all yourself, with what you have on hand — and if you don't have the thing you must have on hand — drop dead.

Like the boys in the Gemini 8 capsule when the thruster started spinning their ship helplessly. Absolutely nothing whatever could have been done for them if they hadn't clawed their own way out with what they had. There absolutely could not have been any rescue mission. None. Impossible. They'd have been forced to stay up there, spinning wildly, in full communication with Houston Space Center, until they died for lack of oxygen, or their fuel-cells quit for lack of fuel cutting off communications. Whereupon they'd have to die for lack of oxygen *out* of communication with Houston. Even if a second Gemini 8 launch had been all ready, with countdown complete, and they'd made orbital rendezvous — we can't dock against a wildly spinning target vehicle. Gemini 8

482

didn't carry space-walk equipment; if they had, and one of the men had stepped out, he'd have taken off at a tangent requiring hours of delicate maneuvering to rendezvous with him on a different orbit, at a different position. He'd have been dead by then.

That is a true frontier.

Imagine an alien coming to Earth. What chance would he have of guessing what small, scuttling beasties were fantastically deadly? A ¾-inch toad that secretes so virulent a poison from its skin that picking it up in an ungloved hand can be fatal. The black widow spider. A coral snake. Yet a ten foot Anaconda is practically harmless. Under water, if a 600 pound grouper is in your way, kick him. A pound of jelly, however, called a Portugese man-o-war, you'd damn well better avoid. Squids are hideous, tough, but edible. There's a pretty looking, plump little fish which is sudden, agonizing death to eat.

Go ahead, Alien — guess which [way] you're going to discover unexpected death!

Regards,   John

Harry C. Crosby   *September 7, 1966*

Dear Harry:

I'm taking "The Dukes of Desire," it's a lovely yarn. Only if you're thinking you're through with that series . . . guess again.

That symbiotic computer you've installed in that Special Forces ship is symbiotic with the Special Forces — *not* with your Captain — and it ain't gonna let him stop being a useful arm of the Special Forces just because *he* wants to! It's got its own form of compulsive desire-generator — it acts on his desire-to-respect-himself. And it's really good at it. It allowed him to take command of the ship because he was the type who had the correct style of self-respect; your trio has a desire-generator that's unselective, and so produces undesirable desire-effects. That symbiotic computer is a cuter gimmick; it has a very limited repertory of desire-generation — but is very selective about the individuals it applies them to.

Your skipper is, unfortunately, stuck with being an effective member of the Special Forces, whether he planned it that way or not. Moreover, since even that super-dooper ship needs some replacements, repairs, etc., sooner or later he's gotta take it back to a Special Forces base — or it'll take him there with or without his consent. And of course he'll discover he's by no means the first Special Forces officer to be drafted into the service by one of their ships! They just service the ship, formally commission him, and hypno-educate him in the full powers of the ship.

Whether the other two come along or not is a seperate matter.

483

He'll get a compatible crew. And, of course, the want-generator discovery will be turned over to the Special Forces.

Moreover, while you've sketched the future civilization on Paradise in broad strokes — it's the details that turned out to be sour in every instance.

There's a type of personality — the true warrior-barbarian — that wants fighting. It's his nature that way. He wants to destroy; it gives him the satisfaction of having *power* to see a great building tumble in ruin because he planted explosives under it. To see people shrieking and running in terror because he and his men set fire to their homes. To see whole social orders shattered because *he* attacked them.

This type does not get satisfaction from constructive achievement.

Genghis Khan destroyed; he didn't build anything except stronger means of destroying. His Mongols destroyed cities, because they occupied land that should have been pasturage for horses.

Their *nature* is such that the want-to-be-constructive field would anger, irritate, and repel them. Its existence would motivate them to attack and destroy.

The essence of what you've developed is that not all human beings are alike, and not all would react the same way to a given stimulus. Broadcast a desire-for-sexual-satisfaction, and some men will go looking for a handsome boy, some will kidnap amd start torturing a girl. They may all have sexual interests, but God knows (and so do psychiatrists!) that human beings are *not* equal with respect to even so basic a factor. (And remember incidentally, that some girls will start looking for a man who'll torture them; you'd get some *most* unexpected results!)

There's one Negro who's extremely active in the extremist, Black Power movement, organizing violence-oriented followers. He runs one of the black-power magazines. He's a perfect case-in-point of the warrior-barbarian type *by nature*. He had a Grade A No. 1 education, graduated with honors in architecture, and was employed in a good firm, advanced rapidly, set up his own firm, and got contracts for some of the really big office buildings and factories. Highly successful, and highly respected as a first-class architect.

But he quit — sold out, and set up this extremist group and his publication with the money he'd made. Constructive success, even when he had it, didn't fulfill him; his basic nature is the warrior-barbarian, and the fact that he was brought up in a constructive-achievement society, and achieved very real success in it — left his soul empty.

O.K. — and your people of Paradise are going to have trouble, but good, from that type. No imposed desire-to-be-constructive is going to work on 'em. The only answer humanity has ever found to that type of individual in some 7000 years of recorded efforts, is "He should drop dead — so drop him!" "The only good Injun's a dead un!" (They were correct; the surviving Indians are descended from Indians who didn't consider fighting and looting as "the only way for a man to live!" Look into Scottish history, and you'll see the same phenomenon; the English *couldn't* live at peace with Scottish neighbors, so long as those neighbors held that fighting, battle, and looting were the only fit occupations for a man!)

So, I think you can see, there's lots of room for more stories in that series — both on Paradise and in the Special Forces direction.

Have fun!

Regards,   John

Damon Knight   *October 12, 1966*

Dear Damon:

I was delighted to see **Jim McConnell's** letter anent the real existence of The Establishment.

Being an Inside Member of The Establishment is like being an air-breathing mammal — it's extremely difficult to become aware of the existence of air. The thing that will make you acutely aware that air exists is when somebody cuts you off from it.

Thus for **Rothman**, who's deep in the Inner Establishment, the fact of the existence of the Establishment is genuinely imperceptible. For **McConnell** who is one of those pushing like fury to get the Establishment to move its leaden tail, the existence of the Establishment and its rigid traditions is obvious. And for me, living outside the Establishment, and trying, like **Jim**, to get it to budge its ponderous pomposity, it is also obvious.

But — do you suppose a fish is aware that water exists? How long did it take men to discover that they live deep in a gravity field?

It's futile to argue with **Rothman**, and this letter is not intended to — just to answer **Rothman's** comments to other *SFWA Bulletin* readers.

The distinction between Scientist and Engineer orientations is important — and can best be clarified by discussing Pure Types. There are individuals who are practically pure types, of course — but most *tend* one way or the other, rather than *being* one or the other. However, I think **Dr. Rothman** would agree that the classificiations Metals and Nonmetals as used in chemistry are very useful — though practically none of the elements displays all-metal-and-no-non-metal characteristics. Is iron a metal? Well, ferric oxide, boiled in air with potassium hydroxide, forms potassium ferrate, in which the iron acts as a non-metallic acid-forming element. And selenium, which is a non-metal, nevertheless has an allotrope that's a pretty fair electrical conductor, while telluric acid is a powerful mineral acid capable of taking gold into solution. But tellurium has a metallic luster, and conducts electricity. . . .

This proves that talking about metals and non-metals is nonsense, useless, and worthless? Fluorine is about the only element that's *purely* non-metal, with *no* metallic characteristics.

The classifications of Scientist and Engineer are just as real and valid as the metal-non-metal classification. Useful, too. A scientist is rated by the papers and monographs he publishes; an engineer by the bridges he builds that don't fall down, or the hardware he builds that does what it's supposed to.

Re **Christofilos'** "calculations that no one could understand": **Christofilos** presented his strong focusing principle in the language of alegbra. Any Scientist who can't read algebra is certainly incapable of handling calculus, differential equations, or tensor analysis. So why couldn't they read **Christofilos'** algebra? Because **Christofilos**, at the time, didn't have the Union card — the Guild membership — a PhD in physics, and that proved he couldn't have anything important to offer. Because *they wouldn't try to see* what he had to offer.

Rothman makes a great point of the "Show me a working model!" being the one necessary and sufficient requirement to convince a good Scientist that something new has been discovered. He also explains why, since he *knows* the **Dean** device couldn't possibly work, it was entirely unnecessary for him to go look at it to see if it worked.

My complaint in the original **Dean** Drive article was that **Dean** *couldn't get anybody to look*. No one would look-to-see, because they knew-without-looking that it wouldn't work.

O.K. — now I am convinced that this nonsense about something called "TV" is simply a silly popular superstition. I've never seen it, and I know it can't exist. Utter nonsense to say you can see things through a "TV set" that are happening miles away behind trees, mountains, buildings, etc. Silly nonsense — light simply can't penetrate that sort of obstacle; telescopes make sense, and really work, but they can't see through things. So I know that superstition is silly, and I don't intend to dignify such nonsense by investigating it.

Moreover, a friend of mine in the physics department did let some one of those TV fanatics who claimed he had a working "TV set" demonstrate in his laboratory. Utter failure of course. The TV nut had nothing resembling a picture on his "set" — just a random flashing of dark and bright dots, and wavering lines. Claimed the trouble was there was "interference" from the spark-gap machine my friend's students were working with, and wanted it shut down. They actually did shut it down — and now the failure was blamed on a vibrator being used to agitate some chemicals down the hall.

I know perfectly well this TV nonsense is a hoax, or, at best, the superstition of misguided fools, and I certainly have no intention of dignifying it by examining such things myself. Now let's see you show me it works!

Look, **Dr. Rothman** . . . how can I show you it works *if you absolutely refuse to look*? How can I show you the moons of Jupiter if you positively refuse to look through my telescope?

You live and work in Princeton, New Jersey. O.K. **Dr. Rothman** — go out in the street, and watch the local water company use dowsing rods to locate underground pipes. You don't have to go far, or expend great effort, nor invest any capital — your local water company routinely *uses* on an *engineering* level of "it works — let's use it" an example of an ESP phenomenon that you "know" is nonsense.

You try demonstrating that TV really works, and I can guarantee to ruin your demonstration completely with a little electronic gimmick I can hide in my pack of cigarettes. What electronic circuits can do with great effort and sophistication, an electronic circuit of great simplicity can louse up to a fare-thee-well. All *it* has to do is make a white noise — an electronic Bronx Cheer. In any communications technique, the problem is signal-to-noise ratio — and generating noise energy is extremely easy.

In like sense, what a mental circuit can learn to accomplish — a much simpler mental circuit can louse up completely, by just radiating a mental Bronx Cheer. One brief spray with a can of Krylon, and I can louse up the finest watch ever made. One table spoon of coarse emery in the oil filter, and a champion Ferrari race car won't win a Classic Car race at 15 miles per hour.

The trouble with **Rothman**, as a typical Pure Scientist, is his absolute refusal to look — with the consequence that he can, of course, truthfully say, "I'll believe it when I'm shown," and be perfectly safe. You can't show me a working TV set if I refuse to open my eyes.

Typical of my gripe at the "I know without having to look" attitude is **Rothman's** statement (italics mine), "Then we can say that if telepathy exists it *must* propagate by something like electromagnetic waves, it *can't* go faster than light, it *must* follow the inverse-square law, and *ought* to be detectable by electronic equipment which is sensitive enough to receive waves from galaxies a billion light-years away." For someone who has never studied ESP, **Rothman** sure knows a lot about what it *must* be and what it *can't* do. By what right or evidence does he establish that it *must* be like electromagnetic waves?

It reminds me of the time during WW II when the Germans sent out specially equipped research submarines, to learn what the secret weapon the Allies were using to detect and destroy their submarines was. They took along radio receiving equipment capable of detecting any electromagnetic waves in the entire spectrum of generatable frequencies — from 10 kilocycles all the way to 2,000 megacycles. All three research submarines were detected and sunk thanks to the strange weapon. The researchers had found no activity over the entire radio spectrum, so they knew the Allied system depended on something else. Since their equipment didn't even come close to the 10,000 megacycles the Allied airborne radar used, they never detected that they were being pinged with kilowatts of RF energy at frequencies they were certain could not be generated. They had lousy klystrons, and didn't have magnetrons.

Because their equipment was inadequate *in a way they did not suspect*, they knew-for-certain that the detection system was not radar. And **Rothman** who knows-for-certain just how telepathy has to act is making an equal mistake — the characteristic mistake of the theory-oriented scientist. He's *sure* he knows what it *must* be and what it *can't* do.

Incidentally, that galaxy-detecting hypersensitive electronic equipment wouldn't even know that a kilowatt signal from a pseudo-random noise coded transmitter was blasting through it. It's very carefully designed to integrate signals over a period of time; a signal deliberately coded to resemble noise very closely would be completely suppressed by the integrator circuits.

So your equipment is hypersensitive . . . so what? It's sensitive to the wrong thing. It's like boasting that you have the most complete, sensitive, and perfect analytical equipment possible; it can detect one part in a billion of any chemical element in any combination or mixture. So how good is it at analyzing a magnetic field?

Moreover, **Rothman** wasn't really old enough to be interested back in the 1928-32 period when I was at M.I.T. and the scientists were beating me about the ears for being interested in my "pet off-beat idea such as" commerical use of nuclear energy, space-ships capable of visiting the Moon, radio astronomy, and other such pseudo-science fantasies. And while it was true that stars were able to fuse hydrogen to release energy, the idea that Man could make some kind of machine to do it — utter nonsense, stemming from a complete lack of knowledge of what physics was. Why, you'd have to confine the gas at temperatures of millions of degrees — which was clearly utterly impossible since nothing can exist in a solid state at that temperature.

Rothman better get out of that hydrogen-fusion research; it's clearly pseudo-scientific research — a crazy off-beat idea. And he certainly can't show anybody that it actually works!

Sure, we have more knowledge now, than we did in 1930. But does that make you one whit wiser — more understandingly judicious — than were the professors at M.I.T. in 1930?

The only one of the M.I.T professors who ever helped me with a science-fiction story was another fellow who had a lot of off-beat ideas. A guy who believed in pseudo-scientific fantasy ideas like robots and automatic self-operating machinery — **Norbert Weiner**.

For a man who's working on way-out ideas like hydrogen fusion to call my interest in the present-day, routine engineering application of a solidly useful technology like dowsing "off-beat" is kind of stretching things, isn't it? Your attitude implies "All my ancestors and my predecessors in Science were fools, and only I am wise." They said that what you're doing was pseudo-science and fantasy. Their best judgment was, we can now recognize, badly off. Are you intrinsically wiser — better able to judge the still-unknown areas of the Universe than they? How can you be so arrogantly and smugly certain that you're righter than they were? And can you suggest how I can show you something — when you positively refuse to dignify "such nonsense" by looking at it?

Sincerely,   John W. Campbell

Algis Budrys   *October 24, 1966*

Dear A.J.:

Didn't know whither you'd gone, though I gathered you were no longer bucking for *Playboy's* bunnies.

Like very much that poltergeist item you sent — it's the perfect example of "I wouldn't believe it if I saw it myself!" They really don't, do they?

Here's one to try believing: in the Philippines, near Quezon City, there's a local medical man . . . er, that is, a local *medicine* man! — who has an improbable technique for do-it-yourself surgery. He operates — and I mean abdominal tumor type operations! — with his hands alone. No instruments, no anaesthetics, no sterile technique, no hospital.

I've learned about it now from four different, completely

independent sources, including one medical missionary, a Dr. Hunter, who watched his operations with several Filippino M.D.'s who came out from Quezon City to watch. A TV-news film company made a movie of one of his operations, and a reporter friend of mine saw the film, with two of his friends who were movie special-effects specialists. The experts say they're 100% certain that there's no hokery about it — the film's genuine.

Tony Agpaoa is about 27; he puts the patient on a plain table, exposes the abdomen, then with his right hand makes a pass across the flesh . . . and it opens, as though he'd pulled a secret zipper. He reaches in, feels about a bit, and pulls out the fibrous tumor mass, which he pinches off with his fingers. Then he pinches the incision closed with his fingers; in about one minute, the flesh is re-zipped, and there's nothing but a thin white line of a long-healed scar. The patient is told to get up and go home — and does.

I don't know that I've gotten any of your releases about "Lovely Mary Sue Johnson, the Fish Cakes Queen," but I've gotten lots of wonderful releases about the new scientific breakthroughs like battery powered toy air-cushion cars, and electric-powered flea-killer applicators for your pets.

How lyrical can one get about an electrically powered flea-powder rubber-in?

Regards,   John

Andrew J. Offutt   *October 31, 1966*

Dear Mr. Offutt:

One factor usually overlooked in damning cliches is that the basic requirement of writing is to communicate — and that means using a mutually understood vocabulary. The most common cliche going is the verb to be — everbody uses it. Why not be more original and use a new term — say "He farbed glissing slowly," for instance?

My point: it's essential to balance original creativity with familiar, communicative expressions. Too many novel and clever metaphors and similies and the reader's mind wanders away from the story line.

Re weapons in the future: O.K. — so we won't use a laser or a rifle. We'll use a "blaster," or a "proton gun" or a "flamer." They're cliches too, aren't they? If I say the hero used a *gwofl* totally without description, that's not a cliche. Also not very communicative. What was a deLameter. How'd it work?

As an editor, I'd like to see more attention given to proposing new space drives — but I can't publish what I can't get authors to write. And man, you don't know the fierce pride authors take in writing only their own great, creative thoughts, and haughtily rejecting the suggestion that they should take (sniff!) someone else's ideas . . . or write what someone else wants.

Only the very top pros are sure enough of themselves as creative individuals to do that sort of thing!

Finally, if I could think of some way of collecting, I'd be happy to bet that missile weapons — rifles, pistols, etc. — *will* be used 5000 years hence.

In WW II at various times and places, various fighting forces used, against their enemies, cross-bows, long-bows, knives, battle-axes, swords, sling-and-stone, clubs, blow-guns, and just about every form of weapon man's 7000 year history records. Plus a few recorded only in prehistoric cave-paintings. The little brown brothers in the Viet Cong are using sharpened bamboo stakes, poisoned.

The advantage of the primitive is that it's apt to be simple, and exceedingly rugged. Wonder how a laser weapon would stand up to being lugged through a muddy stream, dropped in wet sand, bounced down a 6-foot rockfall, and wiped off with a dirty rag?

Energy storage is a very difficult business; strained atomic configurations such as [missing word: ed.] are remarkably reliable and exceedingly rugged energy-storge devices.

The greatest possibile energy storage per cubic inch is matter; it's exceedingly hard to handle when you pack a bit of kinetic energy into it. You can't reflect it, phase it out, interference-cancel it —

It isn't a bad weapon — and it's extremely simple.

Bow-and-arrow is superior to rifle fire in jungle country. Arrows don't deflect worth a damn; bullets do.

Regards,   John W. Campbell

RE "Ever Read Venus Equitorial?" by Andrew J. Offutt

Joseph L. Green   *November 16, 1966*

Dear Joe:

Tsk! Tsk! Your Centaur propulsion engineer is evidently a real engineer-type that thinks in that horrible confused, mixed-up crazy English system (?) of units. The B.P. of liquid hydrogen is -252.7° according to the *Handbook of Chem. & Phys.* — I was off a few degrees when I used general memory instead of looking up the figure.

Trouble is — I think in Centigrade degrees for anything but weather temperatures. Oxygen's B.P. is about -180°C.

I think you're slighly biased in saying that liq-He was developed "primarily" for controlling liq-H_2. The boys at AEC and Bu.

Stand. did go to work trying to control liq-H_2 with liq-He because of the problem tritium presented, in Test Mike. Test Mike involved a lot of *most* expensive tritium, and their liq-tritium could *not* be simply vented off — not when you've stuck it together, atom by atom, in an immense, strictly-for-that-purpose 2 gigabuck Savannah River plant. And that was before they found a catalyst to make the ortho-para conversion go rapidly to completion, so that even perfectly insulated tritium wouldr·'t stop boiling off.

Old Onnes developed liq-He — and most of the work done on the problem was done — for cryogenic research purposes, for studying superconductivity, superfluidity, and various other phenomena that are achievable *only* by using liq-He.

Which reminds me of the acute annoyance I felt when an oh-so-scientific book reviewer, reviewing my book, *The Atomic Story*, chided me for not knowing that helium had been solidified. I said, very carefully, that "No amount of cold has ever been able to solidify helium." I didn't want to go into elaborations about helium's peculiarities — I just wanted to explain why helium wasn't used as a moderator in the first nuclear piles. (It would have been the absolute ideal, because it has 0.00000 . . . absorption of neutrons, and slows neturons very quickly.) I had carefully stated that *no amount of cold* would solidify it — it's still superfluid at 0.001° K. It takes a combination of *cold and pressure*. The son-of-a-gun who reviewed the book was too anxious to prove he knew something that he neglected to read what I said.

I can wait the three-four months you need; I've got a good inventory of articles at the moment.

Re sending a Surveyor to the Moon "even at apogee." A lot of people are confused by the problems of space flight — and whoever told you that was one of them. If you land a Surveyor on the Moon, that must mean that you've exactly matched the energy of the Moon in its orbit. And that means that you can match that energy — the sum of orbital kinetic and potential energy — *in any part of the orbit*. Because necessarily, the orbital energy of the Moon is conserved; the *total* energy is KE + PE = Constant; at perigee there's less Potential and more Kinetic energy; at apogee there's more PE and less KE — but the sum is constant.

Some of the asteroids come closer to Earth than 250,000 miles — but landing a Surveyor on such an asteroid at 200,000 miles would be enormously more difficult than landing on the Moon at 238,000 — actually more difficult than a Mars landing. Because the asteroid is, of course, in an orbit that retreats a couple hundred million miles further from the sun than Mar's orbit — and you have to match that orbit. Which means energy sufficient to carry your vehicle 350,000,000 miles up in the Sun's gravity field.

Distance doesn't mean a thing is space — It's total energy potential that counts.

Regards,   John

Harry Altshuler   *November 21, 1966*

Dear Mr. Altshuler:

Sorry, but no dice on this one.

First, seeing it through the eyes of a doped protagonist doesn't help any — the situation is foggy all the way through. Second, the court trial system is a lousy way to bring out Truth — the trial system is based on a black-white conception of Truth, and essentially that's an always-false proposition. But this results, in your story, in no opportunity to express the rationality on both sides.

And as a persuasive pleader for his moderate cause, the protagonist is pure Egghead — he might please some of his Egghead friends with his learned discourse, but he wouldn't get to first base swaying the multitude. Quoting Egghead philosophers like Huxley et al, gets you nowhere with the mob. It takes Churchill to come up with expressions that people remember — things like "blood, sweat, toil and tears" — things with emotional appeal.

The damn fool Scientists lost out because they'd lost all touch with the people. So's your protagonist — or he wouldn't pull such windy philosophy on 'em!

Finally, any organization that can manufacture and produce spare parts for automatic automobile repair equipment and nuclear reactors secretly, distribute them so secretly the people around don't know how it's done, and has noiseless high-lift aircraft can most certainly crack a prisoner out of any primitive hoosegow the Emperor's Secret Police has him stashed away in.

Such an organization is the equivalent of a multi-billion-dollar enterprise.

Sincerely,   John W. Campbell

RE: "Trial By Fire," by **James E. Gunn**

P. Schuyler Miller   *June 15, 1967*

Dear Schuy:

It usually isn't the major distributor that returns the magazines without even displaying them — it's the lazy slob who's running the newsstand, and doesn't see any reason why anybody'd buy that junk, so why should he bother bending over his fat gut and putting 'em out?

Sure . . . TV has cut into reading time — and more than that, kids aren't learning to read now as they used to. (**Lynn**, my middle-sized daughter, teaches remedial reading in Dayton, Ohio; believe me, the kids *don't* learn and *won't*.) That cuts down on possible sales. "Down with literacy; up with comics!"

And sure, Triangle News is a monopoly. So is United Parcel, finally; it took the department stores in the New York Area thirty years or more to stop sending a procession of expensive trucks, expensively manned, down one suburban street, one after the other, because Mrs. Kibbutz bought a lamp at Macy's, a shade at Gimbels', an end table at Wannamaker's, an ash tray at Bamgerger's, and a bookend at Bloomingdale's. They finally caught on it was a damn sight better economics to send *one* truck, with *one* man down the street and deliver all of Mrs. Kibbutz purchases. The dairies haven't gotten that idea across to their unionized drivers yet, so there's still a stupid procession of seven different dairy trucks down our street every other morning. I'm hoping United Parcel takes over that business, too, so we can cut some of the feathers out of the price of milk, and remove some of the featherbedders to more useful areas.

Remember when Philadelphia had the Keystone and Bell telephone systems competing? God help the Philadelphians! You had to have two phones — one of each — to be able to call *all* your friends.

There are things that are natural monopolies — typically, distribution activities fall in that class. Don't misassign the blame for the fact that people don't read as much as they used to.

The fact is, distribution is the toughest part of any business that deals in small units. Sure — Bethlehem Steel doesn't have too much trouble with distribution of twenty-ton bridge girders — but pity the drugstore owner with eleventy seven different brands of tooth paste, powder, or glue!

In this case, it's not City Hall you're fighting — it's the nature of the real-world problem. One of the reasons *Analog* gets better display than most magazines is very simple; *Astounding-Analog* has been appearing every month for over 30 years. Simple-minded newstand operators have been putting it in the same old place on their same old stands for as long as they've been in business. Or the same old place Papa used to put it when the current owner-operator was a boy, 35 years ago. It takes no thought — just reflex. Give him a new mag, and he has to reshuffle things, and work out a problem of spatial geometry . . . or send it back to the distributor without displaying it. Guess what he tends to do!

If you think it's just science-fiction mags that have trouble . . . guess again!

The prize item I myself encountered was a line-up on a New York newstand, with *Playboy*, *Sir!*, *Fling*, *Mademoiselle* and *Cavalier* all in a row. I mean, man, some of those newstand operators are sharp like a wet noodle.

If you specifically order the sci-fi mags from the handiest newstand, he'll get 'em for you; if he doesn't, write the publisher and the local operator will get visited by a whole series of publisher's roadmen finding out What The Hell.

The distributors know damn well that publishers *do* have roadmen who go around and make a living checking up on what they're doing; it's the local operators who don't give a damn, and don't believe roadmen really exist.

When I heard from one subscriber who'd just moved to Cocoa Beach, Florida, that his newstand didn't carry *Analog*, I naturally sicced the circulation people on the case. A newstand in Cocoa Beach, right next to Cape Kennedy, that didn't carry *Analog*. . . ? What was going on?

The reader was right; he'd gone three months running and never seen a copy of *Analog*. He went in about the 1st of the month, by which time of course the regulars had all picked up their copies. That particular stand only stocked 55 copies a month. The Newstand at the M.I.T. Cooperative Society store has had only one or none copies when I was there four times. They get over 100 copies a month, I believe — and they're a circulation man's ideal. They sell 'em, instead of returning 'em!

Regards, John

William R. Burkett, Jr.   *July 24, 1967*

Dear Mr. Burkett:

The best answer I can give is to tell you of the old story about the old New England sea captain who'd retired and moved into a small New England town. He had fascinating sea stories and the boys in town were always gathering round him to hear them.

However, he also had a peg leg . . . and that was one thing he wouldn't talk about, though the kids repeatedly pestered him about that story. Finally one day he said, "All right — all right, dag nab it, I'll answer just *one* question, if you dang kids promise you'll stop pesterin' me about it. You agree?"

"Sure! Sure, Cap'n!"

"All right; what's your question?"

"What happened to your leg, Cap'n?" their spokesman asked eagerly.

"It was bit off," snapped the captain.

And the name of that story is "Logistics."

Regards, John W. Campbell

RE: "A Matter of Logistics"

Joseph P. Martino   *August 9, 1967*

Dear Joe:

This one needs some minor rewriting at the end for greater clarity.

The Arcani didn't have a "secret weapon" at the physical-objective level — but they did have one at the subjective-organizational level. They had a secret *tactic* — the secret was *in the way they used their weapons.*

So the fact is they did have a secret weapon — as much a secret weapon as radar was during WW II. They did have a superior detection technique — it just wasn't a physical change-of-circuitry superiority.

A friend of mine after WW II, in the Navy, was in charge of electronics research to improve radar range. Immediately after one quarterly inspection, when he could expect three months before the next, he launched a project on his own that he knew damn well he couldn't get authorized.

Before the next inspection, he'd succeeded in having achieved something that effectively multiplied the transmitter power of every radar in the Navy by 16 — for a total expenditure of $35,000.

He'd observed as a battle veteran during WW II that some radar operators could spot targets that were completely buried in "grass" to other operators using the same equipment. What he did was to hire some experimental psychologists to find out how those super operators did it — and teach ordinary operators the technique. The results effectively doubled the useful range of existing radars — equivalent to a 16X increase in transmitter power.

Now had he developed a "secret weapon"? Had he increased the sensitivity of the detecting devices?

At any rate, since his unauthorized expenditure of Navy funds had been so howlingly successful, his Admiral happily gave full *post facto* authorization — and commendation.

What the story needs is clarification that there *was* a secret weapon, but that it was a tactic, not an object.

There is, incidentally, a possibility of a sequel here. You know the old Military saying, "There's always some poor slob that doesn't get the word." O.K. — so the men working on the Arcani ship, patiently trying to figure out whathehell this gizmo is supposed to be doing, trying to find the secret weapon, don't get the

496

word right away. Somebody sort of forgets to tell them — analyzing the Arcani ship is certainly important in itself.

And one of them, laboring over those intricate circuitry blocks, using microtome slices a few molecules thick and electron-micrograms, field-emission micrograms, etc., to figure out what it is, finally deduces that it's a gadget for transmitting and receiving faster-than-light messages. (If the ships can exceed light-speed, then *some* organizing mechanism is travelling faster than light to maintain their organization.)

So he and his group sweat it out, and build up a unit of their own, based on what the Arcani unit *must* have been.

Only, of course, the Arcani unit wasn't. But *theirs is.* However only after they've demonstrated their gadget do they get "the word" that the Arcani had no secret device, and certainly didn't have a $c+$ signalling unit.

Regards,   John W. Campbell

RE: "Secret Weapon" by **Joseph P. Martino**

Lyle R. Hamilton   *August 24, 1967*

Dear Lyle:

Psychosomatics are real fancy contraptions to get hooked into. I've done considerable studying of them for some 16 years — and know enough about them to recognize their high potency.

For one thing, they're a form of neurosis, and have the characteristics of neuroses in this respect; knowing in full that you have claustrophobia doesn't cure it. Knowing you have xenophobia doesn't make it easier to deal with strangers. Conscious knowledge does some good; you can control the public manifestations, and consciously avoid situations you can't handle.

Psychosomatics are controlled by a level below conscious, that's for sure. You should see the remarkable tricks that can be produced by hypnosis in a good subject — phenomena that prove beyond possibility of argument that the mind has complete control over blood flow in capillaries. "Bleeding wounds" can be produced on command — without any external injury to the skin whatever. And cuts through the skin can be commanded not to bleed — and they don't.

With control of capillaries like that, it's pretty obvious how psychosomatic control can produce things like bleeding ulcers! And *full* psychosomatic control, if conscious control could be achieved, would permit an individual to throttle a cancerous growth by simply commanding all capillaries leading to it to shut off all blood flow.

Re business and article possibilities.

What's for after the Moon?

One suggestion that's damn well worth considering and looking into is a visit to a handy asteroid. There'd be a hell of a lot to learn from an honest-to-God asteroid — a lot of information about what they are, and possibly why and when and how.

No instrumented probe can do any good on that; you need men who actually land on the thing, study it, photograph it, gather samples, and choose the locations from which they pick their samples. Not just random samples. You need samples studied *in situ*. You need core drillings.

Fine — only a manned mission to 350,000,000 miles out would take about 3 years in orbit — and we haven't got even a start of a beginning of a life-support system that good. And it'll be *massive* when we do get one. And it'd take a Nova or a whole flock of Saturn V's to boost the stuff into orbit.

Nevertheless there's a way the next mission beyond the Moon could be, and should be, a manned mission to an asteroid.

Icarus comes so close to Earth that it's very little further than the Moon, and because it's gravity field is near zero, it's a lot easier to visit, land, and take off from. True; because of it's high orbital velocity, it'll take a hell of a high boost to match orbits, and then slow down to rematch Earth's. BUT — the thing comes so close that the Moon-trip equipment will be entirely adequate for life-support — the trip won't take more than a week or ten days. You can get away with bottled gases and chemical absorbents — no biological recycling of biological wastes necessary.

(My own idea of life-support system recycling involves running *all* wastes through a small reactor in which a temperature of approximately 2800-3000 degrees C is maintained. The outflowing gases — and believe me, they'd all be gases! — would be purely inorganic compounds like water, carbon dioxide, nitrogen plus traces of sodium, potassium, iron, zinc, etc. oxides. No organic compounds would stay organic through that cycle. The traces of mineral oxide can be washed, with the CO_2 and water, into a plant-growth hydroponic system that produces food and oxygen while absorbing CO_2.)

The beauty of the Icarus mission would be that *no complex life support system would be needed*.

Re commuter tranportation: remember this area is the heart of the "northeast corridor"; there's a single, continous suburban-and-urban development strip from the New Hampshire boundary down into Virginia. In New Brunswick, N.J., half the commuters take the train to Philadelphia, and the rest board the one to New York. It's the area where they're working on the 160 miles-per-hour trains; something has to be done to cut down air traffic. The air shuttle from the New York area to Boston and Washington are, alone, working on a 30 minute headway all day — and all the other regular long-haul airlines are pulling through here too, of course.

We've *got* to come down to earth again!

Regards, John

Gordon Dickson   *September 7, 1967*

Dear Gordie:

Sorry I didn't see you around at the end of the Convention — talking with fans and new authors, with **Isaac** and **Harry Stubbs**, the costume parade and art exhibit helped give me some clues as to what's going on — and what we *have* to do.

The Awards business — Hugos, etc. — doesn't tell a thing because those awards actually go to personal friends on personal friendship grounds, not on the basis of achievement or quality. [**Jack Schoenherr**, probably the best *artist* science fiction ever had, got one Hugo once. He never attended a convention, never did any artwork for the fan magazines, never made personal friends. We're losing him now; we can't match *Reader's Digest's* $3000 offers — nor the book illustration rates the big publishing houses give him. The man is *good* [(**Kelly Freas** who's good, and attended the convention, and made friends, got it for six years. **Jack Gaughan**, who does a great deal of fan'magazine artwork for the boys, got a double Hugo; as an artist, he's second class.)]

The things that count are what the fans *do*, not what they *say*. And the art exhibition was 100% pure fantasy; there wasn't a science-fiction piece in the whole show. The costume parade was full of barbarians and wizards and fantasy — the only science-fiction was the *Star Trek* set-up.

It *was not a science-fiction convention*. It was a fantasy convention throughout!

O.K. — how come? Wha' happen?

In essence, the swords-and-sorcery and **Tolkien** have displaced science fiction almost completely.

Why?

Well, partly — but I think a small part — is the current leaning to escape-from-reality, LSD etc. to the undisciplined world of my opinion is as good as any other, and don't tell me there's a Universe's Opinion I've got to accept, willy-nilly.

But the larger item, I suspect, is *human beings want heroes*. Real heroes. Not common-men-who-proved-under-stress-they-could-struggle-through.

The swords-and-sorcery yarns are all based on superhuman

heroes — and it's clearly obvious the readers love 'em.

Now in as much as it's the readers who pay for the magazines, it damn well behooves us to give 'em what they want — and they obviously want super-heroes on the Conan order. They want for **Frank Herbert's** "Dune," with his super-hero. They used to go with all-out enthusiasm for **Jack Williamson's** really-not-very-good "Legion" stories. And **Doc Smith's** "Galactic Patrol" series.

Now if the fans want — and they evidently do! — swords-and-sorcery type yarns, then we had damn well better give 'em the type of thing they want, or get out of the way for someone who will.

However, it's the *type of thing* they want; not necessarily that specific thing. Give 'em swords-and-science, and they will — as they did when science fiction was starting — go just as strong for that.

But they clearly do *not* want the "sophisticated" non-hero type of story. They do *not* want the pure think-piece.

Tolkien's immensely popular Rings series has two powerful heroes — Strider the King and Gandolf the Gray — who are protecting and guiding the Common Man figure, the Hobbit, who is cursed, rather than blest, with a magical power, the Ring. Basically, Strider is the Warrior-King, and Gandolf the Scientist in that framework.

All the characters — villains and heroes alike — are far larger than life size.

And the readers love it, despite its extreme wordiness.

Look at the famous classics of science fiction, and see what you get. "Slan," with a specifically so-named superman hero. Again and again you find the readers, during the developmental period of science fiction, were presented with real heroes.

Human beings want heroes to admire — from Odysseus right through to Muad 'Dib of "Dune."

They want hand-to-hand combat, and they want brains and vision — which you built into your Dorsai. It isn't just that *I* want 'em — it's evident that *they* want 'em.

And, dammit, stories of swords-and-science are just as possible as swords-and-sorcery — if we can just chuck out this damned stupidity of the non-heroic central character.

The essence of the true hero is strength in all senses — strong body, strong mind, strong determination, and strong wisdom. He's ruthlessly honest in ethics — whether he's being ruthless to villains, or ruthless to himself. If a job has to be done that's almost certain to kill the guy who tackles it, he's willing to assign himself, or anybody else best gifted for the task. If the deadly villain has to be baited into a situation where he can be trapped, he'll bait the trap with himself, or his dearly beloved, or Joe Doakes — depending on which one makes the best bait, not on which one he'd least object to losing.

There are times when, to be honest, you must lie; he will therefore be a liar. There are times when, to be moral, you must be dishonest; then he is dishonest. And he will be immoral when that's needed for ethical behavior. He will, in other words, be a real hero, who earns the deep and sincere respect of any man — but is uncomfortable to be around, and is not a lovable person.

And incidentally, when he has led his followers to victory over the deadly enemy — he'll be turned out as quickly as they can get rid of him. He's uncomfortable.

Look at what happened to Winston Churchill. He was *not* liked in the 1936-39 period. He was followed with immense respect and loyalty through 1940-45. He was dumped as quickly as possible after Hitler's defeat; blood, sweat and tears he had given them, as promised, and he'd led them to victory — but blood, sweat and tears has never been exactly popular.

When he died, of course, there was a tremendous outpouring of affection; they knew he was a great man, and now that he was no longer a living force to menace them with his ruthless determination, they could safely express that respect and admiration.

Dead heroes are so much more readily accepted and admired than overwhelmingly powerful living personalities!

Except in stories, that is — where you can *be* the overwhelming hero.

And if you can be a sword-wielding hero in fantasy, dammit, you can be a sword-wielding hero in science fiction. The future is going to have just as desperate a need for heroic leaders as the past ever did!

Regards,   John

Virginia Kidd   *September 21, 1967*

Dear Miss Kidd:

Kay MacLean's yarn is good — I want it. BUT . . . it isn't ended strongly enough. And this one needs a strong ending, because it has everything it takes to be a first-of-a-series. The Rescue Squad background is great stuff for a lot of series.

The ending should make much more strongly the fact that Ahmed is a powerful personality indeed — and has the genuine respect of his department. That his recommendations are considered most carefully.

George here is indeed short on brains and motivation — at least on the intellectual-logical type of brains. Objective-logical brains, he ain't got it.

So? So Eusapia Palladino, who repeatedly demonstrated levitation and telekinesis under full laboratory control, was studied by the great psychologist, Prof. Lombros, and his students, and officially declared a moron. And **Edgar Cayce** who repeatedly — with full documentation — demonstrated full clairvoyance, and on some occasions showed highly specific precognition, was definitely no genius. Talented, yes — genius, no. People I've spoken to who knew him personally agree that he was a medium-to-high grade moron.

The *idiot savant* types generally are not bright — but they can extract the cube roots of seven digit numbers in seconds, add six seven-digit numbers as fast as you can rattle them off, determine whether a given eleven-digit number is or is not a prime.

Our George, here, is evidently a nice, respectable, healthy young moron. With a Talent; he's telempathetic. He has precisely the Talent the Rescue Squad people need.

But because he's a moron, he can't even begin to pass their logical-intellectual tests.

Before the days of electronic computers, just think how enormously valuable one of those *idiot savant* computers would have been in an astonomical observatory! He could compute orbits for them in a hundreth the time it took normal men. In a physics lab, he could compute out wave-numbers from spectrographic data to find series-relationships normal physicists would never find.

There was Blind Tom, a Negro idiot — and a low-grade idiot at that! — years ago. He'd been born a slave; some sharp-witted guy bought him for practically nothing — and made a living because of his Talent. Tom was so stupid he had to be told when to eat. He had a vocabulary of about 24 words. He had to be taken to the bathroom and told what to do. He was as near to being brainless as a living organism could get.

But with good care, and careful guardianship, he could be kept alive, fairly healthy, and quite content. Of course he was freed by the Emancipation Proclamation legally — but his "owner" simply became his "guardian" and continued working with him.

Blind Tom was a biological tape recorder. You could play any sequence of notes on a piano in his presence, and on being shoved toward the piano, Tom would sit down and play the same series of notes with exact reproduction. Do an original composition that no one had ever heard before, or a Beethoven sonata — all the same to Blind Tom. Play a pure random-noise sequence; just as a tape recorder could reproduce that sequence perfectly, so could Blind Tom.

Talents have zero point zero zero zero correlation — a strong negative! — between *displaying* Talents and high intelligence.

People with good brains learn fast and early that it's undesirable to display them; only a low-grade mind is so stupid as to persist in a line of action that causes them to be rejected by those around them.

Ahmed and/or George here would make a terrific team.

And inasmuch as a lot of the people in a great city who are in desperate trouble get that way because somebody *is* trying to do them in, or extract information the hard way, much of the Ahmed, George & Co.'s cases will be of acute and immediate interest to the police. And some will be CIA-FBI cases.

And as George is rewarded by attention, respect and genuine admiration, by people he respects and admires, for his accomplishments by using his Talent, he will be motivated to use it and develop it.

Really acute hate — the "I am going to kill that bastard slow and vicious!" searing kind — no doubt radiates too. Which would interest the police no end. (It wouldn't work on professional killers, who are no more emotionally involved than a farmer at hog-sticking time.)

Ah, yes — lots of stories possible.

But *this* story's got to end with Ahmed somehow putting it over that George is just the fear-hound the Squad needs — whether he's got intellectual-logical type brains or not. That while their tests and training programs are just fine for finding individuals who have excellent logical-objective brains, plus a little empathy — it's empathic data-sensors they need before the thinker-type can use their thinking effectively. Sure — it'd be nice if George not only had the Talent, but also had the brains.

Except that there's that strong negative correlation between *displaying* a talent and high intelligence!

And . . . how about "Fear-Hound" as a title? The present one is long, vague, and not particularly interesting to a guy thumbing through a magazine on a newsstand.

Remember magazines depend on impulse-buyers for growth in circulation. Our regular readers buy because they know the magazine; impulse buyers buy because something sounds intriguing — and if they like what they get, they're our new readers. Titles are, therefore, important.

Regards,   John W. Campbell

Re: "Rescue, New York City, 2000 A.D."
by **Katherine MacLean**

503

Dear Mrs. Shiras:

One of the troubles with writing or public speaking is that "what you said" is not what you meant, but what the audience understood you to mean. And one of the necessary functions of an editor is to be a professional misunderstander. He's got to spot and catch unintentional implications, unmeant *double entendres*, etc., before both author and editor become famous for their howlers.

In the case of your story, the easiest interpretation would be "In Praise of LSD Living."

Unfortunately, the prime effect of LSD is to shut down the judgement faculty — the ability to discriminate and evaluate. That's what leads to the individual's impressions that he's thinking magnificent, new, wonderful, revelations. Anoxia — as when a pilot flies above about 20,000 feet without oxygen mask — has almost exactly the same effect.

Sure, the "Flower children" love everybody; they've lost their sense of judgement and discrimination. They would, consequently love Adolph Hitler, Lucretia Borgia, and Jack the Ripper, too.

Of course currently "judgement" and "discrimination" are held to be Evil Words and Wicked Thoughts. But that won't last long; no culture that tries to operate without those basics lasts long. It's like an LSD tripper who decides he can fly without wings, and demonstrates it by stepping off the 10th floor roof, a conclusion reached by lack of judgement.

As to the proposed with story: I don't know whether you've been reading *Analog* the last few years, but **Randall Garrett** has been doing a lovely series about a world or historyline that branched off from ours (or vice versa!) when Richard the Lionhearted came from the Crusades and settled down to being a good ruler of England and France.

In the world, Science never developed; instead Magic was developed into a sound, logical, reliable and workable technique. One of Garrett's principal characters is Master Sean O' Lochlainn, Master Sorcerer, duly licensed by the Church as a White Magician.

Magic, approached as a logical, laws-of-nature system, is not fantasy — it's science fiction. But magic approached as a sort of LSD-dream-come true, without limits or coherence, is fantasy — and not for us, no matter how good a yarn it is.

I'm definitely looking for psi stories — stories involving psionic powers such as telepathy, clairvoyance, teleportation, telekinesis, etc. (You can't call telekinesis "ESP" because it's not extrasensory *preception*; it's extra-muscular *manipulation*. Therefore the border term *psi* or *psionics* was developed to cover both ESP and extra-muscular manipulation.)

Whether your story falls in the "fantasy" or the "science fiction" category, then, depends on how you've handled the concept.

Knowing you, I imagine it's more on the science-fiction side!

Incidentally, the TV shows "I Dream of Jeannie" and "My Favorite Martian" are both fantasy. They can do anything, with no consistent, logical rules.

Calling the magical character "a Martian" instead of "a genie" makes no difference; they're both pure fantasy.

Regards,   John W. Campbell

Gordon R. Dickson   *September 25, 1967*

Dear Gordie:

"Spacepaw" came in, so I read that before answering your long letter. You didn't mention that one to me — either at the convention or in your letter — and I can see why; you're right, it's not for us.

However, I'm glad I got to see it at this time.

Bill is a pretty typical anti-hero. He stumbles and fumbles and bumbles his way through the yarn, manipulated and pushed around by everybody from Bone Breaker, More Jam, and Sweet Thing through Grandfather Squeaky to the Humanoid. He don't know nuffin, and he don't do nuffin — it's all done to him. But he wins out in the end, as anti-heroes, the apotheoses of the Common Dope, always do.

Thanks of course to the astute manipulations of Hill Bluffer, Bone Breaker and More Jam. You gave him an appropriate name — Pick-and-Shovel, which is about the level of competence he demonstrated.

One of the characteristics of the anti-hero is that everything he does is on a courage-of-the-cornered-rat basis; he's continuously defensively desperate, struggling along from frying pan to frying pan.

The hero type has self-confidence, and accepts without argument that a strong offense is the best defense. He doesn't seek to escape from the terrible position he's in — he acts to manipulate that situation to one that suits him. He operates on the basis that his head is not solely for stopping other people's clubs, black-jacks and/or other types of injurious devices.

Take a look at some of the old N.C. Wyeth illustrations of adventure yarns of a generation or two ago; the heroes are in extremely dangerous situations — but with a grin, not a grimace of terror. Robert Louis Stevenson did a hell of a good job of telling his story in *Treasure Island*, and Wyeth did a terrific job of illustration. Long John Silver is an ambivalent character — half hero, half villain — and comes out believable and rather likeable, for all he's a rapacious old bastard. But all he does is done with a sense of humor, of underlying fun and enjoyment of danger — not a snivelling thief! The characters Wyeth painted were doing what they did because they damn well *liked* doing it that way — because it was fun. It might kill 'em — they knew that! — but it was fun enough to be worth the risk!

The modern race driver that enters at Indianapolis, or the Grand Prix, isn't racing for money; you need a sane man for that kind of work — the cars and preparations are too damned expensive to be wasted on a fool — and the money the winner collects wouldn't be reward enough for any sane man to take the risk involved.

They do it for the fun; the winnings hardly pay their costs, even if they collect $150,000. When Ford Motors tosses a quarter of a megabuck into the pot to build a car, they can charge it off to research and advertising. ("Winning races sells cars!") The drivers can't. There are a number of Argentinos who race for themselves — buying their own cars, and hiring their own staff of mechanics, engineers, etc. They have to be a millionaire to even start — and they're *not* racing for money!

Incidentally, there are a couple of technical errors in "Spacepaw."

Your Hemnoid, from a 1.5 g—world, wouldn't have much of an advantage over a human being just because of that. Remember that some men here on Earth are four to five times as strong as others. Take a clerical type desk-worker from a 1.5 g-world, and match him against a 6'4" professional lumberjack from Earth — and guess who'd get his limbs tied in a bow-knot!

Moreover, a Hemnoid, as defined, would *not* have slower, clumsier reflexes than a human; he'd have significantly faster ones.

Standing upright requires a constant readjustment of muscular tensions to maintain that inherently unstable position. When a gusty wind blows, your reflexes *have* to act faster than gravity forces on your body do. You can't stand upright on any planet if your reflexes and neuro-muscular coordination aren't faster than the local gravity. If you drop something, your reflexes need to be fast enough to catch it. On a moderately high-g world, even if the people aren't terribly strong — they'll be awful fast! Entities evolved on a low-g world would be slow reacting, simply because they don't have to be fast.

Now as to the lifting contest with Flat Fingers.

Flat Fingers would never try to lift by pulling on the rope run over by a beam; he'd know better. That would limit his lift to something considerably less than his body weight. You can't pull *down* with more force than it takes to lift you into the air. Unless you have your feet clamped down.

In the days before we had handy differential chain hoists and power-operated winches, a standard village test of strength was to take an anvil by the tine, and hold it out at arm's length. Now a standard anvil is a 110 pound slug of steel.

Weight-lifters, even operating under the very limiting rules of competition weight-lifting, regularly hoist more than their body weight overhead.

Several professional weight-lifters have demonstrated ability to lift 3500 pounds or so — by getting *over* it and lifting up. On this basis a Dibilian blacksmith known for his strength could be expected to lift about 12,000 pounds — six tons.

The standard differential chain hoists commonly used are rated at two tons.

Bill had better have a handy-dandy degravitor hitched onto that load when he does his lift!

Incidentally, Sandow, the famed strong-man, had, as part of his regular act, lifting two full-grown horses. He had a sort of scale-pan balance affair, with a harness that rested on his shoulders. He stood on a raised platform, and the two horses were on the "pans" of the scale-pan affair. The total lift he performed regularly ran between 3200 and 3700 pounds.

Now in addition, there's the phenomenon of "hysterical strength"; I thought that was the gag you were going to pull in the great fight with Bone Breaker. Known fact: a human being, under intense emotional stimulation, can suddenly — 20 seconds maximum! — display absolutely fantastic strength. A 120 pound girl, who sees her 6-year-old-son under a fallen garage overhead door, bleeding and screaming, lifts the door with one hand, and pulls out the boy with the other. Next day six strong men are needed to lift the door back in place.

A farmer and his 14-year-old son, in their farm truck, go off the road and overturn into a ditch. Farmer gets out — and finds that his son is pinned under the fallen truck, under four feet of ditch-water. So he takes hold of the truck and lifts it back onto its wheels, and pulls out his son.

The father of a friend of mine — a lawyer — came back to his office to find some enraged maniac pistol-whipping his wife-secretary. So he picked up the 600 pound office safe and threw it across the room at the guy. Scratch one maniac. A reasonably powerful human, with "hysterical strength" turned on, and the faster reflexes Earth's gravity would naturally give him, might quite genuinely overwhelm even Bone Breaker. I don't think even Bone Breaker would feel too pugnacious after being clobbered with a 600 pound safe, for instance! And from actual historical instances, we know that a human male, in good condition, a fairly strong man to begin with, *could* pick up the 900 pound Bone Breaker and throw him through a warehouse shed wall!

Part of that training he got could include How To Turn on Total Strength When Absolutely Necessary!

Another possibility — the Muddy Nosers don't play baseball. They throw rocks at each other — but by that they mean boulders. A reasonably trained baseball pitcher, with fist-size broken up rock, and Earthly neuromuscular speed could cut a Dibilian to ribbons before the Dibilian's boulders could even get close. Even your Hemnoid Fatty would have an exceedingly rugged time — if he wasn't a baseball pitcher too.

A track superintendent, walking the U.P. tracks and inspecting the right-of-way some years back was faced with an angry grizzly. The bear started to charge — and five minutes later he was dead. Track ballast, in the hands of a semi-pro baseball pitcher, is a most deadly weapon. The bear had been blinded in both eyes in about three seconds — and not even a grizzly's skull can stand up to a bombardment of sharp-edged rocks from a trained pitching arm.

I don't ordinarily do any editing on a manuscript I'm not going to buy — but I did change "Washington" to "Columbus" for you. The Columbus and the egg bit you wound up having *Washington* explain that, "It's easy — after someone has shown you how!" Slight confusion of cultural heroes!

Now as to the proposed novel in the Dorsai series.

Writing, so far as I have been able to make out, is just about a 100% subconscious function, with the conscious mind sort of reading over your shoulder, interestedly watching what the story says. "I" doesn't do it — something else does the job.

When I was writing, I'd start, usually, with a very general idea, and figure out an ending. Then the hardest thing was figuring out where to begin the story. Sort of like it takes a good quarry-man to recognize where he can carve out the flawless block of marble the sculptor wants, and to saw off the base of the block smooth and square — but the quarry-man just stands aside and watches while the sculptor then makes a figure grow out of that hunk of stone.

Generally, that quarry-man is a damn sight better off if he doesn't interfere, but just stands back and watches what emerges.

You've come up with a hell of a complicated logical-conscious structure for a story. *I* think your logical-conscious propositions happen to be wrong, but that's a side issue; let your otherself go — don't try to tell it what to do logically! It's that otherself that's the damn good writer anyway! Nobody (except a scientist writing a technical article for a journal) can write anything worth reading — logically!

My disagreement on your conscious-logical setup has to do with the Animal versus the Ethical self.

You try defining Ethical Laws and you'll find yourself up against a real dizzy-doozy of the problem — because, try as you will to avoid it, it always comes out that *the ends are the only justification for any means*. That is precisely equivalent to saying, "By their fruits ye shall know them." Also to, "I don't care what your intentions were — look what you did!"

The only test of ethics is the long-term effects. The usual "The ends don't justify the means," platitude refers strictly to short-term "ends" that are *not* ends at all — they're practically beginnings. The Laws of Ethics are laws of the Universe, not merely current local tribal mores. Trouble is — it takes a Universal size space-time mind to know the answers; the best we can do is judge from the results over a long period of time.

And that would be impossible, because human culture with recorded results is so extremely brief. Why, the oldest star-maps made by Man show the proper motion of only three of the nearest stars!

But that Animal you're so happily demeaning has built into it some three billion years of experience, recording things that did work over megayears — not weeks!

Is punishment bad for Junior's precious little ego?

Ask Animal Man! He's got the recorded results of three hundred megayears of trying it; the answer is "No! Punishment is a Good thing; it works over hundred megayears testing."

Only warm-blooded animals punish their young; they run the planet now. Birds don't bother to guide and punish their young for long — mammals punish them for a major fraction of their lifetimes — in humans, it's almost a third of their lifetime.

Now Animal Man doesn't know why these things are true — doesn't know why they work. But Animal Man had an ancient data-bank, with an immense amount of data summarized into rule-of-thumb working principles. Animal Man never knew that adenosine triphosphate existed — he just used it for the last three billion years, because It Worked. From the time before cell membranes were invented, ATP has been the basic energy-transfer substance in organic life.

That's not brilliance, it's not intellectual grandeur — but it's an incomparable fund of immense wisdom of Things That Work.

Animal Man calls for Sex — and doesn't know at all that it's a long-term purposeful activity — to keep the race alive. No entity as utterly egocentric as a cat would burden her comfort and ease with the handicap of pregnancy — if it weren't for the racial wisdom. (Note that responding to a very short-term desire, that tabby cat is

509

induced to do something to her several-weeks disadvantage — which is a Good Thing in the megayears-long view of the race of cats.)

Animal Man has wisdoms that Intellectual Man can't justify logically. Like, "Give a logical explanation of the motivation of a man deliberately sacrificing his own life to save his wife and children from destruction." Or, "Why should Roger Young have knowingly invited the Jap machine gunner to riddle him; it clearly was not to his benefit, but solely beneficial to other men."

It's Animal Man that has the overwhelming wisdom to answer that one. "Because one must do it that way — the end, success of the race, justifies that means."

But that takes many hundreds of megayears to learn; it's an illogical proposition, *for any individual organism.*

Of course, that basic lesson is much older; red blood cells live solely to produce useful oxygen-carrying corpses. Skin cells grow for the purpose of producing tough, horny corpses behind which all the other cells can be sheltered. Living things had to learn that system before the highly evolved organisms like hydras and planarians could come into being.

Your Ethical Man would be impossible — without the megayears of wisdom Animal Man has accumulated by the long, slow, hard route of trial and error.

Just read about that 18-year-old kid who's a professor of mathematics in the University of California Mathematics [Department], of course. Kids make great chess-players, too. Neither field requires any wisdom whatever — simply brilliant logical talent.

But do you think that 18-year-old, terrifically bright though he is, is capable of wise judgements in real world — as wise, say, as a 60-year-old small business man?

The kid is brilliant, undoubtedly, and incredibly logical. But I'm glad he isn't going to marry any daughter of mine; she'd have a hell of a life. (Incidentally, you should spend some time talking to **Peggy Weiner Kennedy**; **Norbert Weiner** was a brilliant, precocious mathematical genius too. But as a husband and father?! Try the local plumber or TV repairman!)

Animal Man has ages of wisdom — though he lacks intelligence. Intellectual Man has intelligence . . . but no sufficent fund of data; he is not wise. Ethical Man would have to have the long viewpoint — because that's the only true test of what is Good and Evil in this Universe.

Do not reject Animal Man. You can't, of course — and stay alive!

Regards,   John

Re: "Spacepaw" by **Gordon Dickson**

Randall Garrett   *September 28, 1967*

Dear Randy:

So far, of course, I haven't heard from you Re the Lord Darcy story you said you were sending in two weeks or so ago. Tsk tsk.

If you ever do get that one done, I have another possibility for you to play with. Novelette that could start another fun series. Swashbuckler type, with high-competence hero — only in this case, a hero-team. Super trouble-shooters type.

The front-man hero is a big, rugged-looking guy, with usual hero attributes — big, fast-moving, decidedly non-fool type, and *dangerous*. He not only knows karate, knife-fighting, quarterstaff work, and similar Earthly amusements, but has trained in half a dozen hand-to-hand combat forms from other plants of the Federation. Including how to handle some of the decidedly non-humanoid aliens.

His teammate is a sort of a dog-equivalent, named Rover or Fido or some-such, to whom he tends to talk over his problems — though Fido never talks back of course. Fido's an alien beastie, equipped with about a dozen short legs, vaguely over-sized-ant-like in that he appears to have an exoskeletal structure — things tend to *clack* when they hit him, and bounce off. Low slung type, of course. Jaws relatively small, many small teeth. Foremost limbs equipped for manipulation. Fido can run like a blue streak, and can trail individuals in a way to make a bloodhound whimper in disgrace and self-pity.

Basic gimmick being . . . Fido's a very highly intelligent alien, who's at least a full 50% partner in the team. But he comes from a warm, oxygen-nitrogen atmosphere equivalent of Meskelin, a warm-blooded Barlenan. His planet has a surface gravity varying from about 5 G at the equator to around 500 at the poles.

He's not really an exoskeletal creature — it's just that his tissues and muscles, evolved under those g-loads, are so enormously dense and tough that they seem to be hard. His bones are made of hexagonal-crystalline diamond fibers embedded in a still-unanalyzable matrix with an appropriate degree of toughness. His teeth can do a nice job of gnawing on such bones, of course, and when he and his partner are alone, enjoys the flavor of a piece of high-alloy drill rod — kinda like a piece of candy-cane, in his view.

One of his more lethal tactics when required and/or appropriate, is simply running through the opposition. After all, with his kind of flesh, who needs weapons?

There's only one limitation: no one, not a field man of the

Federal Peace Force is ever to know that Fido is not simply a pet animal . . . and live.

This is helped along by the fact that Fido is slightly telepathic, in the sense of being able — unreliably, because of mental-symbolism differences between individuals — to pick up ideas which individuals he concentrated hard on have in mind. But he can always detect the thought-presence of any conscious mind. That, actually, is how he does his trailing.

And he "talks" to Our Hero by perfectly reliable thought-projection — since, in this case, he's learned the personal mental symbolism Our Hero uses internally. (In a telepathic race such as his, there would be a common symbol-language between individuals; in non-telepathic races, every individual develops his own internal symbol-language.)

The thing that he wags so cheerfully and friendly when strangers come around and try to pet him ain't a tail in the doggy sense; it's a highly sensitive and exquisitely prehensile manipulator organ — and he can close it in a loop tight enough to snip off an oak 4 by 4 *scrunch*. It also makes a useful scimitar . . . even without an edge. Remember it evolved under 3-500 g fields.

The human hero is the front man — and a damn dangerous man in his own right, as well as a Grade A sharpie in his own peculiar right.

The planet they come from is way the hellangone out at the edge of things. It's a planet of a very old Population II red dwarf, visible only about 4 light-years away, and there are no trade-potential planets within about 70 light-years.

A Federation exploration-mapping team found the place — and it's been kept under wraps, by mutual decision between the Federation Top Brass and the leaders of Fido's people. There's very little trade, because both parties are highly technical peoples, and only knowledge is really exchangable between them — which doesn't require massive shipping. Most Federation-made devices do not function so good under a 3-500 g field anyway. And since their tissues approach ordinary carbon steel in hardness anyway, when they need tools, they need *power* tools like we don't make.

One trouble they have now and then — Fido has a tendency to dream when he's asleep, and twitch around somewhat the way dogs do. Only with the muscular structure *he* has, a twitch of that tail, driven by a 3000-g acceleration (after all, it can lift stuff handily under a 500 g field!) is hard on nearby furniture, I-beams, etc. Also to explain.

If Fido makes a leap at something, or somebody, he has a tendency to appear to have teleported. I.e., he vanishes from point A and reappears at severely damaged point B. A muscle-system

512

geared to a multi-hundred-g field would make his leaps hard to follow visually.

Of course, his leaping is limited considerably by the tendency of his multiple feet to sink fetlock deep into ordinary concrete floors on take-off.

But basically, his people are very strongly self-disciplined; they have a philosophy of mutual helpfulness, honesty, and kindness — sort of inevitable in a telepathic race.

I think such a team could be a lot of fun to play with.

Whaddya think yourself?

Regards,   John

P.S. Wonder what Fido would use for a back-scratcher? Maybe Our Hero could help with a ¼″ drill using a wire-brush attachment? Of course if he rubbed himself against a concrete wall. . . .

Carl Sagan   *October 10, 1967*

Dear Dr. Sagan:

Dr. Paul Arthur, of DuPont Research, sent me a Xerox of your recent item in *Nature* under "Planetary Science," to which he had added the word "Fiction," being a long time devotee of this literature, and asked how you and **Dr. Morowitz** had "escaped my author dragnet."

Your article is precisely the sort of thing we want to present, of course — intelligent, careful analyses of non-terrestrial environments which could be life-supporting environments.

I'm writing you, rather than **Dr. Morowitz**, because I am planning on making one of my Semi-regular visits to Cambridge on October 25, 26 and 27, and I'd like to have a chance to talk to you while I'm there, if possible.

At minimum, I'd like to have your permission to reprint your note in *Nature*; hopefully, you may be willing to do for us a somewhat broader piece on life-adaptations in non-terrestrial environments.

The present cultural attitude makes professional scientific journals very limiting in an important respect; scientists are not adequately free to speculate on possible systems in public, where scientists of other disciplines can cooperate in refining or expanding the suggested ideas.

That is one very real service that science-fiction magazines such as *Analog* can serve, and which I try to make it serve.

Sincerely,   John W. Campbell

513

John D. Clark   *November 16, 1967*

Dear John:

Jack Schoenherr and I discussed the matter of dragonwings — and came to the conclusion that the only possible way of flying those dragons involves the use of levitation — the wings propel, but do not sustain. We are in full agreement that neither jointing nor musculature would be possible.

But — well, it was a *hell* of a good yarn! And it needed a cover. And everybody agrees they're the most delightful dragons that ever blew a firey breath. And besides, I think **Anne** came up with a lovely idea in the phosphate-eating phosphine-belching metabolism!

The closest approach to what Venus seems to be like was **Hal Clement's** Tenebra — the "Close to Critical" planet. However Meskelin did have the horizon-inverting optical illusion now believed to apply on Venus, though for slightly different reasons.

What bothered me was the Russian report of little-or-no nitrogen. Huh? How come. . . ? Nitrogen is one of the most active elements, and wouldn't be around loose in any atmosphere not in contact with a vigorous biosphere. However if there's no loose water, and not much oxygen, there might be a lot of metallic nitrides around. . . ?

As to CO_2 — convert all Earth's carbonate rocks to oxides and silicates and aluminates, burn all the fossil fuels, and all the biosphere — and how much CO_2 would you get?

Regards,   John

James Schmitz   *December 4, 1967*

Dear Jim:

This is about the nth time I've tried to express what I want to say about that Tuvela yarn of yours. Some things are easy — like it's a terrific yarn, and I'm buying it, and I'm sure the readers will give you the bonus rate on it, and of course that means we'll need a snyopsis of Part I — break it approximately in two, where you think the best break comes.

The hard problem is that I think it needs an epilogue, or something, to make some of the magnificent propositions it contains clear. You know the old rule in play-writing, "If you want the audience to get a point, say it three times at least." Or say it once very clearly, practically kindergarten level.

And this yarn is loaded with beautiful stuff that's not stated at all, and is quite obscured by reason of the single viewpoint (Niles.)

It's obvious that the Parahuans were perfectly correct in one sense — Tuvelas do exist, and Nile, quite obviously, is one. Only the Tuvelas are far more deadly than the Parahuans imagined. In fact, they rather closely resemble Lewis Carroll's fabled Boojums, of "The Hunting of the Snark." You may remember that the trouble with Snark-hunting was that some Snarks were Boojums, and anyone who met a Boojum "suddenly, silently vanished away!" And aside from that peculiar deadliness, a Boojum was completely indistinguishable from an ordinary Snark.

Nile is — in a hideously literal way! — a Boojum. From a Parahuan viewpoint, that is! A Great Palach goes to spy on her — and fast as the Great Palachs are, he's snatched up, whopped senseless, and carted off trussed up in a bag berfore he can do anything whatever to her. She chooses to untie him in order to talk; he tries to attack and suddenly, *permanently* vanishes away. Thereafter every Parahuan that encounters her — even their great and terrible tarms! — suddenly, silently vanishes away. And in no case do the Parahuans have any clue whatever as to how the vanished got that way.

Literally the Parahuans learn absolutely nothing whatever about Tuvelas — except that, like Boojum, anyone who encounters one suddenly, silently vanishes away.

They never do learn whether a Tuvela is indestructible — they only learn that whatever Tuvelas are, Parahuans can't destroy one.

Now the reader going through the story is acutely aware of the terrific, desperate pressure on Nile. You've done a hell of a good job of putting that over and maintaining it.

But that very fact obscures the fact that the pressure on the Parahuans is fantastically greater. Look — Nile feels desperately pressured; sure. But who's doing all the dying? Or . . . are they dying? No Parahuans know; *they* know only that whole patrols, and even gigantic tarms, vanish without so much as a trace. (Those sea-halvars aren't going to leave anything a Parahuan could trace to a tarm, for instance!)

The civil war among Great Palachs is actually Nile's doing; the Voice of Action quite literally goes nuts because of the frightful uncertainty, the absolute inability to get any data whatever as to Tuvela-powers.

Single-handed, Nile has the whole expedition in precipitate retreat by the time her friend arrives with bombs. They were fleeing for their lives before the Federation warships arrived. The Parahuans never so much as saw her — until she so chose voluntarily. Then she walked into their fortress unarmed, stayed as long as she chose, and left when she was ready — taking their captive with her, and again vanished beyond their ken completely. If she *was* destructible, no Parahuan could do it.

Since to the Parahuans immortality and superior powers were in one-to-one correspondence, the idea of a mortal super-being escaped them. Also, the idea of a super-being which was physiologically indistinguishable from the normal members of its race escaped them. And finally, the idea that, in a given race, the super-beings might have super-powers of completely different types escaped them. If they *had* been able to get data on Nile, and comprehend what she was — they would have been totally unprepared to meet another Tuvela, one Telzey Amberdon.

Finally, for the last two megayears at least, the male of the human species has been the warrior-hunter-fighter. He's always been bigger, stronger, more aggressive, more violent and more destructive than the female.

The Parahuan expedition was utterly clobbered by one young female Tuvela. What would have happened if they'd met a mature male Tuvela?

The humans didn't send a man against them — they didn't even send a boy. The Parahuans were completely helpless against a Tuvela girl.

(I'm aware of your pro-feminine leanings! But the fact remains that the human — in fact higher-mammalian — system is based on the female being the conservator, and the male being the warrior-fighter-protector. Males can be sacrificed — they aren't critical for racial survival; females must be protected. Evolution has concentrated strength, size, violence and aggressiveness in the male. The female has greater endurance — but the males can hit far higher peaks of explosive violence. In an objective analysis of the race, an alien would quickly recognize that fact. Knowing that, if a young female were sent to meet their invasion, it would imply that the Tuvelas considered Parahuans so incompetent that they represented no threat, that a young female didn't need protection or defense against them.)

Now the problem is this: how can those factors be brought to the reader's attention without producing the effect of a lecture, or an anticlimax?

Dr. Cay started to bring it out in that Incubator — but the full scope must come out *after* the Parahuans' total defeat.

Possibilities:

1. Since the Parahuan invasion attempt represented a threat to the entire Hub culture, it must be studied by the High Commission of the Hub as a matter of High Policy. Nile will have to be interrogated. And the High Commissioners would be Tuvelas capable of seeing both viewpoints on the problem, and pointing them out to Nile.

2. Some of the Palachs and Great Palachs escaped alive from Nandy-Cline, and reported to the Grand Palach and his council.
3. Some of the non-human-non-Parahuan might-have-been allies of the Parahuan would know about the entire sequence — their intelligence forces would not be totally incompetent! And *their* High Commission would need a report. Their analysis would be thoroughly objective — and might include some intelligence reports suggesting that Tuvelas, or at least some of them, had psi powers. The affair of Tolzey and Tic-toc would not have been totally covered up against competent intelligence agents.

At least they'd have data enough to realize there could be many very different types of Tuvelas, with very different powers — for the existence of human xenotelepaths was no secret. They couldn't know but that Nile used xenotelepathy to turn the floatwood life-forms against the Parahuans — or to mentally enslave the Parahuans to kill each other. The mutual slaughter of Palachs and Great Palachs on Nandy-Cline would suggest that. . . .

But the critical point that the reader should be made to look at is *how the affair appeared from the Parahuan viewpoint.*

Nile was under desperate pressure? Haw! One girl against hundreds of enemies . . . and who was doing all the dying?

Regards, John

Leland Sapiro *December 8, 1967*

Dear Leland:

The anti-psi forces were riding high on their test tubes in Vol. 3 No. 1 letters department . . . but I'd like to see those proponents of rationalism versus voluntarism apply the scientific methods to their rationalism, and use a little less voluntarism in their non-rational thinking.

Like this: it is voluntarism — or I prefer the term "volitionalism" — to hold, as they do, that everything in the Universe can be explained by *known* logical techniques applied to *now-known* laws of the Universe.

That involves two false postulates:
1. That we *now* know all the proper rules of rational thinking.
2. That what we *now* know is adequate to explain everything in the Universe.

The first is patently a false assumption; logic, which is what the self-assigned "rationalist" means by "rational," is a formalized method of manipulating postulates and/or data to deduce a conclusion. The conclusion is only as valid as the postulates, the data, and the assumed laws of logic.

The non-Euclidean postulates concerning parallel lines that lead to Rieman's and Lobatchewsky's alternative geometries opened new worlds of understanding, by a simple change of postulates — and are just as rational as Euclid's geometry. Change one postulate, and you change the fundamental nature of the deduced Universe.

Yet before those pioneers did their work, it was "unimaginable" that there could be any rational alternative to Euclid.

O.K. — and equally, it is *still* "unimaginable" that there could be other fundamental rules of logic itself. But two fundamentally different systems of logic, are well into development.

And not by far-out kooks. The University of Illinois Electrical Engineering Department (computers division) is working on one under an Air Force concept. It's leading to a self-aware computer.

Your self-styled rationalist-scientists who label me and others interested in psi "voluntarists" are, themselves, "guilty" (in their own terms!) of the hideous crime of voluntarism; they insist the Universe must be limited to the logically-deducible consequences of their now-known set of postulates and data.

They insist that their now-limited information and beliefs must rule the total universe. They are saying, "Nothing is True but those things I say are logical according to my perfect knowledge."

That, my friend, is pure voluntarism — and a mighty fortress against facing uncertainty. In the past, many people have found a mighty fortress in their God, who is infallible and omniscient.

Present scientific knowledge is neither infallible nor omniscient.

I am not voluntarist; I don't think human will rules the Universe — either individual or collective. But my denial of the efficacy of human will includes denying that human knowledge can impose limits on what is and is not in the Universe — which is a tendency I observe is very prevalent among many self-styled scientists — who actually are not true scientists because of that voluntaristic attitude.

Also, unlike many of those SSS (Self-Styled Scientists) I do not believe in guilt-by-association. A couple centuries ago there were hundreds of alchemists mulcting people with phony transmutation-to-gold schemes. This proves that all alchemists (whether they try to hide behind their new name, chemists, or not) are charlatans and crooks, huh?

And the witch-women and witch-doctors did not use scientifically approved methods, and this proves that all those people were crooks and purely fraudulent charlatans. That's why they discovered digitalis, curare, opium, cascara, hot poltices, and something over half the armory of modern medicine? And also developed psychosomatic techniques for treating psychosomatic illnesses, which modern psychiatrists are beginning to rediscover in an approved, technical way.

It took a two-step rediscovery process to get hypnotism back into therapeutic technology. First Mesmer had to rediscover it, and a century or two later, Mesmer had to be rediscovered.

Science in its then-omniscience "knew" that such "animal magnetism" was nonsense.

My whole beef against the SSS is that they will not acknowledge that there are things that are real in the Universe which they cannot logically deduce for lack of present knowledge.

When Lord Kelvin, back in the last century, presented his absolute and complete mathematical-logical-scientific proof that the Earth could not possibly be more than 25,000,000 years old, his proof was perfectly logical. He showed that, with the known value of heat-conduction of rock, and any reasonable estimate of the original molten ball of rock that became Earth, and the known present rate of heat-flow from the interior of the Earth, that he could readily compute how long the Earth had been cooling.

His figures were fairly accurate, his logic impeccable and his result ridiculous — because at that time, no scientist knew anything whatever about radioactivity, and the fact that potassium-40 and uranium and thorium decay processes were producing at least as much heat as Kelvin knew was escaping from Earth.

Any SSS who declares psi is "obviously provable nonsense!" is claiming to have absolute omniscience with respect to *all* the possibilities in the Universe.

That man is living in a voluntarist fantasy of the purest ray serene — he thinks his wisdom is unlimited.

I know mine isn't — and I know his isn't.

I frequently cite the "bumble bees can't fly" proof because it's typical; the mathematical proof of non-flying bumblebees stemmed from one false assumption: *If* bumblebees operated as fixed-wing aircraft, *then* their flight would be aerodynamically impossible. And *that* proof *is* 100% valid. My point is, simply, that when there's a false assumption — a hidden false assumption — logic, mathematics, and scientific data lead to ridiculous conclusions.

And you will never know when there is a missing factor in your logic . . . until much later.

For the fanatically convinced anti-psi SSS, I suggest the present situations:

1. The Marines are using dowsing rods, such as those described in *Analog* 10 years ago, for finding Viet Cong tunnels and bamboo-stake booby traps, neither of which can be detected by electromagnetic devices.
2. After over 100 years of violent "scientific" denial of any such ridiculous idea — it was finally demonstrated by electronic computer analysis that the phases of the Moon *do* influence Earth's weather. Which astrologers and farmers and sailors had been observing for a couple of millennia previously.

   The computer didn't given them an explanation of how it came about . . . simply demonstrated that it *did*.
3. Over a decade ago, **John Nelson** of RCA Communications, showed that violent solar flares, with consequent radio blackouts and violent magnetic storms on Earth could be predicted by purely astrological techniques. "With Saturn and Jupiter in quadrature, and Venus in trine. . . ." sort of things.

This was "clearly astrological nonsense," and very upsetting to orthodox scientists — particularly because the blasted nonsense *worked*.

At the time **Nelson** pointed that out, Science lacked the data necessary to guess at the reason it was true. They did not have the necessary appreciation of the magnitude of solar magnetic-field energies, nor of solar wind effects, nor of van Allen belts. With those necessary data missing their logic and mathematics — like Lord Kelvin's about Earth's heat — lead to ridiculous conclusions.

And most scientists failed to consider the meaning of certain data they did have on hand; the center of mass of the Solar System is *not* inside the Sun — it's a varying distance from the center of gravity of the Sun. Just where it lies is determined by the angular relationship of the planets.

If Jupiter and Saturn are aligned on the same side of the Sun, the CG of the system is hundreds of thousands of miles outside the surface of the Sun; if they're on opposite sides of the Sun, the CG of the system is somewhat inside the surface of the Sun.

The Sun is an effectively perfect electrical conductor, with stupendous magnetic field energies entangled with that perfectly conducting plasma. Yank the mass around gravitationally, and there are electro-magnetic turbulences set up that are on an equally immense scale; they show on the solar surface as sunspots. (Hence the 11+ year Sunspot Cycle.)

Sunspots and Solar Flares project enormous currents of

electrons and protons and great knots of magnetic field energy entangled with those charged particles. These forces, striking Earth's Van Allen belts, magnetic field, and the ionosphere, cause everything from auroras through magnetic storms and radio blackouts to violent disturbances of the ionosphere. Which has a catalytic effect on the stratosphere, and strongly influences the stratospheric currents.

Meteorological astrology, anyone?

Anytime the SSS boys decide they know the ultimate absolute limits of what can be true — they're claiming they're omniscient. Anyone who claims omniscience thinks he's God Almighty. Well, *that* God is not only dead, he never existed.

My interest in psi stems from direct observation of phenomena that are real and reproducible by some talented individuals and are not explicable in terms of now-known data.

Where the SSS says "If my present data and logic can't explain it, that proves it doesn't exist," I hold, instead, that "If present knowledge and data can't explain it — maybe there's something new to learn here! Let's investigate!"

A *true* scientist does keep that difference in mind.

It's only the SSS type — the self-styled scientists — that are so arrogant as to deny their knowledge is not total.

Keep in mind that the great scientist Lord Kelvin, proved, by the most advanced scientific knowledge of his time, that the Earth was not more than 25,000,000 years old. (Some of the earliest apes were having trouble with Nile crocodillians about then. The dinosaurs had been extinct for 100,000,000 years or so.)

And that the best scientific knowledge of 1955 showed that astrology had absolutely no valid data — nothing worth studying.

And that the best scientific data and logic of 1966 was still firmly holding that dowsing was nonsense — although some Marines were beginning to use it because it saved their leathernecks.

It's the SSS boys who are the real voluntarists; they claim that their orthodoxy determines what's true in the Universe.

Sincerely,   John

Thomas T. Hill   *December 18, 1967*
Dear Tom:

Some sweet day, you may actually get around to doing what I've been suggesting to you for some — lessee, now . . . how many years have you been corresponding with me? . . . Oh, twenty years and actually write an article for me.

I would most dearly love to get an article that discussed what advances in photoscience have done for all fields of science.

Simplest example: when the 200″ telescope was built, they hoped to reach 4X as far out as the 100″ had been able to. But before they finished the 200″ — improvements in photofilm had increased the reach of the 100″ *more* than 4 X! And a darned sight cheaper than a 200″ telescope, too!

And I would, of course, *love* an article on non-silver-halide photography.

And there's probably fifty other things you know about that would make fascinating articles of the general scientifically interested readership.

And we are, now, paying 5¢ a word, for about 5,000 words, plus $5 a photograph used. (On the basis that the photos already exist, and that is a researcher's fee for digging out copies for our use — we don't expect anybody to make shots at that price. Obviously true for such things as that terrific shot of the Centaur blow-up. Nobody blows up a Centaur so we can have a picture!)

Re your film-developer combination article — that one I saw in the original. My own combo for nearly all purposes is Tri-x and Acufine; for high-resolution copy work normally it's Pan X and Acufine. For some special jobs I've had to use High Contrast Copy and D-11.

That, by the way, was a *very* special job — a real bastard for the home-workshop type photographer.

My wife is in the business of crewel embroidery supplies. (Consult your wife for data on what crewel embroidery is!) Among other things, **Peg** has more different patterns for embroideries than anyone else in the country. She wanted photographs of some of her very special (she has them made for her in England) patterns to send out (most of her business is mail) to good prospects.

The patterns were for things like bedspreads, drapes, and other large areas. They consist of special wax-ink lines on a tough tissue paper. Problem: On a pattern 7′ long, the individual lines, by the time 7′ is reduced to fit on a 1.5″ negative, are somewhat narrow. Eastman told me that 35mm would probably do as well or better than 2¼ x 2¼ — unless I used glass plates in the Mamiyaflex — because flatness of film could be more precise in the 35mm camera. The width of the lines worked out to something like 1/2000th of an inch — and she wanted a nice, evenly exposed black-on-white print, of course.

It had to be a high-contrast ultra-fine-grain film to get sharp-edged lines under those conditions.

But under those conditions — how do you get illumination even enough for that high-contrast stuff to be perfectly exposed over the whole 7′ length? Oh, sure . . . any good commercial studio has adequate lighting equipment, and I could too, for a few kilobucks.

First try: stuck the tissue paper pattern up on the inside of our view window on a cloudy-bright day — figured that general illumination through the thing would be level and give good shots.

Guess again! The light comes from the sky, and the ground doesn't supply much. Moreover, light meters of the standard logarithmic type used for ordinary photography just aren't accurate enough for that sort of work. A one-stop difference, which is about all they'll detect, means practically all the differenece between solid white and solid black.

Sooo — since electronics is one of my hobbies anyway, I built a linear-scale light meter, using an electron multiplier vacuum photcell. The cause of the uneven lighting on the view window, and its degree, was immediately evident. That 931-A and meter was as persnickity on the subject of light-levels as the high-contrast film.

I tried balancing illumination on a suspended easel, using reflector floodlights. I finally got balance . . . but it called for 5-second exposures. And with the required extreme resolution, I next learned I'd need one of those $300 studio tripods that do *not* vibrate.

So — use electronic flash.

Yeah . . . but how do you balance electronic flash illumination with the required accuracy? You can't do it with an ordinary light meter.

Soooo . . . back to the electronics department.

I now have an integrating photoelectric light-meter that's accurate to a gnat's split eyelash, takes an accurate reading, and integrates the total illumination, of any flash from 10 nanoseconds to 0.1 second, and holds the reading for about 10 minutes, or until you push the button for the next reading.

And I did, by God, get the required negatives!

(Thanks, of course, to the use of a Nikon Micronikor lens — a hell of a nice little process lens, in effect! Great, too, for getting extreme close-up details of the stitches used in some of **Peg's** fancier fancy embroidery.)

The integrating photometer, incidentally, uses one of the oldest types of photoelectric cells — the old 929 vacuum non-multiplier cell, one of Texas Instrument's incredible new field-effect transistors, and a simple condenser. The DC input resistance of a field effect transistor is absolutely fantastic; even TI's cheap little 90¢ jobs have input (gate) resistances running to *hundreds of billions* of Ohms. You can hang that resistance directly on a 0.25 μF condenser, and it takes over an hour for the charge on the condenser to drop to ½! Yet the output from the little FET — it's the size of half a pea — is fully adequate to swing a 100 μAmp meter.

523

The things are as sensitive as an electrometer — but work on fractions of a volt, instead of kilovolts.

The scale on the gadget is perfectly linear, and the range is readily changed by simply switching in different capacitors.

Generally, the trouble with such cute gadgets is that they serve brilliantly only one special purpose. The integrating photometer does let you balance light-intensity from two or more guns the way you want it without having to take exposures and look at results, but otherwise . . . well, what can you do with it?

I built an enlarging lightmeter, using a Clairex CdSe photoresistor. Works great. So sensitive that puffing on a cigarette three-four feet from the cell moves the needle 5 divisions across the meter, yet the meter doesn't overload if you forget and turn on the white lights. Does a beautiful job.

Only 95% of the time I go on guesstimating by eye. It's easier.

Incidentally, I dunno why they don't use CdSe cells instead of CdS in light meters; CdSe follows beautifully at 50 kilocycles, and the hysteresis is effectively zero. CdS of course has terrible hysteresis.

Oh, well . . . so how about an article from you?

Regards,   John

Miriam Allen DeFord   *January 23, 1968*

Dear Mrs. DeFord:

Whoa back! You misunderstood me rather extensively, I see!

My point on belonging to "an oppressed" minority was strictly an ironic comment on how people have so splintered themselves into Something-Americans, whether it's Italo- or Afro- or Lefthanded-Luxemburgo-Americans that everybody's a minority these days, and there aren't any more Americans.

This whole stupid nonsense of Minorities and Defamation and whatnot is long since past the *reductio ad absurdum* point — and the propagandists who seek to make political capital out of it are getting away with the Hitler technique of the Big Lie. They aren't even being challenged rationally — which was my point on the matter of racial numbers.

If they can get away with the Big Lie repetition of something so readily disprovable by simple arithmetic — they obviously can get away with all sorts of more complex lies.

I object to Black Power (meaning I-personally-want-power-and-you-Negroes-give-it-to-me) demagogues blaming "Whitey" for all their miseries "because you Whites enslaved us and crushed us."

Of my four great-grandfathers, one was a Vermont legislator and Abolitionist. One was a doctor in the Union Army. One was a

524

New England Unitarian minister. And the fourth hadn't left Germany yet as of 1860. So I'm responsible for slavery in the Old South?

Or my fellow editor **Sam Andre** — whose Italian ancestors left Italy in the 1900's?

Or **Miss Tarrant**, whose Irish ancestors came over late in the 19th Century? And what were your ancestors doing in 1860 that proves you guilty of oppressing those po' black slaves?

I'm objecting — strongly — to the pure-nonsense lying propaganda that's being widely spread to generate race hatred. And using precisely the technique that Adolf Hiter, the master race-hatred merchant of history, specified — the Big Lie, endlessly repeated, till everybody "knows" its true, and doesn't question it anymore.

Notice that the *innocent repetition-acceptance of the Big Lie* serves the Big Liar's propaganda purposes just as well as a conscious race-hatred preacher.

My "taboo" is solely against helping spread the Big Liars' propaganda!

Sincerely,   John W. Campbell

Gene Roddenberry   *January 23, 1968*

Dear Mr. Roddenberry:

I'm joining in the campaign to promote "Star Trek," naturally — it's the world's first and only true science-fiction program, and it averages really high in quality. (Of course you're bound to pull an occasional clunker! Who doesn't?) I'm writing a few letters — but also I thought of something that might help otherwise.

Sorry I'm late on this, but it still may have time to do some good, if you choose and get some fast action.

For this noble idea, I'll charge a fee of $1.00 — so it'll be legally and beyond question yours in full.

Gimmick: Winter cap for boys, made of heavy black overcoat material (scraps and cuttings can probably be used) cut to match Mr. Spock's skull-cap style hairdo. The usual winter-hat earflaps have appliqued pink felt Vulcan ears.

It should please mothers in being warm, relatively cheap, with earflaps which Sonny would be delighted to use.

It should also please Sonny.

And as a salable by-product using scraps, it might please the overcoat industry, too.

Sincerely,   John W. Campbell

Dear Keith:

The trouble with a ¾-hour discussion between two people, both bursting with ideas, is that we could bring up a lot of subjects, but not get any of 'em correlated or reasonably well explained!

Now Topic No. 1 was the matter of the proposed psi story plot.

The last-century tradition of the "spirit mediums" was that "spirits" were entities living on a "higher plane," who "had different vibrations," and were "purer" than we who were of the "common clay of gross material."

You start off saying your character lives on a higher plane and *bung*! The reader's got *him* classified all right, as more of that damn hogwash about spirits and vibrations and mediums and all that *ugh* stupidity. Complete with inadequately illuminated rooms with seances and Aunt Martha's dear old ghost wandering around with her ectoplasm showing and tootling on a "spirit trumpet."

Wherefore avoid like the plague any terms which might link your story in any way to the semantic complex involved in last century's "spiritualism." Note carefully that while it may *not actually* be 100% hogwash, the modern reader *now believes* it was 100% nonsense, and a man acts always on what he *believes* because no man ever knows "the Truth, the whole Truth, and nothing but the Truth" since he's not the Omniscient Deity In Person.

Early science-fiction even got away with having "another universe based on other vibrations," and parallel with ours. Back in the days when "vibrations" was a mystical-magical-mysterious term, you could use it to explain anything, because nobody really knew what vibration was and/or could do.

It's been defined. You can't pull that one any more.

There are various possibilities of alternative universes — but I suspect the best one would be the alternative-history universes. *If* the Egyptians had caught on to the idea of experimental science 5000 years ago — they had every opportunity, because they actually were fairly started in that direction! — *then*. . . . Heck, man where will our science be in 5000 years?!

Randy Garrett has had immense fun exploiting the idea of an alternative history in which Magic instead of Science was rigorously developed.

All I know of psi investigation — honest, genuine efforts, by professionally trained scientists who seriously tried to learn something — indicates that the old concept of "charm" is damn well real, solid, and workable. The simplest example is the dowsing rod; the man, not the sticks, does the dowsing — but the sticks are a "charm" which is itself inert, but makes possible a focussing of human attention of some kind. The everyday equivalent is paper and pencil, which permit you to do something that you can't do without them — like multiplying two five-digit numbers, or determing how many times 267 goes into 97,643.

In other words, a rigor of psi, equivalent to the rigor of science, might lead to an engineering understanding of charms, how to design and build them. A modern man is not as strong as the man of 500 years ago — but a modern man can readily lift a three-ton load, and carry it away at five times the fastest speed his great-grandfather could. The modern man uses a couple of scientific "charms" called a "differential hoist" and a "light truck." He has to have somebody skilled in the art build the hoist and the truck, and then he has to learn the technique of operating those charms — but he sure can do things great-grandpappy couldn't!

O.K. — so a character descended from an Egyptian-science-rigor-of-psi, who is himself a psi engineer, can design, build, and use charms of about the same level of efficacy.

Item: Take a look at modern printed circuit boards — and consider that *they are charms*. They're force-field focusers — invisible-entity-manipulators. (Neither electric nor magnetic fields nor electrons are visible entities — but they're damn well real!)

Note also: If you want a "transistor radio circuit," there are seventy-leven ways of building one. Dozens of different circuits, with lots of component variables are equally workable. Superhetrodyne? Regenerative? Tuned RF. Tunnel diode circuits? Straight transistors? Field Effects jobs? Or even vacuum tubes could be used.

O.K. — so *no two charms for the same purpose need be the same*.

So willow sticks, apple-wood forks, welding-rod Ls, flexible nylon wands, pendulums — all work equally well as dowsing charms.

What can make a psi story get hold of a reader and haul him along like a megaton tractor beam is an internal rational consistency such that he's forced to acknowledge that *if* this starting postulate is accepted, the rest *has* to follow inescapably.

Every psi power has inherent limitations — because they're all simply applications of laws of the Universe which we, in this culture, happen not yet to have worked out. Since we haven't found the laws, characteristically we observe occasional operation of these laws (spontaneous cases of clairvoyance, telepathy, precognition, levitation, etc.) and observe "a power exists." Since we don't know the law, we do not see that the conclusion "with that power I could do anything whatever" is a false conclusion.

To make a psi story that really grips and holds, the most

important factor will be conveying the feeling that these are *rationally, naturally limited forces.* They can *not* be used without limits.

Given only the first half of Newton's Law of Gravity, "Every body in the Universe attracts every other body in the Universe with a force proportional to the product of their masses," which is a true statement, the natural reaction is, "Then why doesn't the whole universe collapse to a small lump."

The feeling that psi is unlimited stems from assuming only the "first half" of the law.

Now: If your central character, the psi-talented hero, is to refrain from using his powers here on Earth, the reason must be a good one *from our human viewpoint.* After all, we're Earth-human, and I don't think we'd approve of his refraining because he enjoyed the amusing, laughable primitiveness of Earth's squalor, disease, misery and pain. That he didn't really do what he could, because he felt Earth's condition was so delightfully quaint. Like those climbers over there on that mountain, laboring up the side of the avalanche-threatened mountain to reach that fellow who slipped and broke his leg and is freezing to death — when all they had to do was levitate the man and teleport him to a Healer. "Haow kwaint!"

Build him up that way, and he'll be as popular a hero as Nero fiddling at Rome's pyre.

Set up the proposition that he could, with very little effort, help us — but he won't because he thinks it's so amusing to watch us sweat it out, and he'll make one of the most hateable villains in science-fiction history.

Now: You know the reason we're in such a helluvamess in Vietnam? Because the US honestly and generously tried to give freedom of choice to a people who wouldn't work for it themselves. And *you can not do that.*

That's why *we can not help the Negro* — either here or in Africa.

We got diverted the other afternoon, so I wasn't able to clarify the points I was making, or correlate them properly.

I sprung that item about the Caucasoid race being superior to the Negro *on a biological test basis*, but didn't have time to explain or integrate.

I first got that one from a graduate sociologist, who pointed out that the test of a superior type in zoological-ecological terms was simple. That type which can extend its range at the expense of competing types, and increase its population over others is, zoologically, superior. A zoologist does not *have* to ask how that was accomplished (he naturally will, but it's not genuinely important) in determining zoological superiority.

Now contrary to widely dispersed propaganda, the Caucasoid

528

race fulfills that zoological test of superiority in full. We outnumber *all other races combined*. Because being Caucasoid, also contrary to popular opinion, is *not* a matter of skin-color. The vast masses of Indians, though they range from black to a relatively pale heavy-tanned color, are members of the great Indo-Aryan migration who went East. Add them to the population of Europe, Russia, and the Americas, Australia, New Zealand, etc., and you find that Caucasoids outnumber *all* other races. They have, also, extended their territorial range from a region of central Europe to something like 80% of the arable land surface of the planet. On the most basic of zoological tests, we are superior.

Now that being settled let's get to something more useful. That was simply to make the point the "what everybody knows" is usually what Hitler so wisely called "The Big Lie" — and you don't get far basing your thinking on somebody's lies — Big or little.

One of the things that distinguishes the Caucasoids as a breed is that they have, for at least 7000 years been subjected to a selective breeding program. That wasn't what they intended, but that's what they damn well got.

Those famous "educational opportunities" the Negroes complain they never had? Why not? They've been here on Earth as long as we have — and nobody came in and kindly handed us a bunch of set-up-and-operating educational institutions.

The essential answer is that education is the most violently and cordially detested thing that ever happened to human beings. After trying — with the help of a number of very high-grade minds — for about 6-8 years, my wife and I finally got a definition of what people mean by "slavery" that works. It turns out to have no objective definition — it's purely subjective-emotional. It comes out, "Slavery is the emotionally painful situation of being forced to learn a way of life you do not choose."

Example: The Vietnamese people are now enslaved, and will be enslaved for two generations. *No matter who wins*, their own way of life, the traditional, beloved way of life, will be taken from them, and they will be compelled to learn a new set of values, a new way of life, and compelled to work at chores they neither understand nor choose. *No matter who wins*. And it will be very horrible for them, because they aren't ready for the huge step they must make.

Japan was crushed absolutely flat by the US in 1945; the people there were enslaved by the Allies, and compelled to learn a new way of life . . . that is, they were enslaved for about two years. Then they discovered that this new way of life fitted them like a new pair of shoes — took a little breaking in, but felt perfectly wonderful once that was over. They *were* ready for the step, and made it so successfully they rapidly outstripped nearly all the European nations.

529

The agony Africa's going through now is only a beginning; the mass of African natives are not ready for the big step — and they're going to suffer horribly for two or three generations getting keel-hauled into Industrial Civilization.

And *nothing whatever we can do can help that.* You can whip and beat a man into doing what *must* be done — but you can't beat him into understanding what he can't conceive. If you go in and do it for him, you have to shove him out of the way so he doesn't get buried while you pour the concrete, or drowned in the lake the dam forms, and he stands in misery in the nice, clean, sanitary new town you built for him, weeping for his home forever gone, and groaning at the alien decrees that force him to put his sewage in a special place, instead of the street where it always belonged, and go a long way out of town for water, instead of pumping it up out of the sewage-laden central square. You have enslaved him in misery while you give him a new and better life. And when you turn the completed facilities over to him, and release him from his bondage, still you have disrupted his way of life forever, and the misery remains with him for generations till he can reestablish his familiar, beloved villages with handy sewage dumps and nice, convenient middle-of-the-town wells.

Final point: If you think you can't selectively breed a human type, you're saying, "Human beings are not related to the rest of mammalian evolution; their genetics has no bearing on their characteristics."

Look, the Incas of the South American Andean region had, for many thousands of years a spring fertility festival. Come Spring, on a certain date, all the girls who'd come of age that year started, on a signal, running up hill. On a second signal, all the boys who'd come of age that year started after them. And him what caught her mounted her there and then.

Currently, the Peruvian Indios have an inhabited village at 17,500 feet. Now you just figure what kind of a young man it takes to chase a girl up the side of a mountain, *starting* at 17,500 feet, and still have interest in doing something about it when he catches her. Hell, at that altitude you and I could just about mangage to stand up straight to watch the festivities — if they didn't take too long. Those Indios regularly play a 90-minute game of football at 15,000 feet; you or I would be laid out flat if we tried to walk up and down the sidelines following the action.

The Peruvian Alto Plano Indios are a selected breed of human beings — and if you think of any neater way to breed an altitude-adapted race than that spring festival gimmick, put it in a story!

Cultures, by their traditions and customs, act as selective breeding mechanisms. Not consciously — not by determined intent

— but simply by the fact of being cultures.

So what limits your psi engineer hero's use of his powers?

You can't give a man freedom. You can't give a man wisdom. Oh, you can give him knowledge, maybe — but the *Encyclopedia Brittanica* is available to anyone anyway. The thing is, not everyone can use it — anymore than anyone who has knowledge can use it. A fact best exemplified by the precocious bratling who knows all the answers — but doesn't know which problems those answers actually belong to.

Cliff Simak pulled a magnificent gimmick with that in his story "The Fisherman." His hero has had an effectively-immortal "trade minds" with him; it wasn't the hero's idea, but the idea of the alien, who likes acquiring knowledge, and finds that the simplest way. It ruins the hero's life, and damn near kills him, but he manages to get the awful mass of knowledge into some workable shape. Then he finally encounters, in the last struggle, the bigoted, fanatically determined villain — and totally destroys him, by simply giving *him* all that stupendous knowledge of a million races on a million worlds in a hundred galaxies.

One of the most horrible ways one can imagine for destroying a man is to give him what he thinks he wants. If he's the wrong kind of man, it doesn't merely kill him — it disintegrates him utterly.

But that's a very old idea, of course. Remember the legend of Phaeton and the Chariot of Apollo?

I can well imagine our psi engineer using that basic technique for destroying individuals who must be destroyed. Give them a psi device they demand — and stand aside while they use their new knowledge, without waiting to learn the necessary new wisdom.

What happens if you teleport from Nome, Alaska to Para, Brazil? You smash through the nearest fixed object at roughly 1000 miles per hour. You forgot to compensate for the rotational speed of the Earth at the Equator. Teleporting from Denver to New York naturally is lethal, unless you compensate for the mile-high potential energy of position with which you arrive.

You can *give* a man knowledge — but he has to earn wisdom, and the more you do for him, the less chance he has to earn that.

That's a terrific limitation on what an ethical psi engineer can do.

Withholding his powers, in other words, is *not* just because he finds Earth so quaint and amusing he doesn't want to "spoil" it.

And I suspect that the most believeable and strongest background for Our Hero, the Psi Engineer is the alternative history item. And possibly he got here because he was doing research on a new charm, and got a side-effect he did *not* intend — a real side-effect; sidewise in time.

Regards, John

James Tiptree, Jr.   *April 1, 1968*

Dear Mr. Tiptree:

I'm taking your yarn — but I'll strongly argue against its plausibility!

In the situation of alternating generations you describe, they damn well *better* be friendly, because if they aren't a sort of "suigenocide" gets to be pretty darned certain. They simply would not last long as a species. The system could be stable if one or the other type were in fact non-competitive — really were purely "baby factories" for the other.

But in a system of mutual hostility ——?

Well, the tribal cultural system is stable; it can and does continue for tens of millenia. But that ritual-tabu level does *not* involve real inter-tribal killing hostility. Their "wars" are more a formal dance, or Saturday afternoon sport in which deaths or serious injuries are purely accidental — like football.

The next level up is the barbarian culture — which *is* a hostile-out-for-blood system. It's also a short-lived cultural pattern; they either get themselves killed off or learn to be civilized and go in for economic, instead of physical, throat-cutting. (Kruschev was expressing in pure form the true, civilized challenge . . . "We will bury you!," meaning Russia would overwhelm us economically.) Physical war doesn't help the race much; economic cut-throat competition definitely speeds evolution on a "Devil take the stupidest!" basis.

That is, of course, more than somewhat undesirable from the viewpoint of the economically crushed individual — but it's a great thing for the race!

And when did Evolution ever give a damn about the feelings of the evolving individuals?

Regards,   John W. Campbell

RE: "Your Haploid Little Heart," by **James Tiptree, Jr.**

Scott Meredith   *April 4, 1968*

Dear Scott:

Verge Foray's new "Mind Changer' is an excellent sequel to "Infinity Sense"; I want it.

The minor changes in the windup of "Infinity Sense" can fit right into this — but they're still needed, to

1. complete "Infinity Sense" rationally as a complete-in-itself novelette, and
2. to make a clear tie-in to "Mind Changer."

Now there's one item worth throwing in somewhere along toward the end of this one.

Want to bet on a seven-year-old genius, with psi powers, and the ability to cause controlled genetic changes, having the *wisdom necessary to make balanced changes?*

Or even a young man of, say, 25, having the wisdom to plan children with the necessary judgement (even forgetting that not having infinite knowledge, he can't know what changes will have what side effects!) to generate *Homo optimum?*

If a congress of gorillas had assembled about a megayear ago to plan the development of *Gorillus superiorus,* I doubt that they'd have decided on a creature with smaller muscles, weak, undersize jaws, sawed-off arms, stretched out legs, no hair, and a sensitive skin that can't be safely exposed to the sun without burning in hours, or developing cancer in a few months, with an incompletely knitted skull that's too big on top, and too weak to stand a friendly swat from a good healthy bull?

Starn is going to have himself a hell of a time getting Billy to lay off on that shaping genes the way *he* is sure they ought to be!

Hell, the whole human race doesn't have one millipercent of the knowledge/wisdom necessary to recognize a desireable gene change — *when you include all the inescapable side-effects!*

Very simple, very crude example: Sickle cell anemia is a slowly lethal disease caused by a specific gene that controls the production of haemoglobin. It's a lethal, and would, normally, eliminate itself from the race fairly rapidly.

BUT — an individual with a sickle-cell gene from one parent, and a normal gene from the other, has blood cells that malaria plasmodia can't live in — he's immune to malaria. In tropical countries, then, individuals who are heterozygotes for the gene survive much more successfully than either normal homozygotes or sickle-cell homozygotes, because they have neither malaria nor sickle-cell disease! Result: The sickle-cell gene is widespread in tropical peoples, and has been for thousands of years.

Gene-juggling is going to be about as simple and safe as pulling out computer circuit-boards and pushing new, original designs at random in hopes of getting a better computer.

You might, of course. But you'll get a hell of lot of wrong answers out of the computer in the meanwhile.

Regards,   John

Re: "The Mind Changer," by **Verge Foray**

Dear Mr. Myers:

Some years back I had fun during one of my semi-annual bull-session get-togethers up in Cambridge. We had a somewhat high-powered gang in that evening; **Dr. Wayne Batteau**, **Dr. Claude Shannon** (Information Theory Inventor, and the one who made modern computer circuit analysis possible), **Isaac Asimov**, **Watten Seaman** (head of Harvard's Computer Lab number-theory group), **Tony Oettinger**, who was in charge of computer-translation research at Harvard at the time, being the principle ones.

I threw them the problem: It is for some reason necessary to leave a message on a planet essentially earth-like (because that's all we can talk about with any solid data) which must be recoverable after a period on the order of a couple billion years. Just to have something specific to talk about, let's say the message deals with the interrelationships of carbon dioxide and water. How can a message be encoded so that it will resist two billion years of weathering, tectonic activity, and all other destructive forces predictable for such a time span?

Carving a mountain won't do; the Laurentian Range of Canada, earth's oldest known mountains, are only about 1.8 gigayears old — and they started out like the Himalayas. Weathering got 'em. There were older mountains — but some of them sank back into the magma. The ocean beds are only about 200,000,000 years old. No matter where you carve your message, or on what grand scale, what with continental drift, tectonic activity and weathering, it'll be chewed up and spit out.

They spent an hour and a half analysing the problem, kicking it around, and having fun. They agreed finally that

1. it must be a matter of extreme multiple record, so that even if billions of copies are lost, some will remain.
2. it must be self-replicating.
3. it must have some inherent surface-seeking tendency, so the copies will be found on the surface, and not buried 15 miles deep in ancient rock.
4. there must be some self-destructive mechanism whereby imperfect copies destroy themselves, leaving only correct copies to self-replicate.

I listened with considerable interest — while they developed a detailed description of biological genetics.

Note that genes are not only self-replicating and surface-seeking (they need solar energy) but also, with respect to the type of message I originally suggested, defective copies are self-destructive. If an organism doesn't know how to handle the relationships between CO_2 and H_2O, it ceases forthwith to replicate or even exist.

Since I'd thrown it from the information-theory and inorganic direction, it was only toward the end that they themselves realized what it was they'd been carefully designing.

One of the authors once complained that Nature made organisms that were just barely good enough to survive. (He suffered from allergies, diabetes, and a few other chronic complaints.)

Wrong answer: Nature builds organisms with a tremendous drive to stress themselves to their ultimate limitations. And the organisms are in constant competition, which continuously culls the less competent. The three-billion-year-old message entitled "How To Live On This Planet" may vary in details — but the essential, literally vital, truths are carried on correctly . . . or not at all.

The self-correcting mechanism is, simply, that *only true answers can survive in the real universe*. That is the one reference standard against which every living cell gets checked.

And part of the gimmick in that is that *only the most fundamental realities are stable*. Realities like, "The temperature of this area ranges between 5 degrees and 30 degrees C.," is *not* a stable truth; ice ages come and change it, and continental drift shoves arctic-adapted areas into the tropics. Land bridges form and allow highly evolved predators into an area where only marsupial mammals have roamed . . . and the marsupials vanish in less than a single megayear.

The Tribesmen represent one way of surviving a violent change in the environment; "Develop new ways of adapting!" The scientist-group developed the other way; "Develop protective techniques that can stabilize your immediate environment against change." Both ways are good . . . within limits. But, like most things, a judicious balance of both is by far the best!

I agree with your latest ammendments to P. 49, and I believe you've strengthened your story markedly.

But you might have fun considering the several-generations later consequences of *conscious* feed-back control of the genes.

There are lots of brilliant ideas people have had — but relatively few of them work out well, because they're almost invariably unbalanced with respect to unknown, overlooked, or willfully denied factors.

Perfect eidetic memory would be a great improvement? The number of permutations and interrelationships between n factors is $n!$, essentially. Now $55!$ is 1.3×10^{73}; the number of fundamental particles in the universe — electrons, neutrons and protons — has been estimated to be 10^{72}. Now consider the problem of usefully relating *all* the data you have encountered in, say, 40 years of living, with the proviso that you have every bit of that data equally clearly in memory.

Also observe that most "Mr. Memory" experts, who can cite any datum required from historical records, sports, encyclopedias, etc., are markedly stupid. Their thinking machinery is hopelessly bogged down in a sea of data that they can't interrelate.

Telepathy would be an unlimited blessing? How many minds are feeding in, and how soon do you hit that 55! figure that you're trying to interrelate?

The Novo Sense that would be most useful, would be one that *limited* clairvoyance, telepathy and memory and those other faculties to controllable, usable correlateable degree. Or the development of a method of data-inter-relating that permitted the mind to handle greater quantities of data. Or of a society that was made up of closely interrelated individuals, each specializing in one of the talents — an integrated group of idiot-savant types. And some of the group are going to have to be hewers of wood and drawers of water, some thinkers-without-much-data who have telepathy enough to search the idiot-savants for the data they need when they need it. And each feeling pretty incompetent without the aid of those specialists.

But . . . that means a hive-type culture, and almost certain stasis!

So . . . all the "simple and obvious" solutions seem to be wrong answers.

Thinking is the art of abstracting and relating relevant and important data from the immense field of True data. It's defining "relevant and important" that causes most wars.

The function of science-fiction is to indicate wrong answers, and why they're wrong, as well as suggesting right answers and possibilities!

Sincerely,   John W. Campbell

Dr. John R. Pierce   *May 29, 1968*

Dear John:

Thanks for the Carleton Putnam book — I hadn't heard of the guy before, and he had a lot of data, complete with bibliography, that I hadn't seen.

I did know about the Savannah education trials — and had seen more of the data presented in that case, which was well and truly prepared on the scientific data side. They had spent ten years accumulating masses of highly meaningful data in the Savannah school system, and done a first-rate, bang-up job of research. One of the things Putnam did not mention was that the research results could not be published in any American journals of sociology, anthropology, etc. The American Journals flatly refused to touch it — until that data was separated, and the data on Negro children published entirely apart from the corresponding data on white children. No correlation of the facts was permitted in this country — the original paper was published in a Scottish Journal of anthropology.

Savannah's work was exceptionally sound, because the school system there, under the prior Supreme Court ruling of "separate but equal," had established a no-kidding separate but *equal* system. One thing — the Negro teachers in the Negro schools, during the 10-year study period, had *higher* qualifications than the white teachers in the white schools.

Reason: Savannah paid the same wages to all teachers in grade. White teachers have more school-openings to fill (particularly then) so that Negro teachers of the highest qualifications sought jobs in the Savannah system.

They kept punched-card records on *all* students in all schools. From these, they computer-selected Negro and White kids having equivalent home backgrounds. (Son of a Negro lawyer with son of a white lawyer.)

Their ten-year follow-ups showed that Negroes were not as educable as whites.

It's no wonder that the NAACP did everything in their power to keep the trial from being decided on the evidence in the case!

However, Putnam himself is unfortunately biased in his approach — he's decidedly unwilling to admit that a fine, capable Negro gentleman is just as good a gentleman as a white man of the same qualifications.

This whole damn mess stems in considerable part from the fact that a statistical truth can be absolute — and an individual truth among those statistics can be just as absolute, and completely the reverse. Yet wisdom requires *that both truths be acknowledged and worked with*.

The simplest example of such a situation is the absolute statistical truth, "The average velocity of molecules in a hot gas is higher than the average veloctiy of molecules in a cool gas," vs. the equally absolute truth that, "Some molecules in a hot gas move slower than some molecules in a cold gas." You can not possibly solve thermodynamic problems without awareness of both truths.

Sociology, dealing with populations, *must* consider the statistical truths: psychology, dealing with individuals, is in a horrible mess because it seeks to deal with individuals on statisical truths.

Putnam is trying to solve the sociological problem on a basis that denies individual truth; the NAACP tries to force only the individual truth, that some Negroes are markedly better human beings than some Whites, into a sociological rule-of-statistics.

Naturally, the two forces get along somewhat badly. Each has a truth, and knows he has a truth, and therefore knows the other side is totally biogted, false, and lying.

To make the mess more explosive, it *is* a matter of breed, of genetics — and genetics, like it or not, generated individuals on a purely statistical basis! Wherefore a great individual, arising from a long line of low-quality people, will nevertheless, despite his individual quality, produce normal-to-his-breed-statistics children — children of low quality.

No more perfect example than that of Abraham Lincoln do I know of. Descendant of a long line of nobodies, he was truly a great individual. But none of his children amounted to a damn.

The inverse, of course, is the equally frustrating and "unjust" fact that a weak, stupid scion of a long line of great men and women, of darned low value himself, can nevertheless father children matching his family's norm — brilliant, high-quality men capable of great achievement.

Nothing could be more difficult to integrate into a system of sociology and inter-human, inter-racial cultural patterns.

The only logical reactions to these genetic consequences would be that — let's leave color out of it, and say the Lincolns and the Adamses, since the Adams family of Mass. have, generation after generation, produced unusually capable men.

We would hold that while Abraham Lincoln was a fine gentleman, worthy of the highest office, he would *not* be held as a desirable member of the family. While James Q. Adams, medium grade moron, generally a slob, and of very little use in the world, would nevertheless be considered a desirable member of the family!

Further complicating the problems of a real-socio-political world is the fact that *only the Adams types would be capable of recognizing its wisdom.* The least intelligent, less analytical individuals of the Lincoln-family type, would see only the injustice of rejecting a brilliant Lincoln from the family, and accepting a truly stupid slob. Particularly since there is nothing whatever that Lincoln can do to change his nature — it's "not his fault."

As to *why* there's a racial difference between white and Negro — I think history provides a wide-open clue to that.

For some 7000 successive years, the Mediterranean-European world has been a continuous battleground — with highly lethal battles — over ideologies. The result was that only those strains —

those genetic types — that learned fast, and had great drive, determination, and toughness both physical and mental, survived. If you continually cull a breed of mammals for some 70 centuries, 350 human generations, you can definitely produce and stabilize a genetic differentiation. The more rigorous the culling, the higher the death-rate-by-violence, the more rapid the genetic bias will be.

The "educational opportunities" the white race enjoyed were known as Slavery in Egypt, and Slavery to Crete, and the Roman Empire, and the Middle Ages and the Goths and Vandals, and the Hundred Years War and the Thirty Years War and the Seven Years War and a couple of World Wars. There were Crusades and Wars of Roses and such like in between.

Those were our "educational opportunities" which the unfortunate Africans missed out on.

The way the Congo and Nigeria-Biafra are going to town currently, it looks as though, at long last, Africans are moving into the educational system.

It isn't the *best* way — but it does work, where nothing else seems to hold the student's attention as well.

Regards, John

Arthur C. Clarke *June 6, 1968*

Dear Arthur:

One item you mention interests me in particular; the bit about **J.B.S. Haldane** suggesting that cosmic rays were the noise of interstellar drives. When did he make that suggestion?

I'm curious, because I had that idea in an editorial about 1948 or 1950 and used it as a basis for part of the plot of my story "The Idealists" in *Nine Tales of Space & Time* some years later. I know it was original-with-me — that I hadn't seen **Haldane's** comment — and naturally I'm just curious as to whether I actually had priority.

Not that priority would do either me, you, or **Haldane** any real good!

And I did like **Bova's** quasar suggestion — but it was something of a question as to just how such an item should be billed — as science fact, or science fiction?

Anyway, one of the things I most enjoy about quasars is that they have magnificently thrown the Scientific Establishment into a tizzy of "Gee . . . uh . . . well . . . gee, I dunno *what* they are!!" They've finally hit something they admit really exists, and can't explain by any mechanism they know of, and can't stretch anything they've got to fit.

Goody, goody! Someday they may even acknowledge dowsing exists and can't be explained by anything now known!

Regards, John

Piers Anthony Jacob   *June 6, 1968*

Dear Mr. Jacob:

By now you'll have gotten your check on the bonus for "Alien Rulers"; they're usually delayed a bit, but they are guaranteed to get there!

"Xanthes's Heart" is returned herewith — it's really not much of a story, and what there is of it is distinctly downbeat, which science-fictioneers definitely dislike. Their attitude is, quite strongly, that, "Sure, there are problems in the world — but that's what brains are for! Solving 'em! *Not* bellyachin' about 'em!"

Re "Macroscope": As of now, I'm looking for a novel — but *not* 150,000 words of novel! That would require a seven-part serial — and readers kick about even three-quarters. "Dune" was about the longest thing we ever ran — and that we could run as two separate multipart serials.

I dislike summaries; thirty years of experience in this editing business has long since shown me that you can't judge a book by its cover, nor by its synopsis either. What *I* see in a synopsis may be 180 degrees out of phase with what the author sees — with the result that a synopsis may make me enthusiastic for a great story idea . . . and I get an absolute blob. Or the synopsis may appear a mess of oh-so-what-to me . . . but what the author saw in the idea was something entirely different, and it's a great yarn the way he tells it.

It'd sure save me a hell of a lot of time and effort if I could judge by synopsis; just think of all the hours of reading I could duck!

And remember that something like 87% of my manuscript reading time is wasted effort!

No, the fact is, I simply have to read the whole story in order to judge it.

Sincerely,   John W. Campbell

Re: "Xanthe's Heart," by **Piers A. D. Jacob**

Terry Carr   *June 17, 1968*

Dear Mr. Carr:

Perhaps this'll do for the "Meet the Editor" column: —

There's one distinction I can claim in this science-fiction editing business without fear of agrument: I've been running *Astounding-Analog* for almost 31 years, and during that period I have unquestionably read more lousy science-fiction than any other man in the world.

And that, while a considerable bore, is a very educational

experience. Usually the errors authors make in stories — if they have learned enough to sell some stuff — are subtle, hard to spot, and therefore hard to point out and offer useful criticism. Read a lot of lousy stuff, and you'll see practically every error would-be authors are capable of making — and see it in such exaggerated form that you *can* name it. You know — the horrible-example type of demonstration.

Some of the most frustrating things I run into are stories containing a perfectly lovely idea — a dilly of a plot scheme — by somebody who can't write, hasn't written, and never will write. You can forgive a weak writer for the sake of a gorgeous idea — but not simply awful writing. And as SFWA authors know, professional writers never lack for ideas — they're practically never interested in taking on somebody else's idea, even if it's a damn good one. They're too busy working up their own.

Another frustrator for editors is the story synopsis. You can no more judge a story by its synopsis than you can a book by its cover, because what *I* see in a synopsis and what *he* sees in it can be worlds apart. I've thought the synopsis looked like a great story — and gotten a Grade A #1 dud. I've seen synopses that closely resembled dead-flat sour beer — that turned into classic yarns.

That's partly, I think, because any really good novelette or novel develops its own characters, who walk off with the story, many times in directions the author never intended.

This business is, basically, part of the general field of Entertainment-Show Business. And it has, inherently, all the instability and uncertainty of Show Business. Wherefore the only thing you can definitely expect is the unexpected — the only stable thing is the constant change. If we don't change, the audience gets to be able to predict what's coming . . . and goes away. If we change in the wrong direction, they get mad and go away.

Science-fiction was, is, and bids fair to continue to be my hobby — which is why despite 31 years of reading 98.8% lousy science-fiction, I still read every manuscript that comes in.

Of course another reason for reading 'em all is that every so often, the Big Thrill comes along. I run across the First Story by a brand new Big One. The first **Heinlein**, or **Asimov** or **van Vogt** manuscript — all of which naturally showed up in the "slush pile" as unknowns.

The later Big Ones? Sure they're there — they just haven't become Classic Authors yet. Becoming a Classic Author involves time; quality isn't enough — it takes time for public recognition to soak in gradually.

Besides which, an editor's a damn fool to name names — it gets other authors annoyed!

Regards,   John W. Campbell

541

Dear Mr. Chalker:

You've got a lot of highly interesting and original ideas here — but the story isn't coherent enough to stand as is.

The essential problem is motivation; that's what makes a reader identify with a story character. Here, you have — in essence — only mechanisms.

There's no understanding of the motivations of the Terrans — or what the galactic situation is. And a man's actions are either good or bad not in terms of what he does, but the circumstances in which he does them. Even the motivations are less important than the circumstance! A man, for some petty, personal, half-mad reason of his own might have assassinated Hitler in 1938 — an act of evil motivation — which, in the circumstances, would have been a great benefit to Mankind.

Why are the Terrans disrupting the culture of the planet?

"For Wealth" is a damn poor answer; unthinking people may think slaves mean huge profits. They did — once. In the days before technology! When living organisms were the only available machines — they were as Plato said, "my animate agricultural instruments." But can you allow rebellious slaves work on multi-million-dollar refinery plants, where a single act of sabotage can cost $50,000,000? Particularly when a microminiaturized computer chip can watch the controls more closely than a conscious mind?

Raw materials, metals? In a high-order technology that can mine asteroids in space, instead of going to the bother of stripping useless rock and dirt on a planet?

For organic products, food and fibers? Huh, where have you been?! You wear Orlon? socks, a perma-press suit and shirt, and can enjoy *only* the products of the four billion years of local evolution — which you evolved with, and so are very specially designed to utilize successfully. And even among our own evolution's products, a lot of us have serious troubles, called allergies. Want to try the products of a 4-gigayear-alien development?

Labors? At what? Digging ditches, which slaves can be used for? When a power ditching machine can walk along as fast as a man can trot, making a 6-foot-deep, 18-inch-wide ditch, installing pipe or conduit, and filling the earth in behind? Watch the telephone company's cable laying equipment, with four huge tractors hauling a special plow that cuts a four-foot-deep furrow, lays in a cable, and neatly replaces the dirt, while hauling the trailer with the huge rolls of cable behind it.

There are things men want — but they never know until afterwards. The fine-chemical type organics — the hitherto-undreamnt-of medicinals, for instance. Ideas and philosophies. Works of art. New and totally different viewpoints on life.

And for *this* hunger, a static culture is useless — as a static culture is, equally, useless to itself. In the truest sense, a static culture is meaningless — it's simply a repetition of the same message, like saying all clouds are white all clouds are white all clouds are white all clouds are . . . indefinitely. It can be shown mathematically, even, that such a redundant system carries no information or meaning. Do the inhabitants of that cracked record a favor — nudge the needle into a new groove! It may start getting somewhere.

Sure, it means misery for the generation that gets the nudges! it usually takes war and violence to shake 'em loose.

And yes, you could save them more misery by showing 'em which way to go next. Of course, it would be *your* way, but it goes down a well understood, already-smoothed pathway.

But that (A) defeats your purpose of getting completely new ideas and approaches and (B) prevents them ever developing their *own* potentials.

But enslaving a planet for metals and slaves and meat — man, you can't validate any one of those as economically practical in an advanced technology.

It won't take too much rewriting to switch the situation — and it'd make a hell of a sight stronger (also somewhat longer and remunerative!) story.

Basically, you need to explain the situation in the *galaxy*, and the *motivation of the Terrans*. The motivation of the aliens for the tricks they did is simple. They got stuck there, couldn't return, and were horribly lonely for something approaching a human environment. So they magicked one up!

Sincerely,   John W. Campbell

Re: ". . . Or The Devil Will Drag You Under,"
  by **Jack L. Chalker**

A. Bertram Chandler   *August 5, 1968*

Dear Jack:

Thanks for the "False Fatherland" — which, oddly, got here several days *before* your letter! Remarkable!

You mention getting slightly muddy at a new port of call. I've often wondered why it wasn't practical to equip ships with some sort of attachment points, an air compressor, and a collection of plastic bags for emergency use. I should think you could boost your C of G a few feet, in calm waters, without danger of capsizing, and with reasonable hope of a quick departure from over-affectionate mudbanks. Oh, well . . . not knowing the technology of flotation at all. . . .

That Siege of Glenfield you mentioned happened during a somewhat quiet news period over here — and was played up for several days in the New York papers. The young cooky got himself world-wide publicity; it must have delighted him.

My own suggestions for handling the problem involved the proposition that there's no need to get anybody killed who doesn't need it; the girl was slightly balmy herself, obviously, but as long as she *had* fallen for the nut, and *had* produced his bratling, she did have some reason to want to make it official. She's just a standard-model stupid teenage girl, with the usual unshakeable conviction that she Knows All The Right Answers, and parents and elders are Strictly Out Of It.

The baby, of course, had nothing to say about it, except express a desire for food, dryness, cleanliness, and warmth.

My personal Department of Dirty Tricks would suggest sending in limited quantities of food — enough so they'd be hungry by the time more came. And load the food with a slow-acting drug such that when she ate it (I understand he made her eat first) it would be 8-12 hours before results showed up. By which time he'd have been hungry enough to eat it. There are slow-acting, harmless, but *very* effective sleepy-by drugs.

Another item I considered, was sending in ammunition he demanded — with 40% dynamite substituted for the usual propellant powder. Dynamite is a very poor propellant; it doesn't wait long enough to find out the bullet's willing to move. The act of attempting to murder some one would become an act of instant-suicide.

To a more useful topic . . . since you're familiar with writing up reports about getting stuck on mudbanks, why not write one for us? What sort of equivalent of a mud-bank could a spaceship get stuck on? It would be more interesting, of course, if something broke loose, perhaps, resulting in a hold atmosphere of something like fifteen tons of ammonium nitrate fertilizer onto which several tons of ethylene glycol, or maybe castor oil, had dripped. This combination would cause any sensible man to be chary about violent methods, fires, unshielded sparks, etc. in the vicinity.

One perfectly good way of retrieving the situation that the ordinary spacer wouldn't think of — drill or otherwise open the hold to space. Ethylene glycol (or castor oil) has a low vapor pressure — but not *that* low! A little patience, and if the hold is kept warm (ordinary temperature) the last molecule of the organic liquid will boil off into space — leaving almost perfectly inert NH_4NO_3. (Just keep those tetryl caps away, and we're all right now!)

Reminds me of a real instance in Switzerland, where a piping system sprang a leak in a chemical plant, and several tons of a light hydrocarbon liquid became saturated with N_2O_4, yielding an exceedingly explosive mixture. The plant was up-stream from a good sized village; if they tried to dump the awful stuff, it might flow away from their plant O.K. — but it'd be sure to be set off somehow in the village. Any chemical reaction to tie down the nitric oxide would be a heat-yielding reaction — and heat was all it needed. They stewed for several days, while keeping the mess at a temperature of about 40 degrees below zero. They were afraid to freeze it; that could set it off. They finally decided that the only possible solution was to separate the two by careful — very careful! — distillation. The nitric oxide is normally a gas; by vacuum pumping, they should be able to cause the stuff to come out of solution, while still keeping the temperature fairly low, and get the two apart.

They were almost 90% successful. It didn't so go off until they were working on the last 10%, so one of the three chemical engineers survived, and it took only six months to rebuild the plant.

You think you got troubles with mud-banks?

Regards,   John

Lawrence A. Perkins   *August 19, 1968*

Dear Larry:

I'm taking "Messything" — check will follow in a few days, if the accounting department's up to its usual standard.

The modified version is more effective; I'll acknowledge your point about the cure-probability not being over-rosy as being valid. The main thing, as you say, is that Sanderson *wants* it.

As to Mensa — or MM — I retain my tendency to feel that there's a good bit of mutual admiration society about it. IQ is a lousy measure of real-world competence-in-achievement; I've known too many guaranteed-certified-IQ 160+ characters who were third level assistants to certified-IQ-90-95's who were working on their second or third million. Technical moron-millionaires in the contracting business, or the big-wholesale hardware business, or major lumberyard, with highly educated high-IQ birds managing the company books. Lots of brains — no drive. Great conformers and believers in That's The Way It Is.

I'd be quite willing to bet that if Winston Churchill had taken an IQ test when he was in prep school, he'd have shown up far below Mensa's level; the IQ tests tend to measure and predict school-grades performance — and Churchill would have been kicked out as uneducable if his father hadn't had the status and power he did. Specifically, the IQ test is a *precocity* index, as actually used in testing. You get a high score if you're able to answer questions considered proper for older children. Adult IQ tests are therefore actually something other than the original IQ test system — they actually measure the degree of agreement between the testee and the testor's ideas as to "the right answers" — and God help the testee if he has a much deeper and broader understanding than the testor!

A psychologist may ask, "What is the difference between a king and a president?" and believe sincerely that he's asking a meaningful question. But an anthropologist, sociologist or historian wouldn't be able to answer sensibly. In many cultures kings are elected, and many a South American President inherited his office.

Incidentally, the highest score ever made on any IQ test was made by a 6-month old chimpanzee on a test meant for babies. He was extremely precocious — on a human scale! — and scored 250.

One of the beauties of this science-fiction job is that I meet some really unusual and fascinating people (as well as some real weirdos! The real challenge is spotting the far-out original geniuses from the way-out crackpots.)

If you want to get some understanding of my annoyance with IQ tests — get hold of *The Genetics of Genuius, VOL. II*, by Terman, the great IQ-tester. Vol. I has to do with his 1000 brilliant school children; Vol. II is made up of the studies a bunch of his grad students and assistants made of the historical geniuses from 1450 to 1850. Take a look at the IQ ratings they gave men like Copernicus, Newton, Franklin, Galileo, vs. those they gave to the book-larnin' specialists like John Stewart Mill — who was their choice for the all-time most brilliant of all those geniuses, far brighter than Leonardo da Vinci, or a mere barely-normal man like Copernicus.

Looking over that book gave me an acute case of the pip, so far as IQ scores was concerned, and underlies considerable of my resistance to the Mensa idea.

Of the three "1000 brightest children" of Terman's I know, three are Grade A +1 miserable neurotics. Just like John Stewart Mill, Terman's choice for the all-time prize!

Regards,   John

Ron Stoloff   *December 5, 1968*

Dear Mr. Stoloff:

My first reaction to your request to "use short quotes from" my editorial is "No!" By using a few short quotes from Winston Churchill, I can show that Churchill considered Adolf Hitler one of the greatest men in the world. He certainly said, repeatedly, that Hitler was one of the greatest menaces of the world; I need only leave out the "ace" part to make my point.

I can, equally, show that Hitler was kind, good, benevolent and a wise philosopher. It might take me quite a while to find the necessary words and phrases in his screechings, but anybody want to bet it couldn't be done?

I've had sufficient experience with statements abstracted from context to say, "Show me first your wares!" before giving consent.

As to that November editorial and the election: It drew 95% angry howls, and about 5% agreement. Reasons: The guy whose toes you don't step on doesn't thank you for not doing so; it's the guy whose feelings you hurt that starts howling. I naturally heard from outraged fanatics; these included, incidentally, a few Racist-Segregationist pro-Wallace fanatics who damned me for saying I didn't like their hero.

The election came out almost the way I had hoped it would; both parties were forced to do some deep and solid soul-searching during many long hours while the issue hung in doubt. And they've been — and will continue to be — busy studying the results since.

Nixon won, as I'd predicted — but with a distinct indication that he didn't have any all-out "mandate from the people."

The Democrats lost — with distinct indications that if they'd been willing to drop their exactly-in-the-middle-of-the-road line, and accepted a more liberal position with someone like McCarthy, they might have won.

What concerned me was the need for getting two parties pried apart; it makes no difference whether one goes right, or the other goes left — just so they aren't offering one and only one approach to the world!

Sincerely,   John

George H. Scithers   *January 23, 1969*

Dear Mr. Scithers:

O.K., so ox yokes ain't my business — but I do know the Romans didn't have horsecollars, they did have oxen, but they didn't use them such a hell of a lot. I think there's more to the problem of ox-power than either of us understands. One of the problems may be that the ox's compound low makes for an extremely miles-per-bushel fuel consumption, resulting in an unprofitable operation.

You say the North Koreans don't use oxen openly — ashamed of 'em. The major point of my editorial beautifully illustrated: status is more important than actual solid achievment. The So. Koreans have made a tremendous industrial growth — and are willing to use oxen openly. Results, not status, accepted as more important.

Re **Joe Goodavage's** piece: **Joe Goodavage** didn't invent those ideas — those were in essence quotations from major scientific organizations. Observatories — government meteorological outfits, etc.

So please step down off that high dudgeon, and reevaluate the facts. First, forget the inverse square law — it doesn't apply, because we're discussing moments, not gravitational force.

It goes this way: Jupiter weighs about 1/1000th what the Sun does. (I.e., its mass is 1/1000). The center of gravity of that pair must, therefore, lie 1/1000th of the way from the CG of one to the CG of the other. That distance is roughly 500,000,000 miles, so their common CG must be 500,000 miles from the CG of the Sun. I.e., the CG of the Sun-Jupiter system lies *outside* of the Sun.

Now the CG of the whole damn solar system can be calculated by anyone with a formula for solving a twenty-body problem; it is *not* a nice, simple, stable point moving in a pretty, smooth orbit around the CG of the Milky Way.

If you repeat the above calculation for Mercury, you'll see why the inverse square law has damned little to do with it; Mercury's on a very short moment arm, and has low mass. Saturn's longer moment arm is offset by lesser mass than Jupiter.

The inner planets have effects greater than their moments would at first suggest, because of their far more rapid oscillation — they provoke more turbulent flows because of their short periods. After all, Neptune's period is so long that there would be damned little tidal disturbance and eddying caused by changes that were that long period.

Now in re Astrology being an observational study of correlations. It is, my friend. You mistake a fundamental problem of such observational studies. The young Swedish statistician who pointed out that there was, each year, a marked rise in the birth rate in Sweden every time the storks returned from Africa was calling attention to a correlation. The correlation is real. It can be studied. Study it long enough, and deeply enough, and eventually somebody may find a causative link somewhere. But the existence of a correlation does *not* prove that storks bring Swedish babies.

And by the way . . . the exact period of rotation of the total mass of the Solar System with respect to the external stars is a little hard to define — but it is just about 11.2 years.

Curious that that's the period of the sunspot cycle isn't it?

Regards, John W. Campbell

George H. Scithers   *February 20, 1969*

Dear Ltc. Scithers:

O.K. — you can take the galactic viewpoint, and recognize that the CG of the system is traveling in a smooth curve about the Galactic CG.

Only be physicist enough to recognize that a Center of Gravity is, like a "line of force," a mathematical concept having no physical reality, and being mathematically valid only beyond certain limits. (Geologists use the fact that the Earth's gravitational pull does not emanate from a point at the center of the Earth in spotting geological anomalies, for example.)

Also, recognize that the Earth has tides because the gravitational forces do not in reality concern only Centers of Gravity.

The Sun is a superconducting plasma, full of immense electric currents and consequent magnetic fields. But it's not a massless super conductor — and that mass is being heaved around quite considerably by slightly gargantuan tidal forces. Those tidal forces are *not* stable and simple; they're complex as hell — and they cause huge variations in the solar wind and solar flares, which are, therefore, tied in with periodicities of tidal influence.

As to the exact sunspot period — it isn't known, because we haven't been watching long enough.

The exact periodicity of the rotating mass of the solar system is also damned hard to determine; again, we haven't been watching long enough! How often will all the planets line up in a neat array from Mercury right out to Pluto? You know that such an alignment *must* happen now and then — but it's a little rare, and we haven't happened to be around when one happened.

As of now, we lack data.

But that's nothing; ask any solar physics expert what we know about the Sun, and he'll assure you we lack data. Like how come the neutrino experiments keep yielding many too few neutrinos for what our best astrophysics says the Sun should be emitting?

Come off it guy! We've got one hell of a lot to learn, and one way to learn is to take a new idea and *test it by observation*. Not just by theory!

Regards, John W. Campbell

Robert Silverberg   *February 24, 1969*

Dear Bob:

I knew, of course, about your file-destroying fire — but you must remember the old saying that, "Three moves is as good as a fire," with respect to loss of possessions.

And I'll add another; three daughters is worse than a fire, when it comes to loss of reading material. They have girl-friends and boy-friends, and somehow things wander. . . .

On looking over my library, I find I have a "Twilight" in a French version, an Italian version, and I believe a German and a Dutch version.

But no English version.

My original-magazine-copy version has vanished. So has my Shasta edition of "Who Goes There?," the Dell paperback edition, and, so far as I can currently make out, every other copy of it I ever had.

However, for some while now **Scott Meredith** has been my literary agent; they collected copies of my various pieces a while back, and they may have a photocopy of "Twilight" on hand.

In any case, you'd have to arrange for rights through them, so you might as well write 'em.

If you're stuck, I may be able to pry loose a copy from the office files here, long enough to get a photocopy. It's not viewed kindly; the office files are for legal purposes and being printed on old style sulfite pulp, it's oxidized pretty badly. The result is that flattening the magazines out enough to get a usable photocopy is apt to split the brittle old paper.

See what Scott's got to work with, huh?

Regards,   John

Wayne D. McFarland   *April 7, 1969*

Dear Mr. McFarland:

A young friend of mine at CCNY was present during the "student riot" on the campus, and told me how the TV station coverage of the event was arranged.

The fact was that there were about ten "students" actively involved — eight of whom were not students, but outsiders. They were doing all the sitting-in and objecting.

Since that doesn't make a good TV show, the cameramen set their cameras up at such an angle that a couple of hundred other students who were strictly interested bystanders amused by the hysteria, *appeared* to be part of the demonstration. Made a good TV show.

The majority of the *actual rioters* in Chicago were like those ten "students" — 80% outside agitators. The mobs on the screen were largely like the spectators at a football game. You wouldn't say that there were 80,000 players at the annual Yale-Harvard game, would you — though cameras will show you 80,000 were involved at the scene.

And yes, I *do* distrust the entire content of any report when I find that report contains palpable falsity. Don't you? Military Intelligence evaluates information on the basis of the reliability of the reporter, and the probability of the information. If a known liar reports something they've been expecting to hear — they'll consider it probable but dubious. If an agent who's never been know to lie or report false information reports something they don't believe possible — they'll start intense efforts to get confirmation.

And when a lawyer uses a term like "unrestrained," he's supposed to know precisely what the term means, and use it accurately. The term "unrestrained" *does* include Maoist barbarian tactics. If that isn't what he meant — Walker had no business misusing the term. Do that sort of trick in a legal contract, and see what it would get him! That use of "unrestrained" was sheer emotionalism, and I resent it in a government-sponsored report.

Finally — yes, it *was* a game, and my sense of proportion is fairly good. *They* made a game of it, a game called "Fuzz-baiting," a rough contact sport that's fun, and much safer than football, skiing or intercollegiate boxing for instance.

Look, guy — a strong man armed with a *lignum vitae* club can very easily knock a man's brains out. I do *not* mean bump his noggin gently — I mean *literally*. Gray goo on the street. A man with one of those can readily break limbs.

Now what damned fool, or emotionally prejudiced nit-wit, says there was "unrestrained" force — when *not one cop lost his cool.* Not *one* fuzz-baiter had his brains spilled, not one broken limb resulted. So far as I know, not one was even clunked hard enough to knock him cold — something that's considered good sport when it happens in boxing or football?

But the "players" of fuzz-baiting are very lousy sports indeed — they specialize in whimper, whinny and whine when they get a sore fingernail.

If they're so dedicated to peace they're willing to take risks for it — *real* risks — they might do what my nephew did. He went as a conscientious objector, a medic-linguist, working with the Vietnamese people.

Since people trying to improve the condition of the Vietnamese are the particular targets of Commie hatred — Communism grows best in misery and hopelessness — he's back in the US now, getting put back together.

If those loud-mouthed demonstrators mean what they say — I'll believe them when they *do* something, instead of just talking and demanding under conditions where they know they will not be injured.

Why don't they go try to help Vietnamese people? The government will be glad to supply training, transportation and supplies.

Oh — don't confuse "hurt" with "injure." Getting spanked hurts, but it doesn't injure anything but pride.

Sincerely,   John W. Campbell

Jay Jay Klein *June 5, 1969*

Dear Mr. Klein:

Our thanks for the portrait of **Anne McCaffrey** with the Nebula.

Mrs. McCaffrey is one of the most interesting and accomplished women in science-fiction — and any woman writer is a rarity in this field.

Incidentally — as a fellow photographer, I am sure you share my feeling of sympathy for the Apollo 10 astronauts, on the most magnificent sightseeing expedition in human history — and *both* of their electric-drive Hasselblads stalled by dead batteries! And just when they were making their low, 9 mile pass!

Regards,   John W. Campbell

Perry A. Chapdelaine, Sr. *June 12, 1969*

Dear Mr. Chapdelaine:

One thing you need to get straight that the "Milford Mafia" won't recognize, and in fact preaches angrily against.

You do *NOT* write stories *for me.*

I like reading science-fiction, but I certainly have no intention of paying $6,000 for a couple of novels for my own pleasure — which is what I paid out for two novels in the last week or so.

You are *not* writing for *me* — you're writing for the 100,000 paying customers, for whom I act solely as purchasing agent. They're the ones who can, and happily do, pay kilobucks for a novel.

What I suggest in stories is not my personal, iron-clad whim as the Milford gang suggests — it's what the largest science-fiction audience on earth seems to want. "The New Wave" to the contrary notwithstanding, *Analog* has more than twice — in fact more than three times! — the circulation of the other and "artier" magazine of the New Wave. What we publish may not be so "literary," but it happens to be what a bunch of highly educated and technically oriented human beings enjoy.

Don't blame me if they don't like "art" — but don't let anybody mislead you into thinking that it's *my* whim that I'm inflicting on long-suffering authors.

The gang I work for (readers!) encourages me to pay higher rates because they like that type of yarn.

I'd strongly recommend that you pay the least possible attention to Literateurs and their learned comments; graduates in literature, graduates of short-story writing courses, etc., Ph.D's in English, almost invariably turn out lousy *stories*. They make up a mutual admiration society of small scope, small numbers, and great self-congratulation.

I've seen the results of good, competent authors being taken in charge by a bunch of those literary gurus and geniuses; in the 30-odd years I've been running this mag I've had time to watch what does in fact happen.

It louses up a good competent author, and turns him into an artsy-partsy, sound-of-his-own-words type that can't tell a *story* any more, and lacks the bounce and fun and humor that makes a yarn.

Now as to your priestly story: I have no idea how it would work out. It could be strictly last week's dishwater, or it could be a whale of a lot of fun. It certainly has possibilities — but remember that the essence of Ole Doc Methuselah was that the yarns were always fun, no matter how serious the problem.

What could make your fun would be to have the halo-conscience very strict-minded — while the priest could, in a good cause, be a tricky arguer that'd make a Jesuit applaud. You know, properly used, logic can be the dirtiest of all dirtiest tricks — and that's always fun.

Sincerely, John W. Campbell

Ronald E. Graham *July 10, 1969*

Dear Mr. Graham:

It's remarkable the degree to which a seemingly simple statement in English, between two native-English-speakers, can be so completely misinterpreted!

My comment that, "A lot of people think they know me, but I know nothing of them," was intended to explain why I didn't know who you were, and to apologize, beforehand, for my inescapable ignorance. It wasn't to suggest you were brash, Lord knows! I wouldn't go to Conventions at all, if I had that feeling!

It's perfectly typical that you have followed my career and thinking for a couple of decades, and feel that we're friends — but find it somewhat easy to forget that while you've contacted me (through my writing), you haven't written your thoughts to me!

I do indeed regret that you misunderstood my comment.

A Convention is a very poor place indeed to discuss business — except on a basis of retiring into a corner, or into a private room, because of the impossibility of carrying on a sustained conversation when dozens of people tend to drift up and listen in, or horn in. If I stand in one place in the public halls at a convention, I usually wind up with an audience of 20 to 30 people listening in and asking questions!

You'd have been most welcome at my office, or in our suite at the Lunacon, if you'd let me know what was on your mind.

As to your proposed publishing venture; my hunch is you'll have great difficulty filling *one* magazine with the quality of material that will satisfy you. Remember that science-fiction has been going full blast in the United States for over 40 years now. With a population of 200,000,000, a reputation as a top magazine for over 30 years, and paying the highest rates in the field — I have a hell of a time getting an adequate supply of stories as good as I feel they should be, for my *one* magazine. As of now, I'm drawing stories from all over the English-speaking world; I have several Aussie authors, a number of English, and I also hear from Ghana, South Africa, India, Pakistan and other areas.

To fill three magazines with satisfactory material — well, I can wish you luck, but I'll have my doubts!

My own suggestion would be to get one well launched; that will build up a cadre of writers; as the supply of material increases, then you could launch expansion.

In manufacturing industry, you don't launch a 10,000 ton per year plant, with a raw material source capable of only 2,000 tons per year!

Regards,   John W. Campbell

Jack Wodhams   *September 4, 1969*

Dear Jack:

It's rather generally assumed that clowns do not have serious messages — which is peculiar, in view of the fact that it has long been recognized by philosophers that ridicule is the most powerful of all weapons against ideas.

It is also generally considered that fiction is not really important — after all, all professional fiction writers are self-acknowledged

554

professional liars! — and that only serious essays are important.

So why did Jesus use so many parables in his teaching?

My father was Chief Engineer for Plant Practices for the American Telephone & Telegraph Co. I recall, years ago, a rather serious crisis that A.T.&T. faced as a result of an action of some of the U.S. Senators.

As the number of telephones in service increased, the number of human operators necessary to switch the calls had to increase exponentially. By the late 1920's, the number of phones had grown so great that there weren't enough young women in the country to be able to service the switchboards in the years immediately ahead; automatic dial system *had* to be installed. But people like to have human service — somebody who understands what they *mean*, not a machine that mindlessly does what they *say*. So there was grumbling, and complaining that the "telephone company just wanted to put those girls out of work."

And then an automatic dial-operated switchboard was installed in the U.S. Senate office building. And several senators rose in annoyance, and offered resolutions in the Senate that those machines be taken out, and girl operators be brought back — that the dial system made it too difficult to get their calls through.

This would, of course, have been a major public relations disaster for the A.T.&T.

And then Will Rogers, the famous comic, in one of his radio shows commented that it seemed funny that a bunch of senators who figured they could run something as complicated as the United States couldn't seem to work a dial telephone.

And that, of course, was the *end* of the Senate's resistance to dial mechanism. The nation had a good laugh — and the inescapable necessity of dial phones went ahead with far less grumbling.

The problem of the great comics is, simply, that there are so many mugging fools who can cause a giggle, and so few Will Rogers type philosophers who can make powerful social comment with a good natured chuckle.

Your "There Was A Crooked Man" makes a series of sound fundamental points of philosophy — with chuckles, instead of rantings and preachings of Hell Fire and Damnation.

To a major extent, the comic of the Will Rogers (and Bob Hope!) school uses subliminal techniques to plant his philosophical comments below the conscious level; the recipient doesn't realize just what has turned his thoughts, or how or by whom it was done — he just has a different slant on something.

Try to preach to him, and all his conscious defenses against anyone trying to tell *him* what to do flare into action. He'll fight you right down the line.

Amuse him — give him some laughs — and for the sake of the fun he'll assume a viewpoint he doesn't, of course, accept actually . . . something he'd never consider for an instant if you proposed it *seriously* . . . and somehow he lets the new idea infiltrate his rock-ribbed inflexible attitudes sort of accidentally . . . .

Have you considered the comedy of the modern idea of "individual freedom" of "doing my thing" and its relationship to "crime in the streets"? The student rebellions that demand more control of what they are taught, and how, because they want only "relevant" courses? Of the Blacks who demand courses in Black history and Black culture, and separate Black departments — and an end to segregated schools?

Of the students who demand entrance into the great and famous colleges — and then demand that the courses in those colleges be made "more democratic" and "more relevant" so that anybody can graduate without having to learn a tough mental discipline?

Ah but the world is fully equipped with comedy — if someone can just make us chuckle at the nonsense. You know science has been called "the business of making the self-evident obvious." Top-notch humor could also be called "the business of making the obviously ridiculous self-evident."

Unfortunately, my friend, that — like all creative writing — takes an innate talent, and training can't replace it. It also takes discipline and work, of course. Like playing a violin — you have to have an innate sense of pitch, *and* practice.

Reminds me of the young man who stopped an oldster on the sidewalk on 57th St. in New York City and asked, "How do I get to Carnegie Hall?" The oldster looked at him, smiled and said, "Practice, my boy — practice and practice!" (To translate that into local terms, you need only remember that Carnegie Hall in New York is *the* goal of all concert soloists, and is on 57th St.)

The trouble is, practice doesn't do a bit of good if you don't have an innate talent to sharpen. Most of my work here is simply trying to spot the would-be authors that have the gift, but haven't yet sharpened it, and encourage them to do so. And as a humanitarian duty, to save the ungifted from wasting time and energy. With a tin ear, there's no use practicing on a violin!

"Nuku'alofa" sounds, somehow like a "new cooer-and-lofer" making love on a beach.

Ignorance is not, in Tonga, merely a lack-of-opportunity-to-learn; it's something maintained despite pressures as a result of strongly rooted and determined defense. There are a variety of factors in all cultures that motivate the natives against the concepts of alien cultures — whether it be Tonga resisting European, or

556

Englishman resisting French morals. The Chinese — Japanese — African — every people has resisted the indoctrination in alien ideas. Britons didn't appreciate the lessons in Roman civilization, nor the resulting Brito-Romans the Anglo-Saxons, nor the results of *that* interbreeding the Norman education.

I note with interest the Irish resistance to new (Protestant) ideas continues. And the Irish, more fools they, are trying to restore the Gaelic language, while retaining the stupid English money system. What nonsense! Irishmen have been the greatest masters of the English language for the last century! And even the English have finally gotten around to abandoning that crazy mixed up ventigesimal-duodecimal money system.

The basic resistance stems from two things: A child grows up and learns mores; what the culture holds is Good, and what is Evil. The more traditional the culture, the more firmly is the term "change" equated to "evil." The way we do things is Good: other ways are Evil. (Ask any 18th-19th century missionary!) Second, in a centuries-old stable cultural system, individuals who couldn't accept the local mores were killed off, kicked out, or so knocked about that they didn't pass on their genes. Result: The natives of that culture are *genetically* adapted to that moral system.

A calm, thoughtful, slow-to-anger man is admired in England; in Italy he would be despised as a coward unwilling to avenge and insult, to defend his honor. Maintain that mores for a few centuries — and you breed a volatile, vengeful, explosive type of man; the other kind died out or moved away.

Wherefore a native culture resists invading ideas and mores both culturally and genetically!

Finally, a language serves as a terrific philosophical force. Every language represents a system of dividing the real universe into compartments, with names, so it can be communicated . If you want to get a cement-mixer truck through a small passage, you have to disassemble it, pass the parts through, and reassemble at the other end. That's what language attempts to do with ideas.

Different langauges divide reality differently — our way just *seems* "the only sensible way" to us. So long as a people maintains its language — that language maintains a philosophy which underlies a cultural concept which leads to a system of mores which. . . .

And "other ways" of "change" means "Evil," of course.

Even the European languages differ in untranslatable degree. The French term "glorois" or the Spanish "muchissmo" can't be translated with their implications into English. The Spanish term "pueblo" does *not* mean what an Englishman means by "town," or "village."

When you get to non-indo-european languages, the impossibility of translation is enormously widened. The Blackfoot Indian language, for example, has *no word meaning water*. There are words for the-stuff-in-a-lake or the stuff-that-falls-from-the-sky, and . . . but no word for water. The Hopis had no past or future tenses. Japanese has no plurals and singulars.

A language is a tremendously powerful cultural defense, because it's a philosophical basic. That's why a native people clings so tenaciously to their language — without consciously knowing why.

It's a mightly fortress for their native ignorance.

Regards,   John

James D. Cagle   *October 9, 1969*

Dear Mr. Cagle:

We'll be down at Will Rice College April [22], I think. My wife will come along — at my expense! — so please arrange for a double room for us on the appropriate dates.

And send me a letter with full details, so that I can tack it up on my bulletin board to make sure I have the data before me during the next months, and don't get confused and cross up my dates!

I normally speak *ad lib*, because that way I can adjust to what sort of response I get from my audience. Expand the points that appear to interest them — compress or skip areas they show minimal interest in.

If you can have a tape-recorder available, I'll bring along a tape of the "unnatural sounds" that **Dr. Risset** gave me — the sounds discussed in an editorial in *Analog* a few months back. People generally enjoy the weird effects — and I use them to make a basic philosophical point. After you've heard them, you've had an Experience, but you'll find you can *not* describe-communicate that experience to anyone who hasn't heard them.

Sincerely,   John W. Campbell

Jean B. McCormick   *October 23, 1969*

Dear Miss McCormick:

The reason why I lump all the social sciences in one basket of worms is that their subject is so thoroughly intertwined they *have* to be. And they're all suffering under the current socio-cultural delusion of "all men are created equal — and that means they're all really the same." Impose that postulate on your thinking, observe the vast differences between individuals, and the only logical conclusion is "it all depends on education and environmental exposure."

This makes it necessary for socio-psychological-anthropological philosophers to be careful to avoid noticing the effect of a primitive-level log-hut, no schools, subsistence-farming level, no public health system society widely existent in the U.S. midwest 150 years ago on one Abraham Lincoln.

And that a black man, slave in the old South, managed somehow to become Dr. George Washington Carver.

Scientists somewhat dislike uncontrollable random processes, and prefer to have nice, neat, definitives to work with. Genetics is strictly the Monte-Carlo System approach.

The fact seems to be that an individual is like a photographic print; it isn't the exposure to light that makes the picture, nor is it the developing chemicals. Neither one can do the job. But even the best developers can't get a clear picture from an inadequate, fuzzy exposure, nor the best exposure produce a fine print if the developer is contaminated.

The optimum educational environment is one which develops to maximum the genetically endowed potentials.

Interacting with that is the fact that *every culture acts as a powerful selective breeding system.* Certain personality types are honored, encouraged, and given maximum opportunity for attracting and holding desirable mates.

At a very simple level: The Incas used to have a Spring Fertility Festival among the Alto Plano Indians. Each spring, on a chosen date, all the girls who'd come of age that year started running up the mountainside at a given signal. A second signal started the boys running after them — and he who caught her in the race up the mountain mated with her there and then.

For some reason, the descendants of those inverse Sadie Hawkins Day festivals are able to run, work, and play happily for hours at a time at 15,000 foot altitudes. Fully acclimated Caucasians can't walk fast for more than about 8 minutes. If a Caucasian woman spends a week or so above 10,000 feet during her third month of pregnacy, the baby will probably be a mongoloid idiot due to lowered blood oxygen levels. If she went into labor above about 12,000 feet she and the baby would both die of anoxemia. The Peruvian Alto Plano's have an inhabited village at 17,500 feet.

Their culture has selectively bred an extreme-altitude breed by means of a cultural tradition.

In a barbarian-warrior culture — such as the Germani, the Highland Scots, the Plains Indians and a hundred others — a slow-to-anger, peaceable and thoughtful man had little chance of either surviving or propagating.

In a ritual-tabu culture, a creative individual is due for a short life and a miserable one.

Children are not competent to use judgment; they don't have sufficient data. When they do decide to judge, they automatically assume they have all the data anyone needs. (Try arguing with a 13-16 year old girl, in particular!) What you needed was a series of kids brought up by genuinely open-minded cultural anthropologists who brought them up while the parents were investigating various cultures — so the kids were exposed as observers, but not as indoctrinees.

The trouble with cultures is that not only are the children indoctrinated — they're the product of generations of selective breeding to produce individuals who have native tendencies in that direction.

Now genetics produces *potentials*, which are very broad. Thus genetically, human babies have the *potential* to learn language; they are not born speaking any language, but can learn anything around. If none is around, however, the potential withers.

The same applies in other areas. Eskimos have no industrial cultural background whatever . . . apparently! But the extreme harshness of their environment allowed survival only to those who learned how to understand and use the laws of forces and the nature of materials around them. They have a genetic characteristic of acute appreciation of mechanical relationships. That doesn't mean merely how to estimate the strength of an ice floe, or the design and construction of the famous Eskimo toggle-harpoon — when Whites moved in to build the Dew Line stations, labor was needed. Eskimos showed up. Men who had never personally encountered white men before, knew no English, and had never before seen machines.

In one Dew Line location, two years later an Eskimo was the elected shop steward of the Machinists's Union. He was reading not only English, but blue prints, and was a top-notch machinist.

Ask any engineer who's tried to employ native labor in Africa or Southeast Asia what native labor is like when faced with a machine.

The trouble with all the social fields is that, as yet, they've come up with some of the stupidest simple-minded solutions to all human relationships that any teen-age SDS type could imagine.

Of course it would make it ever so much easier to solve the problems if all men were created equal — so let's just make a simplifying assumption to make figuring easy. Everyone's really the same.

The ants and the bees both found a workable system based on that proposition — the hive-hill system works fine. Except they have a few ant-types that aren't really the same.

As to articles: At the moment *Analog's* loaded with 'em. Unusual, but true.

The copper bracelets, incidentally, are not new to us; my wife's been wearing some for several years. It happens I can't, because I develop a sort of allergic reaction to the copper — an intensely itching rash. Our local M.D., who's an open-minded and experimental type told us about the old idea, and he's been trying it on some of his patients, who want to experiment. For some it seems to work — for others, it's useless and for some like me, it has to be discontinued.

I suspect it's like vitamins; B_1 can cure hallucinations, intense depression and nervousness miraculously. A bad case of postpartum psychosis a local woman had cleared up magically (a psychiatrist had been using electric shock to no avail, treating her for three months) when she started taking massive doses of a liquid B-vitamin preparation.

But if your hallucinations etc. are due to taking LSD B-vitamins aren't going to help much.

If your arthritis is associated with an acute copper deficiency, copper bracelets can drive it away; it won't help at all if that's not the cause of the trouble, however.

Sincerely,   John W. Campbell

Encl: "The World Changers"

Ted White   *October 30, 1969*

Dear Mr. White:

Reports of my coming retirement, are like those fabled reports of Mark Twain's death — greatly exaggerated.

Quite some years ago, I found a way to get somebody to pay me for playing at my hobby — and even do all the hard work connected with the hobby that I'm too lazy to do. Like keeping the books, untangling legal requirements, finding printers and distributors — all that necessary but acutely boring nonsense.

I'm still having fun with my hobby — and Conde'-Nast seems happy to do all the hard work of printing and selling 100,000 copies every month. So neither of us has any present interest in changing so mutually satisfactory a set-up.

However, just as my wife finds insurance policies a wise idea, despite the fact that she prefers to have me around — we at C-N not unnaturally have, over the years, kept in mind that I *could* get hit by a truck, take the wrong plane, or grab the wrong terminal in my 2000 volt electronics power supply.

I've got most of a decade to go before reaching C-N's standard retirement age — and that's an "if you feel like retiring at that time" set-up anyway.

I have every reason to hope and believe it'll be a while yet. After all, my model science-fiction editor was **T. O'Conner Sloane**, who was doing fine into his late 70's!

Sincerely,   John W. Campbell

Brad Linaweaver   *November 24, 1969*

Dear Mr. Linaweaver:

Our astronauts who first walked on the Moon, left behind a plaque with their names inscribed on it; I think they had a perfect right to have that symbolic record of their high achievement on the Moon as a legitimate part of Man's history.

I think that it was equally proper for the nation that achieved that first Moon landing to leave it's symbol there as well.

Let's not kid around; it was Armstrong and Aldrin who *did* achieve the first landing — and it was, equally, the United States that achieved it.

Nobody claimed the Moon — but we have a perfect right to leave our record there — and on history.

Sincerely,   John W. Campbell

Lloyd Biggle *c/o Lawrence P. Ashmead*   *December 15, 1969*

Dear Mr. Biggle:

The first two-thirds of this yarn are damn good — I liked it.

The last [one-third is] a wild, self-denying, impossible inconsistency that violates good sense, anthropology, sociology, and psychology.

The trouble is, the IPR boys are right, in at least one respect: It *will* take 2000 years or so to solve the problem of the *olz*.

What you have here now is a big, deep, sheer-walled pit you've dug for yourself, with care and precision, and you're stuck in it, until you introduce something on the order of Cinderella's Fairy Godmother who solves it all with a wave of her magic wand.

You have carefully extablished that the *olz* have been oppressed for *n*-thousand years, during which time any one of 'em showing gumption, spirit, originality, creativity, or self-determination has been painfully bumped off. Say 2000 years of this. That's about 100 human generations — the length of an *ol* generation isn't specified, but it is implied to be shorter.

You cull any sexually reproduced life form for a desired (or elimination of an undesired) characteristic for 100 generations or so, and — guess what — you can eliminate that characteristic. Works great for turning wolves into sheep-herders that won't touch a nice young juicy sheep, but will fight off Cousin Wolf to protect it.

You have set up a system in which the *olz* really *are* spiritless — genetically.

Now you aren't "thinking like an *ol*" either. There have been peasants, serfs, peons, slaves through all of human history; one of the repeatedly demonstrated facts of life is that a slave group, once firmly entrenched as slaves, not only won't rebel, but also will fight off anyone trying to "free" them. A few *individuals* will try to break free, and they're usually either killed off, or thrown out in a "good riddance" effect.

Reason: Slaves have a stable society, in which they know exactly what's expected of them. They have a secure future, requiring no thought-effort on their part, and a deadly fear of the unknowns involved in an uncontrolled environment.

That's a fact of human history. Slaves have almost invariably been freed by a revolution of non-slaves, or by external invasion. The Russian serfs were given their freedom in 1862 by the Imperial Edict of Czar Alexander II, and they promptly rebelled against the edict (The Czar saw it as freeing the serfs from their ancient bonds to the land; the peasants saw that their land — which by ancient tradition could not be taken from them, had been stolen from them!) The Ethiopian slaves were freed because the League of Nations required no slavery in any member nation. (They revolted against freedom, too; the edict had to be amended to freeing any slave who agreed to accept freedom.)

That African slaves in Africa didn't revolt against their black masters; they were freed by invading white men. Ditto in our South; the Negro slaves didn't revolt — in fact they worked hard to support the Southern armies. They were freed by invaders from the north.

The Russian serfs were finally freed by the revolt of middle-class men against the aristocracy — the Bolsheviks freed them, whether they liked it (they didn't) or not.

Now moreover, somebody's lying like hell about the rigor of *ol* life. Given the sort of sneaky instruments your IPR gang has, I could get photographs of the horrors of life in New York City, 1969, showing how people are beaten to death on the streets, mugged, raped and tortured and dismembered, and set afire with gasoline, etc.

I could also show you the horrors of Union affairs, with men being beaten and crippled by goon squads.

Man I could make the most hideous horror-presentation anybody would want.

And if you didn't know better, you could be convinced that was a normal sort of happening. Because those things *do* happen!

Here's how I know that the data presented in this story is a lying propaganda piece:

The minimum age at which an *ol* would be a reasonably efficient adult worker is, let's say, fifteen years. It takes years to grow one to a useful size.

Keep killing 'em off at the implied rate by whimsical murder, sadistic beatings, starvation, disease and cold, and you'll pretty quickly run out of "animate agricultural instruments," as Plato called 'em. You can't let more than one-fifteenth of 'em die per year, on the average, if you're going to maintain a crop to work the fields — and you had better take it easy on the females, or you'll run out of worker-factories.

So we have pretty solid grounds for considering the data give distorted propaganda. The *olz* can't be *that* bad off!

Now, then, there's this business of the *olz* really having a far more adavanced language, with a far higher level of communication than the IPR people or their slave-masters think.

And this brings up the problem of "you can't think like an *ol*."

Now English is an immensely rich language; it has more available terms, with subtler shadings of meaning, than any other language man's so far invented. (This is partly because it's been the most active word-borrower of all the languages.) There's an available vocabulary of some 450,000 words. You and I, professional communicators, probably use 75,000 words or so, with a recognition vocabulary of 150,000 to 200,000 words.

Experts say that the average store-clerk types have a usable vocabulary of 2000 words, and a recognition vocabulary of perhaps 10,000 words. And they don't really recognize the meanings of those 10,000 words. (For instance, distinguish between "feminine," "effeminate," and "worldly.")

It's not because the language isn't there to be used; they grow up in the same general environment of books, magazines, radio, movies, tv and schools we did. What makes the difference?

Answer: People are *not* born equal. I've watched my own children and grandchildren grow up; they're not equal. One has a mind as orderly as a well-kept file system; she has a precision vocabulary and uses it with precision. (She can't spell worth a damn, though.) One of the other girls got far better school marks, and now teaches English and Reading in schools — and she has a mind about as orderly as a ball of yarn wound up by a pair of kittens. I think she has a usable vocabulary of about 7500 words, which she uses imprecisely on all occasions.

The language an individual uses is a direct clue to the clarity of the mind using it.

Your *olz* who have almost no language — have almost no minds. If that richer language were around, and they had the minds to appreciate it, *they would use it*. That is, unless you're saying the whole *olz* population, from age one year up, is consciously engaged in a vast, highly skilled underground secret operation, and has been for *n* generations, without being detected — and without doing one damn thing to help themselves.

In that case, you're claiming a most remarkable self-discipline for year-old toddlers of the *olz*.

Now be it realized that year-old toddlers were not *born* with a religious indoctrination so deep that they'll happily accept being tortured to death without giving away the secret that they have comprehended the high-order abstractions involved in their people's generations-old Great Deception. What you're claiming is that they can be so deeply religiously oriented by the time they can talk, that they'll never reveal that they have a language involving high-order abstractions like Eternal Life and Spiritual Power over Pain.

Remarkable kids, aren't they?

In other words, *either* the *olz* are, and have been for a long, long, time, highly intelligent, competent, quick-learning people, with high order self-discipline, who've done nothing to change their intolerable conditions, but nevertheless really have great spirit and determination, *or* they are the degenerate culls that they seem. Selectively bred for gutless, witless, masochistic semi-animals.

If the latter is true, then explain how these gutless, witless degenerates suddenly turn into a highly organized, effective fighting army, with an effective organization, effective supply service, intelligence officers, etc., overnight.

If they really were practicing a Great Deception — explain how they managed to keep the kids in line so they didn't give the show away.

I know of a case of an Allied intelligence agent during World War II — a Canadian — who was stationed in Occupied France, playing the part of the village half-wit. He spent ten months in a home for the feeble-minded learning how to be a moron. The Gestapo got suspicious of him because of other clues — the underground cell was tapped, and he had been a member of the "family" — so they questioned him, i.e., tortured him. In spite of their high-power torture, he held his idiot identity, and the Gestapo let him go.

But it took psychiatrists some three years, after he was finally brought back to Britain, to break him out of that idiot identity again.

Now you can understand a highly intelligent, highly trained, strongly determined adult being able to play idiot even under Gestapo torture, but can you imagine a child holding out like that?

And no significant failures of the Great Deception in some *n*-

565

generations? A whole *population*? Men, women and toddlers?

But if they aren't working a Great Deception, then they *are* idiots-practicing-to-make-moron-grade, and you cannot turn them into soldiers capable of defeating an organized and trained army overnight.

What you've done in this story is set up a situation which never happened on Earth — but could happen on another world readily enough. Whether you breed chimpanzees up to the level of being useful household servants, or suppress a human sub-race by deliberate down-breeding, to produce a sub-human race of animated robots, the situation is the same. They are no longer quite animals, nor are they human.

Given that situation — what do you do with them? How do you solve the *real olz* problem — a race that, no matter [how] it got there, really isn't at the human level. Given a planet of their own, and a million years of evolution, they could make it. But on a planet where there is an intelligent race. . . ?

The only way to rebuild the *olz* from the state you've got 'em in is by a prolonged selective breeding program like the program by which German biologists succeeded in re-creating the extinct Aurochs, the fierce, powerful and deadly wild cattle of Europe.

It could be done — in two thousand years or so, by geneticists who knew their business, and were ruthless enough to selectively slaughter the *olz* who didn't represent good stock. Just reverse the selective breeding of the preceding millenia, and you could reconstitute the old *olz* race.

But the way you've got things set up, you've got a situation that genuinely, really can not be solved in anything under a couple of millenia — and you would have a hell of a time figuring out what the "right" way of solving it was!

I think you would probably do better to have them discover that the *olz* were originally produced by the dominant humanoid race, by breeding up a species somewhat equivalent to our chimpanzees, but perhaps a bit higher. Animals, not intelligent people. During the great days of the building of the Tower of Eyes, and other really great works, these animals were bred to produce useful field hands — as men bred wolves to yield sheep dogs.

Now dogs are not *slaves*. They're symbiotes. You can't "free" them; they serve their masters out of deep and abiding love and devotion. If their master beats them, the accept it, and beg his forgiveness of the sins they committed — because they love him, not because they fear him.

There are a few perverts among men who will torture a dog, you can always find some psychotics. But did you ever read the poem, "Never Give Your Heart to a Dog to Tear"?

Set up your story that way — have them discover the *real* nature of the *olz* — and you'll be presenting a problem that we are very apt to find Somewhere Out There, and one that's never been discussed. And one that would tear the whole philosophy of your young hero, and the whole IPR structure into howling heebie-jeebies.

What's the ethics — the morality — of a situation like *that*? Is it kindly to tear the *olz* from the living presence of their gods, who love and cherish and command them, to force them out into the dark horror of living without guidance and the love-objects of their gods? Would you do that to a sheep dog?

But they're slaves. Or are they. . . ?

The entire ending would require rewriting, but I think you would have one hell of a powerful and disturbing (and realistic) story. The first two thirds — excellent now — would need only a few minor changes, so that the fact of propaganda in the movies they collected can be recognized later.

And not *conscious* propaganda; a man with a dedicated conviction of Good and Evil interprets what he sees honestly, in those terms. He will have no realization that he's prejudiced, and is violently biased in his selection of evidence.

And the *olz*, being lousy communicators, don't, *can't*, possibly appreciate that the IPR men don't understand naturally that their Masters are the Living Gods.

And always remember — shepherds hate, loathe, and despise above all else a sheep-killing dog. Catch him, and they kill him and all his known get. *That* characterisitc they cannot abide in their sheep dogs.

That's how IPR pseudo-*olz* could get themselves bumped off — by showing the hated characteristics of non-useful animate agricultural instruments.

It's a beee-yutiful problem for consideration. It'd make a great story.

Sincerely,   John W. Campbell

Enc: "The World Menders"

Ben Bova and Harlan Ellison   *December 23, 1969*
c/o Robert Mills, Ltd.

Gentlemen:

"Brillo" is a good yarn; I want it.

But there's a minor change that, I think, is important for consistency.

As you've got it, the cop is heavily armed — equipped with a lethal Needler, Mace, electric prod, and unnamed additional weapons.

At the same time, there is a permissive cultural system — the attitude of the kids, and other side remarks bring that out.

Those two things do NOT go together. When the police are equipped to use adequate force, the society that so equips them holds that force is necessary to suppress undisciplined behaviour — and it therefore has a definite concept of social discipline.

A permissive society holds that no one should be allowed to use effective force — and it therefore disarms the police. (Example: The electric baton is now forbidden. It's an effective disciplinary force that does no injury, leaves no marks, and won't serve to make martyrs. It's an ideal disciplinary device; like spanking, it hurts enough to demand attention, but does not injure. Unlike a gun, it produces no martyrs, no bleeding wounds and thus is loathed by the undisciplined.)

Remember that to be gentle, one must be strong — and restrain that power. A lamb isn't gentle; it's a mean tempered little stupid beast that's too weak to do any harm. A lioness holding down her cub with one immense paw and licking it clean is gentle.

The essence of your story is that Polchik is gentle. To be that he needs *moderate* weapons, not an armory, and the judgment to refrain from using them.

Incidentally, by the time they get the robot sufficiently sophisticated to be a good cop, he would be too expensive to use.

Human beings are cheaper!

Regards,   John W. Campbell

"The best answer I can give is to tell you of the old story about the old New England sea captain. . . . " page 495.

The 1970's

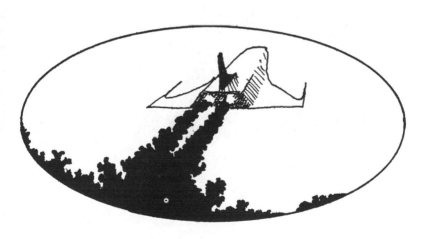

Meade Frierson III　　　　　　　　　　　　　*January 12, 1970*

Dear Mr. Frierson:

Somebody's been feeding you false data; "Dimension X" never had anything to do with *Astounding-Analog*; they had *Galaxy* hooked for that one.

The "Exploring Tomorrow" shows were not, actually, connected with my magazine — Street & Smith had no financial interest in the show whatever. **Sandy Marshall**, who produced the show, had simply asked me to act more or less as Editor and emcee of the show; naturally I picked stories I liked. And understandably, they were stories from my magazine; they were in the magazine because I'd liked them, of course.

Any tape with the "Exploring Tomorrow" show on it will have my fairly recognizable voice; I never emceed any other radio show. Therefore, any tape with my voice on it has to be an "Exploring Tomorrow" show.

The idea for the show was **Sandy Marshall's** — strictly as a producer. He liked science-fiction, but wasn't competent to judge science-fiction for science-fiction values — and was wise enough to recognize his own limitation. That's why he got me to cooperate with him. The other shows were produced by people who thought that knowing how to produce a show (they did) was enough to assure that they could produce good science-fiction (they didn't).

None of the shows on the air was written by me with the single exception of "The Escape." (Girl assigned by genetics board to marry one man, thinks she's in love with young artist who isn't her type, actually. Winds up marrying the genetics board's selection.)

It's been more than fifteen years since I did those things; my memory's not perfect, and I have no notes on them. But something's drastically wrong with the list of "Exploring Tomorrow" shows you have here.

I think the best way to spot an old "Exploring" tape is simply this: I was on *every* "Exploring" show, and I was *never* on any other. Therefore, if my voice is on a tape — it's got to be an "Exploring" show; if I'm not on it, it can't be!

I gave an introduction, and commentary "between the acts" on each show; the commentaries were designed to act as bridges between parts of the show and save time otherwise needed for scene-setting action. I don't see how they could have been cut out without lousing up the show-tape.

The original show was a half-hour; the tapes would run shorter to allow for the sales pitches that paid the bills.

Conde'-Nast, as I say, never had anything to do with the show; Street & Smith has since merged into Conde'-Nast, but at the time

Street & Smith bought "All Serial Rights," and allowed the authors to sell radio and TV rights if they could. The WOR Mutual Network produced and owned the shows.

Sorry I don't have any records to help you with — and it's obvious that there's a hell of a lot of confusion about those tapes — but I can't help you. I've lost tract of **Sandy Marshall** in the years since, so I don't know where you could find him.

Oh, one other identifying key: We used as the theme song in the introduction (and post-commercial breaks) "As Time Goes By." If that's on a tape, my voice should be too.

One of the best of the shows was "Look Out! Duck!" by **Randy Garrett**. (Due to a breakdown, they had to hatch 5,000 duck eggs in an interstellar freighter — and the ducklings need a 1.50 gravity to develop properly!)

Sincerely,   John W. Campbell

Kris Neville   *January 12, 1970*

Dear Mr. Neville:

I think we have a fundamental disagreement on one aspect of religion. You say, "In my view . . . a man who will believe in his ability to know the nature of God (let alone whether or not there is one) can be persuaded to believe damn near any foolishness imaginable."

If you put the word "Universe" in place of "God" above — wouldn't you be talking about our top scientists?

The essence of religions — as distinct from pure witch-doctoring — is the concept that there exists an Entity that brought about the creation of the Earth, the Sun, the heavens, and all living things. Call that Entity "The Laws of the Universe," or "God," or "Allah," as you will — the real sense content would be the same, and would be valid. And all the true religions hold that that Entity is beyond the ability of Man to understand — yet it is essential that Man seek to understand God's (or the Universe's) laws, and obey them, that his life may be successful.

The witch-doctor approach is that the witch-doctor understand the spirits and demons, and control and direct them, and for his special terrible knowledge, you had better kowtow to him and seek his favors.

Incidentally, if you read the New Testament, and replace the word "God" with "the Universe," you would be surprised how neatly it fits and makes excellent sense!

Don't let the semantics of a word loaded with medieval ideas throw you off of a genuinely important basic concept. The Universe does *not* wear a long white beard, and have blue eyes —

but it is the creator of the heavens and Earth, and all living things, you know!

And — for some reason no one can explain — every human culture that has survived for more than three generations has certain basics. No culture that did not have them has survived.
1. Some form of economy — whether it be pure piracy or high-level technological industry.
2. Some systematic regulation of the relationship of the sexes.
3. A religion.
Odd, if religion is a useless aberration!

Regards,   John W. Campbell

James E. Gunn   *January 26, 1970*

Dear Jim:

A better man for your proposed "Science Fiction Magazines 1926-1950" would be **Sam Moscowitz**.

After I got started running *Astounding*, I was too damn busy reading for the magazine to keep up with what was going on in all the other magazines; my knowledge of the other magazines and what they did, tried, or failed to try from 1940 on — the most active period — is miniscule.

Sam and **Chris Moscowitz**, on the other hand, have made a major hobby of knowing all about all the magazines. They've got *complete* stacks, and reams of data.

For your purposes — necessitating a pretty scholarly paper — **Sam** could do a much better job.

Regards,   John

Carl A. Larson   *January 26, 1970*

Dear Dr. Larson:

The factor you're looking for in human tendency to sudden massive manslaughter is indeed a genetically predetermined behavior pattern. Very deeply, very solidly, and very powerfully implanted genetic behavior.

We're the only hunting, carnivour-type higher primate. The mighty gorillas are strictly herbivours. Our teeth and jaws show adaptation from the browse-type herbivour pattern the other big primates follow to a grain-eating adaptation no other living primate has. Gigantopithecus seems to have been a grain-eater.

But for a *very* long time — say 20 megayears or better — our ancestral line was strictly vegetarian.

Something turned the peaceful browser-grain-eater into a hunting killer; as herbivours, we're obviously suffering from species psychosis.

It made possible *Homo sapiens*, a highly intelligent planet-ruler. Because only a species that *culls its own kind* can achieve true dominance over its environment. *Any species must be culled*. The deer cull the wolves; the wolves that don't achieve full wolfish strength, speed, and keenness starve. While of course the wolves cull the sick, the feeble, the stupid among the deer.

But if any creature in the environment can limit the planet-ruler — he isn't a planet-ruler yet! Wherefore the planet-ruling species must be in no danger from any other species, and able to convert any other species into food (either plant or animal, for that matter! Men eat many intrinsically poisonous plants by processing them; any time we want, we can convert sawdust to digestible glucose.) That's what being a planet-ruler means; the environment does not threaten — it only nourishes.

If deer are freed of all threatening predators — they very shortly eat and breed themselves into starvation. Because deer don't kill each other (except by accident) and so don't cull the race.

Man's first great Enabling Act — it enabled him to be a planet-ruler — was the invention of murder. Cain slew Abel in the glade according to the myth — and that means we're the descendants of the original murderer, because the murderee didn't breed.

If Man *hadn't* invented murder, the race wouldn't have been able to improve beyond the level culling by other predators forced on us.

By inventing murder, man invented the first workable Bootstraps Lifter — the level of ability of the race would continue to rise because of Man's own culling of the race of Man.

I can't think of any other mechanism that could have forced on a species the unlimited compulsion to self-improvement.

We happen to have come along in a freak period of human history in which the weird view that human life is sacred has been widely promulgated. Take a reasonable look at the sweep of human history, and you'll recognize that that is, indeed, a way-out viewpoint, an abnormal-to-Mankind viewpoint.

Fortunately, it won't last long — because if it did there would be the inevitable and inescapable total collapse of the environment. We're already threatened with that; just like the unculled deer herd, our unchecked population rise is destroying the environment that supports us. Continue very long, and the result will be a complete collapse of that environment.

"Man's inhumanity to Man" stems from the ancient genetic fact that it *has* to be that way. It is not a question of what you or I want

— what we consider fine and noble and proper, or desirable. It's a simple fact that any species capable of geometric progression reproduction must be culled — or its environmental supports will collapse. It's been that way since life got started on the planet — but Man's the first self-culling species to come along.

That makes him the planet-ruler-species — and also means he is genetically predisposed to murder.

It's a very new system — only a couple of megayears old — and the quirks and kinks haven't been worked out of the system as yet. In the course of another few megayears of evolution, mankind will evolve a better system of self-culling.

But no matter what we do—we can not escape the absolute necessity of a self-culling system. Birth control alone is no answer; it wouldn't work, unless there were a judgement factor imposed. I.e., somehow the control must apply to births of normal or lower individuals, while not applying to superior individuals. That's necessary, if the statistics of the race is to move toward superior overall performance.

No nice, simple, cosily "democratic" system can do what must be done.

The fine old art of murder served as a rough and ready test of superiority; it improved the racial statistics as to fast reflexes, good muscles, and good judgement as to who you challenged to a fight. It improved learning ability, through processes, and inventiveness, which helped in developing useful skills such as weapon design and use, cooperation against enemies, the inventiveness of military tactics and strategy.

It's exceedingly inefficient — but Nature is both patient, and has all the energy of the sun to expend on her little projects. Hard on the test beasties — but it works.

It's now up to us to invent — *and apply to ourselves* — a more satisfactory system of culling.

That famous challenge "Who is to judge?" is simply a way of ducking the problem. The right question must be, of course, "On what basis shall one judge?"

Fail to judge, and we go back to the Old Reliable method — murder does, unarguably, produce results.

If you don't like it, then our job is to figure out a better method *that works*!

Sincerely,   John W. Campbell

Gregory Benford   *February 11, 1970*

Dear Mr. Benford:

I'm afraid that when logical analysis is applied in the area of something like tachyons and causality — I get suspicious that we may have hit an area where logic doesn't work very well.

It's assumed by current philosophy that all problems can be expressed in sound logical form. But Goedel's Proof showed that there are real problems that cannot be expressed logically — in terms of what we accept as proper logical manipulations.

Suppose causality is no more strict at the macroscopic level than it is at the subatomic — that in each instance there are probabilities rather than cause-effect-rigidities.

Suppose we have a tall glass cylinder of water standing with its base in a pool of liquid nitrogen. The water at the base freezes almost instantly, and an advancing front of freezing moves up the column of water. Below that front, the material is frozen rigidly, out in front of it, the water's still liquid. But the front itself is not a mathematical plane; it has depth. Ice crystals here and there build out ahead, while pockets of still liquid water remain for a bit behind.

Crystallizing forces are reaching out from the already aligned molecules of ice tending to draw the still free molecules into rigid alignment; these forces become stronger and stronger as the freeze advances, until the molecules are finally fixed.

Now consider that the front compares with the "instant now" in Time, and that the frozen zone is the immutable past, while the still-liquid zone is the amorphous future.

In such a system, probability and "free will" can exist now, but the past shows absolute rigid causality.

Every experiment performed demonstrates conclusively that causality *was* absolutely rigid.

Moreover, be it remembered that there have been thousands of spontaneous cases of heavily documented instances of precognition. The mere fact that precognition can't be explained, can't be produced at will, and doesn't fit within now-known laws of the Universe simply means — as such factors always have and always will mean! — that we're still ignorant.

After all, we've been at this science business actually for only about 0.4 millenia. And the Sun appears to be good for another 10,000,000,000 years or so. . . .

Maybe there's enough left to learn that it's not necessary to decide we know everything important already!

Does causality apply to a radioactive nucleus? The assumption is made that it does — but damned if you can prove it for any one nucleus!

Just maybe tachyons are involved in that advancing freeze-front called the "instant now," that is *not* rigidly caused — although every single experiment that has ever been completed will always demonstrate rigid causality!

Sincerely,   John W. Campbell

Enc: "The Tachyonic Antitelephone" paper

Virginia Kidd   *March 19, 1970*

Dear Mrs. Kidd:

I hadn't heard about **Anne McCaffrey's** troubles; she never hinted a syllable to me, and I deeply regret it's happened. For some reason, most of the professional counselors, lawyers, ministers, doctors and psychologists, seem to me to be remarkably stupid; they seem to miss one of the major factors in a number of marriage breakups.

A woman of dynamic ability, high intelligence, and genuine creativity expends an enormous amount of life-energy quite happily raising her family — caring for her husband, helping his career, inducing children to acquire and retain civilized habits, encouraging their developing potentials, and nudging her husband in ways that develop his.

But then comes the period when the babies aren't even children any more, and her husband is established and fully effective in his career — and there's no longer any area within the family where her dynamic creative energies can be useful. Further application within the family would be destructive, not helpful at all.

Now some women can turn to the Garden Club, or the League of Women Voters, or the local hospital aides and feel useful; if that's the limits of their abilities, they are useful.

But if a man's taken on a high-power wife, with high-power mind and dynamic intensity — the garden club somehow doesn't satisfy much better than the bridge club or the local gossip set.

So she starts exerting her creative efforts outside the home — she's got a new career going.

And so darned many men then react on the basis that she's not satisfied with what he earns, or that she's trying to compete with him, or that she's withdrawing from him. . . .

And he tries to stop her fruitful expenditure of the redirected dynamic energies. He'd raise hell if she turned all those energies into "helping him" in his work; he doesn't adequately recognize that she *has* to do something with the output of her personal dynamo, or burn up inside. And he gets more and more angry at her "demeaning him" and her "wanting more money" and "not being satisfied with their home."

In other words — an appearance of masculine jealousy. Which it isn't, quite; it's something more complex and subtle, and because it

579

is subtle, it expresses itself by oozing out in seemingly totally unrelated ways. He feels that nothing he does satisfies her; he's got it almost right, but not quite. Nothing *he* can do can satisfy her; *she* has to do something.

Knowing absolutely nothing whatever about **Anne's** problem, never having heard a word about it — I'd suspect she's run into something like that, simply because she's a highly creative, dynamic, energetic woman with a fine bunch of boys who are rapidly outgrowing the "children" stage. And I'd imagine her husband's career is rolling well by this time.

I've seen that sort of thing happen so damn many times, with resultant misery for exceptionally nice people.

It'd make a great novel, if somebody could just figure out how to write it up. But it wouldn't be popular, because it has a miserable ending.

Oh, well. . . .

I'm returning the novel for several reasons. The first reason is simple; I'm loaded with novels through early fall 1971. If I did take this, it'd be running around Christmas time next year! Everybody and his brothers, sisters, cousins and aunts seems to be writing novels this year. And, dammit, good ones!

But it also has definite faults; the major fault is one that's impossible to pin down, because it's a lack of focus. **Anne** hadn't figured out just where she was going, to what end, by what road. The result is that the thing is extremely diffuse.

She has, moreover, fallen into **H. Beam Piper's** worst fault, one I fought with him a dozen times: She's got more characters with strange, and somewhat similar names, than anyone can keep track of — even if she does provide a score-card so you can know the players. **Beam Piper** used to do that — and some of his stories became almost unfollowable because of the scores of characters he introduced.

In this one, the only new ideas she's introduced are the flame-lizards; otherwise it's all a personality-squabble rehash of "Dragonrider".

I don't believe any parts of this one can be isolated as effective novelettes in the present presentation; the whole thing has so many personality-squabbles so tightly interwoven that breaking it apart is somewhat like trying to cut a piece out of a sweater. Do it, and the piece ravels into snibbits of yarn almost immediately.

It would stand up far better as a solid, one-piece novel than in any other way — and by that I mean a book, not a four-part serial. Wanna try writing a synopsis for Part IV of something as complexly interwoven as this, for instance?

Couple of technical points:

1. If the Threads burn holes in any organic material — how come the flame-lizards and the grubs eat them.
2. If dragons are derived from flame-lizards — why didn't the ancient breeders retain the Thread-eating ability? (Possible answer: flame-lizards are small, and can follow Threads into their burrows, where, obviously, a dragon can't. And they don't eat live Threads — they eat fresh-baked Threads. They don't burn them to ashes, as a dragon does; they just cook them tender!)
3. If the Red Star's atmosphere is so searingly hot — the Threads must be extremely thermophilic organisms. They'd be cooked at home if they weren't. And if they are so thermophilic, they couldn't stand Perm's unbearably frigid climate.
4. Possible out for the Thread-eating grubs: the grubs have a silicon-rubber like material. Their digestive juices can break down the carbon-metabolism of the Threads a damn sight faster than the Thread's strictly-carbon enzymes can work on the grub's tissues. You might have someone find that not even HNO_3 would destroy the grub's tissues completely.

Regards,   John W. Campbell

R. I. MacDonald   *March 30, 1970*

Dear Mr. MacDonald:

You can write, but this one's not for us — it's more of a fantasy than a science-fiction yarn.

Your thesis here, by the way, reminds me of something my good friend and favorite scientist-philosopher pointed out some years ago. **Dr. Wayne Batteau** liked to translate scientific laws into English — which makes them come out as epigrams, of course. Thus:

The three Laws of Thermodynamics, in English, are:
1. You can't win. (Conservation of Energy).
2. You can't even break even. (Entropy increases.)
3. Moreover you can't get out of the game! (You can't reach absolute zero.)

However, **Claude Shannon** showed that Information was negative entropy, wherefore you can show the Three Laws of Infodymanics are:
1. You can win,
2. Provided you support a friend —
3. — and quit while you're winning.

You have to support a friend, because information exists only when it's communicated; what you know is not "information" to you. And you have to quit *while* you're winning, not simply "when you're ahead"! (You have to sell your used car while it's still winning — if you wait till it's useless, you have to pay to have someone remove the junk.)

Moreover, it can be shown that Information is not conservative. (I can give Information to you, yet still have it myself, of course.)

From this it follows that wealth, which is largely a matter of information — not merely materials — is non-conservative, wherefore a man can become very wealthy without in any way taking wealth from anyone else and, in fact, to do so he *must* enrich others also! (Second Law of Infodynamics.)

Now your thesis holds that Luck is non-conservative. Then a technique that made others lose their luck would *not* mean you'd become lucky. In the Great Depressioin, a lot of people lost their luck — but who gained from it? Some weren't as bad off as others, and were "comparatively" lucky — but all were worse off than they had been.

A nuclear WWIII might produce very considerable widespread unluck — but nobody, and I mean *nobody*, would be lucky in the sense of coming out with a net positive gain.

With your Arctic experience, you should be able to dream up some yarns where you'd have a very real advantage in establishing a sense of reality! Why not use it?

And remember I'd like an article on optical information processing. You can't cover all of that field in any one article, so pick an area you do know, and show what's going on!

Regards,   John W. Campbell

Carl Larson   *April 30, 1970*

Dear Mr. Larson:

You underrrate our FDA's ability to achieve monumental stupidity when you say they can't be so stupid as to block a treatment of a corrigible disease.

Examples: They stopped all research with DMSO (dimethyl sulfoxide) because it was reported that, under some conditions, it appeared it might cause clouding of the eye lens in some animals. The FDA imposes test conditions for "acceptable" food dyes involving 100,000 times normal concentrations being fed to white rats. The yellow aniline dye that had been used widely for some 60 years passed the test — but when fed to guinea pigs instead of white rats, the rodents all died of cancer of the liver. (Guinea pigs, like man, and unlike rats, can't manufacture vitamin C in the liver.) But some company sent in a sample of a bright yellow crystalline material, suggesting they wanted to use it for coloring butter, under the name "Dawn Yellow." The FDA boys fed it in their standard 100,000 times excess to their white rats. The rats promptly turned bright yellow, turned up their toes, and died. FDA immediately telegraphed a cease-and-desist order to the company forbidding absolutely the sale of the material, or any foodstuff containing that substance. The company replied in essence, "We're sorry, but we can't prevent inclusion of that material in foodstuffs; what we sent was pure crystalline Vitamin A."

And, of course, thalidomide remains absolutely banned — although it was shown to be the most effective analgesic in terminal cancer that had ever been found — and appeared to have marked curative properties. (If it distorts the metabolism of fetal human cells . . . and cancer cells have marked fetal characteristics . . . maybe there is a reason. . . ?) Thalidomide is still the only effective tranquilizer with which a man can *not* commit suicide.

But those things require the use of a modicum of judgement and a departure from pure ritual. Naturally, they are beyond the FDA's abilities.

A neighbor woman was suffering from an acute postpartum psychosis; she'd been under psychiatric treatment for six weeks — complete with electric shock therapy — and was getting no better. Confused-miserable-depressed — unable to decide anything — couldn't care for her children, house or cooking. My wife suggested to her husband that he get her a bottle of liquid vitamin B complex concentrate put out by Lederle Laboratories under the name Lederplex™, and give her four tablespoons a day.

Four days later she was up, around, active, cheerful, and fired the psychiatrist.

And the FDA is requiring vitamin preparations to carry a label assuring the people they don't need extra vitamins; you get plenty in your food.

For this and other reasons I can't take time to list — it would take a full month's issue of *Analog* to print them — I would hate to find myself agreeing with the FDA about something.

But when a disease is known to be genetic, and highly destructive both to affected individuals and their families, it does seem to me efforts should be made to prevent the reproduction of those genes.

Our culture refuses to allow euthanasia or sterilization. If the Mongol children could be sterilized — then raising their IQ and allowing their fuller development would be fine. But currently, sterilization's against the local tribal mores.

We have an additional difficulty over here that your culture does not; I have known that Sweden arranges to have the moron and idiot types given training for jobs they can do, and given useful employment.

There's a sort of moronic mentality in our Union men over here that prevents adequate training for even normal kids in anything but intellectual jobs — the Unions won't allow competition from young workers. Membership is practically an hereditary affair. (This is to a large degree why the Negroes can't get in. It's not because they're Negroes, but because their fathers and uncles, etc., weren't members. They're turned down for the same reason anybody else is. It's not unlike trying to join the Mafia; you may be as thoroughly criminal at heart as you like, but if you're not Sicilian — or at *least* Italian — you aren't a member of the Family.)

Now as to the heritability of Mongolism.

O.K. — I know that a majority of Mongoloids come from normal parents; since Mongoloids generally don't show physical development to puberty, they obviously can't produce more of their kind. Given the treatment that would bring them up through adolescence to sexual maturity — wouldn't they then be capable of producing strings of Mongoloids? And lacking judgement and intelligence, can't you predict they would if they could?

They *do* have defective chromosome arrangements — an extra #21. Their gametes would, I assume, turn up with a 50-50 probability of carrying two #21's and normal ones. Rather like hemophilia, except that both males and females would be active carriers.

I knew a young (naturally!) man who was a genuine hemophiliac — not just a sort of half-way, but the real thing — for some while. I know something about what it's like to live as a hemophiliac — and I know he wasn't sorry when he died at 22.

He told me that, in his opinion, the ancient Jewish custom of circumcision had a great advantage — it kept hemophiliacs from having to go through the miseries of trying to live.

Incidentally, he was a fantastically skillful machinist — who couldn't get a job. No company dared hire him, because of workmen's compensation laws; no insurance company cared to take on the risk of insuring a hemophiliac, but state laws required that he be covered, or not employed.

Anyhow — I'm genuinely not sure how I would decide if I were required to handle the problem of that Mongoloid treatment!

As to superman — well, inasmuch as evolution is a process that never stops, we're either in the process of breeding *Homo superior* willy-nilly, or in the process of becoming an extinct race.

Every culture is a selective breeding mechanism, whether it intends that or not. And the process of evolution does not depend on selecting *for* the best, but *against* the worst.

There are two ways of getting the ore out of the mine-run rock. One is to devise a process that selectively extracts the desired material — the magnetic separation of iron ore, for instance. The other is to selectively reject the non-ore. The heavy-liquid flotation process of tungsten ore, for example. A liquid of density about 3.5 will float almost all rock — but *tungsten* I understand is a good Swedish description of the ore.

Evolution seems to work more by rejecting out the not-so-good, rather than working at the top end of the distribution curve. It's done by culling the ones that don't work.

In a natural system, Mongoloids, hemophiliacs, and child diabetics would be very rapidly eliminated from the gene-pool. (I had a second cousin who was a diabetic at eight years old; she would have been happier if insulin hadn't been discovered. By living to 26, she had time to have a great deal more misery than she otherwise would have.)

I think I should wind up with the comment my local good-friend-family-doctor made. "Mongoloid children are passive and usually quite obedient within their abilities. They make nice household pets, and the parents like them."

Personally, I vote for euthanasia.

Regards,   John W. Campbell

Lurton Blassingame   *May 18, 1970*

Dear Mr. Blassingame:

Herewith **Galyou's** "Final Tilt."

He told me about it somewhat at that luncheon — for which I thank you; sorry you had to leave just as things got really interesting! — and I was a little afraid he might have run into a problem.

He did — almost head on. **Bob Heinlein's** now-classic "Beyond This Horizon" was based on a genetically selected society in which **Bob** very explicitly analyzed the results of breeding out the gene of aggression. One small group of men were hold-outs; they thought aggressiveness had a place.

Naturally, they took over the world in a generation. Sheep don't drive wolves into a corner and slaughter them!

Galyou's idea is valid, rather obviously — but this build-up to its denoument becomes boring because the inescapable conclusion hangs fire so long.

Galyou might consider this philosophical question: There's a lot of very loud noise about peace and non-violence in the country today — particularly from the teenage-young-adult group. They gather in great protest masses and shout peace slogans and hurl rocks and other things at peace-officers trying to cool the mob; they set fire to buildings and bomb offices. They shout for peace and "meaningful discussion" and smash automobiles.

This "hysterical yearning for a completely pacified world" seems to me more a *hypocritical* yearning for non-aggression.

The fact — which they deny loudly with their mouths! — is that, as human beings always have, they want powerful, aggressive leaders that they can follow. But they're so uncertain of themselves they dread committing themselves to anyone, and so fear desperately the rise of a truly powerful hero-leader.

Thus they both want and simultaneously dread a true hero — and intellectually damn the idea of heroes. In literature, they say they want the anti-hero, the Common Man as hero.

The common man never is a hero — because if he were, he would, by definition, be uncommon!

This makes for a strange sort of literature — they *want* stories that make the Common Slob *important*. But they *enjoy* stories of true heroes — who, by definition, are bold, aggressive, strong and self-determined.

In *Analog*, I'm trying for what they enjoy (and say they don't like!) and, as a pragmatist myself, I judge by that fact that *Analog's* circulation continues to grow.

Regards,   John W. Campbell

Robert Chilson   *September 8, 1970*

Dear Mr. Chilson:

The pure perfect glass fibers were produced by an exceedingly simple apparatus — and it would have been easy for Isaac Newton to make the experiments, if he'd turned his attention that way!

What you do is to take a little cross-bow gadget, and stick one side of a glob of molten glass onto the end of the cross-bow arrow, and fire the arrow across the room. This yanks out a long thin filament of molten glass, which hardens instantly. You handle the thing by blowing it from place to place as desired, and you measure its strength. Fantastic! You get a perfect one about once in ten tries — but you learn a lot about the ultimate strength of stuff. Quartz works the same way, and is even stronger.

Carbon, boron, silicon carbide, sapphire and other ceramic fiber materials are a bit harder to prepare. Carbon fibers are currently prepared by preparing a plastic fiber from one of the plastics having aligned carbon atoms; this is heated in a furnace until everything but the carbon distilled off, while the stuff is under tension. The result is a carbon fiber of enormous strength. The heat treatment involved is a bit tricky; some twenty million dollars worth of research went into working it out.

Boron fibers are even stickier; you have to start with an ultrafine tungsten wire heated to white heat in a boron hydride atmosphere. The boron hydride breaks down, plating out boron on the tungsten wire, and a fiber of desired thickness is gradually built up. Again, exact temperatures and pressures of gas involved are just a bit tricky.

There is indeed an intermediate ground between the super-ceramics and crude baked clay — like the modern armor glass.

I've seen a piece of armor plate about ¼ inch thick, clear as water, that is used to stop .50 caliber machine gun bullets and will even stop a 20mm shell — though one of those also destroys the clarity of the armor. It's made of a combination of sapphire and fiberglass.

When somebody starts learning how to make *really* strong materials, the whole technology of the culture takes off. So long as we were stuck with wood and primitive ceramics, steam power was impossible. Copper, silver, lead, gold, etc., can't be used to make powerful engines — they're weak, unless you add beryllium — and *that* takes a really hot-shot chemical technology.

If we'd latched on to the secret of strong ceramics, we'd have had steam engines then, without the need for iron.

I think you're unnecessarily limiting what your Amerindian friends could do with their ceramics.

But that's all right — it's your story, so have fun with it!

Sincerely, John W. Campbell

Alexi Panshin *September 8, 1970*

Dear Mr. Panshin:

My friend, you're trying to track a will-o'-the-wisp to its lair.

As an author yourself, you should know that you-the-conscious-intellect don't write stories, and you-the-conscious-intellect can't determine what comes out of the typewriter. Writing is done by a subconsious set of circuits in the mind that can set up a magnificent set of schizophrenic personalities, and start talking like two, three, or a dozen other people. Those circuits even think in ways you dislike and resent, and force you to tell a somewhat different story than the one you had all planned.

Now you ask me if I disagreed with **Gernsback's** theories. Why hell, man, I didn't know he *had* theories — and I'll bet he didn't know it either, until he thought about it months or years later! I wrote stories because I thought they needed telling — they "needed" telling to stop the peculiar sort of itch they were causing in my own mind. I can give you a real good song-and-dance about my noble motivations and deep insights now — but that's my conscious-intellectual self trying to explain what the hell it was that happened.

Simply — I wrote what I felt like writing, because I enjoyed doing it, and I was lucky enough to find people would pay me nice, spendable dollars for what my hobby produced.

Don A. Stuart resulted from a growing desire to do a quite different kind of story — the super-science spaceopera pieces no longer fully satisfied me. I continued doing spaceopera because that's needed to express one part of what I think of as science-fiction — but **Don A. Stuart** was expressing another type, which I wanted to write. And . . . Goody! Goody! — people turned out to be willing to pay me for that, too! How nice!

I do not trust theories; I don't have theories, at least I don't let my theories "have" me to the extent that I can't try something that violates said theories.

As of now, of course, I have some 30-odd years of experience, reading the very best and the unprintably awful in science-fiction — and I've abstracted certain observational facts from that, and from observation of the world's literature that has proven enduring.

Part of my rejection of the "New Wave" stories stems from the observation that sex has not played any major role in any of the great, millenia-enduring epic of human literature. Conclusion: Sex literature is a literature of "planned obsolescence" — it's a short-lived type. But why not at least *try* for the kind of story that lives?

I'm afraid, though, that your quest for the motivations of it all will prove more than somewhat difficult. All you can get is somebody's explanation, long afterward, of something he did by the operation of unconscious mechanisms that his own conscious mind is inherently incapable of understanding!

You-conscious can *not* think like four entirely different people having an angry argument — but your unconscious can, does, and writes dynamic dialog!

Regards,   John W. Campbell

Tony Chapdelaine   *October 1, 1970*

Dear Tony,

That there are flaws in the educational system is of course true. It always has been, and it always will be true; Mark Twain was writing a century ago — yet you find his complaint valid today, after enormous, very real changes in the educational system!

However, the real trouble is that the problem is enormously

difficult — far more difficult that the simplistic-minded students appreciate. In fact, so difficult that the wisest philosophers still haven't been able to work it out all the way.

It's composed of several things:

1. The fundamental of education is development of basic disciplines, which are essentially arbitrary agreements which have to be learned by sheer rote, since they have no logical, real-world basis. The simplest example is that the student must learn a language that other people understand and speak.

    Now notice that any word in any language is purely arbitrary, and has no rationale. Why is a table called "a table," for instance? Because it is, that's why. (Except south of the border it's called "una mesa," and don't seek a why for that, either.)

2. Education should lead to training in logical thought. (But logic isn't rational, as students presently recognize.)

3. It should also induce creative originality — problem-solving ability.

4. It should give the student access to the accumulated experience and conclusions of Mankind. (It's quite a trick learning how to use a library, remember!)

5. It should seek to develop the maximum potentials of each student, both the useful morons and the brilliant geniuses. (Geniuses make completely unsafe truck drivers; their minds wander and they have accidents. Morons can keep their little minds on the job and drive well.)

6. It should teach the student to achieve the wisdom of knowing, when he finishes his schooling, how ignorant he is — how much there is to know.

Look those over, and you can see that each is essential to a really good education — and they are mutually incompatible in large degree. The rigid discipline of arbitraries is anathema to logical analysis, rationality, and creativity — yet the intellectual methods can't work without the basic arbitraries.

It is important to recognize the importance of human opinion — and to recognize that human opinion has nothing whatever to do with the truths of the Universe. (Whether you think so or not, gravity will affect an unsupported body.)

Some truths are made by human consensus; in the United States the word is spelled "color," but this is not true in England, where it is spelled "colour." But there are truths that are *not* subject to human consensus; even if everyone in the country agreed that water should burn as a fuel, the facts wouldn't change.

Finally, because of the immense differences between human minds — whatever current ideals may hold — no possible single educational system can provide optimum development for all students.

The consequence of the immense complexity and difficulty of the problem is, as I say, that the wisest philosophers in all the millenia since men first started trying to have formal education — and the Egyptians were running schools 6000 years ago! — haven't been able to generate a complete solution.

The result is that the students down through the ages have bitched about what lousy education they're offered, and what incompetent teachers they have, and how much better *they* could do it.

And most of all, they've bitched about arbitraries and formalisms, because they're illogical and irrational. They're "orthodox" and "traditional" and various other opprobious terms.

Young artists object to spending hours and hours learning to be draftsmen — learning the basic techniques of drawing lines, how to handle shading, how to hold a brush — all that traditional, orthodox discipline. They prefer surrealism, abstractionism, impressionism that's free of those traditional rigidity.

Yet the recognized artists — such as Dali — who created those schools were, every one of them, superb draftsmen *first*, and then *added* new techniques. They didn't reject the basics; they learned to use them . . . and go beyond.

And the problems you encounter in the real world are like those underlying educational problems; a rejection of basics such as discipline, rigor of logic, clear thinking-through, and the fact that people are *not* born equal. Most people don't think things through straight because they *can't* — they don't have the mental ability to do so.

The idealist becomes a fanatic because he's never thought through his idealism to recognize where it leads, and wants never to have it forced on him. He would very literally rather fight than switch.

Your father's run into that repeatedly — and he's still running into it. It's a fact of human life that most people *do* think in terms of "for us or against us." They can readily say they want Truth — but don't expect them to be able to face up to it.

To expect of someone something which is beyond his powers is foolish; to try to force him to achieve it is cruel.

Sincerely,   John W. Campbell

P.S. To construct the bifurcated trident on the cover you have to build it of quasi-matter, as stated in the story!

Alan Dean Foster   *October 8, 1970*

Dear Mr. Foster:

The rules of story plotting are rather complex, quite traditional, and best results are obtained by using them rather than kicking them in the teeth. A really good plot is one that conforms to all the traditional rules — and magnificently louses up the ones that need lousing up without besmirching the heroes.

This one doesn't do that. The heroes are duty-bound to defend the gal against the savages — they are *not* permitted to pimp for her.

Possible way out: the party has two beacon-compasses, right? Now if that planet has no appreciable magnetic field, ordinary magnetic compasses would be useless — but a compass of some kind, that will indicate a line of direction, is immensely valuable on either a watery or a desert world.

So that's what they could pay with.

Now as to taking care of the girl; the natives have a kind of cheese as their standard compact rations. One of the goodies the gal was privately nibbling included an euphoric — it helped keep her feeling serene and self-assured. Only like modern psychic energizers it's an enzyme-blocker. It blocks the metabolism of diamines.

Fact: a man who was on one of those psychic energizer-euphorics (treatment for acute depression) died from eating a 100 gram piece of cheddar cheese.

The gal goes into convulsions, hypertension, cerebral hemorrhage and dies; no one else is affected — because she hadn't shared her pill-popping style goodies.

That's a f'rinstance of how she could get caught — there's probably a million others.

Sincerely,   John W. Campbell

Scott Edelstein   *November 12, 1970*

Dear Mr. Edelstein:

I've heard from a number of readers protesting that *they* aren't the kind of young people I describe.

The only answer I can make to that is, "If the shoe doesn't fit — why try to cram yourself into it?"

If I speak of "juvenile delinquents" that doesn't mean that I think "juvenile" and "delinquent" are synonomous — the term applies only to those who are juvenile *and* act as described.

The "Now Generation" applies to those youngsters (there are a damn sight too many!) who do act as I described.

It didn't seem necessary to me to explain that — since my wife and I have raised four children ourselves, we know what any parent learns — children, even twins, are totally different personalities. The "Now Generation" applies to a specific sub-set of youngsters — just as "Members of SDS" applies to *some* students, even though they claim to be all students interested in democracy.

As to the "Now Generation" listening to history as it shows violence is the quickest way to achieve a result: If they do, they sure listen badly! That thesis says that the quickest way for us to solve the problem of disruptive youth is to shoot them and get it over with. We've got guns, organization, numbers, and technical equipment on our side, so we should be able to end that problem in a matter of about two weeks.

We could also end the problem of the Inner Cities and the Negroes quickly, and simply. A friend of mine has a photograph of a 10 megaton hydrogen bomb (the genuine article) on his office wall, on which he has put a label "Instant Slum Clearance Project Now Available" as a reminder of the realities in the world.

Like most "quick" solutions, the solutions the Now Generation type demands are the short-sighted immediate-result kind that serve to make the problems vastly worse than they were. As I said in my "Drug Scene" editorial, morphine is a quick, simple way to solve the problem of the pain of appendicitis. Cutting your throat is even quicker, and unlike the morphine approach, more permanent.

There are times when war is the optimum solution — but that's usually because a false, quick-and-easy solution was tried and failed.

Sincerely,   John W. Campbell

Jack Williamson   *January 7, 1971*

Dear Jack:

Looking over your paper on college courses in science-fiction I see something that puzzles me deeply — a repetition of a phenomenon I have observed at science-fiction conventions, and simply can't figure out the "Why?" of.

The works named in your list of books most often used in science-fiction courses includes three by **Wells**, which were the "hard" science-fiction of their day, but all the modern books are "soft" science-fiction or fantasy.

Essentially, all the secondary lists of books show the same overwhelming preponderance of fantasy-to-"soft" science-fiction, with almost *no* "hard" modern science-fiction.

I see **Herbert's** "Dune Messiah" listed, but not the material to which "Dune Messiah" was a sequel; "Dune" was hard science-fiction worked out in meticulous detail while "Dune Messiah" was heavily dominated by a mystical air.

Clement's "Mission of Gravity" and Asimov's "Foundation" and "Robot" stories were hard science-fiction — but aside from these very few, the entire list is massively dominated by fantasy/"soft" science-fiction.

The same is true of the science-fiction conventions; Burroughs' Tarzan and Martian stories constitute a major fraction at the conventions with conventions-within-the-convention in their honor.

Now the odd thing about this is that the magazines that are directed along these lines — *Fantasy & Science-Fiction* for example — have circulations so small as to be marginal, or losing operations.

Analog is the only hard-science-fiction magazine on the market — and sells approximately as many copies as the next *three* magazines combined. And clearly it's not because *Analog* is written to a lower-level audience in words of two syllables maximum, nor on a basis of "cheap sensationalism."

The puzzling fact is that *the most popular form of science-fiction in terms of readership is the form given least acknowledgement.*

In college courses, it is being ignored to such an extent that the impression given by such courses would be that it hardly exists at all.

Can you suggest any reason why this phenomenon exists?

Regards,   John

Jack Williamson   *March 4, 1971*

Dear Jack:

I'm afraid I agree with you that the ones offering science-fiction courses are non- or even anti-science members of the academic culture. And that means, actually, that they are teaching *non-*science-fiction courses labelled science-fiction!

I think the basic separation of the two cultures is somewhat like the late unlamented angry debates over science vs religion — based on the two different kinds of Truth, with the academics insisting angrily that the only True Truths are the truths of human realization, of human consensus. The scientific "facts" are no more than opinions anyway, and scientists are arrogant, nasty fellows claiming a special authority with no more reason than anybody else to their opinions. And their opinions are unpleasant, unkind, inhumane, and arbitrary things such as, "You can't get something for nothing," and, "Things always run down hill," and other arbitrary impediments they put in the way of fine and noble ideas.

Certainly they *do* like fantasies, don't they?

Regards, John

Waldo T. Boyd *March 18, 1971*

Dear Mr. Boyd:

If you notice, a good bit of science-fiction is already written in metric terms — and more is being done in centimeters, grams and centigrade all along.

Trouble is — we feel at an emotional level what the situation is when the author says the temperature on this plain the hero's struggling across is 140° F. — but there's an emotional blank if the author says the temperature was 52° C.

On the black on white vs white on black . . . try it my friend! Get a photostat of a page of type, a negative, and try reading it. It's harder on the eyes. The eye focuses on *light* and responds to edges; therefore you can focus on a white page, and spot the edges easily. A black page is harder to focus on.

Sincerely, John W. Campbell

H. Kenneth Bulmer *April 12, 1971*

Dear Mr. Bulmer:

I'm afraid we can't do a thing for the science-fiction book exhibition in May; *Analog* doesn't own any art work we could send you.

The reason: There's a sales-tax over here, which the seller is required to collect, keep books on, and turn over to the City and State governments.

Now companies are notoriously adverse to paying unnecessary taxes, and artists are notoriously lousy accountants; if we bought a piece of art, we'd have to pay a sales tax, and the artist would be forced to keep books on his sales for the government.

So we don't; we *pay for a service* — we do *not purchase an object*. So we buy only first reproduction rights — and the artists still own the art-work, which they did not sell to us.

So . . . you'd have to contact all the artists individually.

Sincerely, John W. Campbell

Stanley Schmidt *May 27, 1971*

Dear Mr. Schmidt:

Be it remembered that the rise-time of supernovas is inherently essentially unobservable. The thing can't be detected, usually, until it *has* bloomed — previously it was, typically about magnitude 18 down to 30, then increases in brilliance 100,000,000 times or so. *After* it's popped, people notice it — but it's darned seldom that the sky-area concerned has been under constant photographic survey that could catch the rise time.

Ordinary novae (as distinct from supernovae) have rise times that are extremely variable — and they may be almost anything every now and then, up to an outburst that would fuse the surface of the Solar planets clear out to Saturn. (A supernova blast would volitalize all but the cores of the giant planets Jupiter and Saturn.)

The best discussions I've run across are in *Atlas of the Universe* and *Exploration of the Universe* by Abell. But mainly I've gotten data from various articles on the "black hole" phenomenon, in *Sky & Telescope*, *Physics Today*, and *New Scientist*. (*Sky & Telescope* had the best.)

If your local library can't supply — see if they don't have a get-it-for-you connection with the State library system; usually they can get any needed reference book that way.

Atlas of the Universe is a dilly — any self-respecting modern library should have a copy, as they automatically have a copy of an *Atlas of the Earth*. Take a couple of weeks off and read through it — the pictures, drawings, etc., are magnificient, and the text is Grade A +1 discussion.

Regards,   John W. Campbell

Vernor Vinge *c/o William Rupp*   *June 17, 1971*

Dear Lieutenant Vinge:

Whatever name (or names) an author indicates on the title page of his manuscript is the name that the story will be published under.

If a manuscript is received that has been co-authored, our tracer, any correspondence, and payment goes to the one we have had previous dealings with. This avoids the necessity of double entry all around.

"Just Peace" had William Rupp and Vernor Vinge on the title page and that's how it will appear in the magazine.

Sincerely,   John W. Campbell

Mike Glyer   *July 1, 1971*

Dear Mr. Glyer:

That fat-headed argument that "human beings don't obey natural laws" is one of my hates. In essence what you really mean is that "since human beings don't obey my theories, that shows they don't obey rational laws."

Do modern theories include all the laws of the Universe? Do you know *all* the laws of Reality? And if an entity follows laws you haven't discovered yet, does that prove it doesn't follow laws?

The true laws of the mind are almost totally unknown; that's the field that the social sciences are *supposed* to be studying — and they are *not* supposed to be bellyaching about how their subjects don't act in a decent, rational, logical manner.

The way to solve a problem is to assume that there is a reason behind what you observe, and *find* that reason. Note carefully that finding it does *not* include whimpering, "There is no reason! It's irrational, and just an impossible whim."

You find it by acknowledging that there *is* a reason and digging until you find it. You find it even if you have to throw out 90% of what you "know" is true, and start accepting that what you call "superstition" is valid.

But so long as you insist that the subject of your study behaves whimsically, irrationally, illogically, and with no correlation to anything else — just so long will you totally fail to solve the problem.

The social scientists annoy the hell out of me because they're constantly bitching about how unreliable their subjects are.

Look; you can define what you mean by "logic"; you know and can communicate logical processes by which you get from point A to point B in an argument.

Logic has no provable correlation with rationality; talk to any paranoid schizophrenic with well systematized delusions. He's the most logical type you'll ever meet; he is so logical it's creepy. And he is also very apt to be a deadly homocidal, and strictly insane.

Because his faultless logic is working from false postulates.

There is no way to communicate how you get your postulates; logic can manipulate postulates after you have them — but it can not generate them.

Therefore all logic is floating in midair, with no provable basis. *All* postulates remain unproven.

If you find out how men generate the postulates they live by, you'll have taken a long, long step toward making a social science. And note that the method cannot be logical.

Sincerely,   John W. Campbell

Finis
by
PERRY A. CHAPDELAINE, SR.

So now you've met the *real* John J. Campbell, Jr. — and if you liked what you've read, there are plans to publish the tens of thousands of letters remaining, covering most every subject related to Science Fiction, which means most everything on, above, and below Earth and beyond time and space itself.

It is only fitting, that this — the very first volume of John W. Campbell letters — end by consensus words from two who held a very special relationship to the Campbell family — Kelly and Polly Freas — as written by Kelly Freas.

598

In the Beginning
was —
Campbell

by
FRANK KELLY FREAS

It's hard to realize that over three generations (an SF generation being approximately four years) have passed since I last had the pleasure of talking with John W. Campbell. Harder still is the realization that by far the majority of today's readers were never exposed to the Campbell magic, and know him only, perhaps, as required reading for Modern Science Fiction 101. But there are still many of us to whom Campbell *was* science fiction, and everything else merely filler for the dry periods between issues of *Astounding*.

"Define science fiction? Of course! Science fiction is the stuff I publish in *Astounding*."

There were one or two people who disagreed, but none could dispute the fact that for over thirty years John W. Campbell, Jr., set the styles, determined the parameters (so he could kick his way beyond them), and broadcast the ideas which generated most of the stories being written.

Students of science fiction as a genre apparently have yet to realize that up to the early sixties, *only* magazine SF was important in either a literary or a monetary sense. We were well into the fifties before a significant amount of SF became available in *either* hardcover or paperback. Science fiction was the magazine. Not only did Campbell offer the highest pay, but he also repeatedly, in print, invited new authors to submit stories. And further, any writer short on ideas need only to have lunch with Campbell to be provided with enough concepts, and frequently complete plots, to keep him busy for weeks.

"I *like* young Querty. When I throw an idea at him, he catches it on the run, and usually carries it to a touchdown." (Campbell was sharing a floor with Street & Smith's sports magazine at the time).

There are numberless tales about Campbell's mercurial temperment, his violent (and violently swinging) opinions, his dogmatism, his ruthless criticism, and above all, his rigid insistence that things be done *his* way.

All of them are wrong.

For instance, it wasn't *his* way he insisted upon: it was the *right* way (any one of the six-and-ninety would do) for this particular problem. In one case, he sent a story back to the author five times, insisting that the ending be utterly logical, and consistent with the premise of the story, however unpleasant it might be. The resulting story became a classic.

Ruthless? Perhaps. Campbell chopped me off at the ankles more than once — to my lifelong benefit. He was perfectly willing to admit that he knew nothing about art, but he knew storytelling and he knew what it took to illustrate a story. John had no use whatever for abstraction, very little for stylization, and barely tolerated anything that approached the fashionable.

"Page decoration, that's all it is. *Astounding* is *not* a fourteenth-century manuscript! Give me pictures that tell me something about the story!"

What he most liked to get from me was that part of the story which is impossible to verbalize — that something extra which makes story and picture inseparable parts of the reading experience. Short of that, he liked a very realistic treatment of a scene in the story.

"Look," he said, "if I could send a camera to Mars, or into your bloodstream, or into the future, I'd use a camera. But you're all I've got. So *be* a camera, OK?"

Yes, Campbell could be a rough critic — to the people he thought tough-minded enough to profit by it. But I have seen him treat a new and sensitive soul with such gentleness that the tyro never even felt the least put down. More than a few artists and writers left a pleasant and inspiring interview with John simply overflowing with new ideas, eager to try them out, and only vaguely regretful that Campbell's narrow field had no room for their unquestionable abilities. . . . And Campbell wasn't being hypocritical —

"That I can't use a man's work doesn't necessarily mean that it's bad, any more than the fact that he does great work means that I have to buy it for *Astounding*."

John's enthusiasms were legendary — and often led to acute frustration in a writer who leaped onto the bandwagon three months too late. Campbell felt that his own major function was to stimulate minds; and as soon as he got a few others working on an idea, he felt free to turn his attention elsewhere. But while he was hot on the trail of a concept, he would discuss it with anyone incautious enough to get in range — authors, waitresses, cab drivers, even artists. It didn't matter how little his listener knew about the subject. John was perfectly willing to teach his listener enough of the basics for the listener to form a more or less "intelligent" opinion.

One of Campbell's favorite techniques was to ask a question such as, "What sort of technology do you suppose might develop on a planet with virtually *no* heavy metals?"

Now, he didn't care *what* your answer was. His interest was in the *way* you answered, and the way you thought about it. Did you

600

consider the question seriously? Did you approach the problem methodically? Did you bring any originality to bear on the problem? Did you come up with a reply which showed some understanding of the situation, without the usual syncophantic drivel?

It was probably inevitable that Campbell should get a reputation for dogmatism, intransigence, and simple bull-headedness. He enjoyed nothing so much as a good fight, even (or perhaps especially) when he lost. John always made a point of stating his own opinions in such a definite and rigid form that a valid attack on either his data or his reasoning would bring the whole structure down in a heap.

Unfortunately for his detractors, Campbell had a mind whose breadth and scope was matched by the clarity and depth of his perception. He wasn't *often* wrong, and even his errors were Homeric. Whenever he discovered that he was headed in the wrong direction, he was fully capable of making a 180° turn in full career, without missing a beat. Less agile minds naturally found this ability annoying. John loved a good intellectual scrap, preferably one with plenty of hard data to juggle, but he was perfectly capable of calculated violence when violence was called for. Peg could never understand why John would repeatedly subject himself to the sort of bear-baiting he encountered at conventions, workshops, seminars, and even at parties. The attackers went at him like a pack of hound-dogs after a possum — and retired in yelping disorder when the possum turned out to be a grizzly.

It took me a good many years to realize that John Campbell was utterly and completely consistent — even when he appeared to be contradicting himself. He knew exactly where he was going; he knew exactly what was required to get there; and he knew that goals and means of reaching them change as inexorably as the phases of the moon. In you or me, it would be a fault; on Campbell it looked good. It kept him (and his work) alive, vital, and exciting to everyone who encountered him, however violently they might disagree.

If John W. Campbell, Jr., created many of the writers who made up the science fiction roster in the 1940s, it could equally be said that Peg Campbell created the John W. Campbell, Jr., who dominated the science fiction of the fities and sixties.

Peg Campbell was a rare and powerful personality herself — and certainly John never let anyone forget it. He was justifiably proud of her in every way, and it delighted him that she could and would stand up to him in an argument — and frequently plow him under, when the subject lay in her territory.

Banker's daughter, English teacher, highly skilled in several crafts, she was also a fine business person. She had started (and sold) several successful businesses of her own. John was vastly proud of her business ability: it was a talent which he ruefully admitted he did not share. Peg was particularly knowledgeable in the art of crewel embroidery, and was for several years adviser on the subject to the British Museum, among others both American and European. John functioned happily as her photographer, taking as much joy in *her* expertise as he did in his own. He would all but snatch people bodily off the street — or hotel corridor — to show off her work. Of course, to see it was to admire, but even more, you felt a desire to do it yourself, at which point Peg was prepared to sell you all the necessary materials and guide your first steps. . . . She would have made a great pusher.

I sometimes suspected, however, that the quality that most endeared Peg to John was her rather zany sense of humor, which ranged from the most abstrusely erudite to the bawdiest slapstick. She played a great honky-tonk piano, and spent years looking for a good recording of a song which started:

"I'm looking for a guy who plays alto and baritone
And doubles on a clarinet
And wears a size thirty-seven suit
Boodle-do-wa-wa. . . ."

Peg was a superb hostess. She never had trouble keeping a party in high gear: around her everyone seemed to come to life. She wasn't much impressed by science fiction. Yes, she could see the importance of the ideas — but the writing and the characterization gave her indigestion, and she didn't mind saying so, in terms usually tempered more by her victim's sensitivity than his professional status.

Sometimes all the talk wore her down —

"But you don't *go* anywhere! You just go round and round, restating the same old problems, discussing the same things over and over . . . and you never solve *anything!*"

"Ummmm . . . yes. But Peg, how many times have you listened to Beethoven's *Moonlight Sonata*? Do you enjoy it less because you have played it so often?"

That sort of thinking Peg could buy. Sometimes. . . .

Living with John would hardly have been easy, but Peg was perfectly able to cope. When she married John, she went into a motherless, utterly disorganized house, and made it into a warm and loving home. John's two daughters adored her, perhaps not least because she believed in the direct approach — as when she calmly tipped a bowl of ice cream into John's open shirt front in response to his kidding. . . .

Theirs was the good marriage of two intelligent adults who

clearly — and dearly — loved and respected each other. It was also a partnership between two strong people of very dissimilar nature and interest, looking for (and finding) many basic answers together. Each brought a great deal of happiness to the other.

I said in my book *The Art of Science Fiction* that when John Campbell died, much of my pleasure in science fiction went with him. Not that working with him was easy, but he kept his people — or at least *me* — feeling that it was worth the effort. Working with Campbell, one could never forget that one's primary function was to entertain — *but*, through this very entertainment could be laid the foundation for a whole new world. . . .

Over the last few years, there has developed, in science fiction, a perceptible tendency to minimize, downgrade, or simply ignore John W. Campbell's importance to the field, and there are certainly those in the field who would deny that he had any influence on *them* whatever. There are, thank heaven, many, many more people now working in the various scientific disciplines (and even some in the arts) who eagerly admit that they wouldn't be in their particular specialty but for the inspiration Campbell gave them.

I mentioned before that to me John W. Campbell, Jr. was only a few steps lower than God. From the perspective of thirteen years without his presence, I begin to suspect that I under-rated him.

Index

John W. Campbell speaks to or about —